EXPLORING THE SOCIAL

Readings in Contemporary Sociology

Peter Kivisto

Augustana College

Boston   Burr Ridge, IL   Dubuque, IA   Madison, WI   New York   San Francisco   St. Louis
Bangkok   Bogotá   Caracas   Lisbon   London   Madrid
Mexico City   Milan   New Delhi   Seoul   Singapore   Sydney   Taipei   Toronto

McGraw-Hill Higher Education 🪐

A Division of The McGraw-Hill Companies

EXPLORING THE SOCIAL
Readings in Contemporary Sociology

Some ancillaries, including electronic and print components, may not be available to customers outside the United States.

This book is printed on acid-free paper.

1 2 3 4 5 6 7 8 9 0 DOC/DOC 0 9 8 7 6 5 4 3 2 1 0

ISBN 0-07-238631-2

Publisher: *Phillip Butcher*
Sponsoring editor: *Sally Constable*
Developmental editor: *Katherine Blake*
Marketing manager: *Leslie Kraham*
Project manager: *Craig S. Leonard*
Production supervisor: *Gina Hangos*
Designer: *Pam Verros*
Supplement coordinator: *Jason Greve*
Cover designer: *Crispin Prebys*
Cover illustration: *Robert Neubecker*
Compositor: *Shepherd Incorporated*
Typeface: *10/12 Palatino*
Printer: *R. R. Donnelley & Sons Company*

Library of Congress Cataloging-in-Publication Data

Exploring the social: readings in contemporary sociology/[edited by] Peter Kivisto.
    p.cm.
      ISBN 0-07-238631-2 (softcover: alk. paper).
      1. Sociology. I. Kivisto, Peter, 1948-
HM585 .E86 2001
301—dc21   00-042715

www.mhhe.com

EXPLORING THE SOCIAL

ABOUT THE AUTHOR

PETER KIVISTO is currently professor and chair of sociology at Augustana College, Rock Island, Illinois. After completing his undergraduate studies at the University of Michigan, he received an M.Div. from Yale University and an M.A. and Ph.D. from the New School for Social Research. Among his 14 authored or edited books are *Key Ideas in Sociology, Illuminating Social Life, Americans All,* and *For Democracy.* His publications in scholarly journals focus on race and ethnic relations and social theory, and he has been active in professional organizations in these two fields, including serving recently on the Executive Committee of the Immigration and Ethnic History Society and as Secretary-Treasurer of the American Sociological Association's Theory Section.

To my sisters, Kay and Kathy

CONTENTS

PREFACE

When I began my undergraduate education at the University of Michigan over three decades ago, I knew virtually nothing about sociology. In fact, if a friend of mine had not suggested that I take a sociology course, I may never have encountered the discipline. One semester later, I was hooked. On the basis of the experience of my introductory sociology class, I decided that sociology would become my major. As I look back on that decision, I am able to identify two factors that influenced my enthusiastic response to sociology. One of the reasons was that I had the benefit of being taught by a bright, engaging, and personable professor, an individual who by example showed what it meant to look at the world sociologically. However, in retrospect, I don't think that this was the primary factor in my decision.

Rather, the main reason for seeking to delve further into what sociology was all about was that I quickly learned that it provided me with the tools I needed to make sense of the world around me. Living through and being a part of the tumultuous decade of the 1960s on a campus engulfed by the anti–Vietnam War movement, the civil rights movement, and the counterculture, I was caught up in a period of dramatic social change. I marched in Washington to protest the war, took part in teach-ins and antiwar protests in Ann Arbor, got involved in antipoverty organizing, tutored inner-city youth, worked for migrant farm workers in the California grape boycott campaign, and in a variety of other ways sought to promote social change. It was both an exhilarating and a frustrating time. I found myself wanting to understand more about the nature of the central problems and concerns of the era in order to find constructive ways of responding to them.

What I discovered was that my sociology courses, more than any other classes I took, seemed most capable of addressing these vital concerns. When nearby Detroit was engulfed in urban riots in the summer of 1967, my race and ethnic relations course helped me understand the nature of American race relations and in so doing allowed me to gain insights into this particular event that would otherwise have eluded me. My social stratification course helped me achieve a greater understanding of the impact of endemic poverty on the children I tutored. My course in political sociology helped me in my efforts to evaluate governmental policies and actions, both domestic and foreign. And so it was with the rest of my sociology courses.

Throughout this period, as my appreciation of the value of sociological knowledge grew, I learned that the contemporary sociologists I read were building on a tradition that extends back to the 19th century. Over time, I came to see not only how they built upon the work of their predecessors, but also how, in the process, they adapted and transformed that tradition in their efforts to address the complex and ever-changing social world we inhabit.

Likewise, I also came to appreciate the remarkable range of topics that preoccupy sociologists, from issues involving the most intimate levels of social life, such as those dealing with family and friendship relations, to those concerned with the broadest sorts of social processes, such as deindustrialization, the rise of religious fundamentalism, technological change, ethnic strife, and the globalization of popular culture. I learned that the sociological vision reveals not only how societies change, but also how they manage to persist over time. I learned that it casts light on not only the ways societies constrain people, but also the ways that they enable or make possible various kinds of activities. In short, sociology provided me with the ability to explore the social in all its facets.

Sociology and the Sociological Novice

About a decade after completing my undergraduate studies, I began to teach sociology, and since that time I have had the pleasure of introducing the field that captured my imagination to thousands of undergraduate students. Throughout my teaching career, I have always asked my students to read books and articles by important contemporary sociologists, and I have discovered that they respond to these works much the same way I did as an undergraduate. They, quite simply, appreciate the relevance of sociology to their own lives, as they come to realize that it provides them with compelling descriptions and analyses of social life.

By encountering sociologists directly—and not through the second-hand mediation of a textbook—students get to appreciate how members of the profession go about investigating, describing, and making sense of myriad aspects of social life. They get a flavor for the ways sociologists frame questions, devise methods for exploring those questions, and draw conclusions about whatever it is they are investigating. Students also derive an awareness of just how varied the sociological enterprise actually is, and an enhanced awareness of the diverse array of insights that can be obtained from various modes of sociological inquiry. In short, they are exposed to what C. Wright Mills called "the sociological imagination" in its many guises by seeing it enacted and embodied in the writings of contemporary sociologists and social scientists working in closely related fields.

To this end, I have concluded over time that it is vitally important to expose students to the best that we sociologists have to offer. In their first—and for many only—course in sociology, students should become acquainted with some of the most important practitioners of the sociological vocation. In particular, they should be introduced to scholars who have made valuable contributions to the discipline and who write with a stylistic virtuosity that reflects sociological writing of the highest caliber. I have developed this reader with this conviction in mind.

What Makes This Book Different?

What distinguishes this reader from others on the market is that all of the contributors are, in fact, respected scholars whose work is having a significant impact in their respective areas of expertise. Although most of the contributors are sociologists, the collection also includes selections from people in related social sciences, such as anthropology and political science. Those nonsociologists included herein have also had an impact on sociology proper. Their presence reflects the fact that sociology is increasingly shaped by interdisciplinary encounters.

There are a number of fine readers on the market today, and the question one might reasonably ask is how this one differs from the others. I think the best way to answer this question is to identify a few salient characteristics of this collection.

First, as noted above, the choice of authors is somewhat unique. Part of becoming acquainted with sociology ought to be about learning who is who in the world of sociology. To this end, the authors chosen for inclusion are prominent scholars. For the student choosing to go on in sociology, this is important insofar as it provides them with an introduction to the thought of people they will get to know better as their studies progress. It affords those students—the vast majority—who do not opt to major in sociology the opportunity to be introduced to the people who illuminate in instructive ways the distinctive virtues and possibilities of the discipline. Moreover, they become acquainted with people whose work they may well encounter later in their lives, for these are the kinds of people who are not only prominent scholars, but are public intellectuals as well. They write for newspapers and magazines, participate in radio and television news programs, serve as advisers to government officials and public interest groups, and in other ways are in touch with the general public.

Second, the readings that have been assembled herein are somewhat longer than the selections in most other introductory sociology readers. The reasoning behind this decision is that I want students to come away with an awareness of how sociologists actually go about framing particular topics, and how they make a sociological case by employing a variety of concepts or theories and varied kinds of empirical evidence. When a reading is too short, it does not permit the student reader to examine how it is that sociologists go about drawing conclusions about whatever it is they are exploring. The student does not come away with an understanding about how sociologists develop their arguments, employ a variety of rhetorical strategies and conventions, and infuse their work with creative insight. Thus, it seems to me that there is a very compelling pedagogical reason for longer, more sustained readings. It's my conviction that teachers who are committed to developing their students' critical and analytical abilities will find that these somewhat longer readings help them greatly in this task.

Readings should not simply be engaging; they should also challenge. They should stimulate students to think about subjects that are both difficult and complex, and in so doing, they ought to push students to think in new ways and to develop more critical and nuanced sensibilities about the world around them. If education is about personal transformation—and it ought to be—then students need to be assisted in the process of acquiring the analytical and critical abilities to think in new ways. These readings, I believe, do just that. Far from pandering to students or underestimating their abilities, the readings in this collection have been chosen with the assumption that earnest students are capable of reading them with real insight and are up to the challenge they afford.

Third, I have made a pragmatic decision to limit the number of selections to 46. This number strikes me as a reasonable one, providing sufficient options for instructors who have some flexibility in deciding which readings work best for the courses they teach. On the other hand, one of the frequent complaints we hear from students concerns the rising cost of books. More specifically when it comes to readers, they are often quite unhappy when asked to purchase a book only to discover that they are actually assigned only a small fraction of its contents. An underlying assumption that I made in arriving at the number of readings is that most of this book will be assigned, thereby alleviating this common complaint.

Finally, the readings collectively reflect the full range of concerns that preoccupy contemporary sociologists, revealing to students that our discipline is, indeed, the most expansive and inclusive of the social sciences. At the same time, insofar as the themes of some resonate with those of others, students will come away with a feel for the interconnectedness of the society they inhabit and a greater awareness of their place in it. In other words, at the end of the course, they can look back with a more sophisticated appreciation of what C. Wright Mills referred to as "the promise" of sociology.

ACKNOWLEDGMENTS

It is my conviction that an impressive body of wonderful sociological writing has been produced in recent years. This is not everyone's belief. Sociologists are often criticized for employing an impenetrable jargon or their work is viewed as too methodologically complex and theoretically sophisticated for the ordinary reader. Although plenty of evidence can be cited to support both of these convictions, it is also the case that many sociologists write exceedingly well in a manner that is quite accessible to people without previous exposure to sociology. Indeed, it is not hard to find clean, clear, engaging, and sometimes even elegant prose coming from the pens—or probably from the word processors—of many of today's most important practitioners of the sociological vocation. I note this because in making selections for this book, I was struck by the sheer volume of writing that could have been included in this collection. In other words, I had the rather daunting task of making choices. For every reading selected, dozens of excellent readings were not chosen.

How did I arrive at decisions about what to include and what to exclude? Although the criteria I employed in making selections is discussed in the Preface, what I did would not have been possible without the suggestions, insights, and advice of numerous people. In the end, the decisions for inclusion were mine, but they were made with the influence of others who deserve to be acknowledged. First, I would like to thank a number of current and former students who offered crucial insights into what works and what doesn't work for students. Although many students helped out, I would like to single out for special mention Zubair Ansari, Meagan Bean, Kelly Corley, Liz Davenport, Heather Gordon, Chad McPherson, Kendra Nicholson, Dan Pittman, Bill Pokorny, Shiney Puthusseril, Siiri Rimpila, and Erin Sullivan. Likewise, colleagues have, in ways large and small, helped me. These include Harry Bash, Dave Brown, Steve Dandaneau, John Farley, Beth Hartung, Mike Loukinen, Stan Lyman, Bob Nakamaru, Ben Nefzger, Chris Prendergast, Bill Staudenmeier, Bill Swatos, Bob Wazienski, Dean Wright, and Sue Wright. Finally, I would like to thank the reviewers of various versions of this manuscript, including: Judith Blau, *University of North Carolina–Chapel Hill;* Susan L. Brown, *Bowling Green State University;* Deborah Carr, *University of Michigan–Ann Arbor;* James C. Cavendish, *University of South Florida;* Isaac W. Eberstein, *Florida State University;* John B. Harms, *Southwest Missouri State University;* Paul Higgins, *University of South Carolina–Columbia;* David Kyle, *University of California–Davis;* Joel Nelson, *University of Minnesota;* David Redburn, *Furman University;* Thomas Soltis, *Westmoreland County Community College;* and Juniper Wiley, *California State University–Long Beach.*

Peter Kivisto

INTRODUCTION: EXPLORING THE SOCIAL

Sociology emerged in the 19th century as a new social scientific discipline committed, as the title of this collection suggests, to exploring the social. More explicitly, it arose as a concerted effort on the part of its early practitioners to make sense of the profound changes sweeping the world as a consequence of the rise of modern industrial societies. The classical figures in sociology's formative period—with Karl Marx, Émile Durkheim, Max Weber, and Georg Simmel being the most enduringly important—sought to make sense of the changes they witnessed. They did so with the assumption, to paraphrase Marx, that people create their own social worlds, but they do so in circumstances not of their own choosing. In other words, we are both the creators of our social worlds and the products of our social environments. In different ways and with different foci and emphases, the founders of sociology attempted to find discernible patterns and trends that can be used to explain the impact of modern societies on the people who inhabit them, identifying structures or social forces that shape and act as causal factors in our lives. At the same time, they sought to comprehend the ways that people play a part in shaping or constructing their social worlds, focusing in this instance on people as actors or agents of their own lives.

Though much has changed during the past two centuries, the task of sociology remains the same today as it was during its formative period. Thus, the capitalist industrial societies that Karl Marx attempted to comprehend in the 19th century are in many respects different from the advanced industrial societies of countries such as the United States at the dawn of the 21st century. Likewise, the impact of rationalization and bureaucratization that Max Weber was concerned about in the early part of the 20th century has continuing relevance, whereas the ways these phenomena manifest themselves are not the same as they were during his lifetime. Similarly, the investigations of Émile Durkheim, a contemporary of Weber, into the impact of individualism on community allegiances and loyalties captured concerns about the new bases of social solidarity in the modern world. This topic is a recurring theme in contemporary sociological literature, as we attempt to make sense of phenomena unknown to Durkheim, such as the nature of community in the suburbs and the impact of such technological revolutions as television and the Internet on notions of community. Finally, Georg Simmel's interest in the characteristic features of modern culture at the dawn of the 20th century resonates with contemporary debates about changes that have taken place in modern culture during the ensuing century, particularly those concerned with consumerism and leisure. All four have something to say implicitly about whether or not it is accurate at present to speak about the prospect of entering into a new postmodern cultural era.

The readings in this collection make clear what was noted earlier: that sociologists are interested in a broad array of social phenomena and they go about looking at those phenomena in different ways, making use of differing kinds of data and employing a variety of methodological approaches. Sociologists have cast their net outward over the entire social universe. In fact, it's sometimes hard to figure out what might be excluded from the purview of sociology. Indeed, as prominent sociologist Neil Smelser[1] characterized the situation, this means that sociology's "scope is enormous; in principle there is a sociology of virtually everything under the sun." However, despite differences in topics, data, and methods, sociologists hold in common a particular appreciation of the sociological vocation, which calls for a search for understanding based on a careful and judicious analysis of relevant evidence and on a desire to seek the general or typical in the particular or individual case.

---

[1]Neil J. Smelser, *Sociology* (Cambridge, MA: Blackwell, 1994), p. 8.

Terms that have often been used to describe sociological inquiry include "objective" and "disinterested." This does not mean that the sociologist is not passionately concerned about whatever is being investigated. Indeed, there is no need to suggest that the sociologist cannot be both involved and detached. Involved because what tends to motivate sociological work is a perceived need to make sense of something. This might be in order to find a solution to what one sees as a social problem, but it can also be driven by a desire to know more about how the social arrangements that shape our everyday lives arise, are maintained, and sometimes change. The best sociology reflects a passionate involvement with one's subject matter. However, detachment is also necessary. It is important to be able to step back, to do what one can to prevent one's own beliefs, prejudices, preferences, and desires from clouding or influencing the conclusions one draws. Things might not work as the sociologist initially thought they did. What was once thought possible might not be. The sociologist must, quite simply, be open to surprises—to the possibility that the world is not quite the way it appears at first. The mark of a good sociologist is that she or he is able to balance involvement and detachment, and in so doing, genuinely contributes to advancing our understanding.

If the object of inquiry can define sciences, then sociology can be defined as the science of society. Indeed, this is precisely how William Graham Sumner, one of the earliest sociologists in the United States, described sociology. But this definition reflects the expansive nature of sociology that Smelser noted above. What sociologists actually go about doing is studying slices of society—sometimes large slices, sometimes small slices, but always a part of the whole and not the whole. In so doing, they focus on such facets of the social as culture, patterns of social interaction, groups, collective behavior, organizations, social institutions, social divisions, social movements, and social change. Thus, not surprisingly, sociology as it has evolved as a discipline has been divided into numerous specialty areas. The sections in this reader are a reflection of the major subareas of sociological inquiry.

What does it mean to do sociology or to profess the sociological vocation? The collection begins with two essays that address these issues: C. Wright Mills' discussion of "The Sociological Imagination" and Charles Lemert's recent meditation on sociology as a calling.

Students of culture focus their energies on the beliefs and value systems that shape institutional life and individual behaviors. Culture has been appropriately described as a "tool kit" containing the collective symbols, beliefs, values, and norms that are crucial for interpreting action and interaction and providing meaning to social life. The readings in Section II, Culture and Society, provide the reader with varied aspects of cultural analysis. Sociologists are concerned not only with the cultural character of the society as a whole, but with subcultures within a society and with countercultures intent on challenging the status quo. The reading by Eviatar Zerubavel examines the sociological significance of the week, which is a remarkably fixed and taken-for-granted aspect of our culture. In contrast, the readings by Orlando Patterson and by Andrea Fontana and Stanford Lyman examine changes in aspects of popular culture. The changes Patterson addresses involve the ways contemporary popular cultures transcend national borders. Fontana and Lyman focus on the Hollywood culture industry as a way of getting at what it means to think about a shift from modern culture to postmodern culture. Elijah Anderson examines the values of the subculture of inner-city black males who are part of the culture of the streets, comparing and contrasting their worldviews to that of the society at large.

Section III, The Social Construction of Self and Everyday Life, examines a variety of topics that in one way or another deal with the ways self-identities and the content of various forms of interpersonal interaction are invented, enacted, sustained, subverted, or transformed. The focus in this section is on aspects of the social at the micro level. The sociological frame for investigating these topics involves seeing social construction as something that occurs, not as a result of individual actions, but via processes of social interaction. It is this focus that links the disparate topics considered by the readings in the section: (1) Erving Goffman on the function of embarrassment; (2) Anthony Giddens on the meaning of codependence; (3) Guy Oakes on the importance of trust in social relations; (4) Sherry Turkle on the fluid nature of personal identity and the ways this is revealed in encounters in cyberspace; (5) Gary Alan Fine on the organizational props that are employed in the service of facilitating the pursuit of fun; (6) Claude S. Fischer on the ways in which new modes of communication by people not in physical proximity to each other are rendered meaningful; and (7) Peter Adler and Patti Adler on the impact of role conflict on notions of the self.

The following section, Deviance and Crime, shifts from the normal to the pathological, from social conformity to social deviance, from efforts to shore up the social order to attempts to undermine or threaten it. Despite this difference, what should become obvious after reading the four selections that have been included here is that sociologists approach these topics in the same way they approached the topics addressed in the previous section. We see in Joseph Gusfield's reading that what we come to define as alcohol-related problems vary depending on time and place; in the reading by Eric Dunning and colleagues that fan violence at soccer matches can be understood if one looks into the deeper features of class structure; in Philippe Bourgeois's contribution that drug dealing in inner cities is a job that in many respects is not unlike many jobs in the legal labor market. The reading by Joel Best and Gerald T. Horiuchi indicates how we should look at the underlying factors that contribute to the creation of urban myths.

Sections V, VI, and VII address the broad topic of social divisions and inequalities. Sociologists are particularly sensitive to and concerned about comprehending those forces that divide humankind and in the process lead to a wide variety of inequalities. Although there are many forms of social division—including those based on age, religious affiliation, geographic region, and physical and mental abilities—it is nonetheless the case that three forms of social division loom large in the sociological literature. These are the divisions of race, class, and gender, and it is these particular social divisions that constitute the foci of these three sections.

Joel Feagin and Hernán Vera address the persistence of racial discrimination, in this case institutional discrimination, over a quarter of a century after the civil rights movement. In a parallel fashion, Douglas S. Massey focuses on the segregated world of the black urban underclass—separate and unequal. The section on race is rounded out with William Julius Wilson's attempt to explore, not continuities with the past, but new issues related to economic changes that have eroded the manufacturing jobs that have historically provided poor people with an opportunity for upward social mobility. Although the focus is race, both Massey and Wilson discuss issues in which race and class intersect.

The next section turns explicitly to class divisions. Andrew Hacker provides a brief portrait of three large sectors of the American class structure, identifying them as those who are merely getting by, the poor, and the affluent. Given the large size of the middle class, we would expect to find considerable variation within this particular sector. Although many middle-class people have recently been doing quite well, others have not. Katherine S. Newman looks at this latter group, exploring the anxieties and concerns of members of the middle class threatened by downward social mobility. David Snow and Leon Anderson shift the focus to one of the groups in American society that is truly disadvantaged, the homeless. Their ethnographic study affords an insight into the everyday life of a group of people living on the streets.

The third section addresses gender, including the topic of sexual identity. Arlene Kaplan Daniels' contribution offers an inquiry into the world of uncompensated "women's work," including household labor and volunteer work in the community. By referring to these forms of work as "invisible," she suggests that there is a tendency to fail to appreciate such activities as work. Ruth Horowitz examines the world of teen mothers who are part of a program that helps prepare them for both motherhood and the job market, assuming they will have to juggle child raising and the world of work. Finally, in Arlene Stein's essay, we turn to the topic of sexual identity. Specifically, she addresses the question of what it means to be a lesbian, and in so doing, she raises central issues related to the social construction of sexual identity.

Section VIII concerns social organizations. Here the focus is on the structured associational arrangements, which serve to both constrain and enable various forms of social action and interaction. Diane Vaughan's investigation of NASA looks at the culture and decision-making processes that were at play when the *Challenger* disaster occurred. Her explanation of the tragedy, in contrast to those which placed the blame on individual decisions, points to factors embedded in the organization itself. In a somewhat similar fashion, Robert Jackall looks at the implicit ethical code of a modern corporation, seeing in the demands of organizational efficiency and the quest for profit powerful guides to conduct that tend to trump the ethical standards that employees bring into the bureaucracy. Daniel F. Chambliss also looks at the ethic of personnel in a modern organization, in this case it is nurses in a hospital. He is chiefly concerned with the ways that nurses act to protect their ordinary routines from being undermined by disruptive forces—how order is preserved in the face of possible disorder. Finally, Alan Wolfe turns to the world of neighborhood, community, and voluntary associations. Specifically, he revisits a current debate about whether or not middle-class Americans have withdrawn from civic involvement.

The following section addresses the topic of social institutions, which can be seen as relatively fixed constellations of roles, statuses, groups, and organizations. Sociologists are not in agreement about the precise number of institutions in modern societies, but generally they focus on the economy, politics, the family, education, and religion, with some adding the media, health care, the military, and others. The eight readings in this section address issues related to four of these institutions. Stephanie Coontz and Andrew Cherlin look at the family. Coontz believes that the family today is often compared with a mythic family of the past—particularly the family of the 1950s world of sitcoms—and attempts to offer a corrective. Cherlin reports on research he has been engaged in on the impacts of divorce for the adult and child members of families and on the difficult process of reconstruction involved in remarriage.

The articles by Michael Lienesch and by Roger Finke and Rodney Stark are concerned with issues related to religion in America. Lienesch addresses the impact of Christian fundamentalists who have sought to infuse their religious beliefs into politics, exploring both their current role in public life and the possible future of this movement. Finke and Stark focus on changing denominational membership trends, locating such shifts in terms of longer processes of institutional growth and decline.

With the readings by Richard Sennett and Ruth Milkman, we shift our focus to the economy. More specifically, both readings examine facets of the changing character of work in an advanced capitalist economy. Sennett's reading is devoted to the implications of what has become known as flexible capitalism for middle-class professionals, both in terms of the character of work itself and the increasingly unstable nature of the relationship between employee and employer. Milkman shifts the focus to the blue-collar working class and to the impact that deindustrialization is having on the lives of auto workers experiencing what is euphemistically referred to as downsizing.

This section is rounded out with two selections concerned with aspects of contemporary politics. Todd Gitlin examines the role that television plays in shaping what he sees as a growing antipolitical sensibility, and in the process raises questions about the larger issue of the significance of new communications technologies for citizen participation in the political process. Moskos treats the military as an interesting microcosm of larger societal changes concerning the incorporation of people previously excluded from full participation in various institutions. He assesses the political decision making that has shaped the ways the military has handled racial integration, the expanding role of women, and gays in uniform.

Social movements arise as a result of and are a source of change. Social movements can be defined as collective actors that mobilize to either promote, prevent, or reverse change. Sociologists are particularly interested in issues related to the circumstances in which movements arise, their internal dynamics and tensions, and the likely trajectories of movements over their careers. The four readings in Section X address one or more of these concerns. Craig Calhoun witnessed and herein reports on the Chinese pro-democracy movement in 1989, paying particular attention to the leadership and internal disputes that shaped events. Doug McAdam, in his study of 1960s civil rights activists, is also interested in movement participants. However, in his case he looks at their involvement retrospectively, attempting to ascertain the subsequent impact of their involvement on their personal lives. Arlene Skolnick is also interested in a retrospective assessment of the impact of a movement—in this case the women's movement of the 1960s—but not on the participants themselves. Instead, she is interested in drawing up a balance sheet of what the movement managed to accomplish and what goals remain unfulfilled. The concluding selection in the section, by James Davison Hunter, focuses explicitly on the conflictual character of movement and countermovement in contemporary debates about such controversial topics as abortion and homosexuality.

As the final section reveals, social change is not simply the product of social movements. Rather, it is also important to explore broader dimensions of structural change. This is what the final four readings do. Arlie Hochschild's contribution deals with changes in the connection between work and family life brought about as a result of the single-parent household and the dual-career family. In both instances, what Hochschild discovered is that people are experiencing "time famine" in their constant efforts to balance the demands of home and job. Kai Erikson is concerned about the unintended negative consequences of science and technology. In this reading, he examines the varied ways that the public responds to this new species of risk and hazard. Shifting to a rather different manifestation of change, Mark Gottdiener turns his gaze to the realm of modern consumption. Specifically, he is interested in making sense of the themed character of phenomena such as fast-food chains, shopping malls, and amusement centers. Finally, Daniel Bell attempts to identify three stages of development within the era of industrial society, contending that with the centrality of electronics (making possible the revolution in computers and telecommunications) we have entered a new phase of development that has wide-scale ramifications for all facets of social life.

Taken as a whole, these 46 readings shed light on a wide range of topics that make up aspects of the social world. As such, they testify to Neil Smelser's claim about there being a sociology of virtually everything. These readings are reflective of the best that sociology has to offer to the reader who is not a sociologist. When sociologists speak only to other sociologists they frequently make use of a more arcane language and the methodologies they use and theoretical discussions they engage in are often beyond the comprehension of most people who have not been trained in the discipline. In this respect, sociologists are no different from chemists, biologists, or other natural or social scientists. However, sociologists also have a role to play in helping the general public acquire a deeper, richer understanding of social life. To this end, as the contributors to this book reveal, they also write for general readers in order to offer insights that make society more comprehensible. The readings herein demonstrate an appreciation of the difficulties associated with social inquiry. None of them should be taken as the definitive statement on any particular topic. Rather, all ought to be seen as provisional assessments based on rigorous empirical investigation and the imaginative employment of theories. Building on a long tradition of sociological inquiry, these readings offer a sense of the importance of the science of society today and in the future.

PROFESSING SOCIOLOGY

Why study sociology? What reasons can one point to for spending the time to become acquainted with the theories and research methods employed by sociologists? What can sociology tell us about the society we live in that we don't already know? These questions run through the minds of many students as they embark on their first sociology course. One of the challenges confronting those who teach sociology is to convince the novice that there is something distinctive about the sociological vision and that it is intrinsically rewarding and worthwhile to work at developing that vision. Not surprisingly, sociologists have often looked for ways to invite students into the discipline.

Periodically, sociologists have attempted to articulate what are deeply personal statements about the effect that sociology has had on them in an effort to encourage newcomers to become acquainted with this particular way of knowing. Thus, my generation was offered "an invitation to sociology" and an account of "the sociological imagination." Contemporary students have in addition been presented with "an introduction to the sociological life," a conversation about the "sociologically examined life," and a meditation on "sociology as life, practice, and promise."

In these and other calls to the sociological vocation, students are told that the singularly significant feature of sociology rests with its potential—not always realized—to connect biography, history, and

1

society. Sociology has the capacity to locate individual lives—ranging from your own and those you know intimately to the lives of people you know far less well, and finally including strangers living in places you have never visited—in terms of larger historically embedded social structures and patterns of social change. Sociology supplies us with the ability to see people as creators of their own lives, and at the same time see social structures as constraining and enabling social actors. It reveals both how we construct our social worlds and how we are molded by those worlds.

For example, sociology can offer a new way of examining such a mundane activity as purchasing a baseball cap with the corporate logo emblazoned on it at the local mall. It can help us understand what that purchase means for the consumer, whether that individual is a white suburban teen or a black inner-city youth. But sociology can also connect the consumer to the corporation—to the kinds of decision making that goes on in the boardroom that are intended to influence consumer preferences (for example, by using icons such as sports stars in their advertisements) and to maximize profits. In so doing, it would also inevitably offer connections between the customer in the mall and the garment worker, possibly located in a sweatshop somewhere in an underdeveloped nation. In making these connections, sociology reveals that the simple act of shopping has far more profound implications than the shopper usually realizes.

Those who have developed and nurtured the sociological imagination are capable of thinking in ways that make the move between the familiar and the unfamiliar, between the micro level and the macro level, between the present and the past, between the individual and the social, and between what is and what might be. This constitutes the essence of what it means to think sociologically. The two articles in this section are intended to provide glimpses at what it means to profess sociology.

The Promise

C. Wright Mills

In this classic essay from his book, The Sociological Imagination, *C. Wright Mills makes a powerful case for sociology as a moral science. In contrast to those in the discipline who seek to make sociology into a rigorously objective and morally neutral endeavor, Mills argues that sociology has the potential to assist in not only making sense of the social world, but also finding ways to act constructively in it. Sociology has a vital role to play in redressing social problems and in promoting a more just and humane social order. Key to fulfilling sociology's promise is the development of the "sociological imagination," wherein we comprehend the connections between public issues and private troubles, between history and biography.*

Nowadays men often feel that their private lives are a series of traps. They sense that within their everyday worlds, they cannot overcome their troubles, and in this feeling, they are often quite correct: What ordinary men are directly aware of and what they try to do are bounded by the private orbits in which they live; their visions and their powers are limited to the close-up scenes of job, family, neighborhood; in other milieux, they move vicariously and remain spectators. And the more aware they become, however vaguely, of ambitions and of threats which transcend their immediate locales, the more trapped they seem to feel.

Underlying this sense of being trapped are seemingly impersonal changes in the very structure of continent-wide societies. The facts of contemporary history are also facts about the success and the failure of individual men and women. When a society is industrialized, a peasant becomes a worker; a feudal lord is liquidated or becomes a businessman. When classes rise or fall, a man is employed or unemployed; when the rate of investment goes up or down, a man takes new heart or goes broke. When wars happen, an insurance salesman becomes a rocket launcher; a store clerk, a radar man; a wife lives alone; a child grows up without a father. Neither the life of an individual nor the history of a society can be understood without understanding both.

Yet men do not usually define the troubles they endure in terms of historical change and institutional contradiction. The well-being they enjoy, they do not usually impute to the big ups and downs of the societies in which they live. Seldom aware of the intricate connection between the patterns of their own lives and the course of world history, ordinary men do not usually know what this connection means for the kinds of men they are becoming and for the kinds of history-making in which they might take part. They do not possess the quality of mind essential to grasp the interplay of man and society, of biography and history, of self and world. They cannot cope with their personal troubles in such ways as to control the structural transformations that usually lie behind them.

Surely it is no wonder. In what period have so many men been so totally exposed at so fast a pace to such earthquakes of change? That Americans have not known such catastrophic changes as have the men and women of other societies is due to historical facts that are now quickly becoming "merely history." The history that now affects every man is world history. Within this scene and this period, in the course of a single generation, one sixth of mankind is transformed from all that is feudal and backward into all that is modern, advanced, and fearful. Political colonies are freed; new and less visible forms of imperialism installed. Revolutions occur; men feel the intimate grip of new kinds of authority. Totalitarian societies rise, and are smashed to bits—or succeed fabulously. After two centuries of ascendancy, capitalism is shown up as only one way to make society into an industrial apparatus. After two centuries of hope, even formal democracy is restricted to a quite small portion of mankind.

Everywhere in the underdeveloped world, ancient ways of life are broken up and vague expectations become urgent demands. Everywhere in the overdeveloped world, the means of authority and of violence become total in scope and bureaucratic in form. Humanity itself now lies before us, the super-nation at either pole concentrating its most coordinated and massive efforts upon the preparation of World War Three.

The very shaping of history now outpaces the ability of men to orient themselves in accordance with cherished values. And which values? Even when they do not panic, men often sense that older ways of feeling and thinking have collapsed and that newer beginnings are ambiguous to the point of moral stasis. Is it any wonder that ordinary men feel they cannot cope with the larger worlds with which they are so suddenly confronted? That they cannot understand the meaning of their epoch for their own lives? That—in defense of selfhood—they become morally insensible, trying to remain altogether private men? Is it any wonder that they come to be possessed by a sense of the trap?

It is not only information that they need—in this Age of Fact, information often dominates their attention and overwhelms their capacities to assimilate it. It is not only the skills of reason that they need—although their struggles to acquire these often exhaust their limited moral energy.

What they need, and what they feel they need, is a quality of mind that will help them to use information and to develop reason in order to achieve lucid summations of what is going on in the world and of what may be happening within themselves. It is this quality, I am going to contend, that journalists and scholars, artists and publics, scientists and editors are coming to expect of what may be called the sociological imagination.

1

The sociological imagination enables its possessor to understand the larger historical scene in terms of its meaning for the inner life and the external career of a variety of individuals. It enables him to take into account how individuals, in the welter of their daily experience, often become falsely conscious of their social positions. Within that welter, the framework of modern society is sought, and within that framework the psychologies of a variety of men and women are formulated. By such means the personal uneasiness of individuals is focused upon explicit troubles and the indifference of publics is transformed into involvement with public issues.

The first fruit of this imagination—and the first lesson of the social science that embodies it—is the idea that the individual can understand his own experience and gauge his own fate only by locating himself within his period, that he can know his own chances in life only by becoming aware of those of all individuals in his circumstances. In many ways it is a terrible lesson; in many ways a magnificent one. We do not know the limits of man's capacities for supreme effort or willing degradation, for agony or glee, for pleasurable brutality or the sweetness of reason. But in our time we have come to know that the limits of "human nature" are frighteningly broad. We have come to know that every individual lives, from one generation to the next, in some society; that he lives out a biography, and that he lives it out within some historical sequence. By the fact of his living he contributes, however minutely, to the shaping of this society and to the course of its history, even as he is made by society and by its historical push and shove.

The sociological imagination enables us to grasp history and biography and the relations between the two within society. That is its task and its promise. To recognize this task and this promise is the mark of the classic social analyst. It is characteristic of Herbert Spencer—turgid, polysyllabic, comprehensive; of E. A. Ross—graceful, muckraking, upright; of Auguste Comte and Emile Durkheim; of the intricate and subtle Karl Mannheim. It is the quality of all that is intellectually excellent in Karl Marx; it is the clue to Thorstein Veblen's brilliant and ironic insight, to Joseph Schumpeter's many-sided constructions of reality; it is the basis of the psychological sweep of W. E. H. Lecky no less than of the profundity and clarity of Max Weber. And it is the signal of what is best in contemporary studies of man and society.

No social study that does not come back to the problems of biography, of history and of their intersections within a society has completed its intellectual journey. Whatever the specific problems of the classic social analysts, however limited or however broad the features of social reality they have examined, those who have been imaginatively aware of the promise of their work have consistently asked three sorts of questions:

1. What is the structure of this particular society as a whole? What are its essential components, and how are they related to one another? How does it differ from other varieties of social order? Within it, what is the meaning of any particular feature for its continuance and for its change?

2. Where does this society stand in human history? What are the mechanics by which it is changing? What is its place within and its meaning for the development of humanity as a whole? How does any particular feature we are examining affect, and how is it affected by, the historical period in which it moves? And this period—what are its essential features? How does it differ from other periods? What are its characteristic ways of history-making?

3. What varieties of men and women now prevail in this society and in this period? And what varieties are coming to prevail? In what ways are they selected and formed, liberated and repressed, made sensitive and blunted? What kinds of "human nature" are revealed in the conduct and character we observe in this society in this period? And

what is the meaning for "human nature" of each and every feature of the society we are examining?

Whether the point of interest is a great power state or a minor literary mood, a family, a prison, a creed—these are the kinds of questions the best social analysts have asked. They are the intellectual pivots of classic studies of man in society—and they are the questions inevitably raised by any mind possessing the sociological imagination. For that imagination is the capacity to shift from one perspective to another—from the political to the psychological; from examination of a single family to comparative assessment of the national budgets of the world; from the theological school to the military establishment; from considerations of an oil industry to studies of contemporary poetry. It is the capacity to range from the most impersonal and remote transformations to the most intimate features of the human self—and to see the relations between the two. Back of its use there is always the urge to know the social and historical meaning of the individual in the society and in the period in which he has his quality and his being.

That, in brief, is why it is by means of the sociological imagination that men now hope to grasp what is going on in the world, and to understand what is happening in themselves as minute points of the intersections of biography and history within society. In large part, contemporary man's self-conscious view of himself as at least an outsider, if not a permanent stranger, rests upon an absorbed realization of social relativity and of the transformative power of history. The sociological imagination is the most fruitful form of this self-consciousness. By its use men whose mentalities have swept only a series of limited orbits often come to feel as if suddenly awakened in a house with which they had only supposed themselves to be familiar. Correctly or incorrectly, they often come to feel that they can now provide themselves with adequate summations, cohesive assessments, comprehensive orientations. Older decisions that once appeared sound now seem to them products of a mind unaccountably dense. Their capacity for astonishment is made lively again. They acquire a new way of thinking, they experience a transvaluation of values: in a word, by their reflection and by their sensibility, they realize the cultural meaning of the social sciences.

2

Perhaps the most fruitful distinction with which the sociological imagination works is between "the personal troubles of milieu" and "the public issues of social structure." This distinction is an essential tool of the sociological imagination and a feature of all classic work in social science.

Troubles occur within the character of the individual and within the range of his immediate relations with others; they have to do with his self and with those limited areas of social life of which he is directly and personally aware. Accordingly, the statement and the resolution of troubles properly lie within the individual as a biographical entity and within the scope of his immediate milieu—the social setting that is directly open to his personal experience and to some extent his willful activity. A trouble is a private matter: values cherished by an individual are felt by him to be threatened.

Issues have to do with matters that transcend these local environments of the individual and the range of his inner life. They have to do with the organization of many such milieux into the institutions of an historical society as a whole, with the ways in which various milieux overlap and interpenetrate to form the larger structure of social and historical life. An issue is a public matter: some value cherished by publics is felt to be threatened. Often there is a debate about what that value really is and about what it is that really threatens it. This debate is often without focus if only because it is the very nature of an issue, unlike even widespread trouble, that it

cannot very well be defined in terms of the immediate and everyday environments of ordinary men. An issue, in fact, often involves a crisis in institutional arrangements, and often too it involves what Marxists call "contradictions" or "antagonisms."

In these terms, consider unemployment. When, in a city of 100,000, only one man is unemployed, that is his personal trouble, and for its relief we properly look to the character of the man, his skills, and his immediate opportunities. But when in a nation of 50 million employees, 15 million men are unemployed, that is an issue, and we may not hope to find its solution within the range of opportunities open to any one individual. The very structure of opportunities has collapsed. Both the correct statement of the problem and the range of possible solutions require us to consider the economic and political institutions of the society, and not merely the personal situation and character of a scatter of individuals.

Consider war. The personal problem of war, when it occurs, may be how to survive it or how to die in it with honor; how to make money out of it; how to climb into the higher safety of the military apparatus; or how to contribute to the war's termination. In short, according to one's values, to find a set of milieux and within it to survive the war or make one's death in it meaningful. But the structural issues of war have to do with its causes; with what types of men it throws up into command; with its effects upon economic and political, family and religious institutions, with the unorganized irresponsibility of a world of nation-states.

Consider marriage. Inside a marriage a man and a woman may experience personal troubles, but when the divorce rate during the first four years of marriage is 250 out of every 1,000 attempts, this is an indication of a structural issue having to do with the institutions of marriage and the family and other institutions that bear upon them.

Or consider the metropolis—the horrible, beautiful, ugly, magnificent sprawl of the great city. For many upper-class people, the personal solution to "the problem of the city" is to have an apartment with private garage under it in the heart of the city, and forty miles out, a house by Henry Hill, garden by Garrett Eckbo, on a hundred acres of private land. In these two controlled environments—with a small staff at each end and a private helicopter connection—most people could solve many of the problems of personal milieux caused by the facts of the city. But all this, however splendid, does not solve the public issues that the structural fact of the city poses. What should be done with this wonderful monstrosity? Break it all up into scattered units, combining residence and work? Refurbish it as it stands? Or, after evacuation, dynamite it and build new cities according to new plans in new places? What should those plans be? And who is to decide and to accomplish whatever choice is made? These are structural issues; to confront them and to solve them requires us to consider political and economic issues that affect innumerable milieux.

In so far as an economy is so arranged that slumps occur, the problem of unemployment becomes incapable of personal solution. In so far as war is inherent in the nation-state system and in the uneven industrialization of the world, the ordinary individual in his restricted milieu will be powerless—with or without psychiatric aid—to solve the troubles this system or lack of system imposes upon him. In so far as the family as an institution turns women into darling little slaves and men into their chief providers and unweaned dependents, the problem of a satisfactory marriage remains incapable of purely private solution. In so far as the overdeveloped megalopolis and the overdeveloped automobile are built-in features of the overdeveloped society, the issues of urban living will not be solved by personal ingenuity and private wealth.

What we experience in various and specific milieux, I have noted, is often caused by structural changes. Accordingly, to understand the changes of many personal milieux we are required to look beyond them. And the number and variety of such structural changes increase as the institutions within which we live become more embracing and more intricately connected with one another. To be aware of the idea of social structure and to use it with sensibility is to be capable of tracing such linkages among a great variety of milieux. To be able to do that is to possess the sociological imagination.

3

What are the major issues for publics and the key troubles of private individuals in our time? To formulate issues and troubles, we must ask what values are cherished yet threatened, and what values are cherished and supported, by the characterizing trends of our period. In the case both of threat and of support we must ask what salient contradictions of structure may be involved.

When people cherish some set of values and do not feel any threat to them, they experience *well-being*. When they cherish values but *do* feel them to be threatened, they experience a crisis—either as a personal trouble or as a public issue. And if all their values seem involved, they feel the total threat of panic.

But suppose people are neither aware of any cherished values nor experience any threat? That is the experience of *indifference*, which, if it seems to involve all their values, becomes apathy. Suppose, finally, they are unaware of any cherished values, but still are very much aware of a threat? That is the experience of *uneasiness*, of anxiety, which, if it is total enough, becomes a deadly unspecified malaise.

Ours is a time of uneasiness and indifference—not yet formulated in such ways as to permit the work of reason and the play of sensibility. Instead of troubles—defined in terms of values and threats—there is often the misery of vague uneasiness; instead of explicit issues there is often merely the beat feeling that all is somehow not right. Neither the values threatened nor whatever threatens them has been stated; in short, they have not been carried to the point of decision. Much less have they been formulated as problems of social science.

In the 'thirties there was little doubt—except among certain deluded business circles that there was an economic issue which was also a pack of personal troubles. In these arguments about "the crisis of capitalism," the formulations of Marx and the many unacknowledged re-formulations of his work probably set the leading terms of the issue, and some men came to understand their personal troubles in these terms. The values threatened were plain to see and cherished by all; the structural contradictions that threatened them also seemed plain. Both were widely and deeply experienced. It was a political age.

But the values threatened in the era after World War Two are often neither widely acknowledged as values nor widely felt to be threatened. Much private uneasiness goes unformulated; much public malaise and many decisions of enormous structural relevance never become public issues. For those who accept such inherited values as reason and freedom, it is the uneasiness itself that is the trouble; it is the indifference itself that is the issue. And it is this condition, of uneasiness and indifference, that is the signal feature of our period.

All this is so striking that it is often interpreted by observers as a shift in the very kinds of problems that need now to be formulated. We are frequently told that the problems of our decade, or even the crises of our period, have shifted from the external realm of economics and now have to do with the quality of individual life—in fact with the question of whether there is soon going to be anything that can properly be called individual life. Not child labor but comic books, not poverty but mass leisure, are at the center of concern. Many great public issues as well as many private troubles

are described in terms of "the psychiatric"—often, it seems, in a pathetic attempt to avoid the large issues and problems of modern society. Often this statement seems to rest upon a provincial narrowing of interest to the Western societies, or even to the United States—thus ignoring two-thirds of mankind; often, too, it arbitrarily divorces the individual life from the larger institutions within which that life is enacted, and which on occasion bear upon it more grievously than do the intimate environments of childhood.

Problems of leisure, for example, cannot even be stated without considering problems of work. Family troubles over comic books cannot be formulated as problems without considering the plight of the contemporary family in its new relations with the newer institutions of the social structure. Neither leisure nor its debilitating uses can be understood as problems without recognition of the extent to which malaise and indifference now form the social and personal climate of contemporary American society. In this climate, no problems of "the private life" can be stated and solved without recognition of the crisis of ambition that is part of the very career of men at work in the incorporated economy.

It is true, as psychoanalysts continually point out, that people do often have "the increasing sense of being moved by obscure forces within themselves which they are unable to define." But it is not true, as Ernest Jones asserted, that "man's chief enemy and danger is his own unruly nature and the dark forces pent up within him." On the contrary: "Man's chief danger" today lies in the unruly forces of contemporary society itself, with its alienating methods of production, its enveloping techniques of political domination, its international anarchy—in a word, its pervasive transformations of the very "nature" of man and the conditions and aims of his life.

It is now the social scientist's foremost political and intellectual task—for here the two coincide—to make clear the elements of contemporary uneasiness and indifference. It is the central demand made upon him by other cultural workmen—by physical scientists and artists, by the intellectual community in general. It is because of this task and these demands, I believe, that the social sciences are becoming the common denominator of our cultural period, and the sociological imagination our most needed quality of mind.

DISCUSSION QUESTIONS

1. Identify a current social problem, preferably an issue that appears to be global in nature. Discuss the root causes of this problem and then attempt to relate it to the troubles of individuals closest to the problem. Finally, attempt to determine if this particular problem has any connection to the troubles you have experienced in your everyday life.
2. Think about the students on your campus. Do they possess the sociological imagination? Whether you think they do or don't, provide some evidence to support your assessment.

<hr>

READING 2

Lost Worlds and Modern Sociology

Charles Lemert

We grow up in a world not of our own choosing, and where we end up is in no small part a result of those origins and the social places we find ourselves in throughout our lives. This is the central theme of Charles Lemert's essay, which rearticulates a call for a renewed commitment to the sociological imagination.

What makes his call different in emphasis from C. Wright Mills's is his insistence that we must look to the past, to the lost worlds that continue to shape our lives today. In addition, Lemert makes an implicit case for viewing sociology as something that

often is and should be an activity of ordinary people, and not simply a pursuit of professional sociologists.

All children grow up as best they can, comfortably or miserably, in what sociologists are inclined to call worlds—a term meant to suggest not so much the geographical globe as the force of all the social things into which a child is born. Social worlds, thus, comprise everything from the social events occurring near about a crib or playroom to the larger, hard-for-a-child-to-imagine global structures.

All sociologists, we should remind ourselves, were once children. In the 1940s, Darlene Loving, David Bennett, and I grew up with the playthings set before us by the then rising tide of white, middle-class American affluence. Some seventy years before, in the 1870s, many of the first generation of professional sociologists grew up with what their worlds structured into their lives. Max Weber, as a child in Germany, played with upper-middle-class social toys provided by his demanding but well-off father. Somewhat the same, Charlotte Perkins enjoyed the intellectual and artistic benefits of Providence, Rhode Island. Yet, because her father (Frederick Perkins) essentially abandoned them, Charlotte and her mother suffered economically—a fact of her world which may well have shaped her views of the man-made world, just as little Max Weber's adult interest in authority may have been influenced by his boyhood fears of his father's ugly temper. The worlds, small and big, into which children grow very often determine who they become and how they think about social things.

At about the same time in the 1870s when Max and Charlotte played in Berlin and Providence, a boy of African descent grew up among whites in Great Barrington, a small town in the Berkshires of western Massachusetts. Willie, as he was then known about town,[1] was even less well acquainted with his father than Charlotte had been with hers, and he was decidedly poorer even than she. Nor did Willie and his mother enjoy the bourgeois splendor of the Weber home in Berlin. Just the same, Willie grew up to become a famously disciplined scholar—just as disciplined and just as much a lover of European culture as Max. Like Charlotte and Max, Willie came eventually to practice his sociological competence in public life. Little Willie of Great Barrington grew up to be W. E. B. Du Bois—sociologist and historian, journalist and man of letters, political organizer, and, through much of the twentieth century, for many, the acknowledged spiritual and intellectual leader of black people worldwide.

Kids grow up by coming to understand the worlds of their childhoods. The sociological imagination is first practiced early in life as children try to imagine the meaning of their experiences with others. Their attempts to understand may at first find expression in the way they play. Those frightened children in Poland did not comprehend the structured world of Soviet secret police, but they hugged each other in a game of mutual understanding—a close enough grasp of the situation. Willie Du Bois had such an experience when he was a schoolboy in the 1870s. More than twenty years later, in *The Souls of Black Folk,* his most famous book, Du Bois remembered the story from his world of white children's play, and retold it:

> It is in the early days of rollicking boyhood that the revelation first bursts upon one, all in a day, as it were. I remember well when the shadow swept across me. I was a little thing, away up in the hills of New England, where the dark Housatonic winds between Hoosac and Taghkanic to the sea. In a wee wooden schoolhouse, something put it into the boys' and girls' heads to buy gorgeous visiting cards—ten cents a package—and exchange. The exchange was merry, till one girl, a tall newcomer, refused my card—refused it peremptorily, with a glance. Then it dawned upon me with a certain suddenness that I was different from the others; or like, mayhap, in heart and life and longing, but shut out from their world by a vast veil.[2]

One can only guess what he might have felt at the very moment of the refusal. The first rush of feeling must have been confusion followed by embarrassment, if not quite yet indignation, at this surprising intrusion upon a world in which he had known little of what he later came to call the color line.

You can be sure that Willie the child did not at the time have in mind the ideas with which he would later describe his feelings. Like Charlotte in her sickroom, Du Bois could have been crushed by the terrible force of the dividing lines of late-nineteenth-century America. Like her, he was not. Instead, he grew into indignation and the determination to change the world. After years of schoolwork at Fisk University, then Harvard and the University of Berlin, and experience with life in the world beyond that New England village, Du Bois learned to think through the experience of his childhood. From these reflections and musings came such mature sociological ideas as the famous one with which he began *The Souls of Black Folk:* "The problem of the Twentieth Century is the problem of the color line." Few social ideas have been more true, as we who live close to the end of the twentieth century realize full well. A very great deal of Du Bois's many writings thereafter were devoted, one way or another, to the historical and sociological analysis of the *color line*—of the way arbitrary racial divisions are at the foundation of social organization in the United States and most European and other societies.

The sociological life is a process of many rememberings by which individuals go back deep into their earliest years, even to the days few can remember at all, in order to reconstruct, as Du Bois did, the social meaning of those lost worlds. Lost worlds may seem a strange phrase to use in relation to the sociological imagination. One supposes that the imagination is a kind of dream of the future. But dreams cannot come from nothing. The imagination draws on past, as well as present, experience for its material. Just as it can be said that adult life is a continual retelling of the stories of childhood, so the sociological life is a reliving of the events of the past—an attempt to put into new stories the pains and pleasures that shaped us when we first stepped into the world such as it is. In Du Bois's life, the actual events of that little schoolhouse party may not have occurred exactly as he later retold them. Few of us remember the past exactly. Whatever the precise facts of that party were, they helped make Du Bois who he was to be: "Then it dawned upon me with a certain suddenness that I was different from the others; or like, mayhap, in heart and life and longing, but shut out from their world by a vast veil." The veil by which the color line in many societies shuts out blacks and others is produced throughout, and by, those societies at every level of their organization. But the veil works its effects in such little moments as the childishly vicious refusal of a party card. People thus refused, like those in a position to refuse, begin to understand their social worlds, if they do at all, when they remember the lost worlds of the past, and retell those worlds in stories.

The sociological imagination includes, with rare exception, a coming out from a dark, isolated personal place into the light of possibility. The coming out is easier, and the possibilities are greater, when it occurs in an already somewhat well-developed collective life. Children, including heterosexual ones like Darlene and me, who come out to their adolescent world of sexual feelings present themselves to a world already well advertised. Others, like all those kids of my generation who only later found pleasure in life as gays or lesbians, usually suffer in a dark closet of social shame. For them, especially those who still do not dare to present themselves for what they are or wish to be, coming out is much harder—as it must be for children, even for adults, who face social things they do not fully understand. Great Barrington, white and rural, offered little to Willie Du Bois that would have taught him about the color line, just as Charlotte Perkins Gilman as a girl had

only the vague image of her female relatives, notably Harriet Beecher Stowe, to suggest that women can be in the world on other than manmade terms. This is what makes sociologists like Du Bois and Gilman so amazing to behold. They did what they did with little or no support. Though there were race-men and feminists before them, they were available at best as shadowy forms, as whispers between the lines of adult talk. Du Bois and Gilman learned to recover the lost worlds of their early days largely on their own.

Whether one does it alone or in the company of others, the recollection of the lost worlds of the past is that without which the sociological life cannot move forward. But this, most definitely, is *not* an exercise of the individual alone. Even Du Bois and Gilman learned from the wider social worlds of their times. Du Bois's rejection at the hand of a snotty white girl must have festered inside for years. The imagination arose when he rethought and retold that story in his head, even perhaps years later in Europe, where his black skin made no evident difference, not at least to the German girl who wanted to be his wife and whom he refused out of love because he knew what they would face upon returning to the United States. But the retelling of these rejections can reach the imaginative heights necessary to a sociology of the world in all its powerful social reaches only when the true past is remembered for what it is. This is what Du Bois did. It may be too simple to say that the story of the children's mean little party led to his sociology of racial division in the United States and throughout the world. But it would not be wrong to suppose that that story and many others were the stock in which he stirred subsequent learning and experience. The sociological imagination is a soup boiling up from leftovers. It whets the appetite because it is familiar yet sustaining for the days ahead.

The days of childhood, like all those along the course of life, are people-filled. To speak of our social worlds is to speak of lives with the pals and bigots of our playgrounds, and many others as well. If one is to live the sociological life fully, then it must be lived in the wider worlds. Hence, the surprising, but true, idea that just as the individual life must reimagine the lost worlds of its childhood, so the collective life of even the modern world itself is built out of, and requires, a retelling of stories of *its* collective pasts—of the pasts out of which the modernized and westernizing portions of the globe created the social structures in which, for better or worse, nearly everyone must live.

The social worlds in which we live locally are often several in number and different in kind. Upon encountering the white, excluding world in Great Barrington, Massachusetts, Du Bois realized that he must ever thereafter live in two worlds at once. This experience was at the heart of his most famous line about the twoness of African-American experience:

> One ever feels his twoness,—an American, a Negro; two souls, two thoughts, two unreconciled strivings; two warring ideals in one dark body, whose dogged strength alone keeps it from being torn asunder.[3]

If a person's soul is double, then it is because he must live in two worlds at once. Du Bois's idea of *double consciousness,* or twoness, applies to the experience of many in addition to those who suffered as he did. Though she did not put it the same way, it is plain that Gilman also understood that she lived in two social worlds at once—the man-made one that defined reality for nearly everyone, and the silent one of women confined to their rooms.

It is more common for those who live in the excluded, veiled places of the world to be vividly aware of the twoness or many-ness of their social realities. But even comfortable white boys like Max Weber and Emile Durkheim had the experience. Emile, for example, came from many generations of Orthodox Jewish rabbis. His father wanted him to follow in the tradition.

Yet something in his childhood experience in rural France in the 1870s exposed him to the world of secular learning and nudged him out into the wider world of Paris, and the modern urban world, where he was accorded much respect even while being subject to those who hate Jewish people. Though some have safer passage than others, few are given a free ride through the world that stands outside their childhood streets and villages. The infant is born into a small world surrounding her crib, but soon enough, over the years, she grows into awareness of other worlds—first the worlds of gossipy stories her caretakers chat about as she plays, then the worlds of small differences in early school, then eventually the wider worlds of state and nation, of the global situation. All the great sociologists of the past followed this path of discovery, leaving behind the worlds of their youth in rural France or Massachusetts, or urban Berlin or Providence.

Professional sociology, as it is practiced in the colleges and universities, differs from practical sociology chiefly for having accepted the obligation to speak about the modern world and its powerful structures. Pure, practical people have the option to pretend, at their peril, that the bigger social things won't bother them. The professionals do not. Needless to say, as we know from the stories of Du Bois and Gilman, this does not mean that the professionals ignore the stories of their childhood, any more than it means that the practical cannot understand the modern world. But what distinguishes the professionals is that, one way or another, they come to an understanding of the modern world as a whole. It's their job. That they do this work is what can make the professionals excellent field guides to living the practical sociological life. Professional sociology's dedication to describing the modern world is a constant encouragement and reminder to the rest that the sociological life is also a life in a world of big, usually national or global, social things. Such intimidating worlds as the modern one have their characteristic features about which we must learn to speak.

One of the most unsettling features of the modern world is that, over the last several centuries, Europeans and North Americans have created a vast and complicated social world by imposing their view of social things on many people in most parts of the globe. Another, still less generous, though entirely accurate, way to put this is that the modern world created by Europeans and Americans was organized out of a succession of colonizing adventures. For example, Native Americans (southern and northern) were brought under the sway of European culture and morality through the colonizing world explorations of the late fifteenth and early sixteenth centuries. Americans today very often consider 1492, the year Christopher Columbus landed in the West Indies, as the birth year of their New World civilization and culture.

To refer to the beginnings of the modern world, much less of a proud nation state like the United States, as a process of colonization may offend patriotic feelings, but there is no better word. *Colonization* is, simply put, the process whereby people with power and wealth (usually prestige as well) get the peculiar notion that their idea of how to run things gives them the right to take over the lands, sometimes the properties, and often even the minds of some other people who are usually not in a position to defend themselves. Religious missionaries are a famous example. All those priests and lesser Christians who followed Columbus thought they were doing the Taino people of the West Indies a big favor. Depending on your point of view, they may have. But, for all the good they may have done, slavery and syphilis soon followed. Colonizers are known to rationalize their conquests with the soothing idea that they are bringing the inhabitants of the lands taken a better morality, political system, or way of life. But, more often than not, they skip the niceties. The slave traders who colonized West Africa in order to capture people to be sold to the colonizers of the Americas seemed not to have given the least thought to bettering the lives of the people who suffered the middle passage, transported in deadly ship holds, only to face even worse in the Americas.

Still, there are some ways in which we might speak of colonizing as less than overtly malicious. Parents and a few schoolteachers could be said to be the colonizers of the minds or moral appetites of the children under their charge. Though colonizing is a tricky business wherever and whenever it is done, many parents and some teachers actually do some good. As an adult who remembers his own childish behaviors, I would not, as a rule, want to trust most children to their own devices. Colonizing of this gentle, perhaps necessary, kind may also be at work in the process whereby nations are made out of other people's lands, but, if so, only as an accident of the process. In Connecticut are two Native American tribes who have learned the capitalist trade very well and, hence, have built fabulously successful casinos. All the white folks thereabouts depend on their generosity to pay the state's bills. And things in India proper got no worse, and generally have gotten better, after the British gave up in 1948. Many *post-colonial* people who have survived the colonizers are able to do well with what they learned under colonial rule. But most do not. If child rearing is sometimes the more gentle and necessary sort of colonizing, nation and world building are usually the more harsh. Still, in both, the genteel and the wicked are working their ways.

What is usually called "*the* modern world" (as though there were only one of them) is no less a product of colonizing than any other of the imperial civilizations of the past—the Babylonian, the Roman, the Incan, the Sioux, or the Ottoman. What separates "the" modern world-system from many of the prior ones is that its colonizers indulged themselves the belief that what *they* were doing was much more like raising children than slave trading. In 1804 and 1805, when Lewis and Clark explored the upper Missouri River of the newly acquired Northwest plains of the United States, they were accustomed to addressing the Mandan and Nez Percé Indians as "children" when they spoke on behalf of the great white "father" in Washington, D.C., Thomas Jefferson. Lewis and Clark were actually very nice young men. Their problem was that they thought as all good European and American colonizers thought. Little did even they suspect that the indigenous peoples who saved their lives and opened the riverways to them would soon be victims of American avarice.

Modern world colonizers tend to be caught in a sociological contradiction. Colonizing is dirty business, by any standard—whether it is the taking of slaves and lands or, as today, the hawking of capitalist commodities to third-world villagers who need peace and clean water more than basketball shoes and deadly cigarettes. Yet these modern colonizers generally want to think of themselves as doing good even when it is usually bad they are doing to the people whose worlds they take away. The moral burden of this contradiction is perfectly evident, if sometimes overlooked, in the myths the modern colonizers pass down to their children and other true believers.

One of the most frequently repeated myths of the modern world is one associated with its very beginnings around 1500. Nearly every school-child in the United States (and other places as well) is taught that what made Christopher Columbus such a great explorer was that he set off from Spain in spite of the fact that everyone else believed the world was flat. This is a nice story but one without foundation. Columbus had no fear that he would fall off the edge of the world because those in that day who made it their business to study the subject (explorers most of all) knew very well that the world was spherical.

Where Columbus and most of the New World explorers were innocent was in their naive belief that they had discovered, not America, but a new route to India, China, and Japan. Columbus spent quite a lot of time on his first voyages looking for the great Asian ruler (not to mention their gold) in the forests and mountains of Cuba. As we know, things turned out differently. They found other commodities as good as gold, one of which was smoking tobacco, of which Europeans were ignorant and to which the Taino people of the West Indies were addicted. This single commodity made so much gold over the centuries that today its purveyors are among the most greedy and corrupt capitalists one could imagine.

Capitalism has had better representatives than these, but they will do as an illustration of the addictive effects of the modern world on human consciousness. Such an effect was, in fact, brought to the New World by Columbus himself. He arrived in the new land—which he probably took to be Japan, then widely understood to be a well-developed and mighty civilization. He disembarked on the shore of this world with a laughably puny contingent of three small ships and ninety armed men. As European explorers were inclined to do, upon disembarking from the *Santa Maria,* Columbus, thus meagerly armed, planted the flag of Queen Isabella and proclaimed the land Spain's and himself its governor general (his right by the terms of his contract with the queen). He was saved from this foolishness by the fact that he encountered, not a powerful people of the Indies proper, but the friendly and welcoming Taino "Indians" of the West Indies. But this does not excuse the absurdity of his beliefs. Columbus, and most who followed him, believed that a few good European men had only to present themselves in order to claim their rightful place as the rulers of whoever might be present. Rulers they became in fact, and whatever good has issued from their presumptions, so too has a lot of misery for the original people of the Caribbean and millions of others across the North and South American islands and plains, to say nothing of the peoples of Africa, Asia, the South Seas, and the Arctic.

The myth of Columbus the colonizer, like most of the big stories modern people believe about their history, illustrates the peculiar problem moderns face in coming to a coherent sociology of their world. They want to believe that their world is better than others (most colonizers do), even the best that ever was (as Americans, especially, do). Yet they do the same dirty little deeds that any colonizer must do. It is not just that the Europeans who settled North America stole land from the indigenous people. It is also devastatingly true that they killed, maimed, and infected the bodies and cultures of those people. The color line of racial divisions of which Du Bois wrote is just one of the several disgusting consequences of what is too often called simply "modernization," as though the path of human progress inevitably passed without consequence to others along the westward line of European and American migrations.

Modernization is the customary professional term for the process whereby the far surfaces of the globe come under the influence of modern Western political, economic, and cultural systems. It is a term that attributes an unwarranted inevitability to the course of social things. It suggests that the modern world has come to be what it is out of some deeper moral urging of human history. Even those who prefer to speak of *postmodernism* (the idea that the modern world has broken down of late into not very well organized social fragments) are sometimes inclined to share the view that modernization is so inevitable that whatever succeeds it, succeeds it inevitably. Few human things, and fewer social ones, are so rigidly predetermined. So, whenever one gets the drift of talk about inevitability in human history, it is safe to suppose that some part of the story is not being told. One could say that modernization is one of those sociological concepts that may describe some things superficially well, but fails to expose the dirty underbelly of the societies and histories it describes.

Much like little boys and girls, the culture of the modern world is a culture that never has quite known what to say about the lost worlds upon which it has been, and is being, founded. The lost worlds of modernity are, to be sure, the worlds of the Lakota Sioux and Mandan peoples, of the slaves taken from West Africa, of the immigrant workers from China or Ireland, of the women, and of all the others, and their children, upon whose backs the modern world was built. Had it not been for pioneering writers like Gilman and Du Bois and hundreds of others who, over this century, insisted upon telling the stories of those consigned to labor in the galleys, holds, and engine rooms of the ship of modern progress, we might not today be learning more than any previous generation of their lost worlds.

But there is another sense in which the sociology of the modern world has always had to remember lost worlds. Modern urban and industrial societies all emerged, of course, from a rural past. In the first generations of factory workers of whom Marx wrote, for example, there were those whose parents or grandparents had still lived in rural villages and worked the fields or had settled frontier towns in the American West, the Australian outback, the interior of Africa. The modern world of the industrial system and the urban centers was built, quite literally, upon once open fields and dense forests, with the labors of settlers as well as slaves, ranchers as well as field workers, wheat farmers as well as their silenced women. Just as a number of freed slaves built good lives, so a good many settlers failed. Success and failure do not fall neatly on either side of the walls of injustice. Many people overcame the hardships of the agrarian premodern world. A very good many people whose grandchildren migrated to the new cities in the nineteenth century had good reason to love the simpler life in small villages and towns of late premodern times, and thus to regret, deeply, the passing of this life before the progressive force of the modern world—the railroads, the cities, the factories, the automobile, and worse yet today.

All of us today whether we suffer still the injuries of childhood or have found a way to overcome, must deal with the past of the modern. Whether that past is the lost world of the terrible things done to one's ancestors or the past of social privilege, the collective past of the modern is all those ignored and forgotten miseries of abuse, yes; but it is also longings for the simpler life sacrificed to progress. These all were the worlds through which the modern colonizers marched to make a new world.

Behind its glitter and boasting lie the lost pasts of the modern world. Until the past is remembered and spoken about, no world will be truly better. Modern, or postmodern, sociologies, whether practical or professional, must be able to imagine those lost worlds. Without them there is no way to understand the present or face the future. Without those lost worlds, well remembered, there is no way to imagine the structures of power and inequality that determine the present and frustrate some people's futures. Just as Du Bois's sociology of the color line drew upon his recollection of the lost world of a hurtful party gesture, so what any sociologist today might have to say about the social world in its largest aspect depends on a collective recalling to the social mind of what modernity has wished to forget—the rural pasts some still long for, the man–made world some still struggle to maintain, the forgotten Lakota slaughtered at Wounded Knee, the world of our ancestors who died in filthy ship holds on the middle passage, and all the rest.

The personal courage of sociological work is that of being able to remember what one might wish had never happened. Yet this is what sociology must do, and it is what professional sociology, over the years, has done as well as it knew how. . .

REFERENCES

1. On the use of the name Willie, see David Levering Lewis, *W. E. B. Du Bois: Biography of a Race* (Henry Holt, 1993), chapter 3.
2. *W. E. B. Du Bois, The Souls of Black Folk* (1903; reprint, Bantam Books, 1989), p. 2.
3. Ibid., p. 3.

DISCUSSION QUESTIONS

1. Think back to your own childhood in order to identify and discuss what you consider to be the most significant events or experiences that have shaped your life and contributed to making you who you are.
2. Choose a famous or infamous person who has had a marked impact on some event in the history of the 20th century and discuss how this individual's background can be used to comprehend why it is that they became famous or infamous.

CULTURE AND SOCIETY

Travelers often experience a phenomenon known as culture shock. What this means is that certain taken-for-granted features of everyday life are called into question by a society that, quite simply, functions in ways unfamiliar to the outsider. Culture shock is often startling and uncomfortable. This experience points to two important features of culture: first, that cultures are plastic and diverse; and second, that we tend to accept much about our own culture in a fairly unreflective and habitual manner. Unfamiliar surroundings often result in stimulating people to look at the familiar in a new light. Sometimes it leads to what is known as ethnocentrism, whereby individuals make invidious comparisons between the supposed superiority of their own culture and the shortcomings of the one they are visiting. However, at other times, and this is typically what happens with seasoned travelers, it leads to an appreciation of difference and an ability to see one's own culture in a new and more critical light.

But what exactly do we mean by culture? The term is relatively easy to define. A typical textbook definition of culture describes it as the beliefs, values, norms, behaviors, language, and material artifacts characteristic of a way of life for a particular social group. Culture is generally viewed as that which makes possible the taken-for-granted or habitual character of much of everyday life. For example, most of us were probably not explicitly taught that we should maintain a particular body distance from a person we are speaking to in public. However, when someone violates that space, intruding too closely for comfort, we realize that the person does not share our sense of what we consider to be appropriate body distance. A shared culture is a moral force that serves to regulate and coordinate social interaction. It channels and guides not only our behaviors, but also our desires and our sense of purpose.

In the modern world, culture envelops our lives in a series of concentric circles. Some aspects of culture operate at the civilizational level. Among the things we can point to at this macrocultural level are the ways we structure, perceive, and experience space and time. It can also include the division of the social world into the public and private realms, and the understanding that certain activities are only appropriate in one or the other of these realms, which according to the late German-born sociologist Norbert Elias is part of what he referred to as the "civilizing process."

Culture operates at the societal level as well, as the traveler example suggests. Compare, for example, the United States and Sweden, both affluent, advanced industrial nations with much in common. Nonetheless, whereas the former has a weak welfare state, Sweden has one of the strongest in the world. Why is this the case? Although not the whole story, at least part of the answer rests with the fact that whereas U.S. culture places a premium on individualism, Swedish culture values communal solidarity.

Culture also functions at the intersocietal level as various groups in a particular society respond to the dominant cultural values in a variety of ways. Especially in large and heterogeneous societies, a variety of subcultures exist, being both part of the larger culture and carving out a unique niche within it. At the same time, countercultures, which maintain an adversarial stance toward the larger culture, are also common.

Finally, we can also speak about a culture industry in modern societies. This includes the gatekeepers of elite or high culture as well as the creators of mass or popular culture. It includes those involved in the cultural diffusion and creolization that is leading to cultural spheres no longer simply identified with or limited to particular nations.

The articles in this section afford something of the flavor of the range of topics located under the rubric "culture and society."

Experiencing the Week

Eviatar Zerubavel

Many aspects of our everyday lives are perceived to be unchanging givens that we think little about, if at all. For example, we tend to take for granted the seven-day cycle we call "the week." It appears to be natural and inevitable. However, Eviatar Zerubavel reveals in this excerpt from his book, The Seven Day Circle, *that the week is a human construction, albeit one that has become so deeply implanted in our culture that we rarely think twice about it. In the process of illustrating this claim about the constructed character of the week, he helps us look with a new eye at this important feature of our daily routines.*

We very often think of time in mathematical terms, that is, as homogenous quantities of duration. From this mathematical standpoint, one hour is essentially interchangeable with any other hour, as both consist of precisely sixty minutes. However, as Henri Bergson demonstrated in his seminal work on the psychology of time, mathematically equivalent durations can nevertheless be experienced as having quite different qualitative "intensities" or feeling tones.[1] His work made us aware of our *qualitative experience of time* as a heterogeneous entity.

Bergson's theory, however, was essentially psychological, and obviously lacked a sociological dimension. The necessity of the latter was made clear a few years later, when sociologist Henri Hubert pointed out that the source of the differing feeling tones of mathematically equivalent durations is very often society.[2] Thus, for example, it is only the Church that makes Lent experientially different from any other forty-weekday period within the calendar year, and it is the university that is responsible for making the examinations week "feel" like no other week in the semester. Similarly, it is

American society that, by commemorating the last three decades of the eighteenth century far more intensively than any other thirty-year period in its history, manages to attach different meanings to historical periods of equal duration.[3]

THE WEEKEND

One of the classic manifestations of humans' qualitative experience of time is the cultural differentiation among the seven days of the week. Despite their physical-mathematical equivalence, these twenty-four-hour intervals are socially regarded as seven distinct types of days with entirely different feeling tones.

"Periods of time acquire specific qualities by virtue of association with the activities peculiar to them."[4] First-graders, for example, already associate Tuesday with having to prepare their weekly mathematics home assignment, whereas women whose husbands take evening classes on that day may come to associate it with a less elaborate dinner and longer telephone conversations. Likewise, for parents whose older child has after-school activities on Wednesday, the latter may come to "mean" an exclusive afternoon with their younger child. Yet the days of the week acquire their distinctive meanings not only from the activities occurring within them, but also as parts of a larger pattern,[5] and particularly from their temporal location vis-à-vis other days. Thus, for example, for those who take regular music lessons every Thursday, Wednesday may "mean" the last day on which they can still practice their études. Similarly, for teachers who have a heavy schedule on Mondays, Sunday may "mean" a bad night for going out.

Various days often function as the principal temporal landmark or milestone within the weekly cycle, with respect to which all the other days of the cycle acquire their distinctive meanings. Consider, for example the special significance of Thursday for lovers who meet regularly as well as exclusively on it,[6] or for,

> certain unemployed urban Negro men who bide their time until Thursday night, typically the suburban Negro maid's night off, whereupon they drive to the railroad station, pick up one of the girls, and enjoy a night of revelry and profit. The period between these Thursday nights is defined as "dead" time—a period of social inactivity.[7]

Along similar lines, those who get paid on Friday often regard that day as the pivot on which the entire week turns.[8] By the same token, for those working in a newspaper that is regularly published every Wednesday, Tuesday and Thursday may come to "mean" preparation for Press Day and cleaning after it, respectively.[9] However, all the above idiosyncrasies notwithstanding, it is basically the *weekend* that, for most of us, functions as the principal temporal milestone with respect to which all the other days of the week acquire their distinctive meanings.

Consider, for example, the way we normally experience Monday: "If a person feels blah, acts sluggishly, and cannot easily make decisions, there may not be anything deeply wrong with him or her; it may simply be Monday."[10] Monday's notorious association with gloominess and low morale is so strong in our culture that, upon warning her readers not to expect much passion and melodrama in her novel *Shirley,* Charlotte Brontë simply indicates that "something unromantic as Monday morning" lies before them.[11] The general feelings associated with this day range from anger[12] to melancholy. Cartoonist Jim Davis's cat Garfield defines it as "a day designed to add depression to an otherwise happy week,"[13] and the lover in the song "Monday, Monday" complains that, while "every other day of the week is fine," Monday mornings usually find him crying.[14]

While cartoons and popular songs often provide us with some penetrating insights into the human soul, the "hard" evidence is even more compelling. Consider, for example, the fact that almost half of all sickness spells begin on Monday and that it is the busiest day in hospital emergency rooms.[15] It is quite hard not to take a cynical stance and see this association of Monday with the highest rates of absenteeism from work[16] as a modern version of the so-called "cult of Saint Monday"[17] that has haunted employers at least since the Industrial Revolution. As cultural historian Lawrence Wright has so wittily observed, "viruses seem able to distinguish between shift workers and day workers, and can even understand the calendar. They tend to make day workers go sick on Mondays, but very few shift workers go sick on a Monday which falls in their rest period.[18] At the same time, however, it is impossible to be cynical about clinical evidence such as the excess proportion of cardiac deaths—normally indicative of some serious psychological stress—among men on Monday.[19] Even more compelling is the fact that, of the seven days of the week, Monday is clearly the one with the highest suicide rates.[20]

Only a nonmedical, sociological explanation can account for these findings. That so many people attempt suicide, suffer sudden cardiac death, call in sick, or else are depressed, irritable, and full of complaints on Mondays can be explained only by the latter's temporal location vis-à-vis the weekend. The sharp contrast between Monday and the day immediately preceding it is the most distinctive experiential characteristic of that day. Thus, for example, in the song "Sunday," a lover feels blue every Monday, when thinking over Sunday.[21] Likewise, in another song, it is essentially a "Sunday kind of love" that a lover feels she needs in order to keep her warm "when Mondays are cold."[22] Mondays are experienced as "cold" because they are associated with the transition from the attractive world of rest, playfulness, lack of responsibility, and intensive contact with loved ones to the serious, mundane, and demanding world of work. These experiential characteristics of Monday morning often rub off on parts of Sunday as well. The mere anticipation of the approaching day they dread and regard as their least favorite day of the week leads many people to experience sometimes a sort of "Sunday evening (or even afternoon) blues."

That Monday's distinctive qualities are essentially a function of its temporal location immediately following the weekend becomes even more obvious once we contrast them with those of the day immediately preceding the weekend, Friday. Not surprisingly, these two days, which share no other characteristic in an exclusive manner, are sometimes coupled, as in the following aphoristic allusion to the fundamental contrast between sybaritic hedonists and compulsive workaholics: "There are two kinds of persons—those who look forward to Friday and those who look forward to Monday." The contrasting cultural meanings of these two days are most clearly a function of their contrastive relationship to the weekend. Whereas Monday, the postweekend day, is normally associated with a dreadful sense of "there we go again, back to the same routine," Friday, the preweekend day, is usually associated with an elated feeling of "it's finally over." The complementary cultural counterpart of the notion of "blue Monday"[23] is, thus, the popular expression "Thank God it's Friday" (TGIF).[24] Not surprisingly, in contrast to the "cult of Saint Monday," Friday is the least popular day for sickness spells to begin,[25] and is normally characterized by a considerably cheerful mood.[26] (One Friday afternoon, when I asked one of our secretaries why she was looking so cheerful, she replied "it's Friday" and seemed genuinely astonished at my having asked such a silly question.)

While clearly not a part of the actual weekend (after all, it is a day on which one still goes to work or school), Friday is nevertheless considered by many their favorite day of the week, because it involves an experience many of us evidently cherish, namely, anticipation. For those of us who already as very young children

often found pleasure in counting down the days remaining before the weekend and who possibly even prefer the experience of anticipating the weekend to the experience of the weekend itself, weekends may feel as anticlimactic as are homestretches to runners who have already established their victory long before the race is officially over. After all, on Friday we can experience a feeling that we can never experience on the weekend itself, namely, that there are still a couple of weekend days before us! In fact, some people therefore find Thursday, which involves the anticipation of both the weekend and Friday, even more gratifying than the latter. (The anticipated weekend, however, must be experienced as being within reach, which explains why few people, if any, consider Tuesday or even Wednesday their favorite day of the week.)

Let us not forget, however, that it is basically the attractiveness of the weekend that accounts for that of Friday. It is Saturday that D. Gates has in mind when claiming, in his song "Saturday Child," that there are seven days in a week made to choose from, but only one is right for him.[27] It is Sunday that is portrayed in the song "Sunday in the Park" as the best day, the day we keep on looking forward to all week long.[28] It is Saturday and Sunday that can also boast the lowest suicide rates.[29]

Much of the attractiveness of the weekend can be attributed to the suspension of work-related—or, for the young, school-related—obligations. Admittedly, there are some people who do look forward to Monday rather than Friday and who may even feel a particular sense of accomplishment when they manage to work during the weekend. Workaholics' compulsive need for structure is sometimes so great that they may even develop the syndrome identified by Sándor Ferenczi as "Sunday neurosis."[30] To quote Sebastian De Grazia,

the Sunday neurosis, as it sometimes is called, seems fairly widespread in the milder form as a malady exhibiting a peculiar uneasiness rather than true anxiety on free-time days. The lack of structure to the days opens them up to choice, and choices without a guiding pattern may lead either to temptation or to reflection, which then leads to a feeling of not knowing how to act, of existing without purpose.[31]

Most people, however, prefer Fridays to Mondays and usually seem to resent having to work during the weekend, despite the considerable benefits and advantages it often entails— higher pay, lighter traffic to and from work, and a far more relaxed working atmosphere (less supervision, a rather informal dress code, and so on). That is why hospital staff, for example, who can easily swap a Wednesday shift or night on call for a Tuesday one, can hardly ever do that with a Saturday shift or night on call, and why "fair" hospital administrators do their very best to avoid scheduling them for work two weekends in a row.[32] It has also been demonstrated that the quality of one's work is somewhat lower on weekends than on ordinary weekdays.[33]

Most of us seem to feel that working during the weekend is essentially doing something we are not supposed to be doing. Furthermore, it also involves making an actual sacrifice. Consider, for example, a single woman who, "plans to work at home on Sunday, but she still thinks of Sundays as family days and being alone then is like being a dateless teen-ager on Saturday night."[34] The price one pays for being out of phase with the conventional weekly work/rest cycle is essentially a social one, namely depriving oneself of the opportunity to interact intensively with those whom one can see mainly during the weekend. That is why students, for example, often find it much easier to study during the weekend when their spouses, roommates, or friends are also busy studying! (For precisely the same reason, incidentally, having our weekly time off on days when our family or friends have to work robs us of much of the pleasure of being off work and often involves some sense of waste, not to mention guilt.

Those who work on Sundays and instead take Tuesdays off, for example, still get together with their friends on Saturday nights more than on Monday nights and are often quite at a loss about how they should spend Tuesdays, when most of their immediate social environment is at work.)

The quality of social interaction varies considerably between ordinary weekdays and weekends. The weekend is generally perceived as a relatively exclusive, "private" time period that is usually spent with family, lovers, and friends. (That is why nonintimates usually sound somewhat apologetic when they call us during the weekend.) Given the close relationship between exclusivity and intimacy,[35] weekend social encounters obviously tend to "mean" much more than weekday ones, which accounts for the differential symbolic significance of Saturday night and Wednesday night dates. (After all, even the prostitute portrayed by Melina Mercouri in Jules Dassin's film *Never on Sunday* would restrict her weekend sexual contacts to "nonprofessional" ones!) The link between exclusivity and intimacy also explains why interpersonal barriers are much more permeable and tend to crumble much more easily and rapidly during the weekend.[36] Thus, for example, when they get together during the weekend, even people who normally encounter one another only on businesslike occasions nevertheless interact with each other in a relatively informal manner. Office weekend picnics, usually characterized by a rather casual atmosphere and a relatively informal dress code, are a perfect case in point.

Just as one is not expected to be working during the weekend, one is also "supposed" to date, go out, and generally "have fun" on weekend (that is, Friday and especially Saturday) nights. That makes adolescents and single adults feel particularly embarrassed to be seen in public by themselves (or, still worse for adolescents, with their parents) on those nights.[37] More sadly, it is also on those nights that they tend to feel the loneliest when staying at home by themselves.[38] That is the general message one gets from the popular song with the suggestive title "Saturday Night Is the Loneliest Night of the Week."[39]

THE PULSATING WEEK

Having examined the cultural "qualities" of four of the seven days of the week (Friday, Saturday, Sunday, and Monday), we have ignored the other three. Since most people regard the weekend as the principal "temporal milestone" within the weekly cycle, whatever "qualities" Tuesday, Wednesday, and Thursday might have, they are generally experienced not quite as intensively as the other four days. In order to understand why, we should briefly reexamine the Jewish and astrological weekly cycles. Their superficial resemblance to one another notwithstanding, these two seven-day cycles were of entirely different origins. Thus, they must have also been experienced in rather strikingly different ways.

Having developed within the context of a polytheistic cosmological system, the astrological week essentially consisted of seven days, each of which was assigned to a particular planet-deity. These seven days carried relatively similar "weights," since each of them had its own distinctive cultural significance, quite independently of the others. The Jewish week, by contrast, evolved within the context of a monotheistic cosmological system and, as such, has always entailed the consecration of only one of its seven days to God. Having essentially derived from the periodic observance of the Sabbath, this week revolves entirely around it. As "the pivot on which the entire [Jewish] week turns, the day from which all others are measured,"[40] the Sabbath alone is regarded by Jews as having its own distinctive characteristics, quite independently of the other six days. As for the latter, they are traditionally divided into the three that follow the Sabbath (Sunday, Monday, and Tuesday) and the three that precede it

(Wednesday, Thursday, and Friday),[41] so that they are basically distinguished from one another only in terms of their temporal location vis-à-vis that holy day. Friday, to take one obvious example, derives its entire cultural significance in Judaism from the fact that it is the day of preparation for the Sabbath.

This fundamental difference between the ways these two seven-day cycles were experienced is also evident from the two strikingly different systems used for designating their days. As each one of the seven days of the astrological week had its own distinctive cultural significance, it also had a distinctive name that indicated its association with a particular planet-deity. Not so with the six weekdays of the Jewish week, which are essentially "anonymous."[42] These days were designated, from the very start, by ordinal numbers which indicated their temporal distance from the preceding Sabbath—"first in the Sabbath" (or simply "first day"), "second in the Sabbath," and so on.[43] This serves to remind us that their entire cultural significance in Judaism derives from their temporal location relative to the holy day. As pointed out earlier, the unusual status of the Sabbath is also evident from the fact that, back in antiquity, the same word was used to denote both the Sabbath and the entire weekly cycle as a whole.

This latter Jewish practice has been preserved to this day in Armenian (where Shapat' denotes both Saturday and the week as a whole) and, in a slightly modified form, in Romany and Serbo-Croatian as well (where Koóroki and Nedelja, respectively, denote both Sunday and the week as a whole). Neither is the practice of designating days of the week by ordinal or cardinal numbers that reflect their temporal distance from some pivotal day exclusively Jewish by any means. We have already seen, for example, various West African tribes that designate days as "market day is tomorrow," "second day of the market," and so on. Moreover, in ancient Rome, of the eight days of the market week, seven were designated in terms of their temporal distance from the eighth one—VIII Nundinas ("the eighth day before the coming market day"), VII Nundinas, VI Nundinas, V Nundinas, IIII Nundinas, III Nundinas, and Pridie Nundinas ("the day immediately preceding the market day").[44] The Jewish practice of designating days of the week in terms of their temporal distance from the preceding Sabbath has also been preserved—although, often, only in part or with some modifications—in languages as diverse as Persian, Arabic, Greek, Portuguese, Icelandic, Estonian, Lithuanian, Latvian, Russian, Polish, Slovak, Czech, Serbo-Croatian, Slovene, Hungarian, Romany, and Armenian. Finally, there are instances where the day immediately juxtaposed to the pivotal day is named relative to it. The Greeks, for example, still call Friday, the day immediately preceding the Sabbath, Paraskeyi, which means "preparation." Similarly, as the day following the Sunday rest, Monday is known as "the day after nonwork" in Polish (Poniedziałek), Russian (Ponedel'nik), Serbo-Croatian (Ponedeljak), Slovene (Ponedeljek), Slovak (Pondelok), and Czech (Pondělí).

In all the above instances, the week seems to be experienced as a sort of wave that "peaks" on some pivotal day. [Regarding the topographic imagery of peaking, note that the Basques indeed call Sunday "high" (Igandea).] The Sabbath, the Lord's Day, the market day, and the weekend are all classic examples of such *"peak days."* The Judeo-Christian week and all market weeks are fundamentally different from the astrological seven-day week as well as from most of the weeks constituting the divinatory calendars of Central America and Indonesia. Their most distinctive characteristic is the fact that they include only one day (or possibly two consecutive ones, as in the case of the modern weekend) that is culturally marked as pivotal, whereas all the other days of the cycle derive their entire cultural significance from their temporal location relative to it. In fact, had it not been for their differential temporal location relative to the "peak days," those other days would have probably been experienced as absolutely interchangeable with one another. In other words, had it not been for the "peak day" around which the entire weekly cycle seems to revolve, none of them would have even existed as days with any cultural significance!

The contrast between the astrological and Jewish versions of the seven-day week is quite analogous to the contrast between a musical passage with no clear phrasing and one where the first quarter note within each bar is distinctively accented. (Consider also the difference between eating a different kind of meat on each day of the week and eating meat on Mondays only.) As becomes quite evident from the musical analogy, only in the Jewish version do we encounter the phenomenon to which I have referred throughout this book as a seven-day *beat.* The experience of beat is essentially a sensation of a throbbing pulsation, which is why I shall henceforth refer to weekly cycles with "peak days" as *"pulsating weeks."*

Of the two original versions of the seven-day week, it is clearly the pulsating, Jewish one that has had the most profound impact on the temporal organization of modern life. The two other major monotheistic systems that have sprung out of Judaism followed in its footsteps and also adopted the pattern of consecrating only one of a series of seven days. As a result, the modifications of the identity of the original Sabbath by both Christianity and Islam as well as its more recent transformation into the essentially secularized weekend notwithstanding, the sort of "weekly" life most of us lead today basically derives from the original Jewish model of a seven-day pulsating cycle. None of the distinctive "qualities" of Friday and Monday, for example, would have been possible had we derived our notion of the week from the astrological model of a seven-day nonpulsating cycle.

Note, in this regard, that, colloquially, the words "week" and "day" often refer only to the five weekdays, thus excluding the two weekend days, as when someone inquires whether we should get together "during the week" or on the weekend, or when stores advertise their regular "daily" and weekend hours separately. In other words, of the seven days that constitute the weekly cycle, only five are actually counted as "days" that are part of the "week." The reason for that is that the other two are not considered "ordinary" days: "'The day' . . . refers, of course, only to the five days Monday through Friday: Saturday and Sunday are not counted days in the ordinary sense."[45]

Ironically, the key to a full understanding of the pulsating week as a phenomenon may actually be found in the etymology of the English word "week" (which, in its old Gothic form *wiko,* was first used as early as the fourth century[46]). The Latin word *vicis,* from which it most probably derived (along with such linguistic cousins as the Dutch *week,* the Finnish *viikko,* the Icelandic *vika,* the Swedish *vecka,* the German *woche,* the Norwegian *uke,* and the Danish *uge*), was associated with such notions as movement, change, turnabout, and alternation. The intimate relation between the pulsating week and alternation seems to provide us with the best account of the way in which we experience this phenomenon.

According to Emile Durkheim, any calendrical interruption of the otherwise continuous flow of time is a product of a fundamental human intellectual need to establish differentiation, as well as alternate, among various existential domains: "it was probably the necessity of this alternation which led men to introduce into the continuity and homogeneity of duration, certain distinctions and differentiations which it does not naturally have."[47] The most significant "break of continuity" identified by Durkheim was that between the sacred and the profane domains[48] and, thus, also between sacred and profane time. The insertion of sacred time intervals into the continuum of profane time substantiates the discontinuity between the sacred and profane domains, and

nowhere is this more evident than in the weekly observance of the Sabbath.[49] The ancient Talmudic ruling that travelers who lose count of the days of the week should nevertheless keep observing the Sabbath every seventh day despite the likelihood of its being the "wrong" day makes it quite clear that at the very heart of the institution of the Sabbath lies the periodic alternation between the sacred and the profane along a 6-1 pattern. This structural feature is far more central to Judaism than the actual temporal location of the sacred within historical time.

Durkheim's theory accounts not only for the Jewish experience of the Sabbath, but also for the way most non-Jews, as well as those who are not even particularly religious, experience the modern weekly cycle, which, after all, essentially revolves around a secularized weekend. Durkheim never restricted his notion of "the sacred" to the relatively narrow domain of institutionalized religion and actually referred with it quite broadly to anything that is collectively regarded and treated as "out of the ordinary." Thus, for him, the experience of time essentially involved periodic alternation between the ordinary and the most generally, albeit collectively, defined as "extraordinary." In fact, even his student Henri Hubert, who preceded Durkheim in pioneering the investigation of the rhythmic nature of social life, claimed that all social rhythms are basically products of the interaction between any "critical" (yet not necessarily religiously significant) days and the intervals among them.[50] However, it is Edmund Leach who has probably gone farthest in explicitly reformulating Durkheim's theory of time in this direction, claiming the primacy of our experience of temporality, "as something discontinuous, a repetition of repeated reversal, a sequence of oscillations between polar opposites."[51] According to Leach,

with a *pendulum view of time,* the sequence of things is discontinuous; time is a succession of alternations and full stops. Intervals are distinguished, not as the sequential markings on a tape measure, but as repeated opposites . . . the notion that time is a *"discontinuity of repeated contrasts"* is probably the most elementary and primitive of all ways of regarding time.[52]

We can thus view the pulsating week as a *cycle of periodic alternation between ordinary and extraordinary days.* It is the regular pendulumlike pulsation between the "on" and "off" phases of such a cycle that underlies our very experience of a seven-day "beat." The essence of the experience of the pulsating week is the fundamental cultural binary contrast between the extraordinary and the ordinary. The former is symbolically represented by "critical," "peak" days such as the Sabbath, the Lord's Day, the market day, or the weekend, as well as by such events as the Baha'i Nineteen-Day Feast or the festival dedicated to the patron deity of each Aztec "solar" twenty-day week. The latter is symbolically represented by the ordinary so-called "weekdays." Obviously, had there been no contrast between these two types of days, we would not have had a pulsating week at all.

That would have been the case either if all days were "ordinary" and culturally "unmarked," as in cultures that did not develop a weekly cycle, or if they were all equally "marked," as in nonpulsating cycles such as the astrological week and the weeks of the Central American and Indonesian divinatory calendars. However, the main cultural significance for our weekly "peak days" is the fact that they are not ordinary days. That is why, on many wall calendars, they are printed in red rather than in the ordinary black. At the same time, a concept such as "weekdays" could have evolved only within the context of such a contrast—the word has been used at least since 1477 in contrast to the market day and at least since 1546 specifically in contrast to Sunday.

The rather abstract conceptual contrast between the ordinary and the extraordinary is actually substantiated through our own behavior. It is a "message" that is conveyed quite redundantly through a variety of cultural "codes" that are designed to guarantee that we shall not miss it. Hence its ubiquitous manifestation in so many different aspects of our life. Consider, for example, the extreme, albeit instructive, case of Jewish tradition, which requires believers to walk, sit down, wash themselves, and even move things in a distinctive manner, as well as to avoid uttering any profane words and even thinking about worrisome matters, during the Sabbath.[53] All that is supposed to guarantee that they never confuse the extraordinary sacred with the ordinary profane.

The extraordinariness of certain days of the week can also be "encoded" in distinctive eating patterns. Friday, for example, still means "fast day" in both Icelandic (Föstudagur) and Gaelic (Di-haoine). The abstract conceptual contrast between the ordinary and the extraordinary can thus be manifested in the somewhat "special" nature of "peak day" meals, which often follow a "pattern which is an inversion of the mundane week."[54] Consider again the case of Jewish tradition, which requires that food consumed on the Sabbath be different from food consumed on regular weekdays.[55] The fundamental conceptual contrast between the sacred and the profane is thus substantiated by such contrasts as the one between the white Sabbath *hallah* bread and the dark rye bread of regular weekday meals, or that between the costly fish of the Sabbath and the salt herring of regular weekdays.[56]

An even more conspicuous way of "encoding" the special "qualities" of certain days of the week is through associating them regularly with distinctive types of clothing.[57] Such association is quite conventionalized, as one can learn from a set of recent Evan-Picone ads showing the same model wearing different sets of clothes, each one corresponding to, and even captioned by the name of, one particular day of the week. Sunday, for example, is represented by a formal attire in which one would attend church or family reunions, Saturday by sportive clothing usually associated with informal occasions, and both Friday and Monday (quite interchangeable, as working days) by "business" clothes. This seems to indicate that the fundamental cultural contrast between the ordinary and the extraordinary is often substantiated through a contrast between our outward appearance on regular weekdays and on weekly "peak days."

Jewish tradition, for example, puts much emphasis on the establishment of a distinctive "Sabbath look," and an entire chapter of the *Mishnah* is devoted to detailed instructions regarding one's outward appearance on Saturday.[58] Likewise, after indicating explicitly that "thy Sabbath garments should not be like thy weekday garments," the Talmud proceeds to specify that, if one cannot afford at least two distinct sets of garments, so that one can be used exclusively on the Sabbath, one should at least wear one's garments "somewhat differently" on the holy day![59] Thus, to this day, in traditional Jewish neighborhoods, one can easily recognize Saturday by men's Sabbath caps and caftans as well as by women's special jewelry.[60] Following in the footsteps of Judaism, Christianity has taken a similar stance with regard to the Lord's Day. (The special preparation toward a distinctive Sunday appearance is evident even from the fact that, in most North European languages, Saturday is still called a day of washing and laundry—Laugardagur in Icelandic, Lördag in Swedish, Lørdag in Norwegian and Danish, Lauodag in Lapp, Laupäev in Estonian, and Lauantai in Finnish.)[61] Yet the very same spirit has essentially been preserved even in the secular world of work. The very same individual who always wears well-ironed suits or high-heeled shoes from Monday through Friday is likely to drop that "professional" look and adopt a "casual" (or even "sloppy") one on weekends, wearing sneakers and dungarees and possibly even skipping shaving or putting on makeup. Furthermore, when people occasionally come during the weekend to a workplace that is usually open only between Mondays and Fridays,

one can still easily tell that it is a weekend day by the mere absence of men's ties and women's nylon stockings.

There is no basic difference between a Jew's Sabbath caftan, a Christian's "Sunday best" attire, and a white-collar worker's weekend "workclothes" (e.g., blue jeans). Nor is the common wardrobe of French miners, which consists of one outfit for work and another one for Sundays,[62] fundamentally different from that of Orthodox Jews, where storage space is often divided between weekday and Sabbath clothes.[63] All are manifestations of the symbolic use of clothing for substantiating conceptual contrasts between abstract categories such as the sacred and the profane, work and leisure, public and private, and so on.

The difference between the way we look on Monday and on Sunday is significantly greater than the difference between the way we look on Monday and on Tuesday. That, of course, is also true of the food we eat, the material we read, and even the people with whom we socialize. Ordinary "weekdays" are usually "marked" much less distinctively than "peak days," so that, physionomically speaking, they are often quite interchangeable. Hence the common depictions of days such as Tuesday and Thursday as "a day without distinction, an ordinary weekday"[64] or "the neither here nor there part of the week."[65]

Thus, the fundamental contrast between weekly "peak days" and ordinary weekdays is and needs to be substantiated through actual behavioral patterns. After all, if we were to work, dress "professionally," and eat ordinary meals even on Saturday and Sunday, these days would obviously "feel" just like any other day of the week. Whether we substantiate this contrast by eating only *hallah* bread or reading only "nonserious," "pleasure" material, however, is quite beside the point. The pulsating week is a cycle of periodic alternation between opposites, and whether its "peak" is ritually "marked" through prayer, special meals, or family get-togethers is quite irrelevant. The only significant sensation that needs to be experienced is that of a binary contrast between the ordinary and the extraordinary, regardless of what the actual substance of that contrast might be. As one can tell from a cultural "message" such as the Michelob beer commercial that admonishes the listener to "Put a little weekend in your week," the essence of weekly "peak days" is the fact that they are the precise opposite of ordinary weekdays.

In establishing a contrast between the extraordinary and the ordinary, the pulsating week also introduces some discontinuity between them. Thus, for example, structuring our forty-hour workweek so that we work eight hours a day for five days and then rest on the other two—rather than, say, working only five or six hours a day seven days a week—obviously allows us to experience for two full days the interruption of the continuous routine of working. In regularly disrupting the otherwise continuous flow of our life, the pulsating week also adds more dimensions to it. Both those who work seven days a week and those who do not work at all often commit themselves, either willingly or out of necessity, to a rather unidimensional mode of existence and may miss such experiences as diversity and transition. That, of course, is also true of both those who party every night of the week and those who never attend parties at all. In other words, whether the discontinuity that the pulsating week establishes is one between the sacred and the profane, consumption and production, active socializing and isolation, freedom and obligation, the domestic and the public, or spontaneity and routine is rather insignificant. From an experiential standpoint, the most distinctive feature of this cycle is the fact that it helps to introduce discontinuity into our life and thus promote its multidimensionality. After all, in providing us with the opportunity to both work and rest, save and spend, diet and feast, and stay at home and go out, the pulsating week definitely helps us to experience the world around us as both ordinary and extraordinary!

REFERENCES

1. Henri Bergson, Time and Free Will (New York: Harper Torchbooks, 1960), pp. 98–128, 226–40.
2. Hubert, "Etude Sommaire," pp. 197, 207–10, 226–29. See also Sorokin, *Sociocultural Causality,* pp. 181–225.
3. Schwartz, "The Social Context of Commemoration"; Lloyd W. Warner, *The Living and the Dead* (New Haven, CT; Yale University Press, 1959), pp. 129–35. See also Claude Lévi-Strauss, *The Savage Mind* (Chicago: University of Chicago Press, 1966), pp. 258–61.
4. Pitirim Sorokin and Robert K. Merton, "Social Time: A Methodological and Functional Analysis," *American Journal of Sociology* 42(1937):621.
5. Mary Douglas, *Purity and Danger* (New York: Praeger, 1966), p. 64.
6. Robert H. Rimmer, *Thursday, My Love* (New York: Signet, 1973).
7. Stanford M. Lyman and Marvin B. Scott, "On the Time Track," in *A Sociology of the Absurd* (New York: Appleton-Century-Crofts, 1970), pp. 201–2.
8. John Horton, "Time and Cool People," *Trans-Action* 4(1967), No. 5, p. 8; Dorothy Nelkin, "Unpredictability and Life Style in a Migrant Labor Camp," *Social Problems* 17(1970):479.
9. Loren Reid, *Hurry Home Wednesday* (Columbia: University of Missouri Press, 1978), p. 1.
10. Andrew J. Weigert, *Sociology of Everyday Life* (New York and London: Longman, 1981), p. 210.
11. Charlotte Brontë, *Shirley* (New York: Harper, 1900), p. 1.
12. Vid Pecjak, "Verbal Synesthesiae of Colors, Emotions, and Days of the Week," *Journal of Verbal Learning and Verbal Behavior* 6(1970):625.
13. Jim Davis, *Garfield Sits around the House* (New York: Ballantine, 1983). In many of Davis's cartoons, Garfield is presented as the prototypical Monday-hater.
14. "Monday, Monday," by John Phillips (Duchess Music Publishers, 1965).
15. Cecil Gordon, A. R. Emerson, and D. S. Pugh, "Patterns of Sickness Absence in a Railway Population," *British Journal of Industrial Medicine* 16(1959):237–38; P. J. Taylor, "Shift and Day Work: a Comparison of Sickness Absence, Lateness, and Other Absence Behavior at an Oil Refinery from 1962 to 1965," *British Journal of In-*

dustrial Medicine 24(1967):93–102; Zerubavel, *Patterns of Time,* pp. 16–17.

16. Gordon, Emerson, and Pugh, op. cit., pp. 235–38.

17. Douglas A. Reid, "The Decline of Saint Monday 1766–1876," *Past and Present* 71(1976):76–101; Thompson, "Time, Work-Discipline, and Industrial Capitalism," pp. 73–76.

18. Wright, *Clockwork Man,* p. 211.

19. Simon W. Rabkin, F. A. Mathewson, and R. B. Tate, "Chronobiology of Cardiac Sudden Death in Men," *Journal of the American Medical Association* 244(1980):1357–58.

20. W. Baldamus, *The Structure of Sociological Inference* (London: Martin Robertson, 1976), p. 94; National Center for Health Statistics, "Advance Report," p. 47; Judith Norback (ed.), *The Mental Health Yearbook/Directory* 1979–80 (New York: Van Nostrand Reinhold, 1979), p. 748; Rogot, Fabsitz, and Feinleib, "Daily Variation," p. 205.

21. "Sunday," by Ned Miller, Chester Cohn, Jules Stein, and Bennie Krueger (CBS Songs, 1926).

22. "A Sunday Kind of Love," by Barbara Belle, Louis Prima, Anita Leonard, and Stan Rhodes (MCA, 1946).

23. J. David Lewis and Andrew J. Weigert, "The Structure and Meanings of Social Time," *Social Forces* 60(1981):441.

24. Interestingly enough, in recent years, this expression has penetrated even the traditionally workaholic Japanese society. See Lee Smith, "Cracks in the Japanese Work Ethic," *Fortune,* May 14, 1984, p. 166.

25. Gordon, Emerson, and Pugh, "Patterns of Sickness Absence," pp. 237–38.

26. Loren Reid, *Finally It's Friday* (Columbia: University of Missouri Press, 1981), pp. 96–97; Alice S. Rossi and Peter E. Rossi, "Body Time and Social Time: Mood Patterns by Menstrual Cycle Phase and Day of the Week," *Social Science Research* 6(1977):289.

27. "Saturday Child," by D. Gates (Screen Gems—Columbia Music).

28. "Sunday in the Park," by Harold J. Rome (Mills Music Inc., 1937).

29. Baldamus, *The Structure,* p. 94; Rogot, Fabsitz, and Feinleib, "Daily Variation," p. 205.

30. Sándor Ferenczi, *Further Contributions to the Theory and Technique of Psycho-Analysis* (Vol. 11 of the International Psycho-Analytical Library, edited by Ernest Jones) (London: Hogarth, 1950), pp. 174–76.

31. De Grazia, *Of Time, Work, and Leisure,* p. 260.

32. Zerubavel, *Patterns of Time,* pp. 114, 117–23.

33. R. C. Browne, "The Day and Night Performance of Teleprinter Switchboard Operators," *Occupational Psychology* 23(1949):121–26.

34. Louis Bernikow, "Alone," *The New York Times Magazine,* August 15, 1982, p. 25.

35. Georg Simmel, *The Sociology of Georg Simmel* (New York: Free Press, 1964), pp. 126–32; Eviatar Zerubavel, "Personal Information and Social Life," *Symbolic Interaction* 5(1982), No. 1, pp. 100–102.

36. Zerubavel, Hidden Rhythms, pp. 143–45.

37. See, for example, Erving Goffman, *Behavior in Public Places* (New York: Free Press, 1963), pp. 103–4.

38. Reed Larson et al., "Time Alone in Daily Experience: Loneliness or Renewal?" in Letitia A. Peplau and Daniel Perlman (eds.), *Loneliness* (New York: John Wiley & Sons, 1982), pp. 47–48.

39. "Saturday Night Is the Loneliest Night of the Week," by Sammy Cahn (Barton Music Corp., 1944). See also "Another Saturday Night," by Sam Cooke (ABKCO Industries, Inc., 1963).

40. Colson, *The Week,* p. 29.

41. *Babylonian Talmud: Pesahim* 106a; Solomon Ganzfried (ed.), *The Code of Jewish Law* (New York: Hebrew Publishing Co., 1961), 96.15; Maimonides, *The Book of Seasons* (New Haven, CT: Yale University Press, 1961): *Sabbath* 29.3; Mark Zborowski and Elizabeth Herzog, *Life Is with People* (New York: Schocken, 1962), p. 37.

42. André Neher, "The View of Time and History in Jewish Culture," in *Cultures and Time* (Paris: UNESCO, 1976), p. 160.

43. *Mishnayot: Kethubboth* 1.1, *Megillah* 3.6, 4.1, *Ta'anit* 2.9, *Tamid* 7.4; *Babylonian Talmud: Bava Kamma* 37b, 82a, *Makkot* 5a, *Ta'anit* 27b, 29b.

44. Balsdon, *Life and Leisure,* p. 61; Snyder, "Quinto Nundinas," pp. 15–18.

45. Seeley, Sim, and Loosley, *Crestwood Heights,* p. 75.

46. Menninger, *Number Words,* p. 182.

47. Durkheim, *The Elementary Forms,* p. 347.

48. Ibid., p. 54.

49. Zerubavel, *Hidden Rhythms,* pp. 102–5, 110–37. See also Edmund R. Leach, *Culture and Communication* (Cambridge, England: Cambridge University Press, 1976), p. 83.

50. Hubert, "Etude Sommaire," pp. 201–4.
51. Edmund R. Leach, "Two Essays Concerning the Symbolic Representation of Time," in *Rethinking Anthropology* (London: Athlone, 1961), p. 126.
52. Ibid., pp. 133–34. Emphasis added.
53. *Babylonian Talmud: Shabbath* 113a–113b; Ganzfried, *The Code of Jewish Law* 86, 90.6; Maimonides, *The Book of Seasons: Sabbath* 24.1,4,12–13,30.2; Zborowski and Herzog, *Life Is with People,* pp. 47–50, 56–57, 64; *The Zohar* (London: Soncino, 1949): *Beshalah* 47b.
54. Judith Goode, J. Theophano, and K. Curtis, "A Framework for the Analysis of Continuity and Change in Shared Sociocultural Rules for Food Use: The Italian-American Pattern," in Linda K. Brown and Kay Mussell (eds.), *Ethnic and Regional Foodways in the United States* (Knoxville: University of Tennessee Press, 1984), p. 74. See also Goode, Curtis, and Theophano, "Meal Formats," pp. 177, 183–91.
55. Maimonides, *The Book of Seasons: Sabbath* 30.8.
56. Zborowski and Herzog, *Life Is with People,* p. 60.
57. Barthes, *The Fashion System,* pp. 191–210; Marshall Sahlins, *Culture and Practical Reason* (Chicago and London: University of Chicago Press, 1976), p. 182.
58. *Mishnayot: Shabbath* 6.
59. *Babylonian Talmud: Shabbath* 113a; Ganzfried, *The Code of Jewish Law* 72.16; Maimonides, *The Book of Seasons: Sabbath* 30.3; *The Midrash of Psalms* (New Haven, CT: Yale University Press, 1959) 92.3.
60. Israel Abrahams, *Jewish Life in the Middle Ages* (New York: Atheneum, 1975), pp. 288–89; Samuel M. Segal, *The Sabbath Book* (New York: Thomas Yoseloff, 1957), p. 115; Zborowski and Herzog, *Life Is with People,* pp. 41–42.
61. See also Weigert, *Sociology of Everyday Life,* p. 208.
62. Barthes, *The Fashion System,* p. 251.
63. Zborowski and Herzog, *Life Is with People,* p. 363.
64. Mann, *The Magic Mountain,* p. 188.
65. Rimmer, *Thursday, My Love,* p. 21.

BIBLIOGRAPHY

Abrahams, Israel. *Jewish Life in the Middle Ages.* New York: Atheneum, 1975.
Babylonian Talmud, The. London: Soncino, 1938.
Baldamus, W. *The Structure of Sociological Inference.* London: Martin Robertson, 1976.
Balsdon, J. P. V. D. *Life and Leisure in Ancient Rome.* New York: McGraw-Hill, 1969.
Barthes, Roland. *The Fashion System.* New York: Hill and Wang, 1983.
Bergson, Henri. *Time and Free Will.* New York: Harper Torchbooks, 1960.
Bernikow, Louise. "Alone." *The New York Times Magazine,* August 15, 1982, pp. 24–34.
Brontë, Charlotte. *Shirley.* New York: Harper, 1900.
Browne, R. C. "The Day and Night Performance of Teleprinter Switchboard Operators." *Occupational Psychology* 23(1949):121–26.
Colson, Francis H. *The Week.* Cambridge, England: Cambridge University Press, 1926.
Davis, Jim. *Garfield Sits Around the House.* New York: Ballantine, 1983.
De Grazia, Sebastian. *Of Time, Work, and Leisure.* New York: Doubleday Anchor, 1964.
Douglas, Mary. *Purity and Danger.* New York: Praeger, 1966.
Durkheim, Emile. *The Elementary Forms of the Religious Life.* New York: Free Press, 1965.
Ferenczi, Sándor. *Further Contributions to the Theory and Technique of Psycho-Analysis.* (Vol. 11 of the International Psycho-Analytical Library, edited by Ernest Jones.) London: Hogarth Press, 1950.
Ganzfried, Solomon (ed.). *The Code of Jewish Law.* New York: Hebrew Publishing Co., 1961.
Goffman, Erving. *Behavior in Public Places.* New York: Free Press, 1963.
Goode, Judith, K. Curtis, and J. Theophano. "Meal Formats, Meal Cycles, and Menu Negotiation in the Maintenance of an Italian-American Community." pp. 143–218 in Mary Douglas (ed.), *Food in the Social Order.* New York: Russell Sage, 1984.
Goode, Judith, J. Theophano, and K. Curtis. "A Framework for the Analysis of Continuity and Change in Shared Sociocultural Rules for Food Use: the Italian-American Pattern." Pp. 66–88 in Linda K. Brown and Kay Mussell (eds.), *Ethnic and Regional Foodways in the United States.* Knoxville: The University of Tennessee Press, 1984.
Gordon, Cecil, A. R. Emerson, and D. S. Pugh. "Patterns of Sickness Absence in a Railway Population." *British Journal of Industrial Medicine* 16(1959):230–43.

Horton, John. "Time and Cool People." *Trans-Action* 4(1967), No. 5, pp. 5–12.

Hubert, Henri. "Etude Sommaire de la Représentation du Temps dans la Religion et al Magie." Pp. 189–229 in Henri Hubert and Marcel Mauss, *Mélanges d'Histoire des Religions*. Paris: Félix Alcan and Guillaumin, 1909. (In French.)

Larson, Reed, et al. "Time Alone in Daily Experience: Loneliness or Renewal?" pp. 40–53 in Letitia A. Peplau and Daniel Perlman (eds.), *Loneliness.* New York: John Wiley & Sons, 1982.

Leach, Edmund R. "Two Essays Concerning the Symbolic Representation of Time." Pp. 124–36 in his *Rethinking Anthropology*. London: Athlone, 1961.

———. *Culture and Communication.* Cambridge, England: Cambridge University Press, 1976.

Lévi-Strauss, Claude. *The Savage Mind.* Chicago: University of Chicago Press, 1966.

Lewis, J. David, and Andrew J. Weigert. "The Structures and Meanings of Social Time." *Social Forces* 60(1981):432–62.

Lyman, Stanford M., and Marvin B. Scott. "On the Time Track." Pp. 189–212 in their *A Sociology of the Absurd.* New York: Appleton-Century-Crofts, 1970.

Maimonides. *The Book of Seasons.* New Haven, CT: Yale University Press, 1961.

Mann, Thomas. *The Magic Mountain.* New York: Vintage, 1969.

Menninger, Karl. *Number Words and Number Symbols.* Cambridge, MA: MIT Press, 1977.

Midrash of Psalms, The. New Haven, CT: Yale University Press, 1959.

Mishnah, The. London: Oxford University Press, 1958.

National Center for Health Statistics. "Advance Report, Final Mortality Statistics, 1979." Monthly Vital Statistics Report 31(1982), No. 6. [Suppl. Department of Health and Human Services (DHHS) Publication No. Public Health Service (PHS) 82–1120].

Neher, André. "The View of Time and History in Jewish Culture." Pp. 149–67 in *Cultures and Time.* Paris: UNESCO, 1976.

Nelkin, Dorothy. "Unpredictability and Life Style in a Migrant Labor Camp." *Social Forces* 17(1970):472–87.

Norback, Judith (ed.). *The Mental Health Yearbook/Directory 1979–80.* New York: Van Nostran Reinhold, 1979.

Pecjak, Vid. "Verbal Synesthesiae of Colors, Emotions, and Days of the Week." *Journal of Verbal Learning and Verbal Behavior* 9(1970):623–26.

Rabkin, Simon W., F. A. Mathewson, and R. B. Tate. "Chronobiology of Cardiac Sudden Death in Men." *Journal of the American Medical Association* 244(1980):1357–58.

Reid, Douglas A. "The Decline of Saint Monday 1766–1876." *Past and Present* 71(1976):76–101.

Reid, Loren. *Hurry Home Wednesday.* Columbia: University of Missouri Press, 1978.

———. *Finally It's Friday.* Columbia: University of Missouri Press, 1981.

Rimmer, Robert H. *Thursday, My Love.* New York: Signet, 1973.

Rogot, Eugene, R. Fabsitz, and M. Feinleib. "Daily Variation in USA Mortality." *American Journal of Epidemiology* 103(1976):198–211.

Rossi, Alice S., and Peter E. Rossi. "Body Time and Social Time: Mood Patterns by Menstrual Cycle Phase and Day of the Week." *Social Science Research* 6(1977):273–308.

Sahlins, Marshall. *Culture and Practical Reason.* Chicago and London: University of Chicago Press, 1976.

Schwartz, Barry. "The Social Context of Commemoration: A Study in Collective Memory." *Social Forces* 61(1982):374–402.

Seeley, John R., R. A. Sim, and E. W. Loosley. *Crestwood Heights.* New York: Science Editions, 1963.

Segal, Samual M. *The Sabbath Book.* New York: Thomas Yoseloff, 1957.

Simmel, Georg. *The Sociology of Georg Simmel.* New York: Free Press, 1964.

Smith, Lee. "Cracks in the Japanese Work Ethic." *Fortune,* May 14, 1984, pp. 162–68.

Snyder, Walter F. "Quinto Nundinas Pompeis." *Journal of Roman Studies* 26(1936):12–18.

Sorokin, Pitirim A. *Sociocultural Causality, Space, Time.* Durham, NC: Duke University Press, 1943.

———, and Robert K. Merton. "Social Time: A Methodological and Functional Analysis." *American Journal of Sociology* 42(1937):615–29.

Taylor, P. J. "Shift and Day Work: A Comparison of Sickness Absence, Lateness, and Other Absence Behavior at an Oil Refinery from 1962 to 1965." *British Journal of Industrial Medicine* 24(1967):93–102.

Thompson, E. P. "Time, Work-Discipline, and Industrial Capitalism." *Past and Present* 38(1967):56–97.

Warner, Lloyd W. *The Living and the Dead.* New Haven, CT: Yale University Press, 1959.

Weigert, Andrew J. *Sociology of Everyday Life.* New York and London: Longman, 1981.

Wright, Lawrence. *Clockwork Man.* London: Elek, 1968.

Zborowski, Mark, and Elizabeth Herzog. *Life Is with People.* New York: Schocken, 1962.

Zerubavel, Eviatar. *Patterns of Time in Hospital Life.* Chicago and London: University of Chicago Press, 1979.

———. *Hidden Rhythms.* Chicago and London: University of Chicago Press, 1981.

———. "Personal Information and Social Life." *Symbolic Interaction* 5(1982), No. 1, pp. 97–109.

Zohar, The. London: Soncino, 1949.

DISCUSSION QUESTIONS

1. Describe the way the week is constructed on your campus, paying particular attention to the weekend. When exactly does the weekend begin? When does it end? In what ways is the weekend experienced and defined to distinguish it from the rest of the week?

2. Do we really need the week? Try to imagine a world without the week. Would we need something in its place? Why or why not? Is the fact that our week is seven days long of any significance?

READING 4

Ecumenical America: Global Culture and the American Cosmos

Orlando Patterson

We live increasingly in a global culture, and one of the things this means is that the products of popular culture move back and forth across national boundaries in complex symbiotic relationships. Orlando Patterson, a Jamaican-born Harvard sociologist, describes the emergence of a cosmopolitan and universal culture that he dubs "ecumenical America." He contrasts this cultural orientation to that of both traditional culture and multiculturalism. In suggesting what he means by

ecumenical, he uses as a sustained case study the diffusion of popular music in the West Atlantic regional cosmos. The article also identifies three additional regional cosmoses: Tex-Mex; the Southern California cosmos; and the Northwestern Pacific Rim cosmos.

The modern process of global cultural interaction has repeatedly been subjected to two criticisms. The first is that it threatens the diversity and particularism of the world's cultures, resulting in a deadening homogenization of the human cultural experience. The other is that this growing global uniformity results from the dominance of America's culture—that, in effect, global culture is nothing more than American cultural imperialism. Hannah Arendt's lament that we have been brought to a "global present without a common past [which] threatens to render all traditions and all particular past histories irrelevant," is typical of the first. Theodor Adorno's famous diatribe against American popular music is the *locus classicus* of the second. Both objections are without foundation.

The argument that Americanization is resulting in the homogenization of the world ignores the increased vitality of local cultures and ethnicities in recent times and the complexity of global cultural diffusion, in particular the extent to which so-called peripheral regions are increasingly contributing to American popular culture and to the world music scene. Nor does it explain the emergence of a special kind of regional system, what I shall call the regional cosmos, or the great cultural divisions in America itself. The American cosmos, as we shall see, is not a single cultural space, but is divided among three Americas: a traditional America, multicultural America, and ecumenical America.

THE DIFFUSION OF GLOBAL CULTURE

Industrialization and modernization both entailed the spread of common sets of behaviors and attitudes within the context of economic change. However, the globalization of culture also takes place independent of whatever economic changes are occurring in a particular region or society. Traditionally, the transmission of culture across societies was facilitated by two main media: migration and literacy. People learned about other cultures either through traveling themselves or from travelers, or by reading about other cultures and adopting or adapting what they learned. These traditional media could, under certain circumstances, be effective means for the transmission of cultures across the globe.

The distinctive feature of literary transmissions, and all diffusions through individuals except during mass migrations, is that they tend to be largely confined to elites, or, where not, to enclaves of non-elite persons cut off from the mass of their societies. This was true of the diffusion of Hellenism in the Mediterranean world and was largely true of the imperial influence on the societies of Asia and Africa. Until the end of the Second World War, Westernism was largely confined to a tiny minority of the populations of these continents, largely the educated native elites and urban workers. Since the fifties, however, this has changed radically. The globalization of culture, largely (although by no means solely, as the spread of Islam indicates) through the impact of, and *reaction to,* the diffusion of Western popular and elite culture, has not only greatly increased in reins of its spread over the surface of the world, but in terms of the depth to which it has influenced the populations of other societies.

Four factors account for this sudden change of pace. The first is the spread of mass literacy throughout the world, which resulted from the new nations of the postcolonial era investing vast sums and human energy in their educational systems, the structure and content of which were largely influenced by Western models. The second is the rise of mass communication. The third is the growth of global organizations, both private and public, such as the multinational corporation, the United Nations, the World Bank, the IMF, and the large number of regional agencies, themselves often modeled on and directly influenced and promoted by the former. The fourth is the revolution in long distance transportation, which has resulted in the emergence of an entirely new kind of global, or more properly, subglobal system, the regional cosmos. The most remarkable of these emerging regional cosmoses is the West Atlantic system, encompassed by the eastern seaboard of North America and the circum-Caribbean societies of Central America and the islands.

THE GLOBAL POPULAR MUSIC CULTURE

The emergence of the regional cosmoses provides perhaps the best evidence of the complexity of global cultural diffusion. But before turning to the subject of their development, let us consider one example of global cultural diffusion—namely, how mass communication has facilitated the diffusion and creation of global popular musical culture. I choose to focus on popular music because it is in this area of the globalization process that the strongest claims of homogenization have been made. Its classic statement was given by the musicologist Alan Lomax who, in 1968, lamented the presumed passing of the great local cultures of the world under the impact of American popular culture, which, he feared, would lead to global rootlessness and alienation as the peoples of the earth all sank into the desolate gloom of the great, global "cultural grey-out."[1]

As someone who has studied this process in a Third World society that has perhaps been more exposed to the full glare of American culture than nearly any other—namely, Jamaica—I can say unequivocally that such charges are utter nonsense. It is simply not true that the diffusion of Western culture, especially at the popular level, leads to the homogenization of the culture of the world. Indeed, my research, and that of the best scholars working in this area, suggests that just the opposite is the case. Western-American cultural influence has generated enormous cultural production, in some cases amounting to near hypercreativity in the popular cultures of the world.

If what I say is correct, it must be wondered where the popular misconception of the homogenizing effect of the Western impact came from. One source is the propagandistic reaction of traditional cultural gatekeepers in Third World societies whose monopoly and influence has been threatened by the Western cultural impact. That impact, in generating new cultural forms, invariably stimulates the emergence of new and competing cultural agents and managers. To monopolize the cultural resources of a country is to exercise enormous power, not to mention to control economic resources. What usually upsets traditional cultural gatekeepers about the Western impact on their mass cultures is less the content of Western culture—because this is invariably transformed—and more the choice it immediately offers to the consumers of culture.

The second source of misconceptions about the impact of Westernism comes from important segments of the cultural gatekeepers in the West itself, on both the right and the left, who think and talk about this issue. The more abstract of these complaints about the influence of American global popular culture stem from elitist, postmodernist pessimism, of the sort that stimulates similar complaints about the stultifying effects of popular culture on the working class of the West. Cultural critic Paul Willis has recently taken issue with these pretentious criticisms. He notes that people never simply passively absorb cultural messages. There is always what Willis calls symbolic work at play: "The incandescence is not simply a surface market quality. It produces, is driven by, and reproduces further forms and varieties for everyday symbolic work and creativity, some of which remain in the everyday and in common culture far longer than they do on the market."[2]

There is a great deal of sloppy and ill-informed criticism of Americanization in what passes for serious, empirically based research. It is simply assumed that illiterate and semi-literate Third World peoples are powerless in their responses to Western popular culture. Experts on the subject have in mind a world of passive consumers, homogenized and manipulated into Marx's notorious sack of (Western-ized) potatoes.[3] It is nothing of the sort. The semi- and non-literate masses of the Third World invariably react to Western cultural influence in a nonpassive manner, reinterpreting what they receive in the light of their own cultures and experience. One of my favorite examples of this is the story about the British officer in a remote part of northern Greece following the general elections in Britain at the end of the Second World War. The officer asked a Greek peasant if he knew the results of the elections. "Oh yes," replied the peasant excitedly, "the Labour party has won the elections, the King has been assassinated, and Mr. Churchill and his party have fled to the mountains!"

Either the Western cultural form is reinterpreted in light of traditional meanings, or Western meanings are adapted to traditional patterns. In any case, something new, although still local, emerges. As the musicologist Peter Manuel points out, not only do local cultures "adapt foreign elements in distinctly idiosyncratic ways that substantially alter their function, context and meaning," but even what appears to Western ears and perception to be a major intrusion may, in fact, be so shallow functionally to the native listener as to not even be perceived. This is true, for example, of the influence of American music on the thriving Indian pop culture.[4]

In their comparative analysis of eight cultures, musicologist Deanna Robinson, Elizabeth Buck, and others have demonstrated, in my opinion conclusively, that "world musical homogenization is not occurring." As they put it, "even though information-age economic forces are building an international consumership for centrally produced and distributed popular music, other factors are pulling in the opposite direction. They are encouraging not only what we call "indigenization" of popular music forms and production but also new, eclectic combinations of world musical elements, combinations that contradict the continuing constraints of national boundaries and global capitalism."[5]

Furthermore, the common notion that the globalization of culture, especially on the popular level, is a one-way process, from the Western metropolis to the passive and vulnerable periphery, is simply not the case, although it is certainly true that the major diffusionary source of this culture is a single Western country: the United States.

Not homogenization, then, but the revitalization and generation of new musical forms has been the effect of the global exchange process. Some of these forms remain local, providing greater choice and stimulus to the local culture. Examples of such revitalization include the modernization of the traditional Camerounian *makassi* style with the introduction of the acoustic rhythm guitar; the development of the *highlife* music of Ghana, which fused traditional forms with jazz, rock, and Trinidadian calypso rhythms; the vibrant local modernization of traditional Afro-Arab music in Kenya. Elsewhere, musical forms under Western impact have broken out of their provincial boundaries to become regional currency, as, for example, the Trinidadian and American pop influenced *kru-krio* music of Sierra Leone, which swept West Africa and beyond during the sixties and seventies; the Brazilian *sambo,* the pan-American *salsa; merengue* (the latter of Dominican Republic origin); the originally Cuban *nueva trova,* which became a radical pan-Latin form, stimulating the even more radical and pan-Latin *nueva cancion;* and the Colombian *cumbia,* which has become an important part of the music of the Tex-Mex regional cosmos. And there are those musical forms that experience their fifteen minutes of fame as the latest fad in the "world music" scene: the Argentinean *tango;* the Algerian *rai;* the Zairian *soukous;* the Brazilian *bossa nova.*

OUT OF JAMAICA

One of the most globally successful cultural creations of a Third World people is the musical form know as *reggae.* Indeed, the development of reggae perhaps more than any other musical form illustrates the complexity of global cultural interaction. The creation of the Jamaican working classes and lumpen proletariat, reggae emerged in the late fifties from a variety of influences, especially American. Jamaica had always had a rich musical tradition, originating mainly in the music of West Africa brought over by the slaves, but also influenced in its lyrical and melodic lines by British, especially Celtic, popular music of the late eighteenth and nineteenth centuries. At the turn of the century, a popular secular form, *mento,* ideal for dancing, emerged. Similar to the Trinidad calypso in its topical and satirical lyrics and in its reliance on the guitar for a Latinate ostinato, *mento* soon established itself as the traditional popular music of the island.

By the late fifties, however, young working-class Jamaicans had grown weary of *mento.* What they did like were the rhythm-and-blues records being brought back by farm laborers returning from cutting cane in Florida and the "cowboy music" or bluegrass they picked up on short-wave early in the mornings. Aspiring young Jamaican singers—including the teenage Bob Marley, Peter Tosh, Bob Andy, and numerous others—began singing imitations of American soul songs at the many talent parades that preceded the weekend triple bills at the working-class cinemas. These imitations were, at first, ghastly renditions of the original. (I can still recall hearing a pimpled, short-haired Bob Marley singing an American soul song hopelessly out of tune.) At this point, Jamaica would seem to have had the worst of all possible worlds. A delightful native musical tradition had been abandoned, and in its place the island found its middle class swooning over syrupy white American ballads while its lower class sang imitations of African American music.

What happened next, however, demonstrates just how complex the dialectics between local and foreign influences that generate the global culture are. First of all, the imitations were so bad that they were unwittingly original. Furthermore, the Jamaicans instinctively brought their own local musical cadences and rhythms to bear on the tunes being imitated. This coincided with an infusion of the very African music of the Afro-Jamaican cults, which was lifted straight from the "laboring" movements made by cult celebrants as they worked themselves up to the point of spirit possession. Both the movement and the accompanying rhythm were secularized (in a manner similar to the crossover from gospel to soul music among African Americans), and a wholly new musical form and accompanying dance, known as *ska*, was created.

At the time—the late fifties and early sixties—the vast majority of working-class Jamaicans were still too poor to buy record players or expensive imported records. This led to the formation of the *sound system*, a hi-fidelity system outfitted with enormous bass speakers, which the owners rented out, along with their record collections and themselves in the role of disc jockey. The disc jockeys, partly out of boredom, partly out of increasing dissatisfaction with the rhythmic patterns of the imported African American records, but above all, out of a desire to give a "live" quality to the performance of their systems, started to deliberately play around with the records as they were being played. They voiced over the imported records with their own rhythmic commentary, improving their "riddim" as they understood it, either through grunts and screams, or through an accompanying screed that sometimes made sense, sometimes was mere nonsense lyrics, which mattered little since the voice was actually

being used as an additional bass instrument. This was rapidly to become a distinctive feature of reggae. The disc jockey would also "play" the turntable, stopping and pushing the record as it turned on the platter in order to induce strange new sounds. This, too, was later to become an essential part of the music, except that the strange noises were to be made through the manipulation of sophisticated studio electronics.

What emerged from these activities was another distinctive musical form *dub*. When the disc jockeys were unable to match the love lyrics of the imported black American rhythm-and-blues songs, they resorted to what they knew best, local politics. Thus was born reggae dub, with its strong emphasis on the political, a clear departure from popular American music, black or white.

At about the same time that these developments were taking place, the Ras Tafari cult, a millenarian back-to-Africa movement that was the religious component of the reaction to Western influence, was taking hold among the Jamaican proletariat of the Kingston shanties. The spiritualism and radical racial ideology of the cult—a religious form of negritude, exemplifying Sartre's "anti-racist racism"—greatly appealed to the very people developing the music, and it was not long before the two merged, Rastafarian theology giving substance and ideological content to what were previously soppy imported lyrics or garbled political chatter.

The music swiftly went through several formal changes, first from ska to *rock-steady,* a more complex slow-tempo music, and finally, in response to the demands of the entrepreneurs who ran the weekend dance halls and who wanted music with a faster beat so their patrons would drink more of the Red Stripe beer on which they largely depended for their profits, to reggae.

Reggae swiftly caught on, not only among locals, but with the American tourists who were now visiting Jamaica in increasing numbers. Several major singers emerged in the late sixties and early seventies, the most successful of whom was Bob Marley, whose enormous showmanship and song-writing ability were important in internationalizing the music. However, one other factor was equally important in explaining the rapid spread of reggae and its eventual emergence as a global musical form. This was the mass movements of Jamaican working-class migrants. The first such movement was to Britain, where Jamaicans effectively transformed what was a previously all-white country into a multiracial society. By 1964, a thinly Anglicized version of ska known as *blue beat* was already in vogue.[6] Today, reggae has been completely embraced by white British youth, who now view it as an integral part of their culture.[7] From its British base, it was to spread rapidly throughout continental Europe and north and sub-Saharan Africa.

Similarly, reggae spread to the United States as a result of a second mass migration of the Jamaican working class, which began with the liberalization of American immigration laws in the early 1960s. A new kind of West Indian migrant now entered America, not the relatively well-educated, highly motivated petty-bourgeois migrants of previous generations, but the working-class and lumpen-proletarian people from the Kingston slums. Eventually, the reggae music these new migrants brought over with them, along with their disk jockeys and dance halls (as well as their gangs, the notorious posses), were to influence black American youth, but what is interesting is how long it took to do so. Black Americans, in fact, strongly resisted most versions of reggae. Reggae, however, rapidly caught on among the white college students of America, especially after the enormous success of the reggae movie, *The Harder They Come,* and soon broke out of the campus circuit with the success of Bob Marley and other international stars, such as Jimmy Cliff and Peter Tosh.[8]

Eventually, by the late 1970s and early 1980s, even the underclass African American young began to respond to reggae. They were simply unable to prevent themselves from listening to the version of reggae brought over to the ghettoes by the latest wave of underclass Kingston migrants: the dance-hall music. The fact that they also soon developed a healthy respect for the violent Jamaican posses also explains their changed attitude.

The music had gone full circle, from its beginnings in the crude imitations of 1950s' African American lower-class music, to the late 1970s' and early 1980s' imitations of dance-hall dub by the New York underclass. The American music that emerged from this extraordinary proletarian cross-fertilization was *rap,* the first popular American music to have an explicitly political lyrical content. The Jamaicans had repaid their debt.

THE WEST ATLANTIC REGIONAL COSMOS

The transmission of reggae to the American center from the Jamaican periphery not only illustrates the complexity of global cultural interaction, but was a forerunner of a much more complex process that has now integrated parts of the United States with other countries as deeply or more deeply than those parts are integrated with other regions of America. This aspect of the globalization of culture, which has resulted in the development of regional cosmoses, is entirely new. Indeed, it has emerged only over the past two decades or so, largely because it was dependent upon the revolution in cheap mass transportation.

The regional cosmos is best conceived of as a system of flows between a metropolitan center and a set of politically independent satellite countries within what the urban sociologist Saskia Sassen calls a "transnational space."[9] People, wealth, ideas, and cultural patterns move in both directions, influencing both the metropolitan center as well as the peripheral areas, although asymmetrically. Although they are similar in many respects to other migratory systems, such as those of the Mediterranean, there are several unique features of the regional cosmoses that are of special importance to the problem of the globalization of culture.

In the West Atlantic regional cosmos, made up of eastern America and the circum-Caribbean societies, the peripheral areas are either contiguous with or within easy reach of the dominant metropolitan society.[10] The separate units are legally autonomous, but sovereignty becomes merely a resource to be used in the interaction between the main collective actors. In spite of legal restrictions on the movement of peoples, there is a vast flow in both directions—legal and illegal migrants from the periphery, tourists and investors from the center. There is no simple flow of cheap labor to capital in this system, as in the classic colonial regimes. Skilled and cheap labor flow in both directions. Legal and illegal capital also moves in both directions.

The Third World countries of the periphery are only too eager to attract such capital, but with capitalization their economies become dualized, as is true of the center, between an urban-modern sector and a traditional-rural sector. This disrupts traditional labor patterns at a much faster rate than it provides new job opportunities. The result is massive unemployment, the rise of the urban slums—marking the first stage in the migration process—and from there the mass movement to the center. These migrants rarely compete directly with native workers in the center; instead, a wholly new sector—what sociologist Alejandro Portes calls the immigrant enclave—is created for them.[11] Thus, dualization at the center reinforces, and is reinforced by, dualization in the periphery.

An important aspect of the regional cosmos is the rise of the cosmopolis—a major urban center that shifts from being a major metropolis of the center to being the metropolis of the entire regional cosmos. This is precisely the role that Miami has come to play in the West Atlantic regional cosmos.[12] Miami is no longer an American city: it is a West Atlantic city, more vital to, and more dependent on, the needs of the circum-Caribbean societies and cultures than it is on the other sectors of the U.S. economy. It is the political, cultural, social, and economic hub and heart of the Caribbean.

Culturally, the periphery is greatly influenced by the society of the center, but the reverse is also the case, as the example of reggae demonstrates. Another example of periphery-to-center cultural flows is the transmission of Spanish and Haitian creole, which has resulted not simply in the creation of a multilingual center where English once prevailed but, more broadly, in the Latinization of English and the Anglicization of Spanish. This process of creolization, in turn, has resulted in the creation of wholly new cultural forms in the transnational space, such as "New Yorican" and Miami Spanish. The same process of cosmopolitan creolization can be found in other areas of culture: in the rapid spread of Spanish-American food, Franco-Haitian-American dishes, and the recent diffusion of the Jamaican "jerk" method of cooking in both Jamerican (Jamaican-American) and mainstream American cooking; in the Latin and West Indian carnivals that are now a standard part of the festivals of the cosmopolis; in the infusion and transformation of Afro-West Indian and Afro-Latin cults, whose animal sacrifices were recently offered constitutional protection by the Supreme Court after a major nativist challenge; in the ironic revival of the game of cricket, once an elite sport among the dominant Anglo-Americans, under the impact of the Afro-West Indian working-class immigrants; in the spread of the dreadlocks style of hair grooming among African Americans and, increasingly, among white Americans from the Jamaican Rastafarian immigrants. These are only some of the more visible expressions of this extraordinary process of periphery-induced creolization in the cosmopolis.

AFRO-CARIBBEAN INTELLECTUALISM

One of the most fascinating, and neglected, areas of cultural exchange between the cosmopolis and the West Atlantic periphery is in intellectual and professional life. The British, Spanish, and French academic and professional cultures have traditionally dominated the countries of the periphery, the result of their respective colonial experiences. The ruthlessly selective nature of these European traditions created intellectual cultures that were at once highly sophisticated and elitist. What emerged in the black Caribbean—a vibrant engagement with European intellectualism in which the culture of Europe was critically embraced, dissected, and reintegrated through the filter of a creolized neo-African sensibility and aesthetic—had no parallel on the American mainland. It was possible only because of the overwhelming demographic presence of blacks in the West Indies, in contrast with the minority status of blacks in the mainland cosmopolis. In the periphery, the neo-European culture of the elite was mediated through agents of the hegemonic powers, who were themselves black or light-skinned. Hence race, per se, was muted as a factor in the cultural conflict that accompanied the decolonization process.

The ironic effect was that the European experience could be adjudicated, and dialectically explored, in purely cultural terms, devoid of the confounding effects of racial segregation and rejection. In contrast with the black American condition, where any engagement with the dominant culture always ran the risk of the loss of racial identity and the fear of racial betrayal, resulting in an understandable rejection of all intellectualism, the West Indian intellectual developed a love-hate relationship with the culture of the "mother country" that was mediated through fellow blacks. The paradigmatic challenge in this situation became, not the rejection and suspicion of all intellectualism, but a desperate need to outdo the imperial culture at its own game. Intellectualism, however, went far beyond mere anti-imperial one-up-manship. For the ambitious black West Indian, it was, until recently, the only path to mobility, given the paucity of resources and the monopolization of the limited commercial positions by whites and Asians.

The net result has been a virtual hotbed of intellectualism among Afro-Caribbean peoples. These small, poor islands have, arguably, the highest per capita concentration of scholars, professionals, and real, as well as would-be, intellectuals as any place in the world. It is not Germany, Switzerland, or the United States that has produced the greatest proportion of Nobel laureates per thousand, but the tiny, dirt-poor island nation of St. Lucia. With an at-home population of under 100,000, it has produced two Nobel laureates, the economist Sir A. W. Lewis and the poet Derek Walcott. And they are merely the tip of the iceberg: Trinidad's V. S. Naipaul is generally considered one of the two or three best novelists writing in English; its late scholar-statesman, Eric Williams, was a major historian; its late radical intellectual C. L. R. James one of the foremost Marxist theoreticians. The poet-novelists Edward Brathwaite and George Lamming are only the most recent in a long line of internationally acclaimed writers from Barbados; indeed, Barbados was used by the colonial British as the seedbed for black professionals and missionaries in its cultural penetration of Africa and Asia and still lives to a considerable degree on the remittances of its large number of professional emigrants. What is true of the English-speaking Caribbean holds equally for the French-speaking islands where, to take the most noteworthy example, the poet-statesman Aimé Césaire has long been recognized by French critics as one of the best poets in their language.

This extraordinary intellectual and professional tradition is now being rapidly incorporated into the West Atlantic cosmopolis. American educational aid has been accompanied by American models of education, transforming the elitist nature of these systems. At the same time, there has been a massive redirection of the flow of talent from the region. All roads no longer lead to the old colonial metropoles of London and Paris but increasingly to the great East Coast cosmopolitan centers. Budding West Indian intellectuals now experience their required period of creative exile, not in Europe, but in America, where many take up permanent residence. What is more, a disproportionate number of American academic and other professionals are of West Indian ancestry. Paralleling the cross-fertilization of African American lower-class popular culture by West Indian immigrants is the interaction of Afro-Caribbean and African American traditions within the cosmopolitan academe, which has significant implications not only for the cultures of both traditions, but for the wider culture of the cosmopolis.

The special contribution of West Indian intellectualism in the cosmopolitan context will be a transference of its distinctive strategy of aggressive engagement with the dominant tradition of neo-European civilization—a strategy that, at its worst, generates enormous identity crises and self-destructive emotional and physical violence, but at the same time, and at its best, is the crucible for the explosively competitive syncretism that finds expression in Rastafarianism and *voudon,* reggae and merengue, and negritude, magical realism, *omeros,* and the self-loathing genius of V. S. Naipaul. Such engagement African Americans have independently achieved so far only in the universalizing vitalism of rock music and the jazz aesthetic. My prediction is that the West Indian presence in the cosmopolis will act as a catalyst for the promotion of this transcendent Afro-European contribution to the emerging global culture.

In structural terms, the mass migration of peoples from the periphery in this new context of cheap transportation and communication has produced a wholly different kind of social system. The migrant communities in the center are not ethnic groups in the traditional American

sense. In the interaction between center and periphery, the societies of the periphery are radically changed, but so is the traditional immigrant community of the center. What has emerged is, from the viewpoint of the peripheral states, distinctive transnational societies in which there is no longer any meaningful identification of political and social boundaries. Thus, more than a half of the adult working populations of many of the smaller eastern Caribbean states live outside of these societies, mainly in the immigrant enclaves of the United States. About 40 percent of all Jamaicans, and perhaps half of all Puerto Ricans, live outside of the political boundaries of these societies, mainly in America. The interesting thing about these communities is that their members feel as at home in the mainland segment as in the original politically bounded areas.

These communities are more like self-contained colonies—in this respect, they remind one of the *politeumata* of the Hellenistic cities—within the body politic of the United States, and it is a serious error to confuse them with the traditional ethnic communities, including native African Americans. They are what the Jamaican folk poet, Louise Bennett, calls "colonization in reverse." The former colonies now become the mother country; the imperial metropolis becomes the frontier of infinite resources, only now the resources consist not simply of unexploited land but of underutilized deindustrializing capital and the postindustrial service and professional sectors. There is no traumatic transfer of national loyalty from the home country to the host polity, since home is readily accessible and national loyalty is a waning sentiment in what is increasingly a postnational world. Jamaican, Puerto Rican, Dominican, and Barbadian societies are no longer principally defined by the political-geographical units of Jamaica, Puerto Rico, the Dominican Republic and Barbados but by *both* the populations and cultures of these units and their postnational colonies in the cosmopolis.

OTHER REGIONAL COSMOSES

In addition to the West Atlantic system, there are at least three other emerging multinational spaces within the body politic of contemporary America: the Tex-Mex cosmos of the Southwest, incorporating northern Mexican and Southwestern Euro-Indian cultures, peoples, and economies; the Southern California cosmos, with its volatile, unblended mosaic of Latin, Asian, and Afro-European cultures; and the newly emerged Pacific Rim cosmos of the Northwest, which integrates the economies and bourgeois cultures of industrial Asia and traditional Euro-America.

While the processes of incorporation and creolization are broadly similar in all four regional cosmoses, they differ sharply in their degrees of integration, in the volume and velocity of cultural, economic, and demographic flows, in the levels of asymmetry in the transfer of ideas, cultural products, and skills, in the patterns and stages of creolization, and in the nature and extent of the social and cultural conflicts that inevitably accompany the process of cosmopolitanization.

On all these indices, the West Atlantic cosmos is, in my view, the most advanced, especially in the degree of integration and the extent to which the nation-state has been transcended as a major basis of collective commitment and constraint on livelihood. The major outliers in this system are Haiti and Cuba, but in light of the already large contingent of Cubans and Haitians on the mainland, it is best to see their integration as a temporarily halted process, the one on ideological, the other on racist grounds. It is only a matter of time before both these restraints are eroded.

Next in level of integration is the Tex-Mex cosmos. Although it is the oldest of the four, the Tex-Mex cosmos is confined to a limited range of interactions and, in many respects, is the most asymmetric in its flows. The economic interaction consists largely of cheap, unskilled labor serving labor-intensive agricultural and light-industrial capital. Cultural flows are limited to popular music and the culinary arts. The hegemonic Anglo-American culture has remained strikingly oblivious to any significant Latinization. The architecture of the great cities of the region is aggressively Anglo-American, as is its professional and academic life, which takes account of the Latin presence in well-funded programs of Latin American and Latino studies.

The Southern California cosmos is the most heterogeneous and least integrated of the four and undoubtedly the most volatile. South and East Asian peoples of highly varied provenance meet Latin, Anglo-, and African-Americans at all socioeconomic levels. Economic flows are complex, involving highly skilled, professional, and entrepreneurial Asians, professional and working-class Latinos, as well as blacks of all classes and hegemonic Anglo-Americans. There has, as yet, been surprisingly little cross-fertilization of cultures in the cosmos; the process of creolization remains mainly at the pidgin stage, in language as in other areas of culture. The cultural mix has been correctly described as a salad, and a thoroughly unappetizing one at that. That the nation's worst ethnic riot has recently taken place in this cosmos comes as no surprise. That the riot was not a traditional black-white conflict, as erroneously reported by the press, but a multiethnic conflagration engaging more Latinos than blacks, in spite of its origins in the police beating of a black man, Rodney King, is understandable in light of the extreme differences between the interacting cultures and classes.

The Pacific Rim cosmos is the newest, least complex, and potentially most integrated of the four systems. It is, in effect, the transnational space of the most advanced economic sectors of East Asia and the American mainland. Its boundaries in North America extend beyond the U.S. polity, incorporating the Canadian state of British Columbia. Unlike the other regional cosmoses, it is largely bourgeois in its demographic component, involving a large net flow of entrepreneurial capital and talent from industrial Asia. This asymmetric economic and occupational inflow is counterbalanced by a highly asymmetric cultural and social incorporation of the immigrant population. Nothing better demonstrates the globalization of bourgeois capitalist culture than the ease with which these immigrants have been integrated into the mainland cosmos; the cultural capital they bring with them was already highly Americanized.

THE AMERICAN COSMOS

What are the implications of all this for our understanding of contemporary America? I believe that it is best to conceive of not one, but three Americas, traditional America, multicultural America, and ecumenical America—a vast sociological cosmos bounded by a single, powerful polity. The three are obviously related, but it is important not to confuse them, especially in discussions of multiculturalism.

Multicultural America is made up of the mainland or metropolitan populations of the four "transnational spaces" or regional cosmoses discussed above. It has been called immigrant America by Portes and others, and while this term obviously captures an important dimension of this sector, it is likely to be misleading to the degree that it invites too close a comparison with the immigrant America of earlier years. As I had pointed out, there is something fundamentally different in the relationship between these immigrant communities with both their home societies (to which they remain strongly linked socially and culturally) and the broader American society, with which they are permanently intertwined. Multicultural America is a great socio-cultural concourse, a space where all the cultures from the center's several regional cosmoses meet, resist, embrace, display their cultural wares at annual parades, gawk at, fight, riot, and learn to live with each other, sometimes even learn a little something from each other.

By traditional America, I mean the Euro-African world that emerged from the Puritan North, the industrial smokestacks, the prairie farms, and the slave South. It is the America of the Midwestern main street, of the old and new South, and of the ethnic working classes. It is the America of Richard Nixon, J. Edgar Hoover, and Louis Farrakhan. But it is also the America of Jimmy Carter and the Congressional Black Caucus, of the land grant colleges and the United Negro Colleges. Socially, it is committed to enhanced opportunities and inter-generational mobility, but it is also historically racist, though changing in this regard, and profoundly separatist in its basic orientation. It embraces all races and classes, and today a great many African Americans are as committed to the separatist ideal as their Southern white counterparts. There has been some progress: instead of "separate and unequal," the ethic of this America, as a result of African American pressure, is now "separate but *truly* equal." There is profound disagreement about how such an America is to be achieved—witness the war over affirmative action—but all parties, except for the fringe extremists, are in agreement in their desire to live peacefully and separately.

Ironically, traditional America does have a common culture. At the elite level, it is largely the Anglo-American tradition modified by interactions with the older, more traditional ethnic groups, including main-streaming African Americans, and by continental European influences. At the popular level, traditional America has been deeply influenced by the African American working class: in its language, music, art, and religion, and in many of its attitudes. For a long time, it simply refused to acknowledge this influence, but in recent decades it has come to do so. It does so even while remaining committed to a separatist society, though one less and less rationalized in racist terms. The persisting racial segregation among black and white traditional Americans is today as much a product of class as of race and is in many ways more voluntary than imposed.

Perhaps the strongest unifying cultural feature of traditional America is its Christian heritage. Originally and still largely Protestant, traditional America is rapidly losing its hostility toward Catholicism, as an overriding convergence of conservative religious values becomes more important: the belief in a Christian God and regular church-going; the commitment to patriarchy; the demonization of abortion rights; the preference for punitive law-and-order forms of childrearing and justice; the neo-Puritan fear of sex; uncritical patriotism; reverence for, and for many, dependence on, the military; and the parochial suspicion of the foreign. Even while firmly settled in their separate communities, the many different white ethnic groups and the large core of working- and middle-class blacks who make up traditional America are fully committed to this still thriving system of values.

THE MEANING OF RACE

In one important area, traditional America is under strong pressure from the multicultural sector to change one of its central values, namely, the meaning and conception, though not the significance, of race. Traditionally, race has been defined among both black and white Americans in binary terms: the so-called one-drop rule sociologically excluded any intermediary racial groups on a continuum between blacks and whites. While the binary rule was originally constructed and rigidly imposed by whites out of their commitment to notions of racial purity and exclusion, it is one that traditional African Americans have come to embrace for political and cultural reasons. The rule operated with extraordinary tenacity not only because both the traditional "races" came to accept it, but because later immigrant groups quickly conformed. Jews, dark-skinned southern Europeans, and Caucasoid Hispanics, once re-

jected as "true whites," eagerly struggled for, and eventually won, acceptance within the Caucasian chalk circle of white people—in contrast with the excluded blacks, whose presence is required for the extraordinary valorization of whiteness. (The point is best made by noting that for the average Irishman in non-black Ireland, whiteness has no social meaning; Ireland is, in fact, one of the least racist of European societies, as any well-traveled African American or West Indian tourist will attest; however, whiteness is instantly embraced as a valued social, cultural, and economic asset by the marginal, socially insecure Irish immigrant in America, as the well-documented historical negrophobia of working-class Irish Americans, their liberal politics notwithstanding, will also readily attest.)

The rise of the multicultural sector strongly undermines the binary rule in two important respects, one demographic, the other cultural. One reason why the binary rule worked so well was that African Americans were, by and large, the only significant "other" in the American population for most of the nation's history. Until recently, Asians and dark-skinned Latin and South Asian immigrants were an insignificant demographic presence; and Native Americans—who up to the end of the eighteenth century constituted the second significant racial "other"—were removed from consideration through decimation and confinement on reservations.

All this has changed dramatically with the rise of the regional cosmos and the multicultural sector. Visibly nonwhite Asians and Latin Americans, who by no stretch of the imagination can be socially redefined and incorporated within the social category of "white people," now exist in significant numbers in society; indeed, they will outnumber blacks by the turn of the century. Since these groups are clearly neither whites nor blacks, a serious crisis of racial definition now confronts those clinging to the binary conception of race.

Quite apart from the purely demographic factor, however, is the cultural refusal of most of the new immigrants to play by the binary rule, as early streams of immigrants have done. On the one hand, most of the new Asian immigrants have a strong sense of their own racial identity, are proud of the way they look, and do not wish to be redefined racially as anything else. And this sense of racial pride is further reinforced by the multicultural celebration of ethno-racial differences. On the other hand, most immigrants from Latin America bring with them, in addition to their racial heterogeneity, their own highly developed nonbinary or "interval-type" notions of race. That is, socially significant distinctions are made among persons on a continuum between obviously black and obviously white persons. A visibly nonwhite, but light- or brown-skinned Puerto Rican, Dominican, Jamaican, or Brazilian does not consider himself "black." One only has to observe the elaborate shade gradations and mating and marriage patterns of Cuban, Puerto Rican, and other Latin immigrants to recognize that a wholly different principle of racial classification is at play. A similar nonbinary pattern prevails among South Asians between black-skinned "Dravidian" types and fair-skinned "Aryan" types. And the same holds for East Asians. Indeed, nonbinary racial classification is the norm among the vast majority of non-European peoples.

Added to these two factors is a third challenge to the binary rule: the pre-eminence of Japan as a major economic power. The coincidence of the advanced industrial world with the white world strongly reinforced notions of racial purity and superiority. The challenge to American and European economic hegemony from a clearly nonwhite power, one that until as late as the sixties was castigated as the "yellow peril," its immigrants unashamedly herded into concentration camps during the Second World War, has created confusion for traditional Americans holding fast to their binary notion of race. When one adds to this the out-performance of whites in the educational system by the former "yellow devils"— especially on I.Q. tests, which have functioned so prominently as a "scientific" justification for the binary, purist dogma—it is easy to understand why the binary rule is now in crisis.

ECUMENICAL AMERICA

Ecumenical America is not merely cosmopolitan, for it goes beyond the simple embrace of many cultures maintaining their separate identities. It is, rather, the universal culture that emerged and continues to develop in the great cities and university towns of the nation. This culture is a genuinely ecumenical one: it draws from everywhere, not just from the local cultures of the traditional ethnic and immigrant sectors and the traditional Euro-American culture at its doorstep. The image of the melting pot fails to describe the process by which it emerges, for it does not indiscriminately absorb all and everything into some common stew. There is a complex process of selection and universalization of particular cultural forms and styles generating its great cultural innovations for itself and for the world: in science, technology, literature, dance, painting, music, and cuisine.

Like traditional America, it has both a formal or elite and a popular or vernacular level. English, both of the streets and the academy, is its common language. Its shared art thrives in the works of a Jasper Johns or an Andy Warhol (with their ironic ecumenization of traditional America's most beloved icons) but, perhaps most quintessentially, in the musical form of jazz. On the popular level, the shared art of ecumenical America is also strongly influenced by African Americans. Increasingly, the products of the regional cosmoses are selected out for universalization, as in the ecumenization of Chinese and Mexican cuisine, the poetry of Derek Walcott, the fiction of Saul Bellow and Maxine Hong Kingston, and the drama of Eugene O'Neill. Ecumenical America also draws directly from the wider world in meeting the needs of its art and its technology. The culture it produces, in turn, has become the koine, or common currency, of the world, the first genuinely global culture on the face of the earth.

Ecumenical America is based primarily in the postindustrial economy, with its advanced technological plants, complex services, and multinational corporations. It is no utopia, as the legion of previously secure unemployed workers and managers of the smokestack industrial regions and rapidly obsolescent high-tech sectors can attest. It is almost as class-ridden as traditional America. It is politically mainly liberal, but it includes the politically very conservative elites and middle managers of the multinational corporations and silicon suburbs. It also includes the elite managers, scientists, and intellectuals from all over the world—Indian engineers, Japanese and Hong Kong businessmen, Argentinean doctors, European managers and artists, and Caribbean intellectuals—who enter this sector at the top and are not to be confused with the working-class or sweatshop entrepreneurs of the immigrant enclave economy.

A NEW CULTURAL POLICY

Let me conclude with a few reflections on the kind of cultural policy that this interpretation of the American cosmos implies. In the first place, it seems to me that any attempt at a single policy for all of America is a nonstarter. Any cultural policymaker must begin by recognizing the fundamentally tripartite nature of America. It is a waste of time trying to persuade a traditional American to embrace a Robert Mapplethorpe; it might even be unreasonable. The most we can reasonably expect is that he or she respect the right of ecumenical Americans to publicly view Mapplethorpe's photographs.

Second, it should now be clear that the multicultural social philosophy and approach to the arts and culture is wholly inadequate for the American cosmos. It very adequately addresses the needs of immigrant or multicultural America but is inappropriate as a strategy for the other two cultural systems that embrace the vast majority of Americans.

Indeed, it is questionable whether there can be a single policy even for the multicultural sector itself. In the first place, as we have seen, the American, cosmopolitan parts of the four regional cosmoses that together constitute the social bases of multicultural America are at different stages of development, especially in their degrees of integration. What holds true for the highly integrated West Atlantic cosmos, with its harmonizing processes of creolization, simply does not apply to the fissiparous Southern California cosmos.

But there is a more profound problem with regard to any attempt at a single multicultural policy. This is the inherent self-contradiction of all programs that adhere to the dogma of relativism. If all ideals, all values, and all art in the cultures and subcultures are of equal worth, there is no basis for the view that relativism—the basic value of the multicultural theorists and policy advocates—is of any greater worth than the basic values of any of the celebrated subcultures that deny the worth of others—including that of the relativists—in absolutist terms. Relativism requires the acceptance of its condemnation by the very antirelativists it embraces. This is no academic abstraction, as Americans have already learned in the course of their current bitter culture wars. A multicultural relativist is in no position to condemn the traditionalist fundamentalist's insistence that not only is the Christian God the only true God, but that no one has the right to prevent his children from attending public schools where the day begins and ends with Christian prayers. Similarly, a black nationalist has no moral basis for condemning a white supremacist. Indeed, partly out of recognition of this contradiction, there has been an astonishing recent convergence of interests between several white and black racist nationalists. The present volatile debate over speech codes, and more generally, over the First Amendment, is disturbing testimony to the potentially catastrophic social and cultural implications of an unthinking commitment to the self-contradictions of the relativistic dogma that is basic for multiculturalist theorists.

Traditional America is inherently hostile to such a strategy and rightly complains of its disregard for a common center. In its extreme commitment to relativism, multiculturalism well serves the needs of immigrant peoples and cultures thrown upon each other and who must learn basic principles—often contrary to their own traditions—of tolerance for others. But discrimination is the essence of cultural creation, and this same relativism, when applied to the other two areas of the American cosmos, could be deadening in its impact.

The multicultural ideology, then, is certainly needed, but its limits must be understood. Making it the American creed would be a serious mistake. In general, art within the immigrant sector should be encouraged, preferably by private foundations rather than the government, but only where it looks toward, and strives to become, a part of the shared art of the ecumene. However, where the immigrant artist is atavistic, looking only back at his or her original culture, he or she should be tolerated, respected, and accepted in good faith, but not actively supported. It is not the business of the ecumenical to promote the atavistic.

Ecumenical America is no utopia. Nonetheless, it seems clear to me that this is the future of America, for better or for worse. There is no basis for the commonly heard criticism that associates the ecumenical with a grey, homogenized world. Nor is there any justification for the view that the ecumenical is dominated by a global financial elite having no responsibility to any local community. The ultimate thrust of the ecumenical is indeed transnational and, in many respects, postnational. But this is the way of the world in the twenty-first century, and such postnational orientation is by no means confined to the financial elite. Indeed, as I have shown, it is the migrant peasants, working classes, and intellectuals from the periphery of the world's

transnational spaces who are most postnational in their attitudes and behavior. The typical Jamaican resident of Brooklyn or Mexican resident of Texas has already gone far beyond any transnational capitalist of New York in his or her attitudes, migratory movements, and life-style.

We have no choice but to accept the inevitable; but we do have choices in what we make of it. Ecumenical America and its advocates, among whom I count myself, should recognize its special place, not only as the most advanced part of the American cosmos, but as the vital source of the world's first truly global culture. It should support artists, scientists, and other cultural creators in and out of America whose work resonates and who are dialectically engaged with the emerging shared art and shared ways of the global ecumene, at both the advanced and vernacular levels of social and cultural life.

REFERENCES

1. Alan Lomax, *Folk Song Style and Culture* (Washington, DC: American Association for the Advancement of Science, 1968).
2. Paul E. Willis, *Common Culture* (Boulder, CO: Westview, 1990), p. 26.
3. For the standard Frankfurt School criticisms, see Theodor W. Adorno, *Introduction to the Sociology of Music* (New York: Continuum, 1988); and Herbert Marcuse, *One-Dimensional Man* (Boston: Beacon, 1964).
4. Peter Manuel, *Popular Musics of the Non-Western World* (New York: Oxford University Press, 1988), p. 20.
5. Deanna Robinson, Elizabeth Buck et al., *Music at the Margins: Popular Music and Global Cultural Diversity* (Newbury Park, CA: Sage, 1991), p. 4.
6. Orlando Patterson, "The Dance Invasion of Britain: On the Cultural Diffusion of Jamaican Popular Arts," *New Society,* no. 207 (September 1966).
7. See Simon Jones, *Black Culture, White Youth* (Basingstoke: Macmillan Education, 1988).
8. See Stephen Davis and Peter Simon, *Reggae Bloodlines* (New York: De Capo, 1979).

9. See Saskia Sassen, *The Mobility of Labor and Capital* (New York: Cambridge University Press, 1988).
10. For a detailed analysis of this cosmos, see my essay, "The Emerging West Atlantic System: Migration, Culture and Underdevelopment in the U.S. and Caribbean," in *Population in an Interacting World,* ed. William Alonso (Cambridge, MA: Harvard University Press, 1987).
11. Alejandro Portes and Rubén G. Rumbout, *Immigrant America* (Berkeley: University of California Press, 1990).
12. For a spirited journalistic tour of this regional cosmos and Miami's central role in it, see Joel Garreau, *The Nine Nations of North America* (Boston: Houghton Mifflin, 1981), pp. 167–206.

DISCUSSION QUESTIONS

1. Key to Patterson's argument is a distinction he makes between multiculturalism and ecumenical culture. What is your understanding of that difference? Are you persuaded by Patterson's argument?
2. Take one of the regional cosmoses other than the West Atlantic system and offer as much empirical evidence for cultural diffusion as you can to determine whether these areas are indeed similar to Patterson's portrait of the West Atlantic.

READING 5

Norma Jeane and Jimmy Dean: Nostalgic Signifiers of the Postmodern Era

Andrea Fontana and Stanford Lyman

Goodbye Norma Jeane . . .
Hollywood created a superstar
And pain was the price you paid.

—Elton John, "Candle in the Wind."

James Dean went out to Hollywood and put his picture in a picture show.

—John Prine, "Picture Show."

Marilyn Monroe and James Dean, two Hollywood stars of the 1950s, conjured up larger-than-life screen images: the blond bombshell as sexual icon and the sensitive, angst-ridden rebel without a cause. In our contemporary media-saturated culture, the screen persona of these stars becomes entangled with their real or offscreen lives, such that it often became difficult for star and fan alike to know the difference. Andrea Fontana and Stanford Lyman use the example of these now dead screen idols to raise more general issues about the construction of the postmodern self, beyond issues related to the role of media celebrities in shaping self-images.

Postmodernism claims that the content and context of everyday reality are changed in today's mass-media and mediated society (Baudrillard 1988). Thus images from the silver screen and electronic bleeps from the television become real and create an uneasy and perhaps unholy new sense of self and society. Everyday reality is no longer separate from other realms, such as scientific discourse or dreams (cf. Schutz 1971). The world of media and the everyday obdurate world become intertwined beyond separation. What is real when both sides of the Middle-East conflict watch CNN to learn how the war is going? Or when virtual reality can transport us inside the human body or on Mars as if we "were there" (Rheingold 1991). In this ethos it is fitting for our heroes and heroines to be media characters, who overshadow everyday life individuals. Max Headroom epitomizes this new sense of self, an electronic creation of the screen who both controls and is controlled by the electronic medium.

Postmodernism also states that, disillusioned with the cold, monolithic impersonality of modernism, postmodern society craves a potpourri of experiences, steeped in a myriad of colors and representations, a pastiche of styles combined with a nostalgic yearning for the figures and fads of yesteryears (Jameson 1983). The encroachment of mass media and nostalgic fantasies changes reality, which becomes "hyperreality." Disneyland becomes the ultimate reality of our age, for Baudrillard at least (1988), blurring together the boundaries of the real and the imaginary and becoming a reality of its own. In fact, the reality of Mickey and Co. has crossed the Atlantic (as a fitting American revenge against French elitism) and is staking a claim to what is real in France—it won't be long before scores of locals and tourists alike will gaze with an indiscriminate sense of awe both at Magic Mountain and at Versailles, fusing together nostalgia for the fantasy of what might be with the historicity of what-once-was. Having lost the ability or perhaps the willingness to look beneath the glimmer of the surface, we are satiated with myths.

In this paper we will use Marilyn Monroe and James Dean, two very different yet very similar movie idols of the fifties, whose myths have grown tremendously after their death, to examine the forming of the postmodern self of pastiche and nostalgia. This self becomes ambiguous, not only because different interpretations of it are offered, (cf. Lyman 1984) but because it comes to encompass more than its everyday life renditions—history, myth, and media add to everyday life combining signifiers and signified to create a pastiche self. This is self which never finds closure in the interaction but is always being negotiated and changed, as old fragments fall out and new ones are added, in a forever incomplete puzzle.

DIFFERENT YET SIMILAR ICONS

What happens when two icons meet face to face? In the case of Marilyn Monroe and James Dean they practically had to be restrained from spitting (Riese 1991, p. 340).

No one more than Jimmy Dean and Norma Jeane Baker exemplify the postmodern notion of the hyperreal; long after their death they have not been forgotten but their legend has grown and maintained a nostalgic and tragic mystique. As two rainbows in the leaden darkness of the after-storm Norma Jeane and Jimmy Dean fleet-

ingly provided a glimmer of beauty that captured the public imagination. Their premature vanishing left the world aghast, unsatisfied with what it had barely witnessed. The audience yearned for more but the two were gone. Gloria Steinem captures this feeling:

When the past dies, there is mourning, but when the future dies our imaginations are compelled to carry it on (Steinem, 1988, p. 21).

And the legend grew: signifiers and signified about the lives and characters of Norma Jeane and Jimmy Dean grew larger and more complex. It soon became difficult to draw the line between their real life and their "screen" life, between historically accurate recounting of their lives and fictional, legendary accounts of them. In our postmodern era of media, pastiche and nostalgia, our two heroes have come to represent a dreamy yearning of bygone years which is replicated in the pastiche of postmodern representations, Norma Jeane, né Marilyn, becomes the multiplicity of sensuous faces beckoning at us from the wall, in the famous picture-collage by Andy Warhol or is recreated alive by the pastiche/parody of her embodied in Madonna. Jimmy Dean, becomes James Dean, and looks at us enigmatically from behind dark glasses in the innumerable posters bearing his likeness as if he were looking at the endless string of young hopefuls trying to claim his place—from Martin Sheen to Sean Penn.

Tragedy adds to mystery and the recounting of events becomes blurred and unclear. The passing of time also adds to mystery as new generations no longer have that "first hand" witnessing and remembrance of the events. Oliver Stone's film *J.F.K.* plays on these elements by proving a variety of signifiers that each member of the audience to follow her particular theory about "what really happened."

Why bring Marilyn Monroe and James Dean together? Are they not antithetical? The first, sultry, parted lips beckoning almost obscenely—the sex symbol of mid-America's men, sweet innocence denying what the sensuous body promised. The second deep-seated eyes showing inner angst, the symbol of a rebellious youth alienated from their parents and society, the very parents and society who idolized Marilyn Monroe.

Despite clear differences, Dean and Monroe shared much—they shared hope, the hope of the young American fifties, hope for youth in Dean, hope for glamour and success in Monroe. They also shared the tension of the fifties, of a corporate, bureaucratized society that had brought to reality Max Weber's prophecy of the "iron cage"; a personal tension for Marilyn, trying to prove herself as a worthwhile person and actress, struggling not to be suffocated in the narrowness of the role society gave—a dumb, sexy blonde; a generational tension for James, who epitomized all alienated youth in conflict with their parents. They also share the tragedy of success that comes too fast and is too heady. There is a moral story in both tragedies—the men, the women, the fast cars, the powerful people, the lasciviousness of it all. Or, there is a different moral story to be read—not focusing on their sins but on the sins of society, which used them, exploited them and drove them over the edge, and then continued to shamelessly exploit them with nostalgic memorabilia, movies, books and dozens of "whonna be's." Also, the two were sex symbols. Monroe was *the* sexual symbol of American males but Dean was also a sex symbol in his own way. He was the first superstar to present an androgynous figure (not purely homosexual as Montgomery Cliff's, with whom he has, at times, been linked together). While Marlon Brando reeked of pouting arrogance and bulging muscles, James Dean showed his inner self through his eyes, while his lithe, almost frail figure, was a pretty sight not a powerful one. Finally, Monroe and Dean, over three decades after their death, are linked together by the everchanging, mysterious nature of their myth—they represent the ambiguous self of the media world of postmodernity.

TRAGIC BIOGRAPHIES

> The biography is a kind of "pinball machine": the plot is planned; the supporting cast . . . are positioned beforehand, often "static" in terms of personality; finally "Marilyn" is fired into this narrative by the author, made to bounce off each figure until the game is completed (McCann 1988, p. 38).

Comparison between Dean (1931–1955) and Monroe (1926–1962) extends to their tragic lives: troubled youths, struggling young years toward success, the suddenness of stardom, the quick downfall into death, and the growing myth to follow. The story is narrated over and over, seventy times in Monroe's case and not far behind for Dean, who allegedly, "personally" dictated his life story to over twenty biographers (Dalton 1984). All of the biographers claim to uncover the "real" James or Marilyn, yet by and large their stories are stilted, played off against "set" pieces, (cf. McCann 1988). In an era of deconstructionism what we see in Dean's and Monroe's endless biographical accounts is the opposite, reconstructionism, as the biographers, with authorial license, reconstruct the lives of the two icons against the set backdrop of dead mothers, absent fathers, doting teachers, loving husbands, exploiting moguls, and so on.

The biographers seek different angles at times, such as focusing on Monroe's death (Capell 1969, Hamblett 1966, Hudson 1982); writing a lover's letter to the myth of Monroe (Mailer 1975); using Monroe to exemplify the victimization of women in American society (Steinem 1985); and more. Similarly, for Dean, we are told the "while" story (Martinetti 1975); the "real" story (Gilmore 1975); we see him as an icon (Dalton 1984) or a rebel (Brean 1984); or a giant (Fuchs 1986); or a star (Hoskyns 1990), and so on, at nauseam. The result is an unsettled image of the two icons, in which differences between the persons, Norma Jeane and Jimmy, and the screen personae, Marilyn and James, are blurred together.

The Early Years

Much is made of their young, formative years. Norma Jeane's father was nowhere to be seen from the very beginning and she was abandoned by her mother to a series of orphanages and foster homes, twelve in all. The horrors of a wandering life in poverty and subjugation are told by biographers selectively reconstructing events to draw sympathy to the young girl of trying to show psychic scars setting up the suicide to come. The culmination of horrors and exploitation comes with Norma Jeane's rape by a renter when she was only nine (Hecht 1954). Age nine was also a time of suffering for Jimmy, as his mother died at that time. The father, unable to support his son, had to let relatives raise him in a small town in Indiana, twenty miles north of Muncie, Robert Lynd's *Middletown* (Dalton 1974, p. 28).

Some tried, falsely, to claim that Jimmy had been orphaned, perhaps attempting to duplicate the national swell of sympathy that had taken place a few years earlier in Monroe's case (cf. Riese 1991, p. 371). Yet, Jimmy had a much more average youth than Marilyn as he was excelling in sports and drama in school, although beginning to drive motorcycles and then cars, too fast (as his teachers tell us, years later). Norma Jeane, in the meantime, got married at sixteen; it did not last long. The similarity of their plight to stardom came a bit later, when they moved to Hollywood (Norma Jeane) and New York (Jimmy) and began their careers as hundreds of young performers do, by taking bit parts, whenever in whatever was available. Both had to suffer the indignities of poor budding actors in the big city. Norma accepted $50 for her famous pose when the only thing she had on was "the radio" (Mailer 1975, p. 66) and allegedly suffered from the debauchery of tinsel town:

> The legends . . . have her saying to her lawyer as she signs the papers for a big contract, "Well, that's the last cock I suck" (Mailer 1975, p. 107).

Dean was not faring much better, living in cheap hotels:

> Their room (Jimmy and Bill Bast) was 802, and it cost them ninety dollars a month. . . . . It is still spartan, with no TV and minimal furniture. A chest, a chair. . . . (Dalton 1974, p. 87).

Dean too, had to prostitute himself to the depraved demands of the celluloid life. His friend, Bill Bast, reported that Jimmy once told him, in reference to sexual exploitation: "They [Hollywood's powerful] get these poor kids, saps like me, and make them perform. I did a little dancing myself. I was dumb. I thought it might pay off" (Riese 1991, p. 407).

Stardom

Soon the years of pin up calendars (Monroe) and Pepsi commercials (Dean) were left behind. Marilyn first, and a few years later James, (remember that he was five years younger), came into their own. Norma Jeane first became Marilyn Monroe, went from a brunette to a bombshell blonde and then, after a series of forgettable movies, became a star in 1952 with Gentlemen Prefer Blondes and perfected her screen image of the dumb blonde, playing one seductive role after another, epitomized a few years later by a scene in The Seven Year Itch, with Marilyn standing seductively over a subway grating, her white dress blowing above her hips. Marilyn gave glimpses of real acting talent, in movies such as Bus Stop, but she was becoming the icon of sex for American males and they did not want her to be talented or smart, just a big-breasted, sexy, dumb broad with a sweet, innocent smile:

> So we think of Marilyn who was every man's love affair with America, Marilyn Monroe who was blonde and beautiful and had a little rinky-dink of a voice and all the cleanliness of all the clean American backyards. She was our angel, the sweet angel of sex, and the sugar of sex came up from her like a resonance of sound in the cleanest grain of a violin (Mailer 1975, p. 15).

It is worthy of notice that an interview for the *Ladies' Home Journal* was scuttled, as the reporter, Margaret Parton, actually took Marilyn seriously as an actress. As a person she was also becoming idolized; marriages with Joe Di Maggio and Arthur Miller kept her in the public eye continually. Publicity dominated both her private and public life, bridging the two together and leaving Marilyn little time to be anything but her public persona: "She is her career, and her career is herself" (Mailer 1975, p. 143).

Marilyn's image grew as different gossips about her alleged sexual affairs began to circulate; among others she supposedly had affairs with Frank Sinatra, Yves Montand, John Kennedy and Robert Kennedy. Soon she began to slide downward while rumors swirled wildly. What was going on? Was Marilyn's mood affected by her tormented childhood? Was she suffering psychologically from the alleged twelve abortions she had had? Was she the victim of an establishment that failed to recognize her talents and labeled her as a manipulative bitch who used sex to get what she wanted? Was she a spoiled and uncaring manipulator who, in *Some Like It Hot,* drove Tony Curtis and Jack Lemmon crazy, once making Lemmon stand by in dress and high heels while she muffed the line: "It's me, Sugar" over forty times? Death came to meet her very soon, and the rumors grew and the legend grew, as Marilyn returned to fame as never before.

Jimmy Dean's career as a star was much shorter but not less glamorous. He starred in only three movies: *East of Eden, Rebel Without a Cause,* and *Giant.* At the time of his death only *East of Eden* had been released, with Marilyn Monroe as one of the "usherettes" for the premiere, making him an idol the world over. A month after his death *Rebel Without a Cause* appeared and a year later *Giant* (the dialogue for the last scene had to be dubbed after Dean's death). Dean's legend mushroomed; when they released *Giant* in Japan, huge billboards bore

very large images of Dean, dwarfing smaller pictures of Elizabeth Taylor and Rock Hudson (when he was shown at all).

This young boy from Fairmount, Indiana, touched a nerve among American youth. His performances told them that it was okay to be troubled, to feel alienated, and to disagree with their parents. A fine-featured, smallish (5'8") youth he presented an androgynous image, the first of many performers to do so; some of the more notables to follow in this mold were Mick Jagger, David Bowie, Annie Lennox, Boy George, Grace Jones, and the current non-plus-ultra androgynous superstar, Michael Jackson. Some of the scenes from his movies were cut for possible homosexual overtones:

> Some of the powers-that-be at Warner Brothers apparently perceived homoeroticism in the way Cal (James Dean) wrapped his lips around the recorder and in the way he seemed to caress Aron (Richard Davalos) with his words (Riese 1991, p. 81).

Rebel Without a Cause was banned from Mexico and Spain as James Dean was considered a weak male role model for Latino youth (Riese 1991).

Marlon Brando showed in his eyes an inner conflict, but he still represented a long line of macho performers. This was the era when Gary Cooper had written to Kirk Douglas, chastening him for playing the not-so-macho role of Vincent Van Gogh. James Dean changed male role models, both in movies and in everyday life. This is what Martin Sheen, one of the many "future" James Deans, had to say:

> When I was a young actor in New York, there was a saying that if Marlon Brando had changed the way actors acted, James Dean changed the way people lived. I believe that. No one came before him, and there hasn't been anyone since (Dalton 1984, p. 7).

Dean's personal life was not as glamorized as Monroe's, yet his penchant for, at times, bizarre behavior, won his fame. Among other vignettes of his exploits, there is the time when filming an outdoors scene for *Giant*. Dean walked to the outer edge of the large circle of onlookers, calmly urinated on a tree, and then went about his acting. He later recounted that if he could do that in front of all those people, he would no longer feel intimidated by Liz Taylor. His behavior also won him enemies, such as Truman Capote and Humphrey Bogart, who thought Dean possessed no talent at all. As his legend grew, more stories were circulated, about his bullfighting bravados, his fast cars, glamorous women, and gossips about his male "friends." There was no downside in Dean's career, as in Monroe's, he died on his way up, as his career was soaring, prompting an anonymous producer to say about his death:

"Nice career move, boy" (Riese 1991, p. 23).

DEATH AND NOSTALGIA

Actor James Dean, the surly, brooding Caleb of the movie *East of Eden* was killed last night in the head-on-highway crash of his brand new sport car near here (*Los Angeles Mirror*, October 1, 1955).

All the papers had to say was that Marilyn was found in the nude (Elton John, "Candle in the Wind").

They died suddenly, abruptly. They were the first superstars to die young. A list of others were to follow, most notably John Kennedy, Bob Kennedy, Elvis Presley, Buddy Holly, Janice Joplin, Jim Croce, and John Lennon. A number of elements combined to raise them to legends, creating rumors and counter rumors, drawing almost pathological attention to these dead stars. Americans, and disillusioned youth in particular, were seeking new idols, disappointed in the traditional ones, and the tremendous growth of mass media provided the public with some ready-made ones. Also, the mystery of sudden death lead the public to unconsciously try to mystify a Weberian, rational, demystified society. They were not dead, they had

been disfigured and hidden out of sight! The cry: Dean lives! was fairly common; some even offered rewards for finding James Dean. Dean's death triggered a chain reaction by mourning fans. This was not a mere "Valentino" phenomenon, that is, this was not only about broken-hearted fans of a silver screen idol who had died prematurely: this was a part of the fan's lives, their hopes for a free future, as exemplified by Dean. Youth mourned itself in its mourning of James Dean.

As for Marilyn, the mystery was about the cause of death—had she been killed? Rumors about her connections with Jimmy Hoffa, and his archenemy, Robert Kennedy, circulated. Was poor Marilyn not only a sexual victim of society but had she been unwittingly used for some illicit political scheme and then removed? And, if indeed she had committed suicide, why? Who was responsible? Dean became an icon for he showed youth what they could become; Marilyn, at least partially, became an icon in spite of herself, for the image we had made her become, willingly or not. Dean opened a window of hope against conventional society; Monroe made us shed a tear for witnessing how society could use us.

We could not let go of them and we tried desperately to recreate them in "look-alikes" or "the next Dean or Monroe." Doubles! The notion of dopperganger was either seriously taken or duplicated commercially. There was a series of big breasted sex-pots who were supposed to be the next M. M., such as D. D. (Diana Dors), B. B. (Bridgette Bardot), and J. M. (Jane Mansfield), plus a myriad of minor starlets. Also, there is the single-initialed, postmodern "reincarnation" of Marilyn, Madonna. James Dean has had few true "look alikes" (notably Christopher Jones); however, he has had myriad of aspirants ("The Next") from some of his contemporaries, such as Steve McQueen, to Martin Sheen (esp. in *Badlands*), his son Charlie Sheen, Alain Delon, Anthony Perkins, and many, many more.

Nostalgia for both Monroe and Dean went beyond seeking doubles or looking for their heirs. The American love dream with Marilyn continued, as many biographers, mainly males, tried to capture their own nostalgic view of who she really was, or, at times, more morbidly, how she had really died. Norman Mailer exemplifies the undying American males' love for Monroe, with his "love letter/biography" about Marilyn written in quasi-masturbatory style, followed by another book about her. Finally, he cast his own daughter as Marilyn in a play (McCann 1987).

Dean's fans formed clubs across the world; his greatest fan, Japanese businessman Seita Ohnishi, built a statue near the site of Dean's fatal accident and recently commissioned another one (for $200,000) to be built in France (Riese 1991, p. 369). Dean's gravesite was (and is) swarmed by fans and souvenir hunters, who stole his bust and chipped off pieces from his tombstone.

Postmodern consumerism indulged in nostalgic recreation of its two icons of the fifties, and the stories changed, more and more allegedly based on new found "facts" or newly created rumors. But something went amiss in the new postmodern pastiche of Monroe and Dean. One, the victim of a sexist society and the other, the idol of rebellious youth, were "coopted" into mainstream America, or better, into the Americana of consumerism. Movies and documentaries about the two followed by the dozens, along with posters, mugs, ties, and dozens of other memorabilia items.

Something else, perhaps more important, was lost in the postmodern versions of Marilyn Monroe and James Dean. Innocence in Marilyn and introvertedness in James gave way to brush arrogance and extrovertedness in their latest recreations—Madonna and Sean Penn. Madonna's cynical and calculating recreation of Monroe plays on open sexuality but, despite her name, she does not elicit any images of innocence. Madonna is not raped by society; she rapes it. Her former husband, Sean Penn, touted as the next James Dean (Connelly 1983), exhibits some flashes of the acting talent of a

Dean and a rebellious attitude a la Dean, but Penn shows as much inside angst as a pit bull. Dean and Monroe symbolized the many tensions of society in the fifties and Madonna and Penn are also symbols of the societal tensions of the eighties, but their pastiche reconstruction is a hollow one, it recreates the form but lacks much of the content; in a way it becomes a parody of itself (perhaps intentionally so in Madonna).

THE AMBIGUOUS SELF

Over three decades after the deaths of Dean and Monroe we still speculate and re-write the texts of their selves. *McCall's* magazine (Smith 1992) shows us a model made up to their notion of what Marilyn would look like today, at sixty-six. *Hollywood: Then and Now* magazine (1992) shows side by side pictures of Marilyn and Madonna in which Madonna recreates images of Marilyn by wearing the same costumes and make up from famous shots from the past. Dean still influences clothing, mannerism and, more importantly, feelings in young people; his message to youth: "Hey, it's ok to be scared" (Zavatski 1980, p. 53) is still as relevant today as almost four decades ago.

Who are they really? Steinem tells that Monroe was never able to express her true self since:

> She lived in a time when her body was far more rewarded than the spirit inside. Her body became her prison (Steinem 1988, p. 199).

And McCann:

> When we now think of Marilyn Monroe, we summon up a montage of memories stretching across space and time (McCann 1988, p. 11).

Similarly with James Dean:

> Everything about James Dean was ambiguous: his image *floats* in suspension between child and adult, androgynous and macho, actor and person. . . . Jimmy has a multitude of different images. . . . A fugitive presence that suggests

something distinct *only* when in motion, his genius was in blurring the lines (Dalton 1984, p. 257).

Monroe and Dean inform us about the self. That entity which we call the self is a fleeting, unfinished thing. Goffman (in his early works) convincingly showed us that the self is a process, a continuous social accomplishment:

> This self itself does not derive from its possessor, but from the whole scene of his action . . . this self is a product of a scene that comes off (Goffman 1959, p. 252).

Yet the self is more than a single mask that we wear in front of others, something that we accomplished in everyday interaction.

Marilyn Monroe and James Dean show us that there is not a mere single unit called a self which is accomplished, but that there are many fragments of self provided in different accounts, some based on fact, some on fiction, some on different hermaneutic understanding of accounts. Who are Monroe and Dean? A dumb blonde? A skilled actress? A woman of loose morals? A victim of society? A sex symbol? An icon of consumerism? And he, a talented yet arrogant young actor? An unsurpassed young performer? The symbol of rebellious youth? An amoral character? A fad? An icon?

What is real, what is merely surmised, what is on the screen, in the tabloids, and in real life all loosely blend together, intermeshing and confusing what *are* signifiers and what is signified, in an unfinished, puzzling kaleidoscope. The selves of Marilyn and James are open-ended texts, a pastiche of interpretations in which the authors deconstruct the everyday life person and the screen persona to create an ever-changing, always unfinished, always ambitious self. The irony of the postmodern self, as exemplified by Monroe and Dean is that the self is a pastiche, a continually shifting and renegotiated entity, both real and created, and that no closure is possible, as nostalgic memories and new dreams change it constantly.

BIBLIOGRAPHY

Baudrillard, J. 1988. *America.* Translated by C. Turner. New York: Verso.

Brean. 1984. *Rebels United: The Enduring Reality of James Dean.* Indianapolis, IN: Brean-Jones Publishers.

Capell, F. 1969. *The Strange Death of Marilyn Monroe.* New Jersey: Herald of Freedom Press.

Conelly, C. 1983. "Bad Boy. Slab Boy. Everyboy. Sean Penn Is not Another Pretty Face." *Rolling Stone* (May 26). Pp. 27, 28, 31.

Dalton, D. 1974. *James Dean: The Mutant King.* New York: St. Martin's Press.

Dalton, D. (with R. Cayen). 1984. *James Dean: American Icon.* New York: St. Martin's Press.

Fuchs, W. 1986. *James Dean: Footsteps of a Giant.* Berlin: Taco.

Gilmore, J. 1975. *The Real James Dean.* New York: Pyramid Books.

Goffman, Erving. 1959. *The Presentation of Self in Everyday Life.* New York: Anchor Books.

Hamblett, C. 1966. *Who Killed Marilyn Monroe?* London: Leslie Frewin.

Hecht, B. 1954. "Interview with Monroe" *Empire News.* London. May 2, 1954–August 1, 1954.

Hollywood: Then and Now. 1992. "Marilyn-Madonna: If Marilyn Were Alive Today . . . What Do You Think She Would Tell Madonna?" July: 20–27.

Hoskyns. B. (with D. Loehr). 1990. *James Dean. Shooting Star.* London: Virgin.

Hudson, J. 1982. *The Mysterious Death of Marilyn Monroe.* New York: Volitant.

Jameson, F. 1983. "Postmodernism and Consumer Society." Pp. 11–125 in *The Anti-Aesthetic: Essays on Postmodern Culture,* edited by H. Foster. Port Townsend, WA: Bay Press.

Lyman, S. 1984. "Foreword." Pp. vii–xii in *The Existential Self in Society,* edited by J. Kotarba and A. Fontana. Chicago: University of Chicago Press.

Mailer, N. 1975. *Marilyn: A Biography.* New York: Warner Books.

Martinetti, R. 1975. *The James Dean Story.* New York: Pinnacle Books.

McCann, G. 1988. *Marilyn Monroe.* New Brunswick, NJ: Rutgers University Press.

Rheingold, H. 1991. *Virtual Reality: The Revolutionary Technology of Computer-Generated Artificial Worlds—And How It Promises To Transform Business and Society.* New York: Summit Books.

Riese, R. 1991. *The Unabridged James Dean: His Life and Legacy from A to Z.* Chicago: Contemporary Books.

Schulz, A. 1971. *Collected Papers.* Vol. 1. The Hague: Nijhoff.

Smith, L. 1992. "What Becomes a Legend Most?" *McCall's* (July): 114–117, 154–157.

Steinem, G. (with G. Barris). 1988. *Marilyn: Norma Jeane.* New York: Signet.

Zavatsky, W. 1980. "Reflections on the Life and Death of James Dean." *Rolling Stone* (October 16): 51–55.

DISCUSSION QUESTIONS

1. Choose two contemporary movie stars and use them as "signifiers of the postmodern era" in the manner Fontana and Lyman do with their two examples.
2. Fontana and Lyman view the postmodern self as being inherently ambiguous, provisional, and subject to change. In other words, it is not stable, fixed, and certain. Do you agree or disagree with their assessment?

READING 6

The Code of the Streets

Elijah Anderson

By many measures, inner-city life for poor blacks today has become more bleak and dangerous than in the past. Elijah Anderson argues that as middle-class blacks have found opportunities to exit the inner-city, only the "truly disadvantaged" were left behind, without adequate role models that kept the poor connected culturally to the larger society. Anderson has been engaged in ethnographic research on the lives of the poor for over two decades. Here he focuses on young black males who are part of the hard-core street culture. This culture—with its emphasis on respect—is at odds with not only the values of the larger society, but also the values of "decent" people in their neighborhoods.

Of all the problems besetting the poor inner-city black community, none is more pressing than that of interpersonal violence and aggression. It wreaks havoc daily with the lives of community residents and increasingly spills over into downtown and residential middle-class areas. Muggings, burglaries, carjackings, and drug-related shootings, all of which may leave their victims or innocent bystanders dead, are now common enough to concern all urban and many suburban residents. The inclination to violence springs from the circumstances of life among the ghetto poor—the lack of jobs that pay a living wage, the stigma of race, the fallout from rampant drug use and drug trafficking, and the resulting alienation and lack of hope for the future.

Simply living in such an environment places young people at special risk of falling victim to aggressive behavior. Although there are often forces in the community which can counteract the negative influences, by far the most powerful being a strong, loving, "decent" (as inner-city residents put it) family committed to middle-class values, the despair is pervasive enough to have spawned an oppositional culture, that of "the streets," whose norms are often consciously opposed to those of mainstream society. These two orientations—decent and street—socially organize the community, and their coexistence has important consequences for residents, particularly children growing up in the inner city. Above all, this environment means that even youngsters whose home lives reflect mainstream values—and the majority of homes in the community do—must be able to handle themselves in a street-oriented environment.

This is because the street culture has evolved what may be called a code of the streets, which amounts to a set of informal rules governing interpersonal public behavior, including violence. The rules prescribe both a proper comportment and a proper way to respond if challenged. They regulate the use of violence and so allow those who are inclined to aggression to precipitate violent encounters in an approved way. The rules have been established and are enforced mainly by the street-oriented, but on the streets the distinction between street and decent is often irrelevant; everybody knows that if the rules are violated, there are penalties. Knowledge of the code is thus largely defensive; it is literally necessary for operating in public. Therefore, even though families with a decency orientation are usually opposed to the values of the code, they often reluctantly encourage their children's familiarity with it to enable them to negotiate the inner-city environment.

At the heart of the code is the issue of respect—loosely defined as being treated "right," or granted the deference one deserves. However, in the troublesome public environment of the inner city, as people increasingly feel buffeted by forces beyond their control, what one deserves in the way of respect becomes more and more problematic and uncertain. This in turn further opens the issue of respect to sometimes intense interpersonal negotiation. In the street culture, especially among young people, respect is viewed as almost an external entity that is hard-won but easily lost, and so must constantly be guarded. The rules of the code in fact provide a framework for negotiating respect. The person whose very appearance—including his clothing, demeanor, and way of moving—deters transgressions feels that he possesses, and may be considered by others to possess, a measure of respect. With the right amount of respect, for instance, he can avoid "being bothered" in public. If he is bothered, not only may he be in physical danger but he has been disgraced or "dissed" (disrespected). Many of the forms that dissing can take might seem petty to middle-class people (maintaining eye contact for too long, for example), but to those invested in the street code, these actions become serious indications of the other person's intentions. Consequently, such people become very sensitive to advances and slights, which could well serve as warnings of imminent physical confrontation.

This hard reality can be traced to the profound sense of alienation from mainstream society and its institutions felt by many poor inner-city black people, particularly the young. The code of the streets is actually a cultural adaptation to a profound lack of faith in the police and the judicial system. The police are most often seen as representing the dominant white society and not caring to protect inner-city residents. When called, they may not respond, which is one reason many residents feel they must be prepared to take extraordinary measures to defend themselves and their loved ones against those who are inclined to aggression. Lack of police accountability has in fact been incorporated into the status system: the person who is believed capable of "taking care of himself" is accorded a certain deference, which translates into a sense of physical and psychological control. Thus the street code emerges where the influence of the police ends and personal responsibility for one's safety is felt to begin. Exacerbated by the proliferation of drugs and easy access to guns, this volatile situation results in the ability of the street-oriented minority (or those who effectively "go for bad") to dominate the public spaces.

DECENT AND STREET FAMILIES

Although almost everyone in poor inner-city neighborhoods is struggling financially and therefore feels a certain distance from the rest of America, the decent and the street family in a real sense represent two poles of value orientation, two contrasting conceptual categories. The labels "decent" and "street," which the residents themselves use, amount to evaluative judgments that confer status on local residents. The labeling is often the result of a social contest among individuals and families of the neighborhood. Individuals of the two orientations often coexist in the same extended family. Decent residents judge themselves to be so while judging others to be of the street, and street individuals often present themselves as decent, drawing distinctions between themselves and other people. In addition, there is quite a bit of circumstantial behavior—that is, one person may at different times exhibit both decent and street orientations, depending on the circumstances. Although these designations result from so much social jockeying, there do exist concrete features that define each conceptual category.

Generally, so-called decent families tend to accept mainstream values more fully and attempt to instill them in their children. Whether married couples with children or single-parent (usually female) households, they are generally "working poor" and so tend to be better off financially than their street-oriented neighbors. They value hard work and self-reliance and are willing to sacrifice for their children. Because they have a certain amount of faith in mainstream society, they harbor hopes for a better future for their children, if not for themselves. Many of them go to church and take a strong interest in their children's schooling. Rather than dwelling on the real hardships and inequities facing them, many such decent people, particularly the increasing number of grandmothers raising grandchildren, see their difficult situation as a test from God and derive great support from their faith and from the church community.

Extremely aware of the problematic and often dangerous environment in which they reside, decent parents tend to be strict in their child-rearing practices, encouraging children to respect authority and walk a straight moral line. They have an almost obsessive concern about trouble of any kind and remind their children to be on the lookout for people and situations that might lead to it. At the same time, they are themselves polite and considerate of others, and teach their children to be the same way. At home, at work, and in church, they strive hard to maintain a positive mental attitude and a spirit of cooperation.

So-called street parents, in contrast, often show a lack of consideration for other people

and have a rather superficial sense of family and community. Though they may love their children, many of them are unable to cope with the physical and emotional demands of parenthood, and find it difficult to reconcile their needs with those of their children. These families, who are more fully invested in the code of the streets than the decent people are, may aggressively socialize their children into it in a normative way. They believe in the code and judge themselves and others according to its values.

In fact the overwhelming majority of families in the inner-city community try to approximate the decent-family model, but there are many others who clearly represent the worst fears of the decent family. Not only are their financial resources extremely limited, but what little they have may easily be misused. The lives of the street-oriented are often marked by disorganization. In the most desperate circumstances people frequently have a limited understanding of priorities and consequences, and so frustrations mount over bills, food, and, at times, drink, cigarettes, and drugs. Some tend toward self-destructive behavior, many street-oriented women are crack-addicted ("on the pipe"), alcoholic, or involved in complicated relationships with men who abuse them. In addition, the seeming intractability of their situation, caused in large part by the lack of well-paying jobs and the persistence of racial discrimination, has engendered deep-seated bitterness and anger in many of the most desperate and poorest blacks, especially young people. The need both to exercise a measure of control and to lash out at somebody is often reflected in the adults' relations with their children. At the least, the frustrations of persistent poverty shorten the fuse in such people—contributing to a lack of patience with anyone, child or adult, who irritates them.

In these circumstances a woman—or a man, although men are less consistently present in children's lives—can be quite aggressive with children, yelling at and striking them for the least little infraction of the rules she has set down. Often little if any serious explanation follows the verbal and physical punishment. This response teaches children a particular lesson. They learn that to solve any kind of interpersonal problem one must quickly resort to hitting or other violent behavior. Actual peace and quiet, and also the appearance of calm, respectful children conveyed to her neighbors and friends, are often what the young mother most desires, but at times she will be very aggressive in trying to get them. Thus she may be quick to beat her children, especially if they defy her law, not because she hates them but because this is the way she knows to control them. In fact, many street-oriented women love their children dearly. Many mothers in the community subscribe to the notion that there is a "devil in the boy" that must be beaten out of him or that socially "fast girls need to be whupped." Thus much of what borders on child abuse in the view of social authorities is acceptable parental punishment in the view of these mothers.

Many street-oriented women are sporadic mothers whose children learn to fend for themselves when necessary, foraging for food and money any way they can get it. The children are sometimes employed by drug dealers or become addicted themselves. These children of the street, growing up with little supervision, are said to "come up hard." They often learn to fight at an early age, sometimes using short-tempered adults around them as role models. The street-oriented home may be fraught with anger, verbal disputes, physical aggression, and even mayhem. The children observe these goings-on, learning the lesson that might makes right. They quickly learn to hit those who cross them, and the dog-eat-dog mentality prevails. In order to survive, to protect oneself, it is necessary to marshal inner resources and be ready to deal with adversity in a hands-on way. In these circumstances physical prowess takes on great significance.

In some of the most desperate cases, a street-oriented mother may simply leave her young children alone and unattended while she goes out. The most irresponsible women can be found at local bars and crack houses, getting high and socializing with other adults. Sometimes a troubled woman will leave very young children alone for days at a time. Reports of crack addicts abandoning their children have become common in drug-infested inner-city communities. Neighbors or relatives discover the abandoned children, often hungry and distraught over the absence of their mother. After repeated absences, a friend or relative, particularly a grandmother, will often step in to care for the young children, sometimes petitioning the authorities to send her, as guardian of the children the mother's welfare check, if the mother gets one. By this time, however, the children may well have learned the first lesson of the streets: survival itself, let alone respect, cannot be taken for granted; you have to fight for your place in the world.

CAMPAIGNING FOR RESPECT

These realities of inner-city life are largely absorbed on the streets. At an early age, often even before they start school, children from street-oriented homes gravitate to the streets, where they "hang"—socialize with their peers. Children from these generally permissive homes have a great deal of latitude and are allowed to "rip and run" up and down the street. They often come home from school, put their books down, and go right back out the door. On school nights eight- and nine-year-olds remain out until nine or ten o'clock (and teenagers typically come in whenever they want to). On the streets they play in groups that often become the source of their primary social bonds. Children from decent homes tend to be more carefully supervised and are thus likely to have curfews and to be taught how to stay out of trouble.

When decent and street kids come together, a kind of social shuffle occurs in which children have a chance to go either way. Tension builds as a child comes to realize that he must choose an orientation. The kind of home he comes from influences but does not determine the way he will ultimately turn out—although it is unlikely that a child from a thoroughly street-oriented family will easily absorb decent values on the streets. Youths who emerge from street-oriented families but develop a decency orientation almost always learn those values in another setting-in school, in a youth group, in church. Often it is the result of their involvement with a caring "old head" (adult role model).

In the street, through their play, children pour their individual life experiences into a common knowledge pool, affirming, confirming, and elaborating on what they have observed in the home and matching their skills against those of others. And they learn to fight. Even small children test one another, pushing and shoving, and are ready to hit other children over circumstances not to their liking. In turn, they are readily hit by other children, and the child who is toughest prevails. Thus the violent resolution of disputes, the hitting and cursing, gains social reinforcement. The child in effect is initiated into a system that is really a way of campaigning for respect.

In addition, younger children witness the disputes of older children, which are often resolved through cursing and abusive talk, if not aggression or outright violence. They see that one child succumbs to the greater physical and mental abilities of the other. They are also alert and attentive witnesses to the verbal and physical fights of adults, after which they compare notes and share their interpretations of the event. In almost every case the victor is the person who physically won the altercation, and this person often enjoys the esteem and respect of onlookers. These experiences reinforce the lessons the children have learned at home: might makes right, and toughness is a virtue, while humility is not. In effect they learn the social meaning of fighting. When it is left virtually unchallenged, this understanding becomes an ever more important part of the child's working conception of the

world. Over time the code of the streets becomes refined.

Those street-oriented adults with whom children come in contact—including mothers, fathers, brothers, sisters, boyfriends, cousins, neighbors, and friends—help them along in forming this understanding by verbalizing the messages they are getting through experience: "Watch your back." "Protect yourself." "Don't punk out." "If somebody messes with you, you got to pay them back." "If someone disses you, you got to straighten them out." Many parents actually impose sanctions if a child is not sufficiently aggressive. For example, if a child loses a fight and comes home upset the parent might respond, "Don't you come in here crying that somebody beat you up; you better get back out there and whup his ass. I didn't raise no punks! Get back out there and whup his ass. If you don't whup his ass, I'll whup your ass when you come home." Thus the child obtains reinforcement for being tough and showing nerve.

While fighting, some children cry as though they are doing something they are ambivalent about. The fight may be against their wishes, yet they may feel constrained to fight or face the consequences—not just from peers but also from caretakers or parents, who may administer another beating if they back down. Some adults recall receiving such lessons from their own parents and justify repeating them to their children as a way to toughen them up. Looking capable of taking care of oneself as a form of self-defense is a dominant theme among both street-oriented and decent adults who worry about the safety of their children. There is thus at times a convergence in their child-rearing practices, although the rationales behind them may differ.

SELF-IMAGE BASED ON "JUICE"

By the time they are teenagers, most youths have either internalized the code of the streets or at least learned the need to comport themselves in accordance with its rules, which chiefly have to do with interpersonal communication. The code revolves around the presentation of self. Its basic requirement is the display of a certain predisposition to violence. Accordingly, one's bearing must send the unmistakable if sometimes subtle message to "the next person" in public that one is capable of violence and mayhem when the situation requires it, that one can take care of oneself. The nature of this communication is largely determined by the demands of the circumstances but can include facial expressions, gait, and verbal expressions—all of which are geared mainly to deterring aggression. Physical appearance, including clothes, jewelry, and grooming, also plays an important part in how a person is viewed; to be respected, it is important to have the right look.

Even so, there are no guarantees against challenges, because there are always people around looking for a fight to increase their share of respect—or "juice," as it is sometimes called on the street. Moreover, if a person is assaulted, it is important, not only in the eyes of his opponent but also in the eyes of his "running buddies," for him to avenge himself. Otherwise he risks being "tried" (challenged) or "moved on" by any number of others. To maintain his honor he must show he is not someone to be "messed with" or "dissed." In general, the person must "keep himself straight" by managing his position of respect among others; this involves in part his self-image, which is shaped by what he thinks others are thinking of him in relation to his peers.

Objects play an important and complicated role in establishing self-image. Jackets, sneakers, gold jewelry, reflect not just a person's taste, which tends to be tightly regulated among adolescents of all social classes, but also a willingness to possess things that may require defending. A boy wearing a fashionable, expensive jacket, for example, is vulnerable to attack by another who covets the jacket and either cannot afford to buy one or wants the added satisfaction of depriving someone else of his. However, if the boy forgoes the desirable jacket and wears one that isn't "hip," he runs the risk of being teased and possibly even assaulted as an unworthy person. To be allowed to hang with certain prestigious crowds, a boy must wear a different set of expensive clothes—sneakers and athletic suit—every day. Not to be able to do so might make him appear socially deficient. The youth comes to covet such items—especially when he sees easy prey wearing them.

In acquiring valued things, therefore, a person shores up his identity—but since it is an identity based on having things, it is highly precarious. This very precariousness gives a heightened sense of urgency to staying even with peers, with whom the person is actually competing. Young men and women who are able to command respect through their presentation of self—by allowing their possessions and their body language to speak for them—may not have to campaign for regard but may, rather, gain it by the force of their manner. Those who are unable to command respect in this way must actively campaign for it—and are thus particularly alive to slights.

One way of campaigning for status is by taking the possessions of others. In this context, seemingly ordinary objects can become trophies imbued with symbolic value that far exceeds their monetary worth. Possession of the trophy can symbolize the ability to violate somebody—to "get in his face," to take something of value from him, to "dis" him, and thus to enhance one's own worth by stealing someone else's. The trophy does not have to be something material. It can be another person's sense of honor, snatched away with a derogatory remark. It can be the outcome of a fight. It can be the imposition of a certain standard, such as a girl's getting herself recognized as the most beautiful. Material things, however, fit easily into the pattern. Sneakers, a pistol, even somebody else's girlfriend, can become a trophy. When a person can take something from another and then flaunt it, he gains a certain regard by being the owner, or the controller, of that thing. But this display of ownership can then provoke other people to challenge him. This game of who controls what is thus constantly being played out on inner-city streets, and the trophy—extrinsic or intrinsic, tangible or intangible—identifies the current winner.

An important aspect of this often violent give-and-take is its zero-sum quality. That is, the extent to which one person can raise himself up depends on his ability to put another person down. This underscores the alienation that permeates the inner-city ghetto community. There is a generalized sense that very little respect is to be had, and therefore everyone competes to get what affirmation he can of the little that is available. The craving for respect that results gives people thin skins. Shows of deference by others can be highly soothing, contributing to a sense of security, comfort, self-confidence, and self-respect. Transgressions by others which go unanswered diminish these feelings and are believed to encourage further transgressions. Hence one must be ever vigilant against the transgressions of others or even *appearing* as if transgressions will be tolerated. Among young people, whose sense of self-esteem is particularly vulnerable, there is an especially heightened concern with being disrespected. Many inner-city young men in particular crave respect to such a degree that they will risk their lives to attain and maintain it.

The issue of respect is thus closely tied to whether a person has an inclination to be violent, even as a victim. In the wider society people may not feel required to retaliate physically after an attack, even though they are aware that they have been degraded or taken advantage of. They may feel a great need to defend themselves *during* an attack, or to behave in such a way as to deter aggression (middle-class people certainly can and do become victims of street-oriented youths), but they are much more likely than street-oriented people to feel that they can walk away from a

possible altercation with their self-esteem intact. Some people may even have the strength of character to flee, without any thought that their self-respect or esteem will be diminished.

In impoverished inner-city black communities, however, particularly among young males and perhaps increasingly among females, such flight would be extremely difficult. To run away would likely leave one's self-esteem in tatters. Hence people often feel constrained not only to stand up and at least attempt to resist during an assault but also to "pay back"—to seek revenge—after a successful assault on their person. This may include going to get a weapon or even getting relatives involved. Their very identity and self-respect, their honor, is often intricately tied up with the way they perform on the streets during and after such encounters. This outlook reflects the circumscribed opportunities of the inner-city poor. Generally people outside the ghetto have other ways of gaining status and regard, and thus do not feel so dependent on such physical displays.

BY TRIAL OF MANHOOD

On the street, among males these concerns about things and identity have come to be expressed in the concept of "manhood." Manhood in the inner city means taking the prerogatives of men with respect to strangers, other men, and women—being distinguished as a man. It implies physicality and a certain ruthlessness. Regard and respect are associated with this concept in large part because of its practical application: if others have little or no regard for a person's manhood, his very life and those of his loved ones could be in jeopardy. But there is a chicken-and-egg aspect to this situation: one's physical safety is more likely to be jeopardized in public *because* manhood is associated with respect. In other words, an existential link has been created between the idea of manhood and ones self-esteem, so that it has become hard to say which is primary. For many inner-city youths, manhood and respect are flip sides of the same coin; physical and psychological well-being are inseparable, and both require a sense of control, of being in charge.

The operating assumption is that a man, especially a real man, knows what other men know—the code of the streets. And if one is not a real man, one is somehow diminished as a person, and there are certain valued things one simply does not deserve. There is thus believed to be a certain justice to the code, since it is considered that everyone has the opportunity to know it. Implicit in this is that everybody is held responsible for being familiar with the code. If the victim of a mugging, for example, does not know the code and so responds "wrong," the perpetrator may feel justified even in killing him and may feel no remorse. He may think, "Too bad, but it's his fault. He should have known better."

So when a person ventures outside, he must adapt the code—a kind of shield, really—to prevent others from "messing with" him. In these circumstances it is easy for people to think they are being tried or tested by others even when this is not the case. For it is sensed that something extremely valuable is at stake in every interaction, and people are encouraged to rise to the occasion, particularly with strangers. For people who are unfamiliar with the code—generally people who live outside the inner city—the concern with respect in the most ordinary interactions can be frightening and incomprehensible. But for those who are invested in the code, the clear object of their demeanor is to discourage strangers from even thinking about testing their manhood. And the sense of power that attends the ability to deter others can be alluring even to those who know the code without being heavily invested in it—the decent inner-city youths. Thus a boy who has been leading a basically decent life can, in trying circumstances, suddenly resort to deadly force.

Central to the issue of manhood is the widespread belief that one of the most effective ways

of gaining respect is to manifest "nerve." Nerve is shown, when one takes another person's possessions (the more valuable the better), "messes with" someone's woman, throws the first punch, "gets in someone's face," or pulls a trigger. Its proper display helps on the spot to check others who would violate one's person and also helps to build a reputation that works to prevent future challenges. But since such a show of nerve is a forceful expression of disrespect toward the person on the receiving end, the victim may be greatly offended and seek to retaliate with equal or greater force. A display of nerve, therefore, can easily provoke a life-threatening response, and the background knowledge of that possibility has often been incorporated into the concept of nerve.

True nerve exposes a lack of fear of dying. Many feel that it is acceptable to risk dying over the principle of respect. In fact, among the hard-core street-oriented, the clear risk of violent death may be preferable to being "dissed" by another. The youths who have internalized this attitude and convincingly display it in their public bearing are among the most threatening people of all, for it is commonly assumed that they fear no man. As the people of the community say, "They are the baddest dudes on the street." They often lead an existential life that may acquire meaning only when they are faced with the possibility of imminent death. Not to be afraid to die is by implication to have few compunctions about taking another's life. Not to be afraid to die is the quid pro quo of being able to take somebody else's life—for the right reasons, if the situation demands it. When others believe this is one's position, it gives one a real sense of power on the streets. Such credibility is what many inner-city youths strive to achieve, whether they are decent or street-oriented, both because of its practical defensive value and because of the positive way it makes them feel about themselves. The difference between the decent and the street-oriented youth is often that the decent youth makes a conscious decision to appear tough and manly; in another setting—with teachers, say, or at his part-time job—he can be polite and deferential. The street-oriented youth, on the other hand, has made the concept of manhood a part of his very identity; he has difficulty manipulating it—it often controls him.

GIRLS AND BOYS

Increasingly, teenage girls are mimicking the boys and trying to have their own version of "manhood." Their goal is the same—to get respect, to be recognized as capable of setting or maintaining a certain standard. They try to achieve this end in the ways that have been established by the boys, including posturing, abusive language, and the use of violence to resolve disputes, but the issues for the girls are different. Although conflicts over turf and status exist among the girls, the majority of disputes seem rooted in assessments of beauty (which girl in a group is "the cutest"), competition over boyfriends, and attempts to regulate other people's knowledge of and opinions about a girl's behavior or that of someone close to her, especially her mother.

A major cause of conflicts among girls is "he say, she say." This practice begins in the early school years and continues through high school. It occurs when "people," particularly girls, talk about others, thus putting their "business in the streets." Usually one girl will say something negative about another in the group, most often behind the person's back. The remark will then get back to the person talked about. She may retaliate or her friends may feel required to "take up for" her. In essence this is a form of group gossiping in which individuals are negatively assessed and evaluated. As with much gossip, the things said may or may not be true, but the point is that such imputations can cast aspersions on a person's good name. The accused is required to defend herself against the slander, which can result in arguments and fights, often over little of real substance. Here again is the

problem of low self-esteem, which encourages youngsters to be highly sensitive to slights and to be vulnerable to feeling easily "dissed." To avenge the dissing, a fight is usually necessary.

Because boys are believed to control violence, girls tend to defer to them in situations of conflict. Often if a girl is attacked or feels slighted, she will get a brother, uncle, or cousin to do her fighting for her. Increasingly, however, girls are doing their own fighting and are even asking their male relatives to teach them how to fight. Some girls form groups that attack other girls or take things from them. A hard-core segment of inner-city girls inclined toward violence seems to be developing. As one thirteen-year-old girl in a detention center for youths who have committed violent acts told me, "To get people to leave you alone, you gotta fight. Talking don't always get you out of stuff." One major difference between girls and boys: girls rarely use guns. Their fights are therefore not life-or-death struggles. Girls are not often willing to put their lives on the line for "manhood." The ultimate form of respect on the male-dominated inner-city street is thus reserved for men.

"GOING FOR BAD"

In the most fearsome youths such a cavalier attitude toward death grows out of a very limited view of life. Many are uncertain about how long they are going to live and believe they could die violently at any time. They accept this fate; they live on the edge. Their manner conveys the message that nothing intimidates them; whatever turn the encounter takes, they maintain their attack—rather like a pit bull, whose spirit many such boys admire. The demonstration of such tenacity "shows heart" and earns their respect.

This fearlessness has implications for law enforcement. Many street-oriented boys are much more concerned about the threat of "justice" at the hands of a peer than at the hands of the police. Moreover, many feel not only that they have little to lose by going to prison but that they have something to gain. The toughening-up one experiences in prison can actually enhance one's reputation on the streets. Hence the system loses influence over the hard core who are without jobs, with little perceptible stake in the system. If mainstream society has done nothing *for* them, they counter by making sure it can do nothing *to* them.

At the same time, however, a competing view maintains that true nerve consists in backing down, walking away from a fight, and going on with one's business. One fights only in self-defense. This view emerges from the decent philosophy that life is precious, and it is an important part of the socialization process common in decent homes. It discourages violence as the primary means of resolving disputes and encourages youngsters to accept nonviolence and talk as confrontational strategies. But "If the deal goes down," self-defense is greatly encouraged. When there is enough positive support for this orientation, either in the home or among one's peers, then nonviolence has a chance to prevail. But it prevails at the cost of relinquishing a claim to being bad and tough, and therefore sets a young person up as at the very least alienated from street-oriented peers and quite possibly a target of derision or even violence.

Although the nonviolent orientation rarely overcomes the impulse to strike back in an encounter, it does introduce a certain confusion and so can prompt a measure of soul-searching, or even profound ambivalence. Did the person back down with his respect intact or did he back down only to be judged a "punk"—a person lacking manhood? Should he or she have acted? Should he or she have hit the other person in the mouth? These questions beset many young men and women during public confrontations. What is the "right" thing to do? In the quest for honor, respect, and local status—which few young people are uninterested in—common sense most often prevails, which leads many to opt for the tough approach, enacting their own particular

versions of the display of nerve. The presentation of oneself as rough and tough is very often quite acceptable until one is tested. And then that presentation may help the person pass the test, because it will cause fewer questions to be asked about what he did and why. It is hard for a person to explain why he lost the fight or why he backed down. Hence many will strive to appear to "go for bad" while hoping they will never be tested. But when they are tested, the outcome of the situation may quickly be out of their hands, as they become wrapped up in the circumstances of the moment.

AN OPPOSITIONAL CULTURE

The attitudes of the wider society are deeply implicated in the code of the streets. Most people in inner-city communities are not totally invested in the code, but the significant minority of hard-core street youths who are have to maintain the code in order to establish reputations, because they have—or feel they have—few other ways to assert themselves. For these young people the standards of the street code are the only game in town. The extent to which some children—particularly those who through upbringing have become most alienated and those lacking in strong and conventional social support—experience, feel, and internalize racist rejection and contempt from mainstream society may strongly encourage them to express contempt for the more conventional society in turn. In dealing with this contempt and rejection, some youngsters will consciously invest themselves and their considerable mental resources in what amounts to an oppositional culture to preserve themselves and their self-respect. Once they do, any respect they might be able to garner in the wider system pales in comparison with the respect available in the local system; thus they often lose interest in even attempting to negotiate the mainstream system.

At the same time, many less alienated young blacks have assumed a street-oriented demeanor as a way of expressing their blackness while really embracing a much more moderate way of life; they, too, want a nonviolent setting in which to live and raise a family. These decent people are trying hard to be part of the mainstream culture, but the racism, real and perceived, that they encounter helps to legitimate the oppositional culture. And so on occasion they adopt street behavior. In fact, depending on the demands of the situation, many people in the community slip back and forth between decent and street behavior.

A vicious cycle has thus been formed. The hopelessness and alienation many young inner-city black men and women feel, largely as a result of endemic joblessness and persistent racism, fuels the violence they engage in. This violence serves to confirm the negative feelings many whites and some middle-class blacks harbor toward the ghetto poor, further legitimating the oppositional culture and the code of the streets in the eyes of many poor young blacks. Unless this cycle is broken, attitudes on both sides will become increasingly entrenched, and the violence, which claims victims black and white, poor and affluent, will only escalate.

DISCUSSION QUESTIONS

1. Discuss what you think "respect" means for inner-city males. Why is this such a focal point of street culture? How deeply ingrained do you think the code of the streets actually is?
2. Rap music is often said to represent the voice of those immersed in street culture. To what extent do you think this is the case? Why is rap music so appealing to white suburban youth?

THE SOCIAL CONSTRUCTION OF SELF AND EVERYDAY LIFE

Today's self-help gurus, authors of inspirational books and "motivational speakers," argue that people can be whatever they want to be and can accomplish whatever goals they set for themselves. They contend that people can transform their personal lives in far-ranging ways. Humdrum lives can become exciting lives and dead-end jobs can be replaced by lucrative and enjoyable new careers. All that is needed to make success possible is the price of admission to seminars, or the purchase of a particular how-to book or set of cassettes.

At one fairly obvious level, this example would appear to be consonant with what in sociology has become known as constructionism or, in other words, the claim that people as social actors create their own worlds. However, it would be a mistake to consider self-help gurus applied sociologists. The problem with their view of the world is that it is devoid of a sociological sensibility. They operate without any sense of historical or social structural context. They fail to appreciate the fact that the actions of individuals always occur within the context of social interaction. People don't act in a void; rather their actions take place in social situations that vary in terms of degrees of complexity and uncertainty.

A social constructionist perspective takes such factors into account. It grants to individuals a role in shaping not only their own life trajectories and their own sense of selfhood, but also the social world they inhabit. But it also assumes that in no way do individuals accomplish any of this alone. The beginning of a genuinely sociological notion of social construction can be heard in the words of Karl Marx, who, to paraphrase, once said that people create their social worlds, but not in circumstances of their own choosing. We are all, for better or worse, born into a setting that we did not select; it was thrust upon us. Thus, social construction is best understood in terms of interaction, rather than action.

Sociologists today rather widely embrace the notion that social reality is a construct. This includes at the micro level of lived experience a wide range of phenomena related to personal identities, emotions, statuses, roles, behaviors, and experiences. Thus, beginning with the historian Philippe Aries, who noted that the notion of childhood as a distinct phase in the life course did not exist in the Middle Ages, we speak today about the social construction of childhood. Although emotions have a biological basis, they are also subject to societal influence and thus can be appropriately seen as constructed. For this reason, social scientists can differentiate between shame cultures and guilt cultures. Social statuses are constructed, and thus vary according to time and place. For example, in some societies, older people are accorded respect on the basis of the presumed wisdom they have to impart to younger generations. For a variety of reasons, not the least of which is that the kinds of knowledge valued in contemporary societies are often not possessed by the aged, older people today often suffer a loss, not an elevation, of social status. Some social constructionists employ a dramaturgical perspective. Assuming all the world is a stage, they look at roles in theatrical terms as performances. Thus, a faculty member may appear very "professorial" in the lecture hall, but this role may not be evident in the evening at the local faculty watering hole. Moreover, some faculty members manage to be more convincing in their role performances and in establishing a shared understanding of the classroom experience: they are the ones who receive tenure.

As the articles in this selection nicely illustrate, a social constructionist perspective can shed considerable sociological light on their respective topics.

Embarrassment and Social Organization

Erving Goffman

Erving Goffman offers the perspective of a key exponent of dramaturgical sociology, a theoretical approach that views people as actors performing various roles in an effort to present particular images of the self. In this excerpt from Interaction Ritual, *he explores the phenomenon of embarrassment, beginning with a social psychological account of the images and vocabularies individuals are likely to employ in depicting this experience along with the ways people more or less successfully attempt to respond to moments of embarrassment. The discussion shifts to the social structural level when he enters into an analysis of the causes and social functions of embarrassment.*

An individual may recognize extreme embarrassment in others and even in himself by the objective signs of emotional disturbance: blushing, fumbling, stuttering, an unusually low- or high-pitched voice, quavering speech or breaking of the voice, sweating, blanching, blinking, tremor of the hand, hesitating or vacillating movement, absentmindedness, and malapropisms. As Mark Baldwin remarked about shyness, there may be "a lowering of the eyes, bowing of the head, putting of hands behind the back, nervous fingering of the clothing or twisting of the fingers together, and stammering, with some incoherence of idea as expressed in speech."[1] There are also symptoms of a subjective kind: constriction of the diaphragm, a feeling of wobbliness, consciousness of strained and unnatural gestures, a dazed sensation, dryness of the mouth, and tenseness of the muscles.

In cases of mild discomfiture these visible and invisible flusterings occur but in less perceptible form.

In the popular view it is only natural to be at ease during interaction, embarrassment being a regrettable deviation from the normal state. The individual, in fact, might say he felt "natural" or "unnatural" in the situation, meaning that he felt comfortable in the interaction or embarrassed in it. He who frequently becomes embarrassed in the presence of others is regarded as suffering from a foolish unjustified sense of inferiority and in need of therapy.[2]

To utilize the flustering syndrome in analyzing embarrassment, the two kinds of circumstance in which it occurs must first be distinguished. First, the individual may become flustered while engaged in a task of no particular value to him in itself, except that his long-range interests require him to perform it with safety, competence, or dispatch, and he fears he is inadequate to the task. Discomfort will be felt *in* the situation but in a sense not *for* it; in fact, often the individual will not be able to cope with it just because he is so anxiously taken up with the eventualities lying beyond it. Significantly, the individual may become "rattled" although no others are present.

This paper will not be concerned with those occasions of instrumental chagrin but rather with

---

[1] James Mark Baldwin, *Social and Ethical Interpretations in Mental Development* (London: Macmillan, 1902), p. 212.

[2] A sophisticated version is the psychoanalytical view that uneasiness in social interaction is a result of impossible expectations of attention based on unresolved expectation regarding parental support. Presumably an object of therapy is to bring the individual to see his symptoms in their true psycho-dynamic light, on the assumption that thereafter perhaps he will not need them (see Paul Schilder, "The Social Neurosis," *Psycho-Analytical Review,* XXV (1938), 1–19; Gerhart Piers and Milton Singer, *Shame and Guilt: A Psychoanalytical and a Cultural Study* (Springfield, Ill., Charles C. Thomas, 1953), esp. p. 26; Leo Rangell, "The Psychology of Poise," *International Journal of Psychoanalysis,* XXXV (1954). 313–32; Sandor Ferenczi, "Embarrassed Hands," in *Further Contributions to the Theory and Technique of Psychoanalysis* (London, Hogarth Press, 1950), pp. 315–16.

the kind that occurs in clear-out relation to the real or imagined presence of others. Whatever else, embarrassment has to do with the figure the individual cuts before others felt to be there at the time. The crucial concern is the impression one makes on others in the present—whatever the long-range or unconscious basis of this concern may be. This fluctuating configuration of those present is a most important reference group.

VOCABULARY OF EMBARRASSMENT

A social encounter is an occasion of face-to-face interaction, beginning when individuals recognize that they have moved into one another's immediate presence and ending by an appreciated withdrawal from mutual participation. Encounters differ markedly from one another in purpose, social function, kind and number of personnel, setting, etc., and, while only conversational encounters will be considered here, obviously there are those in which no word is spoken. And yet, in our Anglo-American society, at least, there seems to be no social encounter which cannot become embarrassing to one or more of its participants, giving rise to what is sometimes called an incident or false note. By listening for this dissonance, the sociologist can generalize about the ways in which interaction can go awry and, by implication, the conditions necessary for interaction to be right. At the same time he is given good evidence that all encounters are members of a single natural class, amenable to a single framework of analysis.

By whom is the embarrassing incident caused? *To* whom is it embarrassing? *For* whom is this embarrassment felt? It is not always an individual for whose plight participants feel embarrassment; it may be for pairs of participants who are together having difficulties and even for an encounter as a whole. Further, if the individual for whom embarrassment is felt happens to be perceived as a responsible representative of some faction or subgroup (as is very often the case in three-or-more-person interaction), then

the members of this faction are likely to feel embarrassed and to feel it for themselves. But while a *gaffe* or *faux pas* can mean that a single individual is at one and the same time the cause of an incident, the one who feels embarrassed by it, and the one for whom he feels embarrassment, this is not, perhaps, the typical case, for in these matters ego boundaries seem especially weak. When an individual finds himself in a situation which ought to make him blush, others present usually will blush with and for him, though he may not have sufficient sense of shame or appreciation of the circumstances to blush on his own account.

The words "embarrassment," "discomfiture," and "uneasiness" are used here in a continuum of meanings. Some occasions of embarrassment seem to have an abrupt orgasmic character; a sudden introduction of the disturbing event is followed by an immediate peak in the experience of embarrassment and then by a slow return to the preceding ease, all phases being encompassed in the same encounter. A bad moment thus mars an otherwise euphoric situation.

At the other extreme we find that some occasions of embarrassment are sustained at the same level throughout the encounter, beginning when the interaction begins and lasting until the encounter is terminated. The participants speak of an uncomfortable or uneasy situation, not of an embarrassing incident. In such case, of course, the whole encounter becomes for one or more of the parties an incident that causes embarrassment. Abrupt embarrassment may often be intense, while sustained uneasiness is more commonly mild, involving barely apparent flusterings. An encounter which seems likely to occasion abrupt embarrassment may, because of this, cast a shadow of sustained uneasiness upon the participants, transforming the entire encounter into an incident itself.

In forming a picture of the embarrassed individual, one relies on imagery from mechanics: equilibrium or self-control can be lost, balance can be overthrown. No doubt the physical character of flustering in part evokes this imagery. In any case, a completely flustered individual is one who cannot for the time being mobilize his muscular and intellectual resources for the task at hand, although he would like to; he cannot volunteer a response to those around him that will allow them to sustain the conversation smoothly. He and his flustered actions block the line of activity the others have been pursuing. He is present with them, but he is not "in play." The others may be forced to stop and turn their attention to the impediment; the topic of conversation is neglected, and energies are directed to the task of re-establishing the flustered individual, of studiously ignoring him, or of withdrawing from his presence.

To conduct one's self comfortably in interaction and to be flustered are directly opposed. The more of one, the less, on the whole, of the other; hence through contrast each mode of behavior can throw light upon the characteristics of the other. Face-to-face interaction in *any* culture seems to require just those capacities that flustering seems guaranteed to destroy. Therefore, events which lead to embarrassment and the methods for avoiding and dispelling it may provide a cross-cultural framework of sociological analysis.

The pleasure or displeasure that a social encounter affords an individual, and the affection or hostility that he feels for the participants, can have more than one relation to his composure or lack of it. Compliments, acclaim, and sudden reward may throw the recipient into a state of joyful confusion, while a heated quarrel can be provoked and sustained, although throughout the individual feels composed and has full command of himself. More important there is a kind of comfort which seems a formal property of the situation and which has to do with the coherence and decisiveness with which the individual assumes a well-integrated role and pursues momentary objectives having nothing to do with the content of the actions themselves. A feeling of discomfiture per se seems always to be unpleasant, but the circumstances that arouse

it may have immediate pleasant consequences for the one who is discomfited.

In spite of this variable relation between displeasure and discomfiture, to appear flustered, in our society at least, is considered evidence of weakness, inferiority, low status, moral guilt, defeat, and other unenviable attributes. And, as previously suggested, flustering threatens the encounter itself by disrupting the smooth transmission and reception by which encounters are sustained. When discomfiture arises from any of these sources, understandably the flustered individual will make some effort to conceal his state from the others present. The fixed smile, the nervous hollow laugh, the busy hands, the downward glance that conceals the expression of the eyes, have become famous as signs of attempting to conceal embarrassment. As Lord Chesterfield puts it:

> They are ashamed in company, and so disconcerted that they do not know what they do, and try a thousand tricks to keep themselves in countenance; which tricks afterwards grow habitual to them. Some put their fingers to their nose, others scratch their head, others twirl their hats; in short, every awkward, ill-bred body has his tricks.[3]

These gestures provide the individual with screens to hide behind while he tries to bring his feelings back into tempo and himself back into play.

Given the individual's desire to conceal his embarrassment, given the setting and his skill at handling himself, he may seem poised according to some obvious signs yet prove to be embarrassed according to less apparent ones. Thus, while making a public speech, he may succeed in controlling his voice and give an impression of ease, yet those who sit beside him on the platform may see that his hands are shaking or that facial tics are giving the lie to his composed front.

---

[3]*Letters of Lord Chesterfield to His Son* (Everyman's ed., New York, E. P. Dutton & Co., 1929), p. 80.

Since the individual dislikes to feel or appear embarrassed, tactful persons will avoid placing him in this position. In addition, they will often pretend not to know that he has lost composure or has grounds for losing it. They may try to suppress signs of having recognized his state or hide them behind the same kind of covering gesture that he might employ. Thus they protect his face and his feelings and presumably make it easier for him to regain composure or at least hold on to what he still has. However, just as the flustered individual may fail to conceal his embarrassment, those who perceive his discomfort may fail in their attempt to hide their knowledge, whereupon they all will realize that his embarrassment has been seen and that the seeing of it was something to conceal. When this point is reached, ordinary involvement in the interaction may meet a painful end. In all this dance between the concealer and the concealed-from, embarrassment presents the same problem and is handled in the same ways as any other offense against propriety.

There seems to be a critical point at which the flustered individual gives up trying to conceal or play down his uneasiness: he collapses into tears or paroxysms of laughter, has a temper tantrum, flies into a blind rage, faints, dashes to the nearest exit, or becomes rigidly immobile as when in panic. After that it is very difficult for him to recover composure. He answers to a new set of rhythms, characteristic of deep emotional experience, and can hardly give even a faint impression that he is at one with the others in interaction. In short, he abdicates his role as someone who sustains encounters. The moment of crisis is of course socially determined: the individual's breaking point is that of the group to whose affective standards he adheres. On rare occasions all the participants in an encounter may pass this point and together fail to maintain even a semblance of ordinary interaction. The little social system they created in interaction collapses: they draw apart or hurriedly try to assume a new set of roles.

The terms "poise," *"sang-froid,"* and "aplomb," referring to the capacity to maintain one's own composure, are to be distinguished from what is called "graciousness," "tact," or "social skill," namely, the capacity to avoid causing oneself or others embarrassment. Poise plays an important role in communication, for it guarantees that those present will not fail to play their parts in interaction but will continue as long as they are in one another's presence to receive and transmit disciplined communications. It is no wonder that trial by taunting is a test that every young person passes through until he develops a capacity to maintain composure.[4] Nor should it come as a surprise that many of our games and sports commemorate the themes of composure and embarrassment: in poker, a dubious claim may win money for the player who can present it calmly; in judo, the maintenance and loss of composure are specifically fought over; in cricket, self-command or "style" is supposed to be kept up under tension.

The individual is likely to know that certain special situations always make him uncomfortable and that he has certain "faulty" relationships which always cause him uneasiness. His daily round of social encounters is largely determined, no doubt, by his major social obligations, but he goes a little out of his way to find situations that will not be embarrassing and to bypass those that will. An individual who firmly believes that he has little poise, perhaps even exaggerating his failing, is shy and bashful; dreading all encounters, he seeks always to shorten them or avoid them altogether. The stutterer is a painful in-

---

[4]One interesting form in which this trial has been institutionalized in America, especially in lower-class Negro society, is "playing the dozens" (see John Dollard, "Dialectic of Insult," *American Imago,* I [1939], 3–25; R. F. B. Berdie, "Playing the Dozens," *Journal of Abnormal and Social Psychology,* XLII [1947], 120–21). On teasing in general see S. J. Sperling, "On the Psychodynamics of Teasing," *Journal of the American Psycho-analytical Association,* I (1953), 458–83.

stance of this, showing us the price the individual may be willing to pay for his social life.[5]

CAUSES OF EMBARRASSMENT

Embarrassment has to do with unfulfilled expectations (but not with those of a statistical kind). Given their social identities and the setting, the participants will sense what sort of conduct *ought* to be maintained as the appropriate thing, however much they may despair of its actually occurring. An individual may firmly expect that certain others will make him ill at ease, and yet this knowledge may increase his discomfiture instead of lessening it. An entirely unexpected flash of social engineering may save a situation, all the more effective for it being unanticipated.

The expectations relevant to embarrassment are moral, then, but embarrassment does not arise from the breach of *any* moral expectation, for some infractions give rise to resolute moral indignation and no uneasiness at all. Rather we should look to those moral obligations which surround the individual in only one of his capacities, that of someone who carries on social encounters. The individual, of course, is obliged to remain composed, but this tells us that things are going well, not why. And things go well or badly because of what is perceived about the social identities of those present.

During interaction the individual is expected to possess certain attributes, capacities, and information which, taken together, fit together into a self that is at once coherently unified and appropriate for the occasion. Through the expressive implications of his stream of conduct, through mere participation itself, the individual effectively projects this acceptable self into the interaction, although he may not be aware of it, and the others may not be aware of having so interpreted his conduct. At the same time he must accept and honor the selves projected by the other participants. The elements of a social encounter, then, consist of effectively projected claims to an acceptable self and the confirmation of like claims on the part of the others. The contributions of all are oriented to these and built up on the basis of them.

When an event throws doubt upon or discredits these claims, then the encounter finds itself lodged in assumptions which no longer hold. The responses the parties have made ready are now out of place and must be choked back, and the interaction must be reconstructed. At such times the individual whose self has been threatened (the individual *for* whom embarrassment is felt) and the individual who threatened him may both feel ashamed of what together they have brought about, sharing this sentiment just when they have reason to feel apart. And this joint responsibility is only right. By the standards of the wider society, perhaps only the discredited individual ought to feel ashamed; but, by the standards of the little social system maintained through the interaction, the discreditor is just as guilty as the person he discredits—sometimes more so, for, if he has been posing as a tactful man, in destroying another's image he destroys his own.

But of course the trouble does not stop with the guilty pair or with those who have identified themselves sympathetically with them. Having no settled and legitimate object to which to play out their own unity, the others find themselves unfixed and discomfited. This is why embarrassment seems to be contagious, spreading, once started, in ever widening circles of discomfiture.

There are many classic circumstances under which the self projected by an individual may be discredited, causing him shame and embarrassment over what he has or appears to have done to himself and to the interaction. To experience a sudden change in status, as by marriage or promotion, is to acquire a self that other individuals will not fully admit because of their lingering attachment to the old self. To ask for a job, a loan of money, or a hand in marriage is to project an

[5]Cf. H. J. Heltman, "Psycho-social Phenomena of Stuttering and Their Etiological and Therapeutic Implications," *Journal of Social Psychology,* IX (1938), 79–96.

image of self as worthy, under conditions where the one who can discredit the assumption may have good reason to do so. To affect the style of one's occupational or social betters is to make claims that may well be discredited by one's lack of familiarity with the role.

The physical structure of an encounter itself is usually accorded certain symbolic implications, sometimes leading a participant against his will to project claims about himself that are false and embarrassing. Physical closeness easily implies social closeness, as anyone knows who has happened upon an intimate gathering not meant for him or who has found it necessary to carry on fraternal "small talk" with someone too high or low or strange to ever be a brother. Similarly, if there is to be talk, someone must initiate it, feed it, and terminate it; and these acts may awkwardly suggest rankings and power which are out of line with the facts.

Various kinds of recurrent encounters in a given society may share the assumption that participants have attained certain moral, mental, and physiognomic standards. The person who falls short may everywhere find himself inadvertently trapped into making implicit identity-claims which he cannot fulfil. Compromised in every encounter which he enters, he truly wears the leper's bell. The individual who most isolates himself from social contacts may then be the least insulated from the demands of society. And, if he only imagines that he possesses a disqualifying attribute, his judgment of himself may be in error, but in the light of it his withdrawal from contact is reasonable. In any case, in deciding whether an individual's grounds for shyness are real or imaginary, one should seek not for "justifiable" disqualifications but for the much larger range of characteristics which actually embarrass encounters.

In all these settings the same fundamental thing occurs: the expressive facts at hand threaten or discredit the assumptions a participant finds he

has projected about his identity.[6] Thereafter those present find they can neither do without the assumptions nor base their own responses upon them. The inhabitable reality shrinks until everyone feels "small" or out of place.

An additional complication must be noted. Often important everyday occasions of embarrassment arise when the self projected is somehow confronted with another self which, though valid in other contexts, cannot be here sustained in harmony with the first. Embarrassment, then, leads us to the matter of "role segregation." Each individual has more than one role, but he is saved from role dilemma by "audience segregation," for, ordinarily, those before whom he plays out one of his roles will not be the individuals before whom be plays out another, allowing him to be a different person in each role without discrediting either.

In every social system, however, there are times and places where audience segregation regularly breaks down and where individuals confront one another with selves incompatible with the ones they extend to each other on other occasions. At such times, embarrassment, especially the mild kind, clearly shows itself to be located not in the individual but in the social system wherein he has his several selves.

DOMAIN OF EMBARRASSMENT

Having started with psychological considerations, we have come by stages to a structural sociological point of view. Precedent comes from

---

[6]In addition to his other troubles, he has discredited his implicit claim to poise. He will feel he has cause, then, to become embarrassed over his embarrassment, even though no one present may have perceived the earlier stages of his discomfiture. But a qualification must be made. When an individual, receiving a compliment, blushes from modesty, he may lose his reputation for poise but confirm a more important one, that of being modest. Feeling that his chagrin is nothing to be ashamed of, his embarrassment will not lead him to be embarrassed. On the other hand, when embarrassment is clearly expected as a reasonable response, he who fails to become embarrassed may appear insensitive and thereupon become embarrassed because of this appearance.

social anthropologists and their analyses of joking and avoidance. One assumes that embarrassment is a normal part of normal social life, the individual becoming uneasy not because he is personally maladjusted but rather because he is not; presumably anyone with his combination of statuses would do likewise. In an empirical study of a particular social system, the first object would be to learn what categories of persons become embarrassed in what recurrent situations. And the second object would be to discover what would happen to the social system and the framework of obligations if embarrassment had not come to be systematically built into it.

An illustration may be taken from the social life of large social establishments—office buildings, schools, hospitals, etc. Here, in elevators, halls, and cafeterias, at newsstands, vending machines, snack counters, and entrances, all members are often formally on an equal if distant footing.[7] In Benoit-Smullyan's terms, situs, not status or locus, is expressed.[8] Cutting across these relationships of equality and distance, is another set of relationships, arising in work teams whose members are ranked by such things as prestige and authority and yet drawn together by joint enterprise and personal knowledge of one another.

In many large establishments, staggered work hours, segregated cafeterias, and the like help to insure that those who are ranked and closed in one set of relations will not have to find themselves in physically intimate situations where they are expected to maintain equality and distance.

The democratic orientation of some of our newer establishments, however, tends to throw differently placed members of the same work team together at places such as the cafeteria, causing them uneasiness. There is no way for them to act that does not disturb one of the two basic sets of relations in which they stand to each other. These difficulties are especially likely to occur in elevators, for there individuals who are not quite on chatting terms must remain for a time too close together to ignore the opportunity for informal talk—a problem solved, of course, for some, by special executive elevators. Embarrassment, then, is built into the establishment ecologically.

Because of possessing multiple selves the individual may find he is required both to be present and to not be present on certain occasions. Embarrassment ensues: the individual finds himself being torn apart, however gently. Corresponding to the oscillation of his conduct is the oscillation of his self.

SOCIAL FUNCTION OF EMBARRASSMENT

When an individual's projected self is threatened during interaction, he may with poise suppress all signs of shame and embarrassment. No flusterings, or efforts to conceal having seen them, obtrude upon the smooth flow of the encounter; participants can proceed as if no incident has occurred.

When situations are saved, however, something important may be lost. By showing embarrassment when he can be neither of two people, the individual leaves open the possibility that in the future he may effectively be either.[9]

---

[7]This equal and joint membership in a large organization is often celebrated annually at the office party and in amateur dramatic skits, this being accomplished by pointedly excluding outsiders and scrambling the rank of insiders.

[8]Emile Benoit-Smullyan, "Status, Status Types, and Status Interrelations," *American Sociological Review,* IX (1944), 151–61. In a certain way the claim of equal institutional membership is reinforced by the ruling in our society that males ought to show certain minor courtesies to females; all other principles, such as distinctions between racial groups and occupational categories, must be suppressed. The effect is to stress situs and equality.

[9]A similar argument was presented by Samuel Johnson in his piece "Of Bashfulness," *The Rambler* (1751), No. 139: "It generally happens that assurance keeps an even pace with ability; and the fear of miscarriage, which hinders our first attempts, is gradually dissipated as our skill advances towards certainty of success. The bashfulness, therefore, which prevents disgrace, that short temporary shame which secures us from the danger of lasting reproach, cannot be properly counted among our misfortunes."

His role in the current interaction may be sacrificed, and even the encounter itself, but he demonstrates that, while he cannot present a sustainable and coherent self on this occasion, he is at least disturbed by the fact and may prove worthy at another time. To this extent, embarrassment is not an irrational impulse breaking through socially prescribed behavior but part of this orderly behavior itself. Flusterings are an extreme example of that important class of acts which are usually quite spontaneous and yet no less required and obligatory than ones self-consciously performed.

Behind a conflict in identity lies a more fundamental conflict, one of organizational principle, since the self, for many purposes, consists merely of the application of legitimate organizational principles to one's self. One builds one's identity out of claims which, if denied, give one the right to feel righteously indignant. Behind the apprentice's claims for a full share in the use of certain plant facilities there is the organizational principle: all members of the establishment are equal in certain ways *qua* members. Behind the specialist's demand for suitable financial recognition there is the principle that the type of work, not mere work, determines status. The fumblings of the apprentice and the specialist when they reach the Coca-Cola machine at the same time express an incompatibility of organizational principles.[10]

The principles of organization of any social system are likely to come in conflict at certain points. Instead of permitting the conflict to be expressed in an encounter, the individual places himself between the opposing principles. He sacrifices his identity for a moment, and sometimes the encounter, but the principles are preserved. He may be ground between opposing assumptions, thereby preventing direct friction between them, or he may be almost pulled apart, so that principles with little relation to one another may operate together. Social structure gains elasticity; the individual merely loses composure.

DISCUSSION QUESTIONS

1. Goffman distinguishes poise from tact. Offer concrete examples from your own life or from someone you know to indicate your appreciation of the difference.
2. At the end of the article, Goffman makes a central sociological claim, namely that embarrassment has a social function. Discuss your understanding of what Goffman has in mind in making such a claim.

READING 8

The Sociological Meaning of Codependence

Anthony Giddens

A theorist of late modernity, Anthony Giddens contends that profound changes are occurring at present in the shaping of personal identities and in the development of intimate attachments. He finds evidence of this transformation in the recovery movement. One of the central notions that emerged out of this movement is the idea of codependency. In this selection from The Transformation of Intimacy, *Giddens sets out to offer a sociologically—informed understanding of the term, and from there to indicate its relevance to the emerging notion of intimacy. He concludes with a brief discussion of the implications of this notion for the contemporary family and for children.*

---

[10]At such moments "joshing" sometimes occurs. It is said to be a means of releasing the tension caused either by embarrassment or by whatever caused embarrassment. But in many cases this kind of banter is a way of saying that what occurs now is not serious or real. The exaggeration, the mock insult, the mock claims—all these reduce the seriousness of conflict by denying reality to the situation. And this, of course, in another way, is what embarrassment does. It is natural, then, to find embarrassment and joking together, for both help in denying the same reality.

Womanisers often have qualities which correlate closely with common traits of the romantic love complex—here are men who will sweep women off their feet, or woo them with particular fervour, and perhaps have become very skilled in so doing. Some women—to whom all those things are by now very familiar—might very well opt for a short-term sexual liaison in the pursuit of transitory excitement or pleasure. For such women the appeal of the lady-killer fades quickly or is deliberately kept in check.

Most lady-killers' ladies are not like this at all.[1] On the contrary, they are likely quite quickly to become deeply involved once any relationship starts up. Such women's lives are strewn with disastrous romances, or long, painful involvements with men who in some way or another abuse them. These women, in short, are codependent, and it has become a commonplace of the therapeutic literature that codependence—although by no means limited to females—is a term that in some ways describes what was once called the "female role" in general.[2]

Codependent women are carers, who need to give nurturance to others but, partly or almost entirely on an unconscious level, anticipate that their devotion will be rebuffed. What a painful irony this is! The codependent woman is quite likely to become embroiled in a relationship precisely with a philanderer. She is prepared and perhaps even anxious to "rescue" him; he requires such tolerance because, unless he is wholly duplicitous, and keeps his real attitudes completely concealed, other women will reject him.

THE NATURE OF CODEPENDENCE

The term "codependent" is an example of that "reverse reflexivity" so common in the current era. Instead of being coined by professionals, codependence came from the work of individuals struggling with their own alcoholism. In the early alcoholic self-help groups, alcoholism was understood as a weakness of the person affected. It was supposed that the alcoholic recovered best in the company of others suffering from the same problem, away from a family context. Later it came to be recognised that alcoholism affects others with whom the alcoholic is regularly in contact; but most still believed that the alcoholic would have to be cured before being successfully reintegrated into a domestic context. Eventually, however, it became clear that alcoholics have little chance of staying sober if they return to relationships or families where all else remains the same; usually those entire relationships revolve around the alcoholic's addition.

Others' lives, often in subtle, sometimes in highly damaging, ways, are thus dependent upon the dependency of the addict. One of the first terms coined to interpret this situation was the "enabler"—the person, usually the sexual partner or spouse, and most commonly a woman, who consciously or unconsciously supports the individual's drinking. The idea of the "codependent" came to replace that of enabler as it became apparent that such an individual might be suffering as much as, or more than, the person with the chemical dependency.[3]

Once it had become thus generalised, the term "codependence" was somewhat misleading. It was developed in a context in which there was a clear-cut "addict," to whose behaviour the other responds. The notion tends to imply a priority in who becomes dependent upon whom; it refers, as it were, to a secondary addiction, the enabler facing the alcoholic. As used in this way, the concept mixes two things: the refraction of an addiction on to another, who builds his or her behaviour around it, and the interactional quality of a relationship. To complicate things further, codependence is quite often linked, not to a specific relationship, but to a type of personality. As one author puts it:

> The codependent seeks approval from practically everyone with whom she comes into contact. Instead of building a life around one person, she may have several "golden calves" around whom she

dances—perhaps her mother and father, her women friends, her boss, and the clerk at the supermarket, in addition to her lover. She lives her life around the needs of others.[4]

Let me formulate the concepts at issue in the following way. A codependent *person* is someone who, in order to sustain a sense of ontological security, requires another individual, or set of individuals, to define her (or his) wants; she or he cannot feel self-confident without being devoted to the needs of others. A codependent *relationship* is one in which an individual is tied psychologically to a partner whose activities are governed by compulsiveness of some sort. I shall term a *fixated* relationship one in which the relationship itself is the object of addiction. In fixated relationships, individuals do not build their lives around the pre-existing addictions of others; rather, they need the relationship to cater to a sense of security which they cannot otherwise meet. In their most benign form, fixated relationships are those entrenched in habit. Such relationships are much more fractious when those concerned are linked through modes of mutual antagonism, from which they are unable to extricate themselves.

We may suppose that fixated relationships are more widespread than codependency in any of its principal forms. A fixated relationship is built around compulsive dependence rather than codependence. Neither party is distinctively an addict, yet both are dependent upon a tie which is either a matter of routinised obligation or actually destructive for the parties concerned. Fixated relationships usually presume role separation. Each person depends upon an "alterity" which the partner provides; but neither is able fully to recognise, or come to terms with, the nature of his or her dependence upon the other. Men tend to be in fixated relationships in so far as they are with others to whom they are deeply bound, but where that bondedness is either not understood or is actively disclaimed. In the case of women, compulsive dependence is more often associated with a domestic role that has become a fetish—a ritual involvement, for example, with domestic chores and the demands of children.

The work of those who, on the level of therapy, seek to help individuals escape from addictive relationships again provides clues about the structural transformations influencing such relationships. Here once more we encounter the emerging centrality of the pure relationship, as well as its close connections with the reflexive project of self and with a model of confluent love. Addictive ties: (1) do not allow for the monitoring of self and other so vital to the pure relationship, (2) submerge self-identity either in the other or in fixed routines, (3) prevent that opening out to the other which is the precondition of intimacy, (4) tend to preserve inegalitarian gender differences and sexual practices.

The first injunction of all therapy programmes is a reflexive one: recognise that you have a problem and, by dint of that recognition, begin to do something about it! In alcoholic self-help groups, "bottoming out" is the term often used to describe the state of mind of those who say, "Enough is enough: I am going to change." "Even after the decision has been made at some level, you may still need a jolt to get you to take action. It could be a rejection, a car accident, getting abused by a sexual partner, losing sobriety, or an onslaught of anxiety attacks. Harmful consequences are like a shot of energy to the healthy side."[5] The decision to take action normally involves securing the help of others outside the addictive relationship itself, for this is a key mode of achieving initial distance as well as support.

The development of reflexive attention entails, as a basic beginning point, the recognition of choice. Choice, it is emphasized, means an appraisal of one's limits and the constraints to which one is subject: this is the way to assess opportunities. The reflexive moment is called by one author "self talk." Self talk is a reprogramming, a way of considering how far established routines should be thought of in a new way or, if possible, discarded. Recognition of choice means overcoming "negative programmes" that support addictive patterns. The following are what addictive programming sounds like:

> "I just can't do it";
> "I just know it won't work";
> "I'm not cut out for that";
> "I'm not creative enough";
> "I'll never have enough money";
> "I can't get along with my boss";
> "I never seem to have the time I need to get everything done" . . . and so forth.[6]

We should stand back from the naive, almost totalitarian, ring of the injunction to avoid all such thoughts: for, rather obviously, "I just can't do it," "I just know it won't work" and the rest can often be realistic appraisals of one's opportunities in any given context. Reflexivity is a necessary condition for emancipation from addiction, not a sufficient one. None the less, the behavioural importance of such programming is evident enough.

Choice, it is made clear, reflects directly upon the nature of the self. What a person wants helps define who that person is; and finding a secure self-identity is fundamental to identifying wants. "There may be a thousand little choices in a day. All of them count."[7] But some of them count more than others. Compulsive relationships, as the therapeutic literature repeatedly states, although not always in so many words, preclude the reflexive exploration of self-identity. Thus a codependent individual is seen by Kasl precisely as "someone whose core identity is undeveloped or unknown, and who maintains a false identity built from dependent attachments to external sources."[8]

ADDICTION AND THE QUESTION OF INTIMACY

Codependent individuals are accustomed to finding their identity through the actions or needs of others; but in any addictive relationship the self tends to become merged with the other, because the addiction is a prime source of ontological security. One of the aims often suggested in the early phases of therapy or self-help groups is that of "letting go"—releasing the attempt to control others characteristic of codependence. The individual is encouraged to try to free him- or herself from her "unspoken contract" to put the other to rights. The process is an extremely difficult one to go through, although its surface markers are apparent: her conversations no longer so continually focus upon what "he" thinks or does, what "they" say, "my husband" or "my lover" says. In support groups for the partners of alcoholics, letting go is labelled Loving Detachment, a banal enough phrase for a very real phenomenon—the emerging capability of the codependent to sustain care for the other without shouldering the burden of his or her addiction.[9]

What seems at first blush an encouragement of egoism, even narcissism, should rather be understood as an essential starting-point for the possibility of developing confluent love. It is a prerequisite for recognising the other as an independent being, who can be loved for her or his specific traits and qualities; and also it offers the chance of release from an obsessive involvement with a broken or dying relationship. These are some characteristics, as listed by one therapist, of new habits that might replace the older, more compulsive ones:

> You can listen to a friend's problem—just listen—and not try to rescue him or her.
>
> Instead of being focused solely on one person, you are interested in many people.
>
> Instead of returning to the "scene of the crime"—where your ex-lover lives, or special places the two of you went to—you find more interesting places to visit.
>
> If you desire something or someone who is not available, you enjoy something or someone who is.

Instead of putting up with abuse, you say no to the relationship.

If you have just broken up with a lover, and he always called at a certain time, you find another pleasurable pursuit to do at that time.[10]

Defining personal boundaries is regarded as fundamental for a non-addictive relationship. Why? The answer again directly concerns the self and its reflexivity. Boundaries establish what belongs to whom, psychologically speaking, and thereby counteract the effects of projective identification. Clear boundaries within a relationship are obviously important for confluent love and the sustaining of intimacy. Intimacy is not being absorbed by the other, but knowing his or her characteristics and making available one's own. Opening out to the other, paradoxically, requires personal boundaries, because it is a communicative phenomenon; it also requires sensitivity and tact, since it is not the same as living with no private thoughts at all. The balance of openness, vulnerability and trust developed in a relationship governs whether or not personal boundaries become divisions which obstruct rather than encourage such communication.[11]

This balance also presumes a balance of power—which is why the pure relationship, with its promise of intimacy, depends both upon the increasing autonomy of women and upon plastic sexuality, no longer harnessed to the double standard. The same therapist mentioned above provides a chart identifying characteristics of addictive versus intimate relationships.

Pious psychobabble? Perhaps, at least to some degree. Self-contradictory, in respect of some of the claims made in the right-hand column? Undoubtedly—although to some extent these express real contradictions of personal life. Yet I do not think the possibilities listed are mere wishful thinking; they reflect some of the tendential characteristics of the transformation of intimacy which I seek to document throughout the book. Who could fail to see in them evidence of, and a programme for, the democratisa-

Addictive	Intimate
Obsession with finding "somone to love"	Development of self as a first priority
Need for immediate gratification	Desire for long-term contentment; relationship develops step by step
Pressuring partner for sex or commitment	Freedom of choice
Imbalance of power	Balance and mutuality in the relationship
Power plays for control	Compromise, negotiation or taking turns at leading
No-talk rule, especially if things are not working out	Sharing wants, feelings, and appreciation of what your partner means to you
Manipulation	Directness
Lack of trust	Appropriate trust (that is, knowing that your partner will probably behave according to his or her fundamental nature)
Attempts to change partner to meet one's needs	
Relationship is based on delusion and avoidance of the unpleasant	Embracing of each other's individuality
Relationship is always the same	Relationship deals with all aspects of reality
Expectation that one partner will fix and rescue the other	Relationship is always changing
Fusion (being obsessed with each other's problems and feelings)	Self-care by both partners
Passion confused with fear	Loving detachment (healthy concern about partner's well-being and growth, while letting go)
Blaming self or partner for problems	Sex grows out of friendship and caring
Cycle of pain and despair	Problem-solving together
	Cycle of comfort and contentment[12]

tion of daily life? Comparing the list on the left-hand side with that on the right reveals a picture of emancipation. This is not just a "freeing from": as portrayed here intimacy has a substantive content. We begin to see what a liberated personal domain might look like.

INTIMACY, KINSHIP, PARENTHOOD

The transformation of intimacy is about sex and gender, but it is not limited to them—a fact which supports the thesis, which I shall develop in some detail later, that what is at issue here is a basic transition in the ethics of personal life as a whole. Like gender, kinship was once seen as naturally given, a series of rights and obligations which biological and marriage ties created. Kinship relations, it has been widely argued, have been largely destroyed with the development of modern institutions, which have left the nuclear family standing in splendid isolation. Without taking up the question in any detail, it can be seen that this view is mistaken, or at least misleading. In the separating and divorcing society, the nuclear family generates a diversity of new kin ties associated, for example, with so-called recombinant families. However, the nature of these ties changes as they are subject to greater negotiation than before. Kinship relations often used to be a taken for granted basis of trust; now trust has to be negotiated and bargained for, and commitment is as much of an issue as in sexual relationships.

Janet Finch speaks of a process of "working out" when analysing kinship relations today.[13] People have to work out how to treat relatives and, in so doing, construct novel ethics of day-to-day life. She treats this process explicity in terms of a language of commitment. People tend to organise their kinship connections through "negotiated commitment," whereby they work out the "proper thing to do" for their relatives in a specific range of contexts. For instance, an individual does not decide to lend money to a brother-in-law because this is defined in the family or wider society as an obligation; rather the money is lent because the person has developed a series of commitments to the other which defines it as the right thing to do.

How far do the relations between parents and children differ from this situation? Evidently in adult–child interaction there is a marked imbalance of power, especially in the early years of the life of the child. In the light of this fact, one might suppose that the quality of the relationship has little bearing upon the care provided, since there are pre-given social obligations of a binding kind on both sides. Yet there is good reason to doubt how strong such obligations are among many groups today. The best way to demonstrate this is to work "backwards" from parent–child ties that are clearly negotiated to those characteristic of early childhood. Many parents are now step-parents as well as biological mothers and fathers. Step-parents usually accept some obligations towards, and rights over, children, but these are today generally "negotiated commitments" in Finch's sense, from the side of the children as well as the adults. Or take the case of the obligations adult children assume towards ageing parents. In some circumstances and cultural contexts it is more or less taken for granted that the parents can count on their children for material and social support. But the clear trend of development is for such support to depend upon the quality of relationship forged.

The determining influence seems to be what could be described as the forming of cumulative commitments.[14] In a study of mothers and daughters, for example, one respondent says, "My mother and I lived together because we chose to, we liked each other . . . we shared a common home, we could laugh together . . . I was an independent person, so was my mother. We were living together, I wasn't just looking after her."[15] She felt a commitment to care for her mother, as a result of their long history together; but the element of mutual liking was important. As Finch points out, the notion of cumulative commitments helps us to understand how, over a period of time, it becomes "obvious" to one sibling that various forms of care should be provided for one or both parents, whereas another might feel quite differently.[16]

The picture is more complex in the case of the relation of parents to younger children. Not only are parents much more powerful than very young children; their attitudes and conduct shape the child's personality and dispositions. Yet it would certainly not be right to suppose that childhood has remained unaffected by the world of pure relationships. The social invention of motherhood presaged, and gave concrete form to, the idea that the mother should develop an affectionate relationship with the child, one that gives specific weight to the child's needs. Child-rearing manuals published in the early part of the current century advised parents not to become too friendly with their children on the grounds that their authority would become weakened. Later the view developed that parents should seek to foster close emotional ties with their children, but also give due recognition to the child's autonomy.[17] Just as some have spoken of narcissism to refer to the position of the self in modern society, others have suggested that parent–child interaction has moved towards greater "permissiveness." But this is an inadequate label to refer to the endeavour to develop alternative child-rearing strategies to those of the past. It is the quality of the relationship which comes to the fore, with a stress upon intimacy replacing that of parental authoritativeness. Sensitivity and understanding are asked for on both sides.[18]

REFERENCES

1. Peter Trachtenberg: *The Casanova Complex,* New York: Pocket Books, 1988, pp. 244–8.

2. Cf., for example, Colette Dowling: *The Cinderella Complex,* New York: Pocket Books, 1981, p. 34.

3. Anne Wilson Schaeff: *Codependence. Misunderstood-Mistreated,* San Francisco: Harper and Row, 1986, p. 11.

4. Jody Hayes: *Smart Love,* London: Arrow, 1990, p. 31.

5. Charlotte Kasl: *Women, Sex and Addiction,* London: Mandarin, 1990, p. 340.

6. Shad Helmstetter: *Choices,* New York: Pocket Books, 1989, p. 47.

7. Ibid., p. 97.

8. Kasl: *Women, Sex and Addiction,* p. 36.

9. Hayes: *Smart Love,* pp. 63–4.

10. Ibid., p. 73.

11. C. Edward Crowther: *Intimacy. Strategies for Successful Relationships,* New York: Dell, 1988, pp. 156–8.

12. Hayes: *Smart Love,* pp. 174–5.

13. Janet Finch: *Family Obligations and Social Change,* Cambridge: Polity, 1989, pp. 194–211.

14. Ibid., pp. 204–5.

15. J. Lewis and B. Meredith: *Daughters Who Care,* London: Routledge, 1988, p. 54.

16. Finch: *Family Obligations and Social Change,* p. 205.

17. H. Gadlin: "Child discipline and the pursuit of the self: an historical interpretation." *Advances in Child Development and Behaviour,* vol. 12, 1978.

18. Ibid., pp. 75–82.

DISCUSSION QUESTIONS

1. Offer a definition of codependency in your own words and discuss what the implications of this phenomenon are for creating interpersonal relationships.

2. Giddens concedes that the distinction he presents between addictive and intimate relationships has an element of "pious psychobabble," but he also sees real tendencies that are changing our notions of intimacy. Do you agree or disagree with him?

The Sales Process and the Paradoxes of Trust

Guy Oakes

What are the circumstances that spell success in the world of personal sales? This is the question Guy Oakes attempts to answer in his exploration into the sales process. In answering the question, he relied on both the training documents used in the life insurance business and interviews with sales personnel in the industry. Although a number of impression management issues are addressed in both data sources, Oakes singles out the issue of trust as fundamental to success or failure. If a potential sales client does not trust an agent, a sale will not be made. However, because agents use a variety of dissimulations in order to create a climate of trust, there is an inherent paradox in the sales process: "sincerity produces insincerity."

THE PROBLEMATIC STATUS OF TRUST IN PERSONAL SALES

Much of the literature on trust in personal sales focuses on trust as an essential ethical variable in the sales process. The prospect's willingness to trust the salesperson—or, what amounts to the same thing, the salesperson's ability to demonstrate trustworthiness—is held to be a necessary condition for closing sales (Dwyer et al., 1987; Colvin, 1984; Hawes et al., 1989; Prus, 1989; Schurr and Ozanne, 1985; Swan and Nolan, 1985). By analyzing data from life insurance sales, this essay supports the thesis that the role of the agent and the exigencies of personal sales generate certain antinomies of trust that compromise the sales process. As a result, trust occupies a problematic and apparently paradoxical position in the sales process. On the one hand, success in personal sales is held to depend upon trust. On the other hand, because the techniques required to form trust in personal sales

nullify the conditions under which trust is possible, these instruments of trust formation are self-defeating.

A note on the concept of personal sales, which in the textbook literature on marketing and sales is generally understood as designating any face-to-face contact between salesperson and customer (Buskirk, 1970; Churchill et al., 1981; Marsh, 1972; Schewe and Smith, 1980; Stanton and Buskirk, 1983). In the ensuing analysis, personal sales will be construed somewhat more narrowly. Face-to-face interaction between a salesperson and a potential customer will be understood as falling under the concept of personal sales only if the interaction itself is governed by the multiphased sales process: the several steps of recruiting and qualifying prospects, interviewing potential customers, closing the sale, and servicing clients. This means that a comprehensive range of sales positions will not be considered in this investigation. They include the following: sales personnel whose primary function is to deliver merchandise; sales clerks who work in retail stores and may not even have occasion to speak to customers; retail sales personnel who take orders, close sales, and provide services, but are not responsible for prospecting, wholesalers whose main function is to call on businesses that retail the goods in their inventory and to insure that this stock of goods is maintained at a level sufficient to accommodate consumer demand; "missionary" sales personnel, who are not expected to make sales but only to educate the consumer—usually a retailer—concerning a line of products or build good-will on behalf of a marketing organization; and finally, technical or industrial sales personnel whose main function is to serve as consultants to clients who purchase equipment or raw materials that are not resold to the consumer, but are used in a manufacturing process. In sum, personal sales is defined by the sales process. It can be said that sales personnel are engaged in personal sales only if the interaction between salesperson and consumer is controlled by the principles that govern the performance of this process.

The data employed in this investigation are drawn from two main sources: training programs in life insurance sales and interviews with sales personnel in the life insurance industry. The life insurance industry is a major producer and consumer of training programs in personal sales. The largest companies produce their own programs, either by using in-house specialists from the sales and marketing research staff of the company or by employing consultants who design a "unique" program customized to the needs and image of the company. Smaller companies use generic programs developed by consultants, who are frequently agents with legendary sales records and industry-wide prestige. The Life Insurance Marketing and Research Association (LIMRA), the official marketing research organization of the industry, provides a full line of training materials and services that are available to companies, agencies and individual agents. Finally, industry trade journals regularly feature articles on sales training for both trainees as well as established agents who feel it is time to sharpen their skills.

A collection of interviews conducted in 1987–89 provides a secondary source of data. The interviewees were mainly life insurance agents with territories between New York City and Philadelphia. Also interviewed were general agents—the managers of regional agencies of specific insurance companies—and their sales managers, both of whom are responsible for training agents. Finally, consultants who specialize in lectures and seminars in all fields of personal sales were interviewed. Initial interviews generally lasted from one hour to ninety minutes. From the original group of seventy-four interviewees, thirty-two were interviewed a second time. From this second group, fifteen were interviewed repeatedly and more intensively over the two year period. The fifteen agents in this last group worked for a variety of life insurance companies. Some had only a few

months in the business, others more than twenty-five years. They also represented quite different levels of success in the industry. While some had been terminated by more than one company, others were major producers or "heavy hitters," members of the Million Dollar Roundtable and active in the National Association of Life Underwriters. Finally, an additional set of twenty-five interviews was conducted at a national company convention, where I was able to speak with agents from other parts of the United States. These were brief, somewhat fugitive, and frequently impromptu interviews, usually of fifteen to thirty minutes in duration. All interviews with agents active in the industry were conducted on the condition of anonymity. Accordingly, the names of agents and companies that appear in the interviews reported below are fictions. Interviews were taped on a handheld microcassette recorder and subsequently transcribed by the author.

A few of the interviews took place in agents' offices. However, most were conducted in the field: in restaurants, bars, and coffee shops—waystations to which agents repair when they find themselves between calls to prospects. Industry training programs teach agents that success depends upon their ability to market trust in their own probity: prospects will buy a policy only if they first buy the trustworthiness of the agent. This is why successful agents always attempt to sell themselves and their integrity before they try to sell a product. My limited experience in exploring the workworld of life insurance agents suggests that although they live off the trust they inspire in others, they are extremely parsimonious in the investment of their own trust. As one agent put it, with an excess that is typical of the industry: "In this business, you don't trust anybody." Everyone, it seems, has an angle, a hidden agenda, and ulterior motives that are probably base, indefensible, and calculated to thwart the agent's own interests. It is hardly astonishing that this attitude leads agents to be suspicious and cynical about declarations of intention and statements of purpose. Nor under these circumstances is it surprising that my own motives for interviewing agents were often construed in pecuniary rather than scholarly terms. Thus I was sometimes suspected of compiling data for yet another expose of the life insurance industry or of gathering material for a bestseller that would represent agents as charlatans, cheats, and frauds.

TRUST AS A CONDITION FOR THE SUCCESS OF THE SALES PROCESS

Training in personal sales—from cosmetics, vacuum cleaners, and real estate to mutual funds, higher education, and life insurance—is based on the assumption that prospects can be motivated to make purchasing decisions only by sales personnel whom they trust. In life insurance sales, one of the main tenets of the sales process is that prospects will purchase policies only if they see agents not as sales personnel marketing a product, but as professionals who can be relied upon to provide expertise. Prospects can be closed only if they conceive themselves as clients whose interests are respected and cared for by the agent, not as customers who are being sold. As the training literature consistently stresses, the crucial variable in the relationship between prospect and agent is trust. Trust rests on the expectation that technically competent service will be rendered. Perhaps even more important, it includes the expectation of fiduciary responsibility: the belief that agents will recognize their obligations to the prospect, act on these obligations, and in cases where interests conflict, place the prospect's interests above their own (Barber, 1983: 14–21). "People want more that just a product or service. They want you to be concerned about their needs; they want you to inspire confidence and trust and to communicate that you are strongly committed to their welfare" (Miller, 1986: 15).

Consider trust as a dyadic relation. In that case, it can be understood as a set of expecta-

tions I have concerning your actions. These actions satisfy at least two conditions. They are of some relevance—and may even be vital—to my own choices. And in addition, circumstances are such that I must make these choices without being able to monitor your actions (Dasgupta, 1988). If I could exercise surveillance over your conduct insofar as it is germane to my own choices, it would not be necessary for me to trust you. Therefore, trust is a function of imperfect information. Under conditions of perfect information, I would have no reason to act on trust. Under conditions of perfect ignorance, either I would not act at all or I would be obliged to act on blind trust. Under conditions of imperfect information, I may—given the conditions just described—decide to act on trust. Thus the less I know, the more trust I need. In order to reach an appreciation of the importance of trust in personal sales, several points should be considered.

1. Personal sales is a cooperative venture (Williams, 1988). This means it is a joint undertaking for which contributions from both the salesperson and the prospect must be forthcoming. It also means that the contribution of the prospect cannot be coerced or otherwise directly controlled by the salesperson. It follows from these two considerations that the salesperson and the prospect depend upon one another, although for different things. In life insurance sales, the agent is dependent upon the prospect for the premiums from which commissions are drawn. Once the policy application is signed, the agent relies on the prospect to write the all-important check for the initial premium. The prospect is dependent upon the agent for accurate and reliable information, a comprehensive and valid analysis of his or her financial security needs, and honesty and probity—the performance of the fiduciary obligations that are generally held to govern relationships between clients and their expert advisors. Cooperative projects such as personal sales are impossible if

the parties are unwilling to place themselves in a dependent position. Thus the ability of an agent to gain the cooperation of prospects is linked to the willingness of prospects to make themselves dependent on the agent. In principle, agents could solve this problem by confining their sales efforts to prospects to whom they are known, acquaintances who have some confidence in their assessments of a given agent's intentions. On the basis of their personal knowledge of the agent, prospects could feel satisfied that this agent would do his or her part in the cooperative transaction. Because prospecting is essential to the agent's success, this is usually not a feasible option. Agents are obliged to recruit as potential clients persons who do not know them well, and perhaps do not know them at all. As a result, the agent must work with prospects who have no reason to believe they can rely on his or her competence and veracity. Thus in securing the cooperation of prospects, the agent must convince them to take a dependent position. The agent can expect to succeed in this enterprise only if the prospect believes the agent will not defect from the cooperative venture by failing to perform the actions on which the prospect depends. This is where the need for trust enters a cooperative undertaking such as personal sales.

2. Trust seems to be essential to commercial transactions that are not fully controlled by either the legal constraints of contracts or the economic forces of markets. If there are transactions that slip through the network of these sanctions or are located at their peripheries, then trust is required for their consummation. Such transactions include interactions in which an actor in a cooperative venture incurs risk because of the relative freedom of his or her interlocutors. If the conduct of the interlocutors is not controlled by the threat of legal or market penalties, they can exit without damage to themselves before meeting the conditions on which the actor is dependent. Because the prevailing sanctions do not guarantee the honesty of the in-

terlocutors, trust on the part of the actor is indispensable to the transaction. If everyone were honest, or if the laws of contracts effectively covered all cooperative transactions, or if the penalties of the market were sufficiently comprehensive and severe to prevent dishonesty or noncompliance in such transactions, there would be no need for trust. Thus the risk that is an essential part of the prospect's trust in the agent is a consequence of the underdetermination of the agent's behavior: the freedom of the agent to exit at will, to betray the prospect, and to defect from the interaction without suffering significant penalties. Trust is the prospect's means of coming to terms with the freedom of the agent and the risks this freedom entails for the prospect. The larger the range of realistic choices open to the agent, the more important trust becomes.

3. As the foregoing remarks indicate, acts of trust necessarily include the possibility of disappointment. This is because "trust is a solution for specific problems of risk" (Luhmann, 1988: 95). The predicament of the prospect clearly exhibits the relation between trust and risk. In making a commitment that rests on a belief in the trustworthiness of the agent, prospects risk their financial resources. But if they refuse to assume the risks entailed by this commitment, they risk the loss of payoffs in financial security that they stand to gain by making this decision. What is worse, if the agent violates the trust of prospects, there is a sense in which they have themselves to blame. After all, they made the decision to trust the agent. The literature on sales in the life insurance industry stresses that the prospect is acutely aware of these hazards. Thus the dangers this situation poses for the agent are evident. The agent's success depends upon the prospect's decision to assume the risk involved in trusting the agent. It follows that the agent's main task in the area of sales motivation is to persuade the prospect to take this risk. The agent attempts to convince the prospect either by minimizing—or, more usually, by denying—the risk itself, or by

arguing that in refusing to assume the risk the prospect will lose the benefits to be gained by trusting the agent. While the relations between trust, risk, benefit, and loss constitute a serious problem for the agent, they also open up a tempting opportunity. This is because a prospect who can be persuaded to trust the agent can also be convinced that the advantages of risk outweigh its disadvantages. Such a prospect can be closed without difficulty.

4. In the sales process, the object of trust is the agent's volitions, dispositions, motivations, and intentions—everything that is, or used to be, collected under the rubric of character. If character is the object of trust, the prospect's decision to trust the agent is linked to the prospect's perception and judgment of the agent's reputation. This is a crucial consideration for the agent, since it means that trust cannot be established instantaneously, in one encounter, interaction, or interview. Excluding the case of blind trust—a possibility that is not consistent with a sales process that rejects charismatic sales virtuosity in favor of the systematic routine of standardized, tried and true sales tracks—it is reasonable to expect that trust can be formed only as a result of repeated interactions between agent and prospect. In considering what can be learned from these interactions, the prospect will reach some conclusion concerning what they add up to as evidence of the agent's character. Two factors make this situation disadvantageous and quite risky for the agent. On the one hand, time is the agent's most valuable resource, which means that an agent cannot afford to devote too much of it to any one prospect. On the other hand, the agent can expect to close prospects only by gaining their trust. But in order to decide whether the agent is trustworthy, the prospect, at least in principle, needs more time with the agent than it is in the agent's interest to make available.

5. As a result of this practical dilemma, agents are powerfully motivated to develop strategies for inspiring or creating trust, and thus

accelerating an otherwise time-consuming process they can ill afford. This is the source of the agent's need to supply evidence of reputation that will document his or her trustworthiness. Testimonies to the agent's reputation, such as those provided in referrals, are designed to abbreviate the normal period of trust formation. However, it is also worth noting that it takes time to develop a reputation, and thus to exhibit evidence of its unimpeachable quality. Considerable caution and foresight are required here. Although a reputation can generally be acquired only gradually and laboriously, it can be destroyed with virtually blinding rapidity—by a single false move, a suspicious maneuver, or an act of apparent dishonesty. As one agent notes: "It's amazing how quickly your credibility can be blown. And sometimes it's not even your fault."

> A few years ago, I spent several weeks cultivating a major prospect, the head of a big computer engineering firm in Eatontown. At that point, I hadn't been in the business very long, so I asked my sales manager Ed Stockman to come down and help with the sale. Ed Stockman was a real machine. A very nice man, but a truly classic salesman. You know, a product of years and years of those programs in sales technique. So we go down to Eatontown to see this big computer executive. This is probably the most embarrassing situation I was ever in. We're in this big board room. This guy was very nice. He had his accountants there. We didn't have to wait long. We sit down, Ed came in. He wasn't dressed properly, you know, for these people. I hate to put it this way, but these were real executives, and Ed came dressed like a . . . Well, his pants were too short, and so were his socks. There's a role you have to play, and when you're with professionals, you have to dress like a professional. Anyway, he comes in with this big briefcase, and in this briefcase were flipcharts. This stuff is ridiculous. These were very sophisticated people, and at this stage of the game, you don't sell this way. But before anyone can say anything, he has this huge flipchart on the table. He starts telling them why they should buy this insurance. These two accountants really wanted to just get out of the room. Anyway, to

make a long story short, they said they didn't want it, because they were completely turned off by his way of selling. So he puts down this briefcase and he has this other briefcase that he slams on the table. He opens it up, you know, like a vaudevillian. They didn't want the insurance, but he had something else for them. He was talking faster than I ever could, offering them one thing after the other. They start to get up and leave. But he wouldn't let them leave their own office. They were starting to walk out the door, and he just followed them. I was incredibly embarrassed. And this guy, who I had made the appointment with, when I left told me: "I don't want to see you around here anymore. Don't ever come back here again." He said to my face that he had never been subjected to anything like this in his life. So there you are, I was finished. Needless to say, I never went back to Eatontown.

The agent's lesson is clear. In his efforts to abbreviate the process in which his reputation is confirmed for the prospect, he runs a considerable risk of damaging it or, as in this case, destroying it altogether.

6. Finally, the fabrication or appearance of trust worthiness will not do. A real commitment by the agent is necessary to establish a basis of trust without which the prospect cannot be closed. This is why agents are exhorted to be sincere in all their dealings with prospects and demonstrate a genuine interest in providing service. "If you are insincere, your prospect will sense it" (Miller, 1986: 15). Pretense, theatricalization, role playing, or impression management are out of place here. As the same training program stresses: "You can't fake it. Unless you truly have your prospect's best interests at heart, you will not come across as a trustworthy person" (Walsh, 1986: 15). This is one reason why thorough financial planning is so crucial to the work of an agent. Trust is a product of the interaction between prospect and agent that takes place during the process of planning. The planning process itself is essential to the development of the prospect's trust in the agent. Work-

ing out such a plan calls for comprehensive and candid discussions and close cooperation between agent and prospect. In order to create a successful plan, the agent must convince prospects to share their personal ideals and some of the most intimate details of their lives. This experience of sharing binds the prospect to the agent and establishes a relationship based on trust. Once formed, such a relationship is difficult to shake, since it rests on long hours of joint work and the intimacy of details disclosed by the prospect (Simmel, 1964). It is essential for agents to gain access to this privileged data. Without it, the analysis on which their proposals are based cannot even begin. The process by which the agent gains access to these facts ties the prospect to the agent in a highly personal way. Commenting on the confidentiality of this tie, one agent, perhaps with some exaggeration, claims to know everything about her clients. "We know all about their families. We know details about our clients their wives didn't even know. They've entrusted us with family secrets" (Weiner, 1988: 8). In this manner, prospects reveal themselves to the agent and give their trust, in exchange for which they expect to receive the benefits of the financial security planning process.

THE PARADOXES OF TRUST

Sincerity and Dissimulation

Professional sales personnel have an obligation to see to it that their clients treat their joint relationship in a purely professional fashion. For professionals such as physicians, this requirement is institutionally satisfied, as a result of which they need make no special or personal efforts in this direction. For the salesperson, matters are not so simple. In the life insurance industry, the social mechanisms required to establish and legitimize professional status—institutions comparable to post-graduate, degree-granting faculties associated with major universities and organizations with the tradition, power, and prestige of the American Medical Association or the American Bar Association—are not in place. This is why training manuals instruct agents—inelegantly, bluntly, and with brutal candor—that it is crucial for them to "sell the prospect on their professionalism." Why should this be necessary? It is due to the fact that, in important respects and for a number of evident reasons, life insurance agents are not acknowledged professionals at all.

At the risk of some oversimplification, it can be said that in the life insurance industry, a profession is conceived along three axes: a cognitive dimension grounded in a claim to expert knowledge that requires a formalized period of training; a normative dimension grounded in an ideal of service to clients; and a status dimension grounded in occupational prestige. From the standpoint of the cognitive dimension, agents receive no training comparable to the education of the physician, the attorney, or even the dentist or the accountant. From the standpoint of the status dimension, the agent is notoriously lacking in prestige. Unlike the medical student who acquires instant prestige and the charisma of professionalism simply by becoming an M.D., no one gains prestige merely by virtue of becoming an insurance agent. In fact, given the derision, contempt, and sheer bad manners that must be borne by those who have chosen this occupation, precisely the contrary seems to be the case (*New England Life Associate's Career Track,* 1983; Zelizer, 1979: 134–40). Finally, from the standpoint of the normative dimension, the conduct of the agent is not subject to a guild ethic enforced by gatekeeper organizations. Agents who commit moral or legal lapses in their careers at one company have no difficulty—assuming that they have established a record of high performance in "making their numbers"—moving to another company, or even transferring to another agency within the same organization. Consider the following account of the arrangements made to retain rogue agents.

If you get caught doing something that's really hideous or really embarrassing to the company, they'll fire you outright, ostensibly for "breaking regulations." Otherwise, it doesn't happen. There was one guy who left Covenant Life to work for Verity who was supposedly keeping premiums instead of sending them up to the company. Can you imagine that? Now you're entering the grounds of fraud, felony, you know, stealing. Verity supposedly let him go. But I later found out that they basically suspended him for ninety days and let him do business. No problem. They licensed somebody else to sign all his applications. Of course the reason is the numbers. This guy is a great salesman, and they wanted to keep him. They worked something out. This happens a lot. A first-rate agent doesn't truly get fired from an insurance company unless he's going to jail. Or unless he becomes a total embarrassment.

In sum, the life insurance industry expects agents to appear to be what they are not: namely, professionals. This means that agents must endeavor to act as if they were professionals and prove their professionalism to the prospect. They must say what they know to be false, behave in a way that the prospect is led to believe what is false, and suggest, imply, or intimate—whether by gesture, impression, bearing, or insinuation—what is not true. In other words, agents must act insincerely. It follows that they are obliged to act in ways that encourage mistrust, for sincerity, as the training manuals insist, is a requirement of trust. On this point, the training manuals seem to be correct. It is essential to trust that anyone who signifies or implies that he or she has certain characteristics should in fact have them. Trust depends upon sincerity in the sense that actors should be what they claim to be. It is their obligation to see to it that appearance corresponds to reality and that what they express conforms to what they are. Without this basis in sincerity, trust would be impossible. But this is precisely what agents cannot do, since it would compromise their attempt to prove their professionalism to the prospect. Because of their questionable status as professionals, agents cannot afford to be sincere. On the contrary, the circumstances of their work dictate a posture of prevarication, in which agents evade the truth about themselves, or perhaps dissimulation, in which they conceal their motives by pretending to be what they are not. In consequence, the sales process requires of the agent both sincerity, without which trust is impossible since the prospect will not trust a demonstrably insincere agent, and dissimulation, which destroys the sincerity that is essential to trust.

The Paradox of Sincerity

The sales process demands of agents the appearance of professionalism in order to achieve trustworthiness. This expectation is imposed on a service industry role in which the demonstration of professionalism and trustworthiness is not otherwise guaranteed by criteria that agents can satisfy or desiderata that are at their disposal or under their control. The M.D. degree and its legitimation by traditional institutional power and prestige certify the professional status and trustworthiness of the physician, even though an individual physician may not in fact be a particularly reliable person. It is not necessary for doctors to seem professional. They need only be professional by satisfying the requisite criteria. This does not hold true for insurance agents. Even if they are professionally trustworthy, this is not sufficient to prove their trustworthiness in the eyes of the prospect, nor does it demonstrate their professional status. They must also sell the prospect on their professionalism, managing their conduct in such a way that the prospect reaches the desired conclusion about their trustworthiness—which in this case happens to be true.

As a result, the sincerity of agents about their trustworthiness creates a paradox. It depends upon behavior that casts this very sincerity in doubt: the management of impressions undertaken to convince the prospect to believe in the agent's trustworthiness. If sincerity is a natural and unforced conformity between avowals and actions, then it does not make sense to try to be sincere or to devise strategies for becoming more sincere, both of which require the deliberate attempt to achieve a state that cannot be brought about by calculation (Trilling, 1972). Consider agents who are sincere in their attempt to become worthy of the prospect's trust. Their self-consciousness—their knowledge of the circumstances of their role and the conditions required for its performance—rules out the possibility of sincerity. Sincerity produces insincerity.

This paradox is a result of the fallacy committed by a demonstration, the object of which is to establish the possession of certain qualities: The intentionality of the demonstration is related to its object in such a way that the former nullifies the latter (Elster, 1985). If the desired state of sincerity depends on an absence of intentionality, calculation, or striving, then any attempt to achieve sincerity by intentional effort or deliberation is self-defeating. This is because any such attempt renders impossible the result it proposes to establish. The problem at issue concerns the conditions under which professionalism can be proven. Is it established institutionally, or is it demonstrated by means of efforts undertaken by the claimant to a professional status? In the latter case, impression management is essential. To manage impressions is to create a performance, to produce a show, and thus to dramatize one's attributes or conduct. These efforts depend upon the distinction between the agent and the character he or she represents. They presuppose that agents see themselves both as performers and as the characters that are the product of the performance. By dramatizing their conduct and employing dramaturgic criteria in order to assess their performance, agents make sure that they know they are not what they seem to be. The logic of the dramaturgic situation guarantees that agents self-consciously represent themselves as what they are not, thereby demonstrating their own insincerity (Brown, 1977; Goffman, 1959; Howton and Rosenberg, 1965; Lyman and Scott, 1975; Turner, 1974).

The Paradox of Trust

The theory of the sales process to which the life insurance industry is committed holds that a sale is possible only if the prospect trusts the agent. In the relationship between agent and prospect, prospects allocate trust insofar as they find the claims and conduct of the agent credible and reliable. Trust reduces the complexity that prospects perceive in the sales process. If prospects find the agent trustworthy, they will not be inclined to harbour suspicions or raise doubts about whether the agent really is the professional expert he or she claims to be; nor will they question whether a specific policy is recommended because it best serves their own needs or because it maximizes the agent's commission dollars. They will not consider whether each step of the agent's presentation is an attempt to trick them into a decision that is not in their best interests or an honest attempt to formulate a coherent financial security plan tailored to their specific circumstances. Trust also reduces the number of variables in the sales process that the agent must take into account. Agents who enjoy the trust of the prospect are not burdened by the social technology required to sell themselves. Instead of concentrating on the many factors relevant to impression management and the various strategies by means of which they might gain the confidence and win the respect of the prospect, they can explore the prospect's needs and frame plans designed to meet them. Therefore, if agents can rely on the assumption that prospects trust them, certain advantages to agents are clearly forthcoming. Moreover, if the prospect's belief in the agent's reliability is justified, trust seems to work in the interest of the prospect as well.

Although trust limits the range of variables agents must juggle in the sales process and simplifies their task in moving the prospect to the close, it also places certain limits on the freedom of agents to select strategies and tactics. Trustworthy agents cannot act in ways that call

their reliability into question, nor can they afford to engage in behavior that would cause the prospect to entertain suspicions about their credibility. Agents must make sure that the claims they make suggest no contradictions, real or apparent. They cannot take risks that cast doubt on what they have told the prospect about themselves and their work. In short, they cannot afford any lapses in performance that destroy the conformity between avowals and behavior. This is because trust depends not only on familiarity: the confidence of prospects that they know what to expect in dealing with the agent. It depends on consistency as well: the belief on the part of prospects that agents do not make conflicting claims; that what agents say about themselves corresponds to what they do; and that—in some sense that inspires confidence in the prospect—an agent's actions are all of a piece. Consistency requires that one claim or action not defeat another. On the contrary, allegations and actions must be mutually supporting in such a way that they enhance a belief in the agent's veracity and reliability.

If trust depends upon consistency, two consequences follow. The prospect must believe that the professional identity claimed by the agent is consistent with the agent's conduct; and the management of the sales process by the agent must demonstrate this consistency to the prospect. However, the sales process also requires that agents be radical opportunists. They must exploit every advantage and control every variable in the interaction with the prospect in order to maximize the chances of closing. This strategy defeats trust by destroying the conditions under which it is possible. The principle of opportunism keeps the prospect off-guard. Because opportunistic agents gear their tactics to the psychodynamic contingencies of the situation, the prospect hardly knows what to expect next. Indeed, in the ideal sales interview this is necessarily the case, since the interaction is governed by an instrumental logic in which the agent controls the prospect. As a result, opportunism increases the complexity of the sales process for the prospect by increasing the uncertainty of its outcome. Uncertainty also increases the prospect's perception of risk, and thus encourages mistrust (Luhmann, 1979). In consequence, the opportunistic agent betrays trust and teaches mistrust, thereby nullifying the psychological and moral conditions under which the sale can be consummated.

CONCLUSION

The instrumentalization of life entailed by the exigencies of personal sales requires that agents hone their skills, manage their time, and mold their relationships in order to become pliable instruments of the sales process. Agents must do whatever is required, suffer and commit all manner of indignities, and perform whatever violations of taste and principle are necessary in order to close the sale. This, of course, means that the agent cannot be trusted, for a person who regards all things as allowable is unpredictable and thus unreliable. In sum, the sales process, which requires the agent to conceive all persons and employ all relationships as sources of potential prospects, is inconsistent with the possibility of trust. Since trust is the relationship that agents are trained to exploit most aggressively, it also follows that the sales process is ironically self-defeating. On the one hand, it requires agents to develop relations of trust as sources of prospects. On the other hand, in putting to this use those who trust them, agents jeopardize the very relationships they attempt to exploit, thereby compromising their most important source of prospects.

REFERENCES

Barber, B.: 1983, *The Logic and Limits of Trust* (Rutgers University Press, New Brunswick, NJ).
Brown, R. H.: 1977, *A Poetic for Sociology* (Cambridge University Press, New York).
Buskirk, R: 1970, *Principles of Marketing* (Holt, Rinehart and Winston, New York).

Churchill, G., N. Ford, and O. Walker Jr.: 1981, *Sales Force Management* (Irwin, Homewood, IL).
Colvin, G.: 1984, "Would You Buy Stocks Where You Buy Socks?" *Fortune,* July 9, 130–133.
Dasgupta, P.: 1988, "Trust as a Commodity," in Gambetta, D. (ed.): *Trust* (Cambridge University Press, New York), pp. 49–72.
Dwyer, F. R, P. Schurr, and S. Oh: 1987, "Developing Buyer-Seller Relationships," *Journal of Marketing* 51, 11–27.
Elster, J.: 1985, *Sour Grapes: Studies in the Subversion of Rationality* (Cambridge University Press, New York).
Goffman, E.: 1959, *The Presentation of Self in Everyday Life* (Doubleday, Garden City, NY).
Hawes, J. M., K. Mast, and J. Swan: 1989, "Trust Earning Perceptions of Sellers and Buyers," *Journal of Personal Selling and Sales Management* IX, 1–8.
Howton, F.W. and B. Rosenberg: 1965. "The Salesman: Ideology and Self-Imagery in a Prototypic Occupation," *Social Research* 32, 277–298.
Luhmann, N.: 1979, *Trust and Power* (Wiley, New York).
Luhmann, N.: 1988, "Familiarity, Confidence, Trust: Problems and Alternatives," in Gambetta, D. (ed.): *Trust* (Cambridge University Press, New York), pp. 94–107.
Lyman, S. and M. Scott: 1975, *The Drama of Social Reality* (Oxford University Press, New York).
Marsh, U. G.: 1972, *Salesmanship* (Prentice Hall, Englewood Cliffs, NJ).
Miller, C.: 1986, *Prudential Training Program: The Financial Security Selling System,* Book 1 (Pru-Press, Newark, NJ).
No Author: 1983, *New England Life Associate's Career Track,* unit I, module 1 (New England Life, Boston).
Prus, R.: 1989, *Making Sales: Influence as Interpersonal Accomplishment* (Sage, Newbury Park, CA).
Schewe, C. and R. Smith: 1980, *Marketing: Concepts and Applications* (McGraw-Hill, New York).
Schurr, P. and J. Ozanne: 1985, "Influences on Exchange Processes: Buyers' Preconceptions of a Seller's Trustworthiness and Bargaining Toughness," *Journal of Consumer Research* 11, 939–953.
Simmel, G.: 1964, *The Sociology of Georg Simmel* (The Free Press, New York).

Stanton, W. and R. Buskirk: 1983, *Management of the Sales Force* (Irwin, Homewood, IL).

Swan, J. and J. Nolan: 1985, "Gaining Customer Trust: A Conceptual Guide for the Salesperson," *Journal of Personal Selling and Sales Management* **5**, 39–48.

Trilling, L.: 1972, *Sincerity and Authenticity* (Harvard University Press, Cambridge, MA).

Turner, V.: 1974, *Dramas, Fields, and Metaphors* (Cornell University Press, Ithaca, NY).

Walsh, W.: 1986, *Prudential Training Program: Salesmanship and Selling* (PruPress, Newark, NJ).

Weiner, L.: 1988, "Financial Plan Provides Sales Roadmap," *The Pilot's Log,* Summer, 6–8.

Williams, B.: 1988, "Formal Structures and Social Reality," in Gambetta, D. (ed.): *Trust* (Cambridge University Press, New York), pp. 3–13.

Zelizer, V.: 1979, *Morals and Markets: The Development of Life Insurance in the United States* (Columbia University Press, New York).

DISCUSSION QUESTIONS

1. Oakes uses the life insurance industry as a representative example of the world of personal sales, suggesting that the paradoxes he describes would be found in other types of personal sales as well. Do you agree or disagree?
2. The creation of trust is essential in other realms of life beyond that of personal sales. Select any example of a relationship (for example, student/teacher) and see to what extent the paradoxes of trust are also applicable.

READING 10

Multiple Subjectivity and Virtual Community at the End of the Freudian Century

Sherry Turkle

Sherry Turkle was one of the first sociologists to become involved in the study of the social impact of the Internet. In this essay, she explores the implications of Internet communications for our understanding of the self. More specifically, she is interested in the online personae people create when participating in MUDs (Multi-User Domains), and in the ways such personae operating in the realm of virtual communities are related to the identities of people in real—or non-Internet—life. Turkle connects this discussion to an assessment of the shifting notions clinical psychology has about multiple, or flexible, selves. This leads to Turkle's analysis of a process of ongoing identity formation and re-formation, which she dubs "cycling through."

Online experiences challenge what many have traditionally called "identity"; on the Internet many people recast identity in terms of multiple windows and parallel lives. In this way, today's life on the screen dramatizes and concretizes larger cultural trends that encourage thinking about identity in terms of multiplicity and flexibility.

Long before there were computers, the Internet, or virtual communities, Walt Whitman wrote: "There was a child went forth every day. And the first object he looked upon, that object he became." These few lines speak directly to the theoretical commitment behind my research as I explore the role of technology in shaping individuals and communities: We construct our objects and our objects construct us.[1] In this spirit, it is appropriate to ask what we are becoming when some of the first objects we look upon exist only on computer screens. The objects may exist in the virtual spaces of simulation games or they may be online representations of ourselves in virtual communities on the Internet. In either case, Whitman was prescient about their effects when he further wrote: "Do I contradict myself? Very well then I contradict

Sociological Inquiry. Vol. 67, No. 1, February 1997, 72–84. © 1997 by the University of Texas Press, P.O. Box 7819, Austin, TX 78713-7819.

myself. I am large. I contain multitudes." Online experiences challenge what many people have traditionally called "identity"; a sense of self is recast in terms of multiple windows and parallel lives. Online life is, of course, not the only factor pushing in this direction. Today's life on the screen dramatizes and concretizes larger cultural trends that encourage people to think about identity in terms of multiplicity and flexibility.

ONLINE PERSONAE

Through networked software known as MUDs (short for Multi-User Dungeons or Multi-User Domains), people all over the world, each at his or her individual machine, join online virtual communities that exist only through the space created by the computer. The key element of "MUDding," from the perspective of "identity-effects" is the creation and projection of a "persona" into a virtual space. This element characterizes far more "banal" online communities as well, such as bulletin boards, newsgroups, and chat rooms on commercial services.

You join a MUD through a command that links your networked computer to one on which the MUD software and database reside. When you start, you create a character or several characters; you specify their genders and other physical and psychological attributes. Other players in the MUD can see this description. It becomes your character's self-presentation. The created characters need not be human (you can write and deploy a program in MUD that presents itself as a person or, if you wish, as a robot), and there may be more than two genders.

Players create characters who have casual and romantic sex, hold jobs, attend rituals and celebrations, fall in love and get married. To say the least, such goings-on are gripping: "This is more real than my real life," says a character who turns out to be a man playing a woman who is pretending to be a man. As players participate in MUDs, they become authors not only of text but of themselves, constructing selves through social interaction.

In traditional role-playing games in which one's physical body is present, one steps in and out of a character. MUDs, in contrast, offer a parallel life. The boundaries of the game are fuzzy; the routine of playing them becomes part of their players' everyday lives. MUDs blur the boundaries between self and game, self and role, self and simulation. One player says: "You are what you pretend to be . . . you are what you play." Players sometimes talk about their real selves as a composite of their characters and sometimes talk about their MUD characters as means for working on their "real" lives. An avid participant in the online "talk channels" known as Internet Relay Chat describes a similar feeling: "I go from channel to channel depending. . . . I actually feel a part of several of the channels, several conversations. . . . I'm different in the different chats. They bring out different things in me."

Often the most avid participants in online communities are people who work with computers all day at their "regular" jobs. As they play on MUDs, for example, they will periodically put their characters "to sleep," remaining logged on to the game but pursuing other activities. From time to time they return to the online space. In this way they break up their work days and experience their lives as a "cycling-through" between the real world and a series of simulated ones. This same sort of cycling-through characterizes how people use newsgroups, Internet Relay Chat, bulletin boards, and chat rooms.

This kind of interaction with virtual environments is made possible by the existence on the computer of what have come to be called "windows." Windows are a way of working with a computer that makes it possible for the machine to place you in several contexts at the same time. As a user, you are attentive to only one of the windows on your screen at any given moment, but in a certain sense, you are a presence in all of them at all times. You might be writing a paper for a bacteriology journal and using your computer in several ways to help you: You are "present" to a word-processing program in which you are taking notes and collecting thoughts, you are present to communications software that is in touch with a distant computer for collecting reference materials, and you are present to a program that is charting the growth of simulated bacterial colonies when a new organism enters their ecology. Each of these activities takes place in a window and your identity on the computer is the sum of your distributed presence.

This certainly is the case for Doug, a Dartmouth College junior who plays four characters distributed across three different MUDs. One is a seductive woman. One is a macho, cowboy type whose self-description stresses that he is a "Marlboros rolled in the tee shirt sleeve kind of guy." Then there is "Carrot," a rabbit of unspecified gender who wanders its MUD introducing people to each other. Doug says, "Carrot is so low-key that people let it be around while they are having private conversations. So I think of Carrot as my passive, voyeuristic character."

Doug's fourth character is one that he plays on a FurryMUD (MUDs on which all the characters are furry animals). "I'd rather not even talk about that character because its anonymity there is very important to me," Doug says. "Let's just say that on FurryMUDs I feel like a sexual tourist." Doug talks about playing his characters in windows that have enhanced his ability to "turn pieces of my mind on and off."

> I split my mind. I'm getting better at it. I can see myself as being two or three or more. And I just turn on one part of my mind and then another when I go from window to window. I'm in some kind of argument in one window and trying to come on to a girl in a MUD in another, and another window might be running a spreadsheet program or some other technical thing for school. . . . And then I'll get a real-time message (that flashes on the screen as soon as it is sent

from another system user), and I guess that's RL. It's just one more window.

The development of windows for computer interfaces was a technical innovation motivated by the desire to help people work more efficiently. Windows encourage users to cycle through different applications much as time-sharing computers cycle through the computing needs of different people. In practice, windows are a potent metaphor for thinking about the self as a multiple, distributed, "time-sharing" system. The self is no longer simply playing different roles in different settings, something that people experience when, for example, one wakes up as a lover, makes breakfast as a mother, and drives to work as a lawyer. The life practice of windows is of a distributed self that exists in many worlds and plays many roles at the same time. MUDs extend the metaphor. Now, in Doug's words, "RL" [real life] can be just "one more window."

This particular notion of a distributed self undermines many traditional notions of identity. Identity, after all, from the Latin *idem*, refers to the sameness between two qualities. In MUDs, however, one can be and usually is many.

Online experiences of playing multiple aspects of self are resonant with theories that imagine the self as multiple and fragmented, or as a society of selves. In the late 1960s and early 1970s, I was first exposed to such ideas. I came into contact with the notion that the self is constituted by and through language, that sex is the exchange of signifiers, and that there is no such thing as "the ego." I was taught that each of us is a multiplicity of parts, fragments, and desiring connections. These lessons took place in the hothouse of Parisian intellectual culture whose gurus included Jacques Lacan, Michel Foucault, Gilles Deleuze, and Félix Guattari. But despite such ideal conditions for learning, my "French lessons" remained abstract exercises. These theorists of poststructuralism addressed the history of the body but quite frankly, from my point of view, had little to do with my own.

Today, twenty years later, I use the personal computer and modem on my desk to access MUDs. Anonymously, I travel their rooms and public spaces (a bar, a lounge, a hot tub). I create several characters (some not of my biological gender), who are able to have social and sexual encounters with other characters (some of my virtual gender, others not of my virtual gender). My textual actions are my actions—my words make things happen. In different MUDs I have different routines, different friends, different names.

In this context, the Gallic abstractions of poststructuralist theory seem uncannily concrete. In my computer-mediated worlds, the self is multiple, fluid, constituted by machinelike connectivity; the self is made and transformed by language; sexual congress is an exchange of signification; understanding follows from navigation and tinkering rather than analysis. Maps of MUD cyberspaces are rare and if they exist they are usually out of date. MUDs require active, trial-and-error exploration.

One day on a MUD, I come across a reference to a character named "Dr. Sherry," a cyberpsychotherapist who has an office in the rambling house that constitutes this MUD's virtual geography. There, I am informed, Dr. Sherry administers questionnaires and conducts interviews about the psychology of MUDding. I have every reason to believe that the name Dr. Sherry refers to my fifteen-year career as a student of the psychological impact of technology. But I didn't create this character. Dr. Sherry is a character name someone else created in order to quickly communicate an interest in a certain set of questions about technology and the self. I experience Dr. Sherry as a little piece of my history spinning out of control. I try to quiet my mind; I tell myself that surely one's books, one's public intellectual persona, are pieces of oneself in the world for others to use as they please. Surely this virtual appropriation is flattering. But my disquiet continues. Dr. Sherry, after all, is not an inanimate book, an object placed in the world.

Dr. Sherry is a person, or at least a person behind a character who is meeting with others in the world. Well, in the MUD world at least.

I talk over my disquiet with a friend who poses the conversation-stopping question: "Well, would you prefer if Dr. Sherry were a bot (short for online, virtual robot) trained to interview people about life on the MUD?" This had not occurred to me, but in a flash I realize that this, too, is possible. It is even likely to be the case. Many bots roam this MUD. Characters played by people are mistaken for these little artificial intelligences. I myself have made this mistake several times when a character's responses seemed too automatic. Sometimes bots are mistaken for people. I have made this mistake, too, and been fooled by a bot that offered me directions or flattered me by remembering our last interaction. Dr. Sherry could indeed be one of these. I am confronted with a double that could be a person or a program.

Life on the screen thus offers concrete experiences of the abstract theories that had intrigued yet confused me during my intellectual coming of age. Experiences on the Internet, and more generally with contemporary computing, can serve as objects-to-think-with that encourage the appropriation of poststructuralist ideas.

OBJECTS-TO-THINK-WITH

Appropriable theories, ideas that capture the imagination of the culture at large, tend to be those with which people can become actively involved. They tend to be theories that can be "played" with. So one way to examine the social appropriability of a given theory is to ask whether it is accompanied by its own objects-to-think-with, objects that can help the theory move beyond intellectual circles.[2]

For instance, the popular appropriation of Freudian ideas had little to do with scientific demonstrations of their validity. Freudian ideas passed into the popular culture because they offered robust objects-to-think-with. The objects were almost-tangible ideas such as dreams and slips of the tongue. People were able to play with such Freudian "objects." They became used to looking for them and manipulating them, both seriously and not so seriously. As they did so, the idea that slips and dreams betray the unconscious started to feel natural.

In *Purity and Danger*, the British anthropologist Mary Douglas (1966) examined how the manipulation of food, a concrete material, could organize cultural understandings of the sacred and profane. Other scholars had tried to explain the Jewish dietary laws, the kosher rules, instrumentally in terms of hygiene (i.e., pork carries disease), or in terms of wanting to keep the Jewish people separate from other groups. Douglas argued that the separation of foods taught a fundamental tenet of Judaism: Holiness is order and each thing must have its place. For Douglas, every kosher meal embodies the ordered cosmology, a separation of heaven, earth, and seas. In the story of the Creation, each of these realms is allotted its proper kind of animal life. Two-legged fowls fly with wings, four-legged animals hop or walk, and scaly fish swim with fins. It is acceptable to eat these "pure" creatures, but those that cross categories (such as the lobster that lives in the sea but crawls upon its floor) are unacceptable. The foods themselves carry a theory of unbreachable order.[3]

For Freud's work, dreams and slips of the tongue carried ideas. For Douglas, food carries ideas. Today, computational experiences carry ideas. Take the case of the Internet:[4] People decide that they want to interact with others online. They get an account on a commercial network service. They think that this will provide them with new access to people and information and of course it does. But it does more. They may find themselves in virtual communities taking on multiple roles; they may find themselves playing characters of different ages, attitudes, personalities, and genders. They may be swept up by experiences that enable them to explore previously unexamined aspects of their sexuality or that challenge their ideas about a unitary self.

When people adopt an online persona, they cross a boundary into highly charged territory. Some feel an uncomfortable sense of fragmentation, some a sense of relief. Some sense the possibilities for self-discovery, even self-transformation. A twenty-six-year-old graduate student in history says: "When I log on to a new MUD and I create a character and know I have to start typing my description, I always feel a sense of panic. Like I could find out something I don't want to know." A woman in her late thirties who just got an account with America Online used the fact that she could create five account "names" as a chance to "lay out all the moods I'm in—all the ways I want to be in different places on the system." Another individual named one of her accounts after her yet-to-be-born child. "I got the account right after the amnio, right after I knew it would be a girl. And all of a sudden, I wanted that little girl to have a presence on the net; I wrote her a letter and I realized I was writing a letter to a part of me." A twenty-year-old undergraduate says: "I am always very self-conscious when I create a new character. Usually, I end up creating someone I wouldn't want my parents to know about. It takes me, like, three hours." Online personae are objects-to-think-with when thinking about identity as multiple and decentered rather than unitary.

With this last comment, I am not implying that MUDs or computer bulletin boards or chat rooms are causally implicated in the dramatic increase of people who exhibit symptoms of multiple personality disorder (MPD), or that people on MUDs have MPD, or that participating in a MUD is like having MPD. What I am saying is that the many manifestations of multiplicity in our culture, including the adoption of online personae, are contributing to a general reconsideration of traditional, unitary notions of identity. Online experiences with "parallel lives" are part of the cultural context that supports new theorizations about multiple selves.

TROJAN HORSES: FROM FLEXIBILITY TO MULTIPLICITY

The history of a psychiatric symptom is inextricably tied up with the history of the culture that surrounds it. When I was a graduate student in psychology in the 1970s, clinical psychology texts regarded the symptom of multiple personality as so rare as to be barely worthy of mention. I remember being told that perhaps one in a million people might manifest this symptom. In these rare cases, there was typically one alter personality in addition to the host personality. Today, cases of multiple personality are much more frequent and typically involve up to sixteen alters of different ages, races, genders, and sexual orientation (Hacking, 1995). Many current theories of the genesis of MPD suggest that traumatic events cause various aspects of the self to congeal into virtual personalities. These personalities represent "ones" often hiding from the "others" and hiding too from that privileged alter, the host personality. Sometimes, the alters are known to each other and to the host; some alters may see their roles as actively helping others. Such differences in the transparency of the self system led the philosopher Ian Hacking to write about a "continuum of dissociation." The differences also suggest a continuum of association among the many parts of the self.

If the disorder in MPD stems from a need for rigid walls to block secrets, then the notion of a continuum of association or accessibility helps us conceptualize healthy selves that are not unitary but that have flexible access to their many aspects. "Multiplicity" is a term that carries with it several centuries of negative associations; contemporary American theorists such as Kenneth Gergen (1991), Emily Martin (1994), and Robert Jay Lifton (1993) are having an easier time with descriptions of contemporary iden-

tity that stress the virtue of flexibility. In my view, the notion of a flexible self serves as a kind of Trojan Horse for ideas about identity as multiplicity.

Flexibility is a more acceptable concept; but it definitely introduces the notion of a healthy self as one that cycles-through its multiple states of being. From there, I would argue, the distance to multiplicity as a normal state of self is short—a matter of semantics. For the essence of the "acceptable," flexible self is not unitary; even its aspects are ever-changing. The philosopher Daniel Dennett (1991) speaks of the flexible self in his "multiple drafts" theory of consciousness. Dennett's notion of multiple drafts is analogous to the experience of several versions of a document open on a computer screen where the user is able to move among them at will. Knowledge of these drafts encourages a respect for the many different versions, while it imposes a certain distance from them. The historian and social theorist Donna Haraway (1991) equates a "split and contradictory self" with a "knowing self" and is optimistic about its possibilities: "The knowing self is partial in all its guises, never finished, whole, simply there and original; it is always constructed and stitched together imperfectly and is therefore able to join with another, to see together without claiming to be another." What most characterizes the Dennett and Haraway models of the self is that the lines of communication between its various aspects are always open. This open communication is presented as encouraging an attitude of respect for the many within us and the many within others.

Increasingly, psychoanalytic theorists are also using a notion of flexibility and transparency as a way of introducing nonpathological multiplicity. They are thinking about healthy selves whose resilience and capacity for joy come from having access to their many aspects. For example, the psychoanalyst Philip Bromberg insists that our ways of describing "good parenting" must now shift away from an emphasis on confirming a child in a "core self" and onto helping a child develop the capacity to negotiate fluid transitions between self states. Bromberg believes that dissociation is not fundamentally trauma driven. It is a part of normal psychological development, necessary to the "necessary illusion of being one self." The healthy individual knows how to be many, but smoothes out the moments of transition between states of self. Bromberg (1994) says: "Health is when you are multiple but feel a unity. Health is when different aspects of self can get to know each other and reflect upon each other. Health is being one while being many." Here, within the American psychoanalytic tradition, is a model of multiplicity without dissociation—that is, multiplicity as a conscious, highly articulated cycling-through.

SELF STATES AND AVATARS

Case, a thirty-four-year-old industrial designer, reports that he likes participating in online virtual communities (MUDding) as a female because (some would think paradoxically) it makes it easier for him to be aggressive and confrontational. Case's several online female personae—strong, dynamic, "out there" women—remind him of his mother, whom he describes as a strong, "Katharine Hepburn type." His father was a mild-mannered man, a "Jimmy Stewart type." Case says that in "real life" he has always been more like his father, but he came to feel that he paid a price for his low-key ways. When he discovered MUDs, he saw the possibility to experiment:

> For virtual reality to be interesting it has to emulate the real. But you have to be able to do something in the virtual that you couldn't in the real. For me, my female characters are interesting because I can say and do the sorts of things that I mentally want to do, but if I did them as a man, they would be obnoxious. I see a strong woman as admirable. I see a strong man as a problem. Potentially a bully.

For Case, if you are assertive as a man, it is coded as "being a bastard." If you are assertive as a woman, it is coded as "modern and together."

> My wife and I both design logos for small businesses. But do this thought experiment. If I say "I will design this logo for $3,000, take it or leave it," I'm just a typical pushy businessman. If she says it, I think it sounds like she's a "together" woman. There is too much male power-wielding in society, and so if you use power as a man, that turns you into a stereotypical man. Women can do it more easily.

Case's gender swapping has given him permission to be more assertive within the MUD and more assertive outside of it as well:

> There are aspects of my personality—the more assertive, administrative, bureaucratic ones—that I am able to work on in the MUDs. I've never been good at bureaucratic things, but I'm much better from practicing on MUDs and playing a woman in charge. I am able to do things—in the real, that is—that I couldn't have before because I have played Katharine Hepburn characters.

Case says his Katharine Hepburn personae are "externalizations of a part of myself." In one interview with him, I use the expression "aspects of the self," and he picks it up eagerly, for MUD ding reminds him of how Hindu gods could have different aspects or subpersonalities, all the while having a whole self.

> You may, for example, have an aspect who is a ruthless business person who can negotiate contracts very, very well, and you may call upon that part of yourself while you are in tense negotiation, to do the negotiation, to actually go through and negotiate a really good contract. But you would have to trust this aspect to say something like, "Of course, I will need my lawyers to look over this," when in fact among your "lawyers" is the integrated self who is going to do an ethics vet over the contract, because you don't want to violate your own ethical standards and this (ruthless) aspect of yourself might do something that you wouldn't feel comfortable with later.

Case's gender swapping has enabled the different aspects of his inner world to achieve self-expression without compromising the values he associates with his "whole person." Role playing has given the negotiators practice; Case says he has come to trust them more. In response to my question "Do you feel that you call upon your personae in real life?" Case responds:

Yes, an aspect sort of clears its throat and says, "I can do this. You are being so amazingly conflicted over this and I know exactly what to do. Why don't you just let me do it?" MUDs give me balance. In real life, I tend to be extremely diplomatic, nonconfrontational. I don't like to ram my ideas down anyone's throat. On the MUD, I can be, "Take it or leave it." All of my Hepburn characters are that way. That's probably why I play them. Because they are smartmouthed, they will not sugarcoat their words.

In some ways, Case's description of his inner world of actors who address him and are capable of taking over negotiations is reminiscent of the language of people with MPD. But the contrast is significant: Case's inner actors are not split off from each other or his sense of "himself." He experiences himself very much as a collective self, not feeling that he must goad or repress this or that aspect of himself into conformity. He is at ease, cycling through from Katharine Hepburn to Jimmy Stewart. To use Bromberg's language, online life has helped Case learn how to "stand in the spaces between selves and still feel one, to see the multiplicity and still feel a unity." To use the computer scientist Marvin Minsky's (1987) phrase, Case feels at ease in his "society of mind."

We are dwellers on the threshold between the real and the virtual; we are unsure of how to cycle-through between our online and offline lives. Our experience recalls what the anthropologist Victor Turner (1966) termed a "liminal moment," a moment of cultural passage when new formulations and new meanings are most likely to emerge. Liminal moments are times of tension, extreme reactions, and great opportunity. When Turner talked about liminality, he understood it as a transitional state, but living with flux may no longer be temporary. It is fitting that the story of a technology that is bringing postmodernism down to earth refuses any simple resolutions and requires an openness to multiple viewpoints.

CYCLING-THROUGH

Whether or not the term is used, the idea of cycling-through is increasingly important for thinking about identity in our culture of simulation. As recently as the 1980s, when first confronted with computers and computational objects, children's thoughts about whether these objects were alive did not center on their physical movement, as they had for the objects of Jean Piaget's (1960) day, but on their psychology. Children of that time took a new world of objects and imposed a new world order, constructing a coherent story about what is alive. More recently, computational objects that evoke evolution have strained that order to the breaking point. Faced, for example, with widely available computer programs such as The Blind Watchmaker, Tierra, and SimLife—objects that explicitly evoke the notion of artificial life—children still try to impose strategies and categories, but they do so in the manner of theoretical bricoleurs, making do with whatever materials are at hand, with whatever theory can fit the rapidly changing circumstances. When children confront these new objects and try to construct a theory of what is alive, we see a form of cycling-through, this time cycling-through theories of "aliveness."

My current collection of children's comments about the aliveness of simulation games includes the following: "The 'Tierrans' are not alive because they are just in the computer, could be alive if they got out of the computer, are alive until you turn off the computer and then they're dead, are not alive because nothing in the computer is real." I have also heard, "The 'Sim' creatures are not alive but almost-alive, would be alive if they spoke, would be alive if they traveled, are alive but not real, are not alive because they don't have bodies, are alive because they can have babies, and finally, they're not alive because the babies in the game don't have parents."

These theories about what is alive are strikingly heterogeneous. Different children comfortably hold different theories, and individual children are able to hold different theories at the same time. In the short history of how the computer has changed the way we think, children have often led the way. Today, children are pointing the way toward multiple theories in the presence of the artifacts of artificial life.

One fifth-grade girl jumped back and forth from a psychological to a mechanistic language when she talked about a small robotic creature she had built out of Lego blocks and programmed with the Logo computer language. Sometimes she called it a machine, sometimes a creature. She talked about it in ways that referenced it as a psychological being, as an intentional self, and as an instrument of its programmer's intentions. These perspectives are equally present for her; for different purposes, she finds one or another of them more useful. Adults find themselves in a similar situation. One forty-year-old woman, an interior designer, confronted with a computer program that simulates the evolution of simple creatures, cycled-through views of it as alive, as "alive in a way" but not alive like humans or animals, as information but not body, as body but not the right kind of body for life, as alive but not spiritually alive, or as our creature but not God's creature, thus not alive. A thirty-seven-year-old lawyer found the same software not alive because life "isn't just replicating bits of information"; alive "like a virus"; not alive, because "life in a parallel universe shouldn't count as life"; alive "but not real life."

In his history of artificial life, the author Steven Levy (1992) suggested that when we think about computer programs that can evolve

we might envisage a continuum in which an evolving program would be more alive than a car, but less alive than a bacterium. My observations of how people are dealing with the lifelike properties of computational objects suggest that they are not constructing hierarchies but multiple definitions of life, which they "alternate" through rapid cycling. Multiple and alternating definitions, like thinking comfortably about one's identity in terms of multiple and alternating aspects of self, become a habit of mind.

In *Listening to Prozac*, the psychiatrist Peter Kramer (1993) wrote about an incident in which he prescribed an antidepressant medication for a college student. At the next therapy session, the patient appeared with symptoms of anxiety. Since it is not unusual for patients to respond with jitters to the early stages of treatment with antidepressants, Kramer was not concerned. Sometimes the jitters disappear by themselves; sometimes the prescribing physician changes the antidepressant, or adds a second, sedating medication at bedtime. Kramer says:

> I considered these alternatives and began to discuss them with the young man when he interrupted to correct my misapprehension: He had not taken the antidepressant. He was anxious because he feared my response when I learned he had "disobeyed" me.
>
> As my patient spoke, I was struck by the sudden change in my experience of his anxiety. One moment, the anxiety was a collection of meaningless physical symptoms, of interest only because they had to be suppressed, by other biological means, in order for the treatment to continue. At the next, the anxiety was rich in overtones . . . emotion a psychoanalyst might call Oedipal, anxiety over retribution by the exigent father. The two anxieties were utterly different: the one a simple outpouring of brain chemicals, calling for a scientific response, however diplomatically communicated; the other worthy of empathic exploration of the most delicate sort. (p. xii)

Kramer experienced this alternation of perspective because his patient did not take his medication. Other people experience such alternations when they do take medication. They commonly have moments when they equate their personality with their chemistry. But even as they do so, they do not abandon a sense of themselves as made up of *more than* chemistry. Rather, they cycle through "I am my chemicals" to "I am my history" to "I am my genes."

It may in fact be in the area of genetics that we have become most accustomed to cycling-through. In *Listening to Prozac*, Kramer tells a story about how genetics is causing us to cycle through different views of identity. About to express praise for his friends' two children with a comment such as "Don't the genes breed true?" Kramer stopped himself when he remembered that both children were adopted. "Since when had I—I, who make my living through the presumption that people are shaped by love and loss, and above all by their early family life— begun to assume that personality traits are genetically determined?" [p. xiii]. In fact, Kramer hadn't begun to assume this, he just sometimes did. Cycling-through different and often opposing theories has become how we think about our minds and about what it means to be alive, just as cycling-through different aspects of self have become a way of life as people move through different characters and genders when they move from window to window on their computer screens.

NOTES

1. This essay is drawn from Turkle (1995).
2. And, of course, the traffic does not flow in only one direction. In our current situation, science fiction informs social criticism; theme parks such as Disneyland become not simply objects of analysis, but exemplars of theory. The notion of ideas moving out may be heuristically useful, but it is too simple. Postmodern theory has underscored the traffic between diverse and seemingly separate realms. With it, high culture comes to contemplate advertising, science fiction fandom, and the romance novel.
3. Douglas's, (1966) analysis begins with Genesis and the story of the creation, in which a threefold classification unfolds. There is earth, water, and sky. Leviticus, where the kosher rules are set out, takes up this scheme, says Douglas, and "allots to each element its proper kind of animal life." She states: "Holiness is exemplified by completeness. . . . Holiness means keeping distinct the categories of creation" (p. 53). It follows that "any class of creatures which is not equipped for the right kind of locomotion in its element is contrary to holiness" (p. 55).

   If the proposed interpretation of the forbidden animals is correct, the dietary laws would have been like signs which at every turn inspired meditation on the oneness, purity, and completeness of God. By rules of avoidance holiness was given a physical expression in every encounter with the animal kingdom and at every meal (p. 57).
4. I could also have taken the case of people's relationships with the interfaces of contemporary personal computers. In that case, people decide that they want to buy an easy-to-use computer. They are attracted by a consumer product—say, a computer with a Macintosh-style interface. They think they are getting an instrumentally useful product, and there is little question that they are. But now it is in their home and they interact with it every day. And it turns out they are also getting an object that teaches them a new way of thinking and encourages them to develop new expectations about the kinds of relationship they and their children will have with machines. I see the Macintosh as a concrete emissary for significant elements of postmodern thought, most dramatically for the willingness to accept opacity and dialogue with machines. And it would not be an exaggeration to say that, to date, the Macintosh style of simulated desktop has been our most widely disseminated cultural introduction to virtual reality. The sociologist of science Bruno Latour (1988) stresses the importance of such concrete emissaries or "foot soldiers."

REFERENCES

Bromberg, P. 1994. "Speak That I May See You: Some Reflections on Dissociation, Reality, and Psychoanalytic Listening." *Psychoanalytic Dialogues* 4(4): 517–547.

Dennett, D. 1991. *Consciousness Explained.* Boston: Little, Brown.

Douglas, M. 1966. *Purity and Danger: An Analysis of the Concepts of Pollution and Taboo.* London: Routledge, ARK.

Gergen, Kenneth. 1991. *The Saturated Self: Dilemmas of Identity in Contemporary Life.* New York: Basic Books.

Hacking, I. 1995. *Rewriting the Soul: Multiple Personality and the Sciences of Memory.* Princeton, NJ: Princeton University Press.

Haraway, D. 1991. "The Actors Are Cyborg, Nature Is Coyote, and the Geography Is Elsewhere: Postscript to 'Cyborgs at Large.' " In *Technoculture,* edited by C. Penley and A. Ross. Minneapolis: University of Minnesota Press.

Kramer, P. 1993. *Listening to Prozac: A Psychiatrist Explores Antidepressant Drugs and the Remaking of the Self.* New York: Viking.

Latour, B. 1988. *The Pasteurization of France,* translated by A. Sheridan and J. Law. Cambridge, MA: Harvard University Press.

Levy, S. 1992. *Artificial Life: The Quest for the New Frontier.* New York: Pantheon.

Lifton, Robert Jay. 1993. *The Protean Self: Human Resilience in an Age of Fragmentation.* New York: Basic Books.

Martin, Emily. 1994. *Flexible Bodies.* Boston: Beacon.

Minsky, M. 1987. *The Society of Mind.* New York: Simon and Schuster.

Piaget, J. 1960. *The Child's Conception of the World,* translated by J. Tomlinson and A. Tomlinson. Totowa, NJ: Littlefield, Adams.

Turkle, S. 1995. *Life on the Screen: Identity in the Age of the Internet.* New York: Simon and Schuster.

———. 1984. *The Second Self: Computers and the Human Spirit.* New York: Simon and Schuster.

Turner, V. 1966. *The Ritual Process: Structure and Antistructure.* Chicago: Aldine.

DISCUSSION QUESTIONS

1. On the basis of your experience or that of someone you know, discuss your understanding of the relationship between online selves and "real" selves.
2. What do you think Turkle means by "cycling-through" and how is this related to her discussion of multiple or flexible identities? Do you agree or disagree with her assessment?

READING 11

Mobilizing Fun

Gary Alan Fine

According to Gary Alan Fine, leisure time activities, rather than standing apart from the rest of social life, operate with an organizational base similar to that of other facets of social life. Fine discusses three aspects of the organization of leisure in this excerpt from his article, "Mobilizing Fun": the resource base; copyrighted subcultures; and provisioning leisure. Relying particularly on ethnographic research he has conducted on wild-mushroom collectors and on Little League baseball, he discusses the key elements involved in constituting a resource base before turning to a discussion of two of the most salient features of much leisure activity: the organization of leisure for profit, and thus the trend to attempt to monopolize or control particular pursuits of fun; and connected to this the provision of the means by which one can engage in leisure activities.

PROVISIONING THEORY

In order to integrate the characteristics of leisure organizations with the emphasis on structure presented by resource mobilization theory, I suggest the utility of an approach to leisure that explicitly incorporates the centrality of resources to the possibility of leisure. Provisioning Theory recognizes that leisure worlds depend for their existence and for their tensile strength on the presence of a social infrastructure and on the ability to distribute resources that members desire. These resources can take several forms including knowledge, interpersonal interaction, and identity support; they need not be material resources.

I deemphasize a voluntaristic, personal preference model of leisure subcultures, in which people engage in those activities that they like best or those that serve their personal needs, in favor of a more structural, organizationally conscious perspective in which individuals engage in activities that are more available and that have a reputation for being more fun. What constitutes fun is from this perspective a social result rather than a psychological one. People are free to engage in a virtually unlimited number of leisure activities, but that freedom is possible because others have laid the organizational groundwork that facilitates these choices. Likewise, a lack of organizational opportunities constricts the possibilities for leisure. Leisure opportunities do more than follow communal interests; a structure channels and promotes leisure.[1]

Specifically I suggest a set of assumptions that underlie this approach. I shall not test these assumptions here but use them as the basis of the arguments that will outline a perspective on leisure organizations, admittedly one painted with broad brush strokes. Some of these assumptions are empirically testable, and such tests are desirable for future research.

1. Organizations with greater access to resources will be more successful than those with less access to resources.
2. The extent of participation in leisure organizations depends on the organization's ability to provide desired resources for members.
3. Those organizations that provide the most resources to individual members will be those that succeed.

4. Leisure organizations compete in a market, and those that are more efficient in providing resources will survive better than those that are not.
5. Leisure organizations must make their activities known to a general public; those that publicize themselves most effectively will be most likely to survive. Effective leisure organizations connect themselves to media outlets and forms of interpersonal recruitment.
6. Individuals participating in a leisure activity must have access to credible information; those organizations that are best able to provide this information will survive.
7. Individuals participating in a leisure activity must enjoy their relations with other participants; those organizations that are best able to facilitate this sociability will survive.
8. Individuals participating in a leisure activity need their own personal identity validated; those organizations that are best able to provide for identity validation will survive.

These assumptions are based on a presupposition that most leisure organizations wish to grow or at least maintain a stable steady-state. Attitudes toward growth and recruitment are obviously variable, and some organizations deliberately limit their size by curtailing recruitment or establishing membership requirements. A limited organization can be successful if its resource base is stable. Indeed, some leisure participants—a rather small number, I suspect, given the tendency of organizational structure to become sedimented—may see their group as temporary and express no regret when it is disbanded. Still, even here the organization must distribute resources if leisure is to be facilitated.

THE RESOURCE BASE OF LEISURE ORGANIZATIONS

What must a leisure subculture provide to its members in order to have fulfilled its purpose? What do people look for in a leisure world?

Three elements seem crucial: (a) distribution of knowledge about the leisure activity, (b) opportunities for sociability, and (c) access to identity symbols.

These components of leisure activity are evident in mushroom collecting, a world that might at first seem relatively free of demands for goods and services. In a sense, one needs no more than a bucket to hold fungal specimens. Although a bucket is sufficient for the collecting of mushrooms, it is not sufficient for "mushrooming." Of course, not all of the above-named resources must be provided exclusively by an organization but can also, with some difficulty, be provided through an informal social network.

Knowledge

Involvement in a leisure world presumes a store of knowledge—information that enables the competent doing of that activity.[2] But from where does that knowledge come? Much knowledge swirls around in society; *some* information about many forms of leisure is known widely. Although most Americans are not mushroomers, many are aware that mushrooming is a legitimate hobby. Through newspaper and magazine articles, many people are aware that certain organizations are devoted to the hobby. Almost everyone knows that some mushrooms are poisonous, gourmets are aware that morels and chanterelles are delicious, and so forth. This information comes through friends, relatives, the media, and casual conversations. The outlines of a hobby can be widely known even though this knowledge includes gaps, stereotypes, and misinformation.

The recruit to a hobby comes with knowledge acquired along life's journey. Although this knowledge may be necessary for recruitment, typically it is not sufficient and, more significantly, is not seen as sufficient. The recruit lacks the basic "member's knowledge" that permits the competent doing of the activity, according to subcultural standards, but in many cases also lacks enough formal knowledge to behave

safely. The challenge for the leisure organization is to provide the novice with both knowledge sets to participate in the hobby at whatever level of skill is desired. Ideally the information will be provided conveniently and will be taught in a manner that is emotionally satisfying so that the recruit learns what is necessary to know and feels that he/she belongs to the group.

In amateur mycology a gap in knowledge can be dangerous, and this is frequently expressed as a justification for joining the organization: to acquire protective knowledge. One would be foolish to enter the woods, or the kitchen, ignorant of which mushrooms can be safely consumed. Although this information may be acquired from parents or friends, serious mushroom collectors recognize the need to rely upon authoritative, expert, and privileged information.

Many mushroomers learn about fungi through classes, often taught by self-proclaimed mushroom experts who have no degree in mycology but who have had considerable experience with the hobby. Typically these classes are not entrepreneurial enterprises by the teacher, but are sponsored by an organization—a mushroom society, a school, a local government agency, or a for-profit organization. These classes vary in their extent and orientation. Some last a few hours, others require several hours a week, and still others demand continual attendance for days, weeks, or months at a set location. Some are taught by a single individual and others have a faculty.

An advertisement for the Wild Mushroom Conference at Breitenbush Hot Springs in Oregon, published in the Fall 1988 issue of *Mushroom* magazine, reveals the elaborateness of some of these gatherings:

The conference is expressly designed for mushroomers interested in developing their identification skills and understanding of the taxonomy, cultivation, chemistry and ecology of mushrooms. Emphasis will be placed on edible, poisonous and psychoactive species. There will be comprehensive instruction in contemporary commercial and small scale cultivation practices for mushrooms including shiitake, oyster and wine-red stropharia. Workshops encourage a "hands-on" approach. Other topics include mushrooms in history and cultures, mushroom photography and art, and medicinal possibilities and applications. Extensive forays will bring in many kinds of mushrooms from the Breitenbush forests and meadows. Plus the annual Wild Mushroom Cookout and Dance on Saturday! This year's faculty includes David Arora, Paul Przybylowicz, J. Q. Jacobs, Paul Stamets, Gary Lincoff, Mike Wells, Kent Polowski, Dr. Cal Seeba, Tom O'Dell and other scholars, cultivators and aficionados.

The cost of this fungal experience is $145/person. Although this is a particularly elaborate course, it underlines several features of leisure provisioning. First, it is sponsored by an established organization, a resort. Second, the conference has recruited a faculty of experts, several of whom are well known within the mycological community. By their presence, they represent privileged knowledge. Third, the experience is designed to train mushroomers to improve their technical skills in pursuit of their instrumental goals. Finally, the educational experience, embedded within a leisure activity, combines fun with the acquisition of knowledge: instrumental and expressive needs merge. In leisure worlds, education is not an end in itself but a means to increased satisfaction; the activity must tie members to the hobby.

Courses do not spontaneously emerge; they are created by entrepreneurial organizations. Resources (capital and organizational infrastructure sufficient for planning, marketing, and hiring personnel) and the credibility that the organization can bring to the project are crucial. The existence of educational experiences in many leisure worlds speaks to the desire for expert training. Aerobics classes, "fantasy" baseball camps (Brandmeyer & Alexander, 1986), hockey camps, and birdwatching symposiums are examples of the same phenomenon. Stu-

dents arrive with a modest knowledge base that is to become "expertness" with associated personal satisfaction. The organization provides for the transformation of restricted codes into elaborated ones (Bernstein, 1971).

The physical presence of others is not the only means by which individuals learn. Written resources are equally important in many leisure communities. Looking through books in a typical bookstore, one is impressed by the volume of volumes available to hobbyists. The existence of specialized bookstores and mail-order marketing expands the possibilities for sales. Mushrooming guides are published each year, and the hobby supports *Mushroom* magazine, a quarterly, featuring articles on well-known hobbyists, mushroom forays, weather conditions, evaluations of guidebooks, and other pieces of parochial interest. Among the books advertised in *Mushroom* magazine (Fall 1988) were *Mycological Dictionary in Eight Languages; Celebrating the Wild Mushroom, A Passionate Quest; The Edible Mushroom: A Gourmet Cook's Guide; One Thousand American Fungi; The Audubon Society Field Guide to North American Mushrooms*; and *The Mushroom Cultivator*. Many amateurs purchase several books each year and some of them spend over $100 on books annually. The existence of a recognizable, accessible market and the success of particular works encourages publishers to supply this market.

Each leisure world has its own resource structure. The general argument about the need for available information must be applied variously to different leisure worlds. While some differences might be attributed to the particular needs of the leisure activity, many are a function of the resources to which leisure groups have access and the organizational structure that permits the sharing of these resources. A well-established hobby such as birdwatching has more resources and a more effective structure than a newer or smaller hobby such as observing snakes in the wild. Neither activity is inherently more interesting than the other; the key difference is the organizational base.

Sociability

Not every participant in a leisure activity belongs to an organization. Leisure can be had without organization; however, without an organization many feel that something is missing from their leisure activity (see Mitchell, 1983; Stebbins, 1979). People derive satisfaction from their associations. Mushroomers may join the North American Mycological Association (NAMA), a 30-year-old organization with approximately 1,500 members in 49 states. NAMA lists 60 affiliated state and local organizations.

Although a goal of these organizations is to provide information to amateur mycologists and to arrange for mushroom hunting expeditions, another important goal, particularly of local clubs, is to organize sociable times. They are responsible for the provisioning of community, provisioning that is difficult for the individual. Leisure organizations are in effect topically based fraternal organizations. Like other hobbyists, mushroomers enjoy associating with others who share their interests. They swap stories, narrate memorable experiences, joke about outsiders, and relish participating in a "personal community" (Burch, 1969). Leisure organizations are, in Howard Aldrich's (1971) terms, following Georg Simmel, "sociable organizations"—organizations that have as their goal the providing of settings for sociability.

Successful organizations facilitate interaction, providing staging areas for friendship (Fine, 1981). This occurs primarily by providing the location for contact. Regular meetings are centrally important in cementing members to the organization and the hobby. Publicly committing oneself to an activity is a powerful motivation for continuing to participate. The organizational structure and provisioning of place establishes social psychological allegiance.

The Minnesota Mycological Society holds weekly meetings 4 months during the year at a community center. When a voluntary association draws members from a wide area, the choice of location may be controversial since part of what is being decided is the "cost" of attendance. Any location facilitates the attendance of some members and discourages others. One year the club members contemplated moving their meetings from the usual but somewhat out-of-the-way location to a more central meeting place, a natural history museum on the University of Minnesota campus. However, the plan was rejected when it was learned that free parking would not be available. The benefits were perceived not to be worth the cost, at least by those in attendance at the old location.

Sufficient time at the meetings for informal talk is crucial for member satisfaction. Leisure organizations rarely begin on time and the lights are not turned off until long after the meeting itself ends. Meetings of the Minnesota Mycological Society do not begin until 15 or 20 minutes after their scheduled time in order to allow members to converse; after the meeting members stay and talk. For years the Minnesota Mycological Society has had a post-meeting meeting at a local McDonalds where core members gossip, joke, and informally discuss club business. These meetings often last as long as official meetings.

In addition to routine meetings, other events are designed for celebratory purposes, and through their festive, collective quality they create community (Lavanda, 1988). The Minnesota Mycological Society holds a banquet each winter. In "successful" banquets, the restaurant or hotel provides the club with a private room, serves modestly priced food of general appeal, and permits members to share homemade mushroom dishes. One year the hotel at which the banquet was held refused to permit prepared food (perhaps especially mushrooms!) to be brought in because of fear of liability. The banquet was not a success in that the sociability of club members was not enhanced, thanks to the restrictions on their sharing.

Club forays are other special events whose provisioning is critical to member satisfaction. For many members these forays are the highlight of the year. Each year the club organizes approximately half a dozen short forays on Saturdays (3 to 5 hours) and one or two weekend-long forays. On these forays club members collect mushrooms together and, after several hours, return to a prearranged location to identify the specimens collectively. These events require efficient coordination. A club member (the Foray Chairman) selects locations that are suitable for the forays, determines if mushrooms are likely to be growing, arranges for permission, gives directions, and publicizes the event. If it is a weekend foray, the price must be reasonable and the accommodations and cooking facilities must be adequate. Club members search for mushrooms and hope for fun, but someone in the organization must do the groundwork so that there is a reasonable likelihood this will happen.

Individuals look to organizations to ensure that they will be in a position to enjoy each others' presence in locations in which this presence will be tethered to their interest: they strive for *focused sociability*. Sociability is not pure friendship, but friendship can emerge because the participants have something in common that permits them to realize they might become good friends.

Identity Symbols

Leisure worlds contain styles and fashions that are markers of identity (Hebdige, 1979). Those within the activity, on its edges, or on the outside may provide expressive symbols that are accepted as reflecting how participants wish to be known. To become widely used, these symbols must be defined as self-enhancing.

The identity symbols of leisure participants vary as to their potential market. Some may be limited, in practice if not in fact, to members of a particular leisure world. Who but a mushroomer would put a bumper sticker, "I Brake For Fungi," on his car? Who but a mushroomer would wear a T-shirt with a pair of large morels on her chest? Other accouterments may have a wider set of potential consumers: boots, work shirts, knives, baskets, or whistles. I hypothesize that the more limited the artifact's market, the more likely are leisure participants to consider it central to their identity. Some high quality items aimed at a general market (e.g., fine knives) may also have status within the leisure world, although the owner will not consider himself or herself more of a mushroomer by owning one.

Artifacts of style can be provisioned in several ways. Three analytically distinct types of vendors provide artifacts to hobbyists: the leisure organization itself, individual hobbyists, and outside entrepreneurs.

Organizational Vendors Leisure organizations can provide identity symbols themselves, although typically organizations are not manufacturers. They commission firms to produce the objects while they themselves are responsible for distribution. The organization is a broker. For instance, many mushroom societies publish cookbooks that are typeset by printers. Clubs design and sell T-shirts, bandannas, sweatsuits, or hats. The clubs do not create these objects but provision them through their relations with other organizations.

Peripheral Vendors Identity symbols can be sold by individuals or groups with close familiarity with the leisure subculture. For those leisure activities involving members who have considerable disposable income, small businesses arise on the periphery of the subculture, attempting to satisfy the desires of participants; these businesses may or may not have the approval of the central organization. Many proprietors are closely tied to the hobby, often as prominent members. Success increases one's personal status within the leisure world.

Within the world of mushrooming, individuals and groups sell books, postcards, stationery, bumper stickers, and apparel, and organize tours.[3] For instance, the former president of the Minnesota Mycological Society published a meta-guide (a guide to the listing of mushrooms in other guide books) and distributed it through the mailing lists of the national organization and local clubs. A former winner of the NAMA photo contest printed several of her most impressive photographs as postcards and sold them at forays and through *Mushroom* magazine. Several respected mushroomers organize overseas tours for their colleagues. These individuals choose to earn a profit, albeit a small and sincere one, from friends and acquaintances who are pleased to support them.

Mass Vendors   The third source of products and services for a leisure subsociety is external enterprises. Most of what leisure participants purchase, they purchase in locations open to the general public. While some products are designed specifically for members of the subculture (e.g., mushroom guidebooks), most are also sold to other clients. Sturdy rubber boots are needed by naturalists and fishermen as well as by mushroomers. A high quality wicker basket can be used to hold sewing, berries, or a picnic lunch, as well as being a *ding an sich*.

Manufacturers and distributors can appeal to any size market. General merchandisers are disadvantaged in that they cannot target their audience to communicate with them efficiently and be aware of the audience's needs (e.g., producing baskets with slots for knives or gloves). They also cannot gain that customer loyalty derived from shared community identity. However, such entrepreneurs have advantages of economy of scale and sophistication of production values that smaller and more focused firms may lack.

Around and within each well-developed leisure world, vendors provide identity symbols—items that matter to leisure participants and that they consider important to activity and their sense of self within the activity. The provisioning of identity symbols is particularly sig-

nificant in leisure activities defined as "morally controversial" (Olmstead, 1988), in which the issue of identity display is more problematic. For instance, gun collecting is so controversial that identity symbols may only be available in specialized locations, often linked directly to organizational or peripheral vendors.

COPYRIGHTED SUBCULTURES

So far I have examined the provisioning of goods and activities from the perspective of a freely established (autochthonous) leisure world. I turn now to a special case of provisioning theory: the organization of leisure in social worlds created through entrepreneurial enterprise—what Dayan (1986) terms "copyrighted subcultures," although patents may be involved instead of copyrights.

Some leisure scenes are organized (created) by individuals who hope to profit through this organization. It is not that these individuals are cynical or greedy. They may not see themselves as really involved in the world of commerce, certainly not at first (see Fine, 1983). They prefer to think of themselves as facilitators of leisure: people whose goal is to make others happy. Yet they are tethered to capitalism because they created the leisure world, the resources necessary for participating in that world "belong" to them in terms of copyright or patent, and they "license" these resources to participants. While the boundary of owners' control is not always precise de facto or de jure, it is expected that they will be reimbursed by virtue of their legal status.

Many copyrighted subcultures surround games. The critical element that entrepreneurs provide are rules. Unlike other hobbies, rules structure games and are what make games games. With its lengthy rulebooks, Dungeons & Dragons is a prototypical example, but leisure worlds have also developed around games such as Monopoly, Scrabble, Diplomacy, Rotisserie Baseball, and Trivial Pursuit. Rules must be agreed upon for a game to be possible. Of course many games have traditional rules (e.g., marbles, chess, baseball), but even here organizations (e.g., the U.S. Chess Federation, Little League Baseball, Inc.) must specify these rules, deal with conflicts in serious play, run tournaments, and alter the official rules should dissatisfaction emerge. These organizations appear to have more power and resources than those dealing with leisure activities that are interest-based.

Yet the central organization does not have total control. Groups of players may change the rules. Participants come to feel that *they* own the game, and this claim may create friction with those who maintain the legal and economic rights. The individual player's freedom of expression conflicts with the reality that the proper way of playing was decided by others and was formalized through a set of rules.

This tension of control is particularly true in cases in which the original creators revise the game. Five years after the original publication of the Dungeons & Dragons rulebooks in 1973, the company (TSR Hobbies) published new rulebooks. Although these new rulebooks were clearer, more logical, better organized, and more accessible than the originals, their publication required that players who wanted to play the game properly would purchase them.[4] By changing the rules and by making those changes part of the new reality of the game, the manufacturers asserted their control and created a new demand for their product.

The changes in the rules were inevitable, not only from a desire for control but because of a change in audience. In the early years of many copyrighted subcultures, creators have little idea of their future success. As a consequence, the original version of the game may eventually be defined as inadequate for the expanding market. When E. Gary Gygax and David Arneson developed D & D out of their involvement with the war game miniature subculture, they had in mind a sophisticated group of gamers who would be comfortable with more flexible and complex rules than the dice-based rules of board games (see Fine, 1983). But as the game spread to the younger and less educated and to those without experience in war gaming, confusion arose and the rules needed to be revised.

Manufacturers do not limit their activities to selling (licensing) rules but provide a range of other accessories, which often become popular because of the consumers' loyalty to the game world and to the imprimatur of the creators. Given that these worlds are structured as businesses, expanding the product line comes easy. In the case of fantasy games, TSR Hobbies has expanded far from the publication of rules. They publish a monthly magazine (*The Dragon*), game modules designed to help players structure their fantasy adventures, and computer software. The company also sponsors an annual convention (GenCon) at which gamers meet for several days to play fantasy games, participate in tournaments, hear presentations and, not incidentally, purchase new products of TSR Hobbies and other manufacturers. Game manufacturers typically release their new products during this convention, when agents are not needed, to increase profit, to appeal directly to the opinion leaders of the hobby, and to use the social pressures of the convention to sell products.

The provisioning of resources in copyrighted subcultures represents a special case of provisioning theory. Although much is similar, there are two key differences between the provisioning structure of copyrighted subcultures and those subcultures, such as mushrooming, that are largely autochthonous. First, the rules, procedures, and norms of copyrighted subcultures are more codified and organized than those of most autochthonous activities. In copyrighted subcultures a font of truth exists; in autochthonous worlds the activity is more explicitly negotiable. Even if the source of truth in copyrighted subcultures is not heeded, it must be taken into account.[5] Second, the structure of copyrighted subcultures is based on material concerns—they are economic as well as social

worlds. This reality directs the reactions of entrepreneurs to those they define as infringing on
their copyright. This materialist perspective
angers those who emphasize the communal nature of the leisure. Unlike autochthonous
leisure in which authority is communal, in
copyrighted leisure authority depends on property rights. The judicial system supports the legitimacy of economic control and provides the
power to enforce decisions.

PROVISIONING SPORT

Voluntary sport represents a second special case
of provisioning theory. As is true for leisure
generally, differences between sports may
sometimes seem more impressive than their
similarities. Golf, a sport that can be played in
solitude, contrasts mightily with football, a
sport that demands enormous coordination. The
range of provisioning arrangements in the world
of sport is great, with team sports requiring the
most extensive coordination.

If hobbies such as mushrooming can be typi-
fied as traditional activities that lack the need
for highly technical coordination—in which
anyone can more or less do anything—and
games such as Dungeons & Dragons require adherence to rules for their organization, most
sport is both traditional and dependent upon
rules. Baseball without shared rules is unthinkable, but the extent of these rules and the light-
ness with which they are enforced are negotiated in practice.

Baseball, especially youth baseball, is open
to anyone with a field on which to play and a
few pieces of equipment. Rocks can be used as
bases and sticks as bats, gloves are not needed,
and balls come cheap. Children can play baseball without adult supervision, and in such a situation the provisioning of youth baseball hardly
seems a problem, given complementary schedules, decision-making ability, and open space.
The founding of Little League baseball in 1939
(Fine, 1987b) was based on the recognition that

these seemingly simply provisioned needs are
not easily met; finding a large enough group of
children depends on neighborhood demograph-
ics and ecology, children are known to quarrel
with each other, open space is shrinking, and
open does not necessarily mean safe. Further,
there are material advantages of organized provisioning, particularly in the access to identity
symbols. Only an organization with access to
resources can provide uniforms, manicured
fields, refreshments, and public address systems. Although children are masters at creating
their own identity symbols, such symbols are
not validated by those external to the group. Little League with its legitimacy and access to
publicly recognized symbols provides what a
sandlot game cannot—entrance into the fantasy
of professional baseball.

Over its half century, Little League baseball
has excelled at provisioning resources for play.
This provisioning of space, personnel, training,
and equipment is its raison d'être. To play baseball is easy; to play Little League baseball requires an organization that operates on several
levels—national (Little League Baseball, Inc.),
community (Beanville Little League), and small
group level (the Beanville Rangers). Obviously
organized sport does not require all of these levels, but each level plays a role in the organization of sport and it is this multilevel structure
that distinguishes sport organizations from many
other leisure groups. In general the upper levels
(those closest to the central organization) are
more concerned with provisioning organizational resources, and the lower levels (those closest to the local participants) emphasize the provisioning of identity and sociability. The challenge
for these organizations is to control and motivate
volunteers who are required to carry out the
mandate of the central administration on the
local level. A tension can exist between the efficient provision of resources and the concrete relations of sociability; the central organization
often solves this by allowing the local groups to
operate independently until trouble arises.

Each local Little League contributes a share of the registration fees it receives from players to the national organization.[6] For this the national organization provides rules and procedures as well as suggestions for publicizing the local league. Little League Baseball, Inc., provides guidance for general policy even though it has little impact on daily operational decisions. Perhaps most significantly, the national organization permits the use of its name, generating support in the local community from government, schools, businesses, and parents.

Local leagues are responsible for the provisioning of equipment and personnel (Fine, 1987b, pp. 15–19). They must find fields to play on and the fields must be in excellent condition as they will be commented on critically. Uniforms, equipment, and insurance are provided by the local league. Many leagues sell refreshments and are responsible for the upkeep of toilets and scoreboards as well.

Local leagues are also responsible for the temporal organization of the league: someone must arrange for the schedules of the teams and arrange for practice times and make sure each team is treated fairly in terms of its temporal needs. Team sport requires arrangements to equalize access to time and space.[7] Each team must play every other team the same number of times and each team must play the same amount each week. No team should be given all of the best times. Finally, personnel, both players and coaches, must be distributed between teams equitably—by a method that is not only fair but that also *appears* to be fair. Recruitment is essential to ensure that there is a match between the supply of players and adult coaches. Without adult coaches, organized youth sport could not exist. Further, the league must recruit, and often pay, umpires for that thankless task.

The individual team allocates playing time to each player in a manner that should be deemed as fair. Perhaps more significant than the technical assignment of boys to positions and batting slots is the team's role in providing sociability. If

players are unhappy, the team has failed no matter what its record. The coach has a central role in facilitating satisfaction, occasionally through providing identity symbols. One coach gave his team red-white-and-blue wristbands; others shared cookies or snacks; still others brought in baseball equipment that would otherwise have been unavailable, such as batting stands. Fun is generated through adult resources.

Organized sport shares with hobbies an existence that is formally outside the realm of copyright laws. Sport belongs to everyone, and sport organizations ostensibly are nonprofit organizations. Yet, because organized sport requires a definitive rule structure and tight temporal and spatial organization, sport has some of the themes that are characteristic of copyrighted subcultures. Organized team sport falls between the prototypical hobby and the prototypical game in its provisioning of resources.

CONCLUSION

All leisure worlds are material worlds. In order to engage in virtually any leisure activity (daydreams are perhaps the exception that proves the rule), a wide array of resources must be managed. This includes spatial, temporal, affective, and material concerns. Having fun and having access to resources are linked even in those leisure activities that are separate from organizations. Still, organizations have proven to be, in leisure as elsewhere, efficient means by which resources can be provided for individuals. Leisure organizations with their focus on providing satisfactions to participants can avoid many of the difficulties that come with trying to decide how resources should be allocated between internal and external needs. The external needs of leisure organizations (e.g., publicity) are more explicitly connected to the continuing existence of the group, which in turn connect to the internal goals.

Organizations may be formal or informal; the Minnesota Mycological Society has a constitution and a legal identity. TSR Hobbies is incorporated as a corporation. In contrast, adolescents can regularly play Dungeouns & Dragons every Friday night, find a room (perhaps a rec room), and arrange for money to be collected for soft drinks, the purchase of new games and equipment, or even "recreational" drugs. What is essential is the provisioning of basic resources (equipment, space, and companionship), from which comes a sense that the group is meaningful to the participants and that it should continue.

In this article I have simply presented some ideas that might be drawn upon for the understanding of leisure and sport worlds. I have not systematically tested the assumptions presented above, and this is necessary if this approach is to have credibility. I assume that leisure preferences are pragmatically determined—they are a function of opportunity[8] rather than personality—and that there is a "survival of the fittest" operating in the ecology of leisure organizations (Freeman & Hannon, 1983), where those with the most resources, most efficient use of those resources, and most effective publicity of these resources will survive. Such acquisition and distribution of resources helps establish a sense of belonging, the existence of community in a society where community may be overwhelmed by personal preference.

I believe that Provisioning Theory is useful for the study of leisure in somewhat the same way in which Resource Mobilization Theory has helped to revitalize the examination of social movements. Provisioning Theory forces us to examine the form of the organization and the activity rather than the content. By turning a topic that is often connected to social psychology into a venue in which social organizational forces come to play, this approach can have the tonic effect of forging a linkage between macro and micro approaches.

I have avoided discussing what many consider to be the core of leisure activity, those meanings and actions that make specific forms of leisure *fun*, focusing instead on those exter-

nal features that surround the activity: the penumbra of leisure. Success can be measured in ways other than survival, and an organizational rhetoric does not exhaust the ways leisure can be conceived.

Still, every social world has a material base, even those that seem at first glance to be most ethereal. Leisure is not set apart from the real world; it is the real world.

REFERENCES

Aldrich, H. E. (1971). The sociable organization: A case study of Mensa and some propositions. *Sociology and Social Research*, 55, 429–441.

Banfield, E. (1967). *The moral basis of a backward society*. Glencoe, IL: Free Press.

Bellah, R. N., Madsen, R., Sullivan, W. M., Swidler, A., & Tipton, S. M. (1985). *Habits of the heart: Individualism and commitment in American life*. Berkeley: University of California Press.

Bernstein, Basil. (1971). *Class, Codes and Control: Theoretical Studies Toward a Sociology of Language*. New York: Schocken Books.

Brandmeyer, G. A., & Alexander, L. K. (1986). "I caught the dream": The adult baseball camp as fantasy leisure. *Journal of Leisure Behavior*, 18(1), 26–39.

Burch, W. R. (1969, Spring). The social circles of leisure: Competing explanations. *Journal of Leisure Research*, 1, 125–147.

Dayan, D. (1986). Copyrighted subcultures. *American Journal of Sociology*, 91, 1219–1228.

Fine, G. A. (1981). Friends, impression management, and preadolescent behavior. In S. R. Asher & J. M. Gottman (Eds.), *The development of children's friendships* (pp. 29–52). New York: Cambridge University Press.

Fine, G. A. (1983). *Shared fantasy: Role-playing games as social worlds*. Chicago: University of Chicago Press.

Fine, G. A. (1987a). Community and boundary: Personal experience stories of mushroom collectors. *Journal of Folklore Research*, 24, 223–240.

Fine, G. A. (1987b). *With the boys: Little League baseball and preadolescent culture*. Chicago: University of Chicago Press.

Fine, G. A. (1988). Dying for a laugh: Negotiating risk and creating personas in the humor of mushroom collectors. *Western Folklore*, 47, 177–194.

Freeman, J., & Hannon, M. (1983). Niche width and the dynamics of organizational populations. *American Journal of Sociology*, 88, 1116–1145.

Goffman, E. (1961). Fun in games. In E. Goffman, *Encounters* (pp. 15–81). Indianapolis: Bobbs-Merrill.

Hebdige, D. (1979). *Subcultures: The meaning of style*. London: Methuen.

Hoggett, P., & Bishop, J. (1985). Leisure beyond the individual consumer. *Leisure Studies*, 4(1), 21–35.

Jenkins, J. C. (1983). Resource mobilization theory and the study of social movements. *Annual Review of Sociology*, 9, 527–553.

Knoke, D. (1986). Associations and interest groups. *Annual Review of Sociology*, 10, 1–21.

Lavanda, R. (1988). Minnesota queen pageants: Play, fun, and dead seriousness in a festive mode. *Journal of American Folklore*, 101, 168–175.

Little League Baseball, Inc. (1984). *Official regulations and playing rules*. Williamsport, PA: Author.

McCarthy, J. D., & Zald, M. N. (1977). Resource mobilization and social movements: A partial theory. *American Journal of Sociology*, 82, 1212–1241.

Mitchell, R. (1983). *Mountain experience*. Chicago: University of Chicago Press.

Olmstead, A. D. (1988). Morally controversial leisure: The social world of gun collectors. *Symbolic Interaction*, 11, 277–287.

Olsen, M. (1971). *The logic of collective action*. Cambridge: Harvard University Press.

Smith, D. H., & Pillemer, K. (1983). Self-help and groups as social movement organizations: Social structure and social change. In L. Kriesberg (Ed.), *Research in social movements, conflicts, and change* (Vol. 5) (pp. 203–233). Greenwich, CT: JAI Press.

Stebbins, R. (1979). *Amateurs*. Beverly Hills, CA: Sage.

Warren, R., Jr. (1972). *The community in America* (2nd ed.). Chicago: Rand McNally.

Whitson, D. (1983). Pressures on regional games in a dominant metropolitan culture: The case of shinty. *Leisure Studies*, 2(2), 139–154.

NOTES

1. The existence of the Minnesota Mycological Society in the Twin Cities increases the likelihood of people engaging in that hobby. The club makes itself available to the media and sponsors exhibits at the local natural history museum. Contrast this with the sorry state of butterfly collecting. There is no Lepidopterist Society in Minnesota and thus the media do not report on this hobby. According to the membership lists of the Lepidopterists' Society of America and the North American Mycological Association, the former has a lower proportion of Minnesotans than would be expected by chance while the latter has a greater proportion. One cannot definitively attribute patterns of membership in a national organization or newspaper coverage to the existence of a local organization, but it provides prima facie evidence of this possibility.

2. The extent and formality of this knowledge varies among leisure activities. Some such as mushrooms and fantasy gaming require considerable knowledge, others less so. However, since leisure consists of a sphere of specialized activity, some realm of localized knowledge is inevitable.

3. These can of course extend beyond identity symbols and include knowledge and opportunities for sociability.

4. This new rulebook may also have served a legal purpose. The first set of three rulebooks were written by E. Gary Gygax and his erstwhile partner, David Arneson. However, the two men disagreed about the ownership of the game and the second rulebook was written by Gygax alone (see Fine, 1983).

5. In the case of Dungeons & Dragons many players assume that Gygax and his co-workers at TSR Hobbies have special access to his game world, and consequently ask him all manner of questions about the game. Gygax claims with wry frustration that he once received a letter asking how many eggs a hippogriff lays (Fine, 1983, p. 23). The creator is taken as the expert on all questions relating to his/her game even though the facts requested may have little bearing on the rules.

6. The national Little League organization, while not controlling all youth baseball, is a substantial organization. In 1983 Little League Baseball, Inc., reported total assets of over $10.2 million and total expenses of $3.9 million.

7. In Minnesota this issue is particularly critical in youth hockey where there are not enough rinks for such a popular sport. Some children find themselves practicing late at night or in the very early morning. Hockey can get away with such

temporal outrages because hockey carries with it such status and the leagues themselves are provisioned so well.

8. One testable hypothesis is that individuals with more discretionary income are more likely to join leisure organizations (as has been suggested for social movements). On the societal level, one would expect more leisure organizations and an increase in membership in times of economic expansion, when more discretionary resources are available (Douglas Macadam, personal communication, 1989).

DISCUSSION QUESTIONS

1. Discuss in your own words what you understand Fine to mean by provisioning theory. Do you agree or disagree with his assessment that this theory can offer insights into the form of organized fun? Why or why not?

2. Based on your own experience, identify a sport or other leisure activity you were involved in as a youth and apply Fine's understanding of copyrighted subcultures and provisioning theory to describe this case.

READING 12

The Telephone: Personal Calls, Personal Meaning

Claude S. Fischer

Technology does not determine the ways we use various inventions; rather those uses are socially constructed. This is the lesson derived from Claude Fischer's social history of the telephone. In this excerpt from America Calling, *he reviews some of the concerns that were voiced earlier in the century about the introduction of the telephone, contrasting those concerns with the recollections of old timers who remembered the introduction of the phone into their own homes. Fischer proceeds to discuss the impact of the telephone on face-to-face interaction, and looks at the psychology of telephone use, pointing particularly to the role it played in reducing insecurity and alienation.*

THE NATURE OF TELEPHONE SOCIABILITY

If North Americans prior to World War II—especially women—largely used the home telephone for social calls, how did that use affect the nature of their social ties? Did it, for example, replace face-to-face conversations? Urban planners today frame this question, usually with respect to business, as the "communication-transportation trade-off": Does telephone service reduce in-person travel by allowing business people to accomplish the same tasks by calling instead? Or do such calls actually increase travel by generating more business?[1] Our interest is closer to that of the Knights of Columbus [evident in the following quotation:] "Does the telephone make men . . . lazy? Does the telephone break up . . . the old practice of visiting friends?" To be more precise, did the adoption of the telephone between 1890 and 1940 lead Americans to one or more of three customs: First, did people replace visiting with telephoning, so that their total social intercourse remained the same but more of it was by wire? Or, second, did people have conversations by telephone that they would otherwise not have had at all, so that they added more conversations to a constant number of in-person visits? Or, third, did people, stimulated and aided by their telephone calls, make even *more* in-person visits than they would otherwise have made?*

The first contention, that telephone contacts replaced face-to-face meetings, has both a weaker and a stronger form. The weaker form postulates that people became lazy and began calling neighbors and friends instead of dropping by. The stronger form posits that having the telephone encouraged people to live farther apart from one another. For example, a grown daughter could move to town and leave her elderly parents on the farm once she had the ability to reach

---

*There is another logical but unlikely possibility: that telephone calling disrupted social relations so much that total contacts (face-to-face plus telephone) diminished.

them by telephone. Our fragments of evidence best address the first, weaker form, that people just called instead of visiting.

The Lynds argued that "neighborliness" diminished in Middletown during the years up to 1924 and implied that the telephone was partly responsible. Several women whom they interviewed described a decline in visiting, either in their adulthoods or in comparison to their mothers' day. Two of the women attributed the decrease to having children, others to people being more independent, and one to social clubs, but a few mentioned the telephone. One remarked, "Instead of going to see a person as folks used to, you just telephone nowadays." Another noted, "When the 'phone came, it took up a lot of time, since you were within reach of so many more people, but it saved all the time formerly spent with women who 'ran in' on you while you were trying to do your morning's work."[2] In a different context, some observers thought the telephone had reduced the frequency with which farmers visited town and thus cut down on their community involvement.[3]

Our elderly informants from northern California drew a more complex picture of the connection between calling and visiting. Several implied that people in the early twentieth century substituted telephoning for dropping in. An Antioch woman, born in 1903 and quoted earlier, claimed: "We certainly didn't depend on the phone the way we do nowadays. . . . No, phones weren't used that much, you would go to see people and visit them in person." An Antioch man recalled of the 1920s, "Neighbors and friends always visited over the back fence in those days, so there was no need for a phone." And another Antioch woman, born in 1915, recalled telephone visits between her family on the ranch and grandparents in town: "They would call back and forth. It was easier to do that than to go the five miles just for a short visit." Such comments suggest that the telephone call constituted an alternative to the

face-to-face conversation and, perhaps, that having the telephone inhibited personal visits.*

Other interviewees implied that by calling, people increased their total conversations. Some remembered that they called their friends frequently as youngsters. (Today, one common call is between teenagers who have just seen one another at school[4]—just like the calls of over 80 years ago recounted by the San Francisco doctor's daughter.) Similarly, several remembered their mothers regularly chatting with neighbors on the telephone. Although some of these chats may have been substitutes for dropping in, they were probably often conversations that would otherwise not have happened. A few of our interviewees also noted that their mothers' use of the telephone increased as children moved out on their own. That is, mothers spoke to grown children who were infrequently seen. The common perception that telephones helped break the isolation of rural women also implies that calling added to total social interaction. In addition, many long-distance calls, certainly, were conversations that would not have otherwise occurred.

Finally, recollections of using the telephone to arrange dates, trips, and meetings suggest that calling assisted, even if it did not generate, many in-person encounters. Although these people might have found other means of making arrangements, many meetings would probably never have taken place without the calls. In the same vein, a San Rafael woman born in 1907 commented that with everybody driving, one needed to call ahead to make sure someone would be home for a visit.

All three types of relationships between calling and visits seem to have developed during the period of our concern. People substituted

---

*It could also be argued that extraneous reasons (say, more work commitments) led people to reduce their in-person visiting and telephone instead. Hence, telephone calls were the response to, not the cause of, less visiting. This contention would be hard to document.

telephone visits for some in-person ones; they made or received calls when they would or could not have otherwise met in person; and they used the telephone to arrange face-to-face encounters. We cannot measure from such accounts the relative volume of each of these three changes. The balance would, however, appear to be that the number of total contacts stayed constant or increased.

Researchers nowadays have estimated the communication-transportation trade-off for personal interaction. A few studies show some intersubstitution of telephoning and visiting. For example, in the survey of New York City subscribers who temporarily lost telephone service in 1975, 34 percent reported more frequent visiting during the disruption. After a bridge collapsed between two parts of Hobart, Tasmania, telephone calls increased.[5] But in other studies done in the United States, England, and Chile, people with telephones reported more total social contacts than did those without telephones; subscribers visited and wrote letters more often than did nonsubscribers. These correlations support the claim that telephone use multiplies all forms of contact.[6]

Did the telephone, then, "break up . . . the old practice of visiting"? That is too strong a conclusion. Telephoning probably changed visiting practices moderately during the first half of this century. People forewent some visits that they otherwise would have made, particularly unannounced drop-ins. (The elite practice of "calling" during designated at-home hours, printed card in hand, was probably in decline anyway.) Telephone users altered the character of other visits by telephoning ahead to arrange and confirm them. Finally, people probably made rendezvous they otherwise would not have, particularly appointments at public places, because they could telephone. Thus, telephoning perhaps had a limited effect on visits to another's home but made a greater difference in the ability to arrange an appointment outside the home. Furthermore, different people responded in various ways. Whether the sum total of face-to-face conversations with people outside the household declined because of the telephone we will never know, but it is much likelier that the total volume of social conversation increased notably. The telephone probably meant more talk of all kinds.

Little of the evidence, however, addresses the stronger version of the substitution argument, that over the years the availability of the telephone encouraged people to live farther apart, necessarily transforming face-to-face relations into telephonic, presumably weaker, ones. This is, for instance, sociologist Ron Westrum's charge: Communications technologies "allow the destruction of community because they encourage . . . far-flung relationships."[7] We have no evidence that the telephone encouraged separation. (Residential mobility in the United States has actually decreased over the last century and longer.[8]) None of our interviewees indicated any such tendency, although it may not have been on their minds. Nor does our evidence address the converse to the substitution argument, that people moved apart for other reasons, such as job searches, and the telephone allowed relations that would otherwise have withered to continue.

Nevertheless, the assumption that much face-to-face interaction has become largely telephonic stirs worries that such relations are emotionally thin. Not even a telephone company publicist could assert that telephone calls capture the intimacies conveyed by eye contact and physical touches, or that telephone friendships can plumb the same depths as sharing meals, taking walks, or just being together. But the question is not whether a telephone conversation is as rich as a face-to-face one. It probably is not.[9] The question is, can telephoning sustain a relationship, or does it provide only an "inauthentic" intimacy? Malcolm Willey and Stuart Rice, otherwise cold-blooded analysts, worried that more social contacts had become brief and impersonal (due to the telephone and automobile) and believed that this entailed a loss "of those values that inhere in more intimate, leisurely, protracted personal discussion."[10]

As keen an issue as this is, we cannot directly resolve it with the evidence at hand. Recent studies show that people report feeling "closer" to those friends and relatives who live farther away than to nearby associates, even associates whom they see regularly. Although people depend on those nearby for certain kinds of sociability and practical help, they turn as often to distant kith and kin for critical emotional and practical support. As a final note, Americans say they would just as soon have some distance between themselves and their friends.[11]

The critique contends, however, that even though people may believe that their relationships are intimate, honest, and committed, they do not realize that the relationships they handle by telephone actually lack those qualities and are "inauthentic." Personal testimony cannot, therefore, adjudicate the issue. Yet personal testimony is almost all we have. Lana Rakow concluded from her interviews: "Even for those who do use the telephone for companionship and talk it is not always viewed as an adequate replacement for face-to-face talk." The "always" implies that her interviewees usually viewed it as adequate. In a Canadian survey of middle-aged and elderly telephone users, about two-thirds of those over 55 agreed "a lot" that "I feel I only have to lift the telephone and I can be right there with my family." Among those 54 and younger, 55 percent of the women but only 37 percent of the men agreed. Ann Moyal's Australian interviewees believed that "the telephone played a key and continuing role in building kin and friend relationships."[12]

Assessing the quality of social relations over a half-century ago requires relying even more than these recent studies do on personal testimony. Our own interviewees did not say that they had found telephone relations unfulfilling

in the 1920s and 1930s. Some were critical of too much idle talk on the telephone, but none critiqued the authenticity of telephone relationships. (We did not, however, expressly pursue this question with them.) This issue awaits more subtle research.

Finally, what about too much sociability—having one's home invaded by calls or one's conversations overheard? Busy people, news editors, and, in his old age, Alexander Graham Bell himself, complained of telephone interruptions. Household efficiency expert Lillian Gilbreth encouraged women to organize their lives to avoid or to work around telephone calls.[13] Yet, ordinary people seemed to have few such complaints for the years covered in this study. A few women told Lana Rakow that they had to listen to other women's problems because they were reachable by telephone. A Middletown woman quoted earlier said that more people reached her because she was available (but she also said that this interruption was better than being dropped in on).[14] But complaints about such intrusions were not raised in the general reminiscences about the early telephone previously cited or in our own interviews. Nor were unwanted calls much of an issue for etiquette writers [commenting on telephone manners]; they were more concerned about excessive "chatter" on wanted calls. (The level of concern about unwanted calls might be higher today, of course.)

Eavesdropping, on the other hand, posed a frequent worry, especially on rural lines. From the beginning of telephony, people expressed concern that they were being overheard, at first simply by others in the same room—one had to speak loudly—and then by operators or fellow subscribers on a party line.[15] Several rural Indiana women cheerfully recalled listening in on the farm lines: "I was just as bad to eavesdrop as anybody else was, but I heard a lot that way," said one. Another commented, "We sure did visit and eavesdrop. That eavesdropping was funny. Everybody knew what was happening, and what all the neighbors were doing." One of our interviewees recalled that her aunt who ran the country switchboard listened in on "everything." Another half-joked that although her family didn't call much, they did use the telephone to eavesdrop. Listening-in on rural lines caused some uproar. Eavesdropping may have contributed to the most dramatic case of telephone controversy, the decision of the Pennsylvania Amish to ban the device. According to one account:

> . . . then a couple women got to talking about another woman over the phone and this woman also had the phone in and had the receiver down and heard what they said, this made quite a stink and at last came into the gma (church) to get it straightened out, then the Bishops and ministers made out if that is the way they are going to be used we would better not have them.[16]

Summary

Americans in the early twentieth century did not use the telephone to recreate the personal relations of arcadian villagers, notwithstanding the beliefs of Marshall McLuhan, country life reformers, and AT&T[17] copywriters to the contrary. Still, the adoption of the telephone probably led people to hold more frequent personal conversations with friends and kin than had previously been customary, even if it also led them to curtail some visits. Sustaining personal relations by telephone was probably rare before the turn of the century but became common in the middle class and on farms by the 1910s or early 1920s. Such talk turned torrential after mid-century, when telephones became nearly universal. To this day, some Americans, particularly men, have never become "telephone people" and rarely chat on the telephone. A small proportion probably abhorred the device in its early days; some probably still do.

Middle-class and farm women more often carried on personal relations by telephone; therefore the arrival of the technology probably altered their lives most. (Urban working-class women were not among the heavy callers in these years, and we know much less about their telephone usage.) Although conversations over the telephone do not duplicate face-to-face talks, many people seem to have found it a satisfactory way—sometimes the only way—to keep "in touch." The authenticity of relations that rely on the telephone is much harder to assess, but the claim that it is lacking is, so far, mere assertion—an assertion most callers themselves did not make. On a yet broader point, we have inadequate evidence to judge whether people, sensing the telephone's utility for staying socially close, chose to physically distance themselves from family and friends.

THE PSYCHOLOGY OF THE TELEPHONE

What are the psychological consequences of the telephone? Some analysts argue that it produces feelings of empowerment—as claimed by AT&T*—or alienation, or even infantile sexuality. Psychological characterizations of the telephone have changed historically. According to John Brooks, theatrical and literary authors used the telephone as a symbol of sophistication and wonder before World War II and afterward as a symbol of threat, violence, and powerlessness. (For example, a telephone on stage, like a gun displayed in the first act, goes off before the final curtain.)[17] We will look at two psychological themes common before 1940: briefly, that the telephone was an emblem of modernity and, more fully, that the telephone was a source of tension.

---

*For example, a 1909 advertisement entitled "The Sixth Sense—the Power of Personal Projection" told businessmen that the telephone "extends his personality to its fullest limitations." Another ad that year read: "If *any man* in the Union rings the bell of his Bell Telephone at his desk, any other man *at the most distant point* is at his instant command" (in the Ayer Collection, National Museum of American History).

Being Modern

Advertisers argued that the telephone both exhibited and produced a psychological quality of modernity. A 1905 ad told women that "The Modern Way is to save one's time and temper by telephoning." A 1909 ad called the Bell System sign that hung near pay telephones, "The Sign Board of Civilization." Scenes in advertisements for other goods often included a telephone in order to associate the products with modernity and power. Other people also linked the telephone to modernity. The Amish and Mennonite communities divided over allowing the telephone, in part because it threatened to bring them too much contact with the modern world.[18]

A few of our interviewees described the telephone in tones suggesting awe. The Antioch man quoted at the beginning of this reading indicated such a feeling in his story. A Palo Alto man born in 1892 recalled: "I still remember when the first phone was installed at a neighbor's. Everybody was so anxious to talk on the phone." A Palo Alto woman born in 1895 also said: "I remember distinctly getting a phone. That was really something!" However, the younger among our interviewees, especially those raised in towns, were more nonchalant. They were likelier to say, as did a Palo Alto woman born in 1909, "Seems we always had a telephone." An Antioch woman born in 1903 noted: "Telephones were no big deal. It wasn't like you never saw a telephone. They had one at the store or at the neighbor's."

According to our interviewees, the telephone was, except perhaps for rural households, commonplace in northern California by the early 1910s. It neither frightened nor amazed people, and it symbolized nothing special about subscribers except perhaps that they were well-to-do. [It is surprising] how quickly the local newspapers lost interest in the telephone. At some level, the connection between the telephone and modernity probably remained, subtly and below people's consciousness, available for exploitation by advertisers. A kitchen with a telephone would appear more up-to-the-times than one without it. The evidence suggests, however, that few Americans found the telephone dramatic beyond about 1910.

Pace, Tension, and Anxiety

The telephone, some observers assert, sped up the pace of life, forced people to be alert, and thus created a lasting feeling of tension. In 1899 an English newspaperman argued, "The use of the telephone gives little room for reflection, it does not improve the temper, and it engenders a feverishness which does not make for domestic happiness and comfort." An AT&T-sponsored author asserted in 1910 that the telephone made life "more tense, alert, vivid." In his 1976 history of AT&T, John Brooks claimed that the early telephone "was creating a new habit of mind—a habit of tenseness and alertness, of demanding and expecting immediate results, whether in business, love, or other forms of social intercourse."[19] These judgements make sense intuitively (and will get empathetic nods from busy individuals who feel harassed by telephone calls). If people become anxious when they are eager for someone to answer their call or are constantly on edge because their telephone can ring at any time, then they are probably more tense than they would be without the telephone. We are familiar with people today who seek vacations from their telephones. But what evidence is there to support the proposition that Americans in the first half of the century generally were made tense by telephony?

We can search the comments of old-timers for expressions of anxiety or irritability associated with the telephone. One elderly Indiana woman recalled that the telephone "used to scare me," and another that her mother was afraid of the telephone because she had been knocked down by lightning. Two more Hoosier women simply said that they did not enjoy the telephone and used it only of necessity. A few of our own interviewees expressed some disdain for the telephone—"I am not a telephone person"—but whether that reflected tension is unclear. A San Rafael woman born in 1902 reported that her husband disliked the telephone and hated to find her or their children on it when he came home from work, but again, whether his displeasure stemmed from nervousness or some other source is not evident. Of our three dozen interviewees, only this handful made comments at all implying that the telephone provoked anxiety. For the most part, tension was not a vivid part of people's recollections of the telephone.

One cause of such tension could be the fear of ill tidings. A woman told Lana Rakow that during World War I people who hadn't recently heard from their sons in Europe hated to hear the telephone ring. An AT&T study found that elderly people felt the sound of the telephone bell to be unpleasant because they feared it brought bad news. Yet, middle-aged and young people in that same AT&T study thought of it as stimulating because it "promised relief from boredom."[20] There seem to be more comments of the latter sort in the oral histories of the telephone. An Indiana woman said, "We appreciated [the telephones] so much; we just enjoyed them." Another echoed, "We enjoyed the telephone."[21] A few of our interviewees raised on farms appreciated telephones in the sense that having the devices increased their sense of security. One Antioch man born in 1911 rhapsodized about the machine itself:

> You could [call] from ranch house to ranch house and could get the main phone service in town. I was awestruck with that. My father would open up the phone and I would look at it. He'd open up the box and remember the colors—beautiful colors—that identified the circuits. And he would try to identify this thing for me.

Such positive comments outnumbered the few expressing anxiety.

A rare, systematic survey done in the 1930s examined people's feelings toward three forms of communication. A market research firm,

sponsor unrecorded, interviewed 200 men and women from four American cities. Interviewers first asked respondents how they thought people in general felt and then how they personally felt toward telegrams, telephones, and letters. (Answers to the general and personal questions were similar.) The key probe was: "Without considering expense or time, do you think there are people who feel slightly uncomfortable or mind in any way———?" The following list gives the percentages of affirmative responses:

Making telephone calls	33%
Receiving telephone calls	33%
Sending telegrams	42%
Receiving telegrams	62%
Writing letters	70%
Receiving letters	8%

Of the 66 people who expressed discomfort about making telephone calls, almost half complained that it was difficult to hear or to be heard, or that there were other service problems, such as inconvenience in reaching people; 28 percent felt self-conscious or did not know what to say; and 15 percent thought calling was a waste of time because people talked too much. Of the 66 people who expressed discomfort at receiving calls, several complained about hearing poorly, several felt self-conscious about speaking on the telephone, and 38 said it was "time-wasting, bothersome, disturbing." (The report lumped the last three comments together.) The best estimate is that less than 20 percent of the original 200 respondents expressed anxiety about using the telephone. Add those who felt shy about talking and then perhaps 25 percent, at most, expressed some tension about using the telephone.* By contrast, most people disliked receiving telegrams because they feared bad news; many disliked sending telegrams because

---

*I assume that complaints about sound quality, operators, or other people's gabbiness, although they express irritation, do not show the kind of emotional anxiety that is the subject of this discussion.

they might scare the recipients; and most hated writing letters because of the time and effort required or because they felt inarticulate. Few people objected to receiving letters. Asked their preferred modes of communicating, respondents ranked telephone calling first and writing letters last. (Note, however, that this survey was conducted near the end of our period and may reflect a late-developing comfort with the telephone.)[22]

We can also consider a few recent surveys, but only with some reservations due to the probable change in reactions to the telephone as the technology became more common. The AT&T survey in which young and middle-aged respondents found the telephone ring stimulating was previously mentioned. Benjamin Singer asked 138 residents of London, Ontario, how they reacted when the telephone rang at dinnertime. Forty-four percent said they did not mind, 15 percent were mildly annoyed, and 9 percent said they got angry. For calls that interrupted television watching, fewer than 10 percent reported irritation. Recalling the point made earlier that the proper comparison for the telephone is with face-to-face meetings, considerably more respondents, 30 percent, objected to people dropping in unannounced. Calls in the middle of the night, however, upset or angered 63 percent. When asked what the disadvantages of the telephone were, about half pointed to interruptions or unwanted calls. Thus, in general, even though people labeled nuisance and ill-timed calls as a problem, they expressed only modest amounts of irritation about such interruptions.[23]

We can again consult the interviews from the Manhattan study of 190 people who lost telephone service for three weeks in 1975. Large majorities reported feeling out of control, uneasy, isolated, and frustrated without service. Yet, almost half also reported that "life felt less hectic." A substantial minority, therefore, felt that having a telephone simultaneously made life hectic and enhanced their control over their lives. (Ironically, after reporting these findings the authors concluded that "although it may reduce loneliness and uneasiness, [the telephone's] likely contribution to the malaise of urban depersonalization should not be underestimated"—with no evidence at all demonstrating "the malaise of urban depersonalization.")[24]

We can fit these fragments together into a few tentative conclusions. Most people saw telephoning as accelerating social life, which is another way of saying that telephoning broke isolation and augmented social contacts. A minority felt that telephones served this function *too* well. These people complained about too much gossip, about unwanted calls, or, as did some family patriarchs, about wives and children chatting too much. Most probably sensed that the telephone bell, besides disrupting their activities (as visitors might), could also bring bad news or bothersome requests. Yet only a few seemed to live in a heightened state of alertness, ears cocked for the telephone's ring—no more, perhaps, than sat anxiously alert for a knock on the door. Some Americans not only disliked talking on the telephone but also found having it around disturbing, but they were apparently a small minority.* Perhaps a few of the oldest felt anxious around the telephone, but most people—according to our interviews, perhaps almost all of those born after the turn of the century—seemed to feel comfortable or even joyful around it. (An Australian researcher has suggested that a telephone call also raises recipients' feelings of self-esteem; it shows that someone cares.[25]) Sociologist Sidney Aronson may have captured the feelings of most Americans when he suggested that having the telephone led, in net, to a "reduction of loneliness and anxiety, an increased feeling of psychological and even physical security."[26]

---

*Perhaps today, and perhaps earlier, too, the people who most complain about telephone calls harassing them are those with already packed schedules. While many essayists probably fit in this group—and the author and many readers of this book, too—we do not necessarily represent Americans in general.

NOTES

1. See, for example, Falk and Abler, "Intercommunications, Distance, and Geographical Theory"; Pool, "The Communication/Transportation Tradeoff"; Salomon, "Telecommunications and Travel."

2. Lynd and Lynd, *Middletown*, 273–75, quotations from 275n.

3. E.g., Atwood, "Telephony and Its Cultural Meanings," 360–61. Similarly, Martin suggests that by enlarging women's social contacts in the home, telephoning "may have reduced women's opportunities for socializing outside" it (*"Hello, Central?"* 165).

4. Mayer, "The Telephone and the Uses of Time," 234.

5. Wurtzel and Turner, "Latent Functions," 254; Lee, "The Resilience of Social Networks to Changes in Mobility and Propinquity." William Michelson found in a Toronto survey that people tended to telephone more often during the winter than during the spring, presumably because they used the telephone to avoid making trips into the cold weather (Michelson, "Some Like It Hot").

6. The British and Chilean studies show that people with telephones or who use the telephone more have more contacts of all sorts (Britain: Clark and Unwin, "Telecommunications and Travel," and Miller, "Telecommunications/Transportation Substitution"; Chile: Wellenius, "Telecommunications in Developing Countries," and idem, "The Role of Telecommunications Services in Developing Countries"). The U.S. study found that people who make more long-distance calls also more often write and visit their distant associates (reported in Mahan, "The Demand for Residential Telephone Service"). These studies must be taken with some reserve, of course, since the correlation between telephoning and other contacts may be spurious, the product of personality types, for example. But Barry Wellman's Canadian data show a strong and positive partial association between telephone and face-to-face contacts, holding constant other aspects of relationships (Wellman, "Reach Out," table 8). In the study of grandparents, those who called more often also visited more often, suggesting a synergy between the two modes (Cherlin and Furstenberg, *New American Grandparent*, 115–16).

7. Westrum, *Technologies and Society*, 276.

8. Mid-to late-twentieth century Americans changed homes *less* often than did earlier generations. There may be tendency for the moves to be of greater distance now than before, but even that is uncertain. (See Long, *Migration and Residential Mobility*; Fischer, "Ambivalent Communities.") Americans have moved farther from their jobs, however (see, e.g., Jackson, *Crabgrass Frontier*, Appendix).

9. Experimental studies indicate that voice-only communications are experienced as more psychologically distant than visual ones (Rutter, *Communicating by Telephone*). Most respondents to Synge et al.'s Ontario survey ("Phoning and Writing") said that a telephone conversation was less personal than a face-to-face one. On the other hand, many women who responded to Moyal's Australian survey felt that telephone conversations with friends were franker and more intimate than in-person ones (Moyal, "Feminine Culture," 15).

10. Willey and Rice, *Communication Agencies*, 202. Those who claim that the telephone introduces alienation and inauthenticity are numerous. Historian Susan Strasser, for example, has argued:

   [N]ineteenth century American society, at least as mobile as that of today, had no such technology [as the telephone]; many people moved thousands of miles, never expecting to see or converse with friends and relations again. When they arrived in their new homes, they established new day-to-day intimacies, free of charge: women who hung their laundry outside knew their neighbors, who genuinely filled some of the needs the telephone meets inadequately. (Strasser, Never Done, 305).

11. On distance between people and feelings of closeness, see Fischer et al., *Networks and Places*, chap. 9; Fischer, *To Dwell among Friends*, chap. 13; Fischer, "The Dispersion of Kinship Ties in Modern Society"; Wellman, "The Community Question." In a small survey in northern California, people generally said that they would not like their friends to live next door, but would rather have them within easy driving distance (Silverman, "Negotiated Claim").

12. Rakow, "Gender, Communication, and Technology," 159; Synge et al., "Phoning and Writing"; Moyal, "Woman and the Telephone," 284; see also Moyal, "Feminine Culture."
13. Kenneth Haltman cites several *New York Times* articles complaining about telephone intrusions and one, dated 1922, which revealed that Bell himself would never have a telephone in his study (Haltman, "Reaching Out," 343); Gilbreth, *The Home-Maker and Her Job,* 79–81.
14. Rakow, "Gender, Communication, and Technology," 175; Lynd and Lynd, *Middletown*, 275n.
15. See Katz, "US Telecommunications Privacy Policy"; Martin, "Communication and Social Forms," 128, 279, 370, 380.
16. First-hand account quoted by Umble, "The Telephone Comes to Pennsylvania Amish Country," 12.
17. Brooks, "The First and Only Century of Telephone Literature"; see also Wisener, " 'Put Me on to Edenville.' "
18. Ads from "Advertising and Publicity, 1906–1910, folder 1," Box 1317, AT&THA.* Telephone as advertising symbol: Marchand, *Advertising*, 169, 190, 209, 238–47; Mennonites: Atwood, "Telephony and its Cultural Meanings," 326–47, and Umble, "The Telephone Comes to Pennsylvania Amish Country." See also Atwood, 83, on how rural telephone companies in Iowa used the modernity theme in their marketing.
19. *Chamber's Journal*, "The Telephone"; Casson, *History of the Telephone*, 231; Brooks, *Telephone*, 117–18; see also S. Kern, *Time and Space*, 91.
20. Indiana: E. Arnold, *Party Lines, Pumps and Privies*, 146–53; Rakow, "Gender, Communication, and Technology," 231; AT&T: Mayer, "The Telephone and the Uses of Time," 232. Whether older people were more nervous around the telephone because of their cohort—the telephone was new in their youth—or because of their age—more of their friends might be ill, for example—is not evident.
21. Arnold, *Party Lines, Pumps and Privies*, 146–47.

22. *Sales Management*, "Average Person Finds Letter Writing More Difficult than Telephoning or Wiring."
23. Mayer, "The Telephone and the Uses of Time," 232; Singer, *Social Functions of the Telephone*, 62–63, 26, 14–15.
24. Wurtzel and Turner, "Latent Functions," 253, 256.
25. Noble, "Towards a 'Uses and Gratifications' of the Telephone."
26. Aronson, "The Sociology of the Telephone," 162.

REFERENCES

Arnold, Eleanor, ed. 1985. *Party Lines, Pumps and Privies: Memories of Hoosier Homemakers*. Indianapolis: Indiana Extension Homemakers Association.

Aronson, Sidney H. 1971. "The Sociology of the Telephone." *International Journal of Comparative Sociology* 12 (September): 153–67.

Atwood, Roy Alden. 1984. "Telephony and Its Cultural Meanings in South-eastern Iowa, 1900–1917," Ph.D. diss., University of Iowa.

Brooks, John. 1976. *Telephone: The First Hundred Years*. New York: Harper & Row.

———. 1977. "The First and Only Century of Telephone Literature." In *The Social Impact of the Telephone*, edited by Ithiel de Sola Pool, 208–24. Cambridge, MA: The MIT Press.

Casson, Herbert N. 1910. *The History of the Telephone*. Chicago: A. C. McClurg.

Chamber's Journal. 1899. "The Telephone." 76: 310–13.

Cherlin, Andrew, and Frank F. Furstenberg, Jr. 1986. *The New American Grandparent*. New York: Basic Books.

Clark, D. and K. I. Unwin. 1981. "Telecommunications and Travel: Potential Impact in Rural Areas." *Regional Studies* 15: 47–56.

Falk, Thomas, and Ronald Abler. 1980. "Intercommunications, Distance, and Geographical Theory." *Geografisk Annaler*, 62B (2): 59–67.

Fischer, Claude S. 1982a. "The Dispersion of Kinship Ties in Modern Society: Contemporary Data and Historical Speculation." *Journal of Family History* 7 (Winter): 353–750.

---

*AT&THA: American Telephone and Telegraph, Historical archives, Warren, New Jersey.

————. 1982b. *To Dwell among Friends: Personal Networks in Town and City.* Chicago: University of Chicago Press.

————. 1991. "Ambivalent Communities: How Americans Understand Their Localities." In *America at Century's End*, edited by A. Wolfe, 79–92. Berkeley and Los Angeles: University of California Press.

————, Robert Max Jackson, C. Ann Stueve, Kathleen Gerson, Lynne McCallister Jones, with Mark Baldassare. 1977. *Networks and Places: Social Relations in the Urban Setting.* New York: Free Press.

Gilbreth, Lillian. 1927. *The Home-Maker and Her Job.* New York: D. Appleton.

Haltman, Kenneth. 1990. "Reaching out to Touch Someone? Reflections on a 1923 Candlestick Telephone." *Technology in Society* 12 (3): 333–54.

Jackson, Kenneth C. 1985. *Crabgrass Frontier: The Suburbanization of the United States.* New York: Oxford University Press.

Katz, James E. 1988. "US Telecommunications Privacy Policy." *Telecommunications Policy* (December): 353–67.

Kern, S. 1983. *The Culture of Time and Space, 1880–1918.* Cambridge, MA: Harvard University Press.

Lee, T. R. 1980. "The Resilience of Social Networks to Changes in Mobility and Propinquity." *Social Networks* 2 (December): 423–37.

Long, Larry H. 1988. *Migration and Residential Mobility in the United States.* New York: Russell Sage Foundation.

Lynd, Robert S., and Helen M. Lynd. 1929. *Middletown.* New York: Harcourt Brace Jovanovich.

Mahan, Gary P. 1979. "The Demand for Residential Telephone Service." Public Utilities Paper. Michigan State University.

Marchand, Roland. 1985. *Advertising the American Dream: Making Way for Modernity, 1920–1940.* Berkeley and Los Angeles: University of California Press.

Martin, Michèle. 1987. "Communication and Social Forms: A Study of the Development of the Telephone System, 1876–1920." Ph.D. diss., Department of Sociology, University of Toronto.

————. 1991. *Hello, Central? Gender, Technology and Culture in the Formation of Telephone Systems.* Toronto: University of Toronto Press.

Mayer, M. 1977. "The Telephone and the Uses of Time." In *The Social Impact of the Telephone*, edited by Ithiel de Sola Pool, 225–45. Cambridge, MA: The MIT Press.

Michelson, W. 1971. "Some Like It Hot: Social Participation and Environmental Use as Functions of the Season." *American Journal of Sociology* 76 (May): 1072–83.

Miller, C. E. 1980. "Telecommunications/Transportation Substitution." *Socio-Economic Planning Sciences* 14 (4): 163–66.

Moyal, Ann M. 1989a. "Woman and the Telephone in Australia: Outline of a National Study." In *Telefon und Gesellschaft, Band 1: Beiträge zu einer Soziologie der Telefonkommunikation*, Forschungsgruppe Telefonkommunikation (Hrsg), 283–93. Berlin: Volker Speiss.

————. 1989b. "The Feminine Culture of the Telephone. People, Patterns and Policy." *Prometheus* (Australia) 7 (June): 5–31.

Noble, Grant. 1989. "Towards a 'Uses and Gratifications' of the Telephone." In *Telefon und Gesellschaft, Band 1: Beiträge zu einerSoziologie der Telefonkommunikation, Forschungsgruppe Telefonkommunikation (Hrsg)*, 298–307. Berlin: Volker Speiss.

Pool, Ithiel de Sola. 1977. "The Communication/Transportation Tradeoff." *Policy Studies Journal* 6 (Autumn): 74–83.

Rakow, Lana F. 1987. "Gender, Communication, and Technology: A Case Study of Women and the Telephone." Ph.D. diss., Institute of Communications Research, University of Illinois at Urbana–Champaign.

Rutter, Derek R. 1987. *Communicating by Telephone.* Oxford: Pergamon.

Sales Management. 1937. "Average Person Finds Letter Writing More Difficult than Telephoning or Wiring." 41 (20 October): 60.

Salomon, Ilan. 1985. "Telecommunications and Travel: Substitution or Modified Mobility?" *Journal of Transport Economics and Policy* 19 (September): 219–35.

Silverman, Carol J. 1981. "Negotiated Claim." Ph. D. diss., Department of Sociology, University of California, Berkeley.

Singer, Benjamin D. 1981. *Social Functions of the Telephone.* Palo Alto, CA: R & E Research Associates.

Strasser, Susan. 1982. *Never Done: A History of American Housework*. New York: Pantheon.

Synge, J., C. J. Rosenthal, and V. W. Marshall. 1982. "Phoning and Writing as a Means of Keeping in Touch in the Family of Later Life." Paper presented to the Canadian Association on Gerontology, Toronto.

Umble, Diane Zimmerman. 1989. "The Telephone Comes to Pennsylvania Amish Country: A Study of Resistance to Technology at the Turn of the Century." Paper presented to International Communication Association, San Francisco.

Wellenius, B. 1977. "Telecommunications in Developing Countries." *Telecommunications Policy* 1 (September): 289–97.

———. 1978. "The Role of Telecommunications Services in Developing Countries." Workshop on Special Aspects of Telecommunications Development in Isolated and Underprivileged Areas of Countries, Ottawa, Canada, June.

Wellman, Barry. 1979. "The Community Question: The Intimate Networks of East Yorkers." *American Journal of Sociology* 84 (5): 1201–31.

———. 1989. "Reach Out and Touch Some Bodies: How Telephone Networks Connect Social Networks." Paper presented to the American Sociological Association, San Francisco, August.

Westrum, Ron. 1991. *Technologies and Society: The Shaping of People and Things*. Belmont, CA: Wadsworth.

Willey, Malcolm M., and Stuart A. Rice. 1933. *Communication Agencies and Social Life*. New York: McGraw-Hill.

Wisener, P. 1984. " 'Put Me on to Edenville': One Hundred and Six Years on the Telephone." *Mind and Nature* 3 (1): 23–31.

Wurtzel, A. H., and C. Turner. 1977. "Latent Functions of the Telephone." In *The Social Impact of the Telephone*, edited by Ithiel de Sola Pool, 246–61. Cambridge, MA: The MIT Press.

DISCUSSION QUESTIONS

1. Compare and contrast the responses of Fischer's subjects regarding the use of the telephone to the ways your peers view the use of e-mail communication.

2. In what ways does telephone communication resemble and in what ways does it differ from face-to-face communication?

READING 13

Role Conflict and Identity Salience: College Athletics and the Academic Role

Peter Adler and Patricia A. Adler

Based on a four-year ethnographic study of collegiate basketball, Peter Adler and Patricia Adler explore the conflict inherent in the roles of student and athlete in highly competitive university sports programs. As an example of the symbolic interactionist tradition, the study traces the ways that basketball players come to terms with these two roles. What Adler and Adler found was that despite initial expectations that one could meld these roles into a coherent sense of the student athlete, in fact over time the conflict between the two became more pronounced as the role of athlete progressively took precedence over that of student. In examining the factors that contribute to this typical resolution of role conflict, the Adlers reveal the basic powerlessness of the athletes to challenge this outcome.

Athletes attend colleges and universities for the ostensible purpose of getting an education while they exercise and refine their athletic skills, but recent studies note that this ideal has become increasingly corrupted. Reports by journalists, former athletes, and social scientists note the commercialization of big-time college athletics, where the money and prestige available to universities have turned their athletic programs into business enterprises that emphasize winning at all costs, often neglecting the education goals of their institutions.[1] The equality of the exchange between college athletes and their educational institutions has therefore been sharply questioned, with many critics leveling charges that universities have exploited their athletes by making excessive demands of them and failing to fulfill their educational promises to them.[2] Several studies have suggested that these factors have unfortunate consequences for athletes' academic careers, resulting in their having lower grades and less chance of graduating than other students.[3] In-depth, ethnographic investigation into this arena is needed.[4] Drawing on four years of intensive participant observation with a major college basketball team, this article examines college athletes' academic experiences.

THEORETICAL FRAMEWORK

Identity theory links the individual and the social structure. Drawing on symbolic interactionism, its proponents analyze structural characteristics of individuals' self-conceptions, their behavior, and their social relations with others. These have been located in the roles[5] that constitute the self. Each individual's total constellation of roles forms a role set, characterized by a series of relationships with role-related others, or role-set members.[6]

Individuals do not invest their core feelings of identity or self-involvement in all roles equally, however. Some roles are more salient than others. This analysis draws primarily on Stryker's formulation of role-identity salience, using a simplified definition (similar to Hoelter's): the relative importance or centrality of a given role for defining one's core identity.[7]

Identity theory puts forth two variables as determinants of role-identity salience. Stryker[8] proposed a correlation between role-identity salience and role commitment, positing that those roles that are harder to relinquish have a greater possibility of being invoked in any given situation. To this Turner and Hoelter[9] added the variable of role evaluation, suggesting that the degree to which individuals are positively or negatively evaluated by others in a role affects the salience of that role to their overall self-definition.

METHODS AND SETTING

For four years the authors studied a major college basketball program via participant-observation methods using team field research strategies[10] and differentiated roles. The research was conducted at a medium-size private university with a predominantly white, suburban, and middle-class student body. The university's academic standards were demanding as it was striving to enhance its academic reputation. The athletic department, as a whole, had a recent history of success. Players were generally recruited from the region, were 70% black, and ranged from the lower to the middle classes. The basketball program fit what Coakley and Frey[11] termed *big-time college athletics*. Although it could not compare to the really large universities, its recent success had compensated for its size and lack of historical tradition. The national ranking and past success of the basketball team and other teams in sending graduating members into the professional leagues imbued the entire athletic milieu with a sense of seriousness and purpose.

The basketball players' circle of significant others was largely predetermined by athletic environment. The role-set members fell into three main categories: athletic, academic, and social. Within the athletic realm, in addition to their teammates, athletes related primarily to the coaching staff, trainers, team managers, secretaries, and athletic administrators. Secondary role-set members included boosters, fans, and the news media. Within the academic realm, athletes' role-set members consisted of professors, tutors, classmates, and, to a lesser extent, academic counselors and administrators. Within the social realm, athletes related to girlfriends, local friends, and students (non-athletes), but most especially to their college athlete peers: the teammates and dormmates who were members of their subculture.

ROLE EXPECTATIONS

Most incoming college athletes observed approached their academic role with initial feelings of idealism. They were surrounded by family and cultural messages that college would enhance their upward mobility and benefit their lives in many ways.[12] They never doubted this assertion. Because of their academic experiences in high school, few athletes questioned their ability to succeed in college ("I graduated high school, didn't I?"). Athletes' idealism about their impending academic experience was further strengthened by the positive tone coaches had taken toward academics during the recruiting process.[13] Entering freshmen commonly held the following set of prior expectations about their academic role: (1) they would go to classes and do the work (phrased as "putting the time in"); (2) they would graduate and get a degree, and (3) there would be no problems.

Approximately 47% ($N = 8$) of the entering athletes observed showed their initially high academic aspirations and expectations by requesting to be placed in a preprofessional major in the colleges of business, engineering, or arts and sciences. Despite warnings from coaches and older teammates about how difficult it would be to complete this coursework and play ball, they felt they could easily handle the demands. These individuals planned to use college athletics as a stepping-stone to career opportunities. As one freshman stated:

> I goin' to use basketball to get an education. Sure I'd like to make the NBA someday, but right now I've got to have something to fall back on if I don't.

Another group of freshmen, who had already accorded academics a less salient role (45%, $N = 17$), were enrolled by coaches in more "manageable" majors, such as physical education or recreation. Most of these individuals, though, believed that they too would get a degree. They had few prior expectations about academics, but assumed that they would make it through satisfactorily. Someone had taken care of these matters in high school, and they felt that college would be no different. Only a few individuals from the sample (8%, $N = 3$) entered college expecting to turn professional shortly thereafter. From the beginning these individuals disdained the academic role.

Much of this initial idealism was based on an inaccurate picture of college. Athletes did not anticipate the focus on analytical thinking and writing they would encounter, expecting that college courses would be an extension of their high school experiences. One sophomore reflected back on his expectations:

> I didn't think about it much, but when I did, I thought it'd be more or less the same here as it be back in high school, no big change. I be passin' all my courses there, but I still be goin' out every night.

In their first weeks on campus during their summer program, this early idealism was once again bolstered. Repeatedly the head coach stressed the importance of earning a degree. He cared about his players as people and wanted them to build a future out of their college experience. In fact, one of the main reasons athletes' parents encouraged their sons to attend this university was because of the head coach's integrity and good values. Once the school year began, athletes attended required nightly study halls, were told that tutors were available, and were constantly reminded by the coach to go to class. One freshman, interviewed during the preseason period, showed his idealism through his expectations and impressions:

> I'm here for two reasons: to get my degree and play basketball. I don't think it's goin' to be no problem to get my degree. I want to graduate in four years and I think I will. I think that's really important to Coach, too, because in practice he always mentions how important the degree is and everything.

Contrary to popular sentiment, most of the athletes observed began their college careers with a positive attitude toward academics. While their athletic role was unquestionably the most salient and their social role secondary, the academic role was still a critical dimension of their self-identity. Their behavior in the academic realm reflected this; they missed few classes, and turned in assignments regularly. For most this period lasted anywhere from one semester to two years.

ROLE CONFLICT

After two semesters in school and a full basketball season, athletes began to realize that their academic expectations had not been entirely accurate. Their early naive idealism gave way to disappointment and cynicism as they realized both the structural difficulties inherent in fulfilling the obligations of this role and the entrenched conflict[14] with the athletic and social components of their role set.

A major change athletes encountered in shifting from high school to college basketball lay in their athletic role. In large part this was due to the professionalization process they underwent.[15] As one junior remarked:

> In high school, basketball was fun and games, but now it's a job. We get to the gym, we gotta work. You gotta put your all into it no matter how you feelin' that day. 'Cause this is big business. There's a lotta money ridin' on us.

Compounding the professionalization was a dramatic increase in pressure.[16] The basketball players were all public figures in the local area who received intense news coverage. They clearly knew how important winning was to the coaches, boosters, and fans.

The players' athletic role often encroached on their academic role. They soon discovered that handling both roles was not always possible. A primary reason was the time conflict:

some courses they wanted or needed for their majors were only offered in the afternoons during practice time; road trips caused them to miss key lectures, examinations, or review sessions, and banquets and other booster functions (which occurred at least once a week) cut into their studying time. At some point during this freshman year, most athletes realized that they did not have the time to perform as well as they had originally hoped in the academic role. This perception became acute at the end of the fall semester when the start of their playing season overlapped with the last week of classes and final exams. As one sophomore remarked:

> I got two finals tomorrow, but tomorrow night we play North Carolina. How could anyone tell me they be thinking 'bout school and studying for those tests when you know you got to play Michael Jordan the next day?

Athletes' perceptions of their athletic–academic role conflict was also influenced by the role model of their coaches. While the coaches sincerely cared about their players' academic responsibilities and achievements, they had their own priorities. Once the season began, they were too busy with their athletic work to pay much attention to academics. The pressures of recruiting, funding, and winning absorbed their energy. Despite their best preseason intentions, once practice officially began in October, the coaches became predominantly concerned with their players as athletes and ended up passing on the pressures of their organizational demands and constraints. Like their players, they were faced with a complex situation to which they often reacted, rather than acted. While they verbally stressed the importance of academics, they accorded athletic and team functions higher salience than school obligations: players' athletic time was strictly regulated, but their academic time was not. Players' behavior in practice, at games, at booster events, and on road trips was carefully monitored, yet their performance in class was not. Despite the coaches' concern about academics, the predominant message that athletes received was that, in contrast to academics, athletics had to be strictly adhered to because a powerful role-set member was always present.

ACADEMIC ROLE

During the school year, players began to notice other characteristics of their academic role that undercut their coaches' verbal emphasis on scholarship. One of the first was their lack of autonomy over their course (and sometimes major) selection. An assistant coach picked out classes and registered the athletes without consulting them. Assistant coaches bought their books, added and dropped courses for them, and contacted their professors if they had to be absent or were doing poorly in their work. By taking care of these academic matters for them, the coaches served as intermediaries between players and the academic realm. Consequently, most athletes failed to develop the knowledge, initiative, or the interest to handle these academic matters themselves, or to develop significant relationships with their professors or other academic role-set members. Thus, when the coaches were too busy to attend to these details, the players were unable to manage for themselves. As one senior remarked:

> Most of those guys don't even know how to fill out an add-drop card, so when they want to switch classes they just do it, and they tell the coaches to switch them. They figure it's not their job. But a lot of guys get Fs because the coaches never got around to it. The only reason I got through is that my girlfriend did it for me. I don't even know how to read a schedule of classes or where to get one.

Despite their occasional lapses, the fact that coaches managed these administrative matters gave athletes a false sense of security, a feeling that someone was always looking out for them academically and would make sure that they were given another chance. The athletes believed that they could fail to perform academically and not have to pay the consequences.

They developed the perception that their athletic role-set members dominated their academic role-set members, that they would be taken care of academically, and that they need not overly involve themselves in this arena. This led them to diminish the identity salience of their academic role.

Concomitant with this lack of autonomy came a new freedom. Unlike high school, their attendance at classes was not compulsory. Being able to skip classes placed a greater responsibility for self-motivation on them. When their motivation waned, athletes developed a pattern of slipping behind in their attendance and classwork until their problems compounded. When athletes did attend class, they often encountered another set of difficulties or disillusionments. In the classroom athletes thought that many professors labeled them as jocks. This image was fostered by the fact that they were surrounded in their classes by other athletes (also placed there by assistant coaches), and that they were identified early in the semester to their professor as athletes (because assistant coaches called or sent out reports to monitor their academic progress). They therefore encountered different expectations and treatment than the general student body. Whether they were given greater tolerance (extra tutoring sessions, relaxed deadlines, relaxed academic standards) or less tolerance ("Those guys think they're entitled to special treatment because they're athletes, and I'm going to show them they're wrong"), they were treated as less than full adults. This special treatment reinforced the differentiation between these two roles and their perceptions of themselves as athletes more than students. When they returned to the dormitory rooms at night, exhausted and sore from practicing, it became easier for them to rationalize, procrastinate, and fritter away[17] their time instead of studying.

Athletes also became disinterested in their academic role because of the content of their classes. The level of disinterest varied between the athletes enrolled in arts and sciences, business, or engineering courses, and those taking physical education or recreation courses. Many of those in the latter category had wanted and expected to take courses in college that were either entertaining, vocational, or in some way relevant to their everyday lives. This was not what they found. Instead, they were enrolled in courses that they considered comical and demeaning. One sophomore articulated the commonly held view:

> How could I get into this stuff? They got me taking nutrition, mental retardation, square dancing, and camp counseling. I thought I was goin' to learn something here. It's a bunch o' BS.

Players enrolled in more rigorous academic courses were often unequipped for the demanding calibre of the work. Many did not have the knowledge, interests, skills, or study habits to compete with other students. With their inadequate training, tight schedules, and waning motivation, athletes became frustrated, bored, and disinterested. Players often stopped going to classes they did not like, yet never officially withdrew from them. When they did poorly on the first test, they gave up on the course, figuring "to hell with it, I'm not gonna try." The positive feedback from their academic role that the athletes anticipated often was replaced by a series of disappointments. As a result they often spent their days lying around the dormitory rooms, watching television, and convincing each other not to go to class. Athletes' academic failures then brought them feelings of inadequacy and uncertainty, as one player described:

> When I first came here I thought I'd be goin' to class all the time and I'd study and that'd be it. But I sure didn't think it meant studyin' all the time. Back in high school you just be memorizin' things, but that's not what they want here. Back in high school I thought I be a pretty good student, but now I don't know.

Players' experiences in the classroom were very different from their preconceptions. The work was harder and they were not taken care of to the extent they had imagined. The intense competition of the athletic arena led them to be obsessed with success.[18] Their frequent academic failures (or at best mediocre grades) led athletes to distance themselves from self-involvement in the academic role. It was better not to try than to try and fail. And they derived plenty of support for this tack within the peer subculture.

SOCIAL ROLE

Athletes' social experiences at the university were predominantly with other athletes. Initially they had expected to derive both friendship and status recognition from other students as they had in high school.[19] Instead they found themselves socially isolated.[20] Geographically they were isolated by being housed in an athletic dormitory on a remote side of the campus. Temporally they were cut off by the demands of their practices, games, study halls, and booster functions. Culturally they were racially, socially, and economically different from the rest of the student body. Physically, they were different from other students in size and build, and many students, especially women, found them imposing or occasionally intimidating.

These factors left other athletes as their primary outlets for social relations. Housed together in a dormitory reserved almost exclusively for male athletes (primarily football and basketball players), they bonded together into a reference group and peer subculture. Relations within this group were made especially cohesive by the intensity of their living, playing, and traveling together. A junior described this living situation:

> Living in the jock dorm the privacy is limited. Everybody knows everythin' 'bout what you doin' and who you seein'. You got to live with these same faces twelve months out of the year, they like your brothers, and we all one big family, like it or not. You just got to fit in.

Within the dormitory athletes briefed each other about what to expect from and think about various individuals, and how to handle certain situations. They formed generalized attitudes and beliefs about what things were important and what things were not. The peer subculture provided them with a set of norms that guided their interpretations of and actions within their various roles.

One of the peer subculture's strongest influences lay in its anti-intellectual and anti-academic character.[21] Typically, dormitory conversation centered on athletic and social dimensions of their lives with little reference to academic, cultural, or intellectual pursuits.[22] In fact, individuals who displayed too much interest, effort, or success in academics were often ridiculed, as one player described:

> When most of the other guys are making Ds or Fs, if I work hard and I get a B on a test, if I go back to the dorm and they all see I got a B, then they goin' "snap on" [make fun of] me. So most of the guys, they don't try. They all act like it's a big joke.

The athletes' peer subculture conflicted with their academic role in five ways: (1) by discouraging them from exerting effort in academics; (2) by providing them with distractions that made it harder for them to study; (3) by providing them with role models who appeared to be getting through college while according their academic role negligible identity salience; (4) by discouraging them from seeking out and associating with other students who could have provided greater academic role modeling; and (5) by providing excuses and justifications that legitimated their academic failures.

The conflict between their athletic, academic, and social roles pulled the athletes in too many directions. One junior expressed his continuing distress over this role conflict:

> When I think about it I get tense and frustrated, you just can't be everything they expect you to be and what you want to be. Something's gotta give. It's either cut off my social life, or flunk out of school, or not do the things I have to do to be able to make pro.

ROLE CONFLICT RESOLUTIONS

Athletes' expectations for their academic role were gradually replaced by feelings of anomie as they came to perceive the disparity between the recruiting and cultural rhetoric they had encountered and the reality of college life. In order to successfully negotiate their college experience they had to find some way to resolve this role conflict, which they did by realigning the expectations, priorities, and identity salience of their roles.

The biggest change in their core identity salience lay in the growth of their athletic role. While athletics had always been the first priority for most, it now engulfed them. This shift was brought about by the demands and expectations of their athletic role set and by their own desire to cling to their dreams of making it in the NBA. First, the head coach overwhelmed athletes by the intensity of his power and role demands. He expected them to place basketball before everything else. He influenced their view of their present and future life chances by framing these for them based on athletic priorities. He heard about everything they did and reprimanded them for violations of his behavior code. Yet it was the intensity of the athletic experience itself that ensured their self-immersion in this role. The glamour and excitement of playing for a big-time athletic program offered even the most marginal players their most fulfilling gratification and rewards. One player described the impossibility of maintaining any balance between his athletic and other roles:

> When I go to sleep at night what do you think I be thinking? History? Sociology? No way. I hear coach yelling in my ear, "Run, run, get on the ball, play defense, Robinson. Damn, Robinson, can you move your feet, son?" During the season I sleep, eat, and breathe basketball.

In addition, the athletic role pervaded and dominated the identity of their other roles in social and academic situations. On campus they were recognized as athletes first and students second. Off campus and even out of uniform, they were constantly responsible for "representing the program." Their appearance and demeanor reflected on their teammates, their coaches, their basketball program, and the entire university. They therefore had to relinquish a great deal of privacy and freedom.

The growth of the athletic role's identity salience was further endorsed by their peer subculture. Most of the athletes in their dormitory had reprioritized their roles and become engulfed by athletics. These significant others offered them a model of role conflict resolution that adopted the coach's perspective on the predominance of athletics, maintained the secondary importance of having a social life, and reshuffled academics to an even lower identity salience. All of the athletes realigned the identity salience of these roles in this manner, progressively detaching themselves from academics.

These changes in athletes' identities led to a series of pragmatic adjustments in their academic goals. Of the individuals who began with preprofessional majors, only one-fourth of them stayed with these all the way through college and graduated. They did so primarily without the academic care and concern they had originally anticipated. They ceased attending classes regularly, diminished their efforts to get to know professors, did not bother to get class notes or reading assignments until just before tests, and exerted the minimum amount of effort necessary to get by. More commonly, these individuals reassessed their academic goals and found that some adjustment was necessary. A second group (the remaining three-fourths of this original group) adjusted by both shifting their behavior and by changing from their preprofessional program to a more manageable major. While this shift meant that they had abandoned both their academic idealism and their earlier career goals, they still held to the goal of graduating. The predominant attitude changed to getting a

diploma regardless of the major. As one player commented, "When you apply for a job all that matters is if you have that piece of paper. They don't care what you majored in." Many of the athletes in this group managed to graduate or keep on a steady course toward graduation. Much like Merton's[23] innovators, they retained the socially approved goal but replaced their earlier means with a creative alternative.

Athletes who began their college careers with lower initial academic aspirations and who majored in physical education or recreation from the start made corresponding adjustments. Approximately one-fifth of these in this group originally held on to their initial goal and managed to graduate in one of these fields. Like the preprofessional majors, they did so with less concern than they had displayed on entering. The other four-fifths came to the realization, usually relatively late, that their chances for graduating from college were unrealistic. They therefore shifted their orientation toward maintaining their athletic eligibility. A junior's remarks illustrated how this shift to maintaining eligibility affected his attitude toward his academic role:

> I used to done thought I was goin' to school, but now I know it's not for real. . . . I don't have no academic goals. A player a coach is counting on, that's all he think about is ball. That's what he signed to do. So what you gotta do is show up, show your smilin' face. Try as hard as you can. Don't just lay over in the room. That's all the coach can ask. Or else you may not find yourself playing the next year. Or even that year.

By their senior year, when they had met their final eligibility requirements, many members of this last group abandoned the academic role entirely. They either anticipated going to one of the professional leagues, or they knew that their scholarships would soon expire and they would have to look for a job. In either case, wasting their time in class no longer seemed necessary.

DISCUSSION

In sum, athletes' role conflict resolutions were accomplished by realigning, reducing, or, in extreme cases, dropping their academic role. Once this shift was made, athletes managed to cope better with the many demands made of them. College athletes reconstructed the identity salience of their academic role because of several linked conditions: (1) an overwhelmingly demanding athletic role and powerful role-set members; (2) a peer subculture that emphasized both athletics and recreation while devaluing academics; (3) a series of frustrations and failures in the academic realm caused by their poor academic training, their lack of proper study skills, the perceived irrelevance of their courses, and their gradually diminishing effort; and (4) a paucity of role reinforcing others in the academic sphere.

Several variables emerge as significant for determining both the nature and outcome of these role conflict generated reformulations. First, this study reaffirms the relationship between role evaluation and role identity salience. In their academic role, many college athletes received poor or marginal grades and had to relinquish or readjust the academic goals they held on entering college. This perception awakened them to the conflict between their expectations that college would be much like high school and their realizations that the academic demands at the university were greater than they could achieve. Their emphasis on competition and winning, derived from their athletic role, made the failure especially difficult to accept. When faced with extreme role conflict, individuals doing very poorly in their classes engaged in role distance,[24] diminishing the importance of this role to their self-identity. Individuals from stronger academic backgrounds fared slightly better, however, and did not as greatly diminish their academic role identity salience. As individuals assessed their relative strengths and weaknesses within given roles, they accorded higher salience to those in which they were evaluated

positively and lower salience to those in which they were negatively evaluated.

A related dimension of athletes' role evaluation was their differential role reinforcement. College athletes generally lacked significant academic role-set members. They therefore received little positive reinforcement for academic accomplishments. On the other hand, their athletic role-set members gave them much reinforcement for their athletic achievements but little acknowledgment for even moderate academic success. According to the "choice behavior hypothesis,"[25] individuals experiencing role conflict where role A (the athletic role) is legitimate and sanctioned and role B (the academic role) is legitimate but sanctionless will usually have no difficulty in choosing to follow the prescriptions of role A. This relative lack of reinforcement for their academic role influenced athletes to diminish their efforts and identity salience in this area. Only where athletes received significant academic role reinforcement from social role-set members, their girlfriends and families or individuals in the community promising them jobs on graduation, were they able to overcome the predominant tendency toward academic role devaluation. Without rewards or sanctions it is unlikely that individuals will invest much of their self-identity in a particular role.

Second, this study provides qualitative, processual data to support role commitment as a determinant of role identity salience. Most athletes' initial commitment to the academic role was induced by cultural expectations and by the encouragement of others, but that commitment was not firmly embedded in their self-conceptions. Once they got to college, their commitment to work hard academically was easily dislodged by their first few adverse experiences and by the peer culture's devaluation of academics. In contrast, their commitment to the athletic role was entrenched, because this was their dream since childhood. No matter how little playing time they received or how much the coach criticized them, they clung to the primary self-identification as athletes. As their commitment to their academic role and the possibility of a future career based on their academic pursuits declined, so too did their academic role identity salience. The more committed individuals are to a given role, the more likely they are to accord that role high identity salience. Roles to which they are less deeply attached are not considered as central to their self-conceptions.

Role identification is another variable associated with role commitment and identity salience. As college athletes learned the nature of their new status they learned that they were seen as basketball players by nearly everyone they encountered. Their athletic identity pervaded and dominated the identity of their other roles in almost all other situations. This designation was true in their academic and social lives both on campus and off, and it grew more pervasive as they progressed through their playing careers and advanced to more visible team positions. Their athletic role identification by others was influential in their taking the role of the other and, as labeling theory suggests, accepting this as their master identity. They then displayed secondary self-identification characteristics by acting as athletes in these other situations and by reducing the identity salience of their academic role. When people are constantly identified by one role to the near total exclusion of their others, they become increasingly committed to that role and it is likely to take precedence in influencing their self-conceptions.

Finally, this study found a correlation between role identity salience and a second related dimension of role commitment: role power. As college athletes' preconceptions were shattered by the reality of the role conflict they encountered, they came to perceive a power structure operating among their various roles and role-set members. Athletes' position at the university was characterized by "institutional powerlessness,"[26] as their coaches had the ability to control all aspects of their lives. By influencing their personal time, academic schedules, and playing role on the team, coaches could dominate not only their athletic role, but their social and academic roles as well. Regardless of the players' own goals, expectations, or desires, they had to take into consideration the wishes and demands of the coach. Players also be-

lieved, albeit in a vague and unspecified way, that their athletic role-set members influenced their academic role-set members. They felt that the coach could ultimately keep them eligible to play if he wanted, even if they got into academic difficulty. The omnipotence of their athletic over their academic role influenced them to shift greater identity salience to the role where the apparent power lay. Roles characterized by more powerful role-set members are more likely to command greater role commitment and identity salience.

The role conflict of college athletes is thus resolved through their socialization into the athletic subculture that sets the hierarchical salience of their various roles. This resocialization process and the resultant academic outcomes are structured by the coach and the overarching character of college athletes.

REFERENCES

1. Paul Hoch, *Rip Off The Big Game* (New York: Doubleday, 1972); E. B. Nyquist, "Win, Women and Money," *Educational Record* 60(1979): 374–393; James E. Odenkirk, "Intercollegiate Athletics, Big Business or Sport?" *Academe* 67(1981): 62–66; Allan L. Sack, "Big Time College Football," *Quest* 27(1977): 87–97; Allan L. Sack and Robert Thiel, "College Basketball and Role Conflict," *Sociology of Sport Journal* 2(1985): 195–209.

2. D. Stanley Eitzen and George H. Sage, *The Sociology of American Sport*, 2nd ed. (Dubuque, IA: William C. Brown, 1982); James H. Frey, "The Coming Demise of Intercollegiate Athletics," *Arena Review* 3(1979): 34–43; Dean A. Purdy, D. Stanley Eitzen, and Rick Hufnagel, "Are Athletes Also Students?" *Social Problems* 29(1982): 439–448; Sack, op. cit.; Donald Spivey and Thomas A. Jones, "Intercollegiate Athletic Servitude," *Social Science Quarterly* 55(1975): 939–947.

3. Harry M. Cross, "The College Athlete and the Institution," *Law and Contemporary Problems* 38(1973): 151–171; Harry Edwards, *Sociology of Sport* (Homewood, IL: Dorsey, 1973); James H. Harrison, "Intercollegiate Football Participation and Academic Achievement," paper presented

at the annual meetings of the Southwestern Sociological Association (Dallas, 1976); Nyquist, op. cit.; Purdy, Eitzen, and Hufnagel, op. cit.; Spivey and Jones, op. cit.; H. Webb, "Social Backgrounds of College Athletes," paper presented at the annual meetings of the American Alliance for Health, Physical Education and Recreation (St. Louis, 1968).

4. Jay J. Coakley, *Sport in Society*, 2nd ed. (St. Louis, MO: Mosby, 1982); Gary Alan Fine, "Preadolescent Socialization through Organized Athletics: The Construction of Moral Meanings in Little League Baseball," in *Dimensions of Sport Sociology*, edited by M. Krotee (Corning, NY: Leisure Press, 1979) pp. 79–105; J.W. Loy, Barry D. McPherson, and Gerald Kenyon, *Sport and Social Systems* (Reading, MA: Addison-Wesley, 1978); Purdy, Eitzen, and Hufnagel, op. cit.; Sack and Thiel, op. cit.; Eldon E. Snyder, "A Theoretical Analysis of Academic and Athletic Roles," *Sociology of Sport Journal* 2(1985): 210–217.

5. Ralph H. Turner, "The Role and the Person," *American Journal of Sociology* 84(1978): 1–23.

6. Robert K. Merton, "The Role Set," *British Journal of Sociology* 8(1957): 106–120.

7. Sheldon Stryker, "Identity Salience and Role Performance," *Journal of Marriage and the Family* 30(1968): 558–564; *Symbolic Interactionism: A Social Structural Version* (Menlo Park, CA: Benjamin/Cummings, 1980); "Symbolic Interactionism: Themes and Variations," in *Social Psychology*, edited by Morris Rosenberg and Ralph H. Turner (New York: Basic, 1981), pp. 3–29; Jon W. Hoelter, "The Effects of Role Evaluation and Commitment in Identity Salience," *Social Psychology Quarterly* 30(1983): 140–147.

8. Stryker, 1968, op. cit.

9. Hoelter, op. cit.; Turner, op. cit.

10. Jack D. Douglas, *Investigative Social Research* (Beverly Hills, CA: Sage, 1976).

11. Coakley, op. cit.; Frey, op. cit.

12. Moshe Semyonov and Ephraim Yuchtman-Yaar, "Professional Sports as an Alternative Channel of Social Mobility," *Sociological Inquiry* 1(1981): 47–53.

13. Cross, op. cit.

14. Coakley, op. cit.; Edwards, op. cit.; Purdy, Eitzen, and Hufnagel, op. cit.; Sack and Thiel, op. cit.

15. Coakley, op. cit.; D. Stanley Eitzen, "Sport and Deviance," in *Sport in Contemporary Society*, edited by D. Stanley Eitzen (New York: St. Martin's, 1979), pp. 73–89.

16. Odenkirk, op. cit.

17. Stan Bernstein, "Getting It Done: Notes on Student Fritters," in *Interaction in Everyday Life*, edited by John Lofland (Beverly Hills, CA: Sage, 1978), pp. 17–23.

18. D. S. Harris and D. Stanley Eitzen, "The Consequences of Failure in Sport," *Urban Life* 7(1978): 177–188.

19. James S. Coleman, *The Adolescent Society* (New York: Free Press, 1961); D. Stanley Eitzen, "Athletics in the Status System of Male Adolescents," *Adolescence* 10(1975): 268–276; Richard A. Rehberg and Walter E. Schafer, "Participation in Interscholastic Athletics and College Expectations," *American Journal of Sociology* 73(1968): 732–740; William G. Spady, "Lament for the Letterman," *American Journal of Sociology* 75(1970): 680–702.

20. Ferruccio Antonelli, "Psychological Problems of Top-Level Athletes," *International Journal of Sport Psychology* 1(1970): 34–39.

21. James S. Coleman, "Adolescent Subculture and Academic Achievement," *American Journal of Sociology* 65(1960): 337–347; Allan L. Sack, "Big Time College Football," *Quest* 27(1977): 87–97.

22. Dave Meggysey, *Out of Their League* (Berkeley, CA: Ramparts Press, 1971).

23. Robert K. Merton, "Social Structure and Anomie," *American Sociological Review* 3(1938): 672–682.

24. Donald W. Ball, "Failure in Sport," *American Sociological Review* 41(1976): 726–739.

25. Evert van de Vliert, "A Three-Step Theory of Role Conflict Resolution," *Journal of Social Psychology* 113(1981): 77–83.

26. Edwards, op. cit.

DISCUSSION QUESTIONS

1. In what ways are student athletes on your campus similar to or different from those portrayed by the Adlers? Why is this the case?

2. In your own life, outside of the realm of athletics, think of an instance when you have experienced role conflict. If the conflict persisted over time, why did it? If a resolution was found, what was it?

DEVIANCE AND CRIME

Deviance refers to behaviors that are deemed to be violations of normative expectations, and as such points to activities that are generally forbidden or discouraged, and are subject to various forms of sanction or penalty. Although this seems to be a fairly straightforward definition, if one thinks about specific behaviors, it turns out to contain considerable ambiguity. Part of the problem is that so many different types of people end up under a catch-all term that, as some acerbic commentators have suggested, amounts to the study of "nuts, sluts, and perverts." What does and what does not count as deviant is actually quite elusive. Certainly, there are many acts that most people in our society would likely agree count as deviant. Examples would include bestiality, the sexual abuse of children, public nudity, drunk driving, terrorist bombings, glue sniffing, and cross burning. However, there are other examples that are not so clear cut. Most might agree that using crack cocaine is deviant, but the same degree of consensus is unlikely to be achieved if the drug in question is marijuana.

As some of the examples above suggest, many deviant acts are committed by relatively small numbers of people located at the fringes of society. But large numbers of people commit other violations of societal norms. Binge drinking on college campuses is one example. Adultery is another. Are they also deviant? Are they deviant in the same way? Smoking cigarettes has been banned from many public facilities, but should smokers be viewed as deviants? If we employ a medical model to understand mental illness, should the mentally ill ("nuts") be classified as deviant?

And here is the point: deviance is a social construct. Deviant acts are those that are so defined. What makes the task of studying deviance so complicated is that in a large and heterogeneous society such as the United States, there is considerable debate and contestation regarding what is and what is not deviant. One of the foci of the sociological study of deviance concerns the processes by which some acts end up being defined as deviant whereas others don't. Because deviance is socially constructed, it is not surprising that what is and what is not deviant will vary according to the time and place. It is also not surprising that for many behaviors we can expect to find a wide range of conflicting opinions about whether or not the act is in fact deviant.

Crime is generally seen as a subset of deviance. What gives it a precision lacking in most deviant acts is that what counts as crimes are acts prohibited in laws enacted by the state. Without a law, there is no crime; without a law, there is no punishment. Criminology, thus, has the advantage of having a clearer sense of the subject matter at hand. Prostitution is a crime if it is defined as a crime, but— as is the case in some counties of Nevada—if it is not prohibited, it is not criminal to exchange sex for money. Here, too, it is obvious that crime is thus socially constructed.

Sociologists are interested not only in the processes of social construction, but also in the implications that result when certain acts and persons are defined as deviant or criminal, including the effects of the stigma attached to being labeled deviant or criminal, and the varied types of responses of society to such actions. In varied ways these concerns are evident in the four readings in this section.

The Construction of Alcohol Problems

Joseph R. Gusfield

The ability of people to be self-reflexive and to actively engage in various presentations of self in ordinary life constitutes the theoretical basis for Joseph Gusfield's study of competent drinking. Rather than distinguishing drinking behaviors in terms of the amount of alcohol consumed, he suggests that we should distinguish between competent and incompetent drinking, a distinction predicated on how people behave after drinking. Based on ethnographic research in bars, Gusfield examines some of the varied ways bar patrons present images of competent drinking comportment and behavior, how incompetence is recognized, and the various linguistic techniques used to shore up and protect a sense of a competent self.

COMPETENT DRINKING: THE DEFENSE OF THE SELF

Self-Presentation and Exculpatory Defenses: A Theoretical Perspective

Studies of drinking patterns usually distinguish between quantities consumed, identifying drinkers by some typology of heavy, moderate, light, and abstaining (Cahalan, Cisin, and Crossley 1969). We have found it more useful to utilize a classification that has emerged from our observations. It points not to the amounts that drinkers consume but to how they behave in response to their drinking. This distinction—between competent and incompetent drinkers—first came to the attention of one of us in observing blue-collar workers in Chicago bars and was also apparent to us in the San Diego observations (Katarba 1977). It is a distinction essential to understanding how the people we observed conceived the drinking and driving

event in relation to the investment of the self in that phenomena.

The underlying perspective of this study is derived from a general theoretical perspective in use among sociologists and social psychologists. In part it has arisen during the perusal and discussion of our materials; in part it emerges as I type these words.

The notion of the human self as reflexive, as an object to itself, is an old idea in sociology, captured and elucidated in the "old masters" George Herbert Mead (1934) and Charles Cooley (1902). It has also been given more recent implication in the rising interest in reflexivity discussed in the work of Alfred Schutz (1967). The root idea is that one's self is an object about which the human being can think and feel. One can experience self-love, self-hate, embarrassment, or pride in the imagination of the responses and interpretations of one's behavior as perceived by others. This interactive and reflexive aspect of human life emerges in a web of interpretations of the meaning of events for the maintenance, enhancement, or derogation of the self-conception of the social members involved.

In the 1950s and 1960s sociologists and social psychologists gave this orientation considerable attention by examining how it is that members attempt to control and influence the conceptions that others have about them and how external events impinge on such self-conceptions. The primary influence on both study and thought has been the work of Erving Goffman. The title of his first major work, *The Presentation of the Self in Everyday Life*, indicates the primary thrust of the interest in modes by which social members attempt to manage the self-impressions conveyed by their actions (Goffman 1956): "I shall consider the way in which the individual in ordinary work situations presents himself and his activity to others, the ways in which he guides and controls the impression they form of him, and the kinds of things he may and may not do while sustaining his performance before them" (Goffman 1956, Preface).

This general perspective is linked to the drinking-driving phenomena and the instant study by the concepts of "ordinary risk" and "exculpatory defenses." These provide the theoretical and methodological underpinnings of our study of the bars described earlier.

Drinking—including drinking in bars—is part of the ordinary life situation of many Americans and for almost all of the people we observed. It is not an unusual or exotic event. Neither is driving an automobile, although some of our observees either could not or did not do so. Both drinking and driving, thought about separately, are customarily seen as behaviors involving risk. The drinker may lose control of himself, may embarrass himself or others, may insult others, may endanger health or livelihood. The driver may cause accidents and possibly death and, similarly, may be the victim of another driver's "faulty" driving or the dangers of adverse weather or environment. The fact that action is risk does not deter the competent person from engaging in it. Rather, one determination of the competence of people in American society is their ability to undertake "ordinary risks." The adult American who cannot or does not drive an automobile displays a lack of competence to cope adequately with ordinary risk. The member of a drinking group who refuses drinks displays incompetence in drinking. So too, however, do those who engage in the ordinary risks and fail to deal with the risks competently, who cause accidents, create embarrassment, hurt themselves or others, or are unable to perform the needed and expected routine acts of the daily agenda. It is in how the individual handles the risks of drinking and driving and of drinking-driving that the self is presented and one's moral status performed.

It is evident to me and to those we observed that many people at many times fail at the tasks of social assignments. "To err is human." The self swims in dangerous waters where sharks are ready to destroy it. People drink "too much" and make trouble for themselves and others.

People drive "badly" and create accidents. All of us must face a world of audiences before whom we forget our lines, appear unclothed, and miss cues. We must deal with the fact of "fucking up." It too is a part of the normal and ordinary routines of life.

It is also the case, however, that the self is protected from the onus of incompetence by a series of acceptable excuses for poor performance. Borrowing a legal term, I will call these "exculpatory defenses," defenses which excuse an otherwise illegal act from punishment (Hart 1968, ch. 2). Among these are self-defense, insanity, duress, and, most recently, alcohol addiction. To be able to say, "I wasn't myself" is a normal and ordinary defense against the opprobrium of being labeled an incompetent and unworthy person. Illness in this society is (one form of) acceptable defense against the label of incompetence for not being at work or for performing poorly (Parsons and Fox 1952).

It is essential to recognize at the outset that the combination of drinking and driving is a normal event in our observations and, I assert, in American society. Roadside stop studies indicate that for every motorist arrested for driving under the influence of alcohol there are two thousand others on the road with blood alcohol level scores above the legal limit (U.S. Department of Transportation 1974, 2). In our observations most bar customers, whatever the amount they had consumed or their state of intoxication, drove to and from the site without occasioning comment by themselves, other patrons, or the bartenders. It is a normal event in the lives of bar patrons. The failure to drive after drinking is the event that needs to be explained. The competent drinker faces the risk of drinking *and* driving with safety. It is the failure to do so that needs to be excused.

Listening to excuses is an important methodological "device." It is the nature of norms that, being understood and "taken for granted," they are not verbalized. Excuses are necessarily ways of accounting for behavior as unusual. Therefore they indicate, by inference, what is seen as usual as not needing comment.

Understanding how the self is presented and defended is not only important in its own but is also a needed prelude to understanding how these systems of self-presentation operate in the different settings engendered by the bar types described in the earlier portion of this reading.

The Presentation of Competent Drinking

Our observations of tavern patrons have led me to posit a dual system in the display of competence in drinking. The model of the competent drinker is the person who can drink in accordance with the standards of the setting and the group of which he is a part; he can "hold his own." Having done so he does not create trouble, provide embarrassment for himself or others, and will be able to manage himself and his transportation without causing accident or arrest. But drinking is inherently a risky and even unpredictable action. The drinker gets drunk and risks the loss of his competence. Competent people know when they have become incompetent and display their control and competence by that recognition. It is *not* imcompetent to limit drinking, to avoid driving, or to be drunk as long as the drinker can indicate that the determination of the state of incompetence is *his* self-recognition, that it is not forced upon him. Displaying self-understanding of incompetence is a display of competence. To "know enough to come in out of the rain" is a mark of adequacy of intelligence, just as knowing that one is ill and unable to meet usual obligations is a sign of a capable person in this society.

Drinking is itself evidence of meeting the demands of social membership. The amount and kind of alcohol used testifies to the social adequacy of the member. George is a central figure in the heavy-drinking group that frequents the Club. George comes into the Club almost every night and stays for between three and four hours. Ordinarily a heavy drinker of beer, whiskey, or both, sometimes he leaves early or drinks less than is usual. He says then that he must go to work early the next day. This "excuse" indicates that his norm demands keeping up as the mark of adequacy. George is part of the regulars at the Club who buy drinks by the "round," taking turns ordering and paying for drinks for the whole group. In one case, a "kid," aged twenty-four, enters into the round-buying. The observer reports:

> I was drinking a gin and tonic and George was drinking a screwdriver (orange juice and gin). The kid was getting drunk—it was pretty obvious by his slouching in the chair; he started slurring words and turning beet red. I was getting a backlog of drinks since we were buying rounds and this guy was drinking so fast. My drinks were two-deep and George had one-deep. George noticed the guy was getting drunk and commented that he had better slow down because he was getting drunk and to sort of space it out more. The guy continued to drink although he did slow down and mostly talked about his past in the military and working as a horse trainer.

George sees himself as a person who has the ability to drink a lot and yet "hold his liquor." On another occasion, when the observer fell behind in drinking, George took it as a sign that Paul was getting drunk. It was the occasion for George to insist that he drive Paul's car.

Drinking at the level of the "crowd" without incurring more trouble than your peers is the mark of competence, of "manhood." It is not the total amount consumed but the ability to meet the norm without displaying incompetence that is essential. This consideration makes the issue of the bartender's refusal to serve drinks to a customer a significant source of antagonism and conflict.

Behavior after drinking is another sign of adequacy. Not the fact of drunkenness but the nature of comportment and its possible interpretation as improper drunken behavior constitutes the delinquency. On one occasion a young man came into the Club looking as if he'd slept in his clothes. George said, "Oh, shit. This guy is drunk." He explained that when sober this guy was "the nicest guy you'd ever want to meet" but when drunk he was rude, offensive, and "very embarrassing to the management." Ed, the bartender, talked to him, and he left. Ed then explained that they had an understanding. The customer was allowed to stay for short periods of time as long as he didn't drink. Here is clearly the incompetent drinker. Jim, George's roommate, had decided not to go into the Club again. One night the previous week he had gotten extremely drunk and "made an ass of himself."

Driving after drinking is a part of the test of competence. I have already shown this in the way in which George interpreted Paul's slow drinking as a sign of drunkenness and then "decided" to drive Paul's car. The same condition applied in all the bars we observed. We were struck by the limited discussion of drinking-driving and the normal occurrence of it. The issue arose only in certain situations. When bluntly told that he is in no condition to drive, the drinker is held up to an audience as incompetent. At Friendly Al's one night a couple in their late fifties were leaving at about 1:55 A.M. "The man was making a lot of noise, laughing and hollering on his way out. The young bartender hollered over to him to be careful and to take it easy. The man stoically said that he was okay, that he *'can take care of himself'* [italics mine]. In hearing this, his wife laughed loudly and said that her husband was okay because she was doing the driving. The husband gave her a stern look as if embarrassed at her statement about his condition."

On another occasion at Al's, a customer appeared to people at the bar who knew him as too drunk to drive. He got up to leave. As he staggered off the barstool, one of the women hollered out that he should call a taxi. "Jim insisted that he was okay and able to drive home." The two women at the bar laughed and said that he "was really drunker than he figured." The female bartender entered the conversation and laughingly said that he was "too young a man to

take a cab home." Here age appears as related to norms of competence. As we see later, older people can excuse incompetence in ways younger people cannot; the self is undamaged by that act (or perhaps the self is already damaged by age).

The Recognition of Incompetence

In saying that Jim was drunker than he claimed to be, the women at the bar were also derogating Jim's capacity for self-recognition of his incompetence, declaring him incompetent to recognize risks. The oft-repeated statement, "I know when I've had enough" is the drinker insisting on his ability to manage the risks, to distinguish between health and illness.

The following conversation, overheard in Friendly Al's one night, contains both the ingredient of the norm of competent drinking and the self-recognition that the drinker is in too risky a state to drive and can admit it. Notice how the state of incompetence is used to present the drinker as competent in reaching that state:

First man: You're sure as shit driving home tonight.

Second man: No, I ain't. . . . You're the one who's drinking Seven–up. You gotta take care of your buddy, even when you don't have the balls to take care of him by drinking with him.

First man: Don't worry, I'll get you home. I wouldn't strand you on the street at this time of night, would I?

The bartender at the Hermitage used a similar typology of competence to distinguish inabilities for risk. He differentiated between those customers for whom he feels he has to call cabs and "good customers who know when to quit drinking or know when to call a cab for themselves." In the first case he, the bartender, had to decide on their incompetence. The second are the "cool customers." They can "control their drinking and be aware of their incapacities."

We had expected that the Breathalyzer machine at Friendly Al's would be used extensively to provide self-evaluation of the drinker's risk. That was not so. Several evenings it was not used at all. In three- and four-hour observational periods, we never saw it used more than three or four times. Never did we see it used at closing time. Our understanding of the rejection of the machine is that it threatens the image of self-knowledge by which the drinker presents himself as adequate.

In steering conversation at Al's toward discussion of the Breathalyzer machine, our observer met with a discounting of its value. The machine undermined the display of adequacy self-recognition presents. "I asked Marty if he had ever used the Breathalyzer machine. He laughed at my question. He said that *he doesn't need a machine like that to tell him how much he's had*" [italics mine]. A little later the observer used the machine after his fourth drink. It registered a .11, and the machine displayed a large skull and crossbones in red, accompanied by a loud noise. The observer was embarrassed: "As I sat back down, Frank, a customer, laughed and said to me, 'Well, it looks like you'd better stay off the booze for a while.' Then he told me not to worry about it; that it's only a machine and that I looked as if I could handle a lot more booze than he saw me drink that afternoon."

The machine embarrasses. It contradicts the drinker's self-judgment of his state of risk-acceptance. Here it is important to repeat what I have asserted earlier. Drinking and driving is the normal way in which drinkers deal with the issue of getting to and from sites—from bar to bar or bar to a home. Experience shows the individual that almost all the times he has driven after drinking he has had neither an accident nor an arrest—the two risks that the drinking driver heightens by his action. He demonstrates his competence by recognizing his ability to drive and to know when he is in danger, when he ought not to drive or ought to take special precautions. Even George, at the Club, whose pride in his ability to hold his liquor has been stated, did ask the observer to do the driving one night,

admitting that he had had too much. As one informant at That Place put it, "guys who get themselves in trouble while they're drinking and driving are just plain dumb and don't know how to handle themselves."

Are the studies of drinking and driving on which legislation is based really incorrect? Is drinking and driving not dangerous? In part the distinction must be made between risky events and riskier events. While increased amounts of alcohol, after a point, raise the risks of accident as compared to sobriety, the possibility of any single event ending in accident remains small (Borkenstein et al. 1964; Cameron 1978; Zylman 1975). Faced with practical contingencies, which I will discuss later, the drinker's attitude is not without a rational basis. Faced with the practical problem of getting from one place to another, his experience tells him that most of the time he will make it without adverse outcomes. He displays his competence in showing that he has not gone beyond the state of drunkenness in which the risk is no longer reasonable and that when he has, he can recognize it and act like a reasonably drunken man should in a situation of greatly heightened risk.

There is also another aspect, however. Riding with the San Diego Police Department's drinking-driver squad several years ago, I became aware that one rule of thumb used by some police to "spot" drinking-drivers was to look for the overly careful driver. The premise here is that drivers who know they are "under the influence" adjust their driving to take account of their state of insobriety. This exists among those we observed. In conversations about drinking-driving some maintained that they were good drivers and did nothing special, although one said that he did drive particularly carefully because he is driving his buddy's car. Some take great pride in the ability to drive while under the influence. The bouncer at That Place commented on his customers: he said that he had never called a cab for a customer. ". . . most of the guys who come into That

Place pride themselves on being good drivers, even when they're totally loaded . . . you just have to look at their 'wheels' . . . some of them do a lot of racing, on and off the road . . . it's kind of a touchy thing to talk to a customer about his ability to drive home, whether or not he's drunk or sober. . . ." He thought that even some of the customers who are really drunked up have very little trouble driving home because of their expertise behind the wheel.

In his observations of blue-collar bars in Chicago, Joseph Kotarba had found a great deal of discussion of how to drive after drinking and how to avoid police. We had hoped in the San Diego study to gain knowledge of how the drinker adjusts his or her driving to the self-recognition of being under the influence and how it is that the drinker can recognize when he is competent to drive, when he needs to adjust his driving, and when he is in such danger as to avoid driving. "Taking care" is the term that is in frequent use, but its operational meaning is seldom specified. Minimizing "normal" risks appears in occasional references to driving slower and attending to rules. If there is a culture of the art of drinking-driving we were unable to find it in this study. It is ironic that in all the vast research and writing on drinking-driving, there is no study that has attempted to find out how people *do* drive after drinking.

There is one exception to our failure. We did find some mention of techniques for avoiding police arrest. Given the belief that competent people can "handle" the drinking-driver problem, arrest is a comment on competence. The implicit assumption is that adequate drinkers don't get caught. Driving along side streets, for example, is noted as one way of avoiding detection if the drinker sees himself as "under the influence." Driving slow on streets where traffic makes the presence of police difficult to spot is another. Avoiding "jerkiness" in driving and staying inside the lanes are others.

Throughout our observations we were struck by the general lack of comment about drinking-driving. When it emerges in conversation it does so in response to a particular occasion—a person who is thought to be in an especially dangerous state, a history of arrests, a group (women, aged, handicapped) who require special consideration. Drinking-driving is considered a normal event and adjunct to other activities. The risk is understood, but it is the risk that normal, adequate people cope with.

In the following colloquy between the observer and a twenty-one-year-old sailor at That Place the elements of drinking-driving are subordinated and set within a frame of other activities. To this sailor trouble with driving after drinking is a gross display of incompetence; it is the self derogated:

(Bill comes into That Place once or so a week. He says that he also spends a lot of time at other, smaller bars in the general area. He uses a friend's car.)

Bill said that the sailors are regularly briefed by the brass about problems with police and bars and so forth. He said that very few of the sailors really pay much mind to these briefings . . . the sailors don't really have much choice in either drinking or not drinking or driving or not driving . . . most of the guys had one thing on their minds—pussy. He said that there is really not much else to do around San Diego besides hopefully looking for women and drinking . . . the guys just won't give that up . . . he later said that its no big deal to be concerned about drinking and driving while being stationed in San Diego . . . you just have to be smart and look out for yourself like you have to do in all other places in San Diego . . . a sailor will get ripped off if he just stays down on Broadway [main downtown street] and that the same guy who gets ripped off by the whores on Broadway and the shopkeepers on Broadway are the guys who are going to be stopped by the police for something as dumb as drunk-driving.

Exculpatory Defenses: Protecting the Competent Self

Our method is the reverse of the traditional question in drinking and driving studies. Why do people drink and drive? is not my question. That formulation makes the illegal act the deviant and problematic one. Instead I am operating from the premise which our observations support: *not* driving after drinking is the deviant and problematic act. What is to be explained is: Why *don't* people drink and drive? Action that accords with law and public, official norms is the problem, the behavior that in this case cries for explanation.

It is the problem which those we observed see in the bar interactions. The drinker, his friends, the bartender never were observed explaining their driving unless challenged not to, unless advised to forgo driving. It is the "abnormal" act that has to be defended, the threat to being presented as incompetent that must be coped with. It is here that exculpatory defenses, legitimate excuses, come into use. They permit the user to avoid the drinking-driving situation and yet display himself as an adequate drinker, able to cope with the responsibilities entailed by engaging in the risk of drinking in a sober world.

I want to be clear about the status of our data. We are not presenting behavior. My interest is in the typologies by which those we observe themselves understand and observe behavior, what I refer to as Schutz's first-order typologies, those in use by the actors themselves. In examining excuses I am not concerned with exhaustively describing or counting the situations in which drinkers drive. My interest is in answering the question: Are there ways in which the drinker can avoid driving and yet retain the display of adequate drinking ability? Such ways indicate the existence of typologies within the culture and available to persons. It does not indicate either the range of availability—to whom and where—nor the incidence of the use of such typologies. For example, we found that past arrest for drinking-driving was a legitimate excuse for not driving or for calling a taxi or for allowing others to drive. This does not mean that past offenders do not drink and drive or that past of-

fenders customarily avoid driving. We did observe several situations in which drinkers we knew to be past offenders did drink and drive. What it does mean is that the past offender can preserve the display of self-competence even though he avoids driving.

Some of this discussion of exculpatory defenses has already been presented, and more of it will be presented in the discussion of how intimates and bartenders act to control the drinking-driving situation. Here I present some general types of excuses in use.

In one model case—the competent self—the drinker demonstrates that he can both drink and drive. The bartender at the Hermitage summed it up in explaining why he doesn't have much concern for an older customer who drinks heavily throughout the day: "Men must be responsible for their own drinking." In the second case the drinker recognizes his drinking has made him incompetent and admits it. Samuel is a frequent customer at the Club. He is not a chronic drunk, but when he does get drunk he is close to passing out. He allows himself to be driven home by others and puts up no resistance.

The second model, however, has several difficulties as a display of self and as a practical way of behavior. It depends on self-recognition, and thus ambiguity, and it does lessen the display of competence. It is a second level of competence. Other excuses also exist and are in use.

Responsible people, in the cultures we observed, are able to meet their self-responsibilities in assuming risk. When they are responsible to others, however, the degree of risk to be undertaken changes. The issue of drinking-driving when children are passengers did not, of course, arise in our data. However, within the general culture and within our experience with drinking-driving cases in court, in the mass media, and in the literature of publicity about it, the drinking-driver who takes risks with children is more heinous than one who risks only himself or other adults.

Responsibility to an abstract "society" or to others is too vague and unsituated a concept to emerge in conversation or action. What the drinker owes to others to avoid risk is more specific than that.

One repeated situation in which responsibility is stated is in the relations of men toward women. One of the bartenders at Friendly Al's reports an instance in which the Breathalyzer machine changed behavior. One late Saturday afternoon two young men, in their twenties, tried the Breathalyzer machine in a spirit of fun. Scoring .12 and .14 respectively, one said to the other, "Boy, we've got dates tonight. We'd better cool it." The date as control appears in several other places. The responsibility of wives for husbands and husbands for wives makes the inability of the drinker to carry out that responsibility a particularly notable dereliction of duty. At about 1:45 A.M. a wife was observed trying to get her reluctant husband to go home. She threatened to go home with someone else if he would not let her drive. At the end of their argument she shouted: "You fucking drunk! You're the one who forces me to have to take care of myself."

Another available exculpatory defense is the responsibility to work. It is often unclear whether it is a responsibility to self to avoid unemployment or to others to perform cooperative duties. I have already discussed this as an excuse for minimizing drinking. It also appeared as an excuse for shifting the driving responsibility. A wife was observed to get her husband to let her drive on the grounds that though they are both tired and have been drinking he must get up early the next morning for work. Using a similar logic one of the bartenders at the Hermitage, in describing the daytime and lunchtime drinkers, points out that afternoon work keeps them from drinking too much and can excuse some others because even though they drive they are marvelously able to handle heavy drinking. "Mark said that most of the men do not drink too much during the day because they have to drive, especially the salesmen."

There are special categories of people for whom the norms of competent driving demanded of drinkers are less pressing. Women, the elderly, past convicted offenders for drinking-driving, the "problem drinker" all receive special consideration and can be excused from displaying the level of competence expected of others.

Several such problem drinkers were observed at the Club. These were known to the bartender and to a number of the customers as people who came and drank to the point of passing out, woke up, and drank again. These problem drinkers called a taxi and made no effort to drive. In calling them "problem drinkers" I am using the sense of those in the bar that these people were incompetent, accepted their incompetence, and were given special consideration. Harold illustrates how the display of this persona permits him to handle the drinking-driving problem in a way which maintains his esteem in the eyes of his audience:

> Harold is a guy who's been described as worth several million dollars in property . . . according to what I'd heard he was pretty powerful in local politics. . . .
> Harold claimed that he'd had five arrests on 502s. What he usually does is get drunk in the morning, passes out in the car or takes a taxi home, wakes up and starts drinking until he passes out again . . . tonight he only had five drinks . . . by the time he left he was totally drunk. (There was much joking about how Harold would buy the bar and fire the bartender if he refused to serve him.)
> After Harold left I was the only one in the bar and talked to Frank, the bartender, about Harold, confirming that much of what Harold said was true. I asked him about how he handled Harold's drinking. Frank's attitude was that Harold was basically *a harmless drunk* [italics mine]. He always knew that Harold would not go out and drive drunk but that he would either sleep it off in the car or take a taxi or have a friend drive.

On one evening we observed that Harold drove to the Club in his camper, got drunk as usual, and then slept in the camper parked on the parking lot in front of the bar.

It is also the case that drinkers can use past arrests for drinking-driving as explanations for their concern with the problem in a given situation. It can make their avoidance of driving understandable and reasonable. The principle here appears to be that where the risk is greater or the consequences more detrimental, the competent person recognizes it and acts with greater circumspection than the norm.

Whether or not this principle "explains" the special position of women and older people is not clear. But what is clear is that both groups constitute categories that are excused for the avoidance of driving and that can entail special responsibility on others. Bartenders were observed asking other customers to take an older person or a woman home when they appeared too drunk to drive safely, a less "touchy" situation than suggesting similar help to a young man. Women in the Club have greater license to "choose" how much they want to drink. Both in the Club and in Friendly Al's women received a special status. (That Place was more patently a "pickup" bar and presented a very different kind of status for women.)

An observation at Al's illustrates how categorical differences can operate. One night an "old man" staggered over to the bar from the back of the room and said something to one of the women which caused her anger. Some of the men at the bar told her to ignore him "because he's old and drunked up." A few minutes later the bartender did something that the observer had not seen before. He told the old man he thought he's had enough and should make his way home. The old man did not object, and the bartender said he was going to call a cab, which he did. It was also typical at Friendly Al's for some of the young women not to drive but to take taxis.

In one sense the special status of women is observed in instances of departure from the special role of women drinkers. This is seen in the observation of two women who entered the Club late one evening, one in her late twenties and the other around fifty. They had been drinking elsewhere and had come to the Club when the Shack closed. (One of them said that she'd been "loaded" for the last several nights, would get "loaded" again tonight and call in sick tomorrow.) They annoyed the bartender by their abrasiveness and by demanding that he keep the bar open after 2:00 A.M. Though the men at the Club do not swear in front of women, these women often used words like *fuck* in their conversation. In a bar ordinarily solicitous of women driving when they were drunk, they were permitted to leave without any warning, remarks of concern, or offer of help.

The same independent status of women is seen in That Place. There an offer by a male to drive a woman home is interpreted as a sexual proposal and acceptance considered an assent.

Women and older men constitute major groups toward whom customers and bartenders display a special solicitousness. Children, of course, would probably also be included in such categories, but the prohibition against serving minors (strongly enforced and strongly obeyed by the bars we observed) finesses that problem. There is some hint of a norm of greater solicitousness of men toward young men ("kids") or women toward younger women, in references to the "kid" character of a youngish drinker in explaining his incompetence or in the remark of one woman at That Place about her younger sister. Told that she was in the back throwing up, Jenny laughed at this information and said her sister was "too young to mix in cheap dope with booze." Nonownership or use of cars was seen among older men and women, not among the other men. Harry, a regular bartender at Friendly Al's, worries about the older customers who live nearby and have a long way to walk or are walking along the street at night. Sometimes, he says, he drives them home after closing time.

I want to remark that I have described the display of the competent self without much reference to what the audience of other patrons and bar employees do to structure, or control, the stage of action. Nor have I indicated the shape, size, or limits and opportunities afforded by different kinds of settings. The idea of the competent self, the ways in which display is affected and incompetence excused is not set aside.

REFERENCES

Borkenstein, R. F., et al. 1964. *The role of the drinking driver in traffic accidents.* Department of Police Administration, Indiana University, Bloomington, Indiana.

Cahalan, D., I. H. Cisin, and H. M. Crossley. 1969. *American drinking practices: A national study of drinking behavior and attitudes.* New Brunswick, N.J.: Rutgers Center of Alcohol Studies.

Cameron, T. 1978. Alcohol and traffic. In *Alcohol, casualties and crime: Report C-18*, edited by M. Arrens, et al. Berkeley: Social Research Group.

Cooley, C. H. 1902. *Human nature and the social order.* New York: Charles Scribner's Sons.

Goffman, E. 1956. *The presentation of the self in everyday life.* Edinburgh: University of Edinburgh Social Sciences Research Centre.

Hart, H. L. A. 1968. *Punishment and responsibility: Essays in the philosophy of law.* Oxford: Clarendon Press.

Kotarba, J. 1977. The serious side of tavern sociability. Paper presented to the Society for the Study of Social Problems, August.

Mead, G. H. 1934. *Mind, self, and society: From the standpoint of a social behaviorist.* Chicago: University of Chicago Press.

Parsons, T., and R. Fox. 1952. Illness, therapy and the modern urban American family. *Journal of Social Issues* 8:31–44.

Schutz, A. 1967. *The phenomenology of the social world.* Evanston, IL: Northwestern University Press.

U.S. Department of Transportation. 1974. National Highway Traffic Safety Administration. Office of Driver and Pedestrian Programs. *Alcohol safety action projects, evaluation of operations*, vol. 2. Evaluation of the Enforcement Countermeasure Activities. DOT HS801 77. Washington, D.C.: USGPO.

Zylman, R. 1975. Mass arrests for impaired driving may not prevent traffic deaths. In *Alcohol, drugs and traffic safety*, edited by S. Israelstam and S. Lambert. Toronto: Addiction Research Foundation of Ontario.

DISCUSSION QUESTIONS

1. Using the distinction Gusfield makes between competent and incompetent drinkers, offer examples from campus drinking behavior to create a local typology of the various types of competence and incompetence.
2. On the basis of what Gusfield discovered regarding decisions to drink and drive or refrain from driving, what policies might seem most likely to discourage impaired drinkers from driving?

READING 15

Spectator Violence at Football Matches

Eric Dunning, Patrick Murphy, and John Williams

Soccer has been plagued by spectator violence in a number of countries, but perhaps nowhere has this been more problematic than in England. British sociologists of sport Eric Dunning and his associates explore the phenomenon of "football hooliganism" in this essay in an effort to offer a sociological understanding of who is typically involved in such violence and what are the underlying causes of fan violence. Of central importance to their account is the connection they draw between the lower-working-class origins of hooligans and notions of masculinity.

FOOTBALL HOOLIGANISM AS A SOCIAL PHENOMENON

As a form of behaviour, the disorderliness of football fans that has come to attract the label "football hooliganism" is complex and many sided. In popular usage, for example, the label embraces swearing and behaviour which, in other contexts, would be excused as simple "high spirits" or "horseplay." In fact, many of the fans who are arrested in a football context have only engaged in such relatively minor misdemeanours. In the more serious manifestations, however, the label refers to pitch invasions that appear to be deliberately engineered in order to halt a match and, perhaps most seriously of all, to large-scale fracas between opposing fan groups that are often violent and destructive. It is with this latter form of the phenomenon that we are principally concerned. More specifically, the evidence suggests that, although many fans are *drawn* into hooligan incidents—fans who did not set out for the match with disruptive intent—the hard core, those who engage most persistently in hooligan behaviour in a football context, view fighting and aggressive behaviour as an integral part of "going to the match." Such fans are frequently skilled at evading detection and arrest, and hence do not always appear in the police statistics. "Frank," a 26-year-old lorry driver and self-confessed "football hooligan" who was interviewed by Paul Harrison after the 1974 Cardiff City v. Manchester United game, can serve as an example. He is reported by Harrison as having said:

> I go to a match for one reason only: the aggro. It's an obsession, I can't give it up. I get so much pleasure when I'm having aggro that I nearly wet my pants . . . I go all over the country looking for it . . . every night during the week we go around town looking for trouble. Before a match we go round looking respectable . . . then if we see someone who looks like the enemy we ask him the time; if he answers in a foreign accent, we do him over; and if he's got any money on him we'll roll him as well.[1]

Frank may well have exaggerated the extent of his involvement in and enjoyment of "aggro." Indeed, if all his claims were true, he would probably be dubbed by other fans, even most football hooligans, as a "nutter" or a "loony."[2] Nevertheless, the interest in fighting he displays, the concern with the generation of pleasurable excitement in a fight situation, has features that appear to be common to the lifestyles of "hard-core" football hooligans. Sociologically, the point is to explain why. More specifically, why is it that adolescent and young adult males from particular groups within the socio-economically lowest sections of the working class have come to develop a strong interest in and enjoyment of fighting? Why does openly aggressive behaviour form such an important part of their lifestyle? And why has football come to form such an attractive and persistent venue for its expression? Before we turn to these complex questions, let us first sketch in some of the principal forms that football hooligan confrontations take.

THE FORMS OF FOOTBALL HOOLIGAN CONFRONTATIONS

Football hooligan confrontations take a number of different forms and they can take place in a variety of contexts besides the football ground itself. They can, for example, take the form of hand-to-hand fighting between just two rival supporters or between two small groups of them. Alternatively, they can involve up to several hundred fans on either side. In the most serious incidents, weapons—lightweight and easily concealed Stanley knives are favoured at the moment—are sometimes used. Football hooligan confrontations can also take the form of aerial bombardments using as ammunition missiles that range from innocuous items such as peanuts, bits of orange peel, apple cores and paper cups, to more dangerous, even potentially lethal ones, such as darts, metal discs, coins (sometimes with their edges sharpened), broken seats, bricks, slabs of concrete, ball bearings, fireworks, smoke bombs and, as has happened on one or two occasions, crude petrol bombs.

Missile throwing can take place inside or outside the ground, and, at Leicester City recently, a pitch invasion by some 200 Arsenal fans was sparked off because they were the objects of an attack with bricks and other missiles by Leicester City fans who were *outside* the ground. As a consequence of the official policy of segregating rival fans—a policy introduced in the 1960s as a means of preventing football hooliganism but which appears to have had greater success in enhancing the solidarity of "football ends" and driving the phenomenon outside grounds—large-scale fights on the terraces became relatively rare during the 1970s and early 1980s. Small groups of fans, however, still managed frequently to infiltrate the territories of their rivals in order to start a fight or create a wider disturbance. Participating in a successful "invasion"—"taking" somebody else's "end"—is a source of great kudos in football hooligan circles. More usually nowadays, however, the fighting takes place either in the unsegregated seated sections of grounds or before the match, for instance in and around town centre pubs. It also takes place after the match when the police are trying to keep the rival fans apart and to get the main body of away supporters to the railway or bus station without serious incident. It is then that the largest-scale confrontations tend to occur. These often start with a "run," that is with a rush of as many as 200 or 300 young male fans who charge along the street looking for opposing fans or for a breach in the police defences that will enable them to make contact with their rivals. The "hard-core" hooligans, however, those who are most committed in their desire to engage groups of the opposing team's supporters, often operate apart from the main body and use elaborate tactics in their attempts to outflank the police. If they are successful,

what usually takes place is a series of skirmishes scattered over a relatively large area involving young males from either side, punching, kicking and chasing each other, dodging in and out of moving traffic and, occasionally, attacking vehicles carrying rival supporters. Confrontations can also take place when groups of rival fans *en route* to different matches meet, for instance on trains, the underground and at motorway service stations. In addition, fights also sometimes occur *within* particular fan groups, the participants in such cases being drawn, for example, from different housing estates in the same general locality.

In our research, we have been particularly interested in what the football hooligans themselves and other young fans call "fighting crews," especially those of the 'super-hooligan' groups which have evolved in recent years at some of the larger clubs. Members of such groups—such as the self-styled "Inter City Firm" at West Ham, the "Service Crew" at Leeds, and the comparable groups at clubs like Newcastle United and Chelsea—often support extreme right-wing, racist organizations such as the British Movement and the National Front. They have also developed quite sophisticated forms of organization and become nationally known. One of their main distinguishing marks is the fact that they do not travel to matches on "football specials" and official coaches but tend, instead, to use regular rail and coach services or cars and hired vans. They also eschew the forms of dress—the scarves and favours (and also the club banners)—that still tend to be widely associated with football hooliganism in popular opinion. One of their main objectives in attending matches is to confront and fight opposing fans and to "take their end." Fans of this kind travel without identifying colours in order to avoid advertising themselves too soon to rival fans and the police. This emerged in the case of "Frank," the fan interviewed by Harrison, but it is also clear in the description provided by "Howie," a 20-year-old Leicester "hard case." "Howie" told us:

If you can baffle the coppers you'll win. You've just gotta think how they're gonna think. And you know, half the time you know what they're gonna do, 'cos they're gonna take the same route every week, week in, week out. If you can figure out a way to beat 'em, you're fuckin' laughin', you'll have a good fuckin' raut [Leicester slang for a fight]. That's why I never wear a scarf, in case I go in [the opposition's] side. I used to wear a scarf but [the police] used to fuckin' come and stop me. Used to grab the scarf and go, "bang, bang." I thought, I ain't havin' that. Take it off, they can't grab hold of you.

"Hard cases" such as "Frank" and "Howie" gave up wearing scarves and identifying favours long ago, but it is worth stressing that very few fans nowadays who go to football partly or mainly for "the action" sport such marks of identification. Nor do many of them follow the skinhead style that was so popular in the late 1960s and 1970s. Instead, and although there are regional and "end-specific" variations, they tend to dress according to the dictates of current youth fashion, partly because the older "hooligan uniforms" are regarded as anachronistic and lacking in "style," and partly, as we have said, to avoid advertising themselves too soon to opposing fans and the police.

This general description of some of the main parameters of football hooliganism and some of the changes that aspects of it have recently undergone is consistent with the central point we made earlier, namely that the youths and young men involved in the most serious incidents tend to view fighting and confrontations with opposing supporters as an integral part of attending a football match. The songs and chants which form a conspicuous feature of inter-fan group rivalry, especially inside the stadium, point in the same direction. Although some of the "hardest" lads regard singing and chanting as "soft," and tend not to get involved in it, during a match the rival groups direct their attention as much and sometimes more to one another as they do to the match itself, singing, chanting and gesticulating

en masse and in what one might call spontaneously orchestrated uniformity as expressions of their opposition. Their songs and chants are in part related to the match but they also have as a recurrent theme challenges to fight, threats of violence towards the opposing fans and boasts about past victories. Each fan group has its own repertoire of songs and chants but many of these are local variations on a stock of common themes. Central in this connection is the fact that their lyrics are punctuated with words like "hate," "die," "fight," "kick," "surrender," all of which convey images of battle and conquest.[3] Apart from violence, symbolic demasculinization of the rival fans is another recurrent terrace theme, for example the reference to them and/or the team they support as "poofs" or "wankers," the latter accompanied by a mass gestural representation of the male masturbatory act. Yet another recurring theme is denigration of the community of the opposing fans. Let us turn now to the subject of explanation.

OFFICIAL EXPLANATIONS OF FOOTBALL HOOLIGANISM

Two main official explanations of football hooliganism have been proposed and both seem to be widely accepted, namely that it is caused by drinking and/or by violence on the field of play. Both have severe limitations and, to the extent that they contain partly valid elements, they need to be set within a wider explanatory framework. Drinking, for example, cannot be said to be a significant or "deep" cause of football hooliganism for the simple reason that not every fan who drinks, even heavily, takes part in hooligan acts. Nor does every hooligan drink, though a stress, not only on fighting but also on heavy drinking, is integrally involved in the masculinity norms that are expressed in their behaviour. In fact, such fans tend to be relatively aggressive even without drink. Similarly, violence in a match is not invariably followed by hooligan incidents. Nor are all hooligan incidents preceded by violence on the field—this is obviously the case, for example, with pre-match confrontations. But to say this is not to deny the fact that drinking and on-the-pitch violence are sometimes causally implicated in the sequences of events that are typically involved in football hooligan fighting. In order to see how that is the case, one has to think in terms of a *hierarchy* of causes and, in this sense, violence on the field and drinking can be said to be causally implicated in the generation of football hooliganism in a surface sense. This is a complex issue and we do not have the space to go into details here. It must be enough to say that alcohol consumption is one of a series of conditions that can facilitate football hooligan violence, and that it does so because alcohol is an agent which lowers inhibitions. In the case of hooligan fans, it helps to generate a sense of heightened camaraderie in the group and also aids them in combating, on the one hand, their fear to being hurt in a fight and, on the other, their fear of being apprehended by the police. The latter prospect is a real one since, although football hooliganism does not constitute an offence as such, their behaviour often contravenes specific laws and takes place in public places where there is usually a large police presence designed explicitly to prevent it. In fact, the brush with the authorities—those at various levels of the football world and not just the police—can be a significant source of the excitement generated in football hooligan encounters. Football hooliganism also provides the fans involved with an opportunity to act out hostilities with the police established in a non-football context and gives them a public stage for expressing their disregard for "respectable" values.[4]

Similarly, violence on the pitch can serve as a trigger for football hooliganism, but so can a whole series of other contingencies such as heavy and injudicious policing, a desire to avenge a defeat inflicted in fighting at an earlier match, and the desire of one fan group to knock another off the pedestal onto which the media have placed them. We are referring here to the sort of notoriety given by the media to "Doc's Red Army," that is to Manchester United fans, in the 1970s, and to Chelsea and Leeds United fans today. In fact, the media have played a part in creating a national status hierarchy of football hooligans and a struggle for status between the different "football ends." In other words, there are currently two league tables as far as hooligan fans are concerned: one is official, the other unofficial and in part media-created. The first is about matches won or lost and league points gained. The second is about who ran, where and from whom, and who are currently branded by officialdom and the media as the most "evil" and "destructive" hooligans in the country. In short, what we are suggesting is that, whilst these popularly accepted official explanations in terms of alcohol consumption and violence on the field of play refer to factors that cannot be ruled out as elements in the determination of football hooligan behaviour, they fail to penetrate deeply into the hierarchy of causes, that is to the phenomenon's causal roots. More particularly, they say nothing about the way in which the enjoyment of fighting and a stress on the ability to 'look after oneself' are generated among hooligan fans, about the norms and standards which govern their behaviour, or about the reasons why football has come to form one of the most persistent venues for expressing them. The same is arguably true about the majority of academic explanations that have so far been proposed. It is to some among the more prominent of these academic explanations that our attention will now be turned.

FOOTBALL HOOLIGANISM AND THE LOWER WORKING CLASS: "ORDERED SEGMENTATION" AND THE FORMATION OF FAN-GROUP ALLIANCES

Information on the social origins of the fans who fight at football matches is currently rather scarce, but data on those convicted for football-related offences are consistent with our own from participant observation and suggest that the phenomenon is predominantly the preserve of the lower working class. The Harrington Report, for example, concluded in 1968 that "the present evidence suggests that . . . [football hooligans] are mainly from a working-class background with the special problems inherent in large industrial cities and ports where violent and delinquent subcultures are known to exist."[5] Over a decade later, Trivizas reached a similar conclusion, namely that 80 percent of the persons charged with football-related offences were manual workers or unemployed.[6] Harrison's account of Cardiff City's "committed rowdies" in 1974 had them coming from "Canton and Grangetown, rows of terraced houses with few open spaces, and from Llanrumney, a massive council estate with an appalling record of vandalism."[7] And although, as we suggested earlier, Marsh and his colleagues did not directly address the issue of class background in the course of the Oxford study, some of their informants did provide relevant comments. For example, one of them said:

> If you live up on the Leys [a local council estate], then you have to fight or else people piss you about and think you're a bit soft or something.[8]

In fact, over half of the large contingent of Oxford fans arrested during serious disturbances at the Coventry City v. Oxford United FA Cup match in January 1981 came from the estate in question.[9] Evidence from Leicester supports this general picture, with one local lower working-class council estate accounting for around one-fifth of the local fans arrested at the Filbert Street stadium between January 1976 and April 1980. This raises the question of what it is about the structure of such communities and the position they occupy in society at large that generates and sustains the pattern of aggressive masculinity that some of their members display in a football context and elsewhere?

As we suggested earlier, a useful lead in this connection is provided by the work of Gerald Suttles. His research was carried out in Chicago and focused on communities whose overall pattern, as he put it, was one "where age, sex, ethnic and territorial units are fitted together like building blocks to create a larger structure."[10] He coined the term "ordered segmentation" in order to capture two related features of the pattern of life in such communities: firstly the fact that, while the segments that make up larger neighbourhoods are relatively independent of each other, the members of these segments nevertheless have a tendency regularly to combine in the event of opposition and conflict, and that they do so without central co-ordination; and, secondly, the fact that these group alignments tend to build up according to a fixed sequence.[11] This pattern is similar in certain respects to what happens in the "segmental lineage systems" discussed by anthropologists such as Evans-Pritchard.[12] Robins and Cohen claim to have observed a pattern of this kind on a North London working-class estate,[13] and, more significantly for present purposes, Harrison refers to what he calls "the Bedouin syndrome" in the contemporary football context,[14] namely a pattern in which there is a tendency for ad hoc alliances to be built up according to the following principles: the friend of a friend is a friend; the enemy of an enemy is a friend; the friend of an enemy is an enemy; the enemy of a friend is an enemy.[15]

Our own observations provide some evidence to support the existence of such a pattern both on working-class estates and in the football context. In Leicester, intra-estate conflicts involving groups of young male adolescents regularly give way to the requirements of defending the "good name" of the estate as a whole against rival "gangs" that represent neighbouring estates. However, lads from these estates and others from Leicester and the surrounding area stand side by side on the Filbert Street terraces and outside the ground in the cause of expressing "home end" solidarity in opposition to visiting fans. If the challenge is perceived in regional terms, then, again, enemies may join forces. For example, Northern fans visiting London often complain about confrontations with combined "fighting crews" from a number of metropolitan clubs. Euston Station used to be a favourite venue for encounters of this kind. David Robins even refers to alliances between fans of smaller, neighbouring clubs in London such as QPR and Chelsea, and Orient and West Ham, for purposes of confronting the fans of their larger metropolitan rivals.[16] Southerners and Midlanders visiting the North, especially the larger northern towns, also voice complaints about attacks by inter-end alliances. Finally, at an international level, club and regional rivalries tend to be subordinated to the interests of national reputation. At each of these levels, moreover, particularly if opposing groups are not present in sufficient numbers or if the challenge they offer is not, or is not perceived to be, sufficient to unite otherwise rival fans in common opposition, lower-level rivalries sometimes re-emerge. Having established how it operates in a football context, let us probe the structure of "ordered segmentation" in greater detail.

THE SOCIOGENESIS OF "AGGRESSIVE MASCULINITY"

To the extent that their structures correspond to "ordered segmentation," lower working-class communities tend to generate standards which, relative to those of groups higher in the social hierarchy, are conducive to and/or tolerate a high level of open aggressiveness in social relations. Several aspects of the structure of such communities tend to work in this direction. For example, the comparative freedom from adult control experienced by lower working-class children and adolescents, the fact that so much of their early socialization takes place in the street in the company mainly of their age peers, means that they tend to interact aggressively

among themselves and to develop dominance hierarchies that are based largely on age, strength and physical prowess.[17] This pattern is reinforced by the fact that, relative to the tendency of adults higher up the social scale, lower working-class parents exert less pressure on their growing children to exercise strict and continuous self-control over aggressive behaviour. To the extent that parents in the lower working class do attempt to restrain their children in this regard, there is a greater tendency for them to resort to physical punishment. Moreover, such children become more accustomed from an early age to seeing their parents and other adults, especially males, behave in an aggressive and not infrequently violent way. As a result, they tend to grow up with a more positive attitude towards aggressive behaviour than their counterparts higher up the social scale and to be less inhibited about witnessing and publicly taking part in violent acts.[18]

Also crucial to the formation of this pattern is the tendency towards segregation of the sexes, and male dominance in communities of this sort. This means, on the one hand, that such communities tend to be characterized by a comparatively high rate of male violence towards women, and, on the other, that their male members are not consistently subjected to "softening" female pressure. Indeed, to the extent that the women in such communities grow up to be relatively aggressive themselves and to value many of the *macho* characteristics of their men, the aggressive propensities of the latter are liable to be compounded. Further reinforcement comes from the comparative frequency of feuds and vendettas between families, neighbourhoods and, above all, "street-corner gangs." In short, lower working-class communities of the type we are describing, especially those sections of them to which the adjective "rough" most literally applies, appear to be characterized by "feedback" processes which encourage the resort to aggressive behaviour in many areas of social relations, especially on the part of males.

One of the effects of these processes is the conferring of prestige on males with a proven ability to fight. Correlatively, there is a tendency for such males to enjoy fighting. For them and their peers who strive to emulate them, it is an important source of meaning, status and pleasurable emotional arousal. The central difference in this regard between these "rough" sections of lower working-class communities and their "respectable" counterparts in the upper, middle and working classes appears to be that, in the latter, violence in face-to-face relations tends to be normatively condemned, whilst, in the former, there are a greater number of contexts and situations in which the open expression of aggression and violence is tolerated or positively sanctioned. A further difference is that there is a tendency in the "respectable" classes for violence to be "pushed behind the scenes" and, when it does occur, for it to take, on balance, a more obviously "instrumental" form and to lead to the arousal of feelings of guilt. By contrast, in the communities of the "rough" working class, violence tends to occur to a greater extent in public and to involve, on balance, more pronounced "expressive" or "affectual" qualities, that is qualities more closely associated with the arousal of pleasurable feelings. Furthermore, whilst members of the "respectable" classes, especially "respectable" males, are allowed, indeed expected, to behave aggressively in specific contexts that are defined as "legitimate," such as formal sport, members of the "rough" working class tend either to regard formal sport as too regulated and "tame,"[19] or, when they do take part, they tend, on account of their overly physical, sometimes violent approach, to fall foul of officials and opposing players.[20]

The identities of males from the "rough" sections of the lower working class thus tend to be based on what are, relative to the standards dominant in Britain today, openly aggressive forms of *macho* masculinity. Many males of this kind also have a high emotional investment in the reputations of their families, their communities and, where they are into "the football action," their "ends" as aggressive and tough. This pattern is produced and reproduced, not only by the constituent *internal* elements of "ordered segmentation" but also—and this is equally crucial—by some of the ways in which their communities are locked into the wider society. For example, lower working-class males are typically denied status, meaning and gratification in the educational and occupational spheres, the major sources of identity, meaning and status available to men higher up the social scale. This denial comes about as a result of a combination of factors. For example, the majority of lower working-class males do not have—nor do they typically prize—the characteristics and values that make for educational and occupational success or for striving in these fields. At the same time, they tend to be systematically discriminated against in the worlds of school and work, in part because they find themselves at the bottom of a hierarchical structure which seems to require a relatively permanent and relatively impoverished "underclass" as a constituent feature.[21]

Because it is difficult for males from the "rough" sections of the lower working class to achieve meaning, status and gratification and to form satisfying identities in the fields of school and work, there is a greater tendency for them to rely for these purposes on forms of behaviour that include physical intimidation, fighting, heavy drinking, and exploitative sexual relations. In fact, they tend to have many of the characteristics attributed by Adorno and his colleagues to the "authoritarian personality."[22] It is, of course, possible for these *macho* lower-class males to develop forms of relatively high self-esteem on the basis of local and, above all, peer group acknowledgement of their toughness, their prowess as fighters, their courage, their loyalty to the group, their exploits as drinkers, and generally because they handle themselves in a manner that they and their peers consider to be "streetwise." At the same time, because they stand at the bottom of the overall social hierarchy and because they experience a pattern of early socialization which—relative to the patterns characteristic of more "respectable" groups—is conducive to a lower degree of internalization of stable controls on the use of violence, they are more liable to respond aggressively in situations which they perceive as threatening to their self-esteem. The complex requirements of "street smartness" tend to limit the contexts in which fighting is regarded as appropriate by such groups. However, males of the kind we are describing do tend to rely on physical intimidation and to fight more frequently than males from other groups. On the one hand, they tend rationally to seek out physical confrontations because these are, for them, a source of identity, status, meaning and pleasurable excitement. On the other hand, they tend to respond aggressively in threatening situations because they have learned not to exercise the degree of self-control that is demanded in this regard by the dominant norms of British society.

FOOTBALL AND THE MEDIA

During the inter-war years and, in fact, right up to the 1960s, English football crowds tended to be praised by the media for their good behaviour. More particularly, when incidents of misbehaviour by foreign fans or by fans from the non-English parts of the British Isles were reported in the press, the reports often included statements of the "it couldn't happen here" variety. Take, for example, the following extract from a report in the *Leicester Mercury* describing disorderly incidents that occurred at a match in Belfast in 1928:

> . . . the half-time interval in a cup-tie between Celtic and Linfield was given to a diversion which introduced the stoning of the musicians in the band, and the intervention of the police who used their truncheons to keep the more heated rivals in the crowd apart . . .

> In many centres of England during the next few weeks the big issues at stake in the Cup and the League will unite thousands of people in a single thought. . . . And happily all these things will be duly settled without a single policeman having to raise his truncheon to preserve the peace.[23]

Although the behaviour of English football crowds had grown more orderly since before the First World War, reports such as this ignored the disturbances that continued to occur at and in conjunction with football matches in England throughout the inter-war years. Nevertheless, although they were marginally factually inaccurate in this regard, by praising the "typical" English fan they appear to have reinforced the tendency for crowds to be well behaved and to have drawn "respectable" people into watching football in greater numbers. In other words, media treatment and crowd behaviour around this time seem to have mutually reinforced each other to produce a "feedback cycle" which had the effect of leading to a more or less continuous enhancement in the "respectability" of crowds.[24] In the late 1950s, however, in conjunction with the "teddy boy" scare and the more general moral crisis of those years over working-class youth, the media picked on and amplified the sort of violent incidents that had always from time to time occurred at crowded football grounds. It was the preparations for staging the World Cup in England in 1966, however, that appear to have been of decisive significance in this regard. This event meant that English crowds were about to come under the scrutiny of the *international* media and, in that context, popular newspapers in England began to focus on football hooliganism as a threat to the country's international prestige. For example, in November 1965, when a "dead" hand grenade was thrown onto the pitch by a Millwall fan during the encounter of his team with London rivals Brentford, the *Sun* printed the following story under the headline "Soccer Marches to War":

The Football Association have acted to stamp out this increasing mob violence within 48 hours of the blackest day in British soccer—the grenade day that showed that British supporters can rival anything the South Americans can do.

The World Cup is now less than nine months away. That is all the time we have left to try and restore the once good sporting name of this country. Soccer is sick at the moment. Or better, its crowds seem to have contracted some disease that causes them to break out in fury.[25]

Around the time of the 1966 World Cup too, the popular press started sending reporters to matches to report on crowd behaviour and not simply on the game itself.[26] Not surprisingly, these reporters saw incidents since, although by this time they were probably on the increase, they had always tended to occur at least fairly frequently in and around football grounds. What is more, because it tended to sell papers in an industry that was growing more competitive, and because of the increase in the moral and political panic about youth violence which occurred in the mid-1960s, they tended to report such incidents sensationalistically. In that way, football grounds began increasingly to be "advertised" as places where fighting or "aggro," and not just football, regularly took place. This drew in young males from the "rough" sections of the working class, probably in greater numbers than before, adding to the already existing momentum for "respectable" people to withdraw their support, especially from the goal-end terraces, and contributing to the position that we find ourselves in today: namely a situation where hooligan incidents are larger in scale and a much more regular accompaniment of matches than used to be the case and where the English hooliganism problem has been exported abroad to an extent sufficient to lead the terms "English football fan" and "hooligan" to be widely regarded on the Continent as coterminous. The mass media, of course, cannot be said to have *caused* this process but, by initially exaggerating what were usually only minor incidents and by, in effect, "advertising" football grounds as places where disturbances regularly take place and where local reputations for more than just football are at stake, they can be said, as a kind of self-fulfilling prophecy, to have played an important part in the development of football hooliganism in its distinctively contemporary form.

Once adolescent and young adult males from the "rough" working class had been attracted to the game in larger numbers, they stayed there, largely because football is, in a number of ways, a highly appropriate context for the sorts of activities that they find meaningful, exciting and enjoyable. At a football match, for example, they are able to act in ways that are frowned upon by officialdom and much of "respectable" society, and they can do so in a context that provides relative immunity from censure and arrest. The game, too, can generate high levels of excitement and the focus of this excitement is a contest—a "mock battle" with a ball—between the male representatives of two communities. Though formally controlled, usually less openly violent and, in a sense, more abstract, it is in many ways analogous to the sorts of confrontations which occur between the hooligans themselves. That is, it too is a form of masculinity ritual. Also, to the extent that the away team brings with it large numbers of the supporters, a ready-made group of opponents is provided and, in that context, the rivalries that exist between groups of local "hard cases" can be at least temporarily submerged in the interests of "home end" solidarity.

NOTES

1. Paul Harrison, "Soccer's Tribal Wars," *New Society*, 1974, vol. 29, p. 604.
2. See the discussion in Peter Marsh, Elizabeth Rosser and Rom Harré, *The Rules of Disorder*, London, 1978, pp. 70–2.
3. Simon Jacobson, "Chelsea Rule—OK," *New Society*, 1975, vol. 31, pp. 780–3.

4. It is perhaps worth pointing out that football match duties provide the police with opportunities both for overtime earnings and for obtaining a welcome relief from normal routines. At football matches, too, not only the hooligans but also the police are provided with opportunities for "action" in an exciting context. Moreover, on account of the opprobrium which football hooliganism has attracted, it is a context in which the strategies employed by the police seldom draw public criticism.
5. J. A. Harrington, *Soccer Hooliganism*, Bristol, 1968, p. 25.
6. Eugene Trivizas, "Offences and Offenders in Football Crowd Disorders," *British Journal of Criminology*, vol. 20, no. 3, 1980, p. 282.
7. Harrison, "Soccer's Tribal Wars," p. 602.
8. Marsh et al., *The Rules of Disorder*, p. 69.
9. *Oxford Mail*, 9 January 1981.
10. Gerald Suttles, *The Social Order of the Slum*, Chicago: University of Chicago Press, 1968, p. 10.
11. Ibid.
12. E. E. Evans-Pritchard, *The Nuer*, Oxford, 1940.
13. David Robins and Philip Cohen, *Knuckle Sandwich: Growing Up in a Working-Class City*, New York: Penguin, 1978, pp. 73 ff.
14. Harrison, "Soccer's Tribal Wars."
15. Robins and Cohen, *Knuckle Sandwich*, p. 77.
16. David Robins, *We Hate Humans*, Harmondsworth, 1984, p. 86.
17. The emergence of such a pattern probably depends in large part on the fact that, in common with children generally, lower working-class children have not yet had the chance to develop strong and stable internalized restraints over their emotions and are thus heavily dependent on external controls. Where these are restricted to specific contexts such as the home and discontinuous in their application, there are few checks on the aggressiveness and violence of children's interactions and hence on the emergence of dominance hierarchies of this kind. Such a tendency is liable to be compounded to the extent that violent forms of punishment are used by adults as a means of socialization, and to the extent that children regularly see adults acting aggressively, whether inside or outside the home.
18. Using the term introduced by Norbert Elias, one could say that they have a relatively high "threshold of repugnance" (*Peinlichkeitsschwelle*) with regard to witnessing and taking part in violent acts. See, *The Civilizing Process*, Oxford, 1978; and *State Formation and Civilization*, Oxford, 1982.
19. See Paul Willis, *Profane Culture*, London, 1978, p. 29.
20. Howard J. Parker, *View from the Boys: A Sociology of Downtown Adolescents*, Newton Abbot, 1974, p. 35.
21. See, for example, Herbert J. Gans, "Urbanism and Suburbanism as Ways of Life," in R. E. Pahl (ed.), *Readings in Urban Sociology*, New York: Oxford University Press, 1968, pp. 95–118.
22. This may help, in part, to explain the appeal of the National Front and the British Movement to many of the members of such groups.
23. *Leicester Mercury*, 10 February 1928.
24. This is to some extent an oversimplification for, as we shall show in *The Roots of Football Hooliganism: An Historical and Sociological Study*, (forthcoming), there was a slight tendency for concern over the behaviour of football crowds to grow as the 1930s came to a close.
25. *Sun*, 8 November 1965.
26. Stan Cohen, "Campaigning Against Vandalism," in C. Ward (ed.), *Vandalism*, London, 1973, p. 232.

DISCUSSION QUESTIONS

1. Dunning and his colleagues dispute the official explanations for fan violence by contending that they fail to get at the root causes of the phenomenon. Do you agree or disagree with their assessment?
2. Spectator sports in the United States have not been plagued by the fan violence associated with English soccer. Why do you think this is the case?

READING 16

Selling Crack in El Barrio

Philippe Bourgeois

Over a five-year period, Philippe Bourgeois resided in New York's impoverished and dangerous inner-city neighborhood of East Harlem, where he conducted ethnographic research on the subculture of Puerto Rican crack dealers. Drug dealing is an important part of the underground economy, and Bourgeois offers a detailed portrait of those employed in it, as well as those caught up in a world of addiction. In this selection, he provides a description of the mundane realities of working as a manager in a crackhouse: conflicts with the boss and other employees, the competition, security issues, and the police.

MANAGEMENT—LABOR CONFLICT AT THE GAME ROOM

Primo's options in the legal job market were no better than those of any of his employees, but on the stoop of the Game Room his vulnerability was not visible—especially when contrasted with that of his crack-addicted customers and workers. He looked and behaved like an effective boss. Ultimately, however, Primo's relative autonomy and importance within Ray's network was eroded when Ray expanded his franchises. The Social Club's prime retail location on La Farmacia's corner made it far more profitable than the Game Room. Ray instituted a double shift at the Social Club, keeping it open for sixteen hours every day except Sunday. Perhaps also because of his own personal fondness for the spot—having grown up in the building—he invested in renovating the physical infrastructure. Soon the Social Club had a pool table, a powerful sound system, a flush toilet that worked some of the time, an air conditioner, and a heater. Ray also established an after-hours bar at the site, serving beer and Bacardi. For the upscale customers and for hard-core intravenous cocaine users, in addition to the nickels of crack, he offered half-grams of relatively unadulterated cocaine for twenty dollars.

The expansion and diversification of Ray's network allowed him to be more manipulative in his management of labor relations. He began leveraging increased levels of discipline and higher profit margins from Primo at the Game Room. This initiated a protracted juggle for power between Primo and Ray. Ray's first action was to supersede Primo's right to hire assistants. He imposed his own choice of secondary employees to work as lookouts and sellers side by side with Primo. Primo rebelled against Ray's encroachment on his operational autonomy. He did not want to be demoted from manager to senior salesperson.

Ultimately, Primo lost out in this struggle for workplace autonomy, and his position as "manager" became increasingly ambiguous, until by the last two years of my residence on the block, Primo had lost all fiction of control over Game Room operations. Ray even managed to lower his piece-rate commissions from $1.00 to 75 cents per vial sold, although he did maintain an extra incentive by increasing the commission to $1.75 per vial on nights when seven bundles [175 vials] were sold. Ray claimed that Primo had precipitated the changes because of his tardiness, absenteeism, and ineffectiveness in curbing violence and noise at the Game Room. For one ten-month period, Primo became so marginal that another three-quarters-time senior salesperson, Tony, was hired and Ray limited Primo to only working two night shifts per week.

Primo responded to his lowered wages, reduced work hours, and lost managerial autonomy by escalating his alcohol and substance abuse. He became an even less punctual and more undisciplined worker, provoking Ray on several occasions to lay him off in retaliation for probationary two-week stretches. Part of the problem was rooted in the laws of supply and demand. The competition across the block in the project stairwells had permanently dropped the prices of their vials from three dollars to two dollars, and a conglomerate of companies located on another crack corner two blocks away had cut its prices from five dollars to three dollars, while simultaneously increasing the quality of its product.

Ray made a last-ditch effort to retain market share by upgrading the Game Room's locale.

He moved operations upstairs to the newly vacated premises where three licensed doctors had formerly operated an illegal Medicaid-funded pill mill. This temporarily raised morale among his workers but did not affect sales significantly. We critiqued and debated the boss's management strategies in much the same mundane way that anxious employees in a retail enterprise in the legal sector who are in danger of being laid off, will speculate on the reasons for declining business. Relaxing after the end of the night shift in my apartment living room with Primo and Caesar, I tape-recorded one particularly anxious conversation. For the preceding two weeks, the Game Room had been shut down because of intensified police sweeps, and upon reopening that night, Ray had introduced a lower-quality product. (The Dominican wholesaler who formerly supplied him with cocaine at the kilo level had been arrested and his new connection had provided him with inferior cocaine.)

Before speaking morosely, Caesar opened a glassine envelope of heroin, sniffed from it, and then tossed the packet onto my coffee table. He then immediately reached for the folded dollar bill containing cocaine that Primo had just crushed. Primo pulled the cocaine away from him, saying, "Chill man, let me feed you!" and turned to me for emphasis: "I hate it when this nigga' gets thirsty." Primo then scooped a folded matchbook corner into the pile of cocaine and held it up to Caesar's nose for him to sniff with a grimace that effectively closed off one nostril while opening the other one wide. He repeated the motions three more times until Caesar finally sat back calmly on my couch, nodding a thanks to Primo.

Caesar: [speaking slowly] Tonight was slow, we only made twenty-two dollars and fuckin' fifty cents. And I be risking getting snatched and dirtyin' my [police] record for chump change from that fat-assed nigga'.

Ray's gonna lose a lotta business with no light up there. And no one wants to walk up those stairs.

Primo: No, it's not the place of the business. It's just that we're selling two-dollar bottles for five bucks [sniffing].

Caesar: Yeah, the bottles are too small. [gravely] Lately Ray's been fucking up with the product, man. He's like switching product. It'll be good; then it'll be fucked up; then it'll be good; then it'll be fucked up.

Primo: The real problem is that they be small bottles.

Caesar: Plus it was a major mistake to be closed all that time and then the first time we open we be selling shit.

How you gonna open up and sell fire? 'Cause that's what the customers said it is. The cracks taste like fire. That shit is nasty!

He's fucking us up because a lot of people don't come back, man. And people be complaining that we are selling fire.

[picking up his tempo, feeling a rush of energy from the cocaine] I done told Ray, "What's up? This shit is garbage." But he's like, "Fuck you! I sell it like that."

Primo: [sniffing] I never tell him shit, especially tonight. I think he had a roach up his ass, 'cause it's slow. He was pissed off 'cause the electrician from Con Ed [New York City's electrical utility company] didn't show up today.

When I pushed the conversation into a discussion of how they could tolerate being minimum wage crack dealers, they responded with self-congratulatory, glorifying reminiscences of nights of record sales. Perhaps the same types of dialogue could be tape-recorded after-hours among heavy-drinking used-car salesmen during a recession in the local economy.

Caesar: [sniffing more cocaine from Primo's upheld matchbook] Nah, Felipe, it's not so bad. It's slow tonight because it's Monday, and the end of the month, and nobody ain't got no money.

[excited] Primo left out of here the other day with almost three hundred bucks all by himself.

Primo: [smiling] It was the first of the month and everybody had got paid.

Caesar: [taking more cocaine] It was a huge day for selling. Everything comes on the first of the month: all the checks.

Primo: Yeah! Everybody got paid [grinning]. Because the first of the month is like when welfare checks, rent checks, social security checks, all come. The first of the month is definitely *monneeey* [licking his lips].

Caesar: For everybody! Veterans' checks, pensions, social security, welfare, Jew checks . . . [noting my raised eyebrows] You know, Jews be into crazy scams, making money with papers . . . you know, insurance, real estate, shit like that. The Jews be picking up checks. [wiggling his forefingers greedily with a devious grin]

On the first of the month, money flows.

Primo: Everyone was coming. Welfare recipients and workers. I sold twelve bundles.

Ray's sales remained slow for the next several months and morale among his workers continued to plummet, while tensions mounted. Ray ordered Primo to fire Caesar following a series of loud drunken arguments, but Primo refused. Ray retaliated by switching Primo's schedule to working on Monday and Tuesday nights instead of Thursday and Friday nights. Thursday is an especially coveted night to sell on because it is payday for municipal employees.

In a classic example of the internalization of labor–management antagonisms, Primo and Caesar redoubled their hatred for Tony, the replacement employee whom Ray had hired a few months earlier to discipline Primo and Caesar. Tony reciprocated their antagonism. This escalated into a potentially lethal confrontation when three bundles of crack disappeared from the stash inside the Pac-Man video machine during the interval between Primo's Tuesday night shift and Tony's Wednesday shift. Everyone professed

innocence, but there was no sign of forced entry and Tony and Primo were the only two people besides Ray to have keys to the locale. Ray wanted to kill—or at least break the legs—of the culprit, but he could not decide whom to punish.

The following Thursday, another three bundles were stolen from the overnight stash, which had been rotated to a live electrical socket for protection. Ray was not only furious but also helpless—a condition that made him even more dangerous than he normally is. To save face he began deducting the value of the stolen bundles from both Primo's and Tony's wages on a fifty-fifty basis. Sales on Primo's Monday and Tuesday night shifts, however, were so low that Ray had to set up an installment plan for his reimbursement. Primo and Caesar were allowed to keep their full Monday night commission in return for surrendering all of Tuesday night's receipts until their share of the $450 worth of missing merchandise was accounted for.

Sensing that he was the prime suspect, Caesar was especially vocal in denouncing Tony as the thief. He repeatedly advocated "wasting the motherfucker." Those of us who frequented the Game Room regularly were convinced that Caesar had stolen the crack. Primo could not help but share this suspicion. It depressed him that his best friend and employee—his "main nigga' "—could have disrespected him so profoundly. It was during these tense weeks that I tape-recorded many of Primo's most insightful denunciations of how he was trapped in the crack economy.

The mysterious disappearance of the six bundles was finally resolved with the anticipated life-threatening beating, but neither Tony nor Primo nor even Caesar were the victims. The thief was Gato, Ray's jack-of-all-trades maintenance worker who had renovated the new locale upstairs from the Game Room. In the process he had hollowed out fake paneling under the floor, to which he had access after hours via the abandoned building behind the Game Room. He knew the kinds of places where Ray kept his stashes because he repaired all his video games and maintained his electrical systems. In fact, he was the one who had pirated the electricity to the new crackhouse out of a neighboring bodega. We could not help but feel sorry for Gato when Ray brought him back to the Game Room three days later to start working off the debt he owed by fixing some newly acquired broken machines. Gato climbed awkwardly out of Ray's Lincoln Continental limping heavily from the beating he had received three days earlier. He avoided eye contact with all of us. We all left the premises hurriedly when he started unscrewing the back of a broken video game because he reeked from the acrid smell specific to homeless crack bingers who have no access to showers or clean clothes. That he was still alive with no bones broken was a testimony to his childhood friendship with Ray, whom he had faithfully followed as a teenage member of "The Cheeba Crew" (TCC) some dozen years earlier.

Ray took advantage of the tensions generated by this incident to renegotiate Tony's salary from a piece-rate commission to a set wage of $100 per shift, regardless of how many bundles were sold. This was especially profitable for Ray because Tony worked on the nights when sales were at their highest volume, Wednesday through Saturday. Relations were too strained between Tony and Primo for them to coordinate their demands for a higher proportion of Ray's profits. In fact, in a classic divide-and-conquer scenario, neither worker even knew what kind of payment arrangement his nemesis had negotiated with their mutual boss.

THE CRACKHOUSE CLIQUE: DEALING WITH SECURITY

Primo's subordination to Ray was not immediately visible to the clique of parasitical friends, acquaintances, and wanna-be employees who congregated in front of the Game Room on most nights. When Primo was on duty, he appeared to his hang-out crowd to be well in control. He was exceptionally generous, and he regularly treated his friends to beer, liquor, and occasional sniffs of cocaine. I had assumed originally that Primo cultivated a large hang-out crowd to fulfill a psychological need for power and domination, especially vis-à-vis the teenage women competing for his sexual attention.

It took me several months to realize that the people reclining on car hoods, squatting on neighboring stoops, or tapping their feet to the ubiquitous rap or salsa playing on someone's radio, served several different useful roles for the crackhouse. They provided strategic business information on competing drug spots and on the changing trends in tastes and market shifts in the underground economy. As long as they did not become too rowdy, they also served to camouflage the comings and goings of the emaciated addicts, making the crackhouse look more like a youth center than a place of business. A subtle touch of "normalcy" was added by the presence of Primo's adopted grandfather, Abraham, who was responsible for collecting the quarters from the video machines. Whenever potential undercover narcotic detectives entered the Game Room, this hopelessly alcoholic seventy-two-year-old man pretended to be senile. He exuded an aura of helplessness and gentleness that was accentuated by the homemade black patch covering his left eye, which he had lost when a mugger stabbed him while he was home from his job at the cafeteria of Lenox Hill Hospital in the early 1980s.[1]

Most importantly, the hang-out crowd complemented the lookout's job by protecting the Game Room from excessive violence and aggression. Primo's best and cheapest insurance against physical assault was to surround himself with a network of people who genuinely respected and liked him. His crowd of friends became an effective army of detectives for investigating foul play; for warning him of potential stickup artists who might be casing the premises; or for shielding and witnessing when an attack actually occurred. Indeed, assault by thieves represented Primo's greatest physical danger. Whenever two people walked into the Game Room at the same time or at a fast pace, he always tensed up. He also usually suspected new people who joined his hang-out crowd of being emissaries gathering intelligence for a future holdup crew.

Primo's fears were well founded. During the five and a half years that I documented the Game Room's operations, it was robbed twice by masked men bearing sawed-off shotguns. Primo confided to me that during the first robbery he had urinated in his pants with his attacker's shotgun pressed against his temple while he lied about not having a stash of cash. Nevertheless, when he reported the theft to his boss later that night, Primo had exaggerated how much money and crack was stolen in order to keep the difference.

Primo considered somewhat insulting my functionalist interpretation of why he treated his friends and acquaintances so generously. Nevertheless, in his counterexplanations he reaffirmed the sense of tension and imminent danger he was forced to endure every night. More subtly, he made me realize that the hang-out crew was more than physical protection, it provided a stabilizing social atmosphere for him to counterbalance the anxiety that constantly threatens to disable a lonesome seller. His peers distracted and relaxed him from the dangerous reality of his work site:

Primo: I don't need anyone to protect me, Felipe. Naah. I can handle myself alone. It's just like I want my people to be there for me.

It don't have to be O.D. here. [pointing to Willie, who was working lookout that night] It could be anybody that's keeping me company. It could even be Jackie [his girlfriend at the time].

See, just so long as there's someone I could talk to, to keep me company. It could even be just Maria [his former girlfriend, whom he had temporarily broken up with]. But Ray don't like Maria hanging out; he don't know her all that well. She's not from the block.

You understand? I just want someone to accompany me . . . just for the company. You know, it's hard to just be in this dump by yourself.

Because if you're by yourself you know you feel . . . you be more edgy. It's boring and I need to be more relaxed.

And if anything, you always want a witness or somebody to be there . . . you know.

Ironically, it took me several years to realize that Primo's enthusiastic friendship with me was part of the unconscious logic for why he maintained a hang-out crew in front of the Game Room. The disconcerting presence of a white face at night in an El Barrio crackhouse was probably an even better deterrent to potential stickup artists than Willie's large frame, Caesar's reputation for irrational violence, or any one of the teenage girls flirting with Primo. Stickup artists are simply not willing to take the risk of assaulting anyone who could possibly be confused as an undercover police officer. There are too many other easy targets around.

Another crucial service fulfilled by Primo's hang-out network as well as his lookouts was to screen for narcotics agents. Crack dealers have to have organic ties to the street scene in order to be able to recognize the bona fide addict or user from the undercover impostor. The best lookouts and street sellers are those who have hung out in the streets all their lives and know everyone in the neighborhood. When Primo did not recognize someone or sensed something suspicious about a customer, he checked first with his lookout, or with one of his friends outside on the stoop, before serving them. The most frequent confusion arose over men who had just been released from prison and had not yet destroyed their bodies on crack.

Primo: Yo Caesar, who were those two *morenos*? I didn't even know the motherfuckers. They could be *la jara* [the police].

Caesar: Yeah, it's okay. They were good-looking and dressed well, but I know that big black Alabama. He's cool. I know him. He's walked in the Game Room before, it's just that you don't remember.

He musta just came outta jail because that nigga' looked fresh union. That nigga' was healthy. He was like a Buster Douglas size.

In the five years that I knew Primo he must have made tens of thousands of hand-to-hand crack sales; more than a million dollars probably passed through his fingers. Despite this intense activity, however, he was only arrested twice, and only two other sellers at the Game Room were arrested during this same period. No dealer was ever caught at Ray's other crackhouses, not even at the Social Club on La Farmacia's corner, even though its business was brisker. Ironically, the Social Club was raided half a dozen times, because it doubled as a pool hall and bootleg bar. The large clientele ofomni-present regulars confused the police; they never knew whom to arrest. They could not expropriate the landlord, because the City of New York was the owner. The original proprietor had long since defaulted on his taxes. Instead, on two occasions the police smashed the pool tables into kindling wood, ripped out the electrical fixtures, and boarded over the entrance. On one raid, they ticketed Candy for serving unlicensed liquor to an undercover officer, but they were never able to apprehend the primary seller-manager in the act of a hand-to-hand narcotics sale. The biggest threat to the Social Club came from the New York City fire marshals, who sealed the place on several occasions for violating fire codes following the much publicized arson of a social club in the South Bronx that took the lives of eighty-four people.[2]

The invulnerability of Ray's crackhouses to police control was largely owing to the generalized public sector breakdown of the neighborhood. Inner-city police forces are so demoralized and incompetent that for the most part they do not have to be systematically corrupt—although they often are—in order for street-level drug dealing to flourish in their precincts.[3] The attitude of honest officers is too hostile toward the local community for them to be able to build the networks that would allow them to document the operations of the numerous drug-dealing spots in the neighborhoods they patrol. For example, after five and a half years of being practically the only white person out on the street after dark on a regular basis on my block, which hosted almost a half-dozen drug-selling spots, the police never learned to recognize me. Even after I began attending their community outreach meetings for combating drugs, they continued to fail to recognize me on the street.[4]

Ray and his workers took certain basic precautions to minimize their risk of arrest. They never made sales outside the door on the street, and they usually asked customers to step behind a strategically placed Pac-Man machine at the back of the establishment before touching their money and handing them the vials of crack, in case the police were watching with binoculars from a neighboring apartment building. Most importantly, at no point was there more than twenty-five vials—one bundle—visibly accessible. Depending on the night and the season, additional bundles might be strategically hidden in rotated stashes, such as the live overhead electrical socket, the linoleum wall paneling, or the entrails of one of the video games. Depending on supply and demand, runners periodically delivered extra bundles and picked up cash receipts.

Sellers have to develop the crucial skill of judging when it is necessary to stash their vials in the event of a raid. This was what saved Primo, for example, from four years of incarceration on his last arrest. As the police were battering down the Game Room door with their portable ram he flicked thirteen vials from his current bundle into the back of a Mario Brothers video machine. The police found nothing in their search of the premises. At the same time, if a seller becomes overly paranoid—*petro*—of every suspicious siren and revving car motor, the smooth operations of the crackhouse become excessively disrupted. Dealers have to juggle between relaxation and acute premonition. In Primo's case, strategically dispensing beer and cocaine to his friendly hang-out clique was crucial to maintaining this delicate balance of calm alertness.

Primo, Caesar, and other dealers provided me with dozens of accounts of close calls with the police. They had developed complex, risk-minimization strategies.

Caesar: [drinking from a 16-ounce can of malt liquor] I'm not gonna get caught with the stash on me. I'll pitch it or hide it fast. I got a clean slate. So I don't even think I would even get bail. They'll call it being in the wrong place at the wrong time.

I don't sell to people I don't know, never. Pops only made that mistake a coupla' times in the Game Room, but that was when it was wild man.

Primo: [also drinking from a separate 16-ounce can of malt liquor] Yeah, I only got caught once like that, in a buy-and-bust. But there's been times when cops came to buy but I knew it and I was cool.

Way back when my grandfather Abraham was still hanging out here. I was reading in the newspapers about that guy, Larry Davis, who killed those cops. I was chilling, reading.

Caesar: My cousin's in jail with Larry Davis in Louisiana on some wild federal charge.

Primo: Shut up Caesar, let me finish.

So I was reading that Larry Davis thing out loud to Abraham, because he can't read English, when this guy in an army jacket came in—but he was white.

I don't even know why they sent him. He looked like an obvious cop. I pretended I didn't see him, when he walked in. I kept reading like that [peering deeply into an imaginary newspaper]. So he walked past me, to the back and asked Abraham for the shit. But Abraham realized quick what was up and he just went, "*Wahhhh?*" [imitating a senile old man slobbering at the mouth]. And I was in the front, reading the paper like this [crossing his legs awk-

wardly perched on a milk crate] and there were kids playing, and it was cool.

Then he said to me, "They still sell crack here?" but I just went, "I don't know," and kept reading my paper.

He was a cop because I seen the man in the day, with the regular blue suit on.

Primo attributed to carelessness the one time he was successfully arrested and convicted.

Primo: I got my [criminal] record back when O.D. was hanging with me. Oh man, I got jerked! I was outside with a mirror, trimming my hair like that. It was early in the day; it was like four o'clock. I used to open earlier in them days. Like one or two, because Felix was like, "Gotta be there, boy!" I used to hate that.

So Abraham calls me, because I didn't notice the guy go in because I was talking with O. D., trimming my shit.

So I went in and he was pretending he was playing Pac-Man. So then I didn't even bother to look at him, it was like he had a gold chain, short pants, and everything.

So I took the shit from where we kept it right there in a little thin box [pointing in the direction of the current stash]. He tells me he wants five. And when I was serving him, was when I looked at his face; I said to myself, "Shit, I don't know this motherfucker!" He looked like so clean-cut, *y gordito* [and chubby]; I was like [waving his arms in confusion].

So I tell him, "How do you smoke this? Put it in the pipe; or do you smoke woolas [a crack and marijuana mixture]?" He said, "You got that too?" and I said, "No, I'm just asking." So he left.

And when he left, I told O.D., "Yo, wait a minute. Let me stash the shit." Because I didn't trust that dude. But O.D. followed me. He was talking to me so much shit about his problems that I got distracted [drinking].

And when I turned to put the vials away, like that [going through the motions], right there they pushed me [coming over to me and throwing me against a video machine in a half-nelson]. I thought it was Eddie just fucking around so I continued; but when I finished I looked and the cop was already ready to blow me away like that [holding an imaginary gun up to my temple]—or whatever. He was taking precautions. Them niggas just rushed us, boy [drinking]. He pulled the shit out and said "This is what we're looking for" [holding out a handful of crack vials and grinning cruelly].

I got jerked for selling five vials—two-to-four years probation [shaking his head sadly, drinking, and handing me the bottle].

A year later, as the New York state penal system spiraled into a crisis owing to overcrowding following the precipitous increase in drug arrests and the toughening of drug-sentencing rules, an exasperated judge declared Primo's suspended sentence to be completed a year early, in order to clear his overburdened docket. Primo had been arrested for failing to report to his probation officer, a violation that under normal conditions might have resulted in his incarceration for the full term of his probation sentence.

Following his second arrest for a hand-to-hand sale of ten dollars' worth of crack to an undercover officer, once again the mayhem of New York's drug enforcement strategy in the early 1990s saved Primo from becoming a predicate felon and having to serve four to six years in jail.[5] In their disorganized haste to boost arrest statistics, the Tactical Narcotics Team officers who engineered the buy-and-bust operation on the Game Room confused the identities of Primo and Caesar in the courtroom. The jury was forced to free Primo when Caesar derailed the prosecution's case by insinuating under oath—but with the protection of the Fifth Amendment—that he had actually been the one who had sold the crack to the undercover officers. Ray and several of the crackhouse habitués had the pleasure of watching the judge rebuke the district attorney for having wasted the court's time with a sloppy case. Primo was fully vindicated, and the Game Room stayed in business for another year with no police raids.

NOTES

1. Unfortunately, Abraham dropped the replacement glass eye that the hospital had made for him into a vat of soup he was preparing in the hospital cafeteria. Medicaid subsequently refused to pay for a second replacement glass eye.
2. This arson occurred in January 1990 at the Happy Land social club–dance hall, which was frequented primarily by Honduran immigrants. A heroin company operating around my block renamed its brand "Happy Land" shortly after the fire.
3. The intermittent pattern of arrests of corrupt New York City police officers in inner-city precincts in the late 1980s through the mid-1990s illustrates the prevalent, but fundamentally haphazard, nature of police corruption around narcotics at the street-dealer level. Officers are so alienated from the communities they patrol that rather than take payoffs, they specialize in orchestrating fake raids and pocketing the drugs and money they confiscate (cf. *New York Times*, May 8, 1990:A1, B10; *New York Times*, July 7, 1994:B2). Until mid-1994, New York City police officers were specifically discouraged from arresting drug dealers because of the inherent temptations for petty corruption (*New York Times*, July 7, 1994:B2). Narcotics arrests were supposed to be handled exclusively by specially trained elite units.
4. To illustrate the incompetence of the local police force: When I went to the precinct to report the burglary of my apartment in midwinter, I noticed graffiti scrawled on the blackboard in the main office, saying "No more arrests till we get heat."
5. For accounts of how overwhelmed the New York City courts became in 1989 at the height of the "War on Drugs," see *New York Times*, May 31, 1989:B1.

DISCUSSION QUESTIONS

1. Compare and contrast Primo's job to that of someone managing a store in a shopping mall. In what ways are these jobs similar and how are they different?

2. What do you think are the main factors that prevent people like Primo from finding gainful employment in the mainstream economy?

The Razor Blade in the Apple: The Social Construction of Urban Legends

Joel Best and Gerald T. Horiuchi

Joel Best and Gerald Horiuchi scrutinize the conviction held by many people during the past several decades that sadistic acts such as putting razor blades and other dangerous objects into candy, apples, and other treats had become a significant threat on Halloween. The media in many places have carried warnings about the danger and, in some places, hospitals have opened up their x-ray facilities so treats could be examined. The authors, using data from a content analysis of newspaper accounts for a period from 1958 to 1983, conclude that the public fear is out of proportion to the reality of the danger. They conclude that Halloween sadism is an urban myth, whose origin is located in the fear of crime and other factors contributing to social strain.

The 1970s witnessed the discovery of a frightening new deviant—the Halloween sadist, who gave dangerous, adulterated treats to children. Each year, Halloween's approach brought warnings to parents:

> . . . that plump red apple that Junior gets from a kindly old woman down the block . . . may have a razor blade hidden inside (*New York Times*, 1970).

> If this year's Halloween follows form, a few children will return home with something more than an upset tummy: in recent years, several children have died and hundreds have narrowly escaped injury from razor blades, sewing needles and shards of glass purposefully put into their goodies by adults (*Newsweek*, 1975).

> It's Halloween again and time to remind you that . . . [s]omebody's child will become violently ill or die after eating poisoned candy or an apple containing a razor blade (Van Buren, 1983).

Various authorities responded to the threat: legislatures in California (1971) and New Jersey (1982) passed laws against Halloween sadism; schools trained children to inspect their treats for signs of tampering; and some communities tried to ban trick-or-treating (Trubo, 1974). According to press reports, many parents restricted their children's trick-or-treating, examined their treats, or arranged parties or other indoor celebrations (*New York Times*, 1972; *Los Angeles Times*, 1982). By 1984, the threat of Halloween sadists was apparently taken for granted. Doubts about the threat's reality rarely appeared in print. Several Oregon third graders wrote letters to a newspaper: "I wish people wouldn't put poison in our Halloween treats" (*Times*, 1984). Adults questioned for an Illinois newspaper's "Sidewalk Interview" column (*DeKalb Daily Chronicle*, 1984) expressed concern: ". . . part of it is checking to make sure you know your neighbors and checking the candy. I think it's terrible that people are doing this and I guess people's morals have to be examined." "Dear Abby" printed a letter describing a North Carolina hospital's program to X-ray treats (Van Buren, 1984); radiologists at a Hanford, California hospital checked 500 bags of treats (*Fresno Bee*, 1984). In 1985, 327 students at California State University, Fresno wrote essays for an upper-division writing examination, advocating the abolition of some holiday. Nearly a third (105 students) wrote about Halloween, and 90 percent of those essays mentioned the threat of Halloween sadism.

Halloween sadism is thought to involve random, vicious, unprovoked attacks against small children. The attacks seem irrational, and the attackers are routinely described as disturbed or insane. These "child-haters" are theorized to "have had a really deprived childhood" having been "abused as children," they are now "frustrated and filled with resentment against the world in general" (Isaacs and Royeton, 1982:69; *New York Times*, 1970; *Trubo*, 1974:28). Law enforcement officials and the media reaffirm that the threat is real, urging parents to protect their children against sadistic attacks.

Although Halloween sadism is widely regarded as a serious threat, it has received little scholarly attention. In this paper, we examine the phenomenon from a sociological perspective, addressing three issues. First, we try to assess the incidence of Halloween sadism in order to demonstrate that the threat has been greatly exaggerated. Second, we draw upon a concept from folklore studies to argue that the belief in Halloween sadism is best viewed as an "urban legend." Finally, we suggest that urban legends can be understood as unconstructed social problems. Like collective hysteria and organized claims-making efforts, urban legends are a product of social strain and of the social organization of the response to that strain.

A HOLIDAY FOR SADISTS?

There are no reliable official statistics on Halloween sadism. Minor incidents, particularly those that do not involve injuries, may never be reported to the police. Cases that are reported may be classified under a wide range of offenses, and there is no centralized effort to compile cases from different jurisdictions. Moreover, the circumstances of the crime—the young victim, the unfamiliar assailant, the difficulty in remembering which treats came from which houses—make it unlikely that offenders will be arrested.

While the true incidence of Halloween sadism cannot be measured, newspaper reports reveal changes in public reaction to the threat.

Therefore, we examined the coverage of Halloween sadism in four daily newspapers between 1959 and 1984. For the *New York Times*, we checked all entries under "Halloween" in the paper's annual indexes for information about Halloween sadism. The *New York Times Index* proved to be unusually complete, listing even short items of a sentence or two.[1] The published indexes for two other major regional newspapers, the *Chicago Tribune* and the *Los Angeles Times*, were less thorough, so for each year, we read both papers' issues for the first three days in November. Finally, we examined all Halloween stories in the files of the *Fresno Bee*. Our search found stories about 76 alleged incidents of Halloween sadism, which included at least the community where the incident occurred and the nature of the attack.[2] Table 1 shows the number of incidents reported in each year.

Obviously, the 76 incidents identified through this procedure do not form a complete list of cases of Halloween sadism. However, there are several reasons why it is unlikely that many serious incidents—involving deaths or serious injuries—were overlooked. First, the papers' coverage was national. The 76 reported incidents came from 15 states and two Canadian provinces; while each of the four newspapers concentrated on incidents in its own region, all reported cases from other regions. All four included at least one case from the South—the only major region without a newspaper in the sample. Second, the 76 reported cases were gen-

---

[1]On the reliability of this index, see Troyer and Markle (1983:141–42).

[2]In addition, all entries under "Halloween" in the *Reader's Guide to Periodical Literature* and MEDLINE—the computerized medical data base—were checked. Neither popular magazines nor the medical literature described any additional cases of Halloween sadism. Every case was included if the news report treated it as an instance of Halloween sadism. As noted below, some of the cases included were of questionable authenticity.

TABLE 1

REPORTED INCIDENTS OF HALLOWEEN SADISM, 1958–84

Year	Number of incidents	Year	Number of incidents
1958	0	1972	1
1959	1	1973	4
1960	0	1974	1
1961	0	1975	2
1962	1	1976	2
1963	1	1977	0
1964	3	1978	0
1965	1	1979	3
1966	5	1980	0
1967	4	1981	0
1968	3	1982	12
1969	7	1983	1
1970	10	1984	0
1971	14		

erally not serious. Injuries were reported in only 20 cases, and only two of these involved deaths. It seems unlikely that newspapers would choose to print accounts of minor incidents, while ignoring more serious crimes. This impression is bolstered further by the frequent appearance of stories—often from different states—about other Halloween tragedies: children struck by cars and other accidental deaths; people murdered when they opened their doors, expecting trick-or-treaters; racial disturbances; vandalism; and so on. At least two of the newspapers carried reports on each of the two deaths attributed to Halloween sadists. It is therefore unlikely that the list of 76 incidents excludes any fatal instances of Halloween sadism.

Table 1 reveals two peaks in the pattern of reporting. Thirty-one of the 76 incidents occurred in the three years from 1969 to 1971. This wave of reports encouraged recognition of Halloween sadism as a threat. As a holiday when millions of children venture out at night, Halloween has a long history of tragic accidents. Routinely, newspapers and magazines print lists of safety tips, warning parents against flammable costumes, masks that obscure the wearer's vision, and the like. A systematic review of such lists found no mention of the danger posed by sadists before 1972; but, from that year on, lists of safety tips almost invariably warned parents to inspect their children's treats for signs of tampering. At the same time that these warnings spread, reports of Halloween sadism fell to a few per year until 1982, when there was a dramatic increase. Of course, this reflected the fear caused by the Tylenol murders. A month before Halloween, seven people died after swallowing poisoned Extra-Strength Tylenol capsules. In the weeks that followed, there were hundreds of reports of "copycats" adulterating food, over-the-counter medications, and other household products. As Halloween approached, the media repeatedly warned parents that trick-or-treaters would be in danger. After raising the specter of Halloween sadism, the press naturally covered the incidents that were reported. A year later, however, coverage fell to pre-Tylenol levels.

Examining the reports of the 76 incidents leads to three conclusions. First, the threat of Halloween sadism has been greatly exaggerated. There is simply no basis for *Newsweek's* (1975) claim that "several children have died." The newspapers attributed only two deaths to Halloween sadists, and neither case fit the image of a maniacal killer randomly attacking children. In 1970, five-year-old Kevin Toston died after eating heroin supposedly hidden in his Halloween candy. While this story received considerable publicity, newspapers gave less coverage to the follow-up report that Kevin had found the heroin in his uncle's home, not his treats (*San Francisco Chronicle*, 1970). The second death is more notorious. In 1974, eight-year-old Timothy O'Bryan died after eating Halloween candy contaminated with cyanide. Investigators concluded that his father had contaminated the treat (Grider, 1982). Thus, both boys' deaths were caused by family members, rather than by anonymous sadists.[3] Similarly, while the newspaper reports rarely gave detailed information about the remaining 18 cases in which injuries were reported, most of the victims were not seriously hurt. Several incidents involved minor cuts and puncture wounds; what was apparently the most serious wound required 11 stitches. In short, there were no reports where an anonymous sadist caused death or a life-threatening injury; there is no justification for the claim that Halloween sadism stands as a major threat to U.S. children.[4]

A second conclusion is that many, if not most, reports of Halloween sadism are of questionable authenticity. Children who go trick-or-treating know about Halloween sadism; they have been warned by their parents, teachers, and friends. A child who "discovers" an adulterated treat stands to be rewarded with the concerned attention of parents and, perhaps, police officers and reporters. Such a hoax is consistent with Halloween traditions of trickery, just as the fear of sadists resembles the more traditional dread of ghosts and witches (Santino, 1983). The 76 reported incidents included two cases that were identified as hoaxes at the time, and it seems likely that other cases involved undiscovered fraud. After all, it is remarkable that three-quarters of the children who reported receiving contaminated treats had no injuries. Efforts to systematically follow up reports of Halloween

sadism have concluded that the vast majority were fabrications. After Halloween 1972, *Editor and Publisher* (1973)—the trade magazine of the newspaper industry—examined several papers' efforts to trace all local reports of Halloween sadism; it concluded that virtually all the reports were hoaxes. Ten years later, in the wake of the Tylenol scare, the confectionary industry tried to reassure potential customers in a "white paper" on Halloween candy tampering in 1982 (National Confectioners Association et al., n.d.) The report noted that "more than 95 percent of the 270 potential Halloween 1982 candy adulterations analyzed by the Food and Drug Administration have shown no tampering, which has led one FDA official to characterize the period as one of 'psychosomatic mass hysteria.' " Further, a confectionary industry survey of police departments in "24 of the nation's largest cities, as well as smaller towns in which highly-publicized incidents were alleged to have occurred, found two reports of injuries—neither requiring medical treatment—from among the hundreds of claims of candy tampering." [5] Thus, not only does a survey of press coverage reveal

---

[3]The particulars of these cases are sometimes forgotten, so that the deaths continue to be used as proof that Halloween sadists pose a real threat. Trubo (1974:28) describes Toston as "the victim of a sadistic prankster." Similarly, an anonymous reviewer of an earlier draft of this paper recalled the O'Bryan case but did not mention that it was the boy's father who was convicted.

[4]Certainly other elements of everyday life, while not receiving as much attention, are far more hazardous. In 1980–81, according to the U.S. Consumer Product Safety Commission (1982), 60 children under age five died in "product associated deaths" involving nursery equipment and supplies; another 13 deaths involved toys.

---

[5]In one apparent hoax:

> . . . a youth claimed to have ingested an insecticide-saturated candy bar. . . . Testing showed no traces of any chemicals in the youth's blood. . . . although there was insecticide on one end of the bar, the side of the candy bar that had been bitten into was insecticide-free. (National Confectioners Association et al., n.d.)

Similarly, over 80% of the reports of so-called "copycat" poisonings that followed the Tylenol deaths were apparently fabricated (*Time,* 1982). Some were anonymous pranks, but others involved publicity-seekers or schemes to collect insurance settlements from manufacturers. As in the case of Halloween sadism, the threat was exaggerated: Congressional hearings denounced "a new kind of thug that is stalking the American communities" (U.S. Congress: House of Representatives, 1982:2), while psychiatrists speculated that "copycat criminals may have weak ego structures and 'have difficulty running their lives' " (*New York Times,* 1982).

fewer reports of Halloween sadism than might be expected, but there is good reason to suspect that many of the reports are unfounded.

Third, the press should not be held responsible for the widespread belief that Halloween sadism poses a serious threat. While the news media can manufacture "crime waves" by suddenly focusing on previously ignored offenses (Fishman, 1978), the press has given Halloween sadism relatively little publicity. Many of the 76 reported incidents received minimal coverage, in news stories of only two or three sentences. Often the reports were embedded in larger stories, such as a wire service summary of Halloween news from around the country. Nor did popular magazines highlight Halloween sadism; before 1982, only two short articles focused on the problem. The absence of authentic cases of serious injuries caused by Halloween sadism undoubtedly explains this limited coverage. While the publication of annual warnings to parents to inspect their children's treats, as well as occasional short items reporting minor incidents, may help keep the fear of Halloween sadism alive, the media do not seem to be the principal channel by which people learn of the danger. Rather, knowledge of Halloween sadism apparently spreads by word of mouth.

ROOTS OF AN URBAN LEGEND

The belief in Halloween sadism as a serious threat can be understood using a concept developed by folklorists: Halloween sadism is an *urban legend* (Grider, 1982). Urban legends are contemporary, orally transmitted tales that "often depict a clash between modern conditions and some aspect of a traditional life-style" (Brunvand, 1981:189). Whereas traditional legends often feature supernatural themes, most urban legends "are grounded in human baseness . . ." (Fine, 1980:227). They describe criminal

attacks, contaminated consumer goods, and other risks of modern life.[6] Halloween sadism combines two themes found in several other urban legends: danger to children (e.g., the babysitter who cooks an infant in a microwave oven; the child kidnapped from a department store or an amusement park); and contamination of food (e.g., the mouse in the soft-drink bottle; the Kentucky Fried Rat) (Brunvand, 1981, 1984; Fine, 1979, 1980, 1985). These legends, like that of the Halloween sadist, are typically told as true stories. They "gratify our desire to know about and to try to understand bizarre, frightening, and potentially dangerous or embarrassing events that *may* have happened" (Brunvand, 1981:12). Urban legends may even have a factual basis; soft-drink manufacturers have been sued by people claiming to have found mice in their drinks (Fine, 1979). Whether a legend begins with a real incident or as a fictional tale, it is told and retold, often evolving as it spreads. On occasion, urban legends appear in newspaper stories, reinforcing the tale's credibility (Brunvand, 1981, 1984). The belief in Halloween sadism is maintained through orally transmitted warnings about the dangers contemporary society poses for the traditional custom of trick-or-treating. These warnings, which greatly exaggerate the threat, are an urban legend. That some incidents of Halloween sadism have occurred, and that the media have reported such incidents, does not disqualify the warnings as legends.

---

[6]The term "urban legend" is generally used by folklorists to distinguish modern folk tales from those told in traditional societies; it ignores the differences between contemporary urban and rural communities. Some familiar urban legends include: "The Hook"—a maniac who terrorizes a couple parked in a lover's lane; the black widow spider that nests in a beehive hairdo; the deep-fried rat sold at a fried-chicken franchise; and "The Choking Doberman," that swallows a burglar's fingers. Brunvand's (1981, 1984) books present several dozen such tales.

Viewing Halloween sadism as an urban legend helps explain why the belief became widespread when it did. News reports of Halloween sadism are not new (cf., *New York Times*, 1950).[7] But the general perception that Halloween sadism is a serious threat can be dated to the early 1970s. This was the period when the press began reporting more incidents and warning parents to inspect treats, and legislatures began passing laws against Halloween sadism. In general, urban legends are products of social tension or strain. They express fears that the complexities of modern society threaten the traditional social order (Fine, 1980, 1985). Urban life requires contact with strangers who—the legends suggest—may be homicidal maniacs, unscrupulous merchants, voyeurs, or otherwise threatening. By repeating urban legends, people can respond to social strain, expressing their doubts about the modern world.

While it is obviously impossible to establish a causal link between particular social tensions and the spread of a particular urban legend, folklorists typically examine a legend's elements for clues about its roots (Brunvand, 1981, 1984; Fine, 1980). Some legends feature a transparent message, but others are more difficult to interpret. In the case of Halloween sadism, a plausible argument can be made that the legend's flowering in the early 1970s was tied to the heightened social strains of that period. The late 1960s and early 1970s were years of unparalleled divisiveness in post-World War II America (Carroll, 1982; O'Neill, 1971). The media exposed several serious crises to the public, including an increasingly unpopular war, ghetto riots, student demonstrations, and increased drug use. It was a period of intense social strain. Three forms of strain that emerged or grew during these years seem related to the growing fear of Halloween sadism.

Threats to Children

The form of strain that seems most clearly linked to a belief in Halloween sadism was the growing sense that children were no longer safe in the United States. During the 1960s and early 1970s, physicians and social workers promoted child abuse as a major social problem; the popular press responded with dozens of dramatic stories about children who had been cruelly treated by their parents (Pfohl, 1977). The rhetoric of this campaign emphasized that all children were potential victims, that child abuse occurred in all sectors of society. But even parents who remained confident that their children would never be abused could worry about losing their children to other threats. Older children adopted radical political views and experimented with illegal drugs.[8] Other parents found their grown children facing a less symbolic threat—death in Vietnam. The social conflicts that marked

---

[7]This case involved giving children pennies heated on a skillet. Apparently this was an early image of Halloween sadism; Grider (1982) recalls a heated pennies legend circulating among Texas children in the 1940s. Of course, the fear of Halloween sadism also seems linked to traditional warnings about accepting candy from strangers.

[8]The possibility that their children might adopt disapproved values may have suggested betrayal to some parents, creating another source of strain—ambivalence toward one's children. This ambivalence is nicely revealed in a popular cultural genre which regained popularity during the late 1960s and early 1970s. In popular novels and films (e.g., *The Exorcist* and *Rosemary's Baby*), the horror tale—traditionally associated with Halloween—took on a new emphasis: stories about children with demonic powers.

The concern with growing drug use may have been especially important in fostering the initial fear of Halloween sadism. Although only one of the 76 newspaper reports involved "hippies" giving drugs to children, early oral versions of contaminated-treat tales often took this form. (On a related, early 1970s legend—that LSD was being distributed on pictures of Mickey Mouse, which children might mistake for a lick-on tatoo—see Brunvand, 1984:162–69). Only later did the razor blade in the apple become the standard image for Halloween sadism. Six of the 12 incidents reported before 1967 involved over-the-counter or prescription drugs; only one involved a sharp object. In contrast, 49 of the 64 reports after 1966 involved razors or other sharp objects, while only four involved drugs. Of course, razor blades, pins, and so on are readily available equipment, which would make it easy to carry out hoaxes.

America during these years must have left many parents wondering if their hopes for the next generation would be fulfilled.

Since the emergence of the belief in Halloween sadism, the generation gap seems to have narrowed, but threats to children remain visible. The movement against child abuse continues to spread, receiving still more publicity. And, during the late 1970s and early 1980s, emerging campaigns against incest, child pornography, child molesting, and abortion may have contributed to a larger sense of children in jeopardy. Perhaps the clearest link between threats to children and the fear of Halloween sadism appeared during the series of murders of Atlanta schoolchildren. In 1980, STOP, an organization of the victims' parents, argued that "the city should organize Halloween night events that will minimize dangers to the children" (*New York Times*, 1980).[9]

Fear of Crime

Other forms of strain involved more general threats. Survey data reveal that the fear of crime grew substantially between the mid-1960s and the early 1970s (Erskine, 1974; Stinchcombe et al., 1980). Although violent crimes often involve offenders and victims who are acquainted, the fear of crime focuses on the threat of an anonymous attacker.[10] The threat of an unpredictable, unprovoked criminal attack parallels the Halloween sadist menace.

Mistrust of Others

Survey data also reveal rising expressions of general mistrust during the early 1970s. The proportion of Americans who agreed that

"... you can't be too careful in dealing with people" rose from 45.6 percent in 1966, to 50.0 percent in 1971, to 54.3 percent in 1973 (Converse et al., 1980:28). Studies of urban dwellers in the 1970s found high levels of mistrust for strangers (Fischer, 1982; Merry, 1981; Suttles, 1972). While warnings about the collapse of the neighborhood in the anonymous modern city have proven exaggerated, the belief that people now live in greater isolation remains widespread. The social conflicts of the 1960s and early 1970s may have encouraged doubts about the trustworthiness of other people. Such doubts provided another from of strain during the period when the belief in Halloween sadism spread.

These sources of strain—threats to children, fear of crime, and mistrust of others—provided a context within which the concern about Halloween sadism could flourish. The Halloween sadist emerged as a symbolic expression of this strain: the sadist, like other dangers, attacks children—society's most vulnerable members; the sadist, like the stereotypical criminal, is an anonymous, unprovoked assailant; and the sadist, like other strangers, must be met by doubt, rather than trust.[11] Placed in the context of the late 1960s and early 1970s, the spread of Halloween sadism is easily understood.

If these sources of strain account for the belief's spread, what explains its persistence? The extraordinary social conflicts of the early 1970s have moderated, yet the belief in Halloween sadism remains. Why? First, some of the same sources of strain continue to exist: the media still publicize threats to children (e.g., child abuse), and the fear of crime and strangers remains high.

---

[9]Similarly, the Tylenol poisonings raised the prospect of attacks via product contamination. Like the Atlanta murders, these real crimes by an anonymous sadist led to warnings about Halloween sadists.

[10]This fear also found expression in a popular culture horror genre—the "mad slasher" films in which a maniac stalks and kills a series of high school or college students. Interestingly, the first of these films was *Halloween* (1979).

---

[11]Grider (1982:6) agrees: "The Razor Blades Syndrome expresses a deep-rooted fear of strangers, a distrust of old customs and traditions, an acknowledgement of child abuse and infanticide, and an ambivalence toward random, wanton violence."

Second, and more important, Halloween sadism is an established urban legend; it can remain as a taken-for-granted, if dormant, part of American culture. The survey of newspaper stories found only five reports of Halloween sadism from 1976 to 1981—less than one per year.[12] However, warnings about sadists continued to appear during these years and, of course, the Tylenol poisonings in 1982 led to both predictions and reports of Halloween sadism.

Third, folklorists have traced the evolution of some legends over centuries (Brunvand, 1984). Legends seem most likely to persist when they have a general, underlying message (for instance, warnings about trusting outsiders) which can be tailored to fit new situations. Thus, the dangers of eating commercially prepared food were detailed in nineteenth-century stories about cat meat in baked pies and, more recently, in tales about rats sold at fried-chicken franchises (Fine, 1980; Simpson, 1983). Like other urban legends about homicidal maniacs, the Halloween sadist legend expresses fears about criminal attacks. Given the general nature of this threat, the legend may persist as long as the custom of trick-or-treating.

URBAN LEGENDS AS UNCONSTRUCTED SOCIAL PROBLEMS

Where do urban legends fit within the broader framework of sociological theory? The case of Halloween sadism suggests (1) that urban legends may be viewed as a form of unconstructed social problem, (2) that collective hysteria, urban legends, and social problems construction offer alternative responses to social strain, and

(3) that the emergence of a particular response to strain reflects social organization.

At first glance, the fear of Halloween sadists resembles some of the instances of collective hysteria in the collective behavior literature. The Halloween sadist can stand beside the "phantom anesthetist" of Mattoon (Johnson, 1945), the "phantom slasher" of Taipei (Jacobs, 1965), the "June bug epidemic" in a Southern textile plant (Kerckhoff and Back, 1968), and the windshield pitting in Seattle (Medalia and Larsen, 1958) as a focus of exaggerated fears. Studies of collective hysteria usually account for the emergence of hysterical beliefs as a response to social strain: the Mattoon episode occurred during wartime; the workers in the textile plant were putting in heavy overtime, and so on. In response to this strain, there emerges a belief in some threat, "an ambiguous element in the environment with a generalized power to threaten or destroy" (Smelser, 1962:82). This threat is credible, frightening, and difficult to protect oneself against:

> Instead of simply having a feeling that something is awry, the belief in a tangible threat makes it possible to *explain* and *justify* one's sense of discomfort—instead of anxiety, one experiences fear, and it is then possible to act in some meaningful way with respect to this tangible threat rather than just feeling frustrated and anxious. (Kerckhoff and Back, 1968:160–61—emphasis in original)

However, some of this model's key features do not fit the emergence of the belief in Halloween sadism and other urban legends. Collective hysteria is bounded in time and space. Hysterical beliefs are short-lived; they typically emerge, spread, and die within the space of a few days or weeks. Further, they are typically confined to a restricted locality—a single region, town, or facility (Lofland, 1981). In contrast, the belief in Halloween sadists appears to have spread more slowly, over a period of years, and to have become an established, taken-for-granted part of the culture. Nor has the belief observed the normal

---

[12]Presumably, incidents continued to be reported during this period. The decline in press coverage may have reflected journalists' doubts about the authenticity of the reports (*Editor and Publisher*, 1973), as well as their recognition that the reported incidents were minor and, given the well-established nature of the legend, no longer newsworthy.

geographic limits of collective hysteria—reports of Halloween sadism have come from throughout the country, suggesting that the belief is nationwide. If the Halloween sadist resembles the threats identified in instances of collective hysteria, the dynamics of the belief's spread do not fit the hysterical pattern.

The process of social problems construction offers an alternative perspective for understanding the fear of Halloween sadism. Blumer (1971) and Spector and Kitsuse (1973, 1977) defined social problems as products of claims-making activities, in which people call others' attention to social conditions. Thus, the emergence of a social problem is a political process: ". . . recognition by a society of its social problems is a highly selective process, with many harmful social conditions and arrangements not even making a bid for attention and with others falling by the wayside in what is frequently a fierce competitive struggle" (Blumer, 1971:302). Case studies of claims-making focus on the role of social movements (Tierney, 1982), professionals (Pfohl, 1977), the press (Schoenfeld et al., 1979), and other interested parties in constructing social problems. While these studies demonstrate how some claims-making campaigns succeeded, they do not explain why other social conditions, with the potential to be defined as social problems, never reach this status. Emergent or unconstructed social problems are less often studied (Troyer and Markle, 1983, 1984). Urban legends, such as the Halloween sadist, may be seen in these terms.

While the belief in Halloween sadism is widespread, it has not led to effective claims-making activities. Halloween sadism has, for brief occasions, occupied the attention of legislators, city officials, journalists, and PTA associations, but the belief spread largely outside institutionalized channels.[13] The press never reported more than a

handful of incidents in a given year, and most of these reports were very short; the belief spread informally, by word-of-mouth. Similarly, there was no especially visible response to the threat. By the mid-1970s, the press reported a few organized attempts to thwart sadists—hospitals offering to X-ray treats, communities organizing alternative celebrations, and municipalities passing ordinances against trick-or-treating.[14] But most of these efforts remained localized; they received little publicity and did not lead to a broader, organized response to Halloween sadism. (Similarly, organized campaigns by the confectionary industry to expose fabricated reports of Halloween sadism also failed to attract widespread recognition [*Editor and Publisher*, 1973; National Confectioners Association et al., n.d.].) While it is possible to trace the claims-making activities by which many social problems are constructed, this is not true for Halloween sadism. Although the belief spread widely, it moved largely through informal channels, and the principal reaction—parents restricting their children's trick-or-treating—was equally informal.

This analysis suggests that collective hysteria, urban legends, and social problems construction are alternative responses to social strain, alternatives in which strain is translated into different forms of threat that are spread through different forms of social organization. Strain—discomfort caused by existing social conditions—is made manifest in a perceived threat to the collectivity.[15] This threat may be genuine or false. Commonly, genuine threats

---

[13]Medical professionals, for instance, paid minimal attention to Halloween sadism. MEDLINE listed no articles on the subject from 1966 to 1983.

[14]While the press routinely interpreted these actions as responses to Halloween sadism, many attempts to restrict trick-or-treating were, in fact, prompted by more traditional Halloween problems, e.g., vandalism or children struck by cars (cf. Trubo, 1974).

[15]Social constructionist theorists attack the notion that strain or other objective social conditions offer a sufficient explanation for social problems; they argue that claims-making activities must occur (Blumer, 1971; Spector and Kitsuse, 1977). Troyer and Markle (1983), however, suggest that strain usually, if not always, precedes claims-making.

identify the source of social strain (e.g., pollution endangers the quality of life), while false threats are a more symbolic expression of strain (e.g., a "June bug" attacks people under a heavy work load). The identification of genuine threats often suggests a solution—something that can be done to reduce or eliminate the threat—while false threats are frequently amorphous and difficult or impossible to manage. In general, collective hysteria and urban legends respond to strain through the identification of false threats, while social problems construction deals with genuine threats. Social organization affects the spread of perceptions of threat. In compact, homogeneous collectivities, collective hysteria can spread quickly. In larger, more diffuse collectivities, it takes longer to attract attention to the threat and to mobilize concerned individuals. Typically, in social problems construction, some individuals take the lead in organizing claims-making activities, while urban legends spread through informal contacts.

The example of Halloween sadism suggests some specific factors that may affect the response to social strain. The reports of Halloween sadism did not lead to collective hysteria for two reasons. First, the belief spread throughout the country, rather than within a compact collectivity. Second, this spread could occur relatively slowly, given the limited nature of the threat. Reports of sadistic incidents posed no threat to other children for another year. There was no urgency to the news; the tale could be disseminated slowly, through informal channels. Although a few organizations began claims-making activities directed at Halloween sadism, little came of their efforts. In part, this may have been caused by the absence of serious, documented sadistic incidents; without genuine atrocities to demonstrate the need for action, claims-makers had trouble making a convincing case. Further, potential social movements aimed at Halloween sadism lacked a well-organized natural constituency; while no one approved of Halloween sadism, no group

found it in its interest to mount a sustained campaign against the threat. Again, the fact that the danger was limited to one evening a year may have inhibited the construction of Halloween sadism as a social problem. Nor was it clear how collective action might stop Halloween sadism; parents who worried about the threat found the best protection in individually curtailing their children's trick-or-treating or inspecting their treats. Thus, the diffuse collectivity, the infrequency of the reported attacks, the absence of convincing evidence, the lack of interested individuals willing to commit extensive time to the cause, and the difficulty of devising solutions meant that Halloween sadism became the focus of neither collective hysteria nor successful claims-making. Yet, retaining considerable symbolic power as an expression of social strain, Halloween sadism endured as an urban legend.

IMPLICATIONS: "HALLOWEEN AND THE MASS CHILD" REVISITED

Holiday celebrations reflect the larger culture. The events celebrated, as well as the customary ways of celebrating, reveal the society's values and structure. And, as society changes, its holidays often take on new meanings, consistent with the altered culture. Where earlier American celebrations were communal, ceremonial, and often religious or patriotic, contemporary observances tend to be individualistic, materialistic, secular occasions, marked largely by unstructured leisure time (Caplow, 1982; Caplow and Williamson, 1980; Hatch, 1978).[16]

Gregory P. Stone's (1959) "Halloween and the Mass Child" developed this thesis. Stone traced the evolution of Halloween activities in

---

[16]When they are inconsistent with modern practices, earlier forms of celebrating may be forgotten. On the drunken, riotous Christmas customs of the nineteenth-century working class, see Davis (1982).

his lifetime, from the elaborate pranks of adolescents in the 1930s, to the playful trick-or-
treating of young children in the 1950s. He
found the 1950s children did not understand the
extortionate premise of "trick or treat"; for
them, Halloween was merely an occasion to receive candy. Stone interpreted this shift as consistent with the changes in American values described in Reisman's (1950) *The Lonely Crowd*:

> . . . Reisman's character type of "other-
> direction" may, indeed, be a *prototype* of
> American character and not some strange
> mutation in the northeast. Consumption, tol-
> erance, and conformity were recognizable in
> the Halloween masquerade of a near-south-
> ern town. Production, indignation, and auton-
> omy were not. (Stone, 1959:378—emphasis
> in original)

Twenty-five years after Stone's analysis, the
fear of Halloween sadism has further altered the
meaning of Halloween. While Stone saw trick-
or-treating as a part of the emerging culture of
consumption, folklorists view Halloween as
among the least commercialized of modern holidays (Grider, 1982; Santino, 1983). But this in-
formality has been labeled dangerous by those
who warn against Halloween sadists. Children
are urged to refuse homemade treats and accept
only coupons or mass-produced candy with intact wrappings, as though commercialism offers
protection.[17] Long celebrated through vandalism
and extortion, Halloween has been a symbolic
expression of disorder. Today, the Halloween
sadist has become an annual reminder of the
fragility of the social bond—an expression of
growing doubts about the safety of children, the
trustworthiness of strangers, and the strength of
the modern urban community.

Examining the fear of Halloween sadists reveals topics that deserve further sociological attention. First, urban legends merit more analysis
as expressions of social strain. Second, theories
of social problems construction need to address
the processes by which topics become the focus
of claims-making activities. Most existing case
studies describe relatively successful claims-
making efforts, taking for granted the appropriateness of those efforts. But a complete theory
of social problems construction would also examine the earliest stages in the process, asking
why some social conditions fail to become the
focus for claims-making, how strain, social organization, and other social conditions generate
claims-making, and why some strain is translated into collective hysteria or urban legends,
rather than claims-making. To define social
problems in terms of claims-making without
identifying the roots of that process begs the
question of why some phenomena become social problems.

REFERENCES

Blumer, Herbert
1971 "Social problems as collective behavior." *Social Problems* 18:298–306.
Brunvand, Jan Harold
1981 *The Vanishing Hitchhiker*. New York: Norton.
1984 *The Choking Doberman*. New York: Norton.
Caplow, Theodore
1982 "Christmas gifts and kin networks." *American
Sociological Review* 47:383–92.
Caplow, Theodore and Margaret Holmes Williamson
1980 "Decoding Middletown's Easter Bunny." *Semi-
otica* 32:221–32.
Carroll, Peter N.
1982 *It Seemed Like Nothing Happened*. New York:
Holt, Rinehart, & Winston.
Converse, Philip E., Jean D. Dotson, Wendy J. Hoag
and Williams H. McGee III
1980 *American Social Attitudes Data Sourcebook*.
Cambridge: Harvard University Press.
Davis, Susan G.
1982 " 'Making the night hideous.' " *American
Quarterly* 34:185–99.

---

[17]The intense reaction to the Tylenol murders reflected consumers' dependence on mass-produced food and medications. "The revolt of the product is the ultimate nightmare
for a society like ours" (Spiro, 1982:11). However, new
standards for tamper-resistant packaging apparently
reestablished confidence in product safety.

DeKalb Daily Chronicle
1984 "Sidewalk interview." October 28:10.

Editor and Publisher
1973 "Press finds Halloween sadism rare but warns of danger." 106 (March 3):22.

Erskine, Hazel
1974 "The polls: fear of crime and violence." *Public Opinion Quarterly* 38:131–45.

Fine, Gary Alan
1979 "Cokelore and coke law." *Journal of American Folklore* 92:477–82.
1980 "The Kentucky fried rat." *Journal of the Folklore Institute* 17:222–43.
1985 "The Goliath effect." *Journal of American Folklore* 98:63–84.

Fischer, Claude S.
1982 *To Dwell Among Friends*. Chicago: University of Chicago Press.

Fishman, Mark
1978 "Crime waves as ideology." *Social Problems* 25:531–43.

Fresno Bee
1984 "No tricks found in Fresno treats." November 1:B1.

Grider, Sylvia
1982 "The razor blades in the apples syndrome." Unpublished paper.

Hatch, Jane M. (ed.)
1978 *The American Book of Days*. Third edition. New York: Wilson.

Isaacs, Susan and Robert Royeton
1982 "Witches, goblins, ghosts." *Parents Magazine* 57 (October):66–9.

Jacobs, Norman
1965 "The phantom slasher of Taipei." *Social Problems* 12:318–28.

Johnson, Donald M.
1945 "The 'phantom anesthetist' of Mattoon." *Journal of Abnormal and Social Psychology* 40:175–86.

Kerckhoff, Alan C. and Kurt W. Back
1968 *The June Bug*. New York: Appleton-Century-Crofts.

Lofland, John
1981 "Collective behavior." Pp. 411–46 in Morris Rosenberg and Ralph H. Turner (eds.), *Social Psychology*. New York: Basic Books.

Los Angeles Times

1982 "Trick or treat subdued amid poisoning scares." November 1:1,28.

Medalia, Nahum Z. and Otto N. Larsen
1958 "Diffusion and belief in a collective delusion." *American Sociological Review* 23:180–86.

Merry, Sally Engle
1981 *Urban Danger*. Philadelphia: Temple University Press.

National Confectioners Association, Chocolate Manufacturers Association, and National Candy Wholesalers Association
n.d. "Halloween/1982: an overview." Unpublished paper.

New York Times
1950 "Punish Halloween 'witch,' angry parents demand." November 3:52.
1970 "Those treats may be tricks." October 28:56.
1972 "Trick-or-treating till stroke of 7." November 1:30.
1980 "Atlanta and Miami curbing Halloween." October 31:A14.
1982 "Experts theorize about 'copycat syndrome.'" October 30:6.

Newsweek
1975 "The goblins will getcha. . . ." 86 (November 3):28.

O'Neill, William L.
1971 *Coming Apart*. Chicago: Quadrangle.

Pfohl, Stephen J.
1977 "The 'discovery' of child abuse." *Social Problems* 24:310–23.

Riesman, David
1950 *The Lonely Crowd*. New Haven: Yale University Press.

San Francisco Chronicle
1970 "Capsule caused Halloween death." November 10:3.

Santino, Jack
1983 "Halloween in America." *Western Folklore* 42:1–20.

Schoenfeld, A. Clay, Robert F. Meier and Robert J. Griffin
1979 "Constructing a social problem." *Social Problems* 27:38–61.

Simpson, Jacqueline
1983 "Urban legends in *The Pickwick Papers*." *Journal of American Folklore* 96:462–70.

Smelser, Neil J.

1962 *Theory of Collective Behavior.* New York: Free Press.

Spector, Malcolm, and John I, Kitsuse

1973 "Social problems." *Social Problems* 21:145–59.

1977 *Constructing Social Problems.* Menlo Park, CA: Cummings.

Spiro, Peter

1982 "Chaos by the capsule." *New Republic* 187 (December 6):10–1.

Stinchcombe, Arthur L., Rebecca Adams, Carol A. Heimer, Kim Lane Scheppele, Tom W. Smith and D. Garth Taylor

1980 *Crime and Punishment.* San Francisco: Jossey-Bass.

Stone, Gregory P.

1959 "Halloween and the mass child." *American Quarterly* 11:372–79.

Suttles, Gerald D.

1972 *The Social Construction of Communities.* Chicago: University of Chicago Press.

Tierney, Kathleen J.

1982 "The battered woman movement and the creation of the wife beating problem." *Social Problems* 29:207–20.

Time

1982 "Copycats on the prowl." 120 (November 8):27.

Times (Beaverton, OR)

1984 "Letters." October 25:36.

Troyer, Ronald J. and Gerald E. Markle

1983 *Cigarettes*, New Brunswick, NJ: Rutgers University Press.

1984 "Coffee drinking." *Social Problems* 31:403–16.

Trubo, Richard

1974 "Holiday for sadists." *PTA Magazine* 69:28–9.

U.S. Congress: House of Representatives

1982 Hearing on Tamper-Resistant Packaging for Over-the-Counter Drugs. Committee on Energy and Commerce, Subcommittee on Health and the Environment. 96th Congress, 2nd session. Washington: U.S. Government Printing Office.

U.S. Consumer Product Safety Commission

1982 *Annual Report.* Washington: U.S. Government Printing Office.

Van Buren, Abigail

1983 "Dear Abby." *Fresno Bee* (October 31):D2.

1984 "Dear Abby." *Fresno Bee* (September 30):C4.

DISCUSSION QUESTIONS

1. Think back on your own Halloween experiences as a child. What messages did you receive about the dangers of this holiday from your parents, teacher, peers, and the media?
2. Identify another urban myth and attempt to discern potential reasons for why it emerged and was readily believed by many people.

RACE

This section is concerned with the continuing relevance of racial divisions in American life. Race refers to a category of social division and organization that is based on what are presumed to be socially significant biological differences. Typically, racial categories have been constructed by pointing to differences in skin pigmentation, hair texture, and various other body features. One of the earliest divisions of humankind into racial categories occurred when the Swedish taxonomist Linnaeus defined four races: white, yellow, red, and black. Add brown, and one hears the language of race in the twenty-first century.

The general consensus among social scientists today is that, if defined in biological terms, the physical differences associated with race are irrelevant. However, note the words "socially significant" above. Race is significant if it is so defined. The history of racial discourse is one in which observed biological differences are used to make claims about presumed racial differences in terms of intellectual and moral development. In other words, the language of race has been employed to make invidious comparisons between and among groups.

For this reason, some scholars believe that the term should be discarded. Others argue against this position, following the logic of the early sociologist W. I. Thomas, who once said that if people define a situation as real, the consequences of that belief are, indeed, real. Thus, race is relevant if large numbers of people in a particular society define it as relevant.

In the context of the United States, race has been a powerful—some would say the most powerful—societal division throughout the nation's history. Shaping the successive racial formations throughout the nation's history has been the relationship between blacks and whites. The place of other groups in America has been predicated on who is black, who is white, and where to place those that are neither. This was the case during the centuries-long era of slavery, and after the Civil War during the period of mandated segregation and oppression of blacks—extending from around 1870 until the 1960s—that was known as the Jim Crow era. It is also the case at present, in what has been characterized as the post–civil rights era.

What makes race relations so complicated at present is a consequence of two profound changes that occurred in the 1960s. First, the civil rights movement led to the end of the Jim Crow period and the dawn of a new era in black-white relations. The civil rights movement accomplished some of its goals. Legal segregation is no longer permitted. Levels of prejudice and discrimination have declined. A substantial black middle class has emerged. At the same time, for the poorest blacks living in inner cities—those who should be seen as the "truly disadvantaged"—life remains difficult and dangerous. Racism has not disappeared and many blacks continue to live in segregated neighborhoods. Complicating the situation for blacks further, after four decades during which mass immigration ceased, newcomers began to enter the United States in large numbers once again. The result is that the black community has changed in significant ways, and at the same time the nation has become more racially diverse than it was a relatively short time ago.

In assessing how far we have come and how far we have to go to achieve racial justice, it is important to assess the role of old-fashioned racism, the presence of new forms of racism, and the extent to which American society remains separate and unequal. The three articles in this section address these issues from various angles.

A Tale of Two Restaurant Chains

Joe R. Feagin and Hernán Vera

*Since the end of the civil rights movement,
sociologists have attempted to assess how far
American society has come in ending its long legacy
of racial oppression. Joe Feagin and Hernán Vera
disagree with the claim, made most cogently by
William Julius Wilson, that the significance of race
and the impact of racism have been steadily
declining in America in recent decades. Instead they
contend that prejudice and discrimination are major
problems confronting African Americans today. In
this chapter from* White Racism, *the authors provide
one example to support their case, as they examine
two national restaurant chains that have revealed
persistent patterns of institutional racial
discrimination.*

On February 1, 1960, four African American
college students sat down at a Woolworth lunch
counter in Greensboro, North Carolina. Although black patrons could purchase items in
other areas of the store, they were not served at
the food counter. In a later interview one white
employee said that she would have served the
black students, but her managers would not
allow her to do so. The next day, as word got
around, more than two dozen black students occupied the counter, doing schoolwork when they
were refused service. As their numbers grew
over the next few days, a few whites joined the
students, but most whites heckled them. Whites
across the nation verbally assaulted the student
demonstrators for transgressing the color line.
The protest spread to the rest of Greensboro's
lunch counters, all of which were quickly
closed. The spontaneous actions of these black
students protesting racial discrimination in public accommodations marked the beginning of
the modern sit-in movement.[1]

The Reverend Martin Luther King, Jr., told
the black student leaders "not to forget that the
struggle was justice versus injustice, not black
versus white."[2] The efforts of black customers
to be treated fairly in white-owned restaurants
are but one example in the long history of
African Americans' struggle to overcome injustice. The sit-ins were not just about gaining access to food counters. The rituals of racism at
lunch counters or family restaurants, as well as
in other public accommodations, proclaim a
message of exclusion from the national society
that few other acts of discrimination can deliver
with as much force. For black Americans today,
encounters with discrimination in public accommodations summon up this collective memory
of past degradation. For black and white Americans, discrimination of this type is yet another
marker of the racialized geography of American
towns and cities.

Eating out is often a meaningful social
event and is a frequent activity for many families. The restaurant industry is one with which
most Americans, white and black, have repeated contact. Yet, even though African
Americans spend a quarter of their food budgets eating away from home, some segments
of the restaurant industry, including some
"family restaurants," still discriminate against
black customers.

The idea of the family-restaurant chain originated in the United States, then spread around
the globe. Conrad P. Kottack has noted the behavioral uniformity one finds at such restaurants: people "know how to behave, what to expect, what they will eat, and what they will
pay."[3] The racial uniformity imposed by whites
at public eating places like lunch counters, the
forerunners of fast-food and family restaurants,
was obvious during the days of legal segregation. It was not by chance that these public eating places were selected by civil rights activists
in the 1960s as major targets for desegregation.
This reading examines the continuing reports of
racial discrimination in America's family restaurants, first in employment and then against
black customers.

DISCRIMINATION IN EMPLOYMENT

The restaurant industry is the largest employer of service workers, white and black, in the United States. This institutional arena is filled with opportunities for whites with racist inclinations to victimize blacks. In some cases it is white customers who create problems for black employees, but most publicized complaints in recent years have been against management. Restaurants across the nation have been charged with discrimination against black employees.

Although black workers make up a tenth of all those employed in the United States, they constitute 13 percent of those in food service jobs. Sixteen percent of kitchen workers and 19 percent of cooks are black, compared with only 5 percent of waiters and waitresses and less than 3 percent of bartenders. Black workers are more likely to be in the back of a restaurant than in the front. The food service industry hires more black employees than all other major industries, but few are to be found in the ranks of the industry's management or as owners of franchises.[4] In the District of Columbia in 1993 the lack of black workers in customer contact jobs precipitated organized protests that brought increased opportunities for black workers. The district's 1,500 restaurants employed 30,000 workers, but a 1993 survey found that many of the district's best restaurants employed no black servers or bartenders. Black workers were buspersons or kitchen workers. As a result of the protests, numerous restaurants improved the representation of minority workers in their better-paying jobs.[5]

Very few black entrepreneurs have been able to secure franchises in major family-restaurant chains. Black entrepreneurs have also had great difficulty obtaining bank loans to start restaurants, either on their own or as part of a franchise arrangement. One black businessperson in Los Angeles recently noted that when a black person deals with banks, "a definite barrier [is] set up." In 1992 this man started a Denny's franchise in Watts, a black community in Los Angeles. Until then, no one had succeeded in obtaining money for a new full-service restaurant in the area since the major 1965 Watts riot. In the early 1990s this was the only Denny's owned by an African American.[6]

Shoney's, Inc., and Charges of Employment Discrimination

Headquartered in Nashville, Tennessee, the Shoney's family restaurant chain is one of the largest in the United States. In 1993 it included 1,800 restaurants (under several names) with 30,000 employees in 36 states. During the 1980s a number of individual lawsuits were filed against Shoney's charging employment discrimination, and the federal Equal Employment Opportunity Commission (EEOC) reportedly received hundreds of discrimination complaints involving the firm's hiring practices. In 1989 the chain's national image was damaged when a number of black job applicants along with black employees and former employees, with the aid of NAACP Legal Defense Fund attorneys, filed a class-action job discrimination suit against the company. This case involved the largest number of employees and employment locations of any class-action suit in the history of such workplace litigation.[7]

The suit charged that Shoney's had "turned away black applicants and relegated the few it hired to kitchen chores."[8] Black employees stated that they were assigned the least desirable hours. Even some white supervisors reported that they were fired or threatened with demotion if they refused to obey instructions to restrict black employment in the company. A former assistant manager reported that she was told to darken the "O" in the Shoney's logo on job application forms to indicate that an applicant was black.[9]

According to some reports antiblack attitudes and policies had been common in the company from its beginning. Depositions from job applicants, employees, and managers at all levels of the company implicated numerous restaurant managers, supervisors, and executives in discrimination in hiring, firing, and promotions. A number of executives have described the racial views of Raymond L. Danner, Shoney's cofounder and chair of its board. Former chief executive officer (CEO) Dave Wachtel said Danner's negative views of African Americans were widely known and that Danner had even said that he would match donations by his executives to the Ku Klux Klan.[10] A former personnel director stated, "Danner would say that no one would want to eat at a restaurant where 'a bunch of niggers' were working." A vice president said that Danner believed "Blacks were not qualified to run a store" and that "Blacks should not be employed in any position where they would be seen by customers."[11] Danner was also charged with instructing his managers to fire black employees when they became too numerous and with using racial slurs when talking about his black employees.[12] During lawsuit depositions, Danner himself admitted to having used the "nigger" epithet and also that he had discussed one store's "possible problem area" being the presence of "too many black employees" relative to the "racial mix" in the store's geographical area.[13] In an important investigative report in the *Nation* Steve Watkins noted that Danner had once put into a letter his personal concern over too many black workers at one of his southern restaurants.[14]

The negative views of blacks were not just those of the company's founder. Watkins also reported that the views of some restaurant managers at Shoney's reflected the perspective attributed to Danner. Among the numerous racist code words reportedly used by some managers were "Arnold Schwarzenigger" for a muscular black man; "re-nigging" for rehiring blacks in a restaurant; and "nigger stores" for those in black communities.[15] It seems likely that the opinions attributed to Danner and some of his associates are not unique. The view that white customers dislike black servers, or at least too many black servers, has been found among other whites in

the restaurant industry. Black cooks in the kitchen may be acceptable, but blacks in customer contact positions sometimes are not.[16]

Prior to the class-action suit, less than 2 percent of the managerial and supervisory positions were filled by black employees. Only one of the sixty-eight division directors, and not one of the top executives, was black. The majority of black employees were in positions that did not involve regular contact with customers.[17] The chain's position that the restaurants needed only a small number of black workers, even in the low-wage positions, brings to mind Sidney Willhelm's argument that much black labor is no longer needed by a U.S. economy that is restructuring to take advantage of low-wage immigrants and workers overseas. Corporate disinvestment in the U.S. economy has also created a large group of whites seeking jobs, including lower-wage service jobs that might otherwise have become available to minority Americans.

Henry and Billie Elliott, the white supervisors of a Captain D's restaurant in Florida, part of the Shoney's chain, said that they were dismissed for refusing to terminate black workers and put whites in their place. The Elliotts filed suit to recover lost wages. They and their attorney, Tommy Warren, compiled 200 boxes of company records that reportedly reveal racial discrimination in the Shoney's empire. Eventually the Elliotts, who had taken jobs driving school buses, won their private legal struggle and received a substantial monetary settlement.[18] The Elliott's experience signals a very important aspect of contemporary racial relations—that whites too can be victims if they stand against what they feel to be unfair racial discrimination.

Lawsuits Bring Changes at Shoney's

The lawsuits and related publicity had a major impact on the corporation. White corporate executives usually do worry about the images of their companies, and a steady drumbeat of bad publicity can force them to take action whatever their own personal inclinations may be. This fact is especially true for an industry where an image presented in the media can affect everyday business. In 1989 Shoney's executives made an agreement with the Southern Christian Leadership Conference (SCLC) to hire and promote more black workers and to increase opportunities for blacks to secure business franchises. By the end of 1992 the firm had reportedly spent more than $120 million in black communities as a result of its agreement with the SCLC. Moreover, in the summer of 1993 the SCLC signed another agreement with Shoney's new head, Taylor Henry, Jr., who commented that he had "never seen any other covenant of this type in our industry." This second agreement committed the corporation to spending $60 million over several years to help black entrepreneurs buy land for business franchises and to establish black-owned businesses to supply Shoney's restaurants.[19]

By 1992 Shoney's had also increased its number of black employees, including managers and executives, significantly. Some black applicants were hired at Shoney's Nashville, Tennessee, headquarters. In 1989 a woman hired as vice president of corporate and community relations became the first black senior executive. A half dozen others were subsequently employed at the home office. Shoney's had begun to change its image and was making one of the most aggressive moves to hire minorities in the restaurant industry. By 1992 the firm had also substantially increased its business with black suppliers.[20] Disagreement within the firm arose, however, over the aggressive implementation of the remedial and affirmative action plans. In December 1992 Leonard Roberts, the chair and chief executive hired in 1989 to deal with the charges of racism and affirmative action, resigned his position. Three other top managers working on the remedial plans were fired. According to some sources, Roberts was forced to resign because of his aggressive approach

to affirmative action, although company representatives denied this charge. Roberts was replaced with Taylor Henry, Jr. late in December 1992.[21]

In November 1992, the restaurant chain's executives agreed to settle the major class-action lawsuit out of court. This action did not require that the firm's executives admit to discrimination, and they were also able to avoid the negative publicity of a major court trial. Shoney's agreed to pay $105 million between 1993 and 2000 to the many former and present black employees who had charged the company with discrimination and to some white employees who were fired for protesting what they saw as discriminatory company actions. Although this amount was far less than the $350 million in back pay and $180 million in punitive and compensatory damages that the litigants had originally sought, it was the largest settlement ever in a job discrimination case. The firm also agreed to hire more black local managers and regional directors.[22] Taylor Henry, Jr. stated that the lawsuit had focused the company's "priorities on doing what is right. We are a changed company, and we regret any mistakes we made in the past."[23] After the settlements, Danner resigned from the board charging that the firm had not dealt with him fairly.

The $105 million Shoney's settlement has been discussed in the mass media as an indicator of the high cost of persisting racial discrimination. In a February 7, 1993, column titled "Paying the Price of Racism," columnist Clarence Page made this point and noted that the Shoney's case, among others, shows "how racism is alive and well in America" even in a society with "sweeping anti-discrimination laws."[24] In a restaurant industry publication one writer spoke candidly of "recent discrimination scandals involving the Denny's and Shoney's chains." The writer continued with a lengthy discussion of the "disturbing and costly problems" of racial discrimination "still dogging the restaurant industry."[25]

Remedial responses to reported discrimination such as those made at Shoney's are particularly important because of the difficulty individual victims have in dealing with government enforcement agencies. Employment discrimination in the United States is a major problem for African American workers in all income groups, but U.S. antidiscrimination laws are weakly enforced, and government-aided remedies usually come slowly if at all. The 1964 Civil Rights Act and later amendments officially prohibit racial discrimination in employment; the EEOC was created to enforce the act by investigating complaints, seeking conciliation, and filing suits to end discrimination. For a time, the federal courts and the EEOC played a major role in reducing racial barriers, but under the conservative Reagan and Bush administrations in the 1980s and early 1990s, the number of broad, institutionally focused investigations of discrimination conducted by the agency declined sharply.[26] As reported by the EEOC, black complaints of job discrimination grew from 112,000 in 1990 to 124,000 in 1992, and the pace of resolving complaints was usually slow. As a result, many black victims of discrimination turned to the NAACP for help. The chair of Howard University's Afro-American Studies Department noted: "Folks are turning to them [local NAACP chapters] on the assumption they have the manpower to handle the problems they are talking about, but many branches are just discussion groups."[27] The NAACP's small legal staff has become overwhelmed; this organization cannot replace governmental agencies whose mandates include the eradication of discrimination in employment across the nation.

During their terms Presidents Ronald Reagan and George Bush appointed several conservative justices to the U.S. Supreme Court, which subsequently handed down a number of restrictive decisions that made it more difficult for workers to bring and win discrimination suits.[28] As a result of the court backtracking on enforcement, it became more difficult for the victims of employment discrimination to win in court. An Urban Institute research study that sent matched white and black applicants to the same employers found that a significant proportion of the black applicants suffered discrimination in the hiring process. In addition, the overwhelming majority of black respondents in a late 1980s national survey felt that if an equally qualified black and white were competing for the same job, the black applicant would be likely to suffer racial discrimination.[29]

FAMILY RESTAURANTS AND BLACK CUSTOMERS

The problems African Americans face at family restaurants extend beyond employment to a variety of customer service issues. Indeed, the degrading racial images used by some restaurant chains have caused black customer boycotts and protests. For example, in the late 1970s some critics targeted the Sambo's family restaurant chain, a California-based firm with one thousand locations across the nation, because of the stereotypic "Little Black Sambo" story its name suggested and because some restaurants used that story's cartoon-type character as a logo. Complaints were filed against the firm with the Rhode Island Commission on Human Rights, which ruled that the name made black customers feel unwelcome and ordered the name of Sambo's restaurants in that state to be changed. Subsequently, Sambo's restaurants in a number of states changed their name to Sam's or A Place Like Sam's, although the company denied that these changes were made because of charges of racism. By 1981 the chain was losing millions of dollars and had closed half of its restaurants. By the mid-1980s all of its restaurants were closed or sold.[30] The name controversy and declining black patronage were likely contributors to the chain's demise. Here again black families were major victims of symbolic violence, but they were not the only ones to pay a price. The cost of racial insensitivity for the whites involved was very substantial.

In recent years, the Denny's family restaurant chain has faced numerous charges of racial discrimination against black customers. In the early 1990s this firm had nearly 1,500 restaurants across the nation. About 70 percent were company owned; the rest were mostly white-owned franchises. Denny's parent firm, Flagstar Companies, Inc., of Spartanburg, South Carolina, with 120,000 employees, is one of the largest corporations in the nation. In the early 1990s Denny's reportedly faced more than 4,300 complaints of racial discrimination by black customers. One report from Denny's management noted that among the restaurants under the Flagstar umbrella the Denny's chain had the fewest patrons from black and other minority groups.[31] A lawyer for one group of black plaintiffs who filed a class-action suit against Denny's in the spring of 1993 noted the direct historical connection between the student sit-ins of the 1960s and the discrimination recently reported at Denny's restaurants: "It evokes the memory of segregated lunch counters in the Deep South in the 1950s. And it's appalling to see this kind of 'Jim Crow' discrimination occurring in a California restaurant in the 1990s."[32]

In March 1993, one U.S. Department of Justice lawsuit against the company was resolved by a consent decree in which Denny's acknowledged no discrimination but agreed to conduct sensitivity training for all employees and to place notices in each restaurant indicating that patrons of all racial and ethnic groups would receive good service. The suit had alleged that the firm had a "pattern . . . of discrimination" that included such practices as requiring black customers, and not white customers, to prepay for their orders, demanding special identification, and excluding black patrons.[33] In various interviews about the charges of racial discrimination at Denny's, corporate officials denied that there was a company policy of discrimination but did admit that some Denny's restaurants had been the scene of "isolated" or "individual" instances of racial discrimination from time to time.[34]

In response to the many complaints of discrimination, Jerome J. Richardson, Flagstar's CEO, took an aggressive approach to remedying Denny's racial problems. Richardson met with Benjamin Chavis, NAACP executive director, late in May 1993 to discuss a "fair-share" agreement. Typically, such agreements are privately negotiated and oblige firms to take positive action to address black and other minority concerns. Fair-share agreements between civil rights organizations and businesses have sometimes been effective in channeling investments into minority communities. One NAACP analysis of forty fair-share agreements made by U.S. firms between 1988 and 1993 found that the companies had invested no less than $47 billion in minority employment, service companies, and franchises.[35]

In the summer of 1993, Richardson made a broad agreement with the NAACP that included aggressive minority recruitment, more minority franchises, and more use of minority service and support firms, including insurance and law firms. The agreement also included outside monitoring of the fairness of service at Denny's restaurants.[36] Denny's parent company agreed to invest $1 billion in black- and other minority-owned franchises and restaurant support firms and to place minority workers in 325 new management jobs in its restaurants by the year 2000.[37] The company agreed to substantially increase its purchasing from minority suppliers in this same period.[38] Television ads asserting the company's new image ran in forty-one cities.[39] Impressed by the extent of Richardson's actions, Chavis commented, "In my 30 years in the civil rights movement, I've never seen the commitments made by this CEO today."[40] Richardson said the agreement was "tangible evidence" of Flagstar's intention to end discrimination in its operations.[41] In addition to the NAACP agreement, some Flagstar executives and other representatives made highly visible appearances at NAACP and Urban League conventions, and newspapers reported that the company planned to arrange meetings with minority community groups.[42]

Significantly, however, the company's official position was that it had *not* fostered racial discrimination in its operations in the past or the present. While it is common for employers to refuse to admit past guilt when reaching a settlement, Denny's explicit denial had negative implications for the general public, both black and nonblack. Such a denial reduces the amount of media coverage and public discussion of the reality of discrimination in business settings. In addition, the settlements imply that the problem of antiblack discrimination is not basic to the U.S. economy by suggesting that a few short-range programs will solve whatever racism remains.

A California Class-Action Lawsuit

About the same time that Denny's executives agreed to the aforementioned consent decree with the Justice Department, a class-action suit against Denny's was filed in a California federal court. Thirty-two black plaintiffs alleged that they had faced discrimination at Denny's restaurants,[43] charging that white personnel at Denny's restaurants had discriminated against them in a number of ways.[44] They decided to pursue their case even though the consent decree had dealt with some of the general racial complaints against the firm.

The class-action suit focused on alleged incidents of racial discrimination in several California cities. Several incidents cited in the lawsuit involved prepayment for meals or special cover charges not applied to white patrons. A middle-class black couple had been required to prepay for their meals in a San Diego Denny's. The white manager of a San Jose Denny's had refused to seat a group of eighteen black high school and college students—who entered the restaurant after attending a symposium on what

college life was like for black students—unless they paid a cover charge and prepaid their meals. Reportedly, white students sitting nearby had not been required to prepay. The black students decided to leave, and the incident made the local news.[45] One of the young people said that the incident made him "embarrassed. I was mad that it was happening." Reflecting on the lawsuit, his father added that "We are not concerned with money. We just want to be able to go to a restaurant and order a meal like everyone else."[46]

Another incident cited in the lawsuit involved a free birthday meal. Seeking a pleasant family outing, a black couple had taken their children to a Denny's restaurant to celebrate their daughter's birthday, but the restaurant refused to honor the girl's baptismal certificate as proof and denied her the birthday meal. At a news conference on the events at the restaurant the mother stated, "I felt violated, humiliated and embarrassed, so we didn't eat there. I can't adequately describe the pain that you feel to see this happen to your child."[47] The daughter also reported great embarrassment: "They acted like we were begging for a meal. Everyone was angry after that and it wrecked my birthday night."[48] The goal of these black complainants is clear: to be treated fairly and equally. The cost of the humiliation for the black targets is also evident in their words: pain, frustration, and embarrassment.

The documents provided to the court indicated a range of racial problems. In an affidavit attached to the class-action suit, one Denny's employee documented "repeated instances of racial prejudice" in which employees treated black customers badly or differently from white customers. *Blackout* was used as a code word for too many black customers in a Denny's at one time; managers were expected to prevent these so-called blackouts.[49] In a statement for the media, a Denny's manager in California said his superiors had taught him "to avoid blackouts by requiring black customers to pay for their meals in advance or simply close the restaurant for a few hours." He added that when he objected to such action, his supervisor told him they would have to get another manager.[50]

These events reveal certain important aspects of white thought about black Americans in everyday situations. The code word *blackout* for too many black customers in a store may have originated as an attempt at humor, but the term has significance beyond racist joking. Like the electric blackout for which it is likely named, it represents a loss of proper functioning. White feelings and fears about African Americans can prevent whites from functioning in normal human ways. Concern over the presence of too many blacks relative to the number of whites is common among white Americans in many social settings. The racial geography we noted earlier has its own territorial imperative. Whites are often uncomfortable if the proportion of blacks in a given group—a residential neighborhood, for example—exceeds a modest percentage, perhaps 5–10 percent. One famous Detroit survey in the 1970s found that the proportion of white respondents who said they would be unwilling to move into a hypothetical neighborhood with black families increased as the black proportion increased. If the neighborhood were 8 percent black, just over one-quarter said that they would be unwilling to move in. But if the neighborhood were 36 percent black, three-quarters of the whites expressed an unwillingness to live there.[51] It is probably still true that a majority of whites would refuse to move into a substantially black community if they were faced with that possibility.

Indeed, many whites are uncomfortable with the presence of *any* black people in what they view as white territory, such as historically white restaurants. Why are so many whites uneasy in the presence of black people? One answer may be that these whites reject black people because they project certain fears onto the dark otherness. The work of Joel Kovel and others who suggest that these antiblack fears and

impulses are irrational and that they are rooted in the world of the unconscious.[52] For some whites "blackouts" may symbolize dirt, danger, even the unknown—symbols rooted deeply in the white unconscious. Such reactions mark a breakdown in understanding across the color line.

Because of the consent decree Denny's made with the Justice Department, the firm's lawyers argued that the California class-action lawsuit should be set aside. However, lawyers for the black plaintiffs countered that the many charges of discrimination at Denny's restaurants across the United States provided ample reason to continue the private lawsuit.[53] Referring to Denny's persisting discrimination after the decree, a lawyer for the Washington Lawyers' Committee for Civil Rights and Urban Affairs contended that the U.S. Department of Justice should hold Denny's "in contempt of court for violating the terms of the consent decree."[54]

A Politicized Incident

On April 1, 1993, Dan Rather opened the CBS evening news with a statement about black Secret Service agents. As a Flagstar executive remembered it, Rather said, "They put their lives on the line every day, but they can't get served at Denny's."[55] The six black Secret Service agents had received what they viewed as discriminatory service at a Denny's restaurant in Annapolis, Maryland. They waited for about an hour while fifteen white agents, as well as white customers who entered the restaurant after they did, received speedy and repeated service. The agents made several attempts to get their waitress to serve them, then sought the manager, who did not come out immediately. Both the black and the white agents were in the same section of the restaurant, and all were dressed the same way.[56] This account suggests that any African American, regardless of his or her economic status, can be the victim of discrimination in public accommodations.

One of the black agents later remarked, "I was somewhat invisible that day."[57] He explained that he and the other black agents, like many black Americans, were reluctant to seek redress: "It was very difficult for us to come forth with this information. The question that went through our minds was, 'If not us, who? If not now, when?' And we answered that if we are about social responsibility as well as the Secret Service, we had to step forth."[58] These Secret Service agents felt a responsibility to confront discrimination on behalf of the black community. Denny's officials said that the problem that day was not discrimination but a backup in the kitchen. The manager was fired, but only for not reporting the incident. This well-publicized incident encouraged other black customers of Denny's to complain openly. Within a few months the agents' lawyers had received 250 reports of racial discrimination in service at a number of Denny's restaurants.[59]

The discrimination charges involving Denny's received widespread, albeit brief, national attention. Newspapers and television news shows carried editorials condemning the poor treatment of the agents. At the Annapolis restaurant civil rights organizations held a protest demonstration reminiscent of the 1960s lunch counter protests. Even the White House responded. Bill Clinton's communications director stated that the president "is strongly against discriminatory practices against anyone. Discrimination against black Secret Service agents would be a very serious problem."[60]

Late in May 1994 both the California class-action suit and another class-action suit brought on behalf of the black Secret Service agents were resolved by a consent decree in which Flagstar agreed to pay damages of $46 million to the victims of discrimination as well as $9 million in lawyers' fees.[61] In its report on the court settlement *Business Week* noted that Flagstar had "apologized for apparent racism" in some of its operations.[62] The head of Flagstar, Jerome Richardson, stated that the firm

settled in part to show that Denny's wants black customers: "We deeply regret these individuals feel they were not treated fairly at Denny's. We invite any customers who have perceived discrimination at Denny's to give us another opportunity to serve them."[63] He also indicated that some employees had been terminated because of the discrimination lawsuits.

In a news conference regarding the settlement Assistant Attorney General Deval Patrick stated that the Denny's decree was one type of solution for illegal discrimination in public accommodations: "There will be a high price to pay for unlawful indignities, and the Justice Department will exact that price whenever the law is violated."[64] Patrick indicated that the decree required Denny's to hire an independent monitor to watch over its implementation, the first time such a monitoring requirement had been agreed upon. He noted that in addition to the payment of monetary awards, the settlement required Denny's to advertise nationally that patrons from all racial and ethnic groups were welcome and "to conduct random testing to determine whether black patrons continue to be treated differently, because this testing helps to uncover this particular subtle form of racism."[65] This major U.S. Department of Justice involvement in racial discrimination lawsuits in the early Clinton administration was a clear break from the policies of the previous Reagan and Bush administrations and a hopeful indicator of renewed federal efforts to enforce existing civil rights laws in the area of public accommodations.

PROBLEMS AT OTHER RESTAURANTS

Shoney's and Denny's are not unique. Other family and fast-food restaurants have faced charges of racial and ethnic discrimination. Some are small and local and receive little media attention. A bar in Champaign, Illinois, that refused to admit black customers until compelled to do so by the Justice Department is but one example.[66] Most incidents that have received national media coverage have involved restaurant chains. In the late 1980s, after a number of complaints from potential patrons who represented a number of racial and ethnic groups, the California Department of Alcoholic Beverage Control ruled that the Red Onion chain had discriminated against minority patrons as part of company policy. The firm denied the charge of discrimination, but in the late 1980s it agreed to pay more than two hundred thousand dollars to twenty-nine people of color who charged they had been unfairly denied entry.[67]

In January 1993 another major chain, the International House of Pancakes (IHOP), with more than five hundred restaurants nationwide, agreed to pay $185,000 in settlement of a discrimination lawsuit.[68] The lawsuit charged that the white manager of an IHOP in Milwaukee refused entrance to a group of black college students when the restaurant locked its doors to several groups of black youth on December 28, 1991. The fifteen black plaintiffs, who had just attended a party hosted by Howard University alumni, reported that the IHOP manager and staff told them the twenty-four-hour restaurant was closed, although white customers were being admitted.[69]

Executives at family-restaurant chains, like those at other major U.S. businesses, have reportedly viewed racial and multicultural issues as diversions from their major business goals. Consequently, as some industry analysts have noted, racial and ethnic matters have often been approached in a superficial or too-bureaucratic manner. Company officials may address such issues on paper, but until they are confronted with a crisis most take little significant action. A *Business Week* report concluded that top officials at Flagstar, as well as those at other large firms, "depend too heavily on policy statements instead of active monitoring and training to avoid discrimination complaints."[70] According to the head of Denny's Franchisee Advisory Council, until the late 1980s only ten to twenty minutes of the month-long training provided to franchisees involved learning about problems of discrimination.[71] One analyst of corporate responses to interracial problems has noted that written policies are not the same thing as "the way people really behave." He added that corporate cultures "reflect the behaviors and values that are rewarded."[72]

For a time, the national publicity of the Denny's and Shoney's lawsuits forced the restaurant industry to pay more attention to persisting problems of racial and ethnic discrimination. These two companies and other major chains began to require more racial and ethnic sensitivity training for their employees. It remains to be seen, however, how long this emphasis on multicultural training will last.

REFERENCES

1. David J. Carrow, Bearing the Cross: Martin Luther King, Jr., and the Southern Christian Leadership Conference (New York: Vintage Books, 1986), p. 127.
2. Carrow, *Bearing the Cross,* p. 128.
3. Conrad P. Kottak, "Rituals at McDonald's," *Natural History* 87 (1978): 75.
4. Richard Martin, "Foodservice's Changing Face: Still Grappling with Diversity," *Nation's Restaurant News,* September 20, 1993, p. 1.
5. Calvin W. Rolark, "Let's Talk: Restaurant Justice Is Needed," *Washington Informer,* July 28, 1993, p. 12.
6. Martin, "Foodservice's Changing Face," p. 1.
7. New York Times News Service, "Transformation: Settlement Commits Shoney's to Top-to-Bottom Restructuring," *Dallas Morning News,* February 1, 1993, p. D1; Joan Oleck, "Shoney's Angles for Settlement," *Restaurant Business,* September 20, 1992, p. 26.
8. Darryl Fears, "Shoney's Agrees to Extend Minority Business Investments," *The Atlanta Journal and Constitution,* June 3, 1993, p. G1.
9. Fears, "Shoney's Agrees to Extend Minority Business Investments," p. 1; New York Times News Service, "Transformation," p. D1.
10. Oleck, "Shoney's Angles for Settlement," p. 26.

11. Quoted in Steve Watkins, "Racism Du Jour at Shoney's," *Nation,* October 18, 1993, pp. 426-427.

12. Martin Dyckman, "Lawyers Can Be Heros Too," *St. Petersburg Times,* April 11, 1993, p. 3D.

13. "Shoney's Co. Founder Quits Board, Sells Stock After Multimillion Bias Decision," *Jet,* March 29, 1993, p. 4; Ronald Smothers, "$105 Million Poorer Now, Chain Mends Race Policies," *New York Times,* January 31, 1993, Section 1, p. 16.

14. Watkins, "Racism Du Jour at Shoney's," pp. 426-427.

15. Watkins, "Racism Du Jour at Shoney's," pp. 426-427.

16. See Blair S. Walker and Judith Schroer, "Paralyzing Prejudice: Minority Customers Still Shut Out," *USA Today,* June 11, 1993, p. B1.

17. Watkins, "Racism Du Jour at Shoney's," p. 427.

18. Dyckman, "Lawyers Can Be Heros Too," p. 3D.

19. Fears, "Shoney's Agrees to Extend Minority Business Investments," p. 1.

20. Fears, "Shoney's Agrees to Extend Minority Business Investments," p. 1.

21. Chicago Tribune wireservice, "Shoney's Stock Falls on News of Shakeup," *Chicago Tribune,* December 22, 1992, p. C3.

22. New York Times News Service, "Transformation," p. D1.

23. New York Times News Service, "Transformation," p. D1; "Shoney's Ex-chairman Danner Quits Board," Reuters Limited, BC cycle, June 30, 1993.

24. Clarence Page, "Paying the Price for Racism," *Chicago Tribune,* February 7, 1993, p. C3.

25. Martin, "Foodservice's Changing Face," p. 1.

26. Joe R. Feagin and Clairece B. Feagin, *Racial and Ethnic Relations,* fourth ed. (Englewood Cliffs, N.J.: Prentice Hall, 1993), pp. 232-233.

27. Jerry Thomas, "NAACP's Army Thins as Its Battles Multiply," *Chicago Tribune,* September 27, 1993, Zone N, p. 1.

28. The 1991 Civil Rights Act was designed to countermand these Supreme Court decisions. Congress was more liberal than the court and President Bush.

29. Margery Austin Turner, Michael Fix, and Raymond J. Struyk, *Opportunities Denied: Discrimination in Hiring* (Washington, D.C.: Urban Institute, 1991); James E. Ellis, "The Black Middle Class," *Business Week,* March 14, 1988, p. 65.

30. "Restaurants Ordered to Change Name," UPI, March 18, 1981, BC cycle; Cheryl Devall, "African-Americans Still Suffer Bias When Eating Out," *Weekend Edition,* National Public Radio, May 29, 1993.

31. Calvin Sims, "Giving Denny's a Menu for Change," *New York Times,* January 1, 1994, Section 1, p. 43; Jim Doyle, "32 Blacks Sue Denny's for Bias," *San Francisco Chronicle,* March 25, 1993, p. A17.

32. Doyle, "32 Blacks Sue Denny's for Bias," p. A17.

33. James Vicini, "Denny's Restaurants Settles Race-Bias Charges," *Reuters Asia-Pacific Business Report,* March 26, 1993, BC cycle.

34. Sims, "Giving Denny's a Menu for Change," Section 1, p. 43; Robin Schatz, "Denny's and Others Stumble on Racism Charges," *Newsday,* August 8, 1993, p. 84.

35. Schatz, "Denny's and Others Stumble on Racism Charges," p. 84.

36. Jay Mathews, "Denny's Tackles a Stained Image: Fighting Bias Charges, Chairman Forges Links with Rights Leaders," *Washington Post,* August 1, 1993, p. H1.

37. Susan Christian, "Denny's Hires San Diego Consultant for Civil Rights Job, Liaison," *Los Angeles Times,* July 28, 1993, p. D1.

38. Mark J. McGarry, "Denny's to Spend $1 Billion to Do the Right Thing," *Newsday,* July 2, 1993, p. 47.

39. Mathews, "Denny's Tackles a Stained Image," p. H1.

40. Quoted in Andrea Adelson, "Denny's Parent Vows Larger Role for Blacks," *New York Times,* July 2, 1993, p. D2.

41. Adelson, "Denny's Parent Vows Larger Role for Blacks," p. D2.

42. Sandra Clark, "Denny's Campaigns to Counter Charges," *Plain Dealer,* July 20, 1993, p. F2.

43. Bruce Vielmetti, "More Saying Denny's Discriminates," *St. Petersburg Times,* June 17, 1993, p. A1.

44. Robert L. Jackson, "Denny's Breaks Bias Vow on Day of Accord," *Los Angeles Times,* May 22, 1993, p. A1; Doyle, "32 Blacks Sue Denny's for Bias," p. A17.

45. "Not Yet Free from Racism," *Metro Reporter,* January 26, 1992, p. 3; Chuck Hawkins, "Denny's: The Stain That Isn't Coming Out," *Business Week,*

June 28, 1993, p. 98; "New Race Bias Charges Against Denny's Restaurants," *San Francisco Chronicle,* June 17, 1993, p. A19.

46. Quoted in William D. Murray, "Denny's Charged with Discriminating Against Blacks," UPI, BC cycle, March 24, 1993.

47. Quoted in Calvin Sims, "Restaurant Chain Settles Charges of Racial Bias," *New York Times,* March 26, 1993, p. A14.

48. Quoted in Murray, "Denny's Charged with Discriminating Against Blacks."

49. "Class Action Suit," *Sacramento Observer,* March 31, 1993, p. F1.

50. Quoted in Mathews, "Denny's Tackles a Stained Image," p. H1.

51. Reynolds Farley, Howard Schuman, Suzanne Blanchi, Diane Colasanto, and Shirley Hatchett, "Chocolate City, Vanilla Suburbs," *Sociology and Social Research* 7 (1978): 335-336.

52. Joel Kovel, *White Racism: A Psychohistory* (New York: Columbia University Press, 1984).

53. Washington Post wire services, "Turning Up Heat on Denny's," *Houston Chronicle,* June 17, 1993, p. A10.

54. "New Race Bias Charges Against Denny's Restaurants," p. A19.

55. Quoted in Mathews, "Denny's Tackles a Stained Image," p. H1.

56. Jerry Thomas, "'Invisible' Patrons Demand to Be Seen," *Chicago Tribune,* June 10, 1993, Zone N, p. 1; Mathews, "Denny's Tackles a Stained Image," p. H1.

57. Quoted in Thomas, "'Invisible' Patrons Demand to Be Seen," Zone N, p. 1.

58. Quoted in Devall, "African-Americans Still Suffer Bias When Eating Out."

59. Schatz, "Denny's and Others Stumble on Racism Charges," p. 84.

60. Quoted in Jackson, "Denny's Breaks Bias Vow on Day of Accord," p. A1.

61. Bureau of National Affairs, "Discrimination: Denny's Restaurants to Pay $46 Million, Provide 'Sensitivity' Training to Employees," BNA Management Briefing, May 26, 1994.

62. "Denny's Does Some of the Right Things," *Business Week,* June 6, 1994, p. 42.

63. "Denny's, Blacks Settle Suits: Company to Pay $54.7 Million," *Orlando Sentinel,* May 25, 1994, p. A1.

64. Rupert Cornwell, "Rocketing Cost of Race Bias in the U.S.," *The Independent,* May 28, 1994, p. 8.

65. "Justice Department News Conference with Deval Patrick, Assistant Attorney General, Civil Rights Division," Federal News Service, May 24, 1994.

66. Thomas, "'Invisible' Patrons Demand to Be Seen," Zone N, p. 1.

67. Walker and Schroer, "Paralyzing Prejudice: Minority Customers Still Shut Out," p. B1.

68. Bill Carlino, "IHOP OKs Settlement in Racial Bias Suit," *Nation's Restaurant News,* January 18, 1993, p. 3.

69. Joan Oleck, "Hearings Set in IHOP Discrimination Suit," *Restaurant Business,* October 10, 1992, p. 22.

70. Hawkins, "Denny's: The Stain That Isn't Coming Out," p. 98.

71. Ibid.

72. Quoted in Schatz, "Denny's and Others Stumble on Racism Charges," p. 84.

DISCUSSION QUESTIONS

1. This article highlights the difference between discrimination by individuals and institutional discrimination. In what ways do Shoney's and Denny's illustrate the latter?

2. Discuss the role of the legal system in redressing the discriminatory practices highlighted in this reading. What does this say about American core values and the ways those values are reflected in our laws?

READING 19

America's Apartheid and the Urban Underclass

Douglas S. Massey

Despite the civil rights movement and the legislative and judicial decisions that spelled the end to the Jim Crow era, Douglas Massey contends that residential segregation remains a persistent problem for the black underclass. He indicates that in cities with large black populations, little has changed in terms of patterns of residential segregation, and this even though over 90 percent of whites endorse, in principle, equal opportunities in housing. Massey details the persistence of white prejudice and examines the forms that institutional discrimination takes. The article concludes with a discussion of the role residential segregation plays in shaping economic life chances.

Although the Kerner Commission of 1968 singled out the ghetto as a fundamental structural factor promoting black poverty in the United States, residential segregation has been overlooked in recent academic debates and policy discussions on the urban underclass. Despite the fact that a large share of African Americans continue to be segregated involuntarily on the basis of race, thinking within the policy establishment has drifted toward the view that race is declining in significance and that black poverty is largely a class-based phenomenon.

Given this emphasis, research into the causes of urban black poverty has focused largely on race-neutral factors such as economic restructuring, family dissolution, education, culture, and welfare. Although researchers often use the terms "ghetto," "ghetto poor," and "ghetto poverty," few see the ghetto itself as something problematic, and few have called for dismantling it as part of a broader attack on urban poverty. Despite its absence from policy discussions, however, residential segregation is not a thing of the past or some neutral fact that can be safely ignored. A large share of black America remains involuntarily segregated, and because life chances are so decisively influenced by where one lives, segregation is deeply implicated in the perpetuation of black poverty.

As a result of their residential segregation, African Americans endure a harsh and extremely

Social Service Review (December 1994).

disadvantaged environment where poverty, crime, single parenthood, welfare dependency, and educational failure are not only common but all too frequently the norm. Because of the persistence of white prejudice against black neighbors and the continuation of pervasive discrimination in the real estate and banking industries, a series of barriers is placed in the path of black social and geographic mobility. The federal government has not just tolerated this state of affairs; at key junctures over the past several decades it has intervened actively to sustain it. Residential segregation by race is an embedded feature of American life that is deeply institutionalized at all levels of U.S. society, and as long as high levels of racial segregation persist, black poverty will be endemic, and racial divisions will grow.

TRENDS IN BLACK-WHITE SEGREGATION

In the years following the civil rights movement of the 1960s, urban blacks came to experience one of two basic conditions. Those in metropolitan areas with large black populations experienced extremely high levels of segregation that showed little tendency to decline over time.[1] Levels of black suburbanization lagged well behind those of other groups, and those African Americans who did manage to achieve suburban residence remained racially isolated. In 16 metropolitan areas Nancy Denton and I observed, blacks were so highly segregated across so many dimensions simultaneously that we coined the term "hypersegregation" to describe their situation. Together these metropolitan areas—which included Baltimore, Chicago, Cleveland, Detroit, Los Angeles, Newark, Philadelphia, St. Louis, and Washington—contained more than one-third of all African Americans in the United States.[2]

In urban areas where blacks constituted a relatively small share of the population, such as Tucson, Phoenix, and Seattle, however, levels of black-white segregation *declined* after 1970, at times quite rapidly.[3] In these urban areas,

African Americans dispersed widely throughout the metropolitan environment, and, in contrast to the situation of large urban black communities, suburbanization brought significant integration and interracial contact. Unfortunately, relatively few African Americans experienced these benign conditions.

The dividing line between these contrasting trends is a metropolitan black fraction of 5 percent. Below this level, desegregation occurred; above it, there was little change. Andrew Gross and I developed an index of the degree of segregation required to keep white neighborhoods at 5 percent black or less.[4] The difference between this index and the level of segregation actually observed in 1970 closely predicted the decline in segregation levels over the ensuing decade. During the 1970s, in other words, U.S. urban areas were moving toward precisely that level of segregation needed to keep the likelihood of white-black contact at 5 percent or less. In areas with small black populations, this pattern implied rapid desegregation; in areas with large black communities, it meant continued segregation and racial isolation.

Preliminary work on the 1990 census suggests that this split in the urban black experience has continued.[5] Urban areas with large black populations remain highly segregated and have shown little tendency toward a decline in segregation; areas with small black populations continue their move toward integration. Declines in segregation were especially rapid in urban areas of the South and West that contained sizable Hispanic populations and large military bases, in addition to small black populations. Although black access to suburbs increased, in areas with large African-American populations settlement was restricted to a small number of suburban communities whose racial segregation was increasing; the small number of blacks entering suburbs was not sufficient to affect the overall pattern of high racial segregation within the urban area as a whole. As a result, metropoli-

tan areas that were hypersegregated in 1980 generally remained so in 1990, and some new areas were added to the list.[6]

The high degree of black residential segregation is unprecedented and unique. No other group in the history of the United States has ever experienced such high levels of segregation sustained over such a long period of time. Despite recent declines, the average level of black segregation is still 50 percent greater than that observed among Asians or Hispanics, and the lowest levels of black segregation generally correspond to the highest levels observed for Hispanics and Asians.

THE CAUSES OF RACIAL RESIDENTIAL SEGREGATION

This distinctive pattern of high black segregation cannot be attributed to socioeconomic factors, at least as of 1980 when the last study was carried out.[7] As of that date, black families earning over $50,000 were just as segregated as those earning under $2,500, and in metropolitan areas with large Hispanic as well as black populations, the poorest Hispanic families were *less* segregated than the most affluent blacks. Similar patterns are observed when data are broken down by education and occupation. Controlling for social class makes little difference in considering the level of black segregation: blacks in large cities are segregated no matter how much they earn, learn, or achieve.

Rather than a lack of income, high levels of black segregation are attributable to three other factors: prejudice, discrimination, and public policy. White racial prejudice yields a weak demand for housing in integrated neighborhoods and fuels a process of neighborhood racial transition. Pervasive discrimination in the real estate and banking industries keeps blacks out of most neighborhoods, providing prejudiced whites with an avenue of escape when faced with the prospect of black settlement in their neighborhoods. Finally, the federal government itself institutionalized the practice of mortgage redlining and supported state and local governments in their use of urban renewal and public housing programs as part of a deliberate attempt to segregate urban blacks.

White Prejudice

Although whites have now come to accept open housing in principle, survey data show that they are reluctant to accept it in practice. Whereas almost 90 percent of white respondents to national surveys agree that "black people have a right to live wherever they can afford to," only 40 percent would be willing to vote for a law stating that "a homeowner cannot refuse to sell to someone because of their race or skin color."[8]

When questions are posed about specific neighborhood compositions, moreover, it becomes clear that white tolerance for racial mixing is quite limited. One-third of whites responding to a 1992 Detroit survey said they would feel uncomfortable living in a neighborhood where 20 percent of the residents were black, and about the same percentage would be unwilling to live in such an area.[9] When the racial composition was increased to one-third black, 59 percent of all whites said they would be unwilling to live there, 44 percent would feel uncomfortable, and 29 percent would seek to leave. At a 50–50 racial mixture, neighborhoods become unacceptable to all but a small minority of whites: 73 percent said they would not wish to live there, 53 percent would try to leave, and 65 percent would feel uncomfortable.

In contrast, African Americans express strong support for integration in both principle and practice. Blacks are unanimous in agreeing that "black people have a right to live wherever they can afford to," and 71 percent would vote for a communitywide law to enforce this right.[10] When asked about specific neighborhood racial compositions, they consistently select racially mixed areas as most desirable. Although the most popular choice is a neighborhood that is half-black and half-white, 87 percent would be willing to live in a neighborhood that is only 20 percent black.[11]

Black respondents do express a reluctance to move into all-white neighborhoods; however, this apprehension does not indicate a rejection of integration per se, but stems from a well-founded fear of hostility and violence. Among black respondents to a 1976 Detroit survey who said they would be reluctant to move into an all-white area, 34 percent thought that white neighbors would be unfriendly and make them feel unwelcome, 37 percent thought they would be made to feel uncomfortable, and 17 percent expressed a fear of violence; four-fifths rejected the view that moving into a white neighborhood constituted a desertion of the black community.[12]

If it were up to them, then, blacks would live in racially mixed neighborhoods. But it is not solely up to them because their preferences interact with those of whites to produce the neighborhoods we actually observe. Whereas most blacks pick a 50–50 racial mixture as most desirable, the vast majority of whites are unwilling to live in such a neighborhood, and most would try to leave. This fundamental disparity has been confirmed by surveys conducted in Milwaukee, Omaha, Cincinnati, Kansas City, and Los Angeles, all of which show that blacks strongly prefer a 50–50 mixture and that whites have little tolerance for racial mixtures beyond 20 percent black.[13]

These contrasting attitudes imply a disparity in the demand for housing in integrated neighborhoods. Given the violence, intimidation, and harassment that historically have followed their moving into white areas, blacks are reluctant to be first across the color line. After one or two black families have entered a neighborhood, however, black demand grows rapidly given the high value placed on integrated housing. This demand escalates as the black percentage rises toward 50 percent, the most preferred neighborhood configuration; beyond this point, it stabilizes and falls off as the black percentage rises toward 100 percent.

The pattern of white demand for housing in racially mixed areas follows precisely the opposite trajectory. Demand is strong for homes in all-white areas, but once one or two black families have moved in, white demand begins to falter as some white families leave and others refuse to move in. The acceleration in residential turnover coincides with the expansion of black demand, making it very likely that outgoing white households are replaced by black families. As the black percentage rises, white demand drops more steeply and black demand rises at an increasing rate. By the time black demand peaks at the 50 percent mark, practically no whites are willing to move in and the large majority are trying to leave. Thus, racial segregation is fomented by a process of racial turnover fueled by antiblack prejudice on the part of whites.

Institutional Discrimination

Although prejudice is a necessary condition for black segregation, it alone is insufficient to maintain the residential color line. Active discrimination against black home seekers must also occur; some neighborhoods must be kept nonblack if whites are to have an avenue of retreat following black entry elsewhere. Racial discrimination was institutionalized in the real estate industry during the 1920s and well established in private practice by the 1940s.[14] Discriminatory behavior was open and widespread among real estate agents at least until 1968, when the Fair Housing Act was passed. After this date, outright refusals to rent or sell to blacks became rare, given that overt discrimination could lead to prosecution under the law.

Black home seekers now face a more subtle process of exclusion. Rather than encountering "white only" signs, they encounter a covert series of barriers surreptitiously placed in their way. Although each individual act of discrimination may be small and subtle, together they have a powerful cumulative effect in lowering the probability of black entry into white neighborhoods. Because the discrimination is latent, moreover, it is unobservable, and the only way to confirm whether it has occurred is to compare the treatment of black and white clients with similar social and economic characteristics.

Differences in the treatment of white and black home seekers are measured by means of a housing audit.[15] Teams of white and black auditors are paired and sent to randomly selected real estate agents to pose as clients seeking a home or apartment. The auditors are trained to present comparable housing needs and family characteristics and to express similar tastes; they are assigned equivalent social and economic traits by the investigator. After each encounter, the auditors fill out a report of their experiences, and the results are tabulated and compared to determine the nature and level of discrimination.

In 1987, George Galster wrote to more than 200 local fair housing organizations and obtained written reports of 71 different audit studies carried out during the 1980s: 21 in the home sales market and 50 in the rental market.[16] Despite differences in measures and methods, he concluded that "racial discrimination continues to be a dominant feature of metropolitan housing markets in the 1980s." Using a conservative measure of racial bias, he found that blacks averaged a 20 percent chance of experiencing discrimination in the sales market and a 50 percent chance in the rental market.

He also studied six real estate firms located in Cincinnati and Memphis and found that racial steering occurred in roughly 50 percent of the transactions sampled during the mid-1980s.[17] Racial steering occurs when white and black clients are guided to neighborhoods that differ systematically with respect to social and economic characteristics, especially racial composition. Homes shown to blacks tended to be in racially mixed areas and were more likely to be adjacent to neighborhoods with a high percentage of black residents. Whites were rarely shown homes in integrated neighborhoods unless they specifically requested them, and even then they were guided primarily to homes in white areas. Sales agents made numerous positive comments about white neighborhoods to white clients but said little about these neighborhoods to black home buyers. In a review of 36 different audit studies, Galster discovered that selective comments by agents are probably more common than overt steering.[18]

In 1988, the U.S. Department of Housing and Urban Development (HUD) carried out a nationwide audit survey.[19] Twenty audit sites were randomly selected from among metropolitan areas having a central city population exceeding 100,000 and a black percentage of more than 12 percent. Real estate advertisements in major metropolitan newspapers were randomly sampled, and real estate agents were approached by auditors who inquired about the availability of the advertised unit; they also asked about other units that might be on the market. The Housing Discrimination Study (HDS) covered both the rental and sales markets, and the auditors were given incomes and family characteristics appropriate to the housing unit advertised.

The HDS provides little evidence that discrimination against blacks has declined. Indeed, prior studies appear to have understated both the incidence and severity of housing discrimination in American cities. According to HDS data, housing was made systematically more available to whites in 45 percent of the transactions in the rental market and in 34 percent of those in the sales market. Whites received more favorable credit assistance in 46 percent of sales encounters and were offered more favorable terms in 17 percent of rental transactions. When housing availability and financial assistance were considered together, the likelihood of experiencing racial discrimination was 53 percent in both the rental and sales markets.

In addition to measuring the incidence of discrimination (i.e., the percentage of encounters where discrimination occurs), the HDS study also measured its severity (the number of units made available to whites but not blacks). In stark terms, the severity of housing discrimination is such that blacks are systematically shown, recommended, and invited to inspect far fewer homes than comparably qualified whites. As a result, their access to urban housing is substantially reduced.

Among advertised rental units, the likelihood that an additional unit was shown to whites but not blacks was 65 percent, and the probability that a shown unit was recommended to whites but not blacks was 91 percent.[20] The HDS auditors encountered equally severe bias in the marketing of nonadvertised rental units: the likelihood that an additional unit was inspected by whites only was 62 percent, whereas the probability that whites alone were invited to see another unit was 90 percent.[21] Comparable results were found in urban sales markets, where the severity of discrimination varied from 66 percent to 89 percent. Thus, no matter what index one considers, most of the housing units made available to whites were not brought to the attention of blacks.[22]

Although these audit results are compelling, they do not directly link discrimination to segregation. Using data from an earlier HUD audit study, however, Galster related cross-metropolitan variation in housing discrimination to the degree of racial segregation in different urban areas.[23] He not only confirmed an empirical link between discrimination and segregation, he also discovered that segregation had important feedback effects on socioeconomic status. Not only does discrimination lead to segregation, but segregation, by restricting economic opportunities for blacks, produces interracial economic disparities that incite further discrimination and more segregation.

Galster has also shown that white prejudice and discrimination are connected to patterns of racial change within neighborhoods.[24] In a detailed study of census tracts in the Cleveland area, he found that neighborhoods that were all white or racially changing evinced much higher rates of discrimination than areas that were stably integrated or predominantly black. Moreover, the pace of racial change was strongly predicted by the percentage of whites who agreed that "white people have a right to keep blacks out of their neighborhoods." That is, neighborhoods in which a large share of whites endorsed racial discrimination in principle tended to turn over racially most rapidly.

Public Policy

The final factor responsible for black residential segregation is government policy. During the 1940s and 1950s, the Federal Housing Administration (FHA) invented the practice of redlining and effectively established it as standard practice within the banking industry.[25] As a condition for underwriting a mortgage, the FHA required a neighborhood assessment; neighborhoods that contained black residents, were adjacent to black areas, or were thought to be at risk of attracting blacks at some point in the future were colored red on the agency's Residential Security Maps and systematically denied access to FHA-backed loans. Private lenders originating non-FHA loans took their cue from the government, and the practice of redlining became institutionalized throughout the lending industry.

Black and mixed-race areas were thus denied access to capital, guaranteeing that housing prices would stagnate, dwellings would steadily deteriorate, and whites would be unable to purchase homes in integrated areas. As a result of federal policy, therefore, racial turnover and physical deterioration became inevitable following black entry into a neighborhood. During the early 1970s, lawsuits and pressure from the civil rights community finally forced the FHA to open up its lending program to black participation. Since then, however, whites have deserted the FHA lending program in favor of conventional loans.

Studies show that blacks are still rejected for conventional loans at rates far higher than whites of comparable economic background.[26] Moreover, because of redlining, black and racially mixed areas do not receive the amount of mortgage capital that they would otherwise qualify for on economic criteria alone.[27] Paradoxically, the recent opening up of FHA lending to blacks has only fueled neighborhood racial transition, with FHA loans being used by blacks to buy homes from whites in racially mixed areas, who then flee to all-white neighborhoods using conventional loans that are denied to blacks.

During the period 1950–70, the federal government also promoted segregation through urban renewal and public housing programs administered by HUD. As black in-migration and white suburbanization brought rapid racial turnover to U.S. cities, local elites became alarmed by the threat that expanding ghettos posed to white institutions and business districts. With federal support, they used renewal programs to clear black neighborhoods encroaching on white districts and employed public housing as a means of containing those families displaced by "renewal." White city councils blocked the construction of minority housing projects outside of the ghetto, however, so most were built on cleared land in black areas, thereby driving up the degree of racial and class isolation.[28]

RACIAL SEGREGATION AND SOCIOECONOMIC MOBILITY

If segregation is imposed on African Americans involuntarily through an interlocking set of individual actions, institutional practices, and governmental actions that are prejudicial in their intent and discriminatory in their effect, then significant barriers are placed in the path of black social mobility. Because where one lives is such an important determinant of one's life chances, barriers to residential mobility inevitably end up being barriers to social mobility. If one group of people is denied full access to urban housing markets on the basis of skin color, then it is systematically denied access to the full range of benefits in urban society.

Housing markets are especially important because they distribute much more than a place to live; they also distribute any good or resource that is *correlated* with where one lives. Housing markets do not just distribute houses; they also distribute education, employment, safety, insurance rates, services, and wealth in the form of home equity; they also determine the level of exposure to crime and drugs and the formation of peer groups that children experience. Research consistently shows that, dollar for dollar of income, year for year of schooling, and unit for unit of occupational status, blacks achieve much less in the way of residential benefits than other racial and ethnic groups.[29]

Because of persistent segregation, blacks are far more likely than whites of the same income to experience inferior schools, isolation from jobs, crime and violence, excessive insurance rates, sagging home values, and environments where expectations run to gang membership and teenage pregnancy rather than college attendance. As a result, black families who have improved their lot are much less able than the upwardly mobile of other groups to consolidate their gains, move ahead further, and pass their achievements on to their children.

SEGREGATION AND THE CONCENTRATION OF POVERTY

Segregation not only harms the interests of individual people and families who experience barriers to residential mobility; it also undermines the community as a whole by concentrating poverty at extraordinary levels. Concentrated poverty occurs because segregation confines any general increase in black poverty to a small number of spatially distinct neighborhoods. Rather than being spread uniformly throughout a metropolitan environment, poor families created by an economic downturn are restricted to a small number of densely settled, tightly packed, and geographically isolated areas. Given a high level of residential segregation, any increase in the poverty rate *must* produce a spatial concentration of poverty; no other result is possible.[30]

Because rates of poverty and levels of segregation differ so much between whites, blacks, and Hispanics, individual members of these groups are structurally constrained to experience markedly different levels of neighborhood poverty. The geographic concentration of poverty is built into the experience of blacks but is alien to the experience of whites, even if they are quite poor themselves. Moreover, the basic effect of segregation in concentrating poverty is significantly exacerbated by public housing, which was used during the period 1950–70 in a racially discriminatory manner to confine and isolate urban blacks. Neighborhoods that contain public housing projects have concentrations of poverty that are at least double what they would be otherwise.[31]

In concentrating poverty, segregation acts simultaneously to concentrate anything that is correlated with poverty: crime, drug abuse, welfare dependency, single parenthood, and educational difficulties. To the extent that individual socioeconomic failings follow from prolonged exposure to concentrated poverty and its correlates, therefore, these disadvantages are ultimately produced by the structural organization of U.S. metropolitan areas. The mere fact that blacks are highly segregated as well as poor means that individual African Americans are more likely to suffer joblessness and to experience single parenthood than either Hispanics or whites, quite apart from any disadvantages they may suffer with respect to personal or family characteristics.

A growing body of research has linked individual socioeconomic difficulties to the geographic concentration of socioeconomic disadvantage that people experience in their neighborhoods.[32] One study has directly linked the socioeconomic disadvantages suffered by individual minority members to the degree of segregation their group experiences in urban society. Using individual, community, and metropolitan data from the 50 largest U.S. metropolitan areas in 1980, Andrew Gross, Mitchell Eggers, and I show that segregation and poverty interact to concentrate poverty geographically within neighborhoods and that exposure to neighborhood poverty subsequently increases the probability of male joblessness and single motherhood among individuals.[33] In this fashion, we link the structural condition of segregation to individual behaviors widely associated with the underclass through the intervening factor of neighborhood poverty.

According to our estimates, increasing the black poverty rate from 10 percent to 40 percent under conditions of no segregation has a relatively modest effect on the neighborhood environment that blacks experience, raising it modestly from about 8 percent to 17 percent. Although the probabilities of male joblessness and single motherhood are sensitive to the rate of poverty that people experience in their neighborhood, this modest change in neighborhood poverty is not enough to affect individual outcomes very much. The probability of male joblessness rises only from 36 percent to 40 percent as a result of increased poverty concentration, and the likelihood of single motherhood increases from 23 percent to 28 percent.

In a highly segregated urban area, in contrast, increasing the overall rate of black poverty causes a marked increase in the concentration of poverty within black neighborhoods. As the overall rate of poverty increases from 10 percent to 40 percent, the neighborhood poverty rate likewise goes from 10 percent to 41 percent. This sharp increase in neighborhood poverty has a profound effect on the well-being of individual blacks, even those who have not been pushed into poverty themselves because segregation forces them to live in neighborhoods with many families who are poor. As a result of the increase in neighbor-

hood poverty to which they are exposed, the probability of joblessness among young black males rises from 40 percent to 53 percent, and the likelihood of single motherhood increases from 28 percent to 41 percent.

Thus, increasing the rate of poverty of a segregated group causes its neighborhood environment to deteriorate, which in turn causes individual probabilities of socioeconomic failure to rise. The same rise in poverty without segregation would hardly affect group members at all because it would have marginal effects on the neighborhoods where they live. Segregation, in other words, is directly responsible for the creation of a uniquely harsh and disadvantaged black residential environment, making it likely that individual blacks themselves will fail, no matter what their socioeconomic characteristics or family background. Racial segregation is the institutional nexus that enables the transmission of poverty from person to person and generation to generation and is therefore a primary structural factor behind the perpetuation of the urban underclass.

REFERENCES

This is the seventeenth annual *Social Service Review* lecture delivered at the School of Social Service Administration, the University of Chicago, April 28, 1994.

1. Douglas S. Massey and Nancy A. Denton, *American Apartheid: Segregation and the Making of the Underclass* (Cambridge, Mass: Harvard University Press, 1993), chap. 3.
2. Douglas S. Massey and Nancy A. Denton, "Hypersegregation in U.S. Metropolitan Areas: Black and Hispanic Segregation along Five Dimensions," *Demography* 26, no. 3 (August 1989): 373–93.
3. Douglas S. Massey and Nancy A. Denton, "Trends in the Residential Segregation of Blacks, Hispanics, and Asians," *American Sociological Review* 52, no. 6 (December 1987): 802–25.
4. Douglas S. Massey and Andrew B. Gross, "Explaining Trends in Residential Segregation,

1970–1980," *Urban Affairs Quarterly* 27, no. 1 (September 1991): 13–35.

5. Reynolds Farley and William H. Frey, "Changes in the Segregation of Whites from Blacks during the 1980s: Small Steps toward a More Integrated Society," *American Sociological Review* 59, no. 1 (February 1994): 23–45; Mark Schneider and Thomas Phelan, "Black Suburbanization in the 1980's," *Demography* 30, no. 2 (May 1993): 269–80.

6. Nancy A. Denton, "Are African Americans Still Hypersegregated in 1990?" in *Residential Apartheid: The American Legacy,* ed. Robert Bullard (Newbury Park, Calif.: Sage, in press 1994).

7. Nancy A. Denton and Douglas S. Massey, "Residential Segregation of Blacks, Hispanics, and Asians by Socioeconomic Status and Generation," *Social Science Quarterly* 69, no. 4 (December 1988): 797–817.

8. Howard Schuman, Charlotte Steeh, and Lawrence Bobo, *Racial Attitudes in America: Trends and Interpretations* (Cambridge, Mass.: Harvard University Press, 1985): Howard Schuman and Lawrence Bobo, "Survey-based Experiments on White Racial Attitudes toward Residential Integration," *American Journal of Sociology* 94, no. 2 (September 1988): 273–99.

9. Reynolds Farley, Charlotte Steeh, Tara Jackson, Maria Krysan, and Keith Reeves, The Causes of Continued Racial Residential Segregation: Chocolate City, Vanilla Suburbs Revisited," *Journal of Housing Research* 4, no. 1 (1993): 1–38.

10. Lawrence Bobo, Howard Schuman, and Charlotte Steeh, "Changing Racial Attitudes toward Residential Integration," in *Housing Desegregation and Federal Policy,* ed. John M. Goering (Chapel Hill: University of North Carolina Press, 1986), pp. 152–69.

11. Farley et al. (n. 9 above).

12. Reynolds Farley, Suzanne Bianchi, and Diane Colasanto, "Barriers to the Racial Integration of Neighborhoods: The Detroit Case," *Annals of the American Academy of Political and Social Science* 441 (January 1979): 97–113.

13. William A. V. Clark, "Residential Preferences and Neighborhood Racial Segregation: A Test of the Schelling Segregation Model," *Demography* 28, no. 1 (February 1991): 1–19.

14. Massey and Denton, *American Apartheid* (n. 1 above), chap. 2.

15. John Yinger, "Measuring Racial Discrimination with Fair Housing Audits: Caught in the Act," *American Economic Review* 76, no. 5 (December 1986): 991–93.

16. George C. Galster, "Racial Discrimination in Housing Markets during the 1980s: A Review of the Audit Evidence," *Journal of Planning Education and Research* 9, no. 3 (March 1990): 165–75.

17. George C. Galster, "Racial Steering by Real Estate Agents: Mechanisms and Motives," *Review of Black Political Economy* 19, no. 1 (Summer 1990): 39–63.

18. George C. Galster, "Racial Steering in Urban Housing Markets: A Review of the Audit Evidence," *Review of Black Political Economy* 18, no. 3 (Winter 1990): 105–29.

19. John Yinger, *Housing Discrimination Study: Incidence of Discrimination and Variations in Discriminatory Behavior* (Washington, D.C.: U.S. Department of Housing and Urban Development, Office of Policy Development and Research, 1991), and *Housing Discrimination Study: Incidence and Severity of Unfavorable Treatment* (Washington, D.C.: U.S. Department of Housing and Urban Development, Office of Policy Development and Research, 1991).

20. Yinger, *Housing Discrimination Study: Incidence of Discrimination and Variations in Discriminatory Behavior* (n. 19 above), table 42.

21. Ibid.

22. Ibid., table 44.

23. George C. Galster, "More than Skin Deep: The Effect of Housing Discrimination on the Extent and Pattern of Racial Residential Segregation in the United States," in Goering, ed. (n. 10 above), pp. 119–38; George C. Galster and W. Mark Keeney, "Race, Residence, Discrimination, and Economic Opportunity: Modeling the Nexus of Urban Racial Phenomena," *Urban Affairs Quarterly* 24, no. 1 (September 1988): 87–117.

24. George C. Galster, "The Ecology of Racial Discrimination in Housing: An Exploratory Model," *Urban Affairs Quarterly* 23, no. 1 (September 1987): 84–107, "White Flight from Racially Integrated Neighbourhoods in the 1970s: The Cleveland Experience," *Urban Studies* 27, no. 3 (March 1990): 385–99, "Neighborhood Racial

Change, Segregationist Sentiments, and Affirmative Marketing Policies," *Journal of Urban Economics* 27, no. 3 (March 1990): 344–61.

25. Kenneth T. Jackson, *Crabgrass Frontier: The Suburbanization of the United States* (New York: Oxford University Press, 1985), chap. 11.

26. Harold A. Black and Robert L. Schweitzer, "A Canonical Analysis of Mortgage Lending Terms: Testing for Lending Discrimination at a Commercial Bank," *Urban Studies* 22, no. 1 (January 1985): 13–20.

27. Louis G. Pol, Rebecca F. Guy, and Andrew J. Bush, "Discrimination in the Home Lending Market: A Macro Perspective," *Social Science Quarterly* 63, no. 4 (December 1982): 716–28; Gregory D. Squires, William Velez, and Karl F. Taueber, "Insurance Redlining, Agency Location, and the Process of Urban Disinvestment," *Urban Affairs Quarterly* 26, no. 4 (June 1991): 567–88; Harriet Tee Taggart and Kevin W. Smith, "Redlining: An Assessment of the Evidence of Disinvestment in Metropolitan Boston," *Urban Affairs Quarterly* 17, no. 1 (September 1981): 91–107.

28. Arnold R. Hirsch, *Making the Second Ghetto: Race and Housing in Chicago, 1940–1960* (Cambridge: Cambridge University Press, 1983); John F. Bauman, *Public Housing, Race, and Renewal: Urban Planning in Philadelphia, 1920–1974* (Philadelphia: Temple University Press, 1987); Ira Goldstein and William L. Yancey, "Public Housing Projects, Blacks, and Public Policy: The Historical Ecology of Public Housing in Philadelphia," in Goering, ed. (n. 10 above); Douglas S. Massey and Shawn M. Kanaiaupuni, "Public Housing and the Concentration of Poverty," *Social Science Quarterly* 74, no. 1 (March 1993): 109–22.

29. Richard D. Alba and John R. Logan, "Variations on Two Themes: Racial and Ethnic Patterns in the Attainment of Suburban Residence," *Demography* 28, no. 3 (August 1991): 431–53; Douglas S. Massey and Nancy A. Denton, "Spatial Assimilation as a Socioeconomic Process," *American Sociological Review* 50, no. 1 (February 1985): 94–105; Douglas S. Massey and Eric Fong, "Segregation and Neighborhood Quality: Blacks, Hispanics, and Asians in the San Francisco Metropolitan Area," *Social Forces* 69, no. 1 (September 1990): 15–32; Douglas S. Massey, Gretchen A. Condran, and Nancy A. Denton, "The Effect of Residential Segregation on Black Social and Economic Well-being," *Social Forces* 66, no. 1 (September 1987): 29–57.

30. Douglas S. Massey, "American Apartheid: Segregation and the Making of the Underclass," *American Journal of Sociology* 96, no. 2 (September 1990): 329–58; Massey and Denton, *American Apartheid* (n. 1 above), chap. 5.

31. Massey and Kanaiaupuni (n. 28 above).

32. Christopher Jencks and Susan E. Mayer, "The Social Consequences of Growing Up in a Poor Neighborhood," in *Inner City Poverty in the United States,* ed. Laurence E. Lynn, Jr., and Michael G. H. McGeary (Washington, D.C.: National Academy Press, 1990), pp. 111–86; Dennis P. Hogan and Evelyn M. Kitagawa, "The Impact of Social Status, Family Structure, and Neighborhood on the Fertility of Black Adolescents," *American Journal of Sociology* 90, no. 4 (January 1985): 825–55; Frank F. Furstenburg, Jr., S. Philip Morgan, Kristin A. Moore, and James Peterson, "Race Differences in the Timing of Adolescent Intercourse," *American Sociological Review* 52, no. 4 (August 1987): 511–18; Jonathan Crane, "The Epidemic Theory of Ghettos and Neighborhood Effects on Dropping Out and Teenage Childbearing," *American Journal of Sociology* 96, no. 5 (March 1991): 1226–59.

33. Douglas S. Massey, Andrew B. Gross, and Mitchell L. Eggers, "Segregation, the Concentration of Poverty, and the Life Chances of Individuals," *Social Science Research* 20, no. 4 (December 1991): 397–420.

DISCUSSION QUESTIONS

1. Why do you think so many whites endorse open housing in principle but not in practice? What can be done to overcome this resistance to genuine open housing?

2. What role should the federal government play in combating housing discrimination?

The World of the New Urban Poor

William Julius Wilson

William Julius Wilson is a long-time analyst of inner-city poverty, and Chicago has been his main research site. One of the central themes in his work is the conviction that for the "truly disadvantaged," life is more difficult today than it was in the 1950s and 1960s. In this passage from When Work Disappears, *Wilson discusses the rising number of working-age males from impoverished neighborhoods who are unemployed. He attributes this rise chiefly to the decline in the number of mass-production manufacturing jobs, which only a few decades ago offered the main route for the poor to move out of poverty and into solid blue-collar jobs. As he notes, the alternatives in an era of deindustrialization are fewer jobs in proximity to inner-city neighborhoods and declining wages.*

The disappearance of work in many inner-city neighborhoods is partly related to the nation-wide decline in the fortunes of low-skilled workers. Although the growing wage inequality has hurt both low-skilled men and women, the problem of declining employment has been concentrated among low-skilled men. In 1987–89, a low-skilled male worker was jobless eight and a half weeks longer than he would have been in 1967–69. Moreover, the proportion of men who "permanently" dropped out of the labor force was more than twice as high in the late 1980s than it had been in the late 1960s. A precipitous drop in real wages—that is, wages adjusted for inflation—has accompanied the increases in joblessness among low-income workers. If you arrange all wages into five groups according to wage percentile (from highest to lowest), you see that men in the bottom fifth of this income distribution experienced more than a 30 percent drop in real wages between 1970 and 1989.

Even the low-skilled workers who are consistently employed face problems of economic ad-vancement. Job ladders—opportunities for pro-motion within firms—have eroded, and many less-skilled workers stagnate in dead-end, low-paying positions. This suggests that the chances of improving one's earnings by changing jobs have declined: if jobs inside a firm have become less available to the experienced workers in that firm, they are probably even more difficult for outsiders to obtain.

But there is a paradox here. Despite the increasing economic marginality of low-wage workers, unemployment dipped below 6 percent in 1994 and early 1995, many workers are holding more than one job, and overtime work has reached a record high. Yet while tens of millions of new jobs have been created in the past two decades, men who are well below retirement age are working less than they did two decades ago—and a growing percentage are neither working nor looking for work. The proportion of male workers in the prime of their life (between the ages of 22 and 58) who worked in a given decade full-time, year-round, in at least eight out of ten years declined from 79 percent during the 1970s to 71 percent in the 1980s. While the American economy saw a rapid expansion in high technology and services, especially advanced services, growth in blue-collar factory, transportation, and construction jobs, traditionally held by men, has not kept pace with the rise in the working-age population. These men are working less as a result.

The growth of a nonworking class of prime-age males along with a larger number of those who are often unemployed, who work part-time, or who work in temporary jobs is concentrated among the poorly educated, the school dropouts, and minorities. In the 1970s, two-thirds of prime-age male workers with less than a high school education worked full-time, year-round, in eight out of ten years. During the 1980s, only half did so. Prime-age black men experienced a similar sharp decline. Seven out of ten of all black men worked full-time, year-round, in eight out of ten years in the 1970s, but only half did so in the 1980s. The figures for those who reside in the inner city are obviously even lower.

One study estimates that since 1967 the number of prime-age men who are not in school, not working, and not looking for work for even a single week in a given year has more than doubled for both whites and nonwhites (respectively, from 3.3 to 7.7 percent and 5.8 percent to 13.2 percent). Data from this study also revealed that one-quarter of all male high school dropouts had no official employment at all in 1992. And of those with high school diplomas, one out of ten did not hold a job in 1993, up sharply from 1967 when only one out of fifty reported that he had had no job throughout the year. Among prime-age nonwhite males, the share of those who had no jobs at all in a given year increased from 3 percent to 17 percent during the last quarter century (Buron et al. 1994).

These changes are related to the decline of the mass production system in the United States. The traditional American economy featured rapid growth in productivity and living standards. The mass production system benefited from large quantities of cheap natural resources, economies of scale, and processes that generated higher uses of productivity through shifts in market forces from agriculture to manufacturing and that caused improvements in one industry (for example, reduced steel costs) to lead to advancements in others (for example, higher sales and greater economies of scale in the automobile industry). In this system plenty of blue-collar jobs were available to workers with little formal education. Today, most of the new jobs for workers with limited education and experience are in the service sector, which hires relatively more women. One study found that the U.S. created 27 clerical, sales, and service jobs per thousand of working-age population in the 1980s. During the same period, the country lost 16 production, transportation, and laborer jobs per thousand of working-age population (McKinsey and Co. 1994). In another

study the social scientists Robert Lerman and Martin Rein (forthcoming) revealed that from 1989 to 1993, the period covering the economic downturn, social service industries (health, education, and welfare) added almost 3 million jobs, while 1.4 million jobs were lost in all other industries. The expanding job market in social services offset the recession-linked job loss in other industries.

The movement of lower-educated men into the growth sectors of the economy has been slow. For example, "the fraction of men who have moved into so-called pink-collar jobs like practical nursing or clerical work remains negligible (Nasar 1994, A7)." The large concentration of women in the expanding social service sector partly accounts for the striking gender differences in job growth. Unlike lower-educated men, lower-educated women are working more, not less, than in previous years. The employment patterns among lower-educated women, like those with higher education and training, reflect the dramatic expansion of social service industries. Between 1989 and 1993, jobs held by women increased by 1.3 million, while those held by men barely rose at all (by roughly 100,000).

Although the wages of low-skilled women (those with less than twelve years of education) rose slightly in the 1970s, they flattened out in the 1980s, and continued to remain below those of low-skilled men. The wage gap between low-skilled men and women shrank not because of gains made by female workers but mainly because of the decline in real wages for men. The unemployment rates among low-skilled women are slightly lower than those among their male counterparts. However, over the past decade their rates of participation in the labor force have stagnated and have fallen further behind the labor-force-participation rates among more highly educated women, which continue to rise. The unemployment rates among both low-skilled men and women are five times that among their college-educated counterparts.

Among the factors that have contributed to the growing gap in employment and wages between low-skilled and college-educated workers is the increased internationalization of the U.S. economy. As the economists Richard B. Freeman and Lawrence F. Katz (1994) point out:

In the 1980s, trade imbalances implicitly acted to augment the nation's supply of less educated workers, particularly those with less than a high school education. Many production and routine clerical tasks could be more easily transferred abroad than in the past. The increased supply of less educated workers arising from trade deficits accounted for as much as 15 percent of the increase in college-high school wage differential from the 1970s to the mid-1980s. In contrast, a balanced expansion of international trade, in which growth in exports matches the growth of imports, appears to have fairly neutral effects on relative labor demand. Indeed, balanced growth of trade leads to an upgrading in jobs for workers without college degrees, since export-sector jobs tend to pay higher wages for "comparable" workers than do import-competing jobs (p. 46).

The lowering of unionization rates, which accompanied the decline in the mass production system, has also contributed to shrinking wages and nonwage compensation for less skilled workers. As the economist Rebecca Blank (1994) has pointed out, "unionized workers typically receive not only higher wages, but also more non-wage benefits. As the availability of union jobs has declined for unskilled workers, non-wage benefits have also declined" (p. 17).

Finally, the wage and employment gap between skilled and unskilled workers is growing partly because education and training are considered more important than ever in the new global economy. At the same time that changes in technology are producing new jobs, they are making many others obsolete. The workplace has been revolutionized by technological changes that range from the development of robotics to information highways. While educated workers are benefiting from the pace of techno-

logical change, involving the increased use of computer-based technologies and microcomputers, more routine workers face the growing threat of job displacement in certain industries. For example, highly skilled designers, engineers, and operators are needed for the jobs associated with the creation of a new set of computer-operated machine tools; but these same exciting new opportunities eliminate jobs for those trained only for manual, assembly-line work. Also, in certain businesses, advances in word processing have increased the demand for those who not only know how to type but can operate specialized software as well; at the same time, these advances reduce the need for routine typists and secretaries. In the new global economy, highly educated and thoroughly trained men and women are in demand. This may be seen most dramatically in the sharp differences in employment experiences among men. Unlike men with lower education, college-educated men are working more, not less.

The shift in demand has been especially devastating for those low-skilled workers whose incorporation into the mainstream economy has been marginal or recent. Even before the economic restructuring of the nation's economy, low-skilled African-Americans were at the end of the employment queue. Their economic situation has been further weakened because they tend to reside in communities that not only have higher jobless rates and lower employment growth but lack access to areas of higher employment and employment growth as well. Moreover, they are far more likely than other ethnic and racial groups to face negative employer attitudes.

Of the changes in the economy that have adversely affected low-skilled African-American workers, perhaps the most significant have been those in the manufacturing sector. One study revealed that in the 1970s "up to half of the huge employment declines for less-educated blacks might be explained by industrial shifts away from manufacturing toward other sectors"

(Bound and Holzer 1993, p. 395). Another study reported that since the 1960s "deindustrialization" and the "erosion in job opportunities especially in the Midwest and Northeast . . . bear responsibility for the growth of the ranks of the 'truly disadvantaged' " (Bluestone et al. 1991, p. 25). The manufacturing losses in some northern cities have been staggering. In the twenty-year period from 1967 to 1987, Philadelphia lost 64 percent of its manufacturing jobs; Chicago lost 60 percent; New York City, 58 percent; Detroit, 51 percent. In absolute numbers, these percentages represent the loss of 160,000 jobs in Philadelphia, 326,000 in Chicago, 520,000—over half a million—in New York, and 108,000 in Detroit.

Another study examined the effects of economic restructuring in the 1980s by highlighting the changes in both the variety and the quality of blue-collar employment in general. Jobs were grouped into a small number of relatively homogeneous clusters on the basis of job quality (which was measured in terms of earnings, benefits, union protection, and involuntary part-time employment). The authors found that both the relative earnings and employment rates among unskilled black workers were lower for two reasons: traditional jobs that provide a living wage (high-wage blue-collar cluster, of which roughly 50 percent were manufacturing jobs) declined, as did the quality of secondary jobs on which they increasingly had to rely, leading to lower relative earnings for the remaining workers in the labor market. As employment prospects worsened, rising proportions of low-skilled black workers dropped out of the legitimate labor market (Gittleman and Howell 1993).

Data from the Chicago Urban Poverty and Family Life Survey show that efforts by out-of-school inner-city black men to obtain blue-collar jobs in the industries in which their fathers had been employed have been hampered by industrial restructuring. "The most common occupation reported by respondents at ages 19 to 28 changed from operative and assembler jobs among the oldest cohorts to service jobs (waiters and janitors) among the youngest cohort" (Testa and Krogh 1995, p. 77). Fifty-seven percent of Chicago's employed inner-city black fathers (aged 15 and over and without undergraduate degrees) who were born between 1950 and 1955 worked in manufacturing and construction industries in 1974. By 1987, industrial employment in this group had fallen to 31 percent. Of those born between 1956 and 1960, 52 percent worked in these industries as late as 1978. But again, by 1987 industrial employment in this group fell to 28 percent. No other male ethnic group in the inner city experienced such an overall precipitous drop in manufacturing employment. These employment changes have accompanied the loss of traditional manufacturing and other blue-collar jobs in Chicago. As a result, young black males have turned increasingly to the low-wage service sector and unskilled laboring jobs for employment, or have gone jobless. The strongly held U.S. cultural and economic belief that the son will do at least as well as the father in the labor market does not apply to many young inner-city males. . . .

Joblessness and declining wages are also related to the recent growth in ghetto poverty. The most dramatic increases in ghetto poverty occurred between 1970 and 1980, and they were mostly confined to the large industrial metropolises of the Northeast and Midwest, regions that experienced massive industrial restructuring and loss of blue-collar jobs during that decade. But the rise in ghetto poverty was not the only problem. Industrial restructuring had devastating effects on the social organization of many inner-city neighborhoods in these regions. The fate of the West Side black community of North Lawndale vividly exemplifies the cumulative process of economic and social dislocation that has swept through Chicago's inner city.

After more than a quarter century of continuous deterioration, North Lawndale resembles a war zone. Since 1960, nearly half of its housing stock has disappeared; the remaining units are mostly run-down or dilapidated. Two large factories anchored the economy of this West Side neighborhood in its good days—the Hawthorne plant of Western Electric, which employed over 43,000 workers; and an International Harvester plant with 14,000 workers. The world headquarters for Sears, Roebuck and Company was located there, providing another 10,000 jobs. The neighborhood also had a Copenhagen snuff plant, a Sunbeam factory, and a Zenith factory, a Dell Farm food market, an Alden's catalog store, and a U.S. Post Office bulk station. But conditions rapidly changed. Harvester closed its doors in the late 1960s. Sears moved most of its offices to the Loop in downtown Chicago in 1973; a catalog distribution center with a workforce of 3,000 initially remained in the neighborhood but was relocated outside of the state of Illinois in 1987. The Hawthorne plant gradually phased out its operations and finally shut down in 1984.

The departure of the big plants triggered the demise or exodus of the smaller stores, the banks, and other businesses that relied on the wages paid by the large employers. "To make matters worse, scores of stores were forced out of business or pushed out of the neighborhoods by insurance companies in the wake of the 1968 riots that swept through Chicago's West Side after the assassination of Dr. Martin Luther King, Jr. Others were simply burned or abandoned. It has been estimated that the community lost 75 percent of its business establishments from 1960 to 1970 alone." In 1986, North Lawndale, with a population of over 66,000, had only one bank and one supermarket; but it was also home to forty-eight state lottery agents, fifty currency exchanges, and ninety-nine licensed liquor stores and bars.

The impact of industrial restructuring on inner-city employment is clearly apparent to urban blacks. The UPFLS survey posed the following question: "Over the past five or ten years, how many friends of yours have lost their jobs because the place where they worked shut down—would you say none, a few, some, or most?" Only 26 percent of the black residents in our sample reported that none of their friends had lost jobs because their workplace shut down. Indeed, both black men and black women were more likely to report that their friends had lost jobs because of plant closings than were the Mexicans and the other ethnic groups in our study. Moreover, nearly half of the employed black fathers and mothers in the UPFLS survey stated that they considered themselves to be at high risk of losing their jobs because of plant shutdowns. Significantly fewer Hispanic and white parents felt this way.

Some of the inner-city neighborhoods have experienced more visible job losses than others. But residents of the inner city are keenly aware of the rapid depletion of job opportunities. A 33-year-old unmarried black male of North Lawndale who is employed as a clerical worker stated: "Because of the way the economy is structured, we're losing more jobs. Chicago is losing jobs by the thousands. There just aren't any starting companies here and it's harder to find a job compared to what it was years ago."

A similar view was expressed by a 41-year-old black female, also from North Lawndale, who works as a nurse's aide:

> Chicago is really full of peoples. Everybody can't get a good job. They don't have enough good jobs to provide for everybody. I don't think they have enough jobs period. . . . And all the factories and the places, they closed up and moved out of the city and stuff like that, you know. I guess it's one of the reasons they haven't got too many jobs now, 'cause a lot of the jobs now, factories and business, they're done moved out. So that way it's less jobs for lot of peoples.

Respondents from other neighborhoods also reported on the impact of industrial restructuring. According to a 33-year-old South Side janitor:

> The machines are putting a lot of people out of jobs. I worked for *Time* magazine for seven years

on a videograph printer and they come along with the Abedic printer, it cost them half a million dollars: they did what we did in half the time, eliminated two shifts.

"Jobs were plentiful in the past," stated a 29-year-old unemployed black male who lives in one of the poorest neighborhoods on the South Side.

> You could walk out of the house and get a job. Maybe not what you want but you could get a job. Now, you can't find anything. A lot of people in this neighborhood, they want to work but they can't get work. A few, but a very few, they just don't want to work. The majority they want to work but they can't find work.

Finally, a 41-year-old hospital worker from another impoverished South Side neighborhood associated declining employment opportunities with decreasing skill levels:

> Well, most of the jobs have moved out of Chicago. Factory jobs have moved out. There are no jobs here. Not like it was 20, 30 years ago. And people aren't skilled enough for the jobs that are here. You don't have enough skilled and educated people to fill them.

The increasing suburbanization of employment has accompanied industrial restructuring and has further exacerbated the problems of inner-city joblessness and restricted access to jobs. "Metropolitan areas captured nearly 90 percent of the nation's employment growth; much of this growth occurred in booming 'edge cities' at the metropolitan periphery. By 1990, many of these 'edge cities' had more office space and retail sales than the metropolitan downtowns." Over the last two decades, 60 percent of the new jobs created in the Chicago metropolitan area have been located in the northwest suburbs of Cook and Du Page counties. African-Americans constitute less than 2 percent of the population in these areas.

In *The Truly Disadvantaged,* I maintained that one result of these changes for many urban blacks has been a growing mismatch between the suburban location of employment and minorities' residence in the inner city. Although studies based on data collected before 1970 showed no consistent or convincing effects on black employment as a consequence of this spatial mismatch, the employment of inner-city blacks relative to suburban blacks has clearly deteriorated since then. Recent research, conducted mainly by urban and labor economists, strongly shows that the decentralization of employment is continuing and that employment in manufacturing, most of which is already suburbanized, has decreased in central cities, particularly in the Northeast and Midwest. As Farrell Bloch, an economic and statistical consultant, points out, "Not only has the number of manufacturing jobs been decreasing, but new plants now tend to locate in the suburbs to take advantage of cheap land, access to highways, and low crime rates; in addition, businesses shun urban locations to avoid buying land from several different owners, paying high demolition costs for old buildings, and arranging parking for employees and customers." . . .

The African-Americans surveyed in the UPFLS clearly recognized a spatial mismatch of jobs. Both black men and black women saw greater job prospects outside the city. For example, only one-third of black fathers from areas with poverty rates of at least 30 percent reported that their best opportunities for employment were to be found in the city. Nearly two-thirds of whites and Puerto Ricans and over half of Mexicans living in similar neighborhoods felt this way. Getting to suburban jobs is especially problematic for the jobless individuals in the UPFLS because only 28 percent have access to an automobile. This rate falls even further to 18 percent for those living in the ghetto areas.

Among two-car middle-class and affluent families, commuting is accepted as a fact of life; but it occurs in a context of safe school environments for children, more available and accessible day care, and higher incomes to support mobile, away-from-home lifestyles. In a multitiered job market that requires substantial resources for participation, most inner-city minorities must rely on public transportation systems that rarely provide easy and quick access to suburban locations. A 32-year-old unemployed South Side welfare mother described the problem this way:

> There's not enough jobs. I thinks Chicago's the only city that does not have a lot of opportunities opening in it. There's not enough factories, there's not enough work. Most all the good jobs are in the suburbs. Sometimes it's hard for the people in the city to get to the suburbs, because everybody don't own a car. Everybody don't drive.

After commenting on the lack of jobs in his area, a 29-year-old unemployed South Side black male continued:

> You gotta go out in the suburbs, but I can't get out there. The bus go out there but you don't want to catch the bus out there, going two hours each ways. If you have to be at work at eight that mean you have to leave for work at six, that mean you have to get up at five to be at work at eight. Then when wintertime come you be in trouble.

Another unemployed South Side black male had this to say: "Most of the time . . . the places be too far and you need transportation and I don't have none right now. If I had some I'd probably be able to get one [a job]. If I had a car and went way into the suburbs, 'cause there ain't none in the city." This perception was echoed by an 18-year-old unemployed West Side black male:

> They are most likely hiring in the suburbs. Recently, I think about two years ago, I had a job but they say that I need some transportation and they say that the bus out in the suburbs run at a certain time. So I had to pass that job up because I did not have no transport.

An unemployed unmarried welfare mother of two from the West Side likewise stated:

> Well, I'm goin' to tell you: most jobs, more jobs are in the suburbs. It's where the good jobs and stuff is but you gotta have transportation to get

there and it's hard to be gettin' out there in the suburbs. Some people don't know where the suburbs is, some people get lost out there. It is really hard, but some make a way.

One employed factory worker from the West Side who works a night shift described the situation this way:

> From what I, I see, you know, it's hard to find a good job in the inner city 'cause so many people moving, you know, west to the suburbs and out of state. . . . Some people turn jobs down because they don't have no way of getting out there. . . . I just see some people just going to work—and they seem like they the type who just used to—they coming all the way from the city and go on all the way to the suburbs and, you know, you can see 'em all bundled and—catching one bus and the next bus. They just used to doing that.

Let us again examine the three Bronzeville neighborhoods of Douglas, Grand Boulevard, and Washington Park. As shown in Table 1, the proportion of those in the age categories (20–64) that roughly approximate the prime-age workforce has declined in all three neighborhoods since 1950, whereas the proportion in the age category 65 and over has increased. Of the adults age 20 and over, the proportion in the prime-age categories declined by 17 percent in Grand Boulevard, 16 percent in Douglas, and 12 percent in Washington Park between 1950 and 1990. The smaller the percentage of prime-age adults in a population, the lower the proportion of residents who are likely to be employed. The proportion of residents in the age category 5–19 increased sharply in each neighborhood from 1950 to 1990, suggesting that the growth in the proportion of teenagers also contributed to the rise in the jobless rate. However, if we consider the fact that male employment in these neighborhoods declined by a phenomenal 46 percent between 1950 and 1960, these demographic changes obviously can account

TABLE 1

DEMOGRAPHIC CHANGES IN DOUGLAS, GRAND BOULEVARD, AND WASHINGTON PARK, 1950–1990

Douglas					
	1990	**1980**	**1970**	**1960**	**1950**
Total population	30,652	35,700	41,276	52,325	78,745
% female	58.3	57.6	55.1	52.2	52.3
% male	41.7	42.4	44.9	47.8	47.7
% age 0–4	10.5	9.0	10.2	15.1	11.0
% age 5–19	24.5	26.2	33.3	29.9	21.7
% age 20–44	34.8	36.4	32.0	33.0	43.3
% age 45–64	15.6	16.5	16.8	15.9	18.7
% age 65+	14.7	11.9	7.7	6.1	5.3

Grand Boulevard					
	1990	**1980**	**1970**	**1960**	**1950**
Total population	35,897	58,741	80,150	80,036	114,557
% female	55.9	54.4	53.8	52.3	52.7
% male	44.1	45.6	46.2	47.7	47.3
% age 0–4	11.4	9.5	9.4	11.7	8.3
% age 5–19	30.0	31.5	36.4	21.3	16.8
% age 20–44	30.3	27.9	24.8	32.6	45.3
% age 45–64	14.0	17.5	18.4	25.0	24.0
% age 65+	14.3	13.6	11.0	9.4	5.6

Washington Park					
	1990	**1980**	**1970**	**1960**	**1950**
Total population	19,425	31,935	46,024	43,690	56,865
% female	54.5	54.7	53.0	52.0	52.5
% male	45.5	45.3	47.0	48.0	46.8
% age 0–4	11.8	9.9	9.0	9.7	7.2
% age 5–19	28.8	30.8	31.8	18.1	15.7
% age 20–44	33.7	28.5	28.5	34.9	47.0
% age 45–64	14.9	18.8	20.3	27.6	24.5
% age 65+	10.8	12.0	10.4	9.4	5.6

Source: 1990 Census Population and Housing, File STF₃A; and Local Community Fact Book--Chicago Metropolitan Area.

for only a fraction, albeit a significant fraction, of the high proportion of the area's jobless adults.

The rise in the proportion of jobless adults in the Bronzeville neighborhoods has been accompanied by an incredible depopulation—a decline of 66 percent in the three neighborhoods combined—that magnifies the problems of the new poverty neighborhoods. As the population drops and the proportion of nonworking adults rises, basic neighborhood institutions are more difficult to maintain: stores, banks, credit institutions, restaurants, dry cleaners, gas stations, medical doctors, and so on lose regular and potential patrons. Churches experience dwindling numbers of parishioners and shrinking resources; recreational facilities, block clubs, community groups, and other informal organizations also suffer. As these organizations decline, the means of formal and informal social control in the neighborhood become weaker. Levels of crime and street violence increase as a result, leading to further deterioration of the neighborhood.

The more rapid the neighborhood deterioration, the greater the institutional disinvestment. In the 1960s and 1970s, neighborhoods plagued by heavy abandonment were frequently "redlined" (identified as areas that should not receive or be recommended for mortgage loans or insurance); this paralyzed the housing market, lowered property values, and further encouraged landlord abandonment. The enactment of federal and state community reinvestment legislation in the 1970s curbed the practice of open redlining. Nonetheless, "prudent lenders will exercise increased caution in advancing mortgages, particularly in neighborhoods marked by strong indication of owner disinvestment and early abandonment."

As the neighborhood disintegrates, those who are able to leave depart in increasing numbers; among these are many working- and middle-class families. The lower population density in turn creates additional problems. Abandoned buildings increase and often serve as havens for crack use and other illegal enterprises that give criminals footholds in the community. Precipitous declines in density also make it even more difficult to sustain or develop a sense of community. The feeling of safety in numbers is completely lacking in such neighborhoods.

Although changes in the economy (industrial restructuring and reorganization) and changes in the class, racial, and demographic composition of inner-city ghetto neighborhoods are important factors in the shift from institutional to jobless ghettos since 1970, we ought not to lose sight of the fact that this process actually began immediately following World War II.

The federal government contributed to the early decay of inner-city neighborhoods by withholding mortgage capital and by making it difficult for urban areas to retain or attract families able to purchase their own homes. Spurred on by massive mortgage foreclosures during the Great Depression, the federal government in the 1940s began underwriting mortgages in an effort to enable citizens to become homeowners. But the mortgage program was selectively administered by the Federal Housing Administration (FHA), and urban neighborhoods considered poor risks were redlined—an action that excluded virtually all the black neighborhoods and many neighborhoods with a considerable number of European immigrants. It was not until the 1960s that the FHA discontinued its racial restrictions on mortgages.

By manipulating market incentives, the federal government drew middle-class whites to the suburbs and, in effect, trapped blacks in the inner cities. Beginning in the 1950s, the suburbanization of the middle class was also facilitated by a federal transportation and highway policy, including the building of freeway networks through the hearts of many cities, mortgages for veterans, mortgage-interest tax exemptions, and the quick, cheap production of massive amounts of tract housing.

REFERENCES

Blank, Rebecca. 1994. "Outlook for the U.S. Labor Market and Prospects for Low-Wage Entry Jobs." Working paper, Center for Urban Studies, Northwestern University.

Bluestone, Barry, Mary Stevenson, and Chris Tilly. 1991. "The Deterioration in Labor Market Prospects for Young Men with Limited Schooling." Paper presented at the Eastern Economic Association, March 14, Pittsburgh.

Bound, John, and Harry Holzer. 1993. "Industrial Shifts, Skill Levels, and the Labor Market for White and Black Men. *Review of Economics and Statistics* 75 (August): 387-396.

Buron, Lawrence, Robert Haveman, and Owen O'Donnell. 1994. "Recent Trends in U.S. Male Work and Wage Patterns." Unpublished manuscript, University of Wisconsin at Madison.

Freeman, Richard B., and Lawrence F. Katz. 1994. "Rising Wage Inequality." In *Working Under Different Rules,* ed. Richard B. Freeman. New York: Russell Sage Foundation.

Gittleman, Maury B., and David R. Howell. 1993. "Job Quality and Labor Market Segmentation in the 1980s." Working paper, Bard College.

Lerman, Robert I., and Martin Rein. Forthcoming. *Social Service Employment: An International Perspective.* New York: Russell Sage Foundation.

McKinsey and Company. 1994. *Employment Performance.* Washington, D.C.: McKinsey Global Institute.

Nasar, Sylvia. 1994. "The Men in Prime of Life Spend Less Time Working." *New York Times,* December 1, A7.

Testa, Mark, and Marilyn Krogh. 1995. "The Effect of Employment on Marriage Among Black Males in Inner-City Chicago. In *The Decline in Marriage Among African Americans,* eds., M. Belinda Tucker and Claudia Mitchell-Kernan, pp. 59–95. New York: Russell Sage Foundation.

William Julius Wilson. 1987. *The Truly Disadvantaged: The Inner City, The Underclass, and Public Policy.* Chicago: University of Chicago Press.

DISCUSSION QUESTIONS

1. One problem for inner-city residents is that many jobs have relocated to the suburbs. Why is this a problem and what would have to be done to overcome it?

2. The high-tech area of the economy has grown dramatically in recent years. Why doesn't Wilson turn to jobs in these industries as alternatives to older manufacturing jobs?

CLASS

Class refers to categories of people distinguished from other categories on the basis of differences in income, wealth, status, privilege, and power. Class differences, thus, capture the type of social stratification in a particular society. Although rooted in economic conditions, the impact of class differences transcends the economic. A class-based society—and industrial societies are class based—can be distinguished from caste-based societies. People born into a caste system find themselves stamped with an identity at birth that they cannot cast off. In contrast, class societies make possible the movement of individuals from one class to another. They permit individual achievement to determine class location. The idea of going from rags to riches is an expression of the fluidity of class position. Of course, the reverse is possible, too. If class societies make possible the upward mobility of individuals, it also makes possible downward mobility.

But how many classes are there and how should they be identified? There is no one answer to this question. A Marxist perspective contends that classes ought to be defined in terms of modes and relations of production. Thus, a contemporary Marxist theorist such as Erik Olin Wright will use the terminology derived from Marx in writing about the bourgeoisie, proletariat, petite bourgeoisie, and so forth. On the other hand, other sociologists use class as a classificatory schema for locating people in a stratified social order. Thus, based on some measure such as income, we can divide the population into a variety of slices: upper, middle, and lower class, for example. Or, using a sixfold typology, we can speak of upper upper, lower upper, upper middle, lower middle, upper lower, and lower lower. And we could, as the anthropologist Lloyd Warner did, speak of nine classes by adding to the above a middle upper, middle middle, and middle lower.

However one chooses to divide the population, sociologists are clear about one thing and attentive to its implications: social class location shapes life chances, quality of life, and one's ideas and beliefs. Thus, where people live, the schools they attend, the clubs and community organizations they join, the friends they make, the cars they drive, the clothes they wear, the vacation spots they visit, and so forth, are shaped profoundly by class location. People's social class influences such fundamental factors as the kind of health care they can expect, the kinds of diseases they are likely to contract, and the number of years they can expect to live.

Changes in the American economy during the past two decades have meant a move from an industrial to a postindustrial or advanced industrial economy. One of the consequences of this shift is that jobs in some sectors of the economy, most notably manufacturing, have declined, whereas jobs in other sectors of the economy, and in particular the service and the high-tech sectors, have increased in numbers. With these changes, which have occurred rapidly, come various dislocations. One of the shifts that has occurred during this transition is that levels of inequality have increased. In addition, some people have been the beneficiaries of these changes. For them, these are the best of times. In contrast, for others the changes have resulted in increased economic hardships, with an increase in anxiety about their futures. For these people, these are either the worst of times, or at the least they are troubling times.

Although the three essays in this section cannot possibly afford the reader anything resembling a comprehensive portrait of the contemporary American class structure, they do highlight some of the most salient features of that structure.

Three Nations

Andrew Hacker

America is a society with small sectors of the population located among the ranks of the desperately poor or the very rich. However, within the vast middle there are large differences in terms of earning potential and life chances. In this selection from Money, *Andrew Hacker looks at three broad economic divisions, beginning with people who are, as he puts it, "getting by, barely." This includes not only the working poor employed in minimum-wage jobs, but people working in positions requiring college degrees or other forms of advanced training and making under $30,000 a year. The second category is the poor. Hacker traces changes in the size and character of this income group since the 1960s War on Poverty. Finally, he looks at the growing number of individuals and families who earn more than $100,000 a year—a group, he says, that is far from rich, but lives in very different circumstances from those making less than them.*

GETTING BY, BARELY

In New York's Chenango County, deputy sheriffs start at $16,000. A radio news director in Vermont is offered $17,000, while in Albuquerque, New Mexico, airline reservationists make $14,000. The average salary for lay teachers in Chicago's parochial schools is $21,000. In fact, according to a recent Census survey, a third of all full-time jobs pay below $20,000. Many who hold these jobs are women supplementing the family budget; but for the first time, men account for almost half the workers in this bottom tier. These are working Americans, not individuals who are unemployed or receiving public assistance. The paychecks just mentioned might suggest that a significant segment of the workforce is falling perilously close to the poverty line.

But the $17,000 news director and the $16,000 deputy sheriff will be quick to tell you that they

do not view themselves as poor. They may agree that they are just getting by and sometimes feel the pinch. Yet they are aware of the term *poverty* and in no way do they wish to be associated with it. That they can and do feel this way conveys a lot about how the economy operates.

Just as America remains two nations racially, so it contains equally real economic divisions. Whether or not to call these components "classes" is a matter of ideological taste, and we should be wary of outdated dualities. To draw the divide between "rich" and "poor" fails to mirror current reality, if only because the rich are so small a stratum that the "poor" would have to include the entire middle class. Karl Marx's ideology, which split society into owners and workers, also pushed salaried and professional people into his proletariat. James Madison, the principal author of our Constitution, would have had no major quarrel with Marx. He saw the break, very simply, separating "those who hold and those who are without property." Still, what must be answered is whether that "property" represents impressive holdings, or if it can refer to a more modest stake. If it must mean a business or other assets capable of yielding a comfortable income, then not many Americans can be called persons of property. It was left to Alexis de Tocqueville to illuminate the American way of thinking on this issue. This was the gist of his analysis:

> Among a great democratic people there will always be some members of the community in great poverty and others in great opulence. Between these two extremes stands an innumerable multitude almost alike, without being exactly rich or poor. But the poor, instead of forming the immense majority, are comparatively few in number.

Some commentators have chosen to describe this "multitude" as a large middle class. There is no harm in doing this, so long as we are clear on what kind of income or occupation is needed for inclusion in this stratum. If $30,000 is set as a minimum middle-class income, less than a third of all employed persons will make the cut. Even at $20,000, only about half get included. But things look a bit better for a sizable middle class if we focus on family incomes instead of individuals' earnings. Some 60 percent of all households have incomes of $25,000 or over, and slightly more than half are above $30,000. So even as we aver that a majority of Americans are not poor, many of them are still at a distance from what is usually seen as a middle-class income.

This country still has a considerable working class, which generally means factory jobs or related occupations in transportation and construction. Workers in General Motors plants in Ohio can still draw close to $70,000 a year, although that calls for considerable overtime. But each year, fewer Americans enjoy the safeguards that were common in the days of union protection. When it can, General Motors shifts jobs to North Carolina, where the going rate is nearer to $20,000. Still, even if modestly paid and lacking job security, this group of workers sees itself—and is encouraged to see itself—as distinct and separate from the poor.

America was the first society to essay what was and continues to be an unusual fusion: a politics that expounds the principle of human equality and an economy that produces visible disparities in income and wealth. Such a system will only work if it can induce most of its citizens to believe that they are faring well under its auspices. Thus the way the economy works must have majority support. Of course, citizens can and will be critical, on occasion sharply so. But in the final reckoning, they must feel that all in all they have been treated fairly. The heart of this strategy, as Tocqueville told us, is to ensure that the "multitude" does not see itself as poor.

In a word, the majority must be able to live sufficiently well so that they see themselves as "haves." It is not charity or compassion, but a sense of self-preservation, that led the system to ensure that income is so dispersed that most

people feel they are getting by. The 1995 Roper-Starch survey cited earlier found that seven in ten people felt they could manage decently on less than $35,000 a year and would need only $15,000 more for "reasonable comfort." Indeed, during a stroll through their local shopping mall, the majority of Americans will find that much of what they see is within their means.

Symbols also play a role. Perhaps the most fervid is found in the word *welfare,* which will also be discussed later on. As an object of opprobrium, public assistance serves several functions. For one thing, it allows a distinct group of Americans to be isolated and identified as poor. They are also deemed to be legitimate targets for censure or worse by anyone who pays taxes. And since public funds are involved, taxpayers feel even more entitled to criticize recipients' values and behavior. But perhaps the greatest role of welfare is to heighten the self-image of those not on its rolls. Thus the rest of the population is allowed to congratulate itself by declaring that they work or are otherwise self-supporting. The $14,000 airline reservationist can say that she makes do on even less than welfare recipients, given all of the extra benefits attached to public aid.

How do people get by on $14,000, $16,000, $17,000, or $21,000 a year? The short answer is to double up, if you have not done so already. Among the country's 35 million married couples aged twenty-five to fifty-four, in 73 percent of the households both spouses work. Often, the wife only works part-time or has a less demanding job. In marriages where the husband earns between $20,000 and $30,000, the wife averages $15,954. (However, when he gets to the $50,000 to $75,000 range, her earnings decline to $13,786.) To make do on modest paychecks, young people share quarters with one or more roommates, while those from affluent homes sometimes get subsidies from their parents. A surprisingly large number continue to live at home, since they cannot yet afford a place of their own. The last two Cen-

WHERE AMERICANS LIVE		
1970		1990
66.3%	Detached single-unit homes	59.0%
3.1%	Trailers or mobile homes	7.2%
30.6%	Apartments & other housing	33.8%

suses testify to a visible change in the kinds of roofs Americans have over their heads. As the table on this page shows, fewer Americans can afford to own the traditional dream home. In 1970, such a newly built house cost about twice a young couple's annual income. By 1994, the price tag on a typical new home was almost four times their income.

Perhaps the chief accommodation Americans have made to this new economic fact of life has been to postpone marriage and having children. This can be seen by looking at women aged thirty to thirty-four, first in 1970 and again in the mid-1990s. In 1970, only 6 percent had not yet been married, and only 8 percent had not yet had a child. By the mid-1990s, almost 20 percent had not been married and over a quarter had yet to become mothers, and it seems likely that some will never take those steps. But this does not mean that young people are abjuring sex. More nonmarried couples are living together today than ever before, and in varied pairings of genders and orientations. While affection is what usually binds these households, the fact that both have modest incomes can reinforce the decision to share bed and board.

The number of conceptions is probably as high today as it was in the past, but thanks to *Roe* v. *Wade,* fewer now eventuate in births. However, the fact that abortions are available is not itself the cause of declining reproduction. Rather, it is that for growing numbers of adults, not only in the United States but in most advanced countries, parenthood is a lower priority. If the number of children being born is declining, the chief reason is that raising them is seen as too expensive. Prior to 1970, a typical couple

had already had two children before reaching the age of thirty, and they did not stop to ask if their income was sufficient for that responsibility. In those early postwar days, most fathers made what was then called a "family wage," which was enough to support a full household.

How did a single income do it in 1970? The short answer is that what was seen as an optimal life required fewer amenities. In 1970, for example, only 28 percent of families owned two cars; today, 54 percent do so. In 1970, also, 2.9 million of us traveled to Europe. Last year, 7.1 million did, which signals that jet-setting is no longer confined to an elite. Therefore, the Consumer Price Index, which is based on a typical market basket of purchases, is not a wholly reliable mirror. If wages seemed to go further in 1970, one reason is that shopping lists were simpler. Those were the days of Keds and typewriters and turntables. Today, the Index includes Nikes, laser printers, and multiple-CD changers, which cost more because they do more. Even bread has been upgraded: croissants and exotic grains have replaced blander white loaves; Starbucks costs more than Maxwell House. Since cars have so much high-tech gear, a new one costs about half of a young couple's income, visibly up from 38 percent in 1970. And it is hardly necessary to add that Americans eat out and take out food much more often than was done a generation ago. It may not be gourmet cuisine—Burger King or Taco Bell will do—but even fast-food drive-ins cost more than meals prepared at home.

Much has been made of the disappearance of blue-collar jobs, especially those that paid well even if they entailed enervating work. In fact, though, not much more than the color of the collars has changed. Tens of millions of new jobs are essentially on assembly lines, albeit without the clanking of heavy machinery. An apt example are the polite and well-spoken ordertakers at mail-order merchants such as Lands' End and L. L. Bean, who sit at computer screens and tap in shirt sizes. It has been

WHICH AMERICANS ARE POOR?

Number and percentage in each group who are poor

In total population	36.1 million	13.8%
Children under 18	14.7 million	20.8%
Men 18–64	7.5 million	9.5%
Women 18–64	10.9 million	13.3%
Men 65 and over	0.8 million	6.2%
Women 65 and over	2.5 million	13.6%
White	16.3 million	8.5%
Black	9.9 million	29.3%
Hispanic	8.6 million	30.3%
Asian	1.4 million	14.6%

Below the poverty line, 1960–95

	All families	Persons over 65	Children under 18
1960	18.1%	35.2%	26.9%
1970	10.1%	24.6%	15.1%
1980	10.3%	15.7%	18.3%
1990	10.7%	12.2%	20.6%
1995	10.8%	10.5%	20.8%

claimed that entering such data makes them a part of an "information industry." Perhaps. Certainly, the first requirement for work of this type is to have your fingers trained for QWERTY. So despite all the fretting about subliteracy, it is worth observing how many $14,000 workers can make a keyboard do their bidding and know more than their elders about high-tech appliances. From this arises a feeling that these new occupations belong in the middle class, even if they are poorly paid. America has always tried to wish away the thought that it might have a proletariat. The customer calling L. L. Bean wants to converse with someone who sounds like her favorite niece. Of equal if not more importance is where the person tapping in the order feels she fits in the social scheme.

The important divide, then, is between the poor and those who are not, even if the latter group is not receiving much more than the minimum wage. If the gap is seen as between the have-nots and the haves, what the haves have are manners and skills that give them a decent chance of finding a place in the employment market. Not the least of these attributes has been a readiness to roll with the tide, to understand that they must make the best of the cards being dealt to them. Thus far they seem fairly sure that there will be limits to their descent. The system probably has enough sense not to betray that promise.

THE POOR: ALWAYS WITH US?

Since 1959, the Bureau of the Census has been computing an annual "poverty threshold." This is the level above which you must rise if you wish to escape being defined as poor. In 1995, the threshold for one person living alone was $7,763, or about $150 a week. For a single parent with two children, it came to $12,278, about $236 a week for this family of three. In fact, this poverty income is so low that survival seems problematic without added assistance. At best, one might be more likely to get by in a rural area, where costs tend to be lower and being poor is less evident, since not as much is available for purchase.

On the whole, though, the official poverty figures understate the number of Americans living at a subsistence level. Still, they offer insights into who the poorest Americans are and where they can be found. The highest poverty ratios are for city dwellers (21 percent); women living on their own (25 percent); and families headed by single mothers (53 percent). As hardly needs remarking, the figures for black and Hispanic individuals and families are over twice those recorded for whites.

Many of the programs of Lyndon Johnson's administration were designated as a "war on poverty." As can be seen in the table above, . . . the 1960s did bring a visible decline in the ratio of Americans below the poverty line. How much this was due to government initiatives and how much to broader factors cannot be stated with precision. This was a prosperous period, with opportunities for people who might otherwise have been unemployed. Parents were also having fewer children: two instead of four can make a modest income go a lot further. Relevant, too, was the continuing migration from the Southern states, with workers exchanging rural wages for better-paid factory jobs. Unions were still strong, and immigration was at nominal levels. If the 1960s was a decade of political protest and civil unrest, they also saw more Americans living better than they ever had before.

The bad news, however, was that the downward trend in poverty would be short in duration. The 1970s saw increases in the poverty rates for families and children, a trend that has continued through the 1990s and shows no sign of abating. The only exception has been persons over sixty-five. For them, the role of government has been crucial. Between 1960 and 1994, in dollars adjusted for inflation, the average Social Security payment to a retired worker came close to doubling, rising from $4,347 to $8,089. The average payment for a retired couple now exceeds $15,000. Each year also sees more marriages where both spouses have worked, so checks arrive in each of their names. As of 1996, if both had top earnings records, together they would receive $31,824. A growing number of Social Security recipients also have private pensions, plus savings and investments of their own. Among retired couples, median outside income is slightly over $10,000, and almost a third have $20,000 or more.

Among the aged poor, women outnumber men by a three-to-one margin, putting their poverty rate above the national average. Their numbers consist largely of widows living alone who never had sustained work records and must make do on reduced pensions with their husbands dead. Their median Social Security stipend is $7,693, and their outside income averages $2,000. Many bolster their budgets with food stamps, of which the weekly value for a single person comes to about $15. They are also eligible for Supplemental Security Income, which typically yields $2,923. In addition, the federally funded Nutrition Program for the Elderly serves 3.3 million senior citizens some 250 million meals each year.

The Supplemental Security Income program also gives stipends averaging $4,597 to 4.5 million children and adults who have been classified as physically or mentally disabled. They are then eligible for treatment under the respectable aegis of Medicare, receiving an average of $5,426 in treatment, rather than having to line up at a crowded Medicaid clinic. Another seven hundred thousand or so persons on the SSI rolls are listed as "alien recipients." As is well known, our immigration laws give high priority to "family unification." In many cases, this means young adults come first and then send for older family members. Thus a growing group within the alien recipients consists of grandparents who came here too late to build up pension rights. Until recently, they have been able to receive Supplemental Security Income instead of Social Security. In this way the government relieved their children, most of whom are now citizens and many of whom had comfortable incomes, of having to support the parents they brought here. In 1996, Congress revoked this allowance, on the ground that people who decide to live in the United States should not become a burden on the taxpayers.

The most disheartening trend has been the rise in childhood poverty, from 15 percent of all youngsters in 1970 to 21 percent in 1995. The chief reason is that many more are being raised only by their mothers, which generally means on only her income. Since 1970, their percentage has more than doubled, from 11 to 24. This change has also been the largest single influence on the overall poverty rate: families headed by women now make up 27 percent of all households.

The rise in the number of female-headed households does not mean that disappearing and defaulting fathers are enjoying great bachelor lives. In fact, the poverty rate for single men is also at a new high, although it is not captured in most official statistics. Yet one official figure begins to paint the picture: the nation currently has about 1.5 million of its men incarcerated. At last count, the United States was vying with Russia for leadership in inmate population. Given our current spate of prison construction—this is one bill taxpayers seem willing to foot—we may already be in first place.

America has a growing group of men who have never had steady employment, at least of the legal kind. Many lack a high school level of literacy and the social deportment most employers expect. On the streets of the nation's cities can be seen worn-out men in their forties, begging or searching for soda cans. More than a few are graduates of the prison system, which is hardly a recommendation when seeking a job.

Most of the inmate population will eventually be released. The larger society does not even want to think about what these men will do when they come out. There is, of course, the hope that most will "go straight": rejecting crime for a law-abiding life. But to do so requires employment, and thus far no one has drawn up a list of honest occupations former felons might seek. Indeed, the opposite is often the case. In New York City, an uproar arose when it was discovered that some of its school janitors had served terms in prison. In other cities, people with prison records are barred from becoming taxicab drivers and security guards, even though they are positions suitable for those seeking a fresh start.

At this point, it seems logical to ask whether America would have a much lower incidence of poverty if its economy were able to provide full employment. For example, it has been argued that a key reason why many men do not stay to raise the children they sire is that they lack steady jobs that would make them reliable providers. This idea has an inherent plausibility; the only hitch is that millions of middle-class fathers are also leaving home, but not for economic reasons. In other words, it should not be assumed that steadily employed blue-collar men would be more dutiful spouses than their white-collar counterparts. Still, jobs for all is a salutary goal, even if it can't mend broken marriages, which are a major cause of childhood poverty.

Except during the depths of the 1930s depression, this country has always had more job openings than people available to fill them. This was most graphic during the last century, when employers sent recruiters to Europe to announce that they were hiring. Even today, there are millions of unfilled positions. Hotels in many parts of the country are desperate for chambermaids and kitchen help and offer bonuses to employees who bring in friends or relatives. This is why the country has absorbed so many immigrants. It is almost as if the circulars have been sent out again, but now to Asia and Latin America and the Middle East. There is work waiting to be done, ranging from harvesting crops to designing silicon chips to medical residencies in inner-city clinics. Or services Americans did not realize they wanted until they became available, such as the Korean-owned manicure salons that cater to busy professional women.

The reason why unemployment persists even when jobs are available is quite obvious. The economy has always wanted things done, but is only willing to pay a certain price. And, immigrants, for their part, have been willing to work for wages that citizens of longer lineage would never deign to consider. Nor does it help to tell the long-term unemployed that they should apply for the jobs that immigrants are eager to take. For better or for worse, even poor Americans feel that any work they do must pay what they—like the rest of us—deem to be an American wage.

THE $100,000 LIFE

The real income explosion has been in the topmost brackets. Not only are the rich getting richer, more Americans are becoming affluent or are moving close to that category. For present purposes, an income of $100,000 will be considered sufficient for membership in the comfort class. Of course this is far from being rich; given today's expectations, that takes $1 million or more a year. Nor does comfort connote wealth; that requires having enough in assets to enjoy your prosperity without having to work.

Six-digit incomes were once considered a rarity, indeed an eminence ordinary people could never hope to attain. No longer. The most recent details on Americans in the $100,000 bracket are for 1995. In that year, 6.3 million of the nation's families, 9 percent of the total, were at this level. In 1980, using constant dollars, only 4 percent of families had that kind of purchasing power; while in 1970, less than 3 percent did.

But there's a crucial caveat. Eighty percent of these incomes come from having two or more earners in the family. Indeed, such multiple employment is at an all-time high. Dad may make $52,498, Mom brings in $33,501—this is a typical division—while Sis contributes the $17,221 she earns at the mall. Only one in six of the $100,000 households attains it with a single earner, usually a well-paid husband. Still, this tells us that when wives don't have to work, quite a few choose not to. Almost a tenth of the $100,000 families have one or more members over the age of sixty-five, pointing to a growing class of affluent retirees.

We often hear that families now need two or more paychecks just to keep up with the bills. This rings true for households where one member makes, say, $28,000. But when multiple earnings boost domestic incomes above $100,000, one wants to ask what are all those "necessities" households feel they must have.

Both spouses work in almost 60 percent of the nation's marriages, so two-income homes are now found at all economic levels. Even if the husbands make $100,000, generally enough to support a household, the wives also work in 60 percent of those marriages, which in fact is a

point or so above the national norm. The Census found 120,000 couples where both make at least $75,000, and 45,000 have both passed the $100,000 mark. In this category are Bruce Willis and Demi Moore, who together can command $20 million for a pair of movies. Or Marion and Herbert Sandler, the joint CEOs of Golden Western Financial, who in tandem have been making about $5 million a year.

Washington has always had well-paid couples. During the 1996 presidential campaign, the contenders declared their incomes for the previous year. The Clintons' total was $316,074, which included Bill's $200,000 salary and payments due to Hillary for past professional work. The Doles declared $533,415, to which Bob contributed $148,000 as Senate majority leader and $17,700 for his army disability, while most of the rest came from Elizabeth's $200,675 salary for heading the American Red Cross. (Ross Perot's income was whatever he decided to take as walking-around money from his $3.3 billion fortune.) In some instances, both incomes come courtesy of the taxpayers, as was the case with Anne Bingaman, an assistant attorney general who received $131,400 in 1996, and Sen. Jeffrey Bingaman of New Mexico, whose pay was $133,600.

But there's another $100,000 explosion. Last year's Census study found 2.7 million working Americans—2.4 million men and 300,000 women—who had six or more digits on their paychecks. So if the rich are getting richer, there are also more of them: the group making $100,000 or more now matches the adult population of Los Angeles. For instance, Princeton now pays a star psychology professor $233,546. Pilots at Federal Express average $128,000, earning them the tag of "flying vice presidents." The minimum in major league baseball is $109,000, even for players just out of high school.

Pressure for six-figure salaries extends across a growing array of professions. For example, we were once told the people entered the civil service for security, light work, even to promote the public good. Still, at last count, the federal payroll had 15,266 "senior grade" officials who averaged $102,338. Of course, academics are in it for the love of learning and the joys of stirring young minds. Even so, 5,858 of the nation's 79,323 full professors—7.4 percent—also make over $100,000. Close to half of these prospering scholars are at five schools: Harvard, Stanford, Yale, Princeton, and Cal Tech. MIT pays an ace professor of electrical engineering $321,967, while Wellesley shows that women's colleges also reward their stars, giving $141,023 to an eminent classicist.

Medicine has long been the one field that all but assures a six-figure income. According to the most recent American Medical Association survey, the nation's 407,044 physicians who have their own practices take home a median of $176,000. Fewer than a quarter make less than $100,000, and most of them are just starting out. The AMA also estimates that salaried physicians average about $130,000, with government employment at the low end and some hospitals paying their pathologists and radiologists considerably higher.

It isn't so easy to generalize about what lawyers are getting, since we now have 894,000 attorneys, surpassing the combined adult populations of Atlanta, Pittsburgh, and St. Louis. At the top are liability experts, who take a slice of every multimillion-dollar award and fly to trials in their own Learjets. Chicago starts its public defenders at $32,772, and law clerks for federal judges get $36,426. The Census calculates the lawyers' median at $72,144, with close to 250,000 making over $100,000. According to the *American Lawyer*'s most recent survey, the 13,131 partners in the country's hundred largest firms average $446,000. In New York City, first-year associates can start at $85,000, while in lower-living-costs New Orleans, offers are more like $53,000. Associates in Los Angeles can expect $100,000 by their fifth year.

Corporations prefer not to state what they give upper-middle executives. (Top-tier pay must be shown in stockholders' proxy notices and gets wide publicity.) The Census computes that about 800,000 "managers, executives, and administrators" earn more than $100,000, but that total includes small-business owners who can take what they choose from the till. Texaco has reported that 875 of its people make more than $100,000, while IBM has 1,350 at over $150,000. Leading financial firms now start newly minted MBAs at $100,000. But there's a catch. They are expected to put in twelve hours per day, six days a week. Figured on an hourly basis, the checks look considerably smaller. (Manhattan rents are another shrinkage factor.) But an arduous apprenticeship can pay off. Last year, some 1,500 Wall Streeters made more than $1 million.

Why are so many people paid so much? The most heard answer is that talent is in short supply, so there is fierce competition for the top performers. Derek Bok, who for twenty-two years was president of Harvard, argues that every society contains only "a limited supply of highly talented people." Hence the bidding wars that drive compensations up. In some areas, this hypothesis seems sound. When the major league baseball players went on strike, it was evident that replacement teams from the minors couldn't, well, replace them. Networks ascribe the sad state of prime time to a shortage of good comedy writers. "There's just not enough talent to go around," lamented a CBS executive. Perhaps, although the continued success of soap operas suggest that ways can be found to expand the pool. High-paying law firms say they must compete for a finite fund of brains. At this point, someone might shout, "Whoa!" Each June sees the graduation of forty thousand new J.D.s. True, not all are from Harvard. But could it be that the big firms find it beneath them to scout for prospects at the University of Iowa? After all, Economics 101 taught us that one way to solve talent shortages is by opening doors to new people.

Another claim is that modern work calls for more sophisticated knowledge. Think of investment analysts and their mathematical models. Or lawyers who must become expert in silicon and DNA. But every era says this of its well-paid professions. Tool and die making became a princely craft because it depended on having a head for applied mathematics. (Software does much of the job today.) Novelists of Jane Austen's era may have used quill pens, but it would be hard to argue that they were not as brainy as word-processing writers. True, more of us spend more years in classrooms, ostensibly because our age has more to learn. An alternative reason is that we store people in school since the labor force has little need for workers prior to their twenties.

If Economics 101 said that increased demand should give rise to new sources of supply, it also told us that the equation can work in reverse. Perhaps the strongest force behind all those $100,000 salaries is the increasing supply of things clamoring to be bought. Whether goods or services or entertainments, in recent years the possibilities for purchasing have become more elaborate and intriguing. As always, much is material merchandise, ranging from kitchenware and clothing to cellular phones and powerboats. The economy also highlights new experiences, ranging from sitting at a sushi bar to backpacking in Nepal. Here is a sampling of items advertised during the 1996 Christmas season: a stainless-steel home stove for $13,900; a digitalized putting green costing $1,195; a high-tech desk lamp at $6,800; for him, a polyurethane car coat at $2,145; for her, an alligator briefcase at $7,780; for both, an embroidered cashmere blanket at $3,585; plus a $2,700 reproduction Queen Anne dollhouse for the children. These are just things to have around the house and do not include tough-terrain cars and furnishings for a second home.

These add up to the "new necessities," things to be owned or known in order to lead a full life.

In the past, unions sought a "living wage" for their workers. Today, the process is less overt. The economy and employers tacitly agree that a sizable stratum of Americans should be able to enjoy high-end shopping.

One such expense is college tuition, especially for parents who feel that their offspring must attend a college that has a national reputation. An upscale degree is not wanted simply to open doors to desirable careers. That elite circle of colleges imparts added stature to its graduates, an association that cannot be erased. But simply to attend classes at Amherst costs $22,007 during the current academic year. Harvard is slightly cheaper at $21,900, and Stanford looks like a bargain at $20,500. Even a lower-tier school such as Vanderbilt charges $20,200, while a small college such as Carleton is asking $21,100. But tuition is just the beginning, after which comes bed and board, plus textbooks and travel, not to mention all the gear students must now have during those formative years. To be sure, a car and ski equipment are not absolutely necessary for higher education. Still, such extras help a student make the most of that unique experience. Modestly, having one child at college can exact $35,000 a year. As a result, even families with $100,000 incomes have been known to ask for—and receive—scholarship aid.

In theory, employers do not raise wages because they like playing the role of benefactor, nor even feel obliged to elevate their workers' living standards. But economies are not only guided by economic considerations. During the 1980s, abetted by the Reagan ethos, the expectation emerged of the "the $100,000 life." This was not a pie-in-the-sky dream, depending on a legal settlement or a lottery ticket. Rather, the figure was regarded as a realistic aspiration, approximating how much one had to be paid to enjoy an optimal life.

This is not to argue that employers began to raise salaries to create a new class or to satisfy expensive tastes. Decisions are seldom made in so deliberate a way. Yet it is not totally off base to conclude that law firms and corporations and colleges, even the civil service, all felt that their stature would be enhanced by expanding their echelon of $100,000 people. In return, they would have representing them men and women who could embody a standard of life that was becoming a new national norm. And surely visitors will be impressed by all those BMWs in the corporate parking lot. And aren't investors more likely to trust advice emanating from a $2,000 suit? No wonder clients keep coming to those law firms whose partners average $446,000. That they are paid so much, we tend to reason, even if against our better judgment, must be evidence that they are the best people in the field.

DISCUSSION QUESTIONS

1. In what ways does Hacker think the poor and those who are simply getting by differ in terms of life chances? Do you agree with his assessment?
2. Hacker asks the following question in his section on those who make over $100,000 a year: "Why are so many people paid so much?" How would you answer this question?

<hr>

READING 22

The End of the Social Contract?

Katherine S. Newman

Katherine Newman examines the changing fortunes of those members of the middle class for whom the American Dream appears to be increasingly elusive. The idea that if people work hard, they can expect to achieve occupational security and upward mobility, and can assume that their economic lives will be better than that of their parents has been called into question. Now, with increasing job insecurity and incomes that have not kept pace with the cost of living, purchasing a home, paying for college

educations, and saving for retirement become increasingly difficult goals to realize. In this concluding passage from Declining Fortunes, *Newman asks what this means in terms of an implicit social contract, and suggests what might be done to rekindle the confidence the middle class had during the two decades after World War II.*

It is an article of faith among middle-class Americans that every generation will do better than the one that preceded it and that upward mobility is a birthright for those who work hard. By the same token, nothing is due those who slack off and expect a handout. Indeed, the promise of economic success defines our national identity, but it is a cultural premise built upon shifting sands. Our economy has grown increasingly more fragile, buffeted by forces we barely understand and cannot seem to control. With every day that goes by, these unseen hands seem to interfere more and more in our most intimate decisions: when to marry, when to have children, where to live, how easily we can remain close to our extended families, whether we will be able to enjoy our sunset years or will have to fret over every dime. And on all of these counts, the largest living generation of Americans is doing worse, enjoying less of the good life than those who came before, most notably its own parents.

The baby-boom generation feels strangled by this decline. Decisions that were once left to the vagaries of emotion are now calculated down to the last nickel; risks that could once be taken in education or career are now out of the question. If being careful could cure the disease of downward mobility, baby boomers would at least have a strategy for overcoming the obstacles the economy has placed in their way. But in truth, being careful and making all the right choices is no guarantee that the future will work out well. Indeed, for many of the nation's youngest boomers who put aside risks and dreams in favor of the pragmatic course, economic history has been unkind in the extreme. No amount of deferred gratification will buy them the gratification they want: skyrocketing prices, stagnating wages, dissipating promotion prospects, and the relentless pressure of an economy that just does not seem to work any more—these are the forces and trends that are choking them.

At the very least, sympathy would seem to be in order. After fifty years of sustained expansion in the United States, the bandwagon has come to a screeching halt. The brunt of the slowdown has been born by the baby boomers, with more to come as their own children mature into an economy characterized by fits and starts, weak recoveries, and industrial decline. Surely the country must realize that they are deserving of some concern, some recognition of the price they have had to pay for maturing in the wrong place at the wrong time.

Postwar parents, perhaps more than anyone else, know how steep this slide has been: it is after all their flesh and blood that has been exiled from the places where they were born and raised. Long-awaited grandchildren are growing up many miles away because the boomers in between cannot afford to live near their hometowns. The Ozzies and Harriets of the 1950s would like to be able to point with pride to the material accomplishments of their adult children as a natural extension of their own talents and drive. Instead, they confront boomerang kids who cannot seem to break free and forty-year-old progeny whose life-styles cannot hold a candle to their own, even if they are managers or professionals. The whole program they so believe in seems to have gone sour and no one really knows why. They take some solace, pointing the finger at elites, often those from other countries but some homegrown as well, who have taken unfair advantage and "jumped the line." Expressions of disgust at the urban "other," the underclass that demands tax dollars and affirmative action, creates a sense of moral superiority and a mandate for rejectionist "throw the bums out" politics. In the end, however, postwar parents believe that the boomers

themselves are to blame for wanting it all too soon. They need to "get a new culture," divest themselves of their overblown expectations, and learn to wait their turn.

The problem is, of course, that waiting does not seem to work anymore. Postwar parents who had to wait because their young lives were tangled up in the depression and the war found the pot of gold at the end of the rainbow more by historical chance than anything else. Not that they did not work for it, but their children are working equally hard and are not likely to see the same rewards. They will pay the price for this misfortune for the rest of their lives: delayed entry into the housing market, among other things, will put them at a serious disadvantage from which they are unlikely to recover.

The United States is mired in an economic transformation that may turn out to be as profound as the industrial revolution itself, with consequences that are only vaguely understood by those of us whose lives will be shaped by them. But the decisions we make at this juncture, particularly those that govern the use of federal, state, and local budgets, will shape the very soul of the society we will pass on to the generations yet to come. Will America be a country in which we are our brother's keeper? Or will it be a culture where "every man for himself" summarizes our sense of social responsibility? Will the generations reach across the divides that time and history have placed between them, or will they turn inward and demand their share first, and others be damned? Will our suburban citizens—rapidly becoming the majority—turn their backs on the cities and define the nation's urban problems as someone else's responsibility? There are philosophical questions at issue here that go the heart of the country's national character. But underlying every moral question lies the simple, irreducible, problem of money: who is going to be allowed to lead the good life to which all middle-class Americans believe they are entitled, and who is going to be shut out.

Jim Florio, the ill-fated governor of New Jersey, knows this changing mood all too well. His state budget has been drowning in a sea of red ink, and his every effort to restore solvency through tax increases has met with resounding rejection. Angry middle-class taxpayers have marched on Trenton in protests that looked like the old days of the antiwar movement, save for the Brooks Brothers suits and the silver hair dotting the crowd. Lowell Weicker, independent governor of Connecticut, discovered the same fury in his constituency when he attempted to introduce a state income tax for the first time in order to preserve the public services the budget could no longer cover. All across the nation, starting with the new-age tax revolt in California (Proposition 13) to its companion measure in Massachusetts (Proposition 2-1/2), voters have thrown local government out of their pocketbooks and issued ultimatums to politicians of all persuasions: find the money somewhere else. Not on my back, Jack.

For a nation that professes a firm belief in education as the proving ground for young people, we have been surprisingly mean in our support of public schools throughout the 1980s and early 1990s. School bond issues that passed without a second thought in the expansive years of the 1950s now fail regularly, leaving local school districts no choice but to fire teachers, cut back on extracurricular activities, skimp on supplies, eliminate enrichment courses, and bear down hard in order to meet prefabricated objectives in standardized test scores, hoping to shield themselves against the criticism that they are wasteful. In 1990, 48 percent of the school budgets in the state of New Jersey were rejected by taxpayers,[1] continuing a trend that had been on the upswing since the mid-1980s.

New Jersey residents were hardly alone: school bond failures have become epidemic throughout the nation.[2] Voters charge that there is altogether too much fat in the public schools, and they have served notice that they are not about to pick up the tab. School officials, however, see their districts as skeletal, their mission threatened, and their very value as educators under the gun. Since they make little money to begin with, teachers are beginning to ask themselves whether some other way of making a living might be preferable to the beating they are taking at the hands of the public.

If this were merely a matter of squeezing the funds out of the citizens of Pleasanton to educate their own children, this would be bad enough; in fact, it might be regarded as self-destructive. But the political conflict over school expenditures is everywhere criss-crossed by generational and racial turmoil, by the demands of equity and fairness to distribute whatever resources we have to all comers. Retirees whose own children benefited from public education when they moved to towns like Pleasanton, now turn their backs on the needs of today's young families. And while they often do so in the name of elusive standards of efficiency in public education, underlying their rejection of school budgets is the cold fact that they do not want to pay for services they no longer use. The exile of their own progeny from Pleasanton, fueled by ridiculous real estate prices, has exacerbated the tendency to pull out of the social contract at the local level. After all, what's in it for them?[3] If the same logic were ever applied to social security or Medicare, we would surely see the contract that binds the generations fall apart.

The fiercest debates over school funding have come in states like New Jersey and California, where equalization is the issue. Rich districts fight tooth and nail to prevent their coffers from being tapped in favor of communities with far fewer options for funding the public schools. Supreme Court decisions notwithstanding, the well-to-do have made it clear that they are loath to see their money distributed to those less fortunate, particularly when they are of a different skin color or speak a foreign tongue. Jonathan Kozol's searing account of the nation's inner-city school districts, *Savage Inequalities,*[4] stands as a moral indictment of the consequences: poor kids everywhere attend schools without books, without pencils, and with roofs that are caving in and windows that are broken.

We could chalk these inequities up to racism, and many minority advocates as well as their constituents readily draw this conclusion. There can be little doubt that the fortunate residents of Pleasanton are uncomfortable with minorities who live far away, who come to them through media images of crime and unrest. But racism is far too simplistic a diagnosis of the revolts that have blocked the distribution of middle-class tax dollars to the working poor in the cities and suburbs. It is the sharp edge of declining fortunes, the hoarding mentality that derives from the sense that there is not enough to go around, much less extra to fund the demands of the dispossessed.

The business community is also party to the hue and cry over schools and taxes. It is up in arms over the declining quality of public education, worried about the literacy and numeracy problems of a work force it argues is only marginally able to handle entry-level jobs in banks, stores, insurance companies, and fast-food restaurants. Business leaders bemoan the sliding competence of high school graduates and argue that we have yielded our international economic position to the Japanese and the Germans in part because we have abandoned high standards. Hence, the captains of industry promote highly visible schemes to resurrect the educational enterprise, by adopting schools, promoting voucher systems to stimulate competition, and pushing for more resources to be put in the hands of the educational system.

Yet the business community is caught in the same web of contradictory impulses as the average taxpayer: its market position has eroded, income has plummeted. Hence, business is on the lookout for any means of cutting expenses, including business taxes. Communities hungry for economic stability have traded corporate tax breaks for jobs and in the process have left themselves short of the funds they need to operate the public sector. In Florida $32 million went to public education in 1991, a sizable sum. But the amount is trivial compared with the $500 million claimed by Florida businesses as concessions in sales taxes, machinery, and fuel costs.[5] In Cleveland, Ohio, where the public school system was $34 million in the red for the 1991–92 school year, administrators filed a lawsuit arguing that tax breaks for business have seriously eroded the resource base of public schools. Teachers in Washington State walked off the job in protest against corporate tax breaks, singling out the case of the Boeing Company, which, they charge, was exempted from more than $900 million in sales taxes that could have been used to support public education. In Kansas, Texas, and Minnesota, among other places, legislators have pushed to eliminate property-tax concessions for businesses, since this is the revenue source most directly tied to education.

Businesses themselves point to their losing battle with overseas competitors and argue that their performance will only get worse if they are forced to absorb additional tax burdens. Besides, they argue, the schools should be pushed toward greater efficiencies in the name of accountability. As Forrest Coffey, corporate vice president for government affairs at the Boeing Company in Seattle, put the matter: "First they say, 'Give us more money.' Why should I give [the schools] more money? What do I get?" A powerful rhetoric of efficiency has found a great deal of support in a country skeptical of government and of public sector services: school teachers find themselves having to justify their calling in terms more appropriate for the assembly line. How many widgets were turned out per hour; how high are the reading test scores per hour of invested instruction? Educators lament the increased reliance on these stultifying forms of educational processing, though they have little choice but to prove their merit according to this yardstick. Next to the consumer price index, annual statistics on reading scores have become a major benchmark of mayoral efficacy. Meanwhile, the business world and state governments square off against each other in a fight for resources, while municipalities stand by and pray that they will not have to withstand more plant closings, more defections of firms who can always find other states where the economy is bad enough to extract new concessions.

The nation's colleges and universities have been similarly trapped. Federal contributions toward financial aid declined precipitously throughout the 1980s, leaving just enough for the poorest would-be students and relatively little for the struggling middle-income kids. State budgets for higher education have been slashed, a reflection of the weakened political clout of the education industry. University officials have had no choice but to begin stripping the universities first of their support staff and then of their faculty. No one is going to cry themselves to sleep over these problems, except perhaps the students who will be denied access to a college education, a sheepskin that is irreplaceable in this increasingly credential-oriented climate.[6] Because middle-class children know just how important higher education is for job opportunity, the issue of access has become politicized and, on occasion, ugly. The University of California at Berkeley, the nation's premier public university, has been in the spotlight in recent years because of its admissions policies.[7] High-achieving Asian high school students have squared off against African-American students long denied their turn at the elite schools; affirmative action has been embraced and then reversed as the politics of access heats up. Economic constraints on higher education are turning into blocked opportunities, and when this transpires, conflict inevitably intensifies among those critical credentials.

Private universities, including Brown and Columbia, have seen student protests swell over financial-aid policies that threaten to exclude those who cannot afford to pay the astronomical tuition charges of the Ivy League. On both fronts—the public and the private universities—we are seeing a wrenching end to the period of expansion in higher education that began in earnest in the 1960s, democratizing access to the scientific and humanistic knowledge that is the hallmark of a great nation. The country that bestowed the GI Bill on its deserving soldiers and provided generous student-loan programs to the older boomers is about to let higher education become the province of those to the manor born and the poorest of the poor, leaving everyone else standing at the door.

The 1990s are returning us to an earlier era in which birthright determined one's fortunes. Those who can afford the better things in life will have them from the beginning, and those who do not will find it much harder to lay their hands on a middle-class identity. The issue of schools and taxes makes the cleavage between haves and have nots abundantly clear. Other sources of division are less obvious but have the same destructive potential for undermining the social contract. Generational differences are among the least recognized but most important of these "hidden" conflicts.[8] Richard Lamm, the outspoken former governor of Colorado, now a professor of public policy at the University of Denver, recently spoke out about the age-based inequalities in the way we spend our federal budget:

> Congress . . . has just passed a budget that gives approximately 60 percent of our federal social spending to just 12 percent of our citizens: Americans over sixty-five. Yet the elderly have the highest disposable income and the lowest rates of poverty . . . in America. . . . There is little question that the elderly are the most politically powerful group in America. It's highly questionable whether they are the most deserving.[9]

Lamm goes on to explain that Medicare pays for the health costs of thousands of elderly millionaires, while 20 percent of the nation's children go unvaccinated.[10] We allow Medicare to pay for heart transplants, while thirty-one million Americans lack health insurance of any kind. "We have created an excessive sense of entitlement in the elderly," laments the former governor, "and they are vociferous in defending and enlarging their benefits."[11]

Lamm's warning is the first volley in a generational conflict that is not yet full-blown. His voice is not the only one raised against generational privilege. In the early 1990s the *New York Times* began an opinion series entitled "Voices from a New Generation," a periodic column in which young Americans at least one generation removed from the boomers have the opportunity to speak up. One particularly angry column was written by Mark Featherman, a young man who works in the library of the Jewish Theological Seminary. Mark complained about the colossal national debt racked up in the 1980s by a nation unwilling to live within its means, noting that his generation would end up having to pay for this binge:

America had a party in the 1980's and we—the "twentysomething generation"—weren't invited. While high-flying S & L robber barons were making millions with other people's money, while men of bad conscience were constructing investment houses of paper, we were making our way through college and graduate school, taking out loans to finance our educations. Odd, then, that now that the party's over, we should get stuck with the bill.

People are now speaking of the "new austerity." . . . Those doing most of the talking, of course, are those who can afford to be austere; their income is safely tucked away in tax shelters and investments. But for those of us just entering the work force, austerity is not something we have chosen; it was chosen for us. . . . The baby boomers have a long-term lock on the upper levels of the marketplace, and we face increased competition for entry-level jobs. Who will be made to pay for the good times of the last decade? It doesn't take a genius to figure out that it will be us, the youngest and rawest members of the labor force.[12]

Mark is not a happy camper; his age-mates are likely to be just as upset if their prospects continue to decline and they come to identify the source of their problems as older, more privileged generations of Americans.

The disparate fortunes of these generations may well become so blatant that they will catalyze a new kind of political dialogue. As the stresses and strains evident in the boomer generation become clearer, they may well turn around and ask their politicians (not to mention their own parents) why the country seems so uninterested in their problems. They may well want to know why so little attention has been paid to their concerns, particularly in light of how much attention is given to the problems of other groups: the elderly, the poor, the cities. Boomers are likely to open a generational conversation on the subject of equity and it will not be a pleasant one, for their complaints already evoke countercharges that they are a spoiled generation with inflated expectations, a critique they sometimes level at themselves. If the economic prospects of the boomers continue to sag, the country may hear the sound and fury of promises unfulfilled and hard work gone unrewarded. And this will be just the beginning of the generational debate: in time, the "baby-bust" generation will surely ask why they should have to bear the burden of supporting the boomer generation in retirement.[13]

Until that time, we are left with pressing questions of public policy that cannot wait. Who will pay for the national debt? How are we going to compete in the international arena if we refuse to pay for the school bond issues that will fund quality education? The sky-rocketing cost of health care threatens to bankrupt workers and employers, and there appears to be no end in sight. The nation's inner cities are suffering from massive neglect, severe unemployment, and persistent poverty. Where will the resources come from to speak to these critical issues?

If the experience of the generations of Pleasanton is any guide, the country is in for a rough ride indeed. Even the generation of the

1960s, with its liberal political history, feels economically vulnerable. Their younger counterparts, the boomers of the Reagan era, are that much less inclined to be sympathetic toward the need to be their brother's keeper. Postwar parents who were lucky enough to be in the right country at the right time are now faced with escalating tax bills that are driving them out of towns like Pleasanton. Their need to marshal their resources in order to support themselves through a long retirement, leaves little to help their boomer progeny. The social concerns that no country can afford to ignore, the problems that festered and then exploded in south central Los Angeles in the spring of 1992, flicker on their TV sets and then dissolve into the great beyond of the increasingly distant cities. Suburban dwellers are too preoccupied and too worried about their own problems and those of their children to leave much room for the demands of the inner city. They want someone else to handle that headache, someone else's resources to pay for it.

This does not augur well for the soul of the country in the twenty-first century. Every great nation draws its strength from a social contract, an unspoken agreement to provide for one another, to reach across the narrow self-interests of generations, ethnic groups, races, classes, and genders toward some vision of the common good. Taxes and budgets—the mundane preoccupations of city hall—express this commitment, or lack of it, in the bluntest fashion. Through these mechanistic devices, we are forced to confront some of the most searching philosophical questions that face any country: what do we owe one another as members of a society? Can we sustain a collective sense of purpose in the face of the declining fortunes that are tearing us apart, leaving those who are able to scramble for advantage and those who are not to suffer out of sight?

There will be little left of the nation if we withdraw into our own little corners and refuse to "pay" for anyone else's needs. If the fortunes of the generations diverge to the point where they cannot see each other's legitimate claims

and heartfelt dilemmas, we may well see the development of warring interest groups competing for politically sacred identities: the inviolable elderly, the deserving children, the baby boomers holding IOUs because they have yet to claim their fair share, the burdened baby-bust generation that did not get to "come to the party" in the 1980s. This is a nightmare vision of American politics that we cannot afford to entertain. We cannot allow public policy debates to descend to the level of squabbles over who is spoiled, about which ethnic groups deserve the good life and which should be excluded, about who is really deserving of a decent retirement or adequate medical care. The social contract upon which we all depend required some recognition of the common rights and legitimate aspirations of all Americans for a share of the good life.

In explaining our fate, American culture tends to subtract large forces from our lives—economic trends, historical moments, and even government policies that privilege one group over another—and looks instead to the individual's character traits or values for answers. Ask members of the postwar generation about their extraordinary experience of upward mobility and you are likely to hear a sermon on the importance of hard work and "your own bootstraps." The GI Bill, low-interest mortgages, and the booming economy of the 1950s and 1960s will barely rate a mention in this tale of upward mobility. But the truth is that the hard work paid off only because economic conditions over which no individual had control made it possible and because government policies provided a helping hand.

In the legacy of the GI Bill, the WPA, and a host of other government initiatives lies the kind of active program for recovery we sorely need today. These programs created confidence that we lack at present that there are measures we can take, investments in the well-being of all Americans that will actually make a difference.[14] The Great Depression was a far worse economic calamity than anything we have seen since, and we found our way out of it. It is true that part of that trajectory of success came about because the United States was arming itself for World War II, a catalyst for government spending that few would want to see repeated. But the lesson we might take from the experience of the nation's recovery from the blight of the 1930s is that we need not assume that nothing can be done to move the economy and the generations that depend upon it out of the current malaise. We can ask and should ask what government can do as well as what private industry can do. And when we have finished that agenda, we must ask as well what we must do for one another if the present generations and those that follow are to claim their own share of the American dream.

NOTES

1. "Angry Taxpayers Reject 44% of New Jersey School Budgets," *New York Times,* May 2, 1992, p. B1.
2. See Jean Scandlyn, "When the Social Contract Fails: Inter-Generational and Inter-Ethnic Conflict in an American Suburb" (Ph.D. thesis, Columbia University, 1992).
3. One thing that is "in it for them" is the preservation of the value of their own real estate. The quality of the local public school is essential to property values. On this count, retirees should be concerned to keep quality high. Unfortunately, this interest conflicts with the desire to hold down tax rates, a losing battle in the 1980s.
4. Jonathan Kozol, *Savage Inequalities: Children in American's Schools* (New York: Crown, 1991).
5. "Educators Complain Business Tax Breaks Are Costing Schools," *New York Times,* May 22, 1991, pp. A1, A23.
6. A college degree is an important hedge against wage losses. The wages of college graduates relative to high school graduates were higher in 1987 than at any other time since 1963. But as Lawrence Mishel and David M. Frankel observe, the average college graduate was still earning less in 1987 than in 1971. The increased wage gap between college and high school graduates reflects "a modest increase in the demand for college-educated workers, not an across-the-board, economy-wide trend toward higher skilled and higher wage jobs." See Mishel and

Frankel, *The State of Working America, 1990–91* (Armonk, N.Y.: Economic Policy Institute, M. E. Sharpe, 1991).
7. At the University of California, Berkeley, this was particularly sensitive where the admission of students of Asian origin were concerned. Grade-point averages and test scores would have placed Asian students at the top of the admissions list to such a degree at Berkeley that virtually no room would be left for other ethnic groups, including whites. Responding to this, university officials proposed to rely in part on extracurricular activities, admissions essays, and other unquantifiable characteristics for admissions. Ethnic and racial groups on all sides of this dispute were at each other's throats because access to Berkeley, as well as the rest of the University of California system, is becoming increasingly restricted. See Daniel Seligman, "College in California: The Numbers Game," *Fortune,* February 11, 1991, p. 146; and James S. Gibney, "The Berkeley Squeeze," *New Republic,* April 11, 1988, pp. 15–17.
8. For a look at the favored treatment of the post-war generation by the feds and the comparatively unfavorable plight of the boomers, see Laurence J. Kotlikoff, *Generational Accounting: Knowing Who Pays—and When—for What We Spend* (New York: Free Press, 1992).
9. Richard Lamm, "Again, Age Beats Youth," *New York Times,* Op-Ed, December 2, 1990, p. A32.
10. Lamm is quick to note that Medicare policies were hardly designed for millionaires and that they have been responsible for pulling poverty-stricken seniors out of harm's way far more often than they have been used to coddle the very wealthy. His point, also echoed by H. Ross Perot, is both that a far larger share of our resources go to the elderly than to any other demographic group and that we do not means test the benefits we provide.
11. Perhaps the baby-boom generation should be satisfied with the prospect that they too will one day be the beneficiaries of policies that enhance the lives of the elderly. There is reason to question whether the nation will be able to afford such largesse when this colossal generation is ready for retirement. Yet so little attention has been paid to the problems we are likely to see in the social security system (when a small number of workers—today's children—are paying into a system that will have to care for the enormous

boomer generation) that the conflicts that will undoubtedly emerge over unbearable tax burdens have barely registered in the public mind. See Kotlikoff, *Generational Accounting.*

12. Mark Featherman, "The 80's Party Is Over, . . . " *New York Times,* Op-Ed, September 24, 1990.

13. This particular complaint may have unpleasant racial dimensions as well. The increasing fertility rates of minorities, particularly Hispanics, in the United States may well mean that whites in the boomer generation will be more dependent on racial minorities to pay for their retirement needs than has ever been the case in the past. This is but one more reason for the country to attend to the racial tension growing in the cities and suburbs. For the social security system to work as it was designed, a degree of intergenerational and cross-racial commitment will be needed.

14. Bill Clinton is the only national politician who articulated a program akin to those of the post-war era. He has argued that a national "education bank" should be created that would allow young people to borrow money for college, to be repaid through public service jobs that would rebuild the nation's infrastructure.

DISCUSSION QUESTIONS

1. What, according to Newman, are the major causes of the withering of the American Dream? Do you agree or disagree with her assessment?

2. Not all of the middle class is experiencing "declining fortunes." How are they different from the sector of the middle class that Newman focuses on?

READING 23

Shadow Work

David Snow and Leon Anderson

In this excerpt from Down on Their Luck, *David Snow and Leon Anderson's study of the homeless in Austin, Texas, the reader is afforded a view of the everyday economic survival strategies of street people. Contrary to stereotypical depictions of the homeless as unwilling or unable to work, this reading reveals not only how many homeless actually do work, but that they engage in a wide variety of pursuits, both legal and illegal. To distinguish this work in its various guises from "regular work," Snow and Anderson refer to it collectively as "shadow work." The authors conclude by discussing the worldview of the homeless as it relates to their orientation toward work and their perceptions of their future prospects.*

It's 8:30 on Sunday morning. There are only a few cars on the streets, and even fewer pedestrians, except near the Sally, where some homeless have begun to congregate to await the bus that will take them to the Central Assembly of God Church on the outskirts of town. As we walk toward this pick-up point, we hear some rustling in a large garbage dumpster and then see a head pop up. It's Gypsy, already at work scavenging for salvageable items: food, clothing, tin cans, and other throw-aways he can use directly or sell on the streets or in pawn shops.

On another day, at noon on the Drag, we notice two long-haired hippie tramps panhandling passersby. "Hey, man, you got any spare change? Just a quarter?" they ask. It's Gimpy Dan and a sidekick trying to make ends meet. A bit further down the Drag, in front of the major campus bookstore, sits another homeless person playing a beat-up guitar and singing songs about Jesus. It's Banjo trying to coax passersby to toss some loose change into his guitar case. And just around the corner, by an open crafts area, we spot Rhyming Mike reciting his street poetry in exchange for a few nickels and dimes.

That evening, when we queue up for dinner at the Sally, we observe two rather infirm and weather-beaten men, both in their fifties or sixties, scouring an empty parking lot across the street for aluminum cans. One spots a Coke can, picks it up, and drops it into a plastic garbage bag held open by his partner. It is Indio and his friend JJ. The bag is bulging—they have had a productive day.

While we are still waiting in the dinner line we see two fellows in their mid-twenties leave the queue and scurry across the street to talk to Bill-Bob and his redneck friends. They make a quick exchange and then sprint back to the dinner line. Grinning, they say they got a good deal: "A couple of joints for two bucks each." Across the street Bill-Bob is smiling too, probably because he has just added a dollar or two to his cash supply.

Later, stretched out in the winter warehouse, we hear the barely audible voice of a homeless entrepreneur. Walking through the cavernous room after lights-out, he whispers, just loud enough to be heard over the coughing and muffled conversations, "Joints! Joints! Joints for sale!". . .

In each of the preceding vignettes, we see one or more homeless persons at work. It is not work as traditionally conceived, to be sure. But it is work, for in each case attention and energy are riveted on the procurement of money or other material goods for personal use or exchange. Unlike wage labor, though, in these activities there is little to no regularized exchange of labor for money. Nor are the activities officially sanctioned or their time and place bureaucratically controlled.[1] Instead, they are compensatory subsistence strategies that are fashioned or pursued in the shadow of more conventional work because of exclusion from existing labor markets, because participation in those markets fails to provide a living wage, because public assistance is insufficient, or because such strategies provide a more reliable means of survival. We call these compensatory, non-wage labor subsistence strategies "shadow work."[2] . . .

Four categories of such work were identified during the course of our field research: selling and trading, soliciting donations in public places, scavenging, and theft. We consider each variety in turn, noting, as well, the extent to which the different types of homeless engage in the various kinds of shadow work.

SELLING AND TRADING

As in the domiciled world, so among the homeless, too, the sale and exchange of goods and services are central forms of shadow work. We observed three basic variants of sales work among the homeless in Austin: selling and trading junk and personal possessions, selling illegal goods and services, and selling plasma.

Selling and Trading Junk and Personal Possessions

Sale of junk and personal possessions is not uncommon among most social classes.[3] Among the working and middle classes, these exchanges take the form of weekend garage sales, and among the upper classes they manifest themselves as estate sales.[4] Among the homeless, however, sale of junk and personal possessions takes on a distinctive cast. For one thing, the proceeds are much more fundamental to their subsistence than is typically the case for other strata. If and when the homeless peddle personal items, it is not because they have no use for them or want to clean house, so to speak, but because they need cash. Additionally, the homeless usually have few personal possessions. Their sales thus vary according to what they have recently purchased, scavenged, received as a gift, or stolen. Whatever their source, the sales items most often consist of clothing such as jackets, belts, and shoes, watches and rings, calculators and cassette tapes, and cigarettes and beer.

The asking price for such goods is low, undoubtedly because the other homeless, who make up the primary market, have little money to spend. There are exceptions, though. One afternoon we observed a twenty-eight-year-old male trying to hawk a new pair of jeans his mother had sent him. As he sat on the sidewalk, propped up against a building in the middle of the city's downtown night-life section, he would hold up the jeans as men walked by and yell out, "Man, they're brand new jeans and they're not hot!" They *were* new, too, with the labels still attached. He eventually sold them for $11.00 to a fellow who appeared to be a college student, an extraordinarily good price for a street sale. Sometimes an energetic peddler will attempt to sell his wares to the more affluent university market. For example, when Lance McCay was short of cash he would sell students his gifts from home or items he had purchased with his Social Security money, as when he sold his $400 briefcase for a mere $10 to a college student.

The sales price is usually considerably lower than even $10 or $11, though, not only because the homeless peddle primarily among each other, but also because the goods for sale are often cheap, recycled items in poor condition, items most people would regard as junk. One evening, for instance, we observed an elderly man going from group to group at the Salvation Army, trying to sell a rusty alarm clock he insisted would work even though no one could get it to run. On another occasion a young black man walked beside the Sally dinner line, hawking several old and well-worn *Playboy* magazines. "This is fine stuff," he told the men in line as he tantalizingly showed them the centerfold photos. "And only a buck apiece." He generated obvious interest, but it was Sunday evening, when few of the homeless have any loose change. Consequently, the *Playboy* hawker could find no buyers. . . .

Selling Illegal Goods and Services

An alternative form of selling pursued by some of the homeless is the sale of illegal goods and services, particularly drugs and sex. Not all the homeless are involved in this form of sales work, though. The recently dislocated, whose energies and hopes are still focused on wage labor, tend to shy away from such illicit activity,

as do the mentally ill, who have neither the interactional skills nor the persistence to be much good at it. And the majority of both traditional tramps and traditional bums seem either too old, too rickety, or too inebriated to get involved competitively in either drug trafficking or prostitution. That leaves the regular straddlers, hippie tramps, and redneck bums, all of whom are involved in varying degrees in this illicit form of shadow work, particularly in drug-dealing.

Drug Dealing   Although drug dealing can be readily observed among regular straddlers as well as hippie tramps and redneck bums, it is not as salient to the survival of the straddlers as it is for the other two types. For them, and particularly for the hippie tramps, drug dealing is more commonly a primary subsistence strategy. There are other differences between the groups. Regular straddlers deal drugs predominantly to other homeless individuals, and each deal usually involves only one to three joints of marijuana.[5] Sellers solicit customers in locations where the homeless gather in the downtown area. In the mornings there are usually several people at the Labor Corner and the Labor Pool selling joints at "two bucks apiece, three for five dollars." In the afternoons, individual sellers walk up and down the Sally dinner line soliciting buyers, and in the evenings it is common for sellers to walk along the rows of mats in the Sally's sleeping quarters, calling out in muffled tones, "Joints! Joints!" The number of sales regular straddlers make on a given day is highly dependent on the amount of money being funneled into the street economy from day labor and other forms of shadow work. When the street economy is good, sales are brisk. But when the weather turns bad, curtailing day labor, and on the weekends, when day labor is scarce and the plasma centers are closed, few people have the money for joints.

A few regular straddlers whom we observed selling drugs seemed to engage in this economic activity almost exclusively. One of them, a stocky young man in his mid-twenties who went by the name of Streeter, carried two cigarette cases filled with joints on his daily rounds of the major gathering spots for the homeless. One morning at the Labor Corner we saw him do a particularly good business, making a dozen transactions within half an hour. Except for occasional day labor or, during slow times, the sale of plasma, Streeter did not pursue any other work. A similar repertoire was followed by one of the few Native Americans we met on the streets. Known as "Medicine Man," he worked the same spots as Streeter and a few others, but he was somewhat more proprietary about the Sally dinner line. He could be seen working it vigorously evening after evening, and he did not take kindly to others infringing on "his turf," although there was little he could do about it except make threatening gestures. . . .

Prostitution   The second form of illicit sales work observed among the homeless is prostitution, both homosexual and heterosexual. That some of the homeless would engage in prostitution should be expected, considering their dire economic situation and the fact that prostitution has long been recognized as an activity often pursued by individuals with limited economic prospects.[6]

Our observations indicate that homosexual prostitution is the more prominent, in large part simply because there are more homeless men than women. It is pursued more often by the younger homeless men. How widespread it is among the homeless is unclear, however. Three of our key informants openly admitted to engaging in prostitution, but many more homeless talked about having been approached by men who offered to pay them for sex. Furthermore, when dinner-line conversation among the homeless turned to "rolling queers," it seemed that everyone within earshot chipped in with one or more experiences of having robbed a gay man during a prostitution encounter. One Sunday evening, for instance, a lanky weather-beaten man in his mid-thirties rambled on to an interested gathering about once having gone home with a gay man he had "drugged with three Quaaludes." "Then," he boasted, "I split with his Caddy, a stereo, and a new TV and sold them on the streets for twenty-five hundred bucks." Having the crowd's attention, he continued by recounting an episode with "this other dude who's an accountant here in town who used to give me fifty bucks to tie him up and fuck him. But once I got him tied up I'd just take the rest of his money and split." Another man, who appeared to be about five years younger despite having lost several front teeth, responded, "Let's go find that guy and offer to do a double on him." The younger man then proceeded with a story of his own:

> I went into this bar one time—it was a peter bar, but, hell, I didn't know it—and this guy offered me fifty bucks to go home with him. So we get there and he tells me he wants me to fuck him in the ass, and I told him "Man, I gotta be drunk to do that." So I kept mixing him doubles and me singles until he passed out. Then I swiped his car and took off down the freeway, only I was drunk on my ass and I kept bashing into the other cars, so I pulled off and went to sleep. Next morning I woke up, man, that car was beat to shit.

We suspect that such talk about preying on gay men is not only highly embellished but offers the homeless a relatively safe way to discuss an activity that is fairly common, while still allowing them distance from the stigma of homosexuality. In these stories they can admit contact with homosexuals and even, obliquely, some sexual activity. But by focusing on predation as the central theme of such encounters, they can avoid identification with gays.[7] . . .

Selling Plasma

In a world of limited and irregular opportunities to make a few dollars, an outcropping of economic regularity stands out like a beacon on a dark night. The blood banks or plasma centers are unique in offering the homeless a sure opportunity to pick up a few dollars. Perhaps this certainty helps explain the upbeat ambience of the blood bank compared to the anxious gloom that pervades the day-labor spots. As with most things the homeless do, there is a trade-off to selling plasma—in this case, sitting for an hour and a half with a needle in the arm—but it is a trade-off that many find worthwhile, especially when their pockets are empty. . . .

In *The Gift Relationship: From Human Blood to Social Policy,* Richard Titmuss pointed out the serious ethical implications of developing a system of paid plasma donors drawn to a large degree from the homeless population. "With the great expansion in plasmapheresis programs in recent years," he wrote in the 1970s, "the problem of the effects on the donor's health of frequent and repeated donations has emerged as an important public health issue."[8] He went on to quote a physician who argued that one of the most serious ethical problems of plasmapheresis as it is operated in the United States paid-donor system is "the exploiting for its proteins a population which is least able to donate them—the poorly nourished Skid Row population."[9]

This exploitative process has been even more evident in the 1980s and 1990s, as the ranks of the homeless have expanded to include far more than skid-row alcoholics.[10] One of the more pernicious effects of frequently selling plasma relates to the difficulty many of the homeless have in maintaining their body weight. The plasma centers have weight requirements, but many of the homeless try to circumvent them. Marilyn, who when we met her was no longer healthy enough to sell plasma, told us how she used to deal with the weigh-in at the plasma center: "I'd put rocks in my shoes and my pockets and then I'd go in and get on the scales. It worked for a while, but then one day some rocks fell out of my pocket, and after that they 86'ed me from the plasma center." Tom Fisk, who was 6'1" and weighed only 130 pounds but still donated plasma, told

us of similar problems he faced when living in his car in Killeen, Texas:

> I'd been selling blood all along and it wasn't no problem. Then, one day, I go in—and I'm really needing money bad—and they weigh me and say, "You're too underweight to donate." So I left and drank a lot of water and came back, and they weighed me again and said the same thing. By that time I was getting pretty pissed off, so I left and put some rocks in my pockets and came back. They said, "We're not letting you donate today." Well, I got kinda belligerent about it' cause there weren't no reason not to let me and I was desperate for money. And they called the police on me. . . .

SOLICITING DONATIONS IN PUBLIC PLACES

A somewhat different pattern emerges for the public solicitation of handouts through begging and panhandling.[11] Both strategies are used most frequently by outsiders, and particularly by traditional and hippie tramps and traditional bums, the groups with the longest spans of time on the streets. . . .

The reason for this disparity resides, we suspect, in the nature of begging and panhandling. Both involve fleeting attempts to persuade others to part with a sum of money, usually quite small, without providing anything tangible in return. As such, they are antithetical to the work ethic, which decrees that honorable subsistence involves the exchange of labor for pay or, at the very least, making do without handouts from others. As a consequence, begging and panhandling can engender considerable shame and embarrassment in individuals still imbued with the work ethic as conventionally understood, as are most recently dislocated and many regular straddlers. Tony Jones, who had been on the streets for only two to three weeks when we first met, told us, for example, "I got too much pride to beg. As long as I got my hands and feet, I'll be damned if I'll get on my knees and beg."

And Ron Whitaker, who has been homeless somewhat longer, said that when he first hit the streets he "found panhandling downright embarrassing." He learned to swallow his pride, however, when his pockets were empty and he had exhausted his other options. As he put it, "You can't let pride get in your way. I used to and still do sometimes, but there are times you have to ask people for a couple of quarters because you ain't got a dime."[12]

Apparently the sense of shame that some homeless attach to begging and panhandling is minimal or nonexistent for the outsiders. Most have been on the streets too long or have drifted too far from the world of regular work and its underlying values to permit them to circumscribe survival activities. Moreover, as Ron Whitaker began to realize, the exigencies of street life have a way of withering prior constraints and understandings. . . .

SCAVENGING

Scavenging, the third general form of shadow work, is a salvaging process that entails rummaging through discarded materials to find usable or salable items. Since its material base is the refuse of others, scavenging reflects the location of the homeless at the bottom of the social order. Many of the homeless, not surprisingly, hold scavenging in low regard, and they engage in it only as a last resort. We seldom observed scavenging among the recently dislocated, and only a few straddlers scavenged, and then only when other options were not available, such as on weekends when there was no prospect of day labor. One Sunday morning, for instance, Pat Manchester explained to us, "I couldn't sleep this morning, so I went out looking through dumpsters till I got enough cans to sell so I could buy a breakfast taco and some coffee." The traditional and hippie tramps and the redneck bums also scavenge only rarely, and it is clearly not a favored form of shadow work.

Traditional bums and the mentally ill, by contrast, tend to scavenge fairly regularly. It is the former's primary subsistence activity and the mentally ill's second most important means of survival, next to public assistance. Their patterns of scavenging are quite different, however. Traditional bums often work in a team, whereas the mentally ill engage in solitary scavenging that both reflects and reinforces their social isolation.

The most common items the homeless in Austin scavenge are aluminum beer and pop cans, which they then sell at the going rate. One forty-one-year-old traditional bum, known on the streets as Pushcart, makes almost daily rounds of the student-housing area that surrounds the university campus, pushing an expropriated grocery cart that he loads with aluminum cans he collects from dumpsters, parking lots, and the side of the road. When asked why he engaged in this activity, Pushcart replied, "I've been in the Marines, man, and I've taken too many orders too long. Scrapping for cans, there's nobody telling me what to do. I'm my own boss, and when I want to take a break or call it a day, I can. . . ."

THEFT

The final type of shadow work engaged in by some of the homeless is theft and related criminal activities such as burglary and fencing stolen goods.[13] Although theft is almost always performed surreptitiously, we did learn indirectly that it is fairly commonplace among some of the homeless. A few confessed to having stolen this or that, as when Tom Fisk told us about his theft of a motorcycle, for which he spent thirty-seven days in jail, or when Pushcart admitted to stealing the scavenged cans of other homeless, but only when they are drunk and passed out in public. "I'll say, 'Hey, wake up! I'm gonna take your cans!' If he doesn't wake up, it's 'Sayonara.' Hey, it's happened to me. What goes around, comes around."

Some of the homeless would talk openly with each other about what they had stolen, on occasion even flaunting the stolen item. One afternoon in front of one of the plasma centers, for instance, a homeless woman who was only about eighteen showed Nona a set of earrings she had stolen and then bragged about them until Nona refocused the discussion onto her own exploits at thievery. On other occasions, homeless people would show up inexplicably with new personal possessions, such as radios and tape recorders, or with goods they would try to sell at cut-rate prices. We met a twenty-year-old man, who frequently sold joints around the Sally, one evening several blocks west of the Sally fencing what we took to be stolen goods:

> We were walking toward the Sally when a street acquaintance called to us from across Congress Avenue. We crossed over and he showed us a suitcase full of freshly washed, almost new jeans and asked if we would buy a pair. He sold six pairs for five bucks each while we were hanging around. He told us he had met a guy on the street who sold him the suitcase for fifty cents. "At least I'm making honest money," he said. "And I'm not selling dope either." . . .

SUMMARY

In this reading we have examined an array of non-wage labor subsistence strategies the homeless fashion because they are excluded from existing labor markets, because participation in those markets fails to offer them a living wage, because institutionalized assistance proves inadequate, or because these unconventional strategies provide a more reliable means of survival on the streets. We have called these compensatory subsistence strategies shadow work because they are not traditionally counted as work and because they are pursued in the shadow of regular work—that is, on the sidewalks of urban America and in its back alleys and refuse receptacles. And, just as in the previous chapter we discerned variation in the pursuit of wage labor

and the receipt of public assistance among the different types of homeless, so we have found here variation in the extent to which the various types of homeless engage in the different kinds of shadow work.

These observations, with those in the previous chapter, raise a number of issues that warrant discussion in order to illuminate further the subsistence activities of the homeless. The first concerns the mix of strategies employed by each type of homeless. Although it is clear that the set of subsistence strategies available to the homeless is limited, it is equally clear that each type of homeless has its own peculiar mix of strategies, such that we may speak of type-specific or personalized repertoires of material subsistence. The existence of such repertoires suggests that some degree of selectivity is exercised with respect to the strategies pursued. Yet, the use of one strategy rather than another is not merely a matter of choice. No single strategy can ensure subsistence on the streets, and no matter how strongly one subsistence activity is preferred over another, there is no guarantee from one day to the next that it will still be a viable option. Day labor is not sufficiently abundant to ensure paid work day after day, and it is virtually nonexistent on weekends. Plasma centers, too, are closed on the weekends. And Sundays are particularly bad days for begging and panhandling, because few non-homeless pedestrians are on the streets.

Survival, then, is contingent on the opportunistic fashioning and utilization of a mix of strategies. The recently dislocated and straddlers may frown on scavenging, but, as Pat Manchester discovered when he turned to dumpster-diving in search of funds for breakfast one Sunday, necessity may leave them with little choice but to engage in some subsistence activity they hold in low regard.

These constraints and uncertainties notwithstanding, what is perhaps most noteworthy is that the different types of homeless do have preferred strategies and that they pursue those more regularly than the other strategies. Such selectivity suggests both that the homeless attempt to exercise some autonomy in their lives and that material survival on the streets is more than a random or chaotic affair. Like most spheres of life, it is patterned and ordered, not solely by the network of street institutions that structure the routines and options of the homeless, but also by the preferences and idiosyncrasies of the different types of homeless themselves.

A second and related issue is why outsiders do not pursue wage labor as persistently as the recently dislocated and even the regular straddlers. The traditional tramps are somewhat of an exception to this tendency, but even their mean score for wage labor is lower than that for both the recently dislocated and the straddlers. Thus, the general tendency is that the longer the homeless are on the streets and the more they drift into the world of the outsider, the less salient wage labor becomes as a mode of subsistence for them and the more prominent become one or more forms of shadow work. What accounts for this apparent inverse relationship between time on the streets and pursuit of wage labor? Or, stated differently, why does shadow work figure more prominently in the survival of outsiders?

Two contrasting answers are possible. One, rooted in conventional wisdom, holds simply that the greater salience of shadow work among outsiders is due to a decline in work orientation, which makes them lazy and disinterested in work as traditionally conceptualized. This explanation strikes us as wrongheaded. It resonates neither with the subculture of the homeless as we came to know it nor with the nature of shadow work. As was emphasized earlier, shadow work, like all work, requires the concentration of energy and attention on the procurement of money or other material goods for personal use or exchange. It differs from other work only in that it is neither formally regulated nor sanctioned in terms of time, place, or wage. But to scavenge involves no less toil and

sweat than most kinds of manual labor, and to panhandle effectively requires a certain interactional mettle and the employment of interpersonal skills and lines that are part and parcel of many kinds of sales work. Similar comparisons could be made for the other forms of shadow work.

Such observations suggest an alternative explanation: it is not a decline in work orientation per se that accounts for the greater prominence of shadow work among outsiders, but a change in orientation from the world of regular work to the world of shadow work. Most outsiders retain the incentive to work—they have no choice if they are to survive—but it is directed toward a different order of work. Moreover, it is a shift in orientation that is quite reasonable in light of the demoralizing nature of the wage labor available to the homeless. Its irregularity and low pay prevent wage labor from serving either as a reliable basis for surviving on the streets or a means off the streets. As a consequence, experience with the world of wage labor frequently leads to alienation from it, especially as familiarity is developed with the various forms of shadow work. Thus when Pat Manchester finds a dollar one morning on the way to the Labor Corner and says, "Fuck it, I'll get a cup of coffee and go donate blood," it is not so much a decline in work orientation that prompts him to forego his job-hunting as it is the realization that the attempt is unlikely to succeed and that, with a little luck, he is likely to fare better pursuing shadow work. In either case, time and energy are expended and attention is focused on making do. Unlike the middle-class working person, though, the outsider and slipping straddler, as in Pat's case, cast their bets on the world of shadow work, not because they are disinterested in regular work, but because they have lost faith in its capacity to sustain them.

It might be argued, of course, that if the homeless would only look beyond the moment to the future, if they were not so "impulse-" or "present-oriented," they would come to see the fruits of playing the wage-labor game.[14] But the issue is not so much one of orientation to time or whether the homeless are less future-oriented than those of higher status. Rather, the issue is one of articulation between the present and the future. Elliot Liebow understood this well when he wrote that the difference between black street-corner men of the 1960s and their middle-class counterparts "lies not so much in their different orientations to time as their different orientations to future time or, more specifically, to their different futures."[15] Most people of higher status see a positive articulation between their immediate present and their future. They have a strong sense that what they do today will yield a tomorrow that is just as good as or better than today. The psychiatrist Robert Coles has called this a sense of entitlement and has observed that its salience increases with movement up the status system.[16]

Clearly, such a sense is not pervasive among the homeless. Most of them have little confidence that their actions today will yield a better tomorrow for them. As we have seen, the wage labor that awaits them, if they are lucky enough to secure any, typically involves jobs that lead only to the repetition of their current plight. With this negative articulation between their immediate present and their anticipated future, it is little wonder that many drift from the world of regular work to the world of shadow work. It is not so much because they are present-oriented—although they have good reason to be so, given that their daily survival commands all the resources they can muster. Rather, it is because the tomorrows they can realistically imagine are not ones that inspire either the investment of whatever limited resources they may have scrimped to save or the adoption of lines of action that go beyond the world of shadow work. For many of the homeless, then, the repeated failure of the world of wage labor to yield a fair return on the time and energy invested pushes them into the world of shadow work. Initially, shadow work is seen primarily

as a stop-gap measure, as a kind of supplemental, temporary work. In time, however, as experience and familiarity with it increase, it can become a way of life.

NOTES

1. Although textual discussions of work do not always specify the criteria used to distinguish it from nonwork, three criteria can be culled from most such discussions: remuneration, regulation, and enumeration. Thus, work as conventionally conceived is an activity for which an individual is paid; time, place, and rate of pay are regulated; and it can be enumerated or counted by local, state, and federal governments. These criteria result in a rather "limited set of activities and roles that are deemed legitimate ways of making a living" (Miller, 1981: 133). This narrow focus has begun to expand in recent years, however, with the growing recognition, due in part to the feminist movement, that nonoccupational tasks such as housework and volunteer activities also constitute work, as do various illegal enterprises, such as prostitution, fencing, numbers-running, and drug-dealing, which are typically described as "deviant work." Still, the focus of most textual discussions of work is on jobs, occupations, and professions (Hodson and Sullivan, 1990; Miller, 1981; and Ritzer and Walczak, 1986).

   Moreover, since so much of what we know about conventional work is based on government statistics, it is understandable that some students of work and labor processes emphasize state regulation as the key factor in their conceptualization (Lozano, 1983; Portes and Walton, 1981).

2. The concept of shadow work is borrowed from the philosopher, historian, and social critic Ivan Illich (1981). Illich uses the term for unpaid work that is a necessary requisite for and complement to productive and consumptive activity, such as housework, grocery-shopping, and commuting. We use the term somewhat differently, to refer to unpaid subsistence activities. We do so for several reasons. For one thing, it resonates with the obdurate fact that the subsistence strategies engaged in by the homeless take place in the shadow of regular work. Additionally, it is consistent with the adaptive and behavioral thrust of our conceptual-

ization of the subculture of street life. And, finally, we find *shadow work* preferable to a number of kindred terms. Some labor economists and students of informal sector activity in the Third World have used the term *nonmarket work* to encompass "all work not performed for wages, profits, or rents, including housework and even commuting work" (Uzzell, 1980: 42). But not all shadow work is nonmarket work. As we shall see shortly, some types of shadow work exist only within a market context, but the market is neither officially regulated nor sanctioned. Instead, it is an ephemeral one that exists outside the dominant economic system and thus constitutes part of the "shadow economy" (for a brief discussion of the shadow economy, see Hodson and Sullivan, 1990: 332-36). Another cognate cover term is *hustling work* (Miller, 1981). This term is too broad for our purposes. It encompasses not only what we have called shadow work but other kinds of work that are typically sanctioned and linked to fairly well-defined markets. Even more troublesome, hustling is not peculiar to shadow work but can be relevant to almost any kind of work. Like the panhandler or scavenger, the professional athlete, hot dog vendor, secretary, and floor trader can all hustle. For all these reasons, then, we find the term *shadow work* the most conceptually suitable and resonant cover term for the array of unpaid subsistence strategies engaged in by the homeless.

3. It is important to keep in mind that the distinction between junk and reasonably attractive personal possessions is largely subjective. As symbolic interactionists have reminded us, the meaning of an object resides in its use or function in a given situation (Blumer, 1969). Thus, what is defined as junk and as nonjunk is likely to vary not only from person to person but also from one situation to the next. To the homeless, what is seen as a worthy personal possession one day may be redefined as a salable item or a piece of junk the next day.

4. For an interesting and relevant discussion of garage sales, see Herrmann and Soiffer (1984). They note that although the motives underlying garage sales can be quite varied, often they function as an adaptive survival strategy when times are difficult economically. For a recent analysis of estate sales and auctions, see Smith (1989).

5. We neither observed nor learned of more expensive drugs being sold by regular straddlers to homeless individuals. Some of the homeless might be interested in obtaining such drugs, but most lack the money to buy them. It is also important to note that our research was conducted in 1984 to 1986, before "crack," a relatively new and cheap form of cocaine, was available, at least on the streets of Austin.

6. Writing of sex and prostitution in the nineteenth century, Tannahill observes that "the girls who became prostitutes in [this] century usually did so because they needed the money. At one end of the scale there was the independent-minded career woman who knew that, without any capital other than herself, only prostitution and the stage offered the prospect of making a good living; at the other, the young widow or unmarried mother able to earn little but almost certain to be separated from her child if she applied for the parish relief that would save them both from starvation" (1980: 357-58). Although the character of prostitution may have changed somewhat since the Victorian era, the economic impetus still remains prominent, as Miller's (1986) study of the survival strategies of underclass women in Milwaukee makes clear. Financial considerations also figure heavily in the process of entering male prostitution, but other contextual factors are operative, too, as research on male prostitution demonstrates (Calhoun, 1988; Luckenbill, 1985).

7. Such distancing techniques are not peculiar to the homeless but have also been observed among domiciled male prostitutes (Calhoun, 1988; Reiss, 1961).

8. Titmuss (1971: 115).

9. Titmuss (1971: 124).

10. The plasmapheresis program, as it has operated over the years, is objectionable not only because of its exploitative character but also because it can function as a conduit for the transmission of communicable diseases. This negative, albeit unintended, function has become the focus of increasing public concern as the AIDS epidemic has spread.

11. This distinction is not commonplace in the literature, where *begging* and *panhandling* tend to be used interchangeably. However, we find it useful

to distinguish between the two because our observations in Austin and Tucson indicate that solicitation of money in public places can be arrayed on a continuum, from quite passive gestures or postures intended to elicit sympathy to more aggressive, harassing overtures. For empirically grounded discussions of begging in different contexts, see Wiseman (1970: 30-32) on begging among skid-row alcoholics in a U.S. city in the 1960s, Archard (1979: 39-44) on begging among the same sort of folk in Great Britain, and Gmelch and Gmelch (1978) on begging among Irish tinkers. The latters' analysis comes closest to hinting at the distinction between begging and panhandling. For a more popular discussion of begging that is particularly apropos of today's homeless, see *Time*'s cover story titled "Begging in America: To Give or Not to Give?" (September 5, 1988). Note that much of the activity described as begging in the above works is actually characterized by the aggressive accosting we associate with panhandling.

12. In a recent study of panhandling in Tucson, consisting of field observations and interviews with eighty panhandlers, embarrassment was found to be a powerful impediment. As the study reported, "[T]he most consistent finding regarding how panhandlers felt about panhandling is that it doesn't come easily, and that it is not an enjoyable activity . . . it was repeatedly stated that panhandling is 'embarrassing' and that it takes 'courage and nerve' " (Costello et al., 1990: 31). In her ethnography of skid-row alcoholics, Wiseman also found that shame and embarrassment impeded panhandling. As one of her informants explained, "I can't do it, I just can't. It makes me feel so low. I'd rather do without or even steal. At least, if you steal, you have your self-respect" (1970: 30).

13. As defined by the Federal Bureau of Investigation, theft involves "the unlawful taking, carrying, leading or riding away of property from the possession or constructive possession of another. Examples are thefts of bicycles or automobile accessories, shoplifting, pocket-picking, or the stealing of any property or article that is not taken by force and violence or by fraud." Burglary, in contrast, involves "the unlawful entry of a structure to commit a felony or a theft." (See any re-

cent edition of the *FBI's Uniform Crime Reports in the United States,* Washington, D.C.: U.S. Government Printing Office.)

14. This line of reasoning has been prominently featured in an array of attempts to account for the persistence of poverty. It is a central component of Lewis's "culture of poverty" thesis (1966), which posits a strong present orientation, or the inability to defer immediate gratification and plan for the future, as both a cause and an effect of poverty. It is at the core of Banfield's effort of some twenty years ago to explain the plight of the inner city and its inhabitants in his controversial *The Unheavenly City* (1968). And it is evident in various recent neoconservative tracts that attribute poverty and inner-city "pathologies" to the confluence of aspects of Lewis's culture-of-poverty argument and various dysfunctional "liberal" social policies, as exemplified by Gilder's *Wealth and Poverty* (1981) and Murray's *Losing Ground: American Social Policy, 1950-1980* (1984). Although such works have received a wide hearing, particularly in recent years, they are not without their critics. Thus, see Valentine (1968) and Waxman (1983) for constructive critiques of Lewis's work, and Wilson (1987), Ellwood (1988), and Katz (1989) for reasoned and well-documented counterpoints to the arguments of Banfield, Gilder, and Murray, among others.

15. Liebow (1967: 64-65). This was also a central finding of Stinchcombe's (1964) study of rebellious youth in a California high school. Adolescents who expected to become manual workers in the next labor cohort and who therefore saw no clear relation between what they were doing in school and their future occupational prospects were the ones most inclined toward rebellious behavior. Stinchcombe thus concluded that "the future, not the past, explains adolescent rebellion" (1964: 6).

16. Coles (1977).

REFERENCES

Archard, Peter. 1979. *Vagrancy, Alcoholism and Social Control.* London: Macmillan.

Banfield, Edward C. 1968. *The Unheavenly City.* Boston: Little, Brown.

Blumer, Herbert. 1969. *Symbolic Interactionism: Perspective and Method.* Englewood Cliffs, N.J.: Prentice Hall.

Calhoun, Thomas C. 1988. "Theoretical Considerations on the Entrance and Stabilization of Male Street Prostitutes." Ph.D. dissertation, University of Kentucky.

Coles, Robert. 1977. "The Children of Affluence." *Atlantic Monthly,* September.

Costello, Barbara, Joseph Heirling, Frank Hunsaker, and Terry McCulloch. 1990. "Panhandling in Tucson." Paper, Department of Sociology, University of Arizona.

Ellwood, David T. 1988. *Poor Support: Poverty in the American Family.* New York: Basic Books.

Gilder, George. 1981. *Wealth and Poverty.* New York: Basic Books.

Gmelch, George, and Sharon Bohn Gmelch. 1978. "Begging in Dublin." *Urban Life* 6: 439–454.

Herrmann, Gretchen M., and Stephen M. Soiffer. 1984. "For Fun and Profit: An Analysis of the American Garage Sale." *Urban Life* 12: 397–421.

Hodson, Randy, and Teresa A. Sullivan. 1990. *The Social Organization of Work.* Belmont, Calif.: Wadsworth.

Illich, Ivan. 1981. *Shadow Work.* Boston: Marian Boyars.

Katz, Michael B. 1989. *The Undeserving Poor: From the War on Poverty to the War on Welfare.* New York: Pantheon.

Lewis, Oscar. 1966. "The Culture of Poverty." *Scientific American* 215: 19–25.

Liebow, Elliot. 1967. *Tally's Corner: A Study of Negro Streetcorner Men.* Boston: Little, Brown.

Lozano, Beverly. 1983. "Informal Sector Workers: Walking Out the System's Front Door?" *International Journal of Urban and Regional Research* 7: 340–361.

Luckenbill, David F. 1985. "Entering Male Prostitution." *Urban Life* 14: 131–153.

Miller, Eleanor M. 1986. *Street Women.* Philadelphia: Temple University Press.

Miller, Gale. 1981. *It's a Living: Work in Modern Society.* New York: St. Martin's Press.

Murray, Charles. 1984. *Losing Ground: American Social Policy, 1950–1980.* New York: Basic Books.

Portes, Alejandro, and John Walton. 1981. *Labor, Class and the International System.* New York: Academic Press.

Reiss, Albert J. Jr. 1961. "The Social Integration of Queers and Peers." *Social Problems* 9: 102–119.

Ritzer, George, and David Walczak. 1986. *Working: Conflict and Change.* Englewood Cliffs, N.J.: Prentice Hall.

Smith, Charles W. 1989. *Auctions: The Social Construction of Value.* New York: Free Press.

Stinchcombe, Arthur L. 1964. *Rebellion in a High School.* Chicago: Quadrangle Books.

Tannahill, Reay. 1980. *Sex in History.* New York: Stein and Day.

Time. 1988. "Begging in America: To Give or Not to Give." September 5: 68–74.

Titmuss, Richard M. 1971. *The Gift Relationship: From Human Blood to Social Policy.* New York: Vintage.

Uzzell, J. Douglas. 1980. "Mixed Strategies and the Informal Sector: Three Facts of Reserved Labor." *Human Organization* 39: 40–49.

Valentine, Charles. 1968. *Culture and Poverty: Critique and Counterproposal.* Chicago: University of Chicago Press.

Waxman, Chaim I. 1983. *The Stigma of Poverty: A Critique of Poverty Theories and Policies.* New York: Pergamon.

Wilson, William Julius. 1987. *The Truly Disadvantaged: The Inner City, the Underclass, and Public Policy.* Chicago: University of Chicago Press.

Wiseman, Jacqueline. 1970. *Stations of the Lost: The Treatment of Skid Row Alcoholics.* Chicago: University of Chicago Press.

DISCUSSION QUESTIONS

1. Define shadow work in your own words. How is it similar and how different from regular work? On the basis of these similarities and differences, what do you see as the greatest obstacles the homeless face in moving from shadow work to regular work?

2. The homeless in Snow and Anderson's study constitute a distinct subculture. How do their values and worldview differ from that of the mainstream culture?

GENDER AND SEXUAL IDENTITY

A popular book tells us that *Men Are from Mars, Women Are from Venus*. The title is a reflection of the commonly held belief that men and women think, feel, and act very differently and, as a result, men have trouble understanding women, and vice versa. Certainly, there are significant biological differences between men and women. For example, only women are capable of giving birth to children. But is biology destiny? In what ways is biology relevant and in what ways irrelevant? For example, related to the fact that only women give birth is the widely held assumption that women are more nurturing and caring than men are. Is this true? Consider whether biology can account for the following. Throughout history men and women have tended to do different kinds of work. Furthermore, positions of power and privilege in all realms of social life have overwhelmingly been the domain of men. The appropriate realm for women was seen as the private or domestic arena, whereas men were suited to the tasks associated with public life. At another level, it has frequently been taken for granted that the sexual drives of men and women are fundamentally different.

All of these issues have been investigated by sociologists interested in the topic of gender studies. The dramatic expansion of feminist scholarship beginning in the 1960s has infused and informed this area of sociology in profound ways. Underpinning sociological inquiry is a calling into question the belief that the chief differences between men and women are rooted in biology.

As a starting point, sociologists analytically differentiate the terms "sex" and "gender." Sex refers to the biological (physiological and anatomical) differences between males and females. Gender, by contrast, is a social construct. It refers to the socially learned expectations about behaviors and attitudes defined as consonant with particular images of masculinity and femininity. By making this analytical distinction between sex and gender and by highlighting the socially constructed character of the latter, sociologists point to the possibility that gender need not be posed in simple bimodal terms, but instead ought to be seen on a continuum that does not necessarily neatly coincide with sex differences. Related to these issues is the matter of sexual preference. How should we construe same-sex and opposite-sex orientations? Are these differences hard wired into our brains, the result of distinctive socialization experiences, or are they the result of choices people make?

Sociologists offer angles of vision permitting closer examinations of the social factors that have contributed to gender differences related to such issues as socialization, identities, roles, and inequalities in terms of wealth, income, status, and power. Among the wide-ranging kinds of questions the sociology of gender asks are the following:

- In what ways are boys and girls in the United States socialized differently?
- What are the key features of femininity and masculinity in our culture?
- What is women's work? Why are jobs primarily held by women paid less than jobs primarily held by men? What is the future of economic inequality based on gender?
- In what ways do existing customs, norms, laws, and social policies reinforce gender inequities? What is the future of inequities in social status that are based on gender?
- How are sexual identities constructed? How fixed or fluid are such identities?

These and a variety of related questions fall under the purview of the sociology of gender. Aspects of these questions are addressed in the following three selections.

Invisible Work

Arlene Kaplan Daniels

Arlene Kaplan Daniels contends that various forms of work are often not viewed as work, and she urges a reconsideration. Work done in the private realm, be it childrearing or a variety of tasks involved in maintaining a household, constitutes one important component of what she refers to as "invisible work." Another arena of invisible work is volunteer work conducted in various community service projects. Daniels adds to this the emotional work that, be it in the private or public arenas, constitutes a distinctive and important form of work. What links these three types of work is that the people who perform them are not monetarily compensated. Daniels points to the gendered character of invisible work.

The notion of work as something set apart from the rest of life is a peculiarly modern and Western idea. Cross-cultural studies show us that other peoples are not inclined to make such distinctions. Production, religious practice, and family life are integrated. In our society work is a folk concept (Turner, 1957); we all have a commonsense notion of what work is. It is something that, whatever its status, is hard (it can be arduous, boring, taxing, challenging, stressful), yet we have to do it. Sometimes work is skilled, requiring training and experience. Other work can be monotonous or backbreaking. We usually associate the former with high-status occupations and the latter with low-status jobs. We distinguish work from leisure activity (that we *want* to do because we enjoy it) and from other activities in the private realm of life—personal grooming, child care, homemaking. In modern, industrialized society perhaps the most common understanding of the essential characteristic of work is that it is something for which we get paid. This idea is associated with activity in the public world, which is dominated by men and separated from those private worlds

of family and personal relationships where women predominate. There may be exchanges in households and friendships, but they are not monetary. Even activity in the public sphere, such as volunteering and community service, is not work if it isn't paid. However, any activity we do for pay, wherever it is found, even if we enjoy it, must, by definition, be work. But any effort we make, even if it is arduous, skilled, and recognized as useful—perhaps essential—is still not recognized as work if it is not paid.

I will show how our concept of work is affected by our understanding of three elements in the folk conception: (1) the differences between public and private activity; (2) the importance of financial recompense; and (3) the effects of gender on judgments about the legitimacy of calling an activity work—or if it is recognized as work, giving it a high value. In considering the restrictiveness of these commonsense understandings, I focus on the work that disappears from our observations and reckonings when we limit ourselves to the conception of work that develops from the relationship of these three ideas.

THE DEVALUATION OF UNPAID WORK

It is admittedly difficult to shake free of our folk concept of work. Commonsense understandings about the place of work in social life are reflected and reinforced in our sociological researches. Our studies of stratification, for example, depend on occupation as a key variable in assessing socio-economic status of an individual and his (increasingly, also her) family as well (see Acker, 1972). But the significance of work lies deeper than its importance as an indicator of status. Work provides a clue to a person's worth in society—how others judge and regard him or her. To work—and earn money—is also to gain status as an adult. Thus, working is an important way to develop both a sense of identity and a sense of self esteem. In this process one not only comes to see oneself as an adult and a person of some worth; one comes to appreciate the larger normative order in which we participate. We earn our bread and work to keep society functioning at the same time. The value we place on this reproductive process shows how we participate in the moral order. Study of the division of labor, as social scientists from Emile Durkheim to Everett Hughes have pointed out, is important for what it tells us about the moral order. Any recognition of an activity as work gives it a moral force and dignity—something of importance in a society. In a cash nexus economy like ours, this importance is recognized by payment for doing something. Work in what Illich (1981) calls the "shadow economy" can be included here, for payment can include trading services and goods where money is not—or not officially—exchanged. Payment signals the belief that somehow society needs that something done.

What about all that work outside the economy? The idealized separation of work from the home—the expected distinction between the public world where men went out to work and the private world where women remained at home to raise the family and prepare a place of respite for the working man—sharpened the distinction between productive workers (men doing "real" work for wages) and non-productive workers (women supporting, raising, and rehabilitating those real workers). Of course, lip service is paid to the importance of this work outside the market economy; but it is clear that the work in the private sphere is regarded as less important. It does not figure in the Gross National Product and in the records of divorce settlements. These records indicate that women are sometimes left virtually penniless while husbands keep much of their resources for themselves. Women who have always worked in the home and know no other livelihood become what has come to be called displaced homemakers. The problems of displaced homemakers show the generally low worth placed on the work of women in the home.

One consequence of the lesser esteem given to work in the private realm is that women themselves devalue work in the private world. An early feminist social scientist, Charlotte Perkins Gilman ([1898] 1966), argued that this work should be rationalized and minimized by bringing more of it into the public sphere, e.g., community laundries, eating and child care facilities. She thought stripped-down private houses—composed of little more personal space than bedrooms that individuals would tidy themselves—would solve the problem of completing the work that would otherwise be done in private life. Implicit in her argument is that the work is not significant—it is only mindless drudgery that women should not be asked to undertake individually. Instead the work could be tackled as a societal problem. Then women, like men, could do the important work of society that is economically productive. This support of the commonsense or folk concept of what is important work forces a devaluation of everything that does not fit the definition. Further, since work is associated with adulthood, an implication of the folk concept is that those who do not work are not fully adults.

Today, of course, women who agree that work in the private sphere is not worth their effort have other alternatives. For example, they can hire other (lower-status and lower-paid) women to replace them in the home if they have sufficient means. Other modern, industrialized societies have gone further than our own in providing alternatives to child care at home, though none have made systematic efforts to create communal eating arrangements, with the exception of the Kibbutz experiments—and these experiments have not been widely adopted, even in Israel. Whatever the arrangements, the normative expectation in every industrialized society is that women will coordinate public and purchased services with the private requirements of their families. Even in households where women earn high wages, sometimes higher than their husbands, it is part of a woman's unpaid and uncounted work to tailor these arrangements to fit her circumstances

(Hertz, 1986). This tailoring is thus part of the invisible work in social life. It shows us how gender expectations, and separation between the public and private worlds are mixed together with paid work to create a special type of problem for which women are expected to take responsibility.

The lack of social validation implicit in disregard of all the tailoring required tells women this effort doesn't count as work; and they themselves often discount the effort it requires. Another area where the folk idea of work is too restrictive is in the distinction between paid and unpaid labor commonly associated with work—even in the public world. The work of community service volunteers is useful, but that it is not paid tells others—and the volunteers themselves—that it is not needed, not really important work despite all the lip service about the value of altruistic endeavor. Calling something altruistic is a way of saying it is not work. Since it is not remunerated, and though it may be recognized as a personal benefit—as well as one for society—it is not work. This view does not deny that women's efforts receive ceremonial attention: mothers have mother's days, and volunteers receive awards and other commemorations for faithful service. But these attentions are perfunctory. They are not part of the institutionalized aspects of life represented by salaried jobs and by occupational careers with their expectations of titles and promotions, security and fringe benefits—and by the larger normative framework within which these expectations are embedded. The framework includes the assumption that working activity is important, significant enough for someone to pay for it. A related assumption is that people who receive that pay are important. The pay is both an indicator that they are independent and autonomous, and a resource for making them so. For example, married women find, when they take paying jobs, that individuals making their own money are more independent and have more "say" in families than those who do not make financial con-

tributions (Ferree, 1976). The position of the housewife before she takes a paid position reveals a problem in the definition of work. Many kinds of effort and skill are not recognized in the folk concept. This omission creates an ambiguous position for those in the grey area of working without pay. These people are mostly women—volunteers and housewives—whose efforts are, consequently, not seen as entirely serious, not the significant work of the world.

RECOGNITION OF INVISIBLE WORK AND RESISTANCE TO ITS VALIDATION

The women's movement has called attention to the issue of just what is work by insisting on the importance of all the activities where women predominate. Feminists have argued that, when the housekeeping and childcare activities of women have been ignored or glossed over with vague allusions to "women's work," the real work involved is not appreciated. This neglect arises even though these activities are the most easily observable parts of what I have termed invisible work. One way to draw attention to that work is to show how it is constructed, what effort it involves, and what it would cost if it were purchased in the market. Some of these costs are born by women themselves who go out to work and pay for their replacements out of salary or who work double time—on the job and in the home—to make up the difference. Other costs, like providing long-term care for the sick and elderly, are hard to assign when no women remain at home to provide that care. For example, Nona Glaser (1988) points out that early hospital release for patients depends on whether someone will be at home to care for them. And, as Elizabeth Elliott (1986) notes, home-care programs assume that costs of care can be lowered by replacing hospital-based personnel with someone who will learn how to deliver care to a chronically-ill patient in the family for free. Still other costs involve the replacement of women's volunteer services to the community. Efforts to show the value of this work often involve estimating its dollar value or, if no social arrangements seem feasible for replacing volunteers with paid workers, speculating on how local communities would manage without it and asking what is lost when women no longer volunteer their full-time services.

Efforts to understand the nature of women's work through the analysis of tasks have a long history, stemming from the days of Victorian social reformers who undertook time and motion studies of the work women do in the home. These studies show both the arduousness of the work—especially for the lower classes—and also the pressures under which it is accomplished. The difficulties of work in the home before the advances of modern technology are well documented in such works as Stasser's *Never Done* (1982). But the pressures of the work continue irrespective of technology. For the middle class they involve the boredom and resentment created by mindless routine and the consequent narrowing of vision, ambition, and sense of competence so well-depicted in French's novel *The Women's Room* (1977). For the working class they involve the pressure of making ends meet—often with spouses who are inadequate or sporadic earners and sometimes irresponsible or abusive as well. The studies by Luxton (1980), McKreindle and Rowbotham (1977), and Rubin (1976) highlight the difficulties and disappointments that working-class wives face as they try to manage family responsibilities under these conditions. These women work with inadequate supplies and resources to do the job according to their own performance expectations for such tasks as maintaining cleanliness or providing proper, nourishing meals. For both middle- and working-class wives, the pressures of household work often include isolation. The private work in the home is set off from the public affairs of the world, leaving many women with a sense of alienation and distance that can be oppressive—contributing to what Betty Friedan (1963) called the sickness

without a name. The pressure of isolation is mitigated when women go out to work, but at its own costs. Studies (e.g., Berk, 1985) show that men do very little housework or child care at home and add very little further time when their wives go out to work. When men do work at home, it tends to be the more desirable jobs—reading to the children before bedtime; cleaning up the kitchen at a leisurely pace after the dinner hour. Women, on the other hand, usually undertake the high-pressure tasks with deadlines attached to them—getting children ready for school in the morning; rushing after work to pick up children at day care and then home to prepare dinner.

These problems are exacerbated by the lack of attention to and serious respect for the work in the private sphere. Studies of family life (e.g., Luxton, 1980) show that husbands do not rate the work of their wives as highly as their own. They see the valuable work as that of the breadwinner who can dole out the family allowance to his wife in the manner he chooses. The grim consequences for wives with improvident or unscrupulous husbands are well-known. As the woman's movement has long argued, "most women [with young children to care for] are only one man away from welfare" (Steinem, 1983:8). The problems of displaced homemakers after divorce are also well-known. As Weitzman (1986) points out, divorce settlements are often inequitable and unpredictable. Consequently, women can depend upon neither a fair nor a standardized recompense for years of homemaking. Even in states where community property laws insure a 50–50 split of assets at the time of divorce, men have socially-legitimated human capital—good jobs, training, and experience to further their earning power. These resources are not generally figured into the settlement. Even after equal division, women are not so likely to have these resources, particularly if they have been out of the labor market while raising their children. The recompense of homemaking is correspondingly chancy.

In short, a real pressure underlying the work of the homemaker is lack of validation. The work is private; there is no audience beyond the family and the work is personalized for the family members who rate it as they please. Under these circumstances it is not hard to see why women, family members themselves, do not understand some aspects of their activity as work. DeVault (1987) has pointed out that considerable effort and attention goes into a woman's provisioning the household and preparing meals. The work is "customized," as it were, to pick from the bewildering array of mass-produced products those that suit the budget of the household and the tastes of individual family members. Furthermore, it requires continual checking and policing to note what stocks are running low. Even when tasks can be delegated to others, it is usually the wife and mother who notices what needs to be done and when. The others do not take this responsibility and so do not "see" the task until they are directed. Planning, restocking, improvising, and adapting to family quirks and demands require effort that the housewives themselves do not recognize as work; they say they cannot understand why they become so tired or use so much time in making the effort. The difficulty of recognizing it as work is compounded not only by the realization that no one else will see it as work, but also by a woman's own sense that much of it ought to be offered spontaneously—a gift or expression of love for her family. Yet, the expectation that she ought to provide these services provokes guilt if she slacks off on the extra touches or anxiety if she feels she is not doing enough. The stereotypic picture of the woman idly shopping, of shopping as a leisure-time activity of women, also obscures the work of the woman as consumer (Glaser, 1987). These ideas contradict the folk concept of work as something you *have* to do to receive payment. While, as noted earlier, some of the work women do *can* be translated into paid work equivalents, much of it cannot—the tailoring, planning, and specialized catering,

for instance. Validation of an individual as a worker through this kind of activity is, then, very difficult.

The importance of public validation can be seen from studies of women who do venture from the home. Esther Benjamin (1979) found, in her research on reentry women at Northwestern University, that good grades meant a great deal to them. The grades were universalistic criteria for performance. Women competed for them and won them in an academic marketplace. The grades were a public standard for excellence that these women felt proud to meet. They recognized them as indicators of potential for salaried careers as well. They spoke of a rise in their self-esteem accordingly, a sense of self-esteem that success in raising a family, even maintaining an elaborate home establishment and attaining success in the public world of volunteering, did not create. The grades, as well as the common expectation that they might lead to good jobs, were generally understood and appreciated by a much wider circle of people than the family and volunteer circles where these women had already made their mark. My own research on volunteers who become civic leaders (1988) supports these findings. Even the very successful and prominent among them, if they had no or little experience working for pay, showed signs of self-doubt and anxiousness about their position vis-à-vis paid professionals.

However, the fact that these women have some doubts about their own legitimacy should not deflect us from seeing the skilled, systematic, and persistent effort involved. The women I studied were successful entrepreneurs in civic projects. They were experienced in fundraising, public relations, building organizations, and lobbying as advocates for a cause. Some became community service generalists or brokers sought after for their advice in all areas. Their work is valued in the cities and towns of this country—yet it is always seen as somehow anomalous or idiosyncratic, the work of some unusually talented women with free time on their hands. It is never seen as a widespread pattern of work involving local recruitment, training, and development of skills for women who become capable volunteers leaders in community and civic affairs.

Volunteer work in politics provides another example of hidden or obscured work for women. This example is important, for it overlaps with work in the folk concept in that successful volunteers can move into the prestigious and paid positions available to political appointees. However, men are more likely to be awarded such positions, while women remain in the background as volunteers. Margolis (1979) points out how women help create this obscurity in New England town democracies. The women who are important political leaders send prominent towns*men* (clergy, professionals) to lobby council members on key voting issues in the belief that men will be more persuasive than women. A social scientist who only polled decision makers about which people had lobbied them might never discover how many were directed by the women leaders in the town. This omission raises an important question, not only for political scientists, but also for sociologists of work. Students of work need to understand how the social fabric of life is constructed, how work goes on in areas we have not previously examined; but wherever work is necessary, people have to do it, and put forth skill and effort in its cause. The fabric of life requires this effort—or it is poorer if that work is absent. Most of the people expected to do it—or assumed to do it most easily—are women.

There is increasing recognition of such contributions, of course. Our society is changing, albeit slowly, under the impact of the women's movement. In response to the movement, we now have the examinations of women's lives—and women's work—that I have drawn upon here. But serious discussion of this work that would affect social policy is slow in coming. For instance, changes in inequitable insurance rates, revision of inheritance taxes (for widows

who are not recognized as partners in a family business or farm), redress in patterns of divorce settlements that generally favor husbands, recognition for women in political advancement through their work in organizing and managing campaigns—all these are slow in coming. This slowness reflects a general reluctance to view women's work as a serious work equivalent to that of men, i.e., requiring the same or similar skills and competence to receive the same rewards (Feldberg, 1984). This reluctance is evident even in the area of women's paid work, where it is one of the reasons that comparable worth legislation to reassess the value of and reward for women's occupations to make them equivalent to male occupation standards is still so bitterly resisted (Steinberg, 1986). Where the assumption is prevalent that payment reflects skill, there is still widespread lack of recognition that the skills and education required for typical women's jobs have for so long been under-rewarded.

The lack of validation attendant upon women's work in the family, in volunteer worlds, and in women's occupations affects the definitions women make of their own efforts. If women's work is so hard to conceptualize, and so hard to assess as equal to that of men even when it is recognized as public and paid, it is not surprising that many areas of women's activity receive a low judgment—as of little importance—from women as well as men. The closer the work to the activities of nurturing, comforting, encouraging, or facilitating interaction, the more closely associated it is with women's "natural" or "feminine" proclivities. Such activity is not seen as learned, skilled, required, but only the expression of the character or style of women in general. In the political arena, for example, Margolis (1979) reports that women take responsibility for organizing political meetings: making schedules, sending out flyers, phoning to urge people to come, arranging meeting halls, preparing refreshments. All these activities provide the background and support for (usually male) candidates who appear, speak, and then leave. The women's activities are absolutely essential to the success of campaigns but are not seen, even by the women themselves, as part of "important" political work. They speak of it as "drudge" work instead. The skills required in making decisions and judgments, sizing up prospects, and knowing how to influence and persuade—all these remain invisible. In the volunteer world, as I have noted elsewhere (Daniels, 1985), the women who produce community benefits and parties make the aura of sociability that not only encourages people to give generously to a cause but also develops the esprit to create and shape a sense of community. Yet the work involved in these efforts is colored by the assumption of triviality or frivolity attendant upon such endeavors. The skills needed to do the work and its importance for the community are ambivalently regarded, even, again, by the women themselves. They are, after all, members of the folk who share a concept of what real work is.

The aspect of these activities most difficult for everyone to conceptualize as work involves the warm and caring aspects of the construction and maintenance of interpersonal relations. In the commonsense view, these activities occur spontaneously. They are informal and unregulated—outside of bureaucratic rules and obligations. These activities are what Arlie Hochschild (1979) calls the positive aspects of "emotion work." They involve the following behaviors: (1) attending carefully to how a setting affects others in it—through taking the role of the other and feeling some of the same feelings; (2) focusing attention through ruminating about the past and planning for the future; (3) assessing the reasonableness of preliminary judgments by checking over the behavior of all respondents in an interaction—just as good hostesses do when they look for signs of how well people are enjoying a party, whether or not anyone appears ill at ease or left out; (4) creating a comfortable ambience through expressions of gaiety,

warmth, sympathy, and cheerful, affectionate concern for or interest in another. Emotion work is an example of how gender expectations and the private sphere are interconnected in a job description, for it is women's job in our society to manage these tasks in the family. The behaviors detailed by Hochschild are essential to the support and encouragement of family members—both in their activities in the home and in support for these members as they enter and return from encounters in the public world.

Contradicting commonsense beliefs about these activities as part of the private world of family are other commonsense notions about the way pleasant or even close interpersonal relationships can make certain kinds of work in the public world go more smoothly—team work, for example, or service work where the customer enjoys the pleasant, personalized ambience that workers can create. Hochschild (1983) focuses on this latter kind of work in her study of airline stewardesses to show that emotion work can be rationalized through recruitment and training of women who become adept at making nurturing and encouraging gestures even in the face of resistant or difficult clients. In these situations, emotive skills are developed and focused by the employers much as they might train their workers for any other occupational tasks. But as Hochschild notes, women are not likely to be highly rewarded for a "natural" talent that the airlines have helped them polish into a skill. Women are expected to dispense their interpersonal services in addition to their other services even under trying conditions—such as when greater numbers of customers are added to the workload. When the interpersonal services are an important part of the transaction from the employer's perspective, it is necessary to limit the number of clients each servitor must help—and offer resources and room for autonomy so that the servitors can do so. For example, people willing to pay for seats in the first class cabins of airlines are served by less pressured attendants.

Under what conditions will we pay for such services? Many servitors in first class establishments are men: maitre d's in posh restaurants, porters and concierges in luxury hotels. These are relatively high-status jobs which we "naturally" expect men to fill. They combine authority with their efforts to please, and they are specially rewarded for their combination of interpersonal skills. When we talk about the other area where interpersonal relations make work go smoothly—team work—we think of the work usually assigned to men: leadership. The interpersonal skills involved in leadership are particularly rewarded when men perform them. After all, interpersonal and caring skills are *not* seen as natural for men. They receive more credit for showing these skills accordingly. Part of that credit includes offering men in these high-status jobs the resources (staff, time, independence) to perform at their best advantage. The symphony conductor, the military officer, and the politician or administrator are examples of individuals at work who are recognized as needing to add some important interpersonal skills—understanding and working well with others—to the performance of their tasks.

However, the same interpersonal skills that are rewarded when they are attached to recognized and prestigious occupations in the public sphere are harder to see in the private world of family where women become "specialists" in them. Pamela Fishman (1978) has shown that women engage in a disproportionate amount of the encouraging, facilitating behaviors of communications even in supposedly egalitarian households. When men initiate conversations, women supply the supportive remarks that help channel interactions as men direct. When women initiate, men do not offer the same encouragement; they show by unenthusiastic response, or by ignoring the topic, that they prefer their own topics. Women then drop their own pursuit—sometimes after several tries—to pursue the men's concerns. Sattel (1976) argues that women are expected to perform these interpersonal services for men and are reproached (or men show their disappointment) when women refuse. The expectation that women possess the natural skills for this type of service blend with the expectation that they *should* do them—helping men to express emotions, for example. Sattel confines his argument to the arena of personal relationships, but the expectations that women will facilitate and encourage in interaction spills over into the occupational world. For example, in a study of student evaluations, Norma Wikler (1979) found students to be harder on women than men instructors when an instructor was not readily available, supportive or sympathetic to student problems. The expectations for women in this area were higher and they were sanctioned for not meeting them. A common complaint from women in the business world is that they are expected to show maternal or nurturant behaviors and are berated as hostile or even castrating if they, like male peers, do not.

The resistance to specifying and giving reward to the interpersonal skills of women as legitimate aspects of work is surely an aspect of the pervasive gender stratification noted earlier—i.e., activities, that when women do them, receive less reward than when men do them. The idea that emotional work should be natural for women contributes to the idea that their work is less skilled—or that this part of their work should get less reward. But there is additional resistance inherent in both the lay person's and the economist's perception of the significance of the wage: in general, the effort required to earn money is seen as distinctive and separate from other activity. Even when interchanges do not hinder but aid in the development of esprit, they are rarely seen as the significant skills of work. They are not significant even when what they accomplish is appreciated. As Wadel (1979:367) points out, focusing attention on pay for work and the specific product desired neglects the activities of work that produce such things as "social relations, technical and social skills, attitudes and values."

In addition to the narrow focus on the activities that produce the product for which the wage is granted, resistance to conceptualizing interpersonal activities as work comes from the expectation that emotional interpersonal gestures are natural expressions that come spontaneously. This view fails to recognize that such gestures are not merely expressive but must also be focused or directed so that they communicate the intended emotion. The idea of expressiveness also includes the view that spontaneous gestures that are loving or supportive are given freely and need not be equated with standard units in a monetized economy. The very idea is distasteful. When we speak of a woman "selling" herself in marriage it is a pejorative, repugnant image, although it is a vivid metaphor for a type of exchange that, as theorists since Engels ([1884] 1972) have pointed out, provides a useful insight into family relationships in a bourgeoise economy. Of course, there is a general commonsense understanding that good interpersonal relationships are helpful in work. It meets the opposing understanding that personal relations should not be used for profitable advantage—as seen in the ridicule or disdain sometimes attached to the glad hander and the too obvious, smarmy or oily friendliness of the used car dealer or other high-pressure salesperson.

IMPORTANCE OF RECONCEPTUALIZING WORK

In this discussion of what might be called work, we have moved from activities convertible into commonsense work categories—where a market value can be attached—to those where a wage value is difficult or even repugnant to consider. But the continuum is not a simple one to conceptualize. It is complicated by the mix of exploitive or trading aspects to be found in the most intimate interactions, on the one hand, and spontaneous or altruistic aspects of interaction to be found in work settings, on the other. Even housewives who say they love their hus-

bands sometimes wheedle money or favors from them, trading an especially nice dinner or sex for the desired benefit (Luxton, 1980). The value of a nice ambience and a personal touch is also understood in business. Buttering up the customers so that they will be loyal to a particular service goes better when feelings of warmth or sympathy can actually be summoned by the servitors. If workers summon up the feelings, this behavior is more likely to appear spontaneous. In consequence, supervisors teach airline stewardesses how to get themselves in the right frame of mind to behave this way (Hochschild, 1983). These mixtures raise questions about the idea that spontaneous and altruistic gestures are not part of work as well as the idea that spontaneous and altruistic behavior in the family may not be commingled with calculating and exploitive behaviors.

The mixtures also underline one aspect of the problem of definition: the nature of work changes over time and in various contexts. When, before industrialization, men and women worked together in a productive unit within the home, it was easy to see both as workers. The separation of home and workplace changed the meaning of the work men and women do. Thus, women today may have to bribe or entice their husbands for goods and services when the only way to get things is with money and the husband has sole or primary access to it. At the same time, mass production not only of goods but of services has isolated some of the nurturant activities characteristic of women and placed a market value upon them. Women are expected to produce these activities more readily or easily than men, and include them gratis in whatever labor power the women sell accordingly.

As Wadel (1979:369) notes, market prices can also affect definitions; they can determine what is work and what is not. Once goods and services can be produced both commercially and domestically, our commonsense definitions of work and non-work change to accommodate to the new situation. These changes explain why care of children or of sick and elderly is not real work within a family setting but becomes easier to understand as work once these activities can be bought in the market.

The commonsense understanding of work, despite the importance it attaches to payment for labor, is distinct from an economic perspective; for it has, as Wadel (1979:371) also points out, a moral component. Having a job "is commonly held as a prerequisite for membership in the 'moral community.' " To "earn one's keep" is a commonsense phrase to express an expected common denominator of behavior on the part of any responsible person. Its importance can be seen in the emphasis parents place upon it and their exasperation when young adults don't fulfill it; for it is the *least* they can do. Working is thus an expression of moral values; but it is something more. It is also an arena for their development.

The work of developing and maintaining the moral force of social institutions can be seen in the family, the community, and the workplace. As Wadel (1979:371) instructs us, we need to look not only at "institutions as end results [but also at] the 'work' that has gone into their achievement." In this way we gain a new understanding and appreciation of many activities previously seen as extraneous or trivial—if noticed at all. The work of symbolically *creating family* occurs in the family events—e.g., the dinner hour and special celebrations held at that time—generally made possible by women who plan, provision, and then produce these occasions (DeVault, 1984). Such occasions symbolize the integrity of the family and provide concrete memories of sharing in an activity. The memories help create the sense of solidarity and commitment to the common aims of family that make it a special unit.

The work of *making community* arises through the efforts of many local volunteers who maintain the services and the sense of community required. They organize networks, plan events, get people together to formulate a way—through an organization, a campaign, a social service—to meet hitherto unmet needs in the locality. As people participate in these activities, they develop a sense of commitment to one another, to the purpose of their efforts, and to the community for which the organization or service is constructed. In short, they develop and strengthen moral convictions about what should and should not occur in their community.

The many informal interchanges that make the difference between a tolerable and an unbearable workplace depend upon the efforts of workers and managers to maintain an ambience that encourages commitment and esprit. Again, the work of creating the background for amiable and affiliative interactions can also create a sense of the reasonableness and rightness of work goals, reaffirming the moral necessity to perform at work in order to see oneself as a fully participant citizen in the work group.

In looking at these efforts, one comes to focus on how institutions are changed as well as maintained. For example, when women withhold their services as church workers, they may alter the nature of a religious community. As Susan Stall (1982) reports from her study of women in an agricultural area, fellowship is connected with sociable church activity like church suppers. When the women enter the labor market and have no time to prepare the suppers, the sense of fellowship dissipates, and a different religious institution appears. Similarly, changes in family structure—with more and more female-headed, single-parent households—also bring about changes in the nature and amount of work involved in building family, and a new kind of family appears. Robert Weiss (1979) reports that children take on some of the emotional as well as physical tasks formerly shared by parents. A new distribution of work in the family ensues. These changes call to our attention not only the new work but some of the invisible work—both emotional and physical—that, as Elise Boulding (1990) tells us, children often do in families.

Changes in institutions bring to light not only the earlier work required for their maintenance but also the work implicated in creation of new institutional forms. If we examine changes closely, we can see what has been added or taken away in our society by the presence or absence of efforts that we have come to take for granted. We appreciate and want the efforts that make our institutions more workable though we wouldn't credit most of it as work.

CONCLUSION

I have argued that the concept of work should include all the work in the private world of the home, the volunteer work in the public sphere, and the emotion work in both public and private worlds. All these activities involve real work—only it is work that is sometimes difficult to fit into a commonsense perspective that focuses only on remuneration for effort. We need that other element inherent in both the commonsense and the sociological definition of work: work as a basic element in the moral order. Reconceptualizing work to include all the elements I have suggested does not imply that all aspects of work should be paid—or that all should have a dollar value assigned. Certainly, it is true that assigning monetary value too explicitly to acts which, after all, do contain spontaneous and altruistic elements, does dampen one's enthusiasm about them. For example, reckoning the exact cost of a dinner party, including the time and all labor involved, can put a blight on hospitable impulses. But recognition and validation of the work involved in all this invisible or unattended activity is still possible. What can we give that is more than the perfunctory honors and sentimental accolades we now offer homemakers and volunteers, yet less than (or different from) a regular salary? Some forms of equivalences— e.g., insurance and pension programs for homemakers under various schemes for payment, cash equivalents for volunteer service—

have already been suggested. My own suggestions at this stage are quite tentative. Once we appreciate the significance of all the pieces of emotional and physical work that now do not receive the dignity and moral force of definition as work, we can regard the workers in a new light, appreciating both their effort and their skills.

An analysis of invisible work tells us something about how the fabric of life is woven; it calls attention to what gives life its texture, to continue the metaphor. Should we call this work? Or should we distinguish it from work because it is not remunerated or because of the apparently spontaneous aspects, the appearance of intuitive responses in social settings. I have argued that it is work and that it is important to think of it as work. Even without remuneration, it at least shares one aspect of the commonsense definition in that some people are expected to do it and can be sanctioned for not doing it.

When there is a rift of some kind in the social fabric, public or private, at home or at work, it is often expected either that women *should* or that women *could* weave the fabric back into wholeness because they have the natural talents to do so. My argument is that, whatever their natural propensity, they are trained in these skills. In consequence, women are more likely to be able to do this job. Their practice comes from weaving the fabric together in their friendships, families, and work settings. The skill at this weaving comes from attending to the background comforts that make interaction pleasanter, from watching out for hesitances, likes, and dislikes of others in the social setting and trying to accommodate them. Once these behaviors become habitual, women are just "naturally" better at this work. Of course, social life would run more smoothly if every able-bodied person attended to those matters, rotating some tasks around or shifting them from one to another as a context permitted. Serious attention to the importance of this work in the social construction of reality may make that sharing seem more reasonable.

REFERENCES

Acker, Joan 1972 "Women and social stratification: a case of intellectual sexism." *American Journal of Sociology* 78:936–45.

Benjamin, Esther 1979 "Changing self conceptions and pressures for more egalitarian marriages: women return to school." Paper presented at the annual meetings of the Society for the Study of Social Problems, Boston.

Berk, Sarah Fenstermacher 1985 *The Gender Factory*. New York: Plenum Press.

Boulding, Elise 1990 "Waiting as invisible work: an exploration of waiting in families." In Steven Peter Vallas and Kai Erikson (eds.), *The Nature of work: Sociological Perspectives*. New Haven: Yale University Press.

Daniels, Arlene Kaplan 1985 "Good times and good works: the place of sociability in the work of women volunteers." *Social Problems* 32:363–74.

1988 *Invisible Careers: Women Civic Leaders from the Volunteer World*. Chicago: University of Chicago Press.

DeVault, Marjorie L. 1984 "Women and food: housework and the production of family life." Unpublished Ph.D. Dissertation, Northwestern University, Evanston, IL.

1987 "Doing housework: feeding and family life." Pp. 178–91 in Naomi Gerstel and Harriet Gross (eds.), *Families and Work*. Philadelphia: Temple University Press.

Elliott, Elizabeth 1986 "Who cares and where? The relocation of health care cost, technology and work in the growing business of home health care." Unpublished paper, Northwestern University, Evanston, IL.

Engels, Friedrich [1884] 1972 *The Origins of the Family, Private Property and the State*. New York: International Publishers.

Feldberg, Roslyn L. 1984 "Comparable worth: toward theory and practice in the United States." *Signs* 10:311–28.

Ferree, Myra Marx 1976 "Working-class jobs: housework and paid work as sources of satisfaction." *Social Problems* 23:431–41.

Fishman, Pamela M. 1978 "Interaction: the work women do." *Social Problems* 25:397–406.

French, Marilyn 1977 *The Women's Room*. New York: Summit Books.

Friedan, Betty 1963 *The Feminine Mystique*. New York: Norton.

Gilman, Charlotte Perkins [1898] 1966 *Women and Economics*. New York: Harper Torchbook.

Glaser, Nona Y. 1987 "Servants to capital: unpaid domestic labor and paid work." Pp. 236–55 in Naomi Gerstel and Harriet Gross (eds.), *Families and Work*. Philadelphia: Temple University Press.

1988 "Overlooked, overworked: women's unpaid and paid work in the health services 'cost crisis'." *International Journal of Health Services* 18(1): 26–30.

Hertz, Rosanna 1986 *More Equal Than Others: Women and Men in Dual-Career Marriages*. Berkeley: University of California Press.

Hochschild, Arlie 1979 "Emotion work, feeling rules and social structure." *American Journal of Sociology* 85:551–75.

1983 *The Managed Heart*. Berkeley: University of California Press.

Illich, Ivan 1981 *Shadow Work*. Boston: Boyars.

Luxton, Meg 1980 *More Than A Labour of Love: Three Generations of Women's Work in the Home*. Toronto: Women's Educational Press.

Margolis, Diane Rothbard 1979 "The invisible hands: sex roles and the division of labor in two local political parties." *Social Problems* 26:314–24.

McKreindle, Jean and Sheila Rowbotham 1977 *Dutiful Daughters: Women Talk About Their Lives*. Austin: University of Texas Press.

Rubin, Lillian B. 1976 *Worlds of Pain: Life in the Working-Class Family*. New York: Basic Books.

Sattel, Jack W. 1976 "The inexpressive male: tragedy or sexual politics?" *Social Problems* 23:469–77.

Stall, Susan 1982 "The work women do in a small rural town." Paper presented at the annual meetings of the Midwest Sociological Society, Des Moines.

Stasser, Susan 1982 *Never Done: A History of American Housework*. New York: Pantheon.

Steinberg, Ronnie 1986 "The debate on comparable worth." *New Politics* 1:108–26.

Steinem, Gloria 1983 *Outrageous Acts and Everyday Rebellions*. New York: Holt, Rinehart and Winston.

Turner, Ralph 1957 "The normative coherence of folk concepts." Proceedings of the Pacific Sociological Society. *Research Studies of the State College of Washington* 25:127–36.

Wadel, Cato 1979 "The Hidden Work of Everyday Life." Pp. 365–84 in Sandra Wallman (ed.), *Social Anthropology of Work.* New York: Academic Press.

Weiss, Robert S. 1979 *Going It Alone.* New York: Basic Books.

Weitzman, Lenore 1986 *The Divorce Revolution: The Unexpected Social and Economic Consequences for Women and Children in America.* New York: Free Press.

Wikler, Norma 1979 "Sexism in the classroom." Paper presented at the annual meetings of the American Sociological Association, Boston.

DISCUSSION QUESTIONS

1. Look at the kinds of invisible work that take place among the adult members of your family. To what extent is this work "women's work"?
2. At the end of the article, Daniels raises the issue of how we might compensate people for invisible work. Should such work be compensated, and if so, how?

READING 25

Social Service Providers and Teen Mothers

Ruth Horowitz

Compared to all other advanced industrial societies, the Unites States has by far the highest rate of teenage mothers. Why young women become pregnant and decide to have children are questions raised by Ruth Horowitz in her book, Teen Mothers. *As a participant observer, she followed a group of teen mothers through a year of Project GED, a government program designed to assist teen mothers obtain high school equivalency diplomas and to provide job training. As part of her research, she listened attentively to the accounts the young mothers provided about their self-identities as they proceeded from unplanned pregnancies to motherhood.*

FROM FORTUITY TO AUTHENTIC SELF: PREGNANCY TO MOTHERHOOD

Some people attribute intentionality (desire for welfare, wanting to keep their boyfriends, someone to love, everyone else has one) to the teens becoming mothers, while others claim that the young do not intend to become pregnant (lack of knowledge of sex or birth control, or lack of accessibility of birth control, boyfriend does not want to use birth control) and cannot or do not want to obtain abortions. Intentionality is a complex process of negotiation and renegotiation during talk among the local social networks made up of female peers and family, both young and mature. Accounts of intention and lack of intention are closely related to the young women's position in the social structure and their own efforts to develop their authenticity as people in the world that they know and in which they feel comfortable. Without an understanding of the young women's notions of authenticity and its relationship to motherhood, staff could not communicate effectively with them.

The creative experiences of pregnancy and motherhood are also the experiences that unite participants as women. These are the topics they talked about most and which drew them together. Rarely did the participants discuss the program, clothes or makeup (they had no money to buy them), or possible employment. Before classes started, at lunch, or while waiting for the bus, they often discussed pregnancy, the birth experience, and sometimes how "spoilt" their children were. This was always said with some degree of pride but also inferred that the child was difficult to handle. They all enjoyed discussing their experiences when pregnant, particularly how everyone catered to them; how their mother, grandmother, or sister would go out in the middle of the night to buy them some delicacy. The birth of the child was often described in a very positive light despite the pain and, for several, dangerous medical complications. Typically, several female relatives attended the births and lavished attention on the young mothers. They did, however, receive many messages from the society around them that they had become mothers too early and without the necessary marriage. They are all acutely aware that much of society does not approve of their motherhood.

Lack of Intention: Getting Pregnant

In talk it appears that the majority of pregnancies were unintended. Most of the discussions concerning pregnancy occurred when no staff were present, such as during lunch or while waiting for the bus. Val told me she had just started her period and thought she could not get pregnant yet. June, now pregnant with her second, said she wished she had not gotten pregnant again and had been on the pill and, when she stopped taking it, had immediately gotten pregnant again. Sharon, pregnant now, said she had not meant to and did not want the responsibility. In a discussion on responsibility and bringing a child into the world with David, whose presence was sponsored by Jenna, Kim said she was on the pill when she unintentionally became pregnant with her third baby. Darleen, who was eight months pregnant with her second baby, said she had not even wanted to be pregnant the first time. She was using the pill after her first, but it was making her sick. When the doctor would not change it, she stopped taking it and got pregnant. She said her mother would not let her get an abortion. The other young women concurred with these accounts and never challenged accounts of lack of intention to become pregnant.

Developing Intention: Being Pregnant

Denying the possibility of abortion or adoption begins the transformation from fortuity to inten-

tion. When pregnant, it is time to begin to take responsibility for your actions. Their mothers were not pleased when they discovered that their daughters were pregnant, but, according to the young women, many were opposed to abortion. One mother told her daughter that she could only have an abortion if the daughter paid for it herself. At fourteen she could not get a job and the state would not pay, so she was forced to have the child. None accepted the appropriateness of giving a baby up for adoption and all were critical of one young mother, known by several of the participants, who had considered it seriously. If you were grown up enough to get pregnant, they explained, you should be responsible for the baby. This, they claimed, was also what their mothers told them. In one conversation, Gay asked, "Why get pregnant if you are going to give up the baby? That's stupid. If you don't want a baby you shouldn't get pregnant." Marian added that "no one could get as close to an adopted baby as you would your own." While most expressed lack of intention to get pregnant, they were instructed by peers and mothers that they were expected to "intend" to become mothers.

The shift from lack of intention in becoming pregnant to intending to become a mother often occurred within the context of a redefinition of the mother-daughter relationship and the strengthening of the ties with other young mothers. A common bond of experience developed during pregnancy. For many of the young women, pregnancy created a very significant shift in their relationships with their mothers and was also a time when they were the center of attention. Many of their mothers had been teen parents themselves and several were in their early thirties at the time of the birth of their first grandchild.

Martha's situation was atypical. While her mother threw her out when Martha became pregnant, most mothers and daughters appeared to resolve their differences fairly rapidly and mothers began to treat their teenage daughters more as equals. Ramona told the others that her mother began to allow her to play cards with her mother's friends and to hear all of the interesting gossip. Several reported that their mothers did not care as much when they came in, so they were freer to do what they wanted. Not only did mothers begin to include them in adult activities and supervise them less, but often catered to their eating desires. Favorite stories involved midnight trips to the store for fruits, cookies, and shrimp when they had a craving for such goodies. Relationships, though rocky at times, appeared to improve for many of them as the pregnancy continued.

The new stage in the mother/daughter relationship during pregnancy was not without tension. During one discussion with Lena, Sandy told the group that after getting pregnant her mother allowed her to have guys over and said that they were more like sisters now. However, she did admit that her mother would not let her go out at night and she left using the fire escape. Later that day at lunch Sara said that she wanted to do things differently than her mother, but her mother was always telling her what to do and undermining her authority. Her mother liked to slap her around and wrestle, and now they were friends and "kind of like we growed up together."

Some took the "intention" of motherhood less seriously than others. A few during pregnancy remained embedded in the impulsive self and had not taken much care of themselves through the pregnancy, continuing to smoke and drink. For some, this resulted in elevated blood pressure exacerbated by consumption of too much salt from a constant diet of potato chips, fried food, and too few vitamins. Most actively changed their behavior, which demonstrated their intention to become good mothers. They ate well, stopped smoking and drinking, and had relatively easy births. Most started smoking again after the birth and smoked rather constantly in the program. One of the participants who was pregnant and smoking was criticized by several others.

The birth was the culmination in the creation of another life and involved the participation of a number of female relatives. Only a few of the fathers of the babies attended. It was a women's celebration and a sister, an aunt, and/or her mother accompanied the young woman to the hospital. For most of the young mothers, looking back on it later, the birth was an exciting and wonderful event, despite all of the problems and pain. As the young women progressed in their pregnancies with the help of their friends and relatives, they began to talk about the births of their babies as planned and desirable. They meant to have the baby, even if they did not intend to get pregnant.

Intention: Being a Mother

Intention is necessary if one is going to claim that motherhood is an expression of one's authentic self. To be authentic infers choice, yet motherhood is an expected and often normatively required role for women. Motherhood, however, when achieved as a teenager and outside of the bonds of matrimony is often regarded as problematic by outsiders. These young women stepped outside of the expectations for their age and marital status and, according to their own accounts, *chose* to do something they were not supposed to. However, the stigma is somewhat mitigated because it is expected and approved for most women—at least when they are older and married. Having made an independent decision to become a mother over the objections of their own mothers and the wider society, they are able to claim that motherhood is a reflection of their authentic selves and, as an approved status for women, it is only deviant because of their age and marital status. As Lofland (1969, 110) argues, the lure of deviance "is all the stronger when prohibition is not against the activity per se but against engagement in it by particular categories of persons." Sex and motherhood are valued activities and only prohibited for the underaged and unmarried.

The young mothers were aware that representatives of the wider society thought they had become mothers too early and that they were deviant because they were unmarried. These mothers attempted to justify these categorical deviations. They were able to develop a rationale that attempted to resolve the dilemma of doing something that one knew was approved of for women during a certain stage of their lives, yet was disapproved of for them. They said, "I will be able to grow up with my children." This expression was heard over and over in different contexts and served as an explanation for moving back and forth between the demands of adulthood and the pleasures of youth. Several argued that if they had not had children now, they would never have had any.

Motherhood continually posed dilemmas for these young mothers. It was a positive creative act but it also constrained their behavior. Often they said they wished they had waited. Motherhood has an element of permanence: it cannot be taken away, yet there is always a terrifying risk that social workers may take away the child. Motherhood linked the young women to other women in the wider society, yet they were aware that others condemned them for having children as teenagers. With motherhood came financial independence from their own mothers but financial dependence on the welfare system and frequent social and emotional reliance on their mothers, from whom they wished to be independent. With independence came great responsibility and the end of the freedom to come and go as desired. Real tension exists between self-sacrifice to children (institutional locus) and giving in to the desire to hang out on the street or in a bar with friends and with inhibitions lowered (impulse locus) (Turner 1976).

Moreover, relationships with their own mothers are not without conflict. While that relationship changes as they are both mothers now, it is often the case that the children call their grandmothers "mother" and that the young women are called by their names and leave their chil-

dren with their mothers, who sometimes resent that they have to begin again with the raising of babies while they are still raising their own.[1] Selma said her mother claimed that she was mother to both Selma and her son.

Childraising as a Natural Process: Mothering

Being a mother is viewed as a natural phenomenon that all "normal" women have the skills to do successfully with help from those with more experience—grandmothers or mothers. It is possible to do the job reasonably flawlessly and not reveal human frailties (Turner 1976). Mothering is not viewed the same as being a student or worker, where one is subject to many rules and regulations and technical training is necessary and failure is easy. Mothers and grandmothers have no special training for motherhood and do well, so none is necessary beyond advice from the experienced.

Advice about childrearing is sometimes partially summarized by frequently used phrases such as "she be grown," "she's spoilt," "that girl looks ugly," "she be smart," "he be bad," and "I got an attitude." On a number of occasions when asked about their relationships with their children, the young women responded, "I spoilt her, she won't go to any one else," which is often modified by saying that the child will go to her grandmother too. It appears the young mothers feel children need to be disciplined from a very early age, but they have failed to do enough of it. They believe their children have been permitted to do whatever they want when visiting a father's family or another relative and worry that fathers spoil their daughters. Most of the time these young women were talking about children under the age of three.

Some believe that their children understand more than they probably do and argue that the way to achieve discipline is to "bust his butt."

---

[1]This has been documented elsewhere (Anderson 1990).

This is different than abuse, which has no goal but to hurt the child. Kim explained that she was toilet training her two-year-old. He sat on the pot for a half hour, but a few minutes after he got up, he "shit in his pants, so I hit him. He knew what he was supposed to do and he disobeyed me." Most explained that it was all right to slap their wrists or hit them on the rear but not to hit on the face.

Being a mother is viewed as natural and one does not need schooling or book learning to be one. Life experiences are generally considered necessary for knowledge. Their mothers never had lessons and they turned out all right. For example, Cindy, who was pregnant with her first child, finally admitted she was afraid about the delivery and had no idea of what labor would be like. Liz responded, "How would you know? You've never had a baby." Amy tried to describe the process, but the young women, all of whom had had at least one child, were not convinced that anyone could adequately describe the experience. One had to actually deliver the baby. As experience is viewed as the best teacher, it places enormous difficulties on someone who is trying to teach, in a formal manner, the young women to do things differently than they do currently.

Childrearing as Responsibility

Regardless of the age of the child or with whom a child lives, that son or daughter belongs to the mother and is her responsibility. A child is one's future and no one can say that child is not of the mother. All the young women believe this and talk about the responsibility that they have for the welfare and upbringing of their babies. They know that they are held accountable for their children and think they should already know how to bring them up. Their mothers said that they must be held accountable for their pregnancies and then they must take care of their own children and give up much of the desirable partying. Many of them see themselves as making sacrifices for their children.

Being a woman is not the same as having kids but having kids is taking responsibility, argued Rachel in response to David's question "What is a woman?" David replied, "The key word is responsibility. Raising the baby you must stand alone and take responsibility, that is the responsible job as a parent."

Kim: We had too much [responsibility].

David: I'm not talking about biology. I'm not expressing my views on women's lib but responsibility of a woman to her kids. They only have you to look up to.

Kim: My kids look up to me.

David: You got to select good role models— not drug addicts or pimps.

Ramona: My son models me. He always rolls his eyes like me.

David: You got to look toward the future. I ended up with my daughter and am raising her alone.

Ramona: I can raise my child better than those bums out there—I got a bad attitude sometimes.

Despite their discussions of the importance of responsibility and intending to become a mother, when they talked during lunch, they were more ambivalent about whether they wanted or could adequately meet the responsibilities that motherhood entailed. Sharon, after talking about trying to return to school after the birth of her baby and failing to find a sitter on a regular basis, said that her mother wanted her in school because she had never returned to school after she had had Sharon at fourteen. Sharon said that she is still a kid and likes to run around outside and does not want to be a mother. "I don't want any responsibilities . . . I want my freedom."

Childrearing: The Dream of Independence, the Reality of Dependence on Others

Not all remain equally dependent on family members. Some live entirely on their own. This puts a very heavy burden on the young mothers who have no one to help them out, even in an emergency. Judy, at eighteen, had two children under three. She was living alone when she caught a very bad throat infection from her baby. She was alone with the two sick babies for over a week with only one friend, who had two of her own, to help her.

Most are not unaware of their dependence on others and often try to fight it. While not all rely on older family members, some rely heavily on their mothers and a few on their grandmothers. A frequent topic of informal discussion among the young mothers was leaving children with grandmothers, telling them that they (the mothers) are just going to buy something at the corner store but disappearing for several hours. Although the young women were often upset when their boyfriends did the same to them, they often did not see their own behavior in the same light. On other occasions they left children with a family member to "party" all night, just as other family members did to them. Some took greater responsibility, rarely leaving their children with others.

They often worried about who had authority at home and some saw that their own mothers had taken most of it. Sarah said she wanted to do things differently than her mother did, but her mother was always telling her what to do and undermining what she told her child. Another worried that her mother was too harsh with her child, but felt she could not do anything about it. Few sat down and discussed responsibility and authority with their mothers, though they did discuss it in the program.

Resolutions to the dilemma faced between the dream and desire for independence and responsibility and the everyday reality of dependence and irresponsibility are difficult but possible. There are a number of accounts used. First, the expression "me and my mom are like sisters now" is used to indicate that each takes some responsibility and justifies the help the young women receive without experiencing too much dependence. This is not an individual resolution

as it was discussed among the young mothers informally and in classes and existed prior to the program. Second, some of the young mothers expressed their independence from others through the names they gave their children. One young woman chose the name of a French perfume but spelled it the way she heard it. Another chose a name because she liked the sound it made. Several expressed real pleasure that they had created these names independently.

While the image they try to maintain of themselves is one of sole responsibility for their children—they are entirely accountable morally, legally, and mentally—they must depend on the state to provide economic resources and are subject to the state's rules and regulations. Moreover, their mothers help out and interfere. In a discussion with Jenna and Lena about what they wanted for themselves and their children, they argued about whether they should turn in the names of the fathers of their babies to the welfare system. When Lena asked what welfare meant, Sara responded, "The baby is supporting you." Lena reemphasized the point, "Parents are living on their children." Moreover, most place some of the burden on their mothers. In reality they are partially dependent on the state and their mothers.

While the young women developed means to partially resolve their dilemmas, they often found they faced a reality they did not particularly like and over which they felt they had little control. Their mothers treated them as children; their children did not obey them and were sometimes out of control; no one was around to help them on occasions when they thought that they needed it; and welfare workers appeared to threaten them with taking away their children or publicly embarrassing them. This was the experience of their daily lives. The young women discovered that they often had to work hard and they did not always like the fact that motherhood frequently conflicted with what they wanted to do. Nevertheless, motherhood still revealed to them their most authentic side: something they could accomplish well.

Distance from the Unsuccessful: The Dilemma of Naturalism and Failure to Take Responsibility

If mothering is a natural skill, how can mothers fail? They often saw, however, expressions of disapproval of their mothering by the people who controlled the resources and appeared to the young women as having status in society. Many of the young women were terrified that representatives of the wider society would turn them in as "bad mothers" and take away their children. Being a bad mother to them did not imply lack of skill; all should have the skills naturally. It means she does not care enough and may be of poor moral character.

The young women worked very hard to distance themselves from those whom they saw as bad mothers. In their discussions they separated the good mothers from the bad ones and worried about what others would say about them. Dressing the child nicely was critical to being seen as a good mother. One of the most vehement discussions in the family life class with Amy concerned what to do if your child wanted to dress herself and put on something that did not match. Randy said that she would try to bribe the kid not to go out like that. Shawn said she would be embarrassed that others might see a child like that. Ronda was adamant that the child should not leave the house prior to changing her clothes because of what other people would think. Ronda exclaimed, "Others would think that the mother doesn't care." Shawn added, "People would blame you." Most of the participants agreed with her and only a few saw the answer that Amy wanted: the merits of praising a child for doing something on her own—dressing herself.

They frequently brought up examples of bad mothers. Poor mothers included those who did not get their children dressed until noon because they were too lazy, those who never had clean clothes for their kids, those who did not change diapers often enough, and abusers. They discussed articles from the newspapers about women who abused their children. During a lunch break several became very upset while discussing one particular case of a local mother leaving her newborn baby at a bus stop in the middle of the winter. They could not understand her cruelty and lack of feeling for her baby. Two participants cried. Another news story that concerned them deeply was of a mother who killed her four children. Several argued that she should get the electric chair. It was incomprehensible that some women do not appear to love their children and, in extreme cases, either abandon or kill them. Marge was very upset when the local newspaper reported that an eight-year-old was raped and could describe the perpetrator perfectly. She was convinced that it was the mother's boyfriend and that the mother was covering up for him. Marge talked about nothing else for several days. According to the newspaper several days later, she was correct; the boyfriend was charged. The mother had violated everything that a mother was supposed to be by jeopardizing the welfare of her child. All of the others agreed strongly with Marge. Some of the longest discussions occurred over these events and they were unyielding in their negative evaluations of these women. There were no acceptable excuses for these mothers.

A moral stigma is attached to interaction with the agency in charge of protecting children, which has the right to initiate termination of parental rights. Not only is anyone who is being served by it considered a bad mother, but the young women fear this agency, as it is the one that can legally evaluate their success at mothering and has the power to jeopardize the permanency of motherhood. While a program that provides supplemental food for pregnant mothers and young children can be regarded as merely providing additional resources to someone without sufficient money, the child agency is regarded as questioning the mother's moral qualities should it become involved with the family. Such a thought strikes terror into the hearts of these young women, though they joked about the mothers who had workers. Perhaps that is why they joked.

The fear is so great that a few were afraid to take their children to the emergency room or to a doctor because they had heard that they would be turned over immediately to the children's agency. Ronda's son fell down and, while afraid that he had done something to his ankle, she did not take him to the hospital because she said she might be blamed for the injury. The validity of this fear was confirmed by others' stories. This real fear of the authorities limited the choices that the young mothers felt they could make. By embedding their authentic selves in fulfilling the role of mother, not only were they finding meaning in this role, they were also protecting themselves from the authorities. However, they were extremely sensitive to any comments that they were not fulfilling that role in an approved manner.

REFERENCES

Anderson, Elijah. 1990. *Streetwise*. Chicago: University of Chicago Press.

Lofland, John. 1969. *Deviance and Identity*. New York: Prentice Hall.

Turner, Ralph. 1976. "The Real Self: From Institution to Impulse." *American Journal of Sociology* 81: 989–1016.

DISCUSSION QUESTIONS

1. Many teen mothers see having a child as a way of becoming independent. Discuss those factors that make it unlikely that they will achieve their goal of independence, and describe what kinds of dependency often result from having a child while still a teen.

2. Horowitz thinks that most teen pregnancies are unintended. Do you agree or disagree? If you were asked to design a program to reduce the number of teen pregnancies, what would be its main objectives and strategies for achieving those objectives?

READING 26

Sleeping with the Enemy?

Arlene Stein

What does it mean to be a lesbian? To what extent is lesbianism a socially constructed identity? These questions are explored in Arlene Stein's interviews with lesbians who wrestle with these and related questions. Thus the excerpt begins by examining what it means to a sense of lesbian identity when a woman sleeps with a man. When can a woman sleep with a man and still be a lesbian, and when does this become problematic? This leads to a debate over what it means when a woman becomes an "ex-lesbian." The selection concludes with accounts of ex-lesbians describing the process of moving from same-sex to opposite-sex relationships.

If heterosexual involvements by lesbian-identified women were once taboo, by 1990, the time of my interviews, a greater tolerance for slippages of identity seemed to be in evidence. Many women I spoke with, including some of the most politically engaged lesbian feminists, acknowledged that lesbians occasionally stray from homosexuality, and they felt this to be acceptable, as long as it didn't happen so often as to threaten their lesbian identities. They had come to believe that behavioral inconsistencies do not necessarily pose a threat to lesbian identity, that a lesbian could sleep with men and still be a lesbian. Many acknowledged that the dividing line between homosexuality and heterosexuality was highly variable and subjective, and that for some women a sexual involvement with a man could actually confirm their lesbian identity.

Several women reported to me that they had had affairs with men long after they had come out as lesbians, sometimes out of curiosity about heterosexuality. This was particularly true if they had come out very young, when they had little or no prior heterosexual experience. Meg Dunn came out in south Florida when she was seventeen, and she quickly became part of the lesbian subculture. Fifteen years later, when she was in her early thirties, she began to wonder, "What is all the fuss about men?" By that time, she felt freer to experiment. "It was interesting," she said of her affair with a man, even if it only served to affirm her sense of lesbian self. "I found that I can't get emotionally close to men. I can sleep with them and have an okay time, but not great, and I can be friends with them, but I can't get any closer."

Sometimes it was precisely this lack of connection, coupled with the fact that men were more sexually available, that made such affairs attractive. It was easier to meet men than women, several interviewees observed. Lesbians were, after all, women first, and thus treated as potential sexual partners by men, particularly by strangers who assumed they were heterosexual. As they aged, life cycle changes drew more and more women, even those who had lived their early adulthood in a largely homosexual world, into mixed settings at work and into heterosexual networks. Taking advantage of these networks, sometimes lesbians had affairs with men because potential lesbian partners were difficult to find.

"Lesbians don't know how to date," forty-year-old Muriel Pepper, an office administrator, complained. "They're either too scared of rejection, or they want to marry you right away." This attitude is captured in an often-repeated lesbian joke: "What does a lesbian bring on her first date?" Answer: "A U-Haul." Gay men commonly had little trouble finding casual sex, but found it difficult to establish intimacy and long-term relationships. Lesbians generally had the opposite problem: they reported having difficulties initiating relationships, particularly casual ones. But once established, such relationships became intimate very rapidly.[1] Indeed, lesbians who had affairs with men often reported that they found them enjoyable simply because they perceived them to be free of the emotional demands of relationships with women.

Meg Dunn told me that she often had short affairs with men—even at her "most extreme lesbian feminist stage," in the mid-1970s—simply because "they were quick and easy." Throughout her twenties and thirties, she met men at bars about once or twice a year, particularly if she was between lesbian relationships. It is difficult to know exactly who among my interviewees pursued such affairs; my sense is that only a small minority had. But in view of the stigma attached to such activities—even if now somewhat lessened—it is unclear how many would have admitted to similar affairs, despite my efforts to let them know that I would in no way condemn them for such a revelation. While several women described having affairs with men "for the sex," a few had a rather different experience: they had a connection with men that was emotional and indeed largely devoid of sexual pleasure.

Muriel Pepper recounted how she had recently rekindled a relationship with a fellow she had dated when she was in her twenties. When he visited from out of town, they ended up in bed together: "We didn't have intercourse, but we were kind of sexual with one another." Muriel was forced to reintegrate that experience into her sense of lesbian self. "I was totally flipped out for about a week after that. I felt that I had to turn my whole life around. I wondered, what does this mean? Does this mean I'm not a lesbian? It seemed to call into question who I was." But after a few days, Muriel said she began to realize that because they had known each other so long, and had gone through "so many changes" together, she and her friend had a "unique" relationship. The affair left her sexually dissatisfied but with deep emotional connections to him. Recognizing this, she "calmed down," because "it doesn't mean that you have to come out or go in or whatever." By thinking of a particular involvement as an aberration and labeling a particular man an "exception," some lesbians were able to integrate occasional involvements with men into their sense of lesbian self.

Though tolerating temporary violations of identity, most women I spoke with perceived a hierarchy of transgression; a high frequency of heterosexual involvements could threaten one's lesbian identity. When asked if women who sleep with men are in fact lesbians, Judy Orr responded, "It depends how many times. The people I knew did it once in ten years. If they're still relating to women, and they still feel very much inside that they're a woman's woman, then they're a lesbian. . . . In my heart of hearts, I'm a lesbian." For others, it was a matter of subjective experience. Sunny Connelly differentiated between her own experience of having occasional affairs with men and the experience of her ex-lover, who now identifies as a bisexual. Her ex-lover, she said, was "more open to her sexual feelings about men. . . . For me, being sexual with men is about having sex. I don't want to cook breakfast for them in the morning. And I don't want to go to the movies with them, and I don't want to know their whole life story. I just want sex. That's not true with [my ex-lover]. She wants the whole package." In this understanding, valuing a man as a "whole person" threatens one's lesbianism, while objectifying men does not. However, few women admitted to telling close lesbian friends about these affairs until after they were over, a reticence that reveals the extent to which, among many lesbians, such behaviors continued to be stigmatized. Heterosexual involvements that happened suddenly and unexpectedly were more tolerated than those that resulted after women "went out looking for it." A particular spontaneous affair could be attributed to an attraction to a particular man or could be written off as situational, as "experimentation." But a prolonged affair with a particular man or discussions about attractions to men were viewed as more serious, as posing a possible threat to identity.

Can a lesbian sleep with men and still be a lesbian? By the late 1980s, the answer seemed to be a qualified "yes." Several women managed to embrace a certain degree of inconsistency between sexual identification and behavior, if one or more of the following conditions were met: (1) such affairs were kept private, (2) they were isolated occurrences and not long-term liaisons, and (3) it was understood that individuals were "in it for the sex" only—and not emotionally attached. However, if those whose behavior demonstrated such occasional lapses were often tolerated, women who had a prolonged relationship with a man were generally not.

FAKERS, TURNCOATS, AND SEEKERS

Very few of those couples had stayed together. Of course, that could really be said about anyone who fell in love idealistically. Love with political implications had always interested her from a distance.

> Sarah Schulman,
> *People in Trouble* (1990)

Among lesbian-identified women, views of the "ex-lesbian," generally defined as a woman who had a "primary" or prolonged relationship with a man (or men), varied widely. Some women saw ex-lesbians as having been inauthentic or "fake" lesbians. Others imagined that they were once "real" lesbians but had abandoned lesbianism for an easier life and for the privileges heterosexuality affords. A third group believed that they were sexual seekers whose desires had simply shifted over time.

The first group mobilized an essentialist argument, suggesting that ex-lesbians were *fakers*. Contrasting their experiences with her own, Shirley Alvarez told me, "I've known since childhood that I was a lesbian and I struggled through the pain and fear of this in order to find my dignity and to live my life openly. The greatest number of us have no choice." In her view, the only "true" lesbian is the woman who experiences her sexuality as involuntary, as beyond "choice." It was not at all surprising that many feminists had reneged upon their lesbian identities—they were never "real" lesbians to begin with. Many were "really" bisexual.

Some were quick to note the high percentage of former separatists among the group of women who "turned straight." As Shirley told me, "The women who were the biggest man-haters, the women who would have nothing to do with men for years—those were the women who went straight. It was true every single time. Nearly every single time. They were the ones that raised the biggest fuss about men. The harder they come, the harder they fall." Other women agreed that many of the women who had been the most adamant ideologues were now with men. In the course of my interviews, I heard numerous similar stories. In view of the attractiveness of separatist ideologies to many formerly heterosexual women who had "become" lesbians, this account is somewhat plausible. The embrace of separatist ideas, and the concomitant exclusion of men from one's life, was a form of identity work, a way to reshape the self and consolidate a lesbian identity. As such, it was a stage.

Whether or not the interviewees' perceptions were accurate is less important than what their comments seem to suggest: real lesbians did not become lesbians for political purposes; their feminist politics did not predate their lesbian desires. Real lesbians did not have to engage in identity work to "become" lesbians—they simply had to be "true to themselves." In this formulation, the "ex-lesbian" becomes a kind of contradiction in terms. Former lesbians had never "really" been lesbians; they were "straight women masquerading as lesbians," as Sue Hammond put it. Their lesbian experiences are instances of "dabbling," of heterosexual "tourism," or ideological "play." The belief that feminist ideology produced "fake" lesbians implies an essentialist understanding of lesbianism, which declares that the only "true" lesbian is the lifelong lesbian who never strays, the woman for whom desires, behavior, and identity are perfectly congruent.

In contrast, a second group of women were resolute social constructionists. They believed that ex-lesbians were no different from currently identified lesbians, except that they were *turncoats*—they had "gone back into the closet" and renounced their lesbian commitments. In the most extreme formulation of this view, ex-lesbians were seen as sellouts, defectors from the ranks, women who "got going once the going got tough." They embodied a metaphor of disintegration, a testament to the difficulties of maintaining a lesbian identity over time. Margaret Berg told me that in the late 1970s she had heard of a woman who, upon hearing of several women who had "gone straight," characterized them as "rats leaving a sinking ship."

Another woman had once lit a *yahrzeit* candle, a Jewish memorial ritual, in memory of a formerly lesbian woman she had been close to. In her view, leaving the lesbian community was a kind of symbolic death, and her actions mirrored those of orthodox Jews who mourn the death of a child who "marries out" of the Jewish community.[2] This mode of explanation was most popular among women who attributed their own coming out to feminism. Having framed the coming out process as a "progress narrative," as a challenge to patriarchal norms, they viewed those who left the lesbian community as turncoats or, as a contributor to one feminist periodical put it, "hasbians."[3] Only the strongest, most politically committed women were able to resist the allure of familial approval, material benefits, and other privileges that accrue to heterosexuals, they believed.

These two ways of framing the ex-lesbian—as faker or as turncoat—rest on two very different explanations for why women might move from homosexuality to heterosexuality. Both assume a binary conception of sexual identity, the belief that individuals must forever and always be *either* homosexual or heterosexual. And both assume that lesbian identities are not to be taken lightly, that they entail important commitments—personal, political, or both. The first mode of explanation stresses personal commitments and the importance of authenticity, of being "true to oneself." The second emphasizes the importance of collective, political commitments and the belief that lesbians, as an oppressed group, should "stick together" and make common cause against the dominant heterosexual society.

However, a third group of interviewees saw former lesbians as sexual *seekers;* these women acknowledged the possibility of sexual fluidity and inconsistency, as well as the limits of sexual binarism. They imagined that there may be inconsistencies among sexual desires, identities, and practices, and that one's identity—the way one presents oneself to others—may not always perfectly reflect one's desires. As one reader of *Out/Look* observed, "The fact is that many lesbian-identified women do sleep with men. Some of us identify as bisexual, and many others as lesbian. We are by no means a homogeneous community."[4] Those who embraced this position saw sexual categories as partial, individual lives as complex. Some suggested that desires may change over time: sexuality might be experienced at an earlier age as essentially fixed—that is, invariably focused on women— but later in one's development as more fluid.[5] Sometimes, such fluidity was the result of specific conditions and events, as Joan Salton's comments suggest: "I think that what happened was that a lot of women opened up to the possibility of sexual relations with other women. And some of them found that they were really happy that way. Others found that it just didn't work for them because they were more sexually driven toward relations with men. Like anything else, some people are happy with it, some got burned, hurt pretty badly." Insofar as it affirms the importance of individual choice, the move away from lesbianism is in this view analogous to the process of coming out as a lesbian.

Having heard how women currently self-identified as lesbians talked about ex-lesbians, I became interested in the ways in which ex-lesbians saw themselves. It seemed likely that they would depict their situation and their choices differently, more sympathetically. What, I wondered, might their experiences tell us about lesbian identities and about the formation of sexual identity more generally? I decided to seek out women who came out in the 1970s but who have since decided that the label *lesbian* may not fully describe their sense of self.

BECOMING AN EX

Should I stay or should I go?
If I go, there will be trouble.
If I stay, it will be double.
        The Clash,
            "Should I Stay or Should I Go?"

If this study had been a cohort analysis that traced individual identities over time, chances are good that a number of women who originally identified as lesbians would have, over time, given up that label. Because my study instead focused upon those who currently identified as lesbians, I needed to locate some former lesbians.

Finding them through word of mouth, I interviewed ten women, ranging in age from thirty-four to forty-six, who came out in the 1970s but who, for any number of reasons, no longer consider themselves to be lesbians. Five were interviewed individually, five more as a group. All were white; six out of the ten had at least attended college; several held professional degrees, and the greatest number worked in psychotherapy and social services. On the whole, they were a better educated and more homogeneous group than my larger sample of current lesbians. They were also far more articulate and self-conscious about their sexual choices than the other groups of women in my study, at least in part because of their high levels of education and their training in psychology, which led them to value introspection and self-analysis.

All had identified strongly with the ideas of lesbian feminism. They were somewhat more likely to identify themselves as originally bisexual or heterosexual than were the lesbian-identified women whom I interviewed. But they were not merely "political lesbians," if that label signifies women who took on the lesbian label without engaging in lesbian activity or fully claiming a lesbian identity. Most *believed* they were lesbians, and they lived as such for anywhere from eight to fifteen years (the average was ten years). Half said that they had experienced their lesbianism as wholly authentic; the other half reported that they had sometimes secretly wondered if they were "really" lesbians. However, this sense of "role distance" was not in itself an accurate predictor of eventual heterosexuality. Many women in my larger sample who reported that they sometimes questioned whether they were "real" lesbians lived successfully with this sense of ambivalence; for others, this ambivalence receded with time.

Forty-one-year-old Laura Stone, was perhaps typical of this group of women. Laura was of middle-class origin and worked as a therapist. She had come out as a lesbian in the early 1970s. For Laura, becoming a lesbian was not, as she put it, a "coming home" experience. Before the women's movement, she felt that she was "completely straight." But as she spent more time around women, her desires for women strengthened. With time, Laura believed that she had firmly established an authentic lesbian identity. She raised a child in a lesbian relationship and was part of a lesbian community in California for fifteen years. But in the early 1980s, she had, in her words, "gone straight." She settled down with a man, married him, and had her first biological child. Today she thinks of her lesbianism as a thing of the past, yet she does not deny its authenticity. She says she was once a lesbian, and now she is heterosexual.

Laura didn't simply wake up one day and discover that she was heterosexual. Rather, she, like the other women who moved from lesbian to heterosexual identities, proceeded through what I call the "ex-lesbian trajectory," a process

that was roughly the opposite of coming out. In sociological terms, it was a type of "role exit," a highly patterned process that occurred over time—not unlike the experiences of former nuns described by sociologist Helen Ebaugh, herself an ex-nun. Like devotees who move away from the Catholic Church, lesbians, particularly those heavily influenced by feminist ideology, disengaged from a role that was "central to their self-identity" and reestablished an identity "in a new role that takes into account one's ex-role."[6]

Laura welcomed me into her home and was eager to speak with me about her life, particularly her "transition away from lesbianism," as she put it. Indeed, to my surprise, most of the former lesbians I contacted enthusiastically shared their stories with me. Many of them were very self-aware of how they had disengaged from a lesbian identity and established a new identity. Coming out had been a highly reflexive process for many women who first identified as lesbians in the 1970s, and so too was the process of "becoming an ex." For Laura and other women, the transitions both to and away from homosexuality were highly self-conscious. As Laura put it, "I was a lesbian who thought a lot about lesbianism. Now I'm a straight woman who thinks a lot about heterosexuality. I processed everything. I still do. But I have to tell you that the end of the story is that I have no idea of this stuff at all any more." In the dominant culture, heterosexuality operates as a social norm, the unmarked category against the pathologized, homosexuality. Though acutely aware of the difficulties involved in *being* heterosexual, and maintaining relationships with men, straight women tend to be less self-reflexive than lesbians about the "constructedness" of sexual categories—including their own heterosexuality.[7] Former lesbians, even those who came to call themselves heterosexual, were an exception to the rule.

Laura said she started having "first doubts" about her lesbianism in the early 1980s. She and her partner were not getting along well, and she was not getting along with their child, her lover's biological offspring. She described herself as being "kind of dead" in the relationship. For many women, this questioning of a particular relationship would have simply resulted in a new lesbian relationship, not a wholesale change in sexual object choice and identity. But in becoming disillusioned with her life, Laura also became disillusioned with her lesbianism. This is at least partly because her lesbianism figured so prominently in her life. Most of her friends were lesbians; her political involvements were generally feminist, and largely lesbian; she worked mainly with feminists and with lesbians.

> I remember saying to other people, saying that if I wasn't with Vicki, I don't know if I would be with a woman. So I knew the question was up. But I also knew that there was no way I was going to find out the answer to that question, given that my life was entirely involved with women. I worked with women, played with women, everything. I was completely in the women's community. I had maintained some relations with the left, the straight left, but minimal.

With time, the lesbian community had begun to feel "very stifling" to her. Lesbian feminism had idealized women's relationships, and while she acknowledged that they were often much more egalitarian than heterosexual relationships, "they were certainly not as egalitarian as the feminist vision had promised."

> There were moments when I hated the lesbian community and hated lesbian relationships, so I became less "we're all superior to those straight couples and straight people" and more feeling that there were advantages and disadvantages to straight relationships. I began to wonder whether I needed the straight kind more than I needed the gay kind. I was feeling very distraught. I had a kid, I was working my ass off, she was depressed, she couldn't get a job. I never thought I could get out of the relationship. But divorce was not part of my repertoire.

Former lesbians often framed their emergent heterosexuality in the language of desire, longing, and "internal" selves, contrasting this newer understanding of themselves with that of their former, lesbian self, which had been forged within a lesbian subculture.[8] Some saw heterosexuality as providing a release from the intimate demands of relationships with women. Toby Miller spoke of having a couple of brief affairs with men "to test the waters": "I was at the point of breaking up with my [female] ex, a long-term relationship. It was a little step into the sexual twilight zone. Emotionally, there was nothing in it. It took my mind off a relationship where there was a lot of emotion going on. It was some kind of weird escape." The libertarian "pro-sex" discourse that emerged among some feminists in the 1980s publicly sanctioned the pursuit of pleasure. Though unaware of these "sex debates," as they had come to be called, Laura recalled her realization at the time that "maybe penises weren't so bad after all." The fact that heterosexual love was so forbidden in her friendship circle made it even more powerful. When she eventually became involved with a man, it had "some of the flavor" of her first relationship with a woman—precisely because "it was so not right": "It had the power that I realize was the power that lesbians had when they came out. That's what I think is so frightening to me. It's that here I had come into the situation thinking: I want to try this and see. I expected the same thing to happen to me when I tried women. But instead what happened was this incredibly powerful falling-in-love experience that I didn't know how to interpret." The taboo aspects of that longing made it even more attractive, rekindling a passion that had been missing from her lesbian relationship after the initial few years. "I knew that it might mean that I was straight," she laughed. "I don't think I expected that experience."

But, ultimately, there was much more at stake than simply erotic pleasures. When discussing their relationships with women, many former lesbians mentioned that the differences that once elicited desire had proved to be problematic in the long run.[9] Some ex-lesbians described a dynamic of having been drawn to female lovers who were very different from themselves in terms of class, race, gendered roles, and so forth. Sally Kirk found that in her relationships with women, she "always had to be attracted to people who were really different." But over time, "it was too hard to sustain a relationship" with a woman who was "so different" from herself. In a striking reversal of feminist ideology, which claimed that lesbian relationships offered an intimacy founded upon the pairing of equals, Sally came to believe that a male lover could provide a "better mix" of qualities than a female lover. Her description of her current male partner illustrates her point:

> The thing that feels great about being with him, and that's related to his being a man, is that he's so much like me. The thing that is really great about being with Henry is that he's interested in all the same things. So there is a lot of it that is very validating, but it doesn't feel like I'm relating to myself because he has this penis. It makes him different enough, that there's this dynamic. His being a man enables me to be with him for a long time in terms of our values and our worldview, which is so much more similar.

By becoming involved with a man, according to Sally, she has been able to find a good mix of "sameness and difference" in a partner.

Toby Miller told a similar story. She met a man who, like her, "is very gay-identified": "He identifies as bisexual but he's really more gay than straight. He's primarily had relationships with men and has really been entrenched in gay culture. He's really into drag and stuff. He told me he had crushes on me when he was in total drag. There's actually a picture of him in drag, you can see . . . the odd couple. He told me that he had a crush on me. Anyway, I said that's nice but I'm a lesbian. But we eventually fell in love." While heterosexual, Toby described her relationship as affording an extraordinary reversal of roles. "We're not your average straight couple . . . . With Sandy, I'm the man. He's much more in touch with how he feels at any minute, at every second. He's an unusual man. He's also very

good when I have feelings. It's more balanced than many of my other relationships. [My woman lover] could hear me only after huge, dramatic, gigantic fights. Sandy and I never get that far."

Many women spoke of life cycle changes, which also introduced the question of children. In the 1980s some lesbians of the baby boom came to raise children within lesbian relationships, but others doubted that these couples could provide the sort of security and stability they believed was necessary to raise a child. Lacking strong cultural and institutional supports, lesbian relationships were in flux, perhaps more than heterosexual ones (which were by no means terribly stable). More important, perhaps, was the continuing appeal of respectability and social legitimacy, or "heterosexual privilege": having a child with a partner of the opposite sex linked one to the larger heterosexual society and fulfilled romantic dreams of reproducing life with one's lover.

I heard about one woman who very much wanted to have a child after having engaged in serial monogamy for many years with women. This woman, I was told, was bisexual, but always "much more attracted to women." She was nearing her mid-thirties and had not found a woman to "settle down" with. A former lover, a woman, introduced her to a heterosexual man who also wanted children, but who was not in a long-term relationship. They embarked upon an informal arrangement to parent a child together, outside of a relationship, initially through donor insemination. Facing the added difficulties of that procedure, they decided to have sexual intercourse, and physical intimacy led to emotional closeness. They eventually married, parenting four children together.

A friend of the woman in question told me this story, as if to suggest that "external" identities do not always do justice to "internal" realities. The woman was someone who was deeply committed to other women and who continues to be attracted to women, even if, on the surface, her life is quite conventionally heterosexual. But this story reveals much about the attractions of parenting in a heterosexual context. For one thing, from a purely technical standpoint, it was easier to "do it" with a man who was one's regular sexual partner. One did not have such worries as coordinating monthly cycles to ensure fertility, as did women who used artificial insemination. Some women went to great lengths in their attempts to conceive a child through donor insemination, only to fail. Moreover, for many women for whom lesbianism was at least partially a matter of choice, women who were always bisexual in terms of desire, the allure of heterosexual romantic love and partnership, sanctified and idealized by the dominant culture, was powerful.

NOTES

1. Psychodynamic explanations rooted in object relations psychoanalysis suggest that lesbians, like women in general, are better suited to relationality than to sexual individualism. But there may also be an economic structural reason for lesbians' dating patterns. Gay male communities tend to be relatively wealthy, and their members have had more access to wealth and have invested more heavily in sex-related commerce—bars, clubs, and the like—than have lesbians.
2. Hillary Freeman, "Tears at the Wedding," *Guardian* (U.K.), 26 July 1994, p. 19.
3. Patricia Roth Schwartz, "On the Hasbian Phenomenon," *off our backs,* June 1989, p. 11.
4. Robyn Ochs, letter to the editor, *Out/Look,* Summer 1990, p. 78.
5. In an informal survey conducted among undergraduates, Carla Golden (1987) interviewed lesbians in their late twenties, thirties, and forties who described shifts in their thinking about the nature of their lesbianism. See also Kinsey, Pomeroy, and Martin 1948; Kinsey et al. 1953.
6. Ebaugh 1988, 1. However, like all stage theories (including those that focus on coming out) the "role exit" notion tends to overstate the extent to which the phenomenon is sequentially patterned and to understate the effect of cohort and individual influences.

7. Several years ago, in an undergraduate seminar on the sociology of sexuality at the University of California, Berkeley, I asked students to write a personal narrative about the formation of their sexual identities. The lesbian and bisexual students found the essay relatively easy to write, as they had struggled with their homosexuality and had access to the cultural template of the "coming out" story. But most of the heterosexual students had difficulty understanding the assignment, and a few were unable to complete it.

   A small but growing number of heterosexual feminists are beginning to theorize heterosexuality as a social construction. See, for example, Chodorow 1994; Segal 1994; and many of the essays contained in Wilkinson and Kitzinger 1993. For a historical look at the emergence of "heterosexuality," see Katz 1990.
8. As Hewitt 1989 points out, "social and personal identity are fundamentally different, and in some sense opposite modes of personal organization." While one is always conscious of oneself as an individual, as a separate person, "social identity becomes something of which the individual is conscious only when it is somewhat problematic" (17).
9. Despite the ostensible sameness of two women in love, differences among women were a salient part of many relationships. Butch-femme role identification, sexual orientation, class, race, and ethnicity were all pervasive differences that were eroticized in lesbian relationships. At the same time, lesbian relationships tended to entail varying degrees of merger, as individual differences were muted and partners became similar to one another in various respects. Difference and sameness could each be seen as pleasurable or threatening, depending upon the particular experience of the individuals involved.

REFERENCES

Chodorow, Nancy. 1994. *Feminities, Masculinities, Sexualities: Freud and Beyond.* Lexington: University Press of Kentucky.

Ebaugh, Helen Rose Fuchs. 1988. *Becoming an Ex: The Process of Role Exit.* Chicago: University of Chicago Press.

Golden, Carla. 1987. "Diversity and Variability in Women's Sexual Identities." In *Lesbian Psychologies: Explorations and Challenges,* ed. Boston Lesbian Psychologies Collective. Urbana: University of Illinois Press.

Hewitt, John P. 1989. *Dilemmas of the American Self.* Philadelphia: Temple University Press.

Katz, Jonathan. 1990. "The Invention of Heterosexuality," *Socialist Review* 20(1): 7–34.

Kinsey, Alfred, Wardell Pomeroy, and Clyde Martin. 1948. *Sexual Behavior in the Human Male.* Philadelphia: Saunders.

Kinsey, Alfred, et al. 1953. *Sexual Behavior in the Human Female.* Philadelphia: Saunders.

Schulman, Sarah. 1990. *People in Trouble.* New York: Plume Books.

Segal, Lynne. 1994. *Straight Sex: Rethinking the Politics of Pleasure.* Berkeley: University of California Press.

Wilkinson, Sue, and Celia Kitzinger, eds. 1993. *Heterosexuality: A Feminism and Psychology Reader.* Newbury Park, Calif.: Sage.

DISCUSSION QUESTIONS

1. Compare and contrast the essentialist view of ex-lesbians as fakers to the social constructionists' view of them as turncoats.

2. On the basis of what you have read, do you think the essentialist or the social constructionist account of lesbianism is more convincing?

SOCIAL ORGANIZATIONS

Students on hundreds of campuses gather regularly to write letters to government officials from places around the globe on behalf of someone whom they think has been jailed unjustly, tortured, and/or faces the threat of execution. They do so as members of Amnesty International, a human rights organization that was once the recipient of the Nobel Peace Prize. Based in London, AI has formal operations in many countries and volunteer chapters in even more. At the volunteer member level, such as the campus chapters of AI, the organization appears quite informal, with students and faculty determining their respective levels of involvement and the issues to which they choose to devote themselves. At another level, it is a large formal or bureaucratic organization, characterized by precisely defined operating rules and regulations, an emphasis on written rather than oral communication, a hierarchical chain of command, a highly developed division of labor with considerable job specialization and technical expertise, and (in spite of the fact that the purpose of the organization is saving flesh-and-blood humans from oftentimes horrific abuse) a certain level of impersonality, wherein individuals are treated as cases. AI is but one example of a certain type of organization: the large formal organization, created to accomplish a particular goal or task in an efficient and effective manner.

Another type of organization is smaller, more intimate, and less instrumental. These are informal organizations, groups that rely primarily on personal relationships and tend to be enduring. What are known as primary groups—family, friends, and neighbors—are key examples of this type of organization. They are not bureaucratic, and thus don't have a vertical ranking of positions, a clearly defined division of labor, or formal operational procedures. Informal organizations rely on talk rather than written communication.

Both formal and informal organizations constitute major areas of interest for sociologists. Without devaluing the importance of informal organizations, beginning with Max Weber, sociologists have been convinced that modern society is different from traditional society because of its increased reliance on formal organizations. Weber described this process as bureaucratization. He was highly critical of bureaucracies for their undermining of individual freedom and creativity, referring to them as "iron cages." At the same time, he thought that bureaucracies were here to stay. This was due to the fact that compared to the alternatives, they constituted the most rational and efficient form of social organization possible, and thus were essential to the working of industrial society.

From Weber's original analyses a substantial body of scholarship has subsequently been produced. Taken as a whole, it attempts to examine the manner in which the very structure of these organizations influences the ways objectives are defined, plans are formulated for achieving those objectives, and strategies are devised to handle problems when they arise. The purpose of this research is to describe and analyze the bureaucratic worldview, treating it as different from the worldviews outside such organizations. At the same time, other scholars have found that people sometimes import perspectives from outside these organizations and as such they introduce a kind of ad hoc behavior not unlike the behavior one typically finds in informal organizations. A flavor of these various research foci can be found in this section's four essays.

The *Challenger* Disaster: Lessons Learned

Diane Vaughan

The Challenger *disaster called into question the idea promoted for years by NASA that space flights were routine, and that the risks were sufficiently contained that it was reasonable to send a school teacher on a flight watched by millions of the nation's schoolchildren. For 10 years after this tragedy, Diane Vaughan poured over tens of thousands of documents pertaining to the* Challenger *in an attempt to understand what went wrong and why. Not content with the report of the Presidential Commission which laid the blame on the decisions of middle managers, Vaughan outlines a thesis that refocuses the issue at the level of the cultural and structural factors within which the mistakes that led up to the disaster can be understood.*

The sorrow of mistakes is sometimes very diffuse and sometimes very pointed. It is sometimes the sorrow of failed action and sometimes the sorrow of failed conduct. The sorrow of mistakes has been expressed as *the too-lateness of human understanding* as it lies along the continuum of time, and as a wish that it might have been different both then and now.

Marianne A. Paget, *The Unity of Mistakes*

In *American Technological Sublime,* David Nye argues that the American reverence for technology is such that we have invested technological masterworks with transcendent, near-religious significance.[1] Almost at its inception, NASA's space program became a cultural icon. For many citizens, it represented and glorified American enterprise, cutting-edge technology and science, pioneering adventurism, and national and international power. Each awesome space achievement was a celebration of technological advance that reaffirmed the spiritual and moral values that supposedly underlay it. Keeping our eyes on the skies got us through hard times. The achievements of the space program offered hope during the tumultuous, cruel 1960s and 1970s, as the country was torn by racial conflict, the assassinations of John Kennedy, Martin Luther King, Jr., and Robert Kennedy, protests against the Vietnam war and for the rights of women and minorities, Watergate. In an era of despair for heroes lost, silver-suited astronauts were endowed with heroic stature.

During the 1980s, the symbolic meaning of NASA and its programs sustained the myth of American superiority through times of urban unrest, homelessness, violent crime, drug wars, and the decline of the cities, education, and international power. But skepticism and opposition grew. Spending money for a space station to explore other planets when the needs of this one were great seemed ludicrous. Even for NASA supporters, some of the excitement waned. Apparently, the public bought the definition of routine space flight that was conveyed when the Space Shuttle was declared operational by top NASA administrators and the White House in 1982. Daily work routines were no longer disrupted for space missions as they had been earlier in NASA history, when the first astronauts orbited the earth and set foot on the moon. This change did not substantially alter the symbolic meaning of the space agency and its programs: every vehicle launched still carried the extra weight of the American Dream going awry. But for many citizens, shuttle launches had become routine and taken-for-granted.

Perhaps more than any mission for years, the *Challenger* mission captured the attention of the public. Diverse in race, sex, ethnicity, and religion, the *Challenger* crew was a symbolic reminder that the all-too-elusive possibilities of equal opportunity and unity from diversity could still be attained. Christa McAuliffe was included to give this mission symbolic meaning of another sort. As a woman and professional teacher, she was chosen not because children learned more about space from a teacher orbiting the earth, but because her presence reinforced NASA's message that Space Shuttle flight was routine and the President Reagan image as proeducation at a time when education funds were being slashed. Symbolism notwithstanding, NASA believers, skeptics, and opponents alike developed a personal interest in this mission. Because Christa McAuliffe was among the crew, the media informed us not only of their names, but about their families and their histories. We witnessed their training. When the disaster occurred, we knew these astronauts. Americans had to come to grips with both personal and symbolic loss: the deaths of the astronauts and the anguish of their families as well as the destruction of all the space program represented.

We needed an explanation. The immediate appointment of a Presidential Commission, headed by a politician, to investigate the tragedy underscored the very real political and economic consequences of this event. This action, which usurped and upstaged the oversight responsibility of the House Committee on Science and Technology, stands in stark contrast to reaction to the deaths of three astronauts in the 1967 Apollo launch pad fire, after which NASA conducted its own investigation. In 1967, NASA was a powerful agency with a powerful leader able to stave off an outside inquiry. In 1986, a weakened NASA, essentially leaderless, could not. A Presidential Commission was appointed because of the greater visibility and public attention this event attracted. Christa McAuliffe made this mission special. An explanation had to be found for the deaths of the *Challenger* crew and corrective actions implemented in order to restore the legitimacy of NASA and guarantee the survival of the space program.

In moving language, the reports of both the Presidential Commission and the House Committee emphasized the need to get the program going again. The Commission wrote: "Each member of the Commission shared the pain and anguish the nation felt at the loss of seven brave Americans in the *Challenger* accident on January 28, 1986. The nation's task now is to move ahead to return to safe space flight and to its recognized position of leadership in space. There could be no more fitting tribute to the *Challenger* crew than to do so."[2] The House Committee wrote: "We are at a watershed in NASA's history and the Nation's space program. NASA's 28-year existence represents its infancy. We must use the knowledge and experience from this time to insure a strong future for NASA and the US space program throughout the 21st century. . . . Though we grieve at the loss of the *Challenger* crew, we do not believe that their sacrifice was in vain. They would not want us to stop reaching into the unknown. Instead, they would want us to learn from our mistakes, correct any problems that have been identified, and then once again reach out to expand the boundaries of our experience in living and working in outer space."[3]

To their great credit, both investigations made it clear that the disaster was not merely a technical failure; the NASA organization was implicated. Moreover, both were critical of the economic and political environment that were the structural origins of disaster. But the distillation of the complex and far-reaching findings of these two official investigations in more popular accounts focused public attention—and blame—on the middle managers who made the decisions and allegedly concealed technical problems from top administrators. This focus created the impression that the outcome could have been different had middle managers behaved differently. This historically accepted explanation not only masked the complex structural causes of the disaster, it obscured the fact that individual responsibility spanned hierarchical levels. First, it deflected attention from the powerful elites, far removed from the hands-on risk assessment process, who made decisions and took actions that compromised both the shuttle design and the environment of technical decision making for work groups throughout the

NASA-contractor system. Congress and the White House established goals and made resource decisions that transformed the R&D space agency into a quasi-competitive business operation, complete with repeating production cycles, deadlines, and cost and efficiency goals. While both the Presidential Commission and the House Committee emphasized pressure as a contributing cause of the tragedy, only the House Committee located political elites outside the space agency as the source: "The Committee, the Congress, and the Administration have played a contributing role in creating this pressure. Congressional and Administration policy and posture indicated that a reliable flight schedule with internationally competitive flight costs was a near-term objective."[4]

Second, the conventional explanation disguised NASA's own top administrators' contribution to the tragedy. In order to maintain their own power and that of their threatened institution, they made bargains that altered the organization's goals, structure, and culture. These changes had enormous repercussions. They altered the consciousness and actions of technical decision makers, ultimately affecting the *Challenger* launch deliberations. Also, NASA top administrators responded to an environment of scarcity by promulgating the myth of routine, operational space flight. Perpetuating that myth, they established a policy that allowed nonastronauts on shuttle missions. Neither official investigation pursued the question of who actually decided that a teacher should fly on the *Challenger* mission. By limiting their agenda to the technical failure and decision making about the technology, the investigations effectively prevented the NASA–White House negotiations that culminated in the Teacher in Space mission from becoming a matter of public concern.

Finally, the focus after the disaster on managerial wrongdoing also removed from the public spotlight the difficulty of making engineering decisions about the shuttle technology. Although both official investigations repeatedly

and publicly emphasized that the technology was developmental, not operational, the attention to managers marginalized the role of skilled working people, daily engineering routine, and the technology. Thus, the public remained largely ignorant of the difficulty of decision making about a joint that was invisible once the segments were stacked, the complexity of the sealing dynamics, and the inability of known tests to replicate the environmental forces on the booster joints during a mission. Little publicity was given the conclusion shared by the Presidental Commission and the House Committee on Science and Technology that no one at NASA nor Thiokol fully understood the operation of the joint prior to the accident.[5] The public did not learn that competent technical experts doing the risk assessments, following rules and using all the usual precautions, made a mistake.

It was, as Presidential Commission member Astronaut Neil Armstrong remarked, "a tender design."[6] After the tragedy, Solid Rocket Booster work group members continued to learn about the technology. Previously convinced that they had understood the joint, now they were forced to agree that they had not. It was not just temperature effects that they did not understand. The failure analysis showed that other factors, previously not taken into account, had contributed to the technical failure: the potential for ice in the joint, putty behavior, and effects of violent wind shear.[7] As the postdisaster analysis taught them more and more, explanations about the technical cause changed. They learned that the O-rings had been badly burned, but the charred material had sealed the joint, avoiding a launch pad debacle. The seal might have held had not unpredicted, unprecedented wind shear buffeted the vehicle, dislodging the material and allowing the hot gases to penetrate the joint. More testing was done. They discovered that overcompression of the O-rings was a contributing cause.[8] Prior to STS 51-L, they had worried about undercompression, shimming the joints to increase it. The outside referee tests, authorized in 1985 to settle the seven-year dispute between Thiokol and Marshall engineers about the size of the gap during joint rotation, were completed. The referee testing found a gap size even smaller than Thiokol's measurement, affirming Thiokol's assertion that the joint was fully redundant throughout the ignition transient, and therefore the design ought to have remained in the C 1R category.[9]

Most serious was the discovery that misunderstanding about the most critical technical rule used had contributed to a flawed decision. The temperature specifications had been misread, misinterpreted, and misused by both Thiokol and Marshall for years. The 31°F–99°F ambient temperature requirement for launching the entire shuttle system was created early in the program by other engineers. In a palpable demonstration of structural secrecy, many teleconference participants had jobs that did not require them to know Cape launch requirements and so were unaware that this temperature specification existed.[10] More profoundly disturbing, however, was that for Mulloy, Hardy, and many others who used it regularly in launch decision making at the Cape, this launch decision rule had become dissociated from its creators and the engineering process behind its creation. They had followed it repeatedly, taking for granted the interpretative work that other engineers had done.[11] They did not know that Thiokol had not tested the boosters to the 31°F lower limit.[12] Instead, Thiokol (with NASA engineering oversight) had established the limit using the military temperature specification for Viton O-rings.[13] Pondering the 31°F lower limit, which he and others believed was a legitimate decision rule on the eve of the launch, Mulloy later testified, "I was referencing a non-existent data base."[14] Worse, a close reading of that complex original temperature document showed that launching based on ambient temperature alone was wrong: the temperature of the boosters had to be calculated each time, taking into account

heat from the sun and proximity to the External Tank.[15] None of the teleconference participants understood that prior to the tragedy.

When asked why all the factors influencing joint behavior were not known prior to STS 51-L, Mulloy responded: "I guess it is difficult for me to answer this way, but I was not smart enough to know it before hand. The people, Morton Thiokol and the [S&E] engineers that we have, had been looking at this problem over the last 7 to 8 years. They were looking at the observations and making judgments and making recommendations to continue flying, based on those data, and they were not smart enough to recommend the additional testing, and the people who reviewed that at levels above me were not smart enough to say that we need to do more than what we are doing. It is tough for me to say that, but I don't know any other way in hindsight."[16]

All causal explanations have implications for control. The benefit of explanations that locate the immediate cause of organizational failure in individual decision makers is that quick remedies are possible. Responsible individuals can be fired, transferred, or retired. New rules that regulate decision making can be instituted. Having made these changes, the slate is clean. Organizations can go on. In *The Limits of Safety,* Scott Sagan alerts us to the politics of blame.[17] Both for easy public digestion and for NASA's survival, the myth of production-oriented, success-blinded middle managers was the best of all possible worlds. It removed from public scrutiny the contributions to the disaster made by top NASA officials, Congress, and the White House; it minimized awareness of the difficulty of diagnosing the risky technology. Locating blame in the actions of powerful elites was not in NASA's interest. And focusing attention on the fact that, after all this time, the technology still could defy understanding would destroy the NASA-cultivated image of routine, economical spaceflight and with it the Space Shuttle Program. The myth of managerial wrongdoing made the strategy for control straightforward: fix the technology and change the managerial cast of characters, implement decision controls, and proceed with shuttle launches.

Invariably, the politics of blame directs our attention to certain individuals and not others when organizations have failures. Invariably, the accepted explanation is some form of "operator error," isolating in the media spotlight someone responsible for the hands-on work: the captain of the ship, a political functionary, a technician, or middle-level managers.[18] To a great extent, we are unwitting participants because without extraordinary expenditure of time and energy we cannot get beyond appearances. But we are also complicitious, for we bring to our interpretation of public failures a wish to blame, a penchant for psychological explanations, an inability to identify the structural and cultural causes, and a need for a straightforward, simple answer that can be quickly grasped. But the answer is seldom simple. Even when our hindsight is clear and we acknowledge the players omitted from the media spotlight, as long as we see organizational failures as the result of individual actions our strategies for control will be ineffective, and dangerously so. Consequently, it becomes important to examine the lessons we can draw from the *Challenger* tragedy.

Perhaps the most obvious lesson is about the manufacture of news and the social construction of history in an age when most people are distanced from events and depend on published accounts for information. Even when incredible resources are brought to bear on understanding a public failure involving an organization, the explanation is likely to be more tangled and complex than it appears. Both the consumers and producers of information about public events should beware of the retrospective fallacy.[19] Retrospection corrects history, altering the past to make it consistent with the present, implying that errors should have been anticipated. Understanding organizational failure depends on systematic research that avoids the ret-rospective fallacy by going beyond secondary sources and summaries, relying instead on personal expertise based on original sources that reveal all the complexity, the culture of the task environment, and the meanings of actions to insiders at the time.

Beyond this general caveat are many lessons from the case itself. The point of this book is to provide a revisionist history of this event and, at the same time, to explain it. That done, we now consider what else it teaches us. Anthropologist Clifford Geertz reminds us that having gained access to an unfamiliar universe, put ourselves in touch with the lives of strangers, and considered what the knowledge thus attained tells us about that society, cultural analysts must extrapolate the significance for social life as such, drawing "large conclusions from small, but very densely textured facts."[20] Embedded in the *Challenger* case are general lessons, both theoretical and practical. In order better to explore them, I first will bring into sharp focus the causes of the tragedy. I then consider what the case teaches us about science, technology, and risk; decision making in organizations; and organizational deviance and misconduct. Finally, I demonstrate the significance of the new territory it introduces: the normalization of deviance and its implications for mistake, mishap, and disaster.

THE SOCIAL ORGANIZATION OF A MISTAKE

The *Challenger* disaster was an accident, the result of a mistake. What is important to remember from this case is not that individuals in organizations make mistakes, but that mistakes themselves are socially organized and systematically produced. Contradicting the rational choice theory behind the hypothesis of managers as amoral calculators, the tragedy had systemic origins that transcended individuals, organization, time, and geography. Its sources were neither extraordinary nor necessarily peculiar to NASA, as the amoral calculator hypothesis would lead us to believe. Instead, its origins were in routine and taken-for-granted aspects of organizational life that created a way of seeing that was simultaneously a way of not seeing. The normalization of deviant joint performance is the answer. Why did NASA continue to launch shuttles prior to 1986 with a design that was not performing as predicted? Why was the *Challenger* launched over the objections of engineers? The salient environmental condition was NASA's institutional history of competition and scarcity. We want to know how it affected decision making. The normalization of deviance was the outcome of three social forces: the production of culture in the SRB work group, the culture of production, and structural secrecy. What is important about these three elements is that each, taken alone, is insufficient as an explanation. Combined, they constitute a nascent theory of the normalization of deviance in organizations.

Production of Culture In the history of decision making, we saw a decision sequence whose repetition indicated the development of a work group culture. The decision-making process itself was a key factor in the normalization of technical deviation. As the Level III and IV Marshall and Thiokol managers and engineers assigned to work on the SRB joints interacted about booster joint performance, they developed norms, values, and procedures that constituted a scientific paradigm. That paradigm supported a belief that was central to their worldview: the belief in redundancy. It developed incrementally, the product of learning by doing. It was based on operating standards consisting of numerous ad hoc judgments and assumptions that they developed in daily engineering practice. Each time a signal of potential danger occurred, it challenged the scientific paradigm and the cultural construction of risk that was its product. Each time, the work group analyzed the new information, weighing it against their definition of the situation and the scientific paradigm that un-

derlay it. Each time they elaborated the original paradigm, based on tests and mathematical models that advanced their understanding, coming forward with engineering determinations of acceptable risk and recommendations to fly.

The technology mattered. An unprecedented joint design and the uncertainty that accompanied it were fundamental to the production of the work group culture. More accurately, it was the repeated cycles of uncertainty/certainty that were fundamental. Signals of potential danger sent the working engineers scrambling to unravel the evidence and compare tests and flight experience. Prior to each launch, uncertainty had to be converted to certainty—and it was. But it was always temporary, for indubitably new information surfaced from tests or flight experience that was again a signal of potential danger, challenging the prevailing construction of risk and calling for renegotiation. The five-step decision sequence would again follow. With no formal rules to guide them initially about how to respond to the deviant performance of the SRB joints, the SRB work group evolved a set of solutions to a problem they faced in common: norms, beliefs, and procedures relevant to their specific task. Initially without guidelines, the work group evolved an unobtrusive normative structure that was reinforced over time and did, in fact, guide. A fundamental sociological notion is that choice creates structure, which in turn feeds back, influencing choice. In the history of decision making about the SRBs, we see this principle at work, as work group participants created a cultural construction of risk that, once created, influenced subsequent choices.

The formal aspects of their decision making stabilized their definition of the situation. Of course, using engineering principles and practice to convert uncertainty to certainty was their job. But in addition, each time a launch recommendation was required, diverse opinions had to be pulled together into a collective public position. Creating documents that solidified the group stance committed group members to that stance. Their technical analysis and corrective actions were then subjected to the often painfully adversarial scrutiny of FRR. The challenges raised in FRR drove them back to the labs for further work. Engineering positions that withstood the challenges, as the risk assessments of the SRB joints did, gained in stability primarily because of the engineering analysis behind them, but also because of social affirmation: attacked and defended in a public forum, they received official certification. The capstone, of course, was the feedback from the postflight engineering analysis that showed that their prelaunch corrective actions and performance predictions in response to the most recent anomaly had been correct. Alone, however, the social affirmation and commitment generated as work group decisions were processed are insufficient to explain the normalization of deviance. The culture of production and structural secrecy were environmental and organizational contingencies that caused the work group culture to persist.

Culture of Production Cultural beliefs in the environment affirmed the work group's definition of the situation, informing their sensemaking in common directions. These cultural scripts were part of the worldview that work group participants brought to decision making, providing taken-for-granted sets of invisible rules about how to act in the situations that they faced. Their actions conformed to the culture of production in which they worked; thus, they were acceptable and not deviant in that context. As trained engineers, the situations they faced were consistent with what they understood to be normal technology in large-scale technical systems. Interpretive flexibility, disagreement, crafted decision rules, recurring anomalies, the maxim "Change is bad," and the discipline and methods of scientific positivism all were aspects of the engineering worldview that endowed their decision making with legitimacy. Simi-

larly, their actions conformed to the culture of a profession customarily located in bureaucratic technical production systems. Throughout the history of decision making, the work group's behavior demonstrated a belief in the legitimacy of bureaucratic authority relations and conformity to rules as well as the taken-for-granted nature of cost, schedule, and safety satisficing.

What made this professional culture so powerful as a legitimating force was its nested quality: it was reproduced in the NASA organization and Marshall Space Flight Center, reinforcing the normalcy of their decisions. The workplace was dominated by three cultural imperatives: the original technical culture, bureaucratic accountability, and political accountability. We saw how NASA's environment changed, so that the original technical culture struggled to survive amid institutionalized production concerns and bureaupathology. We saw how the performance pressure at Marshall mandated conformity to all three cultural imperatives, and that the work group did, in fact, conform to all three. Not only did the correspondence of their actions with these cultural scripts normalize their actions, in their view, but their *awareness* of their conformity had a separate effect. The fact that they did everything they were supposed to do reinforced the technical choices they made. For these technical experts at the bottom of the launch decision chain, conformity was the source of the NASA "can do" attitude.

Structural Secrecy To understand why the SRB work group's construction of risk persisted, a final factor is necessary. The culture of production existed for all work groups in the NASA-contractor system. Yet many times work groups did not normalize signals of potential danger: the outcome was a decision of unacceptable risk. Why, in this case, did a work group routinely normalize the technical deviation? Structural secrecy not only prevented a reversal of the scientific paradigm, it perpetuated their view that the O-rings were an acceptable risk: patterns of information, organizational structure, processes, and transactions, and the structure of regulatory relations contributed to a collective organizational construction of risk.

Signals of potential danger were embedded in patterns of information that affected the work group's definition of the situation. Signals lost their salience as a result of the risk assessment process. Signals were mixed: information indicating trouble was interspersed with and/or followed by information signaling that all was well. Signals were weak: the initial threat posed by an anomaly was neutralized as its consequences for performance were measured and understood. Signals were routine: recurring anomalies that were within predictions assured work group participants that they understood the joint and that it was safe to fly. As the work group conveyed information up the hierarchy, organizational structure, processes, and transactions perpetuated the construction of risk created in the work group. Many mechanisms were built into the process so that people outside the work group could (and did) challenge the group's risk assessment. Nonetheless, limiting informational dependencies remained that restricted challenges. The ability of others to intervene, altering the work group's paradigmatic worldview, was inhibited by systematic censorship of information: its patterned reduction due to official organizational practices, specialization, and the tendency of top decision makers to rely on signals when unable to discriminate in decision-making situations.

Finally, structural secrecy originating in the structure of regulatory relationships interfered with safety regulators' capability to contradict the work group's cultural construction of risk. Autonomy and interdependence were its sources. Even Safety, Reliability, & Quality Assurance, the one regulatory unit with personnel who worked closely with the NASA and Thiokol engineers on a daily basis, did not challenge the work group's definition of the situation. Their job was to review, not to produce,

data and conduct tests as an independent check. Dependent on the work group for information and its interpretation, they became enculturated. They reviewed the engineering analysis and agreed. Similarly situated in the culture of production and exposed to the engineering analysis, incremental decision making, patterns of information, decision streams, commitment process, and paradigm development, they also normalized joint performance that deviated from expectations.

On the eve of the *Challenger* launch, the production of culture, the culture of production, and structural secrecy combined in epitome of the history of decision making. The teleconference was a microcosm through which we watched these patterns of the past reproduced in a single, dynamic exchange. In a situation of perhaps unparalleled uncertainty for those assembled, all participants' behavior was scripted in advance by the triumvirate of cultural imperatives that shaped their previous choices. The preexisting scientific paradigm and its dominant ideology, the belief in redundancy, formed the all-important frame of reference for the information that was presented. This decision frame was neither latent nor arbitrary, but manifest and in keeping with the tenets of the original technical culture: the Acceptable Risk Process required that all new information be weighed against the preexisting technical rationale for flying with a component. The original technical culture also was manifest in the selection of people from various specializations to attend and in the stringent FRR standards for adversarial challenges and solid, science-based, engineering analyses.

The engineering discussion was undermined by structural secrecy at the outset because participants were in three locations. As the teleconference got underway, the original technical culture, bureaucratic accountability, and political accountability exacerbated this structural secrecy by affecting both the production and exchange of information. Instead of an irrefutable signal that matched the engineers' sense of "lying down in the bucket," the result was weak and missing signals incapable of altering the scientific paradigm supporting the belief in acceptable risk. The charts the Thiokol engineers prepared contained patterns of information that consisted of mixed, weak, and routine signals, thus the engineering argument failed because it did not meet the standards of scientific excellence prescribed by the original technical culture. In cultural terms, the engineering rationale for delay was a weak signal. Bureaucratic and political accountability were responsible for missing signals. Verbal opposition was undermined because all participants conformed to common understandings about talk and bureaucratic accountability in FRR that silenced people. Political accountability, and the production pressure that was its result, had its impact on both the production of information and its exchange. Again guided by unspoken shared understandings, the Thiokol engineers set a time limit for their preparations, possibly sabotaging their own opportunity to put together an engineering presentation capable of reversing the scientific paradigm. And managers, themselves responsible for bureaucratic, political, and technical accountability, experienced performance pressure in all three areas that resulted in actions that silenced people. The scientific paradigm prevailed.

The historically accepted explanation of the launch that has production goals dominating managerial actions, resulting in rule violations and individual wrongdoing, gives way to a complex imagery of bounded rationality exacerbated by additional environmental and organizational contingencies. What is compelling is how the interweaving of structure, process, and layered cultures that affected all participants' behavior at a subtle, prerational level combined to produce the outcome. Although the discussion itself was adversarial, in keeping with the tradition of FRR, the outcome was a cooperative endeavor: all participants followed agreed-upon, taken-for-

granted understandings that dictated how they were to proceed. Like the history of decision making, the eve of the launch was characterized by conformity, not deviance. Socially organized and history-dependent, it is unlikely that the decision they reached could have been otherwise, given the multilayered cultures to which they all belonged.

Having made explicit the social organization of mistake that resulted in the *Challenger* launch decision and the theory of the normalization of deviance that it generates, we turn to the lessons the case holds about science, technology, and risk; decision making in organizations; and organizational deviance and misconduct.

NOTES

1. David E. Nye, *American Technological Sublime* (Cambridge: MIT Press, 1994).
2. Presidential Commission, *Report* 1:ii.
3. U.S. Congress, House, *Investigation: Report,* 7.
4. Ibid., 3.
5. Presidential Commission, *Report* 1:148; 2:117; U.S. Congress, House, *Investigation: Report,* 4.
6. Russell, interview transcript, 19 March 1986, 60.
7. Presidential Commission, *Report* 1:60–66; U.S. Congress, House, *Investigation: Hearings* 1:341.
8. U.S. Congress, House, *Investigation: Hearings* 1:445.
9. Presidential Commission, *Report* 1:140; U.S. Congress, House, *Investigation: Hearings* 1:517; McIntosh, interview transcript, 2 April 1986, 69.
10. Presidential Commission, *Report* 4:723.
11. Hawkins, "Use of Legal Discretion," 35.
12. Presidential Commission, *Report* 2:K3.
13. U.S. Congress, House, *Investigation: Hearings* 1:447–50.
14. Ibid., 449.
15. Wear, personal interview, 2 June 1992; see, e.g., U.S. Congress, House, *Investigation: Hearings* 1:405, 447–48, 528–29, 534–37.
16. U.S. Congress, House, *Investigation: Hearings* 1:445.
17. Scott D. Sagan, *The Limits of Safety: Organizations, Accidents, and Nuclear Weapons* (Princeton, N.J.: Princeton University Press 1993), 278.

18. See also Perrow, "The President's Commission and the Normal Accident."
19. Starbuck and Milliken, "Executives' Perceptual Filters."
20. Geertz, *Interpretation of Cultures,* 27–28.

REFERENCES

Geertz, Clifford. *The Interpretation of Cultures.* New York: Basic Books, 1973.

Hawkins, Keith. ed. *The Uses of Discretion.* Oxford: Clarendon, 1992.

Nye, David E. *American Technological Sublime.* Cambridge: MIT Press, 1994.

Paget, Marianne A. *The Unity of Mistakes,* Philadelphia: Temple University Press, 1988.

Perrow, Charles. "The President's Commission and the Normal Accident." In *The Accident at Three Mile Island: The Human Dimensions.* Boulder, Colo.: Westview Press, 1981.

Presidential Commission on the Space Shuttle *Challenger* Accident. *Report to the President by the Presidential Commission on the Space Shuttle Challenger Accident,* 5 vols. Washington, D.C.: Government Printing Office, 1986.

Sagan, Scott D. *The Limits of Safety: Organizations, Accidents, and Nuclear Weapons.* Princeton, N.J.: Princeton University Press, 1993.

Starbuck, William H., and Frances J. Milliken. "Executives' Perceptual Filters: What They Notice and How They Make Sense." In *The Executive Effect,* ed. Donald C. Hambrick. Greenwich, Conn.: JAI, 1988.

U.S. Congress. House. Committee on Science and Astronautics. *Hearings on H.R. 4450, H.R. 6470 (Superseded by H.R. 10340).* 90th Cong., 1st sess., 1967.

———*Investigation of the Challenger Accident: Hearings,* 2 vols. Washington, D.C.: Government Printing Office, 1986.

DISCUSSION QUESTIONS

1. Why did NASA want to convey the impression that space flight had become routine? What was the political climate that served to reinforce this belief?
2. In shifting the focus of the causes of the disaster from individuals to organizations, among the factors Vaughan discusses is what she terms "structural secrecy." What does she mean by this term, and what role did it play in the *Challenger* disaster?

READING 28

The Moral Ethos of Bureaucracy

Robert Jackall

Robert Jackall offers a portrait of the moral codes of large-scale bureaucratic organizations based on the results of participant observation research into Chemical Company, a pseudonym for a branch of a large corporate conglomerate. His key point is that bureaucracy, the form of large-scale modern organization first analyzed by Max Weber and depicted in his potent metaphor as the "iron cage," shapes the moral ethos of the organization. It does so by suspending conventional moral codes and making use of a variety of specific and "flexible" moralities that constitute "moral mazes" for the people employed in such organizations. Jackall discusses the central role of managers and the need of subordinates to align themselves strategically with managers if their careers are to flourish. He then discusses what happens when someone—a "whistle-blower"—attempts to import conventional morality into the bureaucracy.

Business ethics is rapidly becoming big business. The last decade has seen the publication of a great number of books and articles on ethical issues in business,[1] the emergence of several centers and institutes either wholly or partly dedicated to the subject,[2] the proliferation of business ethics courses in college and business school curricula,[3] and, in some corporations, the development of seminars on ethics for executives. This ground swell of attention to ethical issues in business continues a historic tradition dating at least to the turn of this century, when the big corporation began its ascendency in our society.[4] The recent upsurge has been, of course, a boon to moral philosophers, a precariously positioned occupational group. With the titles of "ethicist" or even "ethician," they have applied their considerable mental acumen to analyzing the conundrums of the hurly-burly worlds of commerce and industry. In doing so they have extended the much longer tradition of moral casuistry in quite new directions.[5] Unfortunately, most of this analysis has been of hypothetical cases, or real-life cases abstracted from their intricate organizational contexts, or of the well-publicized corporate scandals in recent years. There has been little detailed analysis of the day-to-day structure and meaning of work in business or of how the conditions of that work shape moral consciousness.[6]

In particular, there has been among ethicists little appreciation of how bureaucracy, the dominant organizational form of our epoch, shapes the very rhythm and tempo of our society and indeed, to borrow Emil Lederer's phrase, its very sociopsychic constitution.[7] The thorough bureaucratization of our society in the last century, beginning with industry and commerce, extending later to government, and now reaching every nook and cranny of the occupational structure, has profoundly reshaped our class system, shredded and reknit whole communities in new patterns, and made individual life-chances largely dependent on bureaucratically constructed careers. It has also, as I have argued elsewhere, swept away older ethics of behavior and ways of seeing and evaluating social reality and its moral issues.[8] A focus on business ethics without an analysis of how bureaucracy shapes those ethics is somewhat like producing *Hamlet* without the role of the Prince of Denmark.

MANAGERS

Corporate managers are the quintessential bureaucratic work group in our bureaucratic society. They not only fashion bureaucratic rules but they are also bound by them. Typically, they are not only *in* big organizations; because their ad-

ministrative expertise constitutes their livelihood, they are also *of* the organization. They need maintain no pretenses of allegiances to civil service codes nor to an ethic of public service. Their allegiances are to the principle of organization itself and to the market, itself bureaucratically organized. Their conservative public and personal style and conventional demeanor belie their thoroughgoing transforming role in our society. They are, rather, the principal carriers of the bureaucratic ethos in our era. Their pivotal institutional position not only gives their decisions great reach but also links them to other important elites; as a result, their occupational ethics set both the framework and the vocabularies of discourse for a great many public issues in our society. In this essay, I want to examine how the social and political context of managerial work shapes managers' moral rules-in-use and the way they come to see the world. To do this, I will discuss materials gathered during field work in several large corporations.[9]

"What is right in the corporation," a former vice president of a large company says, "is not what is right in a man's home or in his church. What is right in the corporation is what the guy above you wants from you. That's what morality is in the corporation." The hierarchical authority structure central to bureaucracy comes to dominate the way managers think about their world and about themselves. Managers do not see or experience authority in any abstract way; rather, authority is embodied in their personal relationships with their immediate bosses and in their perceptions of similar links between other managers up and down the hierarchy. When managers describe their work to an outsider, they first say: "I work for Bill James" or "I report to Harry Mills" of "I'm in Joe Bell's group," and only then proceed to describe their official functions. Such a personalized statement of authority relationships exactly reflects the way authority is structured, exercised, and experienced in corporate hierarchies.

American businesses, typically, both centralize and decentralize authority; responsibility for reaching objectives—say, profit targets—is pushed as far down the ladder as possible, while the basic direction of the corporation is set from the top. In the large corporations that I studied, this results in a structure where there are independent divisions or companies, each headed by its own president with his own staff and line hierarchy, all monitored by a central corporate staff that reports directly to the chief executive officer (CEO) of the whole corporation. The system is linked together by an intricate series of "commitments" to specific objectives; each subordinate pledges the accomplishment of certain goals to his own boss, who gathers up the commitments of all his subordinates and makes his own commitment to his boss, and so on up the ladder. Each president of each division or company finally makes his own commitment to the CEO based on the promises of his vice-presidents. The CEO locks the entire system into place not only symbolically but also because he has the power to determine whether or not these commitments have been satisfactorily met. In practice, of course, the CEO frames and paces the whole process by nearly always applying pressure for higher goals and greater commitments; the decentralized structure, in fact, actually increases the CEO's centralized power.

This interlocking series of commitments shapes not only a pyramid of promises but also an intricate system of fealty between bosses and subordinates. Bosses depend on subordinates for realistic estimates of goals to avoid "getting on the hook" for commitments that cannot be met and for crucial information to avoid being "blindsided," especially in public. They extend to subordinates, in return, a measure of protection and to a favored few the promise of promotion when and if their own fortunes improve. In this sense the commitment system also constitutes a series of conspiracies between bosses and subordinates. Bosses are, of course, subordinates to still other bosses; thus, the personal

links and ties of reciprocal obligation extend from the bottom of the managerial ladder right up to the chief executive officer. Overlaying and intertwined with this formal monocratic system of authority are patron-client relationships. Patrons are usually powerful figures in the higher echelons of management. Depending on one's location in the hierarchy, one's patron might be one's boss. If, however, one is farther down the ladder, one's patron can be several levels higher up the chain of command. In such cases, one is still bound by the immediate formal authority and fealty patterns of one's position, but one also acquires new—though more ambiguous fealty relationships with one's highest ranking patron.

This system of fealty, of patrimony, thus meshes intimately with formal bureaucratic authority. It is important to note that a managers' fealty is *not* to offices as such, as Weber argued in contrasting bureaucracy with feudalism, but to persons who hold offices. This seems to be a peculiar characteristic of business hierarchies, at least in the United States; I do not wish to make a general statement about other, say governmental, bureaucracies, though there is some evidence that similar structures prevail there as well. These fealty relationships in business need not be accompanied by affection or other personal sentiment, though they sometimes are; they do, however, seem to require a degree of personal comfort between boss and subordinate or between patron and client—that is, a meshing of personal styles and the familiarity, predictability, and ease that come from a sharing of taken-for-granted frameworks about how the world works.

Managers draw elaborate cognitive maps to guide them through the thickets of their organizations. Because they see authority in such personal terms, the singular feature of these maps is their biographical emphasis. Managers carry in their heads a thumbnail sketch of the occupational history of virtually every other manager, of their own rank or above, in their particular organization. If a rising star appears below them, they take care to "get a fix" on him, to discover and add to their knowledge all important items about him. Such knowledge begins with the star's occupational expertise but focuses especially on his previous and present reporting relationships, his patrons higher in the organization, his alliances among his peers, and the general estimate of his abilities and prospects. This is not to say that these sketches are accurate or fair; they are, in fact, often based on the flimsiest of evidence. Managers trade sketches of others within their circles and often color the sketches to suit their own purposes. This is one reason why it is crucial for the aspiring young manager to project the right image to the right people who can influence others' sketches of him. Whatever the accuracy of these vocabularies of description, managers' penchant for biographical detail and personal histories is quite remarkable, especially since they evince little inclination for other kinds of history and still less for details in general. Details are usually pushed down to subordinates, and a concern with history, even of one's own organization, constrains the cheerful optimism highly valued in most corporations. Biographical detail is, however, crucial knowledge because managers know that, in the rough-and-tumble politics of the corporate world, individual fates are made and broken not by one's accomplishments but by other people.

Political struggles are central to managerial work and shape managers' consciousness and outlook in fundamental ways. The political structure of organizations is most observable during periods of internal upheaval, a regularly recurring phenomenon in American business. The large conglomerate, of which the Chemical Company that I studied is a part, has been in turmoil for the last few years and presents a focused, indeed sharply drawn, case study of political processes basic to all big corporations. I have taken liberties with dates and with some details.

THE CHEMICAL COMPANY: A CASE STUDY

In 1979 a new CEO took power in the conglomerate. His first move was to restructure the organization into five free-standing companies, each with a different business area—energy, chemicals, metals, electronic equipment, and precision instruments. He dismissed the top leadership of the old organization and personally selected the new presidents for each of the five independent companies. The new presidents each had a relatively free hand in restructuring their organizations, although it seems, in retrospect, that the CEO insisted on certain high-level appointments. What happened in the Chemical Company in this early stage was typical of the pattern in the other companies. The newly appointed president—let's call him Smith—came from a marketing background in a small but important product group in a specialty chemicals division of the old organization. Upon ascending to the presidency, he reached back into his old division, indeed back into his old product group, and systematically elevated his old colleagues, friends, and allies. Powerful managers in a rival process chemical group were demoted, sidetracked, or fired outright. Hundreds of people throughout the whole corporation, a great many in the Chemical Company, lost their jobs in what became known as the "October Revolution" or, in some circles, the "Octoberfest."

The Chemical Company had a good financial year in 1980. Smith consolidated his power and, through his top subordinates, further weeded out or undercut managers with whom he felt uncomfortable. At the end of the year, the mood in the company was buoyant, not only because of high profits but also because of the expectation of massive deregulation and good times for business following President Reagan's election. The day after Reagan's election, by the way, saw managers, in an unusual break from normal decorum, literally dancing in the corridors.

Financial disaster struck the Chemical Company in 1981, however, as it did much of American industry. Smith, elated by his success in 1980 and eager to please the CEO, was, it seems, the victim of his own marketing optimism. He overcommitted himself and his company, and the Chemical Company reached only 60 percent of its profit target for the year. By the end of 1981, then, a sense of gloom and incipient panic pervaded the organization. Rumors of every sort flourished: Smith was on his way out and would take the whole structure of the Chemical Company with him. In fact, it was said, one of the CEO's most trusted troubleshooters, a man who "eats people for breakfast," was gunning for Smith and his job. Smith would survive but would be forced to sacrifice all of his top people, alter his organization's structure, and buckle under to the now vigorous demands of the CEO. The CEO was about to put the whole Chemical Company on the block; at the least, large portions of the company would be sold, wreaking havoc with support staff at corporate headquarters. There were disturbing rumors, too, about growing personal tension and animosity between Smith and the CEO; managers up and down the line knew instinctively that, if the personal relationship between Smith and the CEO were to erode, the inevitable period of blame and retribution for 1981 might engulf everyone, not just well-targeted individuals. Managers mobilized their subordinates to arrange their defenses, tried to cement crucial alliances, and waited. In the meantime, they updated their resumés and responded graciously to the phone calls of headhunters.

The next act of the drama unfolded in February of 1982 with a new reorganization. Smith got rid of his executive vice president—let's call him Brown—who was something of an anomaly in the higher circles of the company. His occupational expertise was in finance, rather than in marketing, like Smith and the rest of Smith's circle. Moreover, although his principal rise had been through the old specialty chemicals division, his original roots in the corporation were in the energy division, where he had been a friend and associate of the man who later rose to the presidency of that company in the 1979 shakeup. This history made Brown suspect, especially when the tension between Smith and the CEO intensified and the presidents of the other companies saw a chance to extend their influence. Brown's strait-laced personal style was also an anomaly amidst the bonhomie that marked the Chemical Company's upper circle. The CEO, himself a financial man, saved Brown, however, and appointed him president of the declining Electronics Company, known by this time as a graveyard—that is, a place with decaying businesses that one buries by selling off. Many managers were amused at Brown's reassignment; despite a nominal promotion, he was being told, they felt, to dig his own grave in an appropriate location. Some were more wary and saw the move as a gambit, in fact as a cover-up by the CEO himself, who had invested heavily in several businesses in Electronics only to have them expire. Brown had not been popular in the Chemical Company, and his departure was greeted, as one manager describes it, "by a lot of people standing on the sidelines, hooting, and hollering and stamping our feet. We never thought we'd see old Brown again." In Brown's place, Smith appointed two executive vice-presidents, one a trusted aide from the old specialty chemicals division and the other an outsider with expertise in selling off commodity businesses—that is, what was left of the old process chemicals division. Blame for 1981 was apportioned to a few general managers, all from that division, and Smith fired them. Other managers felt that not only had Smith reasserted the supremacy of his specialty chemicals alliances, but he had, in addition, bought himself eight months in the process—time enough, perhaps, for the economy to turn around.

As it happened, the economy worsened, and by the fall of 1982, the CEO's pressure on

Smith had increased. Smith's men privately referred to the CEO as a "tinhorn tyrant" and muttered about his "henchmen" being sent to extract information from them to be used against Smith. In addition to demanding that some businesses be sold, others cut back, and costs in general reduced, the CEO wanted Smith to dismantle large sections of his staff, particularly in the environmental protection area. In response to a specific environmental disaster in the late 1970s and to the public outrage about chemical pollution in general, Smith had erected upon his ascendency in 1979 an elaborate and relatively free-roaming environmental staff. He felt that this apparatus, though costly, was the best defense against another severely embarrassing and even more costly environmental debacle. The company had, in fact, won an industrial award and wide recognition for its program. The CEO himself had benefited from the public praise for the program on first taking office, and he basked in that attention. Within the Chemical Company, however, as the political atmosphere in the country changed with the conservative legislative, budgetary, and regulatory triumphs in 1981, line managers were chafing under staff intrusions. They blamed the environmental staff for creating extra work and needless costs during a period of economic crisis. The CEO apparently agreed with these sentiments. Smith faced not only relentless pressure because of the company's declining fortunes but public capitulation to the CEO on his preferred organizational design. He chose instead to resign to "pursue other interests," pulling, of course, the cord on his "Golden Parachute" as he left.

The Chemical Company was in a state of shock after Smith's resignation, and the rumor mills churned out names of possible replacements, each tied to a scenario of the future. In such a period, the fealty system of the organization begins to loosen even as it binds people to their pasts. Managers know that others' cognitive maps afford them little escape from their old alliances and associations; at the same time,

they realize that they must be poised to form new alliances in a hurry if their areas are targeted for "restructuring."

As it happened, a great many managers found themselves in just that position. To almost everyone's astonishment, and to a great many people's trepidation, the CEO brought Brown back from the Electronics graveyard, after a "thorough assessment of all the candidates," which took two days, and made him the new president of Chemicals. No laughter or jeering was heard in the corridors. Whatever Brown's previous affiliations, there was now no doubt where his fealty lay. He became known throughout the corporation as the "CEO's boy," and people recognized that he had a mandate to wreak whatever mayhem was necessary to prune the Chemical organization and reduce expenditures. Within a short time, he had fired 150 people, most at the managerial level, slashing in the process the environmental staff by 75 percent. Those environmental staff that survived were subordinated to business areas and effectively neutralized. The official rationale was that the company had gone through an extraordinary learning period on environmental issues, benefited greatly from the expertise of the environmental staff, but had by now fully integrated and institutionalized that knowledge into its normal operations. There were, it was argued, no longer any environmental problems facing the company and therefore a modest reduction in this area made good business sense. Privately, among some managers, the assessment is that good staff people simply create work to justify their own existence. Moreover, they feel that work on environmental issues is doubly unnecessary because the only real threat to corporations on environmental issues in the new Reagan era is in the courts; for the most part, however, the courts judge past actions not present practices. By the time the courts get to cases generated by contemporary practices, typically in fifteen years, present executives will have moved on, leaving any problems their policies might create to others.

Brown's purge created extreme anxiety throughout the Chemical organization, even among those who agreed with his attacks on the staff and his pruning of other areas. Some managers expressed astonishment, and indeed outrage, that mostly persons of managerial rank were fired. The normal rule of management is, of course, to fire Indians, not Chiefs. Brown's action seemed to be an unwarranted and ominous violation of the managerial code that management takes care of itself in good times and bad. Those that survived were "looking over their shoulders" and "listening for footsteps behind them." Bitter jokes circulated freely like: "Opening Day at the Chemical Company: Brown comes in and throws out the first employee."

The company staggered into the Spring of 1983, and six months after the national economy began to pick up, its own fortunes began to improve, a typical pattern for industrial supply businesses. Suddenly, the CEO announced another major reorganization, once again dividing the entire corporation into several broad sectors. This time the Industrial Supplies Sector, as it is now called, incorporated Chemicals, Metals, and Plastics. Brown did not get the call to head the whole Industrial Supplies Sector but retained the presidency of chemicals. The leadership of the whole sector was allotted to a man who emerged out of the Metals Company, where he had been president in the old order. He, in turn, gave the presidencies of the other two divisions of the new sector to Metals people, and a new cycle of ascendancy, with its own patterns of fealty, patronage, and power cliques, seems to have begun. Managers noted, with some satisfaction, the irony of Brown being passed over by the CEO for the sector presidency after performing the CEO's dirty work. . . .

FIXITY AND FAILURE

Bureaucracies place a great premium on "flexibility," as it is called. This comes into sharper focus when we analyze, on one hand, a counter case, that of a man who, holding to a different sort of ethic, tried to "blow the whistle" on practices in his firm and, on the other, corporate managers' appraisals of what he did. Here I am using materials drawn from a substudy I am doing on whistleblowers and interviews with some managers in the Chemical Company to whom the case was presented.[10]

Brady (a pseudonym) was educated in England as a Chartered Public Accountant, a profession that he values highly and one that carries considerably more status, respect, and public trust in Britain than the American equivalent—that is, Certified Public Accountant. After a stint with a major auditing firm in England and then in Canada, Brady got a job in the United States as vice president of finance for the international division of a large processed food company. The CEO of the whole corporation was himself a financial man and had initiated a dual reporting system for all of his firm's divisions. All major financial officers, like Brady, had to report not only directly up the line to the president of his division but also laterally to the corporate vice president for finance who in turn reported to the CEO himself. The fundamental rule of the reporting system required any discrepancy in financial figures—budgets exceeded, irregularities in payments, unplanned raises, and so on—to be documented through a Treasurer's Report (TR) that would, in due course, end up on the CEO's desk. The system was stringent and quite unusual in the detail that it required be sent up to the latter. The CEO relished financial detail and, it is said, reviewed every TR carefully.

Brady is a very conscientious man, one deeply imbued with the ethics of his profession. He was disturbed to discover, upon taking office, a number of irregularities in his division, including a bribery payment of some size made to an official of a developing country and, closer to home, a set of doctored invoices done by his peer on the managerial ladder, the vice president of marketing. With the pressure of a federal investigation aiding him, Brady was able to clear up the bribery issue, but when he submitted a TR on the doctored invoices, with his immediate boss's approval, he found that his boss's boss refused to sign off on the report, the requisite procedure before the TR could go over to the corporate vice president for finance on its way to the CEO. The matter languished for some time, despite Brady's repeated efforts to have it go forward. In the meantime, Brady was approached on different occasions by three people in the company, including one friend, and told to drop the whole affair. Brady felt that he was himself in jeopardy from the CEO's scrutiny because he had no verifiable numbers to put in the book to cover the amount. While the matter was unresolved, Brady's immediate boss retired, leaving him in a direct relationship with the man blocking the TR.

Suddenly, Brady found himself demoted, broken in grade and salary, and transferred to the Corporate Division, where he now reported directly to the corporate vice president for finance as assistant treasurer. The change, he feels, was intended basically to keep him under control. As it happened, he soon came across much more serious and potentially more damaging information. Key people in the corporation—at this stage, Brady was not sure just who—were using millions of dollars of the employee pension fund as a profit slush fund—that is, money was not declared as an asset, but concealed. It was moved in and out of the corporation's earning statements each year, as needed, so that the firm always came in exactly on target; in fact, key members of the hierarchy could predict each October the exact earnings per share of the company for the year even though a third of all earnings were in foreign currency. This uncanny accuracy, of course, assured top executives of completely reliable bonus payments, which were tied to meeting profit targets.

This knowledge deeply upset Brady because he saw it as a direct violation of stockholders'

trust, a misuse of other people's money for personal gain, and one that could, in hard times, jeopardize the employees' pension fund. He felt that he now had no way of reporting the matter through normal channels; his boss, the corporate vice president for finance, had been hostile to him ever since Brady had come under his control, distrusting Brady, it seems, because of his attempted reporting of the doctored invoices. Brady felt that if the CEO were informed about the manipulation of the funds, he would act decisively to end the violation. Brady discussed the matter with a close friend, a man who had no defined position but considerable influence in the company because of his role as lobbyist, front man, and fixer—in short, an all-around factotum. Brady's information alarmed this man, and with a detailed memo on the slush fund written anonymously by Brady, he approached a key director of the corporation who chaired the Directors' Audit Committee. The director took the memo into a meeting with the CEO and his top aides. Immediately after the meeting, Brady's friend was fired and escorted from the building by guards.

It was only at this point that Brady realized that it was the CEO himself who was manipulating the numbers. The entire dual reporting system that the CEO had personally initiated was, in part, a spy network to guard against discovery of the slush fund manipulation, and perhaps other finagling, rather than a system to ensure financial honesty. The top people still did not know that Brady had written the memo, but he was under suspicion. In time, the pressure on him mounted, and Brady had had enough; he went to the chief lawyer in the whole corporation and laid out the case for him. At that point, Brady was summarily fired, and he and his belongings were literally thrown out of the company building.

It is important to note the sharp contrast between Brady's reasons for acting as he did and corporate managers' analysis of his actions. For Brady, the kinds of issues he confronted at work were distinctly *moral* issues, seen through the prism of his professional code. He says:

> So what I'm saying is that at bottom, I was in jeopardy of violating my professional code. And I felt that you have to stick up for that. If your profession has standing, it has that standing because *someone stood up for it.* If the SEC [the Securities and Exchange Commission] had come in and did an analysis and then went into the detail of the case and put me up on the stand and asked me—What is your profession? Was this action right or wrong? Why did you do it then? I would really be in trouble. . . . with myself most of all. I am frightened of losing respect, my self-respect in particular. And since that was tied with my respect for my profession, the two things were joined together.

He goes on to comment further about his relation to professional standards and how those standards contrast with the prevailing ethos of corporate life.

> I have fears in a situation like that. . . . It's not exactly a fear of what could happen to me, although that certainly crossed my mind. What it is is a fear of being found out not to stand up to standards that I have claimed as my own. It is a fear of falling down in a place where you have stuck a flag in the ground and said: "This is where I stand." I mean, why is it in life today that we have to deny any morality at all? But this is exactly the situation here. I was just too honest for that company. What is right in the corporation is not what's right in a man's home or in his church. *What is right in the corporation is what the guy above you wants from you.* That's what morality is in the corporation.

For Chemical Company managers, Brady's dilemma is devoid of moral or ethical content. For them, first of all, the issues he raises are simply practical matters, and his basic failing was that he violated the fundamental rules of bureaucratic life: (1) You never go around your boss; (2) you tell your boss what he wants to hear; (3) if your boss wants something dropped, you drop it; (4) you are sensitive to your boss's wishes so that you anticipate what he wants—you don't force him, in other words, to act as boss; (5) your job is not to report something that your boss doesn't want reported, but rather to cover it up. You do what your job requires and keep your mouth shut. Further, these managers feel that Brady had plenty of available legitimations to justify his *not* acting. Clearly, they feel, a great many other executives knew about the pension fund scam and did nothing; everybody, especially the top bosses, were playing the game. There were, besides, a number of ways out of the situation for Brady if he found the situation intolerable, including resigning. Also, whatever action he took would be insignificant anyway, so why bother to act at all? Third, managers see the violations that disturbed Brady—doctored invoices, irregular payments, shuffling numbers in accounts—as small potatoes indeed, commonplaces of corporate life. For them, juggling inventories, post- or pre-dating memos or invoices, tucking large sums of money away for a rainy day are part and parcel of managing in a large corporation where social interpretations, not necessarily performance itself, decide one's fate. Finally, managers feel that Brady's biggest error was in insisting on a moral code—his professional ethics—that had no relevance to his organizational situation. In doing so, he called others' organizational morality—that is, their acceptance of the bureaucratic ethos—into question and made them uncomfortable. They see this as the key reason why Brady's bosses did him in. And they too would do him in, without any qualms. Managers, they say, do not want evangelists working for them.

The finale to the story is worth recounting. After Brady was fired, the CEO of the firm retired and elevated to his position a man known as Loyal Sam who had tracked the CEO throughout his career. The CEO took an emeritus position with the company: Chief of Internal Audit. When the Chemical Company managers hear the outcome, they laugh softly and nod their heads and give even an outsider one of the knowing looks usually reserved only for trusted others in their world.

CONCLUSION

Karl Mannheim points out that bureaucracy turns all political issues into matters of administration.[11] One can see a parallel alchemy in managers' response to Brady's dilemma. Bureaucracy transforms all moral issues into practical concerns. A moral judgment based on a professional ethos has no meaning in a world where the etiquette of authority relationships, nonaccountability for actions, and the necessity for protecting and covering for one's boss, one's network, and oneself supersede all other considerations. As a matter of survival, not to mention advancement, corporate managers keep their eyes fixed on the social framework of their world and its requirements. Thus, they simply do not see most issues that confront them as moral concerns, even when problems might be posed by others in moral terms.

Managers' essential pragmatism, perhaps their most striking characteristic, stems from the priority they assign to the social rules of their bureaucratic context. This pragmatism is the root of the flexibility that I mentioned earlier, and it constitutes a principal criterion for advancement in a corporation. The higher one goes in the corporate world, the more one must rationalize one's self to the norms of flexibility. On one hand, flexibility means a great adeptness at inconsistency, a dexterity at symbolic manipulation. Those adept at inconsistency can freely, and with no qualms, manipulate a variety of rhetorics and vocabularies to meet, as required, the divergent expectations of diverse audiences. On the other hand, flexibility means the capacity to extend the transformation of moral issues into practical concerns to quite far reaches. One might call this an alertness to expediency. In effect, those alert to expediency externalize the objectification of self learned in the course of self-rationalization; they learn to appraise all sit-

uations and all people as they come to see themselves, that is, as objects, as commodities, to be rearranged and tinkered with. This is the nub of the moral ethos of bureaucracy and how it affects managers. Some managers pose this "trade-off" between morality and expedience as a question: Where do you draw the line?

Some managers find drawing the line a difficult and anxiety-laden process. They worry in very personal terms about the damage to others' careers caused by purges; they agonize about truth-telling and promise-keeping; they are concerned about the safety of their products and about their corporations' compliance with federal regulations; they find the nonaccountability of the corporation unsettling and troublesome. There is little escape from such anxieties for those who experience them because the press of managerial work, and uncontrollable events as well, always bring new problems to be confronted. More particularly, less-questioning managers intensify the anxiety for those who are uneasy. For these managers, who respond more fully to bureaucratic premiums, alertness to expediency means examining issues not on their intrinsic merits but from the perspective of one's organizational advantage. It means stripping away the emotional and any stated moral aspects of a troublesome problem and asking what outcome will best serve oneself and one's social network. It means, then, working to bring about that outcome without regard for other considerations. They invoke as necessary the numerous vocabularies of accounts that bureaucracy provides managers to excuse or justify nearly any action—whether these are meritocratic ideologies, the need for secrecy or team play, disputed scientific evidence, public ignorance, the myth of better informed and wiser superiors—in short, whatever account is organizationally available and ready at hand. The manager alert to expediency sees his bureaucratic world through a lens that may seem blurred to those outside the corporation; it is, however, a lens that enables him to bring into exact focus the relationships and rules of his world. The alert manager comes to see the misfortunes of others as opportunities for himself. More generally, he measures relationships with others with a utilitarian calculus and forms or breaks friendships or alliances accordingly. He comes, too, to see that the nonaccountability of the corporation is really a license to exert one's own will and to improve one's own fortunes as long as one carefully maintains alliances and does not get caught.

The logical result of alterness to expediency is the elimination of any lines at all. As a practical matter, however, bureaucracies are not self-contained—particularly commercial organizations. They operate in the public arena and are subject to the vagaries and pressures of public opinion. Public outrage about numerous corporate practices can and has posed public issues in specifically moral terms—for instance, on the environment or on worker health and safety—often creating costly dilemmas and public embarrassment for corporate leaders. Public opinion constitutes, in fact, one of the only effective checks on the bureaucratic impulse to translate all moral issues into practical concerns. As one might expect, then, those who have attained the upper reaches of corporations and are imbued with the bureaucratic ethos make every effort to mold public opinion to allow continued uninterrupted operation of business. In this sense, moral issues become issues of public relations.

This equation also emerges directly out of the social context of the corporation that we have described. The politics of the corporation, with its system of fealty, patronage, cliques, and endless power struggles, produces in managers a conception of the public that at bottom is closely akin to the way they see rival managerial groups. For the most part, this view consists of a guarded wariness and a bitterly sardonic appraisal of the shifts in public opinion. Managers are acutely aware of how powerful public opinion can be in turning their world upside down—of how, in fact, it can be used by rival manager-

ial groups for their own ends. Every corporation that I studied has had major confrontations with some outraged publics in the last few years. The big fear is that some action, policy, practice, or product of a corporation will suddenly get caught up in what are seen as unpredictable and irrational waves of hysteria stirred up by self-styled public interest groups. When this kind of catastrophe occurs, not only are huge amounts of time and money wasted, but blame time can suddenly fall like the night within a corporation, bringing shakeups and reprisals with it.

The goal then is to get one's story out to important publics in such a way that the main parameters of public opinion can be shaped and controlled. Most corporations do this on a regular sustained basis, intensifying their efforts during crisis periods. For the most part, corporations allot this work to special practitioners of public relations within the corporation who consult regularly with the highest officials of the firm; these practitioners and, quite often, the highest officials themselves, also work with public relations (PR) specialists based in agencies. The views of PR specialists both in corporations and in agencies correspond closely to views held by corporate managers and executives; generally, specialists are, however, somewhat broader, often more sophisticated, and more detached. In particular, their work gives them a finer appreciation for how the drama of social reality is constructed since they are themselves the stagehands. I will restrict my comments here to how PR people, as a sophisticated proxy for corporate managers, approach all issues, including those fraught with moral implications.

In the world of public relations, there is no ascertainable truth; there are only stories. One takes care to report facts, at least some facts, but one feels free to put any interpretation on facts that one wishes. The task is to work with facts at hand and devise plausible stories that will command the assent, or at least the lack of dissent, of important sectors of the public. It is important to remember that sometimes confusion, as long as it is credibly generated confusion, will serve the same purpose. This means seeing the world as popular novelists do, essentially in broad brushstrokes, boiling down all events to simple understandable drama. Most people's understanding of the world, after all, consists precisely of such little stories. The job then is to present a euphemistically told tale that will enable the corporation to function without undue disruption. Truth and, for that matter, morality are all a matter of perception. One tries, therefore, to engineer moral acquiescence, if not consent, by arranging other's perceptions to suit one's own interest. In short, public relations elevates the bureaucratic virtue of alertness to expedience into a professional calling.

Within this bureaucratic framework, an older ethos like the professional code that Brady tried to assert seems merely quaint, and whistleblowers like him, men engaged in a quixotic search for evanescent absolutist ideals. Bureaucracy makes its own internal rules and social context the principal moral gauges for action. It turns principles into guidelines, ethics into etiquette, responsibility into an agility at avoiding blame, and truth into credibility. Corporate managers who become imbued with the bureaucratic ethos take their world as they find it and pursue their careers as best they can by the rules of that ethos. As it happens—given their pivotal institutional role in our epoch—they help create, as one consequence of their personal striving, a society where morality becomes indistinguishable from the quest for one's own survival and advantage.[12]

NOTES

1. For a comprehensive listing of these works, see D. Jones, 1977; D. Jones and Troy, 1982.
2. These include the Center for the Study of Applied Ethics at the Darden Graduate Business School, University of Virginia; the Center for the Study of Values at the University of Delaware; the Center for Business Ethics at Bentley College; the Center for the Study of Ethics in the

Professions at the Illinois Institute of Technology; the Ethics Resource Center in Washington, D.C.; and the Center for Applied Philosophy at the University of Florida.
3. See, for instance, the *Report of the Committee for Education in Business Ethics,* sponsored by the National Endowment for the Humanities (1980).
4. For a useful listing of some of the main works in this tradition going back to 1900, see Christian and Hicks, 1970.
5. Casuistry emerges whenever men and women try to establish rules to guide themselves through the moral quandries of everyday life; it is, of course, as ancient as human thought itself. For two fine summaries of the main historical developments in moral cauistry, see Wenley, 1910; Nelson, 1973.
6. The exception to this in the sociological literature is Bensman, 1967.
7. Lederer, 1918–19.
8. Jackall, 1983.
9. During 1980–1983, I did field work in several corporate settings. These included: the chemical company of a large conglomerate, a large textile firm, a small chemical firm, a large defense contractor, and a large public relations firm. My basic methodology was semi-structured interviews with managers and executives at every level of management. The interviews usually lasted between two and three hours, but, especially with reinterviews, some went on much longer. I interviewed more than 125 managers. In addition, I gathered material in more informal ways—for example, through nonparticipant observation, over meals, and by attending various managerial seminars in the companies studied. I am indebted to the National Endowment for the Humanities, which provided me with a Fellowship for Independent Research in 1980–1981 and to Williams College for several small research grants that have facilitated my work.
10. The field work with organizational dissenters or whistleblowers began in the summer of 1982 and is still continuing. To date, I have completed nine case studies, interviewing thirteen dissenters in the process. I have also done a number of other case studies, which have proved to be too ambiguous to help much in understanding the

nature and motivation of organizational dissent. I am indebted to the Wenner-Gren Foundation for Anthropological Research for its financial support of this phase of my research. The Educational Fund for Individual Rights in New York City and the Governmental Accountability Project in Washington, D.C., have given me considerable help in this project.

11. Mannheim, 1936: 118.

12. I wish to thank Joseph Bensman, Arthur Vidich, Stanford Lyman, Michael Hughey, and Janice Hirota for reading a draft of this paper and for making many helpful comments on it.

REFERENCES

Bensman, Joseph. 1967. *Dollars and Sense*. New York: Macmillan.

Christian, Portia, with Richard Hicks. 1970. *Ethics in Business Conduct: Selected References from the Record—Problems, Attempted Solutions, Ethics in Business Education*. Detroit: Gale Research.

Jackall, Robert, 1983. "Moral mazes: Bureaucracy and managerial work." *Harvard Business Review* 61 (September/October): 118–30.

Jones, Donald G. 1977. *A Bibliography of Business Ethics, 1971–1975*. Charlottesville: University of Virginia Press.

————, and Helen Troy (eds.). 1982. *A Bibliography of Business Ethics, 1976–1980*. Charlottesville: University of Virginia Press.

Lederer, Emil. 1918–19. "On the socio-psychic constitution of the present time." *Archiv für Sozialwissenschaft und Sozialpolitik* 56: 114–39.

Mannheim, Karl. 1936. *Ideology and Utopia*. New York: Harcourt, Brace and World.

Nelson, Benjamin 1973. "Casuistry." *Encyclopedia Britannica* 5: 51–52.

Report of the Committee for Education in Business Ethics, 1980. Washington, DC: National Endowment for the Humanities.

Wenley, R. M. 1910. "Casuistry." *Encyclopedia of Religion and Ethics* 3. Edinburgh: Clark.

DISCUSSION QUESTIONS

1. What does Jackall mean when he says, "Political struggles are central to managerial work"? What are the implications of such struggles for managers and for employees working for them?

2. Jackall provides a negative portrait of what might be seen as the "amoral" ethos of bureaucracy. On the basis of his case study, do you agree or disagree with this assessment?

READING 29

Protecting the Routine from Chaos

Daniel F. Chambliss

In this participation observation study, Daniel Chambliss explores the social ethic operating among the staff, and particularly the nursing staff, in a hospital setting. In this excerpt from Beyond Caring, *he discusses the importance that staff members attach to maintaining a routine in order to perform their central duties. A premium is placed on keeping going, on continuing to act in ways defined as normal in the face of challenges to business as usual. Chambliss identifies challenges to the routine that have the potential to create chaos, which largely revolve around the intrusion of outsiders and the potential for one's emotions to undermine routine. He proceeds to identify and discuss four ways in which nurses seek to protect themselves and others from these disruptive possibilities.*

Every unit in the hospital, then, has its own normality, its own typical patients, number of deaths, and crises to be faced. But just as predictably, every unit has its emergencies that threaten the routine and challenge the staff's ability to maintain workaday attitudes and practices. Emergencies threaten the staff's ability to carry on as usual, to maintain their own distance from the patient's suffering, and to hold at bay their awe at the enormity of events. Occasionally breakdowns occur in unit discipline or the ability to do the required work.

Staff follow several strategies when trying to manage the threat of breakdowns: they will keep outsiders outside, follow routinization rituals, or use humor to distance themselves. Finally, even when all efforts fail, they will keep going, no matter what. Consider in turn each of these implicit maxims:

1. Keep Outsiders Outside

Every hospital has policies about visiting hours, designed not only to "let patients rest" but also to protect staff from outsiders' interference in their work. Visitors are limited to certain hours, perhaps two to a patient room for fifteen-minute visits; they may have to be announced before entering the unit or may be kept waiting in a room down the hall. No doubt many such policies are good for the patient. No doubt, too, they keep visitors out of the nurse's way, prevent too many obtrusive questions or requests for small services, and prevent curious laypersons from seeing the messier, less presentable sides of nursing care.

When visitors cannot be physically excluded, they can still be cognitively controlled, that is, prevented from knowing that something untoward is happening. Typically, the staff behave in such episodes as if everything were OK, even when it is not. This is similar to what Erving Goffman observed in conversations: when the shared flow of interaction is threatened by an accidental insult or a body failure such as a sneeze or flatulence, people simply try to ignore the break in reality and carry on as if nothing has happened. Such "reality maintenance" is often well-orchestrated, requiring cooperation on the part of several parties. For Goffman, normal people in normal interactions accept at face value each other's presentation of who they are:

A state where everyone temporarily accepts everyone else's line is established. This kind of mutual acceptance seems to be a basic structural feature of interaction, especially the interaction of face-to-face talk. It is typically a "working" acceptance, not a "real" one.[1]

And when this routine breaks down, the immediate strategy is simple denial:

When a person fails to prevent an incident, he can still attempt to maintain the fiction that no threat to face has occurred. The most blatant example of this is found where the person acts as if an event that contains a threatening expression has not occurred at all.[2]

In the hospital, the unexpected entrance of outsiders into a delicate situation can disrupt the staff's routine activities and create unmanageable chaos. To avoid this, the staff may pretend to outsiders that nothing special is happening; this pretense itself can be part of the routine. During a code (resuscitation) effort I witnessed, there were three such potential disruptions by outsiders: another patient calling for help, a new incoming patient being wheeled in, and the new patient's family members entering the unit. All three challenges were handled by the staff diverting the outsiders from the code with a show, as if nothing were happening:

Code in CCU [Cardiac Care Unit] . . . woman patient, asystole [abnormal ventricle contractions]. Doc (res[ident]) pumping chest—*deep* pumps, I'm struck by how far down they push. Serious stuff. Matter of factness of process is striking. This was a surprise code, not expected. Patient was in Vtak [ventricular fibrillation], pulse started slowing, then asystole. N[urse]s pumping for a while, RT [Respiratory Therapist] ambu-bagging [pumping air into lungs]. Maybe 7–8 people in patient's room working. Calm, but busy. Occasionally a laugh.

Pt in next room (no more than 10 feet away) called for nurse—a doc went in, real loose and casual, strolled in, pt said something; doc said, "There's something going on next door that's taking people's time; we'll get to you"—real easy,

---

[1]Erving Goffman, "On Face-Work," in *Interaction Ritual: Essays on Face-to-Face Behavior* (New York: Pantheon Books, 1967), p. 11.
[2]Ibid., pp. 17–18.

like nothing at all happening. Then strolls back to code room. Very calm . . .

Two N[urse]s came into unit wheeling a new patient. One said, "Uh, oh, bad time," very quietly as she realized, going in the door, that a code was on. Somebody said, "Close the door"—the outside door to the unit, which the Ns with the new pt were holding open . . .

When the new pt was brought in and rolled into his room, the family with him was stopped at unit door, told to stay in waiting room and "we'll call you" with a casual wave of hand, as if this is routine. [No one said a code was on. Patient lying on gurney was wheeled in, went right by the code room and never knew a thing.] [Field Notes]

This is a simple example of protecting the routine from the chaos of a panicking patient or a horrified family; the outsiders never knew that a resuscitation was occurring fifteen feet away. The staff's work was, in their own eyes, routine; their challenge was protecting that routine from outside disruption.

2. Follow Routinization Rituals

The staff's sense of routine is maintained by the protective rituals of hospital life. Under stress, one may use them more and more compulsively, falling back on the old forms to reconvince oneself that order is still present. Frantic prayers in the foxhole are the prototype cases.

Most prominent of such rituals in hospitals are "rounds," the standard ritual for the routine handling of patient disasters in the hospital. "Rounds" is the generic term for almost any organized staff group discussion of patients' conditions. "Walking rounds" refers to a physician walking through the hospital, usually trailed by various residents and interns, going from patient to patient and reviewing their condition. "Grand rounds" are large meetings of the medical staff featuring the presentation of an interesting case, with elaborate discussion and questions, for the purpose of education and review of standard practices. Nursing rounds usually consist of a meeting between the staff for one (outgoing)

shift reporting to the staff of the next (incoming) shift on the condition of all patients on the floor. Here the staff collectively explains what has happened and why, bringing every case into the staff's framework of thinking, and systematically enforcing the system's capability for handling medical problems without falling to pieces. In rounds, the staff confirm to each other that things are under control. Once a week, for instance, the Burn Unit at one hospital holds rounds in their conference room with a group of residents, one or two attendings, several nurses, the social workers, dieticians, and physical therapists. The patients here are in terrible shape; one can sometimes hear moans in the hallway outside as patients are taken for walks by the nurses. But rounds continue:

Macho style of the docs very evident. . . . Resident will present a case, then the attendings take rapid-fire shots at what he [the resident] had done: wrong dressing, wrong feeding schedule, failure to note some abnormality in the lab results. Much of the talk was a flurry of physiological jargon, many numbers and abbreviations. The intensity of the presentation, the mercilessness of the grilling, is surprising. . . . Focus is on no errors made in situation of extreme pressure—i.e., both in patient treatment and then here in rounds presenting the case. Goal here is to be predictable, *controlled*, nothing left out. [Field Notes]

3. Use Humor to Distance Yourself

Keeping outsiders away and following the standard rituals for maintaining normality can help, but sometimes the pathos of hospital life becomes psychologically threatening to staff members. One response is to break down, cry, and run out, but this is what they are trying to avoid; the more common reaction is the sort of black humor that notoriously characterizes hospitals and armies everywhere. Humor provides an outlet; when physical space is not available, humor is a way to separate oneself psychologically from what is happening. It says both that I am not involved and that this really isn't so important. (In brain surgery, when parts of that organ are, essentially, vacuumed away, one may hear comments like "There goes 2d grade, there go the piano lessons," etc.) With laughter, things seem less consequential, less of a burden. What has been ghastly can perhaps be made funny:

Today they got a 600-gram baby in the Newborn Unit. When Ns heard [the baby] was in Delivery, they were praying, "Please God let it be under 500 grams"—because that's the definite cutoff under which they won't try to save it—but the doc said admit it anyway. Ns unhappy.

I came in the unit tonight; N came up to me and said brightly, with a big smile, "Have you seen our fetus?" Ns on the Newborn Unit have nicknames for some. There's "Fetus," the 600-gram one; "Munchkin"; and "Thrasher," in the corner, the one with constant seizures. Grim humor, but common. ["Fetus" was born at 24 weeks, "Munchkin" at 28.] [Field Notes]

The functions of such humor for medical workers have been described in a number of classic works of medical sociology. Renée Fox, writing in her book *Experiment Perilous* about physicians on a metabolic research unit, says, "The members of the group were especially inclined to make jokes about events that disturbed them a good deal," and she summarizes that

by freeing them from some of the tension to which they were subject, enabling them to achieve greater detachment and equipoise, and strengthening their resolve to do something about the problems with which they were faced, the grim medical humor of the Metabolic Group helped them to come to terms with their situation in a useful and professionally acceptable way.[3]

Fox and other students of hospital culture (notably Rose Coser)[4] have emphasized that

humor fills a functional purpose of "tension release," allowing medical workers to get on with the job in the face of trauma; their analyses usually focus on jokes explicitly told in medical settings. This analysis is correct as far as it goes, but in a sense I think it almost "explains away" hospital humor—as if to say that "these people are under a lot of strain, so it's understandable that they tell these gruesome jokes." It suggests, in a functionalist fallacy, that jokes are made because of the strain and that things somehow aren't "really" funny.

But they are. An appreciation of hospital life must recognize that funny things—genuinely funny, even if sometimes simultaneously horrible—do happen. Hospitals are scenes of irony, where good and bad are inseparably blended, where funny things happen, where to analytically excuse laughter as a defense mechanism is simultaneously to deny the human reality, the experience, that even to a nonstressed outsider *this is funny*.[5] The humor isn't found only in contrived jokes but in the scenes one witnesses; laughter can be spontaneous, and it's not always nervous. True, one must usually have a fairly normalized sense of the hospital to laugh here, but laugh one does.

Certainly, the staff make jokes:

In the OR:
"This is his [pt's] 6th time [for a hernia repair]."
"After two, I hear you're officially disabled."
"Oh good, does that mean he gets a special parking place?"
[Field Notes]
In the ICU, two Ns—one male, one female—working on pt.
Nurse 1 (male): "This guy has bowel sounds in his scrotum."
Nurse 2 (female): "In his scrotum?"
Nurse 1: "Yeah, didn't you pick that up?"

[3]Renée C. Fox, *Experiment Perilous* (New York: Free Press, 1959; reprint ed., Philadelphia: University of Pennsylvania Press, 1974), pp. 80–82.
[4]Rose Laub Coser, "Some Social Functions of Laughter," in Lewis Coser, *The Pleasures of Sociology,* edited and with an introduction and notes by Lewis Coser (New York: New American Library, 1980), pp. 81–97.

[5]The genius of Shem's *House of God* is that it accepts this fact and presents it honestly.

Nurse 2: "I didn't put my stethoscope there!" (Big laughs.) [Field Notes]

Sometimes jokes are more elaborate and are obviously derived from the tragedy of the situation:

In another ICU, staff member taped a stick to the door of the unit, symbolizing (for them) "The Stake," a sign of some form of euthanasia [perhaps the expression sometimes used, "to stake" a patient, derives from the myth that vampires can only be killed by driving a stake through the heart]. Periodically word went around that a resident had just won the "Green Stake Award," meaning that he or she had, for the first time, allowed or helped a patient to die. [Field Notes]

Some colorful balloons with "Get Well Soon" were delivered to a patient's room. The patient died the following night. Someone on the staff moved the balloons to the door of another patient's room; that patient died! Now the staff has put the balloons at the door of the patient they believe is "most likely to die next." [Field Notes]

But jokes have to be contrived; they are deliberate efforts at humor and so make a good example of efforts to distance oneself, or to make the tragic funny. But the inherent irony of the hospital is better seen in situations that spontaneously provoke laughter. These things are funny in themselves; even an outsider can laugh at them:

Nurse preparing to wheel a patient into the OR tells him, "Take out your false teeth, take off your glasses . . . ," and continuing, trying to make a joke, "Take off your leg, take out your eyes." The patient said, "Oh, I almost forgot—" and pulled out his [false] eye! [Interview]

Or:

Lady patient [Geriatric floor] is upset because she called home, there's no answer; she's afraid her husband has died. Sylvia [a nurse] told her he probably just went somewhere for lunch, but patient said he would have called. She's afraid.

[Later] Sylvia went back in lady's room— she's crying. Husband called! Sylvia happy, smiling, "You should be happy!" "But," says the old lady, "he called to say he was out burying the dog!"

Sylvia had to leave the room because she was starting to laugh; she and Janie laughing at this at the N's station, saying it's really sad but funny at the same time. [Field Notes]

Or:

In looking at X-rays of a patient's colon, the resident explains to the team a shadow on the film: "Radiology says it could be a tumor, or it might just be stool." Jokes all around about how "helpful" Rays [Radiology] is. [Field Notes]

One needn't be under pressure to find such things funny. People do laugh to ease pressure or to distance oneself. But sometimes the distance comes first: laughter is made possible by the routinization that has gone before.

4. When Things Fall Apart, Keep Going

Sometimes routinization fails: outsiders come into the room and, seeing their dead mother, break down, screaming and wailing; or a longtime, cared-for patient begins irretrievably to "decompensate" and lose blood pressure, sliding quickly to death; or emergency surgery goes bad, the trauma shakes the staff, and there are other patients coming in from the ambulances. Any of these can destroy the staff's sense of "work as usual." In such cases, the typical practice seems to be, remarkably: just keep going. Trauma teams specialize in the psychological strength (or cold-bloodedness, perhaps) to continue working when the world seems to be falling apart. Finally, nurses and physicians are notable for continuing to work even, in the final case, after the patient is for almost all purposes dead, or will be soon.

A resident said to the attending on one floor, discussing a terminal patient: "If we transfuse him, he might get hepatitis."

Another resident: "By the time he gets hepatitis he'll be dead."

Attending: "OK, so let's transfuse." [Field Notes]

Perseverance is a habit; it's also a moral imperative, a way of managing disaster as if it were routine.

In every unit there are nurses known for being good under pressure. These are people who, whatever their other skills (and, typically, their other skills are quite good), are able to maintain their presence of mind in any crisis. Whereas "being organized" is a key quality for nurses in routine situations, staying calm is crucial in emergency situations. Compare two nurses known for remaining calm (Mavis and Anna) to two others who are prone to alarm (Linda and Julie):

> Mavis [in Neonatal ICU] is cited as a good nurse (great starting IVs, e.g.) who doesn't get shook, even in a code, even if her pt is dying, she still keeps doing what you're supposed to do. Linda, by contrast, is real smart, very good technically, but can freak out, start yelling, etc., if things are going badly. [Field Notes]
>
> Julie [in Medical ICU], hurrying around, looks just one step ahead of disaster, can't keep up, etc. Doc says something about the patient in room 1. Julie says, walking past, "He's not mine," keeps going. But Anna, calm, walks in pt's room—pt with oxygen mask, wants something. Anna goes out, calmly, comes back in a minute w/cup of crushed ice, gives pt a spoonful to ease thirst. She *always* seems to be doing that little thing that others "don't have time for"—never flustered and yet seems to get more done than anyone else. [Field Notes, Interview]

But to "keep going" depends not so much on the individual fortitude of nurses such Mavis and Anna, but on the professional and institutional habits of the nursing staff and the hospital. The continuance of care even in the face of obvious failure of efforts is itself a norm. Whatever one's personal disposition, one keeps working; the staff keep working, often when the patient is all but dead, or "dead" but not officially recognized as such:

> Dr. K., walking rounds with four residents, discussing a 30-year-old male patient, HIV-positive, gone totally septic [has bloodstream infection, a deadly problem], no hope at all of recovery— Dr. K. says this is a "100 percent mortality" case; so they decide how to proceed with minimal treatment, at the end of which Dr. K. says brightly, "And if he codes—code him!" [Field Notes]

Coding such a patient is an exercise in technique; there is no hope entailed, no optimism, no idea that he might be saved. There is only the institutional habit which substitutes for hope, which in many cases obviates the staff's pessimism or lack of interest. When standard procedure is followed, courage is unnecessary. It is one thing to be routinely busy, caring for vegetative patients; it happens every day. It is quite another to handle emergency surgery with no time and a life at stake. Sometimes such a case will challenge all the staff's resources—their personal fortitude, their habitualization of procedures, the self-protection offered by an indefatigable sense of humor. To maintain one's composure while under tremendous pressures of time and fatefulness requires all the courage a staff can muster.

One such case was that of emergency surgery on a thirty-five-year-old woman who came to Southwestern Regional hospital in severe abdominal pain; she was diagnosed with a ruptured ectopic pregnancy estimated at sixteen weeks. The case provides us with a dramatic example of the pressure placed on the staff to retain their composure in the face of disaster.

The long description which follows is graphic. The scene was more than bloody; it was grotesque. More than one staff member—including one member of the surgical team itself—left the room during the operation, sickened. Other nurses, even very experienced ones, told me they have never witnessed such a scene and hope never to witness one. I include it here, in some detail, to exemplify both what health professionals face in their work and how, incredibly, some of them can carry on. The description is reconstructed from Field Notes (some written at the time on the inside of a surgical mask, some on sheets of paper carried in a pocket), and from interviews afterward with participants:

Saturday night OR suite; hasn't been busy. Only one case so far, a guy who got beat up with a tire iron (drug deal), finished about 8:30 P.M. It's about 10:00. 2 Ns—the Saturday night staff—sitting around in the conference room, just chatting and waiting for anything that happens.

Call comes over intercom: ruptured tubal (pregnancy) just came in OR, bringing to the crash room. 35-year-old black woman, very heavy—250 pounds maybe—apparently pregnant for 16 weeks, which means she's been in pain for 10 weeks or more without coming in. Friends brought her to ER screaming in pain. Blood pressure is at "60 over palpable," i.e., the diastolic doesn't even register on the manometer. She's obviously bleeding bad internally, will die fast if not opened up. Ns run to OR and set up fast. I've never seen people work so quickly here, no wasted motion at all. This is full speed *emergency*.

When patient is rolled in, fully conscious, there are more than a dozen staff people in the room, including three gynecological surgery residents, who will operate; all three are women. The surgeons are scrubbed and gowned and stand in a line, back from the table, watching without moving, the one in charge periodically giving orders to the nurses who are setting up. At one point there are twelve separate people working on the patient—IVs going into both arms, anesthesiologist putting mask on pt to gas, nurse inserting a Foley [bladder] catheter, others tying pt's arms to the straightout arms of the table, others scrubbing the huge belly, an incredible scene. The patient is shaking terribly, in pain and fear. Her eyes are bugging out, looking around terribly fast. She's whimpering, groaning as needles go in, crying out softly. No one has time even to speak to her; one nurse briefly leans over and speaks into her ear something like "try not to worry, we're going to take care of you," but there is no time for this. I've never seen anyone so afraid, sweating and crying and the violent shaking.

As soon as they have prepped her—the belly cleansed and covered with Opsite, in a matter of minutes, very, very fast, the anesthesiologist says, "All set?" And someone says "yes," and they gas her. I'm standing right by her head, looking to the head side of the drape which separates her head from her body; the instant that her eyes close, I look to the other side—and the surgeon has already slit her belly open. No hesitation at all, maybe before the patient was out.

What happened next, more extraordinary than the very fast prep, was the opening. Usually in surgery the scalpel makes the skin cut, then slowly scissors are used, snipping piece by piece at muscle, the Bovie cauterizing each blood vessel on the way, very methodical and painstaking. This was nothing like that. It was an entirely different style. They cut fast and deep, sliced her open deep, just chopped through everything, in a—not a panic, but something like a "blitzkrieg," maybe—to get down into the Fallopian tube that had burst and was shooting blood into the abdomen.

When they first got into the abdominal cavity, usually there would be some oozing blood; here as they opened blood splattered out all over the draping on the belly. It was a godawful mess, blood everywhere. They had one surgeon mopping up with gauze sponges, another using a suction pump, a little plastic hose, trying to clean the way. Unbelievable. They got down to the tubes, reaching down and digging around with their hands. And then they found it—suddenly out of this bloody mess down in the abdomen, with the surgeons groping around trying to feel where things were, out of this popped up, right out of the patient and, literally, onto the sheet covering her, the 16-week fetus itself. Immediately one surgeon said mock-cheerfully, "It's a boy!" "God, don't do that," said the scrub tech, turning her head away.

The scrub tech then began to lose it, tears running down her cheeks. Two other people on the team—there were maybe six around the table—said about the same time, nearly together, "Damien!" and "Alien!" recalling recent horror movies, "children of the devil" themes. The fetus lay on the sheet just below the open abdomen for a few moments. The head surgery resident, working, just kept working. The scrub tech should have put the fetus into a specimen tray, but she was falling to pieces fast, crying, and starting to have trouble handing the proper tools to the surgeon, who said something like, "What are you doing?" At this point the circulating nurse, a man, said, "If nobody else will do it," picked up the fetus and put it in a specimen tray, which he then covered with a towel and put aside. He then told another nurse to help him into a gown—he wasn't scrubbed. This violates sterile technique badly, for him to start handling tools, but the scrub tech was becoming a problem. The circulating nurse then quickly gowned and gloved, gently pulled the scrub tech aside and said, "I'll do it." The scrub tech ran out of the room in tears. And the circulating nurse began passing tools to the surgeons himself. It is the circulating nurse's responsibility to handle problems this way, and he did. Another nurse had gone out to scrub properly, and when she came back, maybe ten minutes later, she gowned and gloved and relieved him; so he (the circulating nurse) went back to his regular job of charting the procedure, answering the phone, etc.

By this time, things were under control; the bleeding was stopped, the tube tied off. The other tube was OK and left alone so the pt can get pregnant again. The blood in the abdomen was cleaned up—over 1500 cc's were lost, that's just under a half-gallon of blood. The pt would have died fast if they hadn't gotten in there.

Within two hours after the patient had first rolled in, the room was quiet, only three staff members left, two surgeons and the scrub nurse closing up and talking quietly. Most of the mess—the bloody sponges, the used tools, and all—was gone, cleared away, and all the other staff people, including the chief surgeon, had left. Very calm. The patient, who two hours ago was on the end of a fast terrible death, will be out of the hospital in two days with no permanent damage beyond the loss of one Fallopian tube. [Field Notes, Interviews]

In this situation, we can see two somewhat distinct problems in maintaining the routine order of things: first, the challenge simply in getting the work done; and second, the challenge of upholding the moral order of the hospital.[6] The

first issue was resolved by replacing the scrub tech so the operation could continue. The second issue is trickier. The scrub tech's response appeared to be set off not by the horror of what she saw—the bloody fetus—but by the reaction of the assisting surgeon—"It's a boy!" I can only guess that the joke was too much for her. In continuing to work without her, and continuing without noticeable change of demeanor, the surgical team was asserting not only the imperative to protect the operational routine but also, I think, to protect the moral order of emergency surgery as well. That order includes:

1. The job comes first, before personal reactions of fear or disgust.
2. Cynicism is an acceptable form of expression if it helps to maintain composure and distance.
3. The medical team is rightfully in charge and above what may be happening in the OR.
4. Preserving life is the central value; others (such as niceties of language or etiquette) fall far behind.

There is clearly a morality here. Just as clearly, it is not the morality of everyday life.

DISCUSSION QUESTIONS

1. The threat of chaos is not unique to hospitals. Think about another institutional setting and describe in what ways the methods Chambliss depicts apply in attempting to ward off chaos.
2. Chambliss contends at the end of the selection that although there is a morality operative in the hospital, it differs from "the morality of everyday life." Do you agree or disagree with this assessment? Why?

---

[6]I am indebted to Robert Zussman, who suggested these in his review of the manuscript.

READING 30

Instrumental Ties

Alan Wolfe

Since the early nineteenth century, analysts of American society beginning with Alexis de Tocqueville have described America as a nation of joiners. Community life has been predicated on the willingness of the citizenry to be involved in a wide array of civic involvements. Recently, some social scientists have claimed to detect a decline in such involvements, believing that individualism has produced this withdrawal. Wolfe challenges this pessimistic assessment on the basis of the results of his study of middle-class Americans, which focused on four urban areas—Boston, Atlanta, Tulsa, and San Diego. In this passage from One Nation, After All, *he attempts to indicate not only that middle-class Americans remained active in their communities, but also that they do so with an eye to finding the proper balance between their private and civic lives.*

Treatments of suburban life in the 1950s featured a sharp contrast between the world of work and the world of community. The former, populated by men, emphasized hierarchy, obedience, material rewards, and formal procedures, while the latter, dominated by women, was characterized by voluntarism, friendships, talk, leisure, and—at least in the account of feminist social critic Betty Friedan—great unhappiness.[1] Now that the proverbial commuter railroad platform is crowded not only with men but with women, and now that the trains run earlier in the morning and later in the evening to accommodate the frenetic work schedules of a more competitive capitalism, the ties of trust and mutual dependence upon which communities rely have been as radically transformed as company loyalties and employer-employee relations.

As they talked to us about their perceptions of their suburban communities, middle-class Americans painted portraits of their community ties that give strong support to the idea that America is depleting its social capital. Here is a sprinkling of their comments:

"It's almost as if we set up our own islands. It's a street full of islands. And, you know, we would love to have a great relationship and great neighbors and that sort of thing, but it has just never evolved."

"We don't know who those people are or how they spend their time. We pass them on the street. We talk across the fence, but socially we don't do things with our neighbors to speak of."

"People are a lot more isolated."

"I've been living eight years over here and I still don't know my neighbor."

"There's absolutely no sense of community here whatsoever. I've never found it anywhere."

"Strangely enough, I am unbelievably and sadly disconnected from the community that I live in. Do I identify with Brookline? I do not."

"The way the suburbs are built today, I don't think there's a sense of backyard barbecue communities."

From comments such as these, America's suburban communities do seem to be chilly places. Devoid of people during the day, they are filled with people sitting in front of television or computer screens in the evenings, too self-preoccupied to live a Tocquevillian life of civic engagement.

Nor is it difficult for middle-class Americans to find a cause for the lack of community they feel: everyone is working too hard. "People just have less time," said Rachel Benjamin, the Brookline dentist. "When you look at the number of hours people spend at work now, the whole issue of living in the suburbs has cut time off people's days. Having dual career families cuts time out of the day." Asked why in his opinion communities seem less active, Derek Langer of Cobb said, "I think the big companies transplanting people have something to do with that. . . . A lot of executives are moved around the country. [People] were transferred every two years, no matter what. When two years came around, time to go somewhere else." If there has been an eclipse of community, the cause is the workplace. So great have become the demands of the job that the obligations of the neighborhood have had to give way.

Even among more traditional families in which women remain at home during the day, a deep feeling exists that life has simply become too busy to accommodate a strong sense of community. Ashley George of DeKalb, a homemaker, would like to interact more with her neighbors, but nobody, including herself, has the time. Cobb County's Judy Vogel remembers enough of her college sociology to offer us a short course in Durkheim's theory of anomie. Although she, too, is a homemaker, she feels special concern for her female neighbors who hold jobs: "There's nobody for backup. You're working. You're expected to work. Your child has an ear infection. There isn't a grandmother or an aunt or a cousin to call." That's why, according to her reading of the situation, "people are more isolated . . . you're into your big house with the door closed, and you're not out there with your neighbors." Suburban housewives find themselves facing demands on their time little different from the workaholic schedules of their husbands, and, as they do, something has to give. Brookline's Alexandra Onafri, who does work, wonders "how volunteer organizations in communities survive" these days now that so many women, who once staffed them, are in paying jobs.

There is one exception to this generally dismal picture of life in the local community: the church. Especially in Oklahoma and Georgia, Sunday is the day for socializing and church is the place around which it is organized. "Church is your biggest strongpoint," as DeKalb's Laurie Shepard put it. "Most people that work together really don't socialize outside of work. First of all, because you're probably living in a million different areas. They may do formal things, baby showers, weddings, and all that little stuff. Church is probably gonna be your biggest social [activity] outside of family." But even church at-

tendance has been hit by the way life is organized in modern America. "You can go to church and then just go home," Mylene Santos of Eastlake pointed out. "I wouldn't put church too high. My impression is that those that go and attend services regularly, they probably don't have a whole lot of time to get involved."

Although comments such as these lend substantial support to the notion that the vibrancy of American civic life is in decline, there are nonetheless important qualifications that need to be introduced. For one thing, the estimates of group membership cited by Robert Putnam turn out not to be correct; the GSS excluded memberships in service clubs and PTAs between 1989 and 1994, and when those are added back in, the recalculations show "only a slight decline over the period 1974–1994."[2] Our experience with the Middle Class Morality Project suggests an additional reason why declines may be exaggerated. Sociologists know that Americans overestimate their church attendance.[3] I believe, by contrast, that people often underestimate their group memberships. "I don't belong to any organizations. We don't go to church on Sundays," Dolores Wales of Sand Springs told us, before proceeding to tell us all about her enormously time-consuming experiences in a league devoted to auto racing. Cathy Peterson of Cobb County—who complained that everyone was too busy to have block parties and told us that she and her husband "don't do anything socially"—also said of her neighbors that "if I have a Super Bowl party, I invite them over . . . ; they're very good neighbors." It is quite possible that middle-class Americans, when asked about the kinds of civic organizations to which they belong, assume the questioner is interested in "serious" ones, such as the League of Women Voters or the Masons, and do not talk about the everyday groups in which they may be quite active.

We also discovered yet another reason to qualify the Putnam thesis. The notion that people are not that active in their communities seems especially inappropriate for one group of middle-class Americans: blacks in the Atlanta suburbs. Most middle-class people in this country develop their social networks at work and have fewer social contacts in their neighborhoods. But black suburbanites work with whites and live with blacks, and for them, the situation is quite different. "The majority of my social life involves social interaction with people of this community, who are predominantly black," we were told by Linda Clay-Johnson. If it is true that recent African-American suburbanization is similar to the wave of post–World War II suburbanization among so many white ethnics, then black suburbanites are now building local ties in ways not dissimilar to the Levittowners of the 1950s and 1960s. On the slope of civic decline, they are a generation behind.

When these qualifications are added together, it should come as no surprise that, despite the oft-expressed sense of alienation from their local communities, middle-class Americans remain civically active; even if there has been a decline, it started from a high peak, which means there still is a great deal left. Sybil Ross of Cobb County has lived in her present home all of one year, so, she explains apologetically, "I don't know everyone yet. I probably won't know everybody, it's so big." But because she is a mother, involvement follows automatically:

> The people that I do know are pretty active in their children's lives and in the family as far as school involvement, after-school activities. I'm very involved as far as getting my son involved in things with other kids, gymnastics, sports, music, stuff like that. I've found that the people here are also pretty involved with setting up play groups and then we'll share sitters and we'll all go out together, throw neighborhood parties. We try to have a lot of neighborhood get-togethers.

Just as we thought she was about to stop, Mrs. Ross found a fresh breath of energy:

> I am also a neighborhood watch leader here. I'm also a block captain, which means I distribute all the newsletters to a section. God, there's I don't know how many sections we've got. I have seventeen in mine, so there's probably fifty sections. I distribute newsletters every month, and I give welcome packages to new members telling them everything we have. In the neighborhood watch, there's one coordinator that when something's called in to the police, they're notified, then they call all the leaders, and then we call everybody in our area and let them know what type of a crime has taken place. There's not many. I think I've made two phone calls in a year, and they've been for like somebody was in somebody's garage, and the other one was a house broken into during construction. It seems to work. You'll find a lot of people involved in that.

When she reached this point in describing her community life, she still was not finished:

> We also have safe houses where they paint little houses. In fact, I'm supposed to pick up my stencil. It's for people that are home . . . a pretty good amount of time during the day. They'll put a safe house on their driveway so that if any child gets off a bus or is coming home and feels threatened or anything they know there are people there to welcome them. They can go into them and not be afraid. What else do we have? We have a lot of stuff like that. . . . They have a big sale here that we get involved in where we work the sales. Some of them are charity and some of them are garage sales for the subdivision. We do a lot of family activities. Like Halloween, there's a big parade. There's a big thing at Christmas for the kids with Santa. You know, we'll make things, make contributions of food or money or volunteer, dress up.

One can only wonder what Mrs. Ross's community life will look like after she has lived in her subdivision a little longer! There really are "soccer moms"—media shorthand for civically active suburban women like Mrs. Ross—in America.

Mrs. Ross was clearly atypical, but she was by no means the only person with whom we spoke who was civically active. Our 200 respondents belonged to 308 organizations in all, which means an average of roughly one and a half organizations per person.

Although one-fourth of our sample indicated that they belonged to no civic organizations, the majority claimed membership in at least one and often more than one.

Among the groups in which people were active were many voluntary associations and organizations, such as Habitat for Humanity, City Year, the National Association for the Advancement of Colored People, the Masons, the Rotary, the Optimists, the American Civil Liberties Union, Black Men of Cobb, the Red Cross, the Lions Club, the American Heart Association, the American Association of University Women, the Navy League, Up with Trees, and AIDS Walk Day. Parent-teacher organizations, sports leagues, country clubs, church groups, library support groups, bridge clubs, professional organizations, ethnic associations, unions, and block associations were the focus of their social and civic engagements. Fred Richards, a retired construction company owner in Rancho Bernardo, was on the Missouri State Council for the Arts, serving as vice president, and on the Missouri historical preservation committee. J. W. Cotton is president of an association to which 185 "retired"—by which he means victims of downsizing—men belong. Even childless families in America's suburbs are civically engaged. Samina Hoque of Medford, for example, who emigrated from Bangladesh in 1972, not only works in one of the leading cancer research institutes in the country, she also organizes poetry readings in New England, started a Bengali school in her basement, and is writing a play, inspired by her experience with church after-school programs, about inner-city youth. Henry Pearson of Eastlake, the former history professor, spends considerable time "on-line" in various discussion groups, is also active in the San Diego Zoological Society, and retains his membership in the American Historical Association, besides belonging to numerous other professional and civic organizations.

To some degree, then, Americans are still "joiners." Moreover, the organizations to which they belong, as Table 1 shows, still tend to be civic and religious rather than purely social. By themselves, these membership figures cannot answer the question of whether our respondents are less civically active than similar suburbanites a generation ago. Certainly, many of those with whom we spoke, by emphasizing how little sense of community participation they felt around them, were indicating support for the idea that some thinning out of American social life has taken place. Still, one final comment needs to be added before concluding that America's social capital has been depleted to seriously low levels. The figures in Table 1 suggest that work-related organizations are more common in American middle-class life than social and fraternal ones. To the degree that we look at the place in which people live for evidence of the decline of social capital rather than where they work, we may be looking in the wrong place.[4]

One of the sharpest criticisms made of the "Putnam" thesis is that it idealized a world dominated by men and left the impression that the decision of so many women to enter the workforce was responsible for the decline of civic involvement in the community.[5] Putnam, in subsequent formulations of his thesis,[6] responded by suggesting that no verdict could be given to the question of whether working women were responsible for declining social capital. Our interviews suggest that because women are working, they are not quite as available for civic duties in their communities as they once were. But, at the

TABLE 1			
ORGANIZATIONAL MEMBERSHIPS **MIDDLE CLASS MORALITY PROJECT**			
No organizations	52	Civic organizations	96
1 or 2 organizations	117	Church-related	83
3 or 4 organizations	16	Work-related	66
4 or more organizations	15	Social/fraternal	52
		Other	11
Total	200	Total	308

same time, like men, they are more available to engage in civic activity at work. Jeremy Toole thinks that these days people get about 90 percent of their social connections from the workplace. Most of his friends come from the office, and he thinks his wife may be jealous of that fact. Then he pauses before adding that she, too, works and 90 percent of her friends come from her job.

For every middle-class American woman who may not be involved in a local organization, there are many more who are involved in their workplace settings. "I think people's lives revolve around their work. They make their friends at work, they do their community service through work," says Diana Hamilton of Sand Springs. Elizabeth Tyler no longer feels part of Brookline because its liberal politics conflict with her increasingly conservative sensibilities. But, she adds, "I feel very much like I belong to a community of work. I very much belong to a community with my own office, with my own company, within my own industry, and I am very much involved in community affairs in Cambridge, where my office is, and in Boston." Groups like City Year and Read San Diego work with employers to find ways in which employees can take a day off work to become involved in tutoring inner-city children or cleaning vacant lots. Caroline Carlson of Brookline was "flabbergasted" from her City Year experience to learn what it was like to live in a neighborhood without parks, while Diane Sveressen just thinks there has to be somebody to offer reading opportunities to those who have too few of them. The Hudson Institute's John Clark has written that "although most discussions of civic engagement, eroding social capital, failing trust and so on refer in passing to the workplace, no one examines closely the relationship between work and community."[7] While the Middle Class Morality Project did not observe people at work at the close level he recommends, it did find that workplace involvement has to be

taken into account in any effort to portray the state of civic America.

Work-related civic activity was also important for African-Americans. Linda Clay-Johnson, who noted the ways in which black suburbanites in the Atlanta area feel closer to their black neighbors than to their white coworkers, still found that the workplace offered her a number of white friends with whom she goes to ball games or office parties. It is at work that she spends time on the activities of Habitat for Humanity, one of the organizations to which she belongs. Her husband, Henry Johnson, uses his experience at the workplace to make a point about race relations in America:

> One of the things in my office I try and push. We sometimes have social get-togethers, Christmas parties, a picnic in the summer and so forth. I always welcome these opportunities, especially to bring my wife and kids to these gatherings. A lot of times society has a problem seeing black males as family men. Any opportunity I get I do that, where I bring in my family and say, "Here's my wife and kids."

Despite the fact that social and civic engagement continues to flourish in America, if often in places different from where people live, there is reason to question whether the quality of ties made at the workplace can be compared with those we generally associate with the local community. Different spheres of social life tend to be associated with different kinds of social relationships: family ties reflect a level of intimacy, and can promote a level of anger, that we would never expect of ties between members of a parent-teacher organization. Of all the various kinds of dependencies we develop with each other, economic ties have always been the most suspect from an ethical or moral point of view. Because we form such ties to promote the highly secular activities of getting and spending, friendships and connections developed at work generally are assumed to have an instrumental character: we use people, and they use us, to solicit more business, advance our careers, sell more products, or demonstrate our popularity.

Economic ties are therefore often dismissed as not quite real, authentic, or genuine enough. This is a point that can be traced to the great theorist of capitalism: Adam Smith. In *The Theory of Moral Sentiments,* Smith pointed out that the patron-client relationships associated with feudalism, because they were based on necessity, could not be equated with friendship, a relationship that should be premised on sympathy.[8] Although the implication of Smith's point is that free-market relations will not be characterized by feudalistic necessity, a case could be made that modern capitalism requires that people give to their company, and to their coworkers, not only their physical labor, but their emotional labor as well.[9] If so, it follows that even if the decline of civil ties in the neighborhood is being compensated by new ties formed at work, the instrumental character of the latter cannot be an adequate substitute for the loss of the former.

This may well be true: our middle-class respondents thought of the social ties they developed at work in very instrumental terms. Jane Kates of Sand Springs, who is now a homemaker, is extremely down-to-earth and practical in her thoughts about her social contacts. "I think it depends on probably where you spend most of your time," she said. "When I worked, my friendships were work-related. When I quit working and started doing more schoolwork with the kids, my friendships became school-related. . . . I can see that as I progress through age here, that as I get into more volunteer things, that my friendships are formed around them." Shortly after we talked with her, we talked with Toni Cartwright, an administrative assistant. "I think most people get most of their socializing out of their work experience, just because it's a must situation. You have to go to work, and it's the only place you have a group of people." For these women, work is simply where they are, so, making the best of

it, that is where they form their connections with others.

Brian Fischer, a regional sales vice president in Cobb County, was one of those who wondered whether such instrumental ties could ever be truly satisfactory. Asked where people form their most important social networks, he at first responded in a way typical of many with whom we spoke: "It used to be the family. And then to a lesser degree residential. But it has become business." This trend bothers him. He told us:

> It has become watered down, because we have two categories of friends. We have real friends that you share stuff with, that you care about and will help. And you have all the other people that are friends. They're just people you know. We've kind of lost that . . . a real friend is someone that you bond with and you have a bond with two or three other people in the world. . . . We don't have hundreds of friends. You have hundreds of acquaintances that you call friends. . . . People don't connect over their lives anymore, people's lives are so transient that you connect for times and places. Now the question is: Does that diminish the relationship because it's on a temporary basis?

Mr. Fischer has clearly answered his own question: Something has gone out of the world because so little is left in the world to make the kinds of truly meaningful ties that give life its depth and meaning.

One way to interpret Mr. Fischer's comments is to suggest that the literature dealing with civic decline has tracked something important, but not necessarily in the right way: it is not the overall decline in group membership that is crucial—for, when added up properly, there may not be that much of a decline—but a change in the qualitative nature of those ties that matters. Active engagement in social and civic life is important, not as an end in itself, but because it expresses an altruistic desire to do something for others. If, instead, people are joining groups to do something for themselves—to win friends and influence people—then society could experience a *rise* in organization memberships and still be facing a situation of depleting social capital. Only a handful of our respondents, it turns out, indicated any particular attachment to self-help, twelve-step recovery groups, often pictured as exemplifying an obsession with the self.[10] Still, the fact that, in spite of their organizational activities, so many of them believed that selfishness in America has increased suggests that, in their view of the world, the quality of the social ties they experience are not as rich as they ought to be.

Since it is much harder to measure quality than quantity, we may never have the final word on this important subject. Still, we can be certain of how middle-class Americans frame the debate over what these qualitative changes mean. For the fact is that while people like Mr. Fischer offered eloquent statements of what is increasingly missing in American life due to its increasingly instrumental character, others took the opposite position: instrumental ties, however "thin" they may be with respect to classic ideals of friendship and loyalty, also give individuals greater choice in fashioning their social lives in ways they see fit.

Just as a significant number of middle-class Americans lament the passing of the traditional family but welcome the new freedoms they increasingly have, they also see something positive in obligations undertaken out of individual choice. Middle-class Americans often form their community ties in ways similar to the formation of their family ties. Rather than starting with an ideal of community into which individual needs should be fit, they begin with individual needs and shape their community involvements accordingly. Joseph Palumbo, for example, would rather choose those with whom he will associate than have them determined by the fact that he lives in a particular place. Some of his neighbors are community-oriented. "People are pursuing those things because they find it to their advantage. It works for them," he comments in the spirit of rational choice theory. But not for him. "I can drive thirty miles and be in any number of different communities. My life is not restricted to Medford. The people with whom I choose to associate do not have to live in a three-block radius of my home. It's the disappearance of boundaries," he claims, and he likes it. "I have transportation. I have a telephone. I can do anything I want with almost anyone instantaneously. It's a virtual society now."

The same kind of reasoning applies at the workplace. Guided by their belief in individualism, middle-class Americans assume a kind of moral division of labor: the right balance between work and civic obligation has to be found by each individual. Some people will always want to work hard while others will not. As Cobb Country's Tommy Stevens memorably put it, "If you sit there eating bonbons and watching *As the World Turns,* the world is going to turn without you." Let those who want to work "daylight to dark," as Marcus Ward, also of Cobb, put it, do so and let others do something else: "There's a place for everybody here." Alisa Rice added her thoughts: "I think people have different talents," she told us: some people have a special gift for being involved and others do not, so it makes perfect sense to encourage the former and discourage the latter. This moral division of labor may not be the most attractive vision, and it may not even be a workable one, but it is one that corresponds with strong American adherence to individualistic values.

NOTES

1. Betty Friedan, *The Feminine Mystique* (New York: Norton, 1963).
2. John F. Helliwell and Robert D. Putnam, "Correction," circulated by the authors.
3. C. Kirk Hadaway, Penny L. Marler, and Mark Chaves, "What the Polls Don't Show: A Closer Look at U.S. Church Attendance," *American Sociological Review* 58 (December 1993): 741–52.
4. This is the subject of the doctoral dissertation written by Maria Poarch as part of the Middle Class Morality Project. Maria T. Poarch, "Civic Life and Work: A Qualitative Study of Changing

Patterns of Sociability and Civic Engagement in Everyday Life," Ph.D. dissertation, Department of Sociology, Boston University, 1997.

5. Katha Pollitt, "For Whom the Ball Rolls," *Nation,* April 15, 1996, 9.

6. Robert Putnam, "The Strange Disappearance of Civic America." *American Prospect* 24 (Winter 1996):34–38.

7. John Clark, "Shifting Engagements: Lessons from the 'Bowling Alone' Debate." *Hudson Brief Papers* 196 (Indianapolis: Hudson Institute, October 1996).

8. Adam Smith, *The Theory of Moral Sentiments* (Chicago: Regnery Publishers, 1999). For more on this point, see Allan Silver, " 'Two Different Sorts of Commerce'—Friendship and Strangership in Civil Society," in Jeff Weintraub and Krishan Kumar, eds., *Public and Private in Thought and Practice: Perspectives on a Grand Dichotomy* (Chicago: University of Chicago Press, 1997), 43–74.

9. Arlie Hochschild, *The Managed Heart: Commercialization of Human Feeling* (Berkeley and Los Angeles: University of California Press, 1983).

10. John Steadman Rice, *A Disease of One's Own: Psychotherapy, Addiction, and the Emergence of Co-Dependency* (New Brunswick: Transaction, 1996).

DISCUSSION QUESTIONS

1. Think about the kinds of civic involvements of adults you know, such as your parents and neighbors. Do they resemble the people Wolfe describes, or are they more like the people others have characterized as withdrawing from active participation in their community's voluntary organizations?

2. What is Wolfe's argument about the role that gender plays in civic involvements? Do you agree or disagree with his conclusions?

SOCIAL INSTITUTIONS

Social institutions are major societal subsystems that function to meet the needs of the society at large and the needs of its members. They are normatively defined and composed of relatively stable rule-guided behaviors that, in a smoothly working society, are performed by a majority of the society's members. Institutions constitute the larger social structural framework, within which organizations, groups, and individuals are located. They provide a major force for societal continuity and stability over time.

The general assumption is that it is possible, especially in large, complex modern societies, to divide the social whole into a variety of component institutional parts. However, there is no agreement about the precise number of institutions in a society. There is general agreement that the following five institutions characterize modern industrial societies: political, economic, religious, educational, and family. However, some sociologists are inclined to add others to this list, such as the military, the mass media, leisure, and health care systems. Other sociologists think that these and other possibilities can be located within one or another of the five listed above.

From a functionalist theoretical perspective, each institution has a distinctive role to play in maintaining social order and in helping promote change or adaptation to change. Thus political institutions are responsible for the allocation of power, which is necessary in establishing and acting on societal agendas. For example, it is within the political arena that decisions are made about how to deal with the enemies of social order via its policing function. The political arena likewise is responsible for responding to external threats through its capacity to mobilize for war. Political institutions define what constitutes the common good and act on those definitions with, for example, the promotion of public works projects such as the construction of highways, airports, dams, and so forth.

In similar fashion, the primary function of economic institutions revolves around the need to organize labor, materials, resources, and technologies in the interest of ensuring the production of necessary societal goods and services. The functional significance of religious institutions revolves around the ability of religious belief systems to offer compelling accounts regarding the ultimate meaning of life in the face of evil, suffering, and death. In offering these accounts, religion is a major vehicle in the transmission of cultural values. Educational institutions also impart values. In particular, they play an important role in the socialization of children. What makes this institutional sphere distinctive is that the primary purpose of such activities is to train new generations so that they will be prepared to assume roles in the other major institutional arenas. Finally, the family is an institution with a primary responsibility for nurturing and caring. A chief responsibility involves the care and socialization of children.

Collectively, each of these institutions is crucial for the well-being of the society as a whole. Moreover, they are interdependent. Changes in one have an impact on the others. For instance, given the uncertainty of life in postcommunist Russia, many married couples are deciding not to have children. From their perspective this makes sense, including economic sense. However, from the perspective of the Russian economy, this means that the nation will experience a shortage of labor in the future, thereby setting the stage for a new economic problem. In a slightly different way, conscious decisions in one institution may be designed to have an explicit impact on another. For example, changes in divorce laws can have an impact on the number of single-parent households.

Given the all-encompassing and intertwined character of social institutions, eight articles are included in this section—more than any other section. Despite that, it can only possibly manage to provide a partial portrait of the sorts of topics that fall under the rubric "social institutions."

"Leave It to Beaver" and "Ozzie and Harriet": American Families in the 1950s

Stephanie Coontz

Stephanie Coontz contends that in thinking about changes in the contemporary family, we have a tendency to use images from the 1950s as representations of the typical American nuclear family. This is the family many know today through reruns of popular situation comedies of the era such as "Leave It to Beaver" and "Ozzie and Harriet." In this passage from The Way We Never Were, *Coontz argues that it is a mistake to do so, for two reasons. First, the nuclear family in the 1950s was in many ways different from the typical American family from earlier historical periods, and can in fact be seen as something of an anomaly. Second, beneath the surface of tranquility there were more problems and a greater level of unhappiness than romanticized portraits of this era suggest.*

Our most powerful visions of traditional families derive from images that are still delivered to our homes in countless reruns of 1950s television sit-coms. When liberals and conservatives debate family policy, for example, the issue is often framed in terms of how many "Ozzie and Harriet" families are left in America. Liberals compute the percentage of total households that contain a breadwinner father, a full-time homemaker mother, and dependent children, proclaiming that fewer than 10 percent of American families meet the "Ozzie and Harriet"or "Leave It to Beaver" model. Conservatives counter that more than half of all mothers with preschool children either are not employed or are employed only part-time. They cite polls showing that most working mothers would like to spend more time with their children and periodically announce that the Nelsons are "making a comeback," in popular opinion if not in real numbers.[1]

Since everyone admits that nontraditional families are now a majority, why this obsessive concern to establish a higher or a lower figure? Liberals seem to think that unless they can prove the "Leave It to Beaver" family is on an irreversible slide toward extinction, they cannot justify introducing new family definitions and social policies. Conservatives believe that if they can demonstrate the traditional family is alive and well, although endangered by policies that reward two-earner families and single parents, they can pass measures to revive the seeming placidity and prosperity of the 1950s, associated in many people's minds with the relative stability of marriage, gender roles, and family life in that decade. If the 1950s family existed today, both sides seem to assume, we would not have the contemporary social dilemmas that cause such debate.

At first glance, the figures seem to justify this assumption. The 1950s was a profamily period if there ever was one. Rates of divorce and illegitimacy were half what they are today; marriage was almost universally praised; the family was everywhere hailed as the most basic institution in society; and a massive baby boom, among all classes and ethnic groups, made America a "child-centered" society. Births rose from a low of 18.4 per 1,000 women during the Depression to a high of 25.3 per 1,000 in 1957. "The birth rate for third children doubled between 1940 and 1960, and that for fourth children tripled."[2]

In retrospect, the 1950s also seem a time of innocence and consensus: Gang warfare among youths did not lead to drive-by shootings; the crack epidemic had not yet hit; discipline problems in the schools were minor; no "secular humanist" movement opposed the 1954 addition of the words *under God* to the Pledge of Allegiance; and 90 percent of all school levies were approved by voters. Introduction of the polio vaccine in 1954 was the most dramatic of many medical advances that improved the quality of life for children.

The profamily features of this decade were bolstered by impressive economic improvements for vast numbers of Americans. Between 1945 and 1960, the gross national product grew by almost 250 percent and per capita income by 35 percent. Housing starts exploded after the war, peaking at 1.65 million in 1955 and remaining above 1.5 million a year for the rest of the decade; the increase in single-family home-ownership between 1946 and 1956 outstripped the increase during the entire preceding century and a half. By 1960, 62 percent of American families owned their own homes, in contrast to 43 percent in 1940. Eighty-five percent of the new homes were built in the suburbs, where the nuclear family found new possibilities for privacy and togetherness. While middle-class Americans were the prime beneficiaries of the building boom, substantial numbers of white working-class Americans moved out of the cities into affordable developments, such as Levittown.[3]

Many working-class families also moved into the middle class. The number of salaried workers increased by 61 percent between 1947 and 1957. By the mid-1950s, nearly 60 percent of the population had what was labeled a middle-class income level (between $3,000 and $10,000 in constant dollars), compared to only 31 percent in the "prosperous twenties," before the Great Depression. By 1960, thirty-one million of the nation's forty-four million families owned their own home, 87 percent had a television, and 75 percent possessed a car. The number of people with discretionary income doubled during the 1950s.[4]

For most Americans, the most salient symbol and immediate beneficiary of their newfound prosperity was the nuclear family. The biggest boom in consumer spending, for example, was in household goods. Food spending rose by only 33 percent in the five years following the Second World War, and clothing expenditures rose by 20 percent, but purchases of household furnishings and appliances climbed 240 percent.

"Nearly the entire increase in the gross national product in the mid-1950s was due to increased spending on consumer durables and residential construction," most of it oriented toward the nuclear family.[5]

Putting their mouths where their money was, Americans consistently told pollsters that home and family were the wellsprings of their happiness and self-esteem. Cultural historian David Marc argues that prewar fantasies of sophisticated urban "elegance," epitomized by the high-rise penthouse apartment, gave way in the 1950s to a more modest vision of utopia: a single-family house and a car. The emotional dimensions of utopia, however, were unbounded. When respondents to a 1955 marriage study "were asked what they thought they had sacrificed by marrying and raising a family, an overwhelming majority of them replied, 'Nothing.'" Less than 10 percent of Americans believed that an unmarried person could be happy. As one popular advice book intoned: "The family is the center of your living. If it isn't, you've gone far astray."[6]

THE NOVELTY OF THE 1950S FAMILY

In fact, the "traditional" family of the 1950s was a qualitatively new phenomenon. At the end of the 1940s, all the trends characterizing the rest of the twentieth century suddenly reversed themselves: For the first time in more than one hundred years, the age for marriage and motherhood fell, fertility increased, divorce rates declined, and women's degree of educational parity with men dropped sharply. In a period of less than ten years, the proportion of never-married persons declined by as much as it had during the entire previous half century.[7]

At the time, most people understood the 1950s family to be a new invention. The Great Depression and the Second World War had reinforced extended family ties, but in ways that were experienced by most people as stultifying and oppressive. As one child of the Depression later put it, "The Waltons" television series of the 1970s did not show what family life in the 1930s was really like: "It wasn't a big family sitting around a table radio and everybody saying goodnight while Bing Crosby crooned 'Pennies from Heaven.'" On top of Depression-era family tensions had come the painful family separations and housing shortages of the war years: By 1947, six million American families were sharing housing, and postwar family counselors warned of a widespread marital crisis caused by conflicts between the generations. A 1948 *March of Time* film, "Marriage and Divorce," declared: "No home is big enough to house two families, particularly two of different generations, with opposite theories on child training."[8]

During the 1950s, films and television plays, such as "Marty," showed people working through conflicts between marital loyalties and older kin, peer group, or community ties; regretfully but decisively, these conflicts were almost invariably "resolved in favor of the heterosexual couple rather than the claims of extended kinship networks, . . . homosociability and friendship." Talcott Parsons and other sociologists argued that modern industrial society required the family to jettison traditional productive functions and wider kin ties in order to specialize in emotional nurturance, childrearing, and production of a modern personality. Social workers "endorsed nuclear family separateness and looked suspiciously on active extended-family networks."[9]

Popular commentators urged young families to adopt a "modern" stance and strike out on their own, and with the return of prosperity, most did. By the early 1950s, newlyweds not only were establishing single-family homes at an earlier age and a more rapid rate than ever before but also were increasingly moving to the suburbs, away from the close scrutiny of the elder generation.

For the first time in American history, moreover, such average trends did not disguise sharp variations by class, race, and ethnic group. People married at a younger age, bore their children earlier and closer together, completed their families by the time they were in their late twenties, and experienced a longer period living together as a couple after their children left home. The traditional range of acceptable family behaviors—even the range in the acceptable number and timing of children—narrowed substantially.[10]

The values of 1950s families also were new. The emphasis on producing a whole world of satisfaction, amusement, and inventiveness within the nuclear family had no precedents. Historian Elaine Tyler May comments: "The legendary family of the 1950s . . . was not, as common wisdom tells us, the last gasp of 'traditional' family life with deep roots in the past. Rather, it was the first wholehearted effort to create a home that would fulfill virtually all its members' personal needs through an energized and expressive personal life."[11]

Beneath a superficial revival of Victorian domesticity and gender distinctions, a novel rearrangement of family ideals and male-female relations was accomplished. For women, this involved a reduction in the moral aspect of domesticity and an expansion of its orientation toward personal service. Nineteenth-century middle-class women had cheerfully left housework to servants, yet 1950s women of all classes created makework in their homes and felt guilty when they did not do everything for themselves. The amount of time women spent doing housework actually *increased* during the 1950s, despite the advent of convenience foods and new, labor-saving appliances; child care absorbed more than twice as much time as it had in the 1920s. By the mid-1950s, advertisers' surveys reported on a growing tendency among women to find "housework a medium of expression for . . . [their] femininity and individuality."[12]

For the first time, men as well as women were encouraged to root their identity and self-image in familial and parental roles. The novelty of these family and gender values can be seen in the dramatic postwar transformation of movie themes. Historian Peter Biskind writes that almost every major male star who had played tough loners in the 1930s and 1940s "took the roles with which he was synonymous and transformed them, in the fifties, into neurotics or psychotics." In these films, "men belonged at home, not on the streets or out on the prairie, . . . not alone or hanging out with other men." The women who got men to settle down had to promise enough sex to compete with "bad" women, but ultimately they provided it only in the marital bedroom and only in return for some help fixing up the house.[13]

Public images of Hollywood stars were consciously reworked to show their commitment to marriage and stability. After 1947, for example, the Actors' Guild organized "a series of unprecedented speeches . . . to be given to civic groups around the country, emphasizing that the stars now embodied the rejuvenated family life unfolding in the suburbs." Ronald Reagan's defense of actors' family values was especially "stirring," noted one reporter, but female stars, unlike Reagan and other male stars, were obliged to *live* the new values as well as propagandize them. Joan Crawford, for example, one of the brash, tough, independent leading ladies of the prewar era, was now pictured as a devoted mother whose sex appeal and glamour did not prevent her from doing her own housework. She posed for pictures mopping floors and gave interviews about her childrearing philosophy.[14]

The "good life" in the 1950s, historian Clifford Clark points out, made the family "the focus of fun and recreation." The ranch house, architectural embodiment of this new ideal, discarded the older privacy of the kitchen, den, and sewing room (representative of separate spheres for men and women) but introduced new privacy and luxury into the master bedroom. There was an unprecedented "glorification of self-indulgence" in family life. Formality was discarded in favor of "livability," "comfort," and "convenience." A contradiction in terms in earlier periods, "the sexually charged, child-centered family took its place at the center of the postwar American dream."[15]

On television, David Marc comments, all the "normal" families moved to the suburbs during the 1950s. Popular culture turned such suburban families into capitalism's answer to the Communist threat. In his famous "kitchen debate" with Nikita Khrushchev in 1959, Richard Nixon asserted that the superiority of capitalism over communism was embodied not in ideology or military might but in the comforts of the suburban home, "designed to make things easier for our women."[16]

Acceptance of domesticity was the mark of middle-class status and upward mobility. In sitcom families, a middle-class man's work was totally irrelevant to his identity; by the same token, the problems of working-class families did not lie in their economic situation but in their failure to create harmonious gender roles. Working-class and ethnic men on television had one defining characteristic: They were unable to control their wives. The families of middle-class men, by contrast, were generally well behaved.[17]

Not only was the 1950s family a new invention; it was also a historical fluke, based on a unique and temporary conjuncture of economic, social, and political factors. During the war, Americans had saved at a rate more than three times higher than that in the decades before or since. Their buying power was further enhanced by America's extraordinary competitive advantage at the end of the war, when every other industrial power was devastated by the experience. This privileged economic position sustained both a tremendous expansion of middle-class management occupations and a new honeymoon between management and organized labor: During the 1950s, real wages increased by more than they had in the entire previous half century.[18]

The impact of such prosperity on family formation and stability was magnified by the role of government, which could afford to be generous with education benefits, housing loans, highway and sewer construction, and job training. All this allowed most middle-class Americans, and a large number of working-class ones, to adopt family values and strategies that assumed the availability of cheap energy, low-interest home loans, expanding educational and occupational opportunities, and steady employment. These expectations encouraged early marriage, early childbearing, expansion of consumer debt, and residential patterns that required long commutes to work—all patterns that would become highly problematic by the 1970s. . . .

MORE COMPLEXITIES: REPRESSION, ANXIETY, UNHAPPINESS, AND CONFLICT

The happy, homogeneous families that we "remember" from the 1950s were thus partly a result of the media's denial of diversity. But even among sectors of the population where the "least objectionable" families did prevail, their values and behaviors were not entirely a spontaneous, joyful reaction to prosperity. If suburban ranch houses and family barbecues were the carrots offered to white middle-class families that adopted the new norms, there was also a stick.

Women's retreat to housewifery, for example, was in many cases not freely chosen. During the war, thousands of women had entered new jobs, gained new skills, joined unions, and fought against job discrimination. Although 95 percent of the new women employees had expected when they were first hired to quit work at the end of the war, by 1945 almost an equally overwhelming majority did not want to give up their independence, responsibility, and income, and expressed the desire to continue working.[19]

After the war, however, writes one recent student of postwar reconstruction, "management went to extraordinary lengths to purge women

workers from the auto plants," as well as from other high-paying and nontraditional jobs. As it turned out, in most cases women were not permanently expelled from the labor force but were merely downgraded to lower-paid, "female" jobs. Even at the end of the purge, there were more women working than before the war, and by 1952 there were two million more wives at work than at the peak of wartime production. The jobs available to these women, however, lacked the pay and the challenges that had made wartime work so satisfying, encouraging women to define themselves in terms of home and family even when they were working.[20]

Vehement attacks were launched against women who did not accept such self-definitions. In the 1947 bestseller, *The Modern Woman: The Lost Sex,* Marynia Farnham and Ferdinand Lundberg described feminism as a "deep illness," called the notion of an independent woman a "contradiction in terms," and accused women who sought educational or employment equality of engaging in symbolic "castration" of men. As sociologist David Riesman noted, a woman's failure to bear children went from being "a social disadvantage and sometimes a personal tragedy" in the nineteenth century to being a "quasi-perversion" in the 1950s. The conflicting messages aimed at women seemed almost calculated to demoralize: At the same time as they labeled women "unnatural" if they did not seek fulfillment in motherhood, psychologists and popular writers insisted that most modern social ills could be traced to domineering mothers who invested too much energy and emotion in their children. Women were told that "no other experience in life . . . will provide the same sense of fulfillment, of happiness, of complete pervading contentment" as motherhood. But soon after delivery they were asked, "Which are you first of all, Wife or Mother?" and warned against the tendency to be "too much mother, too little wife."[21]

Women who could not walk the fine line between nurturing motherhood and castrating "momism," or who had trouble adjusting to "creative homemaking," were labeled neurotic, perverted, or schizophrenic. A recent study of hospitalized "schizophrenic" women in the San Francisco Bay Area during the 1950s concludes that institutionalization and sometimes electric shock treatments were used to force women to accept their domestic roles and their husbands' dictates. Shock treatments also were recommended for women who sought abortion, on the assumption that failure to want a baby signified dangerous emotional disturbance.[22]

All women, even seemingly docile ones, were deeply mistrusted. They were frequently denied the right to serve on juries, convey property, make contracts, take out credit cards in their own name, or establish residence. A 1954 article in *Esquire* called working wives a "menace"; a *Life* author termed married women's employment a "disease." Women were excluded from several professions, and some states even gave husbands total control over family finances.[23] There were not many permissible alternatives to baking brownies, experimenting with new canned soups, and getting rid of stains around the collar.

Men were also pressured into acceptable family roles, since lack of a suitable wife could mean the loss of a job or promotion for a middle-class man. Bachelors were categorized as "immature," "infantile," "narcissistic," "deviant," or even "pathological." Family advice expert Paul Landis argued: "Except for the sick, the badly crippled, the deformed, the emotionally warped and the mentally defective, almost everyone has an opportunity [and, by clear implication, a duty] to marry."[24]

Families in the 1950s were products of even more direct repression. Cold war anxieties merged with concerns about the expanded sexuality of family life and the commercial world to create what one authority calls the domestic version of George F. Kennan's containment policy toward the Soviet Union: A "normal" family and vigilant mother became the "front line" of defense against treason; anticommunists linked deviant family or sexual behavior to sedition. The FBI and other government agencies instituted unprecedented state intrusion into private life under the guise of investigating subversives. Gay baiting was almost as widespread and every bit as vicious as red baiting.[25]

The Civil Service Commission fired 2,611 persons as "security risks" and reported that 4,315 others resigned under the pressure of investigations that asked leading questions of their neighbors and inquired into the books they read or the music to which they listened. In this atmosphere, movie producer Joel Schumacher recalls, "No one told the truth. . . . People pretended they weren't unfaithful. They pretended that they weren't homosexual. They pretended that they weren't horrible."[26]

Even for people not directly coerced into conformity by racial, political, or personal repression, the turn toward families was in many cases more a defensive move than a purely affirmative act. Some men and women entered loveless marriages in order to forestall attacks about real or suspected homosexuality or lesbianism. Growing numbers of people saw the family, in the words of one husband, as the one "group that in spite of many disagreements internally always will face its external enemies together." Conservative families warned children to beware of communists who might masquerade as friendly neighbors; liberal children learned to confine their opinions to the family for fear that their father's job or reputation might be threatened.[27]

Americans were far more ambivalent about the 1950s than later retrospectives, such as "Happy Days," suggest. Plays by Tennessee Williams, Eugene O'Neill, and Arthur Miller explored the underside of family life. Movies such as *Rebel Without a Cause* (1955) expressed fears about youths whose parents had failed them. There was an almost obsessive concern with the idea that the mass media had broken down parental control, thus provoking an outburst of "delinquency and youthful vicious-ness." In 1954, psychiatrist Fredric Wertham's *Seduction of the Innocents* warned: "The atmos-phere of crime comic books is unparalleled in the history of children's literature of any time or any nation." In 1955, Congress discussed nearly 200 bills relating to delinquency. If some of these anxieties seem almost charmingly naive to our more hardened age, they were no less real for all that.[28]

Many families, of course, managed to hold such fears at bay—and it must be admitted that the suburbs and small towns of America were exceptionally good places for doing so. Shielded from the multiplying problems and growing diversity of the rest of society, residents of these areas could afford to be neighborly. Church attendance and membership in volun-tary associations tended to be higher in the sub-urbs than in the cities, although contact with ex-tended kin was less frequent. Children played in the neighborhoods and cul-de-sacs with only cursory warnings about strangers.[29]

In her autobiographical account of a 1950s adolescence, Susan Allen Toth remembers growing up "gradually" and "quietly" in a small town of the period: "We were not seared by fierce poverty, racial tensions, drug abuse, street crimes." Perhaps this innocence was "constrict-ing," she admitted, but it also gave a child "shel-ter and space to grow." For Toth, insulation from external problems meant that growing up was a process of being "cossetted, gently warmed, transmuted by slow degrees."[30]

For many other children, however, growing up in 1950s families was not so much a matter of being protected from the harsh realities of the outside world as preventing the outside world from learning the harsh realities of family life. Few would have guessed that radiant Marilyn Van Derbur, crowned Miss America in 1958, had been sexually violated by her wealthy, re-spectable father from the time she was five until she was eighteen, when she moved away to col-lege.[31] While not all family secrets were quite

so shocking, author Benita Eisler recalls a com-mon middle-class experience:

> As college classmates became close friends, I heard sagas of life at home that were Gothic hor-ror stories. Behind the hedges and driveways of upper-middle-class suburbia were tragedies of madness, suicide, and—most prevalent of all—chronic and severe alcoholism. . . .
>
> The real revelation for me was the role played by children in . . . keeping up appearances. Many of my new friends had been pressed into service early as happy smiling fronts, emissaries of fam-ily normalcy, cheerful proof that "nothing was re-ally wrong" at the Joneses.[32]

Beneath the polished facades of many "ideal" families, suburban as well as urban, was vio-lence, terror, or simply grinding misery that only occasionally came to light. Although Col-orado researchers found 302 battered-child cases, including 33 deaths, in their state during one year alone, the major journal of American family sociology did not carry a single article on family violence between 1939 and 1969. Wife battering was not even considred a "real" crime by most people. Psychiatrists in the 1950s, fol-lowing Helene Deutsch, "regarded the battered woman as a masochist who provoked her hus-band into beating her."[33]

Historian Elizabeth Pleck describes how one Family Service Association translated this psy-chological approach into patient counseling dur-ing the 1950s. Mrs. K came to the Association because her husband was an alcoholic who re-peatedly abused her, both physically and sexu-ally. The agency felt, however, that it was sim-plistic to blame the couple's problems on his drinking. When counselors learned that Mrs. K refused her husband's demands for sex after he came home from working the night shift, they decided that they had found a deeper difficulty: Mrs. K needed therapy to "bring out some of her anxiety about sex activities."[34]

We will probably never know how prevalent incest and sexual abuse were in the 1950s, but we do know that when girls or women reported incidents of such abuse to therapists, they were frequently told that they were "fantasizing" their unconscious oedipal desires. Although incest cases were common throughout the records of caseworkers from 1880 to 1960, according to historian Linda Gordon's study of these documents, the problem was increasingly redefined as one of female "sex delinquency." By 1960, despite overwhelming evidence to the contrary, experts described incest as a "one-in-a-million occurrence." Not until the 1970s, heartened by a supportive women's movement, were many women able to speak out about the sexual abuse they had suffered in silent agony during the 1950s; others, such as Marilyn Van Derbur, are only now coming forward.[35]

Less dramatic but more widespread was the existence of significant marital unhappiness. Between one-quarter and one-third of the marriages contracted in the 1950s eventually ended in divorce; during that decade two million legally married people lived apart from each other. Many more couples simply toughed it out. Sociologist Mirra Komarovsky concluded that of the working-class couples she interviewed in the 1950s, "slightly less than one-third [were] happily or very happily married."[36]

National polls found that 20 percent of all couples considered their marriages unhappy, and another 20 percent reported only "medium happiness." In the middle-class sample studied by Elaine Tyler May, two-thirds of the husbands and wives rated their marriages "decidedly happier than average," but an outside observer might well have scaled this back to a percentage much like Komarovsky's, for even the happiest couples reported many dissatisfactions and communication problems. "The idea of a 'working marriage' was one that often included constant day-to-day misery for one or both partners."[37]

A successful 1950s family, moreover, was often achieved at enormous cost to the wife, who was expected to subordinate her own needs and aspirations to those of both her husband and

her children. In consequence, no sooner was the ideal of the postwar family accepted than observers began to comment perplexedly on how discontented women seemed in the very roles they supposedly desired most. In 1949, *Life* magazine reported that "suddenly and for no plain reason" American women were "seized with an eerie restlessness." Under a "mask of placidity" and an outwardly feminine appearance, one physician wrote in 1953, there was often "an inwardly tense and emotionally unstable individual seething with hidden aggressiveness and resentment."[38]

Some women took this resentment out on their families. Surely some of the bizarre behaviors that Joan Crawford exhibited toward her children, according to her daughter's bitter remembrance, *Mommie Dearest,* flowed from the frustration of being forced into a domestic role about which she was intensely ambivalent. Other women tried to dull the pain with alcohol or drugs. Tranquilizers were developed in the 1950s in response to a need that physicians explicitly saw as female: Virtually nonexistent in 1955, tranquilizer consumption reached 462,000 pounds in 1958 and soared to 1.15 million pounds merely a year later. Commentators noted a sharp increase in women's drinking during the decade, even though many middle-class housewives kept their liquor stash hidden and thought no one knew that they needed a couple of drinks to face an evening of family "togetherness."[39]

But not even "the four *b*'s," as the mother of a colleague of mine used to label her life in the 1950s—"booze, bowling, bridge, and boredom"—could entirely conceal the discontents. In 1956, the *Ladies' Home Journal* devoted an issue to "The Plight of the Young Mother." When *McCall's* ran an article entitled "The Mother Who Ran Away" in the same year, the magazine set a new record for readership. A former editor commented: "We suddenly realized that all those women at home with their three and a half children were miserably unhappy." By 1960, almost every major news journal was using the word *trapped* to describe the feelings of the American housewife. When *Redbook*'s editors asked readers to provide them with examples of "Why Young Mothers Feel Trapped," they received 24,000 replies.[40]

Although Betty Friedan's bestseller *The Feminine Mystique* did not appear until 1963, it was a product of the 1950s, originating in the discontented responses Friedan received in 1957 when she surveyed fellow college classmates from the class of 1942. The heartfelt identification of other 1950s women with "the problem that has no name" is preserved in the letters Friedan received after her book was published, letters now at the Schlesinger Library at Radcliffe.[41]

Men tended to be more satisfied with marriage than were women, especially over time, but they, too, had their discontents. Even the most successful strivers after the American dream sometimes muttered about "mindless conformity." The titles of books such as *The Organization Man,* by William Whyte (1956), and *The Lonely Crowd,* by David Riesman (1958), summarized a widespread critique of 1950s culture. Male resentments against women were expressed in the only partly humorous diatribes of *Playboy* magazine (founded in 1953) against "money-hungry" gold diggers or lazy "parasites" trying to trap men into commitment.[42]

CONTRADICTIONS OF THE 1950s FAMILY BOOM

Happy memories of 1950s family life are not all illusion, of course—there were good times for many families. But even the most positive aspects had another side. One reason that the 1950s family model was so fleeting was that it contained the seeds of its own destruction. It was during the 1950s, not the 1960s, that the youth market was first produced, then institutionalized into the youth culture. It was through such innocuous shows as "Howdy Doody" and "The Disney Hour" that advertisers first discov-

ered the riches to be gained by bypassing parents and appealing directly to youth. It was also during this period that advertising and consumerism became saturated with sex.[43]

In the 1950s, family life was financed by economic practices that were to have unanticipated consequences in the 1970s. Wives and mothers first started to work in great numbers during the 1950s in order to supplement their families' purchasing power; expansion of household comforts came "at the cost of an astronomical increase of indebtedness." The labor-management accord of the 1950s helped erode the union movement's ability to oppose the takebacks and runaway shops that destroyed the "family wage system" during the 1970s and 1980s.[44]

Family and gender strategies also contained some time bombs. Women who "played dumb" to catch a man, as 40 percent of Barnard College women admitted to doing, sometimes despised their husbands for not living up to the fiction of male superiority they had worked so hard to promote. Commitment to improving the quality of family life by manipulating the timing and spacing of childbearing led to the social acceptability of family planning and the spread of birth-control techniques. Concentration of childbearing in early marriage meant that growing numbers of women had years to spare for paid work after the bulk of their child-care duties were finished. Finally, 1950s families fostered intense feelings and values that produced young people with a sharp eye for hypocrisy; many of the so-called rebels of the 1960s were simply acting on values that they had internalized in the bosom of their families.[45]

NOTES

1. *Boston Globe,* 11 April 1989; David Blankenhorn, "Ozzie and Harriet, Alive and Well," *Washington Post,* 11 June 1989; "Ozzie and Harriet Redux," *Fortune,* 25 March 1991; Richard Morin, "Family Life Makes a Comeback: Maybe Ozzie and

Harriet Had a Point," *Washington Post National Weekly Edition,* 25 November–1 December 1991.

2. William Chafe, *The American Woman: Her Changing Social, Economic, and Political Roles, 1920–1970* (New York: Oxford University Press, 1974), p. 217.

3. Joseph Mason, *History of Housing in the U.S., 1930–1980* (Houston: Gulf, 1982); Martin Mayer, *The Builders* (New York: Gulf, 1978), p. 132.

4. William Chafe, *The Unfinished Journey: America Since World War II* (New York: Oxford University Press, 1986), pp. 111–18; Stephen Mintz and Susan Kellogg, *Domestic Revolutions: A Social History of American Family Life* (New York: Free Press, 1988), pp. 182–83; Elaine Tyler May, *Homeward Bound: American Families in the Cold War Era* (New York: Basic Books, 1988), p. 165.

5. May, *Homeward Bound,* p. 167; Clifford Clark, Jr., "Ranch-House Suburbia: Ideals and Realities," in *Recasting America: Culture and Politics in the Age of Cold War,* ed. Lary May (Chicago: University of Chicago Press, 1989), p. 188.

6. David Marc, *Comic Visions: Television Comedy and American Culture* (Boston: Unwin Hyman, 1989), p. 50; May, *Homeward Bound,* p. 28; Mintz and Kellogg, *Domestic Revolutions,* p. 180.

7. Steven D. McLaughlin et al., *The Changing Lives of American Women* (Chapel Hill: University of North Carolina Press, 1988), p. 7; Donald Brogue, *The Population of the United States* (Glencoe, Ill.: Free Press, 1959).

8. Susan Ware, *Holding Their Own: American Women in the 1930s* (Boston: Twayne, 1982); Ruth Milkman, "Women's Work and Economic Crisis: Some Lessons from the Great Depression," *Review of Radical Political Economics* 8 (1976): 84; "Marriage and Divorce," a *March of Time* film, vol. 14, no. 7, 1948.

9. Talcott Parsons and Robert Bales, *Family, Socialization, and Interaction Process* (Glencoe: Free Press, 1955); Judith E. Smith, "The Marrying Kind: Working Class Courtship and Marriage in Postwar Popular Culture" (Paper presented at American Studies Association Conference, New Orleans, October 1990), p. 3; Linda Gordon, *Heroes of Their Own Lives: The Politics and History of Family Violence, 1880–1960* (New York: Viking, 1988), p. 161.

10. May, *Homeward Bound,* p. 137; Mary Ryan, *Womanhood in America from Colonial Times to the Present* (New York: Franklin Watts, 1983), pp. 271–72; Susan Householder Van Horn, *Women, Work, and Fertility, 1900–1986* (New York: New York University Press, 1988); Landon Jones, *Great Expectations: America and the Baby Boom Generation* (New York: Ballantine, 1980), p. 34.

11. May, *Homeward Bound,* p. 11.

12. Glenna Mathews, *"Just a Housewife": The Rise and Fall of Domesticity in America* (New York: Oxford University Press, 1987); Betty Friedan, *The Feminine Mystique* (New York: Dell, 1963), p. 204.

13. Peter Biskind, *Seeing Is Believing: How Hollywood Taught Us to Stop Worrying and Love the Fifties* (New York: Pantheon, 1983), pp. 252, 255.

14. Lary May, "Movie Star Politics," in *Recasting America: Culture and Politics in the Age of Cold War,* ed. Lary May (Chicago: University of Chicago Press, 1989), p. 146; May, *Homeward Bound,* pp. 64, 140–42.

15. Clifford Clark, *The American Family Home, 1800–1960* (Chapel Hill: University of North Carolina Press, 1986), pp. 209, 216; Clifford Clark, "Ranch-House Suburbia: Ideals and Realities," in *Recasting America,* ed. Lary May, pp. 171, 182; May, *Homeward Bound,* p. 162.

16. Marc, *Comic Visions,* p. 81; May, *Homeward Bound,* p. 18.

17. Lynda Glennon and Richard Bustch, "The Family as Portrayed on Television, 1949–1978," in *Television and Behavior: Ten Years of Scientific Progress and Implications for the Eighties,* ed. David Pearle et al. (Washington, D.C.: U.S. Department of Health and Human Services, 1982); May, *Homeward Bound,* p. 146; Ella Taylor, *Prime-Time Families: Television Culture in Postwar America* (Berkeley: University of California Press, 1989).

18. Samuel Bowles, David Gordon, and Thomas Weisskopf, *Beyond the Wasteland: A Democratic Alternative to Economic Decline* (Garden City, N.Y.: Doubleday, 1983), pp. 66–67, 74; Chafe, *Unfinished Journey,* pp. 111–18; James A. Henretta et al., *America's History,* vol. 2

(Chicago: Dorsey Press, 1987), p. 852; David Potter, *People of Plenty* (Chicago: University of Chicago Press, 1959).

19. Joan Ellen Trey, "Women in the World War II Economy," *Review of Radical Political Economics,* July 1972; Chafe, *American Woman,* pp. 178–79.

20. Ruth Milkman, *Gender at Work: The Dynamics of Job Segregation by Sex During World War II* (Urbana: University of Illinois Press, 1987), p. 102; Sheila Tobias and Lisa Anderson, "What Really Happened to Rosie the Riveter" *MSS Modular Publications* 9 (1973); Steven D. McLaughlin et al., *The Changing Lives of American Women* (Chapel Hill: University of North Carolina, 1988), p. 24.

21. Marynia Farnham and Ferdinand Lundberg, *Modern Woman: The Lost Sex* (New York: Harper and Brothers, 1947), p. 24; Susan Hartmann, *The Home Front and Beyond: American Women in the 1940s* (Boston: Twayne Publishers, 1982), pp. 173, 179–80; May, *Homeward Bound,* pp. 96–97.

22. Carol Warren, *Madwives: Schizophrenic Women in the 1950s* (New Brunswick: Rutgers University Press, 1987); Hartmann, *Home Front,* p. 174.

23. Douglas Miller and Marion Nowak, *The Fifties: The Way We Really Were* (Garden City, N.Y.: Doubleday, 1977), pp. 164–65.

24. Mintz and Kellogg, *Domestic Revolutions,* p. 181; Barbara Ehrenreich, *The Hearts of Men: American Dreams and the Flight from Commitment* (Garden City, N.Y.: Anchor Press, 1983), pp. 14–28; Miller and Nowak, *The Fifties,* p. 154.

25. Paul Boyer, *By the Bomb's Early Light: American Thought and Culture at the Dawn of the Atomic Age* (New York: Pantheon, 1985); Roger Morris, *Richard Milhous Nixon: The Rise of an American Politician* (New York: Holt, 1990); Ellen Schrecker, *No Ivory Tower: McCarthyism and the Universities* (New York: Oxford University Press, 1986); David Caute, *The Great Fear: The Anti-Communist Purge Under Truman and Eisenhower* (New York: Simon & Schuster, 1978); Henretta et al., *America's History,* p. 867; May, *Homeward Bound,* pp. 13–14, 94–95.

26. Benita Eisler, *Private Lives: Men and Women of the Fifties* (New York: Franklin Watts, 1986), p. 341.

27. May, *Homeward Bound,* p. 91.

28. May, *Homeward Bound,* p. 109; James B. Gilbert, *A Cycle of Outrage: America's Reaction to the Juvenile Delinquent in the 1950s* (New York: Oxford University Press, 1986), pp. 3, 8, 66.

29. For a defense of the suburbs, see Scott Donaldson, *The Suburban Myth* (New York: Columbia University Press, 1969). See also John Seeley, R. Alexander Sim, and E. W. Loosely, *Crestwood Heights: A Study of Culture in Suburban Life* (New York: Basic Books, 1956); and William H. Whyte, *The Organization Man* (New York: Simon & Schuster, 1956). Though Whyte criticized the lack of individualism in the suburbs he described, his description of boring group life might sound rather comforting to many alienated modern Americans.

30. Susan Allen Toth, *Blooming: A Small-Town Girlhood* (Boston: Little, Brown, 1978), pp. 3, 4.

31. Marilyn Van Derbur Atler, "The Darkest Secret," *People,* 6 July 1991.

32. Eisler, *Private Lives,* p. 170. See also Nancy Hall, *A True Story of a Drunken Mother* (Boston: South End Press, 1990).

33. Mintz and Kellogg, *Domestic Revolutions,* p. 194; C. Henry Kempe et al., "The Battered Child Syndrome," *Journal of the American Medical Association* (1962): 181; Elizabeth Pleck, *Domestic Tyranny: The Making of Social Policy Against Family Violence from Colonial Times to the Present* (New York: Oxford University Press, 1987), pp. 169, 182.

34. Pleck, *Domestic Tyranny,* pp. 162–63.

35. Pleck, *Domestic Tyranny,* pp. 156–57; Gordon, *Heroes of Their Own Lives,* pp. 206–22.

36. Mirra Komarovsky, *Blue-Collar Marriage* (New Haven: Vintage, 1962), p. 331.

37. Mintz and Kellogg, *Domestic Revolutions,* p. 194; May, *Homeward Bound,* p. 202.

38. Mintz and Kellogg, *Domestic Revolutions,* p. 195; Miller and Nowak, *The Fifties,* p. 174. The physician reported that most of these women had fulfilled their wifely and motherly roles for years, in seemingly irreproachable ways, but were nevertheless unfulfilled. Unable to accept the logic of his own evidence, the doctor concluded that their problems were a result of their "intense strivings for masculinity."

39. Christina Crawford, *Mommie Dearest* (New York: William Morrow, 1978), especially pp. 51–56, 82–88; Chafe, *Unfinished Journey,* p. 126; Edith Lisansky, "The Woman Alcoholic," *Annals of the American Academy of Political and Social Sciences* (1958): 315.

40. Eisler, *Private Lives,* pp. 209–10; Friedan, *The Feminine Mystique,* pp. 44, 59.

41. Mathews, *"Just a Housewife,"* pp. 219–20.

42. Ehrenreich, *The Hearts of Men.*

43. Jones, *Great Expectations,* pp. 41–49; Betty Friedan, *Feminine Mystique,* New York: W. W. Norton, 1997, pp. 250–51.

44. Chafe, *Unfinished Journey,* p. 144.

45. Chafe, *Unfinished Journey,* p. 125; Eisler, *Private Lives,* p. 369; Chafe, *American Woman,* p. 218; Ryan, *Womanhood in America,* p. 277; May, *Homeward Bound,* pp. 149–52; Joseph Demartini, "Change Agents and Generational Relationships: A Reevaluation of Mannheim's Problem of Generations," *Social Forces* 64 (1985).

DISCUSSION QUESTIONS

1. Why do you think so many young people today are avid viewers of the reruns of television portrayals of the family from the 1950s? Do they have an ironic attitude or are they genuinely nostalgic for what they think is a bygone world?

2. Based on Coontz's review of the problems with the 1950s family, what were the major forces that served to challenge it? What role did women play in the reconsideration of this form of family structure?

READING 32

Divorce and Remarriage

Andrew J. Cherlin

What are the consequences of divorce and remarriage for all the parties involved—spouses and children? These are the questions that Andrew Cherlin raises in this selection from Marriage, Divorce, Remarriage. *He notes at the outset that the state of social scientific knowledge about divorce was until recently quite underdeveloped, but as his discussion illustrates, our understanding of the toll that divorces often take has expanded considerably. Cherlin presents a tempered and nuanced review of the economic and both the short-term and long-term psychological impacts of divorce. Turning to remarriage, he suggests that it entails a complicated renegotiation of social relations, often without a very clear road map. The selection concludes with an overview of some typical forms of familial relationships resulting from remarriage.*

Although social scientists have long been concerned about divorce, they produced little empirical research about its consequences until the 1970s. Since then, they have begun to establish a body of knowledge about its effects on adults and children. On the one hand, recent studies lend qualified support to the view that divorce can be beneficial in the long run for some of those involved. For instance, researchers have produced findings in support of the oft-stated claim that children function better in a single-parent family than in a conflict-ridden nuclear family.[1] On the other hand, the studies also show that divorce is a traumatic process that can cause serious short-term psychological distress. There is evidence that for some adults and children, the harmful effects may be longer lasting.

Developmental psychologists P. Lindsay Chase-Lansdale and E. Mavis Hetherington suggest that the first two years following the breakup of a marriage constitute a "crisis period."[2] During this difficult time adults and children typically face intense emotional upset, continuing family conflict, and adjustments to new living arrangements. When children are involved—as they are in more than half of all divorces—they usually live with their mothers, whose daily routine is often disrupted during the first year after divorce. Hetherington followed for six years a group of middle-class families who had recently divorced and a comparison group of two-parent families. All of the families initially had preschool-aged children. She reported the predominance just after the divorce of a "chaotic lifestyle," as one participant called it, which seemed to persist throughout the first year after divorce and then improve in the second year. Single mothers and their children in the divorced families were more likely to eat pickup meals at irregular times, the children's bedtimes were erratic, the children were more likely to arrive at school late, and so forth.[3]

Saddled with sole or primary responsibility for supporting themselves and their children, single mothers frequently have too little time and too few resources to manage effectively. Robert S. Weiss, after several years of observing single parents, identified three common sources of strain. One is responsibility overload: single parents must make all the decisions and provide for all the needs of their families, a responsibility that at times can be overwhelming. Another is task overload: many single parents simply have too much to do, with working, housekeeping, and parenting; consequently, there is no slack time to meet unexpected demands. A third is emotional overload: single parents are always on call to give emotional support to their children, whether or not their own emotional resources are temporarily depleted.[4]

Moreover, divorced and separated women who are raising children often find that their economic position has deteriorated. Many of those who were not employed in the years preceding their separation have difficulty reentering the job market. Others who were employed find that their wages are too low to support a family. In theory, divorced fathers should continue to help support their children, but in practice only a minority do so adequately. Some avoid a legal agreement altogether: in a 1989 Bureau of the Census survey, 19 percent of all divorced and separated women living with children under 21 reported that they wanted child support but couldn't obtain an award for reasons such as the inability to find their ex-husbands. Even among divorced and separated women who were supposed to receive child support payments, 22 percent reported receiving nothing in 1989. And among those who were fortunate

enough to receive any payments in 1989, the average amount received was just $3,322 for the divorced and $3,060 for the separated.[5]

As a result of their limited earning power and of the low level of child support, single mothers and their children often experience a sharp decline in their standard of living after a separation. In the Panel Study of Income Dynamics (PSID), a national study of families who were interviewed annually beginning in 1968, separated and divorced women suffered an average drop of about 30 percent in their standard of living in the year following a marital break-up. Men, in contrast, experienced a rise of 10 to 15 percent because they no longer fully supported their wives and children.[6] Middle-class homemakers suffered the largest average declines. They had agreed to take care of the home and the children full time in return for their husbands' provision of all financial support. When that bargain broke down, they became dependent on meager child support payments and whatever low-paying jobs their neglected labor market skills could command. Among women in the PSID who had above-average family incomes just prior to the separation, 31 percent saw their standard of living in the year after the separation plunge by more than half.[7]

Many single parents, particularly those with low incomes, receive assistance from a network of kin, but the resources of these networks usually are limited and spread thin. Economic pressure on the mother means that she has less time for child care and for her personal life. Harried and overburdened, some single mothers fail to provide the attention and care children need, especially during the first year or two after the separation.

To be sure, life in a single-parent family, despite economic pressures, also has its rewards, foremost the relief from marital conflict. In addition, single parents may gain increased self-esteem from their ability to manage the demands of work life and family life by themselves. They may enjoy their independence and their close relationships to their children.[8] Some writers argue that women are particularly likely to develop an increased sense of self-worth from the independence and greater control over their life they achieve after divorce.[9]

Psychologically, the period following the separation is likely to be very stressful for both spouses, regardless of who initiated the break-up. Both spouses commonly retain ambivalent feelings toward their partners even if they were relieved to have ended an unhappy marriage. For example, Weiss studied adults who came to a series of eight-week discussion and counseling sessions he organized in Boston for persons separated less than one year. Most reported a persistent feeling of attachment to their spouse, a sense of bonding that continued for several months whether the participant had initiated the separation or not. Thus many of the separated adults who attended Weiss's seminars felt an intermittent longing for their husbands or wives and an accompanying anxiety that Weiss labeled "separation distress." Only after the first year of separation did this attachment fade.[10]

Overall, then, the first year after divorce or separation is often a time when the separated spouses experience ambivalence about the separation, increased anxiety, occasional depression, and personal disorganization—even if they were the ones who chose to end their marriages. And it is a time when the income of mothers with custody of their children often drops sharply. Within a year, however, most separated adults have begun the process of reorganizing their lives, although it may take a few years more to establish a stable identity and a new life situation.[11]

Children too experience an initial period of intense emotional upset after their parents separate. Judith S. Wallerstein and Joan B. Kelly studied 131 children from 60 recently separated families who sought the services of a counseling center in Marin County, California. They met with the children at the time of the divorce action and then again eighteen months, five years,

and ten years later. At first, according to their study, almost all the children were profoundly upset. Their reactions varied according to age. Preschool children tended to be frightened and bewildered by the separation and to blame themselves for what had occurred; older children often expressed great anger. Adolescents were better able to comprehend the reasons for the divorce, but they often were deeply worried about the effects of the separation on their own future.[12]

A number of studies suggest that the short-term adjustment to divorce is different for boys than for girls. Boys in conflict-ridden families—whether or not a separation has occurred—show more aggressive and antisocial behavior, whereas girls are less prone to do so.[13] Hetherington and others have identified "coercive cycles" between mothers and their preschool sons that can occur soon after a divorce: mothers, who may be overburdened, angry, and depressed, respond irritably to the whining and difficult behavior of their distressed sons, only to aggravate the very behavior they try to quell.[14] Girls appear to adjust to a separation more rapidly and to exhibit more "good" behavior. But there is some evidence that they internalize their distress more and, despite outward adjustment, may suffer from depression or lowered self-esteem.[15]

Less is known about long-term adjustment to divorce. Hetherington found marked improvement in the relations between many of the parents and their preschool children between the first and second year after the divorce. One-half of the mothers and one-fourth of the fathers reported that by two years after the divorce their relationships with their children had improved over the tension-filled last days of their marriages.[16] The majority of the children had resumed normal development. But in one type of family, problems tended to linger: six years after the divorce, when the children in Hetherington's study were ten, mothers who had not remarried reported more loneliness and depression and a lower sense of control over the course of their lives. Their relationships with their sons were more likely to include the ineffective parenting and coercive cycles found between mothers and sons during the crisis period. In contrast, relationships between non-remarried mothers and their daughters were similar to mother-daughter relationships in families in which no divorce had occurred.[17]

Wallerstein paints a very pessimistic picture of long-term adjustment. The older males, who were 19 to 29 at the ten-year follow-up, were said to be "unhappy and lonely" and to have had "few, if any, lasting relationships with young women." Many of the older girls, she and her co-author Sandra Blakeslee stated, appeared well adjusted at first but encountered problems years later. At the ten-year mark, most of the 19-to-23-year-old women were said to be overcome by fear and anxiety at the prospect of making an emotional commitment to a man.[18] But although Wallerstein's clinical study contains many insights, the prevalence of long-term problems in the general population of divorced children almost certainly is lower than she reports for her sample. Families were referred to her clinic for short-term therapy by lawyers, clergy, and occasionally court authorities. Many of the parents had prior mental health problems.[19] In addition, Wallerstein didn't compare her children with a control group of children in families that were not disrupted, so it is difficult to judge how many of the problems exhibited by her subjects are common to all children, whether or not their parents have divorced. Given the nature of the study, then, it is perhaps surprising to discover that nearly half of the children survived the divorce with little or no lasting impairment. Sixty-eight percent of the younger children and somewhat less than 40 percent of the older children were said to be doing well at the ten-year follow-up.

Nevertheless, there is evidence from national surveys that growing up in a single-parent family is associated with diminished chances for a successful adult life. Using data from several national surveys of adults, Sara McLanahan and her colleagues have shown that those who report living in a single-parent family as a child are more likely subsequently to drop out of high school, marry during their teenage years, have a child before marrying, and experience the disruption of their own marriages.[20] Part of the association is due to the lower income in single-parent families, which itself increases the risk of undesirable outcomes such as dropping out of school. But McLanahan estimates that low income accounts for only about half of the story. What is behind the other half isn't clear, but it may include inadequate supervision and discipline by some single parents, the influence of the kinds of disadvantaged neighborhoods that many single parents tend to live in, or other family characteristics that make both living in a single-parent family and experiencing negative outcomes more likely.[21]

Still, most persons who grow up in a single-parent family don't drop out of high school, don't marry as teenagers, and don't have a first child before marrying. For example, McLanahan and Bumpass report that in one national survey of women age 15 to 44, 25 percent of marriages had been disrupted among those who had lived with only one natural parent at age 14, compared to about 14 percent among those who had lived with both parents, controlling for other factors. These percentages can be interpreted in two ways. On the one hand, adults from single-parent families are more likely to experience the disruption of their own marriages. On the other hand, most adults from single-parent families are still in their first marriages. So although growing up in a single-parent family increases the risk of detrimental outcomes later in life, it is not true that most adults who grew up in single-parent families will experience those outcomes.[22]

Nationally representative studies of children produce a similar pattern of findings: the negative effects of divorce are real and persistent, but only a minority experience severe negative consequences. One such study is the 1981 National Survey of Children (NSC), which included a random sample of 227 young adolescents from maritally disrupted families and a larger sample from intact, two-parent families. Paul Allison and Frank Furstenberg found that adolescents who had experienced the divorce or separation of their parents differed only modestly, on average, from those whose parents remained married on a wide variety of outcomes such as school achievement, delinquency, and psychological well-being.

The national surveys provide samples that are much more representative of the average child's experience of marital disruption than do the small-scale studies of white middle-class families that constitute the psychological literature. But the brief, structured interviews in the national surveys cannot yield the kind of in-depth information provided by the intensive, repeated testing and observation of studies such as Hetherington's. Consequently, even with the results of national surveys in hand, there are still no firm estimates of the proportion of children who experience harmful psychological effects from parental divorce. It seems unlikely to me that nearly as many will flounder in the long run as Wallerstein predicts. But taking into account what is known from recent studies, we might conclude that: (1) almost all children experience an initial period of great emotional upset following a parental separation; (2) most return to a normal developmental course within one or two years following the separation, and (3) a minority of children experience some long-term psychological problems as a result of the break-up that may persist into adulthood.

Not all children respond similarly to divorce. There are important differences among children, even within the same family, in temperament and in relations with other family members. Some children are simply more resilient to stress than others. Some manage to find safe niches that insulate them from the trauma of divorce. For example, they may have a special relationship with another adult, or they may be buffered from the conflict by one parent.[23] Furthermore, not all divorces have the same consequences for children. This latter statement might seem obvious, but until recently there wasn't enough research evidence to determine the different pathways that help or hinder children's adjustment to parental divorce.

Nevertheless, I think that two conclusions can be drawn: First, children do better when the custodial parent—usually the mother—can reestablish an orderly and supportive household routine. Hetherington refers to the benefits for children of an "authoritative" parenting style, which combines warmth and involvement with supervision and "moderately high but responsive" control.[24] When the custodial parent can keep the house in order, get the children to school and to bed on time, maintain disciplinary standards consistently but without undue harshness, and provide love and warmth, children can draw support from the parent and from the structure of their daily routine. But carrying out these childrearing tasks can be difficult for overburdened, financially strapped, emotionally upset single parents. During the crisis period, when the parent may be anxiety-ridden, harried, or depressed and the household may be disorganized, the children lose another pillar—often the last remaining pillar—of support. The custodial parent, then, can help children by functioning effectively as a parent.

Second, children do better when there is less conflict between their parents. This principle applies to intact two-parent homes as well as to families of divorce. In fact, studies show that children living with a single parent show fewer behavioral problems than do children living in homes in which two angry parents argue persistently.[25] When conflict remains after the break-up, children do better if they are shielded from the disputes. If parents can communicate, despite the conflict, and can cooperate on childrearing tasks, their children benefit. Parents who use their children as pawns or who urge their children to take sides in the battle between the mother and father often increase the child's difficulties.[26]

It is less clear whether children do better, on average, when they have a continuing relationship with both parents after the separation. The Hetherington and Wallerstein studies found that regular visits by the noncustodial parent—usually the father—helped the child greatly.[27] But other recent observational studies have not found this relationship.[28] Moreover, in the 1981 NSC, children who had regular visits with their noncustodial fathers were just as likely as those with infrequent visits to have problems in school or to engage in delinquent behavior or early sexual activity.[29] In any case, the amount of contact between children and their noncustodial fathers is shockingly low. In the NSC, half of the children from maritally disrupted homes who were living with their mothers had not seen their fathers in the last year. Just one-sixth of these children, who were then age 12 to 16, were seeing their fathers as often as once a week.[30] Much of the drop-off in contact occurred in the first two years after the disruption. Why so many fathers fade away is still unclear. Some remarry and form new families; others move away, or their ex-wife and children move away from them; still others may find that frequent visits produce too much guilt and sadness. Whatever the case, most children are deprived of a valuable continuing relationship that might help them develop and adjust.

FAMILY LIFE AFTER REMARRIAGE

For most divorced men and women, living as a single adult is a temporary phase in a process of decoupling and recoupling. Most divorced persons remarry—about two-thirds of the women and three-fourths of the men. It appears that most people who remarry cohabit with their partners first. Indeed, cohabitation after divorce has become so common that rates of union formation—cohabiting or marital—have remained roughly constant despite declines in the rate of remarriage.

In the United States and other western societies, remarriage has been the traditional answer to many of the problems faced by single parents. In the Plymouth Colony, for example, it was not unusual for one parent to die before the children reached adulthood. Most of the widows and widowers remarried within a short time, according to a study by John Demos, often within one year. The surviving parent, Demos emphasized, remarried quickly not out of any lack of respect for the deceased spouse but rather because it took two parents to meet the demands of raising a family in the harsh environment of the colony.[31] Today, despite the changes in American society, many divorced parents remarry because they need assistance in similar ways. Remarriage improves the financial situation of a divorced mother and provides another adult to share the household tasks and responsibilities. In addition, remarrying is a way to end the loneliness and isolation many divorced persons experience.

Whereas divorce often weakens the ties between children and their relatives on the side of the noncustodial parent (usually the father), remarriage creates a new set of relationships with a stepparent and his or her kin. When at least one spouse has children from a previous marriage, the family of remarriage can extend far beyond the bounds of the family of first marriage. Stepparents, stepchildren, stepsiblings, stepgrandparents, the new spouses of noncustodial parents, and other kin all may play a role in family life. This expanded set of family relationships in a remarriage can help compensate children for the loss of kin they may suffer after their parents divorce. Children whose custodial parent remarries often seem to inherit not only a stepparent but also a set of stepgrandparents and other step-kin. And since many children retain some contact with their noncustodial parent and

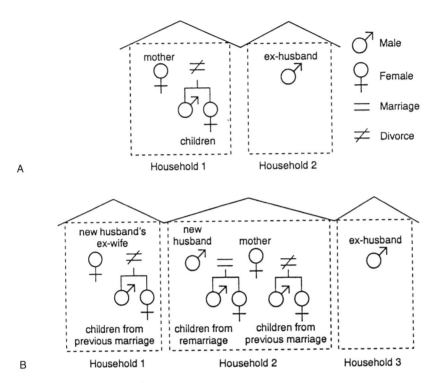

FIGURE 1 Kinship relations and household structure after divorce (A) and after the mother's remarriage (B).

grandparents, some children whose parents remarry may have contact with more kin than they did before their father and mother separated. But the introduction of these new relationships can also cause at least temporary problems for parents and children.

When children retain contact with their non-custodial parents, they create links between households; their visits can require communication among the divorced parents, the new step-parent, and the noncustodial parent's new spouse. In practice, most children have only infrequent contact with their noncustodial parent. Nevertheless, the great increases in divorce and remarriage have made these links across households so common that conceptions of family and kinship have been altered. To illustrate, let us consider the case in which a married couple

with two children divorces and the wife retains custody of the children, as shown in panel A of Figure 1. If we ask the divorced mother who is in her immediate family, she certainly would include her children, but she might well exclude her ex-husband, who now lives elsewhere. If we ask her children who is in their immediate family, however, we might get a different answer. If the children still see their father regularly, they probably would include both their father and their mother as part of their family.[32] And if we ask the ex-husband who is in his immediate family, he might include his children, whom he continues to see, but not his ex-wife. Thus, after divorce, mother, father, and children each may have a different conception of who is in their immediate family. In fact, one can no longer define "the family" or "the immediate family" except in relation to a particular person.

The situation becomes more complicated in a remarriage that involves children from previous marriages. Let us suppose that the mother remarries someone who also has children from a previous marriage and that the mother then has additional children with her new spouse, as diagramed in panel B of Figure 1. Now the mother's household contains persons in four different positions—the mother herself, the father/stepfather, the children from her first marriage, and the children from her remarriage. The persons in each of these four positions may have a different conception of who is in their family. The children from the remarriage are likely to include all the members of their household and no one else. The mother's new husband may well include three sets of children: those from his previous marriage, from his new marriage, and from his wife's previous marriage. In reality, few remarriages involve family structures this complex; just 6 percent of remarried couples under age 40 in 1980 had three sets of children.[33] But whenever children are present from previous marriages, multiple definitions arise.

A household formed by divorce or remarriage that involves children from a previous marriage becomes the intersection of an overlapping set of relationships, each of which constitutes an immediate family for one or more members of the household. Although each person in a post-divorce household may have a clear idea of who belongs to his or her immediate family, the definitions of the immediate family are likely to vary widely among persons in the same structural positions in different households.

It also is unclear exactly who a person's more distant relatives are. In many households linked by the ties of broken marriages, there can be considerable interaction among people whose only relationship is through the broken marriage, such as between a husband's second wife and his ex-wife's second husband. Anthropologist Paul Bohannan has labeled these linked households "divorce chains" and the persons related through the ties of broken marriages "quasi-kin."[34] For example, in panel B of Figure 1, the children from the mother's previous marriage might play with the children from her new husband's previous marriage when the husband's children come to visit. Over time, these two sets of children might begin to consider themselves relatives, although they have no formal ties to each other.

In practice, it appears that even ex-spouses who share the task of childrearing often have little to do with each other. Furstenberg and Christine Winquist Nord found surprisingly little coordination and consultation between custodial and noncustodial parents, even when the noncustodial parent saw the child frequently. The dominant style, they state, was more like "parallel parenting" than co-parenting: each parent operated as independently as possible. This strategy served to minimize parental conflict.[35] Similarly, a study of divorced families in Northern California by Stanford University researchers found that, by three-and-one-half years after the separation, the most common pattern of interaction between the parents was "disengaged"—low communication and low conflict.[36]

When at least one spouse has children from a previous marriage, the addition of a new adult to the household alters the entire system of relationships among family members. But our society, oriented toward first marriages, provides little guidance to currently divorced adults, to remarried adults, and to their children as to how they should manage their unfamiliar and complex family lives. The lack of institutionalized—that is, generally accepted—ways of resolving problems is particularly noticeable for the families of remarriages following divorce.[37] To be sure, many aspects of remarried life are similar to life in a first marriage and are subject to established rules of behavior. And remarriage itself is an institutionalized solution to the ambiguous status of the divorced parent. But for remarried adults and their children, day-to-day life includes many problems for which institutionalized solutions are just beginning to emerge.

Consider the problem of what a stepchild who calls his father "Dad" should call his stepfather. There is still no general rule, but my observations suggest that the most common answer is to call him by his first name. Note, however, that this practice, if accepted, will institutionalize the ambiguous position of the stepparent. An adult whom a child addresses by his first name is neither a parent nor a stranger. Rather, that adult is more like a friend or a companion. The relationship between stepparents and the stepchildren can vary greatly from family to family. Stepparents must create relationships and negotiate with the biological parents and the stepchildren what each person's rights and obligations will be. Consequently, during the first year or two of a remarriage, adults must work carefully and gradually at establishing a coherent system of relationships among kin, step-kin, and quasi-kin.

The first years of life in a stepfamily are also a time of adjustment for children. Many have adapted painfully but successfully to the departure of the father from the household. The arrival of a stepfather necessitates further adjustment. One might think that children's psychological well-being would improve quickly, because stepfathers can provide the family with additional income, emotional support, warmth, and discipline. But studies show that the overall level of well-being of children in stepfamilies is about the same as that of children living with their mothers.[38]

Among children who have not yet entered adolescence, the addition of a stepfather to the home appears to create more problems for girls than for boys. In contrast, the behavior of young boys seems to improve, or at least doesn't deteriorate, when their mothers remarry.[39] These sex differences are just the opposite of what occurs,

according to the psychological studies at least, when marriages break up and young children remain with their mothers alone: boys show more behavior problems and girls are perhaps more depressed and withdrawn. Hetherington and her collaborators speculate that young girls, who tend to form close relationships with their divorced mothers, may view the stepfathers as intruders. Young boys, who are more likely to engage in persistent "coercive cycles" of bad behavior with non-remarried mothers, may benefit from the introduction of a stepfather.

In one study of children aged six to nine in stepfamilies, the authors report that boys were doing better when there was more cohesion and emotional bonding between their mothers and their stepfathers, which presumably reflected a greater integration of the stepfather into the life of the family. But girls were doing better when there was *less* cohesion and bonding between the mother and stepfather. The authors argue that the involvement of the stepfather threatens the close relationship that daughters have developed with their mothers.[40] Moreover, several studies have found evidence that children appear to fare better when they are in the custody of the same-sex parent—boys with their fathers and girls with their mothers.[41] But fathers have custody of their children rarely and often under special circumstances, such as when the mother is unfit or the father has been unusually involved in childrearing. So it is very risky to generalize from the existing studies of same-sex custody.

A recent study of somewhat older children by Hetherington and her collaborators reported that both boys and girls had persistent difficulties in adjusting to the presence of a stepfather. The researchers followed nine-to-thirteen-year-old children in recently formed stepfamilies for two years. They speculated that the developmental tasks of early adolescence—particularly coming to terms with emerging sexuality and developing a sense of autonomy—may make the addition of a stepfather to the home problematic for boys and girls. It may be unavoidably distressing, they argue, for an early adolescent to think of his or her mother and stepfather as sexually active.[42]

It also appears that the role of the stepmother is more problematic than the role of the stepfather. Stepmothers have more competition from absent mothers than stepfathers do from absent fathers because absent mothers are less likely to withdraw from their children's lives. In the NSC, the small number of children in father-custody homes reported substantially more contact with their absent mothers than did children in mother-custody homes with their absent fathers.[43] It may be more difficult, then, for stepmothers to establish a workable role in the family. And because of the selective nature of father custody, children in stepmother-father families may be more troubled. That is, children sometimes may be sent to live with their fathers when their problems are greater than the mother feels she can deal with. In the National Health Interview Survey, parents in stepmother-father families were more likely to feel that their child needed psychological help than were parents in mother-stepfather families.[44] Regardless, there are far fewer resident stepmothers than stepfathers because most mothers retain custody of their children. In 1985 there were 740,000 children under 18 living with a stepmother and a biological father, compared to 6.05 million children who were living with a biological mother and a stepfather.[45]

Finally, the divorce rate for remarried persons is modestly but consistently higher than for persons in first marriages, largely because of the sharply higher risk of divorce during the first few years. Some observers believe that the rate is higher because the remarried population contains a higher proportion of people who, for one reason or another, are likely to resort to divorce if their marriage falters.[46] Furstenberg and Graham Spanier argue, more specifically, that the experience of divorce makes people more averse to remaining in a second unhappy marriage.[47] These

arguments were raised initially in reaction to a hypothesis of mine, namely that many of the difficulties of families of remarriage, including the higher divorce rate, stem from the lack of institutionalized support. Without accepted guidelines, solving everyday problems can engender conflict and confusion among family members.[48] The evidence tying second divorces to the incomplete institutionalization of remarriage is mixed, however, and a lesser aversion to divorce among remarried partners is undoubtedly a factor.[49]

NOTES

1. See, for example, James L. Peterson and Nicholas Zill, "Marital Disruption, Parent-Child Relationships, and Behavior Problems in Children," *Journal of Marriage and the Family* 48 (May 1986): 295–307.

2. P. Lindsay Chase-Lansdale and E. Mavis Hetherington, "The Impact of Divorce on Life-Span Development: Short and Longterm Effects," in Paul B. Baltes, David L. Featherman, and Richard M. Lerner, eds., *Life-Span Development and Behavior,* vol. 10 (Hillsdale, N.J.: Lawrence Erlbaum Associates, 1990), pp. 105–150.

3. E. Mavis Hetherington, Martha Cox, and Roger Cox, "The Aftermath of Divorce," in J. H. Stevens, Jr., and M. Matthews, eds., *Mother-Child, Father-Child Relations* (Washington: National Association for the Education of Young Children, 1978), pp. 146–176.

4. Robert S. Weiss, *Going It Alone: The Family Life and Social Situation of the Single Parent* (New York: Basic Books, 1979).

5. U.S. Bureau of the Census, Current Population Reports, series P-60, no. 173, "Child Support and Alimony: 1989" (Washington: U.S. Government Printing Office, 1991), Tables 1 and 3. The proportion of never-married women who receive any child support payments is even lower.

6. Saul D. Hoffman and Greg J. Duncan, "What *Are* the Economic Consequences of Divorce?" *Demography* 25 (November 1988): 641–645. Hoffman and Duncan demonstrate convincingly that Lenore J. Weitzman's widely cited estimate of the decline in women's standard of living after

the breakup (73 percent, on average) is exaggerated and inconsistent with other figures in her book, *The Divorce Revolution: The Unexpected Social and Economic Consequences for Women and Children in America* (New York: Free Press, 1985). Her estimate of the rise in men's standard of living (42 percent) is almost certainly exaggerated also.

7. Greg J. Duncan and Saul D. Hoffman, "Economic Consequences of Marital Instability," in Martin David and Timothy Smeeding, eds., *Horizontal Equity, Uncertainty, and Economic Well-Being* (Chicago: University of Chicago Press, 1985), pp. 427–467. See Table 14.A.5.

8. Weiss, *Going It Alone.*

9. Janet A. Kohen, Carol A. Brown, and Roslyn Feldberg, "Divorced Mothers: The Costs and Benefits of Female Family Control," in George Levinger and Oliver C. Moles, eds., *Divorce and Separation: Context, Causes, and Consequences* (New York: Basic Books, 1979), pp. 228–245.

10. Robert S. Weiss, *Marital Separation* (New York: Basic Books, 1975).

11. Ibid.

12. Judith S. Wallerstein and Joan Berlin Kelly, *Surviving the Breakup: How Children and Parents Cope with Divorce* (New York: Basic Books, 1980).

13. Chase-Lansdale and Hetherington, "The Impact of Divorce." See also Peterson and Zill, "Marital Disruption."

14. G. R. Patterson, *Coercive Family Process* (Eugene, Oregon: Castalia Publishing Company, 1982).

15. Chase-Lansdale and Hetherington, "The Impact of Divorce."

16. Hetherington, Cox, and Cox, "Aftermath of Divorce."

17. E. Mavis Hetherington, "Family Relations Six Years after Divorce," in Kay Pasley and Marilyn Ihinger-Tallman, eds., *Remarriage and Stepparenting: Current Research and Theory* (New York: Guilford Press, 1987), pp. 185–205.

18. Judith S. Wallerstein and Sandra Blakeslee, *Second Chances: Men, Women, and Children a Decade after Divorce* (New York: Ticknor and Fields, 1989).

19. Families with children who had severe psychiatric problems were excluded, but parents often entered the study with a long history of psychiatric problems. As Wallerstein acknowledges in an earlier book, nearly 50 percent were "moderately disturbed or frequently incapacitated by disabling neuroses and addictions." Some were "chronically depressed" or "sometimes suicidal." Another 15 to 20 percent were characterized as "severely disturbed," with long histories of mental illness and chronic inability to cope with the demands of life (Wallerstein and Kelly, *Surviving the Breakup,* p. 328). Only a third of the sample were deemed to possess "adequate psychological functioning" prior to the divorce. We are never told what, if any, bearing parents' psychological histories had on their capacity to cope with divorce or to respond to the challenges of being a parent. Wallerstein and Blakeslee express great surprise at how many of the couples had difficulty adjusting to life after divorce, how many entered troubled second marriages, and how many had serious problems as parents. But given their psychological histories, the difficulties should have been anticipated. See Andrew Cherlin and Frank F. Furstenberg, Jr., "Divorce Doesn't Always Hurt the Kids," *The Washington Post,* March 19, 1989, p. C3.

20. Sara McLanahan, "Family Structure and the Reproduction of Poverty," *American Journal of Sociology* 90 (January 1985): 873–901; and Sara McLanahan and Larry L. Bumpass, "Intergenerational Consequences of Family Disruption," *American Journal of Sociology* 94 (July 1988): 130–152.

21. McLanahan summarizes her research findings in the newsletter of the Institute for Research on Poverty at the University of Wisconsin: Sara McLanahan, "The Consequences of Single Parenthood for Subsequent Generations," *Focus* 11 (Fall 1988): 16–21.

22. The 14 and 25 percent figures are estimates derived from the results in McLanahan and Bumpass, "Intergenerational Consequences," and are only illustrative. The authors also combine the experience of parental marital disruption with the experience of living with a never-married mother; further results suggest that the difference between these two groups is small.

23. E. Mavis Hetherington, "Coping with Family Transitions: Winners, Losers, and Survivors," *Child Development* 60 (1989): 1–14.

24. Hetherington, "Family Relations Six Years after Divorce," and "Coping with Family Transitions."

25. Peterson and Zill, "Marital Disruption."

26. Christy M. Buchanan, "Variation in Adjustment to Divorce: The Role of Feeling Caught in the Middle between Parents," paper presented at the biennial meeting of the Society for Research in Child Development, Seattle, April 18, 1991.

27. Chase-Lansdale and Hetherington, "Impact of Divorce."

28. For a review see Robert E. Emery, *Marriage, Divorce, and Children's Adjustment* (Beverly Hills: Sage Publications, 1988), pp. 85–86.

29. The payment of child support by noncustodial fathers, however, was associated with fewer behavioral problems. See Frank F. Furstenberg, Jr., S. Philip Morgan, and Paul D. Allison, "Paternal Participation and Children's Well-Being after Marital Dissolution," *American Sociological Review* 52 (October 1987): 695–701.

30. Frank F. Furstenberg, Jr., Christine Winquist Nord, James L. Peterson, and Nicholas Zill, "The Life Course of Children of Divorce," *American Sociological Review* 48 (October 1983): 656–668.

31. John Demos, *A Little Commonwealth: Family Life in Plymouth Colony* (New York: Oxford University Press, 1970).

32. Wallerstein and Kelly, *Surviving the Breakup*, reported that the inclusion of the noncustodial father in the child's view of his family is common when the father continues to see the child.

33. Andrew Cherlin and James McCarthy, "Remarried Couple Households: Data from the June 1980 Current Population Survey," *Journal of Marriage and the Family* 47 (February 1985): 23–30.

34. Paul Bohannan, "Divorce Chains, Households of Remarriage, and Multiple Divorces," in Paul Bohannan, ed., *Divorce and After* (New York: Doubleday, 1970), pp. 127–139.

35. Frank F. Furstenberg, Jr., and Christine Winquist Nord, "Parenting Apart: Patterns of Childrearing after Marital Dissolution," *Journal of Marriage and the Family* 47 (November 1985): 893–904.

36. Eleanor E. Maccoby, Charlene E. Depner, and Robert H. Mnookin, "Coparenting in the Second and Fourth Years Following Parental Separation," unpublished manuscript, Stanford University, 1990. See also Eleanor E. Maccoby and Robert H. Mnookin, *Dividing the Child: Social and Legal Dilemmas of Custody* (Cambridge, Mass.: Harvard University Press, 1992).

37. See my article, "Remarriage as an Incomplete Institution," *American Journal of Sociology* 84 (Nov. 1978): 634–650, from which I draw heavily in this section.

38. See, for example, Nicholas Zill, "Behavior, Achievement, and Health Problems among Children in Stepfamilies: Findings from a National Survey of Child Health," in E. Mavis Hetherington and Joseph D. Arasteh, eds., *Impact of Divorce, Single Parenting, and Stepparenting on Children* (Hillsdale, N.J.: Lawrence Erlbaum Associates, 1988); pp. 325–368.

39. See the following reports on small-scale, intensive studies by psychologists: James H. Bray, "Children's Development during Early Remarriage," in Hetherington and Arasteh, *Impact of Divorce*; Hetherington, "Family Relations Six Years after Divorce;" Eulalee Brand, Glenn Clingempeel, and Kathryn Bowen-Woodward, "Family Relationships and Children's Psychological Adjustment in Stepmother and Stepfather Families," in Hetherington and Arasteh, *Impact of Divorce*; and J. W. Santrock, R. A. Warshak, C. Lindberg, and L. Meadows, "Children's and Parents' Observed Social Behavior in Stepfather Families," *Child Development* 53 (1982): 472–480. Two reports on the 1981 National Survey of Children provide at least partial confirmation that girls seem to react more negatively to the introduction of a stepparent than do boys: Paul Allison and Frank F. Furstenberg, Jr., "How Marital Dissolution Affects Children," *Developmental Psychology* 25 (1989): 540–549; and Peterson and Zill, "Marital Disruption." An analysis of the 1981 Child Health Supplement to the National Health Interview Survey, however, found only small differences between girls and boys: Zill, "Behavior, Achievement, and Health Problems."

40. Bray, "Children's Development during Early Remarriage."

41. See Chase-Lansdale and Hetherington, "The Impact of Divorce," for a review.

42. E. Mavis Hetherington and W. Glenn Clingempeel, *Coping with Marital Transitions: A Family*

Systems Perspective (Chicago: University Chicago Press, 1992).

43. Furstenberg et al., "The Life Course of Children of Divorce."

44. Zill, "Behavior, Achievement, and Health Problems."

45. U.S. Bureau of the Census, Current Population Reports, Series P-23, No. 162, "Studies in Marriage and the Family: Married-Couple Families with Children" (Washington: U.S. Government Printing Office, 1989), Table A.

46. See, for example, Terence C. Halliday, "Remarriage: The More Complete Institution?" *American Journal of Sociology* 86 (Nov. 1980): 630–635.

47. Frank F. Furstenberg, Jr., and Graham B. Spanier, "The Risk of Dissolution in Remarriage: An Examination of Cherlin's Hypothesis of Incomplete Institutionalization," *Family Process* 33 (1984): 433–442. See also, by the same authors, *Recycling the Family: Remarriage after Divorce* (Beverly Hills: Sage Publications, 1984).

48. See Cherlin, "Remarriage as an Incomplete Institution."

49. Some support for my position came from a national study of married persons who were interviewed in 1980 and reinterviewed in 1983. The probability of divorce during the interval was higher among remarried couples, and it increased with the complexity of the remarriage. For example, the probability was higher when both spouses had been remarried than when just one had been; and it was higher when stepchildren were present than when they were not. See Lynn K. White and Alan Booth, "The Quality and Stability of Remarriages: The Role of Stepchildren," *American Sociological Review* (October 1985): 689–698.

DISCUSSION QUESTIONS

1. Based on Cherlin's account of the impact of divorce on adults and children alike, do you think it is wise social policy to revise divorce laws to make it more difficult to terminate a marriage?
2. Discuss some of the dilemmas involved when a stepparent moves into the home. What kinds of relationships and what types of family authority patterns are most realistic and beneficial in this setting?

READING 33

Piety and Politics

Michael Lienesch

Christian fundamentalists have throughout much of the 20th century avoided getting embroiled in American politics. This changed in the 1970s as fundamentalists mobilized to "bring God back into public life," and in so doing created the New Christian Right, a religiously motivated political movement. Communism provided a powerful foreign policy issue, but the grassroots movement paid particular attention to domestic issues, with abortion and prayer in schools heading the list. Michael Lienesch, in this selection from Redeeming America, *discusses the dilemmas that the movement's limited success and its ongoing role as a factor in the Republican Party have meant for those who want to avoid becoming just another special-interest group.*

During the decade of the 1980s, the New Christian Right rose to prominence in American politics. Appearing on the scene suddenly, building its influence with surprising speed, the movement startled many observers, including many scholars, who seemed unprepared to understand this new kind of social movement. Announcing a platform of religious and political renewal, and claiming millions of contributors and members, armies of activists marched forth under a banner of moral reform to save secular society from its humanist and liberal vices. For several years these religious conservatives did battle against a host of enemies, with some significant successes. Then, almost as suddenly as it had risen to prominence, the movement fell into oblivion, battered by scandal and disarmed by its own success. By the close of the decade, it had all but disappeared, and many were declaring its demise.

In its wake, observers sought to make sense of the movement, offering reasons for its successes and explaining its eventual failure. According to most of them, the New Christian Right was an example of radical rightist politics, an intense and intolerant movement that refused to play by the rules of the American political system. Committed but uncompromising, answering only to the agenda of a surprisingly small body of true believers, the movement became increasingly isolated over time, a victim of its extreme and exclusionary views. Thus it fell to earth harmlessly, like a spectacular but short-lived meteor, consumed by its own terrible heat.[1]

At the same time, at least a few observers saw the phenomenon as not quite so transitory. They pointed out that religious conservatism has existed more or less continuously since at least the early nineteenth century. While changing constantly in character, the Christian right has nonetheless been notable for its continuity, including its consistent commitment to traditional moral values and its uncompromising opposition to secular trends. Surfacing periodically, it has been a constant, if somewhat submerged, segment of society, as well as a self-perpetuating part of American politics. According to this interpretation, the Christian right, far from being a flaming meteor, is a permanent aspect of the American scene, a fixed star in the national firmament.[2]

In truth, both of these perspectives are partly right. They are also partly wrong, for the movement is more complicated than either of them, being more consistent than the first and more contradictory than the second. Periodically, as in its most recent manifestation, religious conservatism has been known for its furious forays into the political realm. At the same time, when considered over a longer period, it has been a movement which has managed to protect and perpetuate itself, separating from secular society and developing its own distinctive political views. When taken together, these alternating but complementary characteristics create a cyclical pattern in which the movement seems to appear and retreat, adapting to changing contexts while always staying the same. Thus the Christian right is less like a meteor or a fixed star than a comet that appears and retreats along a more-or-less regular path, attracting our attention periodically and then seeming to disappear, retreating but always returning.[3]

Interestingly, some of those inside the movement see it in this way. At the close of the 1980s, as outside observers rushed to offer their views on the New Christian Right, several writers who had been active in the movement set themselves to the same task. Their books, most of which are based on considerable experience, are frank and insightful. Admitting failures and attempting to learn from them, the authors are critical, and sometimes surprisingly self-critical, but they are also constructive in their criticism, for the purpose of these books is less to look back than to look ahead, suggesting new agendas for the 1990s. Thus they provide a final perspective on the New Christian Right, a kind of postscript, while at the same time serving as a prologue to a restructured Christian right.

LEARNING LESSONS

Among those who have written books that look back over the course of the decade, Ed Dobson and Ed Hindson have been two of the most thoughtful. In their book *The Seduction of Power,* written in 1988, they take an approach to analyzing the New Christian Right that comes close to the political mainstream in its pragmatism and its commitment to pluralist values. Like most observers, including almost all of the movement's secular critics, they describe the pragmatism of the movement as its greatest strength, while singling out its impracticality as its most troubling weakness. They describe the "basic practicality" of the New Christian Right:

> Conservative evangelicals have shown a great ability to make the political system work for them. Unlike left wing evangelicals who espouse lofty but impractical visions of political involvement or noninvolvement, right wing evangelicals have learned very quickly how to get voters registered, platforms adopted, and candidates into office.

As these authors see it, the New Christian Right was most effective when it concentrated on clearly defined issues and sought specific goals. Here they cite a series of successes, including campaigns to prevent passage of the Equal Rights Amendment and various gay rights bills. Recalling voter registration drives from the early 1980s, they claim a role in electing and re-electing conservative candidates, including Ronald Reagan. In each case, they emphasize the pragmatic character of these campaigns. The New Christian Right, Dobson and Hindson sum up, saw their "results-oriented campaigns produce those results very successfully."[4]

Conversely, the authors describe the failures of the movement as coming about when it went beyond the bounds of this pragmatism, venturing into the traps of "fanaticism," "triumphalism," and "naive idealism." In elaborating on the "fanaticism" of the New Christian Right, Dobson and Hindson take Pat Robertson to be an example, denouncing him for the "extremist statements" and "irresponsible remarks" that caused his ill-fated presidential campaign to "lose credibility with the general public." As to "triumphalism," a falling that they attribute in particular to "Southern evangelicals," the authors describe it as "that mentality that overstates one's success or influence . . . the attitude of wanting to announce the score when our team has won and to change the conversation when we have lost."[5] They also comment on the dangers of idealism, which they see as endemic among evangelicals of both the left and the right, causing them to "cling to idealistic concepts which cannot be translated very easily into political action." Once again criticizing Robertson for his impractical proposals, while at the same time deriding left-wing evangelical dreams of disarmament and the elimination of all military expenditures, the authors advocate the advantages of a pragmatic middle position. They write realistically, "Just because we espouse

certain ideals does not mean that they can be effectively legislated through Congress."[6]

Others in the movement take a very different view. In his 1987 book *The Changing of the Guard*, George Grant contends that the successes of the New Christian Right came from its uncompromising commitment to its basic beliefs. Unlike Dobson and Hindson, who advocate pragmatism, the activist and grass roots organizer Grant argues for a politics of principle. Concentrating on the theory of pluralism, and distinguishing it from the practical politics that takes place amid a plurality of differing groups, he warns against mistaking means for ends:

> If the preservation of heathen plural*ism* (as opposed to truly Christian plural*ity* and tolerance) is our grand and glorious desire, then we'd best retreat once again behind the fortress security of the evangelical ghetto whence we came. Political action, for such reasons, is entirely illegitimate.[7]

Grant sees the willingness of the New Christian Right to play by the pluralist rules of the political system not as a virtue but as a vice which led religious conservatives into ill-advised alliances with those who were their enemies rather than their friends:

> All too often naive, inexperienced, and uninitiated, the religious right often found itself allied with the old line traditionalists and conservatives. And it found itself being used. It found itself yoked together with Belial (2 Corinthians 6:14 18). Rushing headlong into established partisan politics, Christian failed to recognize until late in the game that a conservative humanism is little better than a liberal humanism.[8]

By making such alliances, sacrificing principle for the sake of pragmatism, the religious right did achieve short-term successes. Yet while winning victories it lost the courage of its convictions. Says Grant sarcastically, "The religious right did little more than domesticate its own steadfastness." Reminding his readers that compromise has more than one meaning, and that it often comes at some cost, he concludes that the movement "wound up compromised by default."[9]

Almost all of the analysts agree that the most telling failure of the New Christian Right during the decade of the 1980s was its inability to create a positive program of its own. Among those who make this case most strongly is Colonel Doner, who, after eight years of work with the lobbying group Christian Voice, found himself exhausted and frustrated. Upon leaving the organization, and after taking time for rest and reflection, Doner wrote *The Samaritan Strategy,* a 1988 book in which he reflects on the record of the movement and on his own shortcomings. According to Doner, what the New Christian Right lacked most was a sense of positive purpose. He writes, "Our movement did not know where it was going, how to get there, or what to do if we ever did get there." Inexperienced and idealistic, religious conservatives found themselves acting incrementally, dealing in a desultory way with single issues rather than pursuing a unified vision of the whole. Doner comments: "When the Christian Right attempted to substitute isolated planks in place of a cohesive vision, we quickly discovered that one cannot mobilize an army with a disparate collage of single issues." Because of their incremental approach to politics, they were left responding to policies rather than initiating them, reacting rather than acting to carry out a positive plan. The result was a movement that appeared to be carping and critical, constantly complaining rather than offering solutions. Indeed, even its victories, including the defeat of the Equal Rights Amendment and the blocking of the gay rights bills, were essentially negative. Doner sums up: "Lacking a vision of our own, all we could do was react in a negative way to the vision or programs of those with non-Christian or anti-Christian visions and agendas. In this sense, we were guilty of being 'reactionaries.' "[10]

SEEKING STRATEGIES

In addition to analyzing the failures of the last decade, the authors of these books are also seeking strategies for the next one. Learning from their mistakes while building on their successes, they attempt to lay out an agenda for the 1990s. For those like Dobson and Hindson, the agenda follows from their criticism and requires avoiding the extremist excesses of the 1980s: "We must reject hit lists, name-calling, manipulation, and other coercive attempts to hijack the political process. We stand opposed to those who make imprecatory prayers, bomb abortion clinics, and call opponents 'satanic devils.' " Dobson and Hindson stress the dangers of separatism, the tendency of evangelicals and fundamentalists to separate themselves from society and to retreat to the fringes of the political system, and they call on religious conservatives to remain active in the political system. Moreover, having learned from the mistakes of the past decade, they advocate a more sophisticated form of participation, in which activists ally themselves with others but are not used by them. Here the authors warn in particular about the lure of party labels. They write: "We must be willing to back a conservative Democrat who supports the issues in which we believe. We must be willing to criticize wrong actions or policies on the part of Republicans." Chiding the activists of the 1980s for their adversarial approach to politics, the authors contend that responsible religious reformers must adopt an attitude of toleration toward those who disagree with them. While it is unclear how far this tolerance is to extend—the authors appear to limit it to tolerating other religious groups, such as Mormons—they do call on their readers to respect the rights of other citizens. "We need to be sure that we are making our presence felt," they write in this regard, "without limiting the freedoms of others."[11] Thus cautioning against absolutism and idealism, Dobson and Hindson make the case for a more conciliatory pose, as well as a more pragmatic one. "Politics," they remind their readers, "involves the art of compromise." Seeking a cooperative stance, the authors offer an analogy: "If a fire were to break out and we began throwing buckets of water on it and someone came along to help us put out the fire, we would not ask him to enumerate all his personal beliefs. We would most likely accept his help until the fire was out."[12]

Other authors, having learned different lessons from the 1980s, suggest different strategies. George Grant's prescriptions seem to be diametrically opposed to those of his more pragmatic counterparts. Thus, where Dobson and Hindson denounce separatist solutions, Grant embraces them, arguing that the most effective means for religious conservatives to achieve reform is to act alone:

> If the religious right is ever to accomplish its stated goal of returning our nation to moral sanity and spiritual stability, it must humbly but determinedly *set its own course* according to the wind of the Spirit of God. It must no longer be the pawn of powers and principalities, of godless men and institutions be they left or right. In short, the religious right must not compromise.[13]

Grant suggests several possibilities for political reform. In contrast to Dobson and Hindson, who advise activists to build coalitions, he tells them to concentrate their support on single candidates. He explains the logic of the strategy: "Since only about 60% of the people are registered to vote and only about 35% of those actually bother to go to the polls, a candidate only needs to get the support of a *small, elite* group of citizens to win."[14] At the same time, Grant does not rely exclusively on electoral institutions. Arguing that citizenship requires more than casting a periodic vote, he advocates grassroots action, advising readers to practice politics from the ground up by participating in neighborhood groups, PTAs, and the like. Furthermore, he suggests that they work not only within the system but also outside it, relying on a wide range of strategies that include "wise appeal, lawyer delay, lobbying, legislative reform, suffering servanthood, and public protest."[15]

Above all, Grant denies the benefits of compromise, arguing that contrary to the contentions of those like Dobson and Hindson, the experience of the 1980s made it clear that the most successful strategies, such as those in opposition to abortion, were the ones in which religious conservatives took the most uncompromising stances. Cautioning his readers not to take a short-term view of success, he contends that even when these stances appeared to fall short, they were often serving as precursors of subsequent successes. Pointing to a long line of biblical precedents, Grant goes so far as to suggest that even persecution is sometimes required for eventual victory:

> We must recognize, as Daniel did, that God is sovereign, that opposition is inevitable, and that even the worst persecution offers with it promise and privilege. If we do, then we will not fear. The reaction-repression-resurrection pattern in Scripture gives us the assurance that an uncompromising stand will ultimately be blessed and used by God.

Besides, says Grant, even when failure appears certain, the potential for some kind of providential intervention is always present. He writes, "An uncompromising stand is worth the risk. Risk offers resurrection."[16]

Colonel Doner presents another view altogether. Without either endorsing or rejecting the other perspectives, Doner makes the case for a strategy of service. Borrowing from the biblical story of the Good Samaritan, the stranger who stops to aid an injured traveler by the side of the road, he advocates a "new agenda for Christian activism" that he calls the "Samaritan strategy." According to Doner, the principal shortcoming of organizations like Christian Voice, and his own weakness as well, was the failure to see the personal face behind the political issue. In particular, he argues that those in the New Christian Right demonstrated a lack of compassion, an inability or unwillingness to admit that politics is about meeting the needs of others. Focusing in particular on the problems of the poor, he faults the activists of the 1980s for their blindness toward poverty and calls on contemporary religious conservatives to open their eyes to social problems and to do something about them. Doner suggests a strategy of using private and market-oriented approaches to solving the problems of the poor. But he also makes the case for a combination of private and public efforts:

> The most effective methods of service might be a combination of a personalized one-to-one approach, along with working toward structural political or social reform. If we wish to help the poor or oppressed, let us do so directly by giving them a helping hand today. But then let us address the long-term solutions to their misfortune by reforming social or government policies for tomorrow.

Encouraging religious conservatives to concern themselves with issues such as AIDS, care for the elderly, and homelessness, while at the same time continuing to oppose abortion and pornography, Doner seems to be seeking an approach to politics that concentrates on human problems. Avoiding both compromise and confrontation, and looking more to local than national needs, he takes what might be considered a personalistic view of politics. He writes about leadership: "One invaluable lesson I learned was that leadership is earned through the hard work of serving those in our community. It is not won by one political combatant out-maneuvering the other. In short, leaders are not elected, they are made." Thus Doner outlines a strategy of service in which responsible religious conservatives earn their way to political power by meeting the needs of those around them. He sums up: "We must learn to earn our right to lead by first serving those whom we ask to follow us."[17]

PLURALISM, PROTEST, PERSONALISM

These different strategies suggest markedly different stances toward the existing political system. For most religious conservatives, the commitment to democratic values runs strong. As representatives of this democratic majority, Dobson and Hindson make the case for participation within the present pluralist system, calling on those in the Christian right to make alliances and build coalitions in order to bring about changes in public policy:

> When political platforms converge with our agenda, we support them. When they do not, we oppose them. We advocate cobelligerency with others who share our moral, social, and political concerns. We are exercising our American citizenship and doing what other special interest and minority groups have been doing for years.

While strongly supporting their own positions, they insist that those taking other positions be able to do the same. They assume that rights, including the right to the free exercise of one's faith, are universal. Say Dobson and Hindson, "While we may verbally battle with others in the process, we must live with them in peace as fellow Americans." Thus they place themselves squarely within the political mainstream. The authors continue: "One of the greatest strengths of conservative evangelicals is their appeal to a populist audience. These are middle Americans who appeal to middle Americans. Their language, ideals, values, and moral beliefs are those of the vast majority of the American public." They criticize theocratic thinkers for their hostility to democracy and single out Reconstructionist writers in particular for their view that democracy is a heretical political system. While they admit that theocracy is in theory the best of all possible systems, Dobson and Hindson see it as unrealizable in practice, at least prior to the millennium. For now, they argue along Augustinian and Aristotelian lines that democracy remains the best of the second-best systems. Short of the coming of Christ's kingdom, they conclude, "it is the one great hope of freedom in a sin-cursed world."[18]

Nevertheless, the majority notwithstanding, there remain a committed minority within the movement who insist on more extensive reforms. Among these is Grant, who makes the argument that religious conservatives should use democratic means to bring about theocratic ends. For Grant, the idea is not as paradoxical as it seems, since he assumes that America is in fact a theocratic system that has come to be captured in relatively recent times by the anti-American principles of democratic pluralism. Thus he sees the mission of a revived Christian right as reasserting theocratic principles. He writes, "It is to reinstitute the authority of God's Word as supreme over all judgments, over all legislation, over all declarations, constitutions, and confederations." Although his plans appear to be ambitious, Grant considers them less radical than they might seem, since he believes that beneath contemporary democratic institutions lies the firm foundation of theocracy. He explains, "Fortunately, because of the theocratic orientation of our founding fathers, our nation has virtually all the apparatus extant to implement such a reclamation." Grant concludes by calling on religious conservatives to reclaim this theocratic system, to "return this nation to a decentralized, confederated, and theocratic social structure."[19]

In order to carry out such sweeping reforms, Grant outlines a strategy of protest. At the center of this strategy is the church, which he describes as playing a primary role both religiously and politically. Thus, in addition to serving as a center for worship, it is also to be a place of political education: "The Church should teach classes on the Biblical principles of political action. The pulpit should become relevant to the issues. Pamphleteering should begin again in earnest. Candidate score cards should be distributed." While insisting that Christian conservatives remain true to theocratic principles, Grant advises them to concentrate on developing the skills of practical politics. He writes, "The Church should train young men and women for political action through activism: picketing the death clinics of abortion-ists, demonstrating against the distribution of pornography, testifying at State Board of Education meetings, protesting IRS harassment of ministers and ministries, fighting for parental rights in the courts, etc." Above all, he says, the church should involve itself, reasserting its rightful political role. Not only must the church do everything in its power to change the direction of present politics, Grant concludes, "it must *do it now*."[20]

Perhaps most interesting is the small but growing group of religious conservatives who make the case for social service. Neither pluralist nor theocratic, this segment seems to be in the process of defining a more personalized political theology. While participating in democratic processes, and while protesting against them, they appear to be pointing in another direction altogether, toward a politics not of power but of responsibility. Taking himself as a symbol of many of the mistakes made by the New Christian Right, Doner tells how his own pursuit of power over the course of the last decade became an end in itself, leaving him with feelings of frustration and failure. Only after leaving his position in the movement did he gain some perspective on this problem. By studying Scripture, along with praying and fasting, he came to the realization that power could be used effectively only when its purpose was not prideful self-service but a humble concern for others. Thus he calls on religious conservatives to seek power through service. He concludes:

> We must pray that our motivation in wanting to serve God will be pure. We must be led and empowered by the Holy Spirit. We must develop a spirit of service so that people see Jesus, not us—not our "big sacrifice" or our "great deed." This is true evangelism! And true servant-leadership.[21]

PROBLEMATIC PROSPECTS

To play the prophet, predicting the role of the Christian right in the 1990s and beyond, is to envision the same blend of contradiction and continuity that has characterized the movement in the past. On the one hand, it is clear that the movement will continue to be active politically. Continuing to follow recent trends, religious conservatives will in all likelihood be less prominent in national politics, while more visible at the state and local level and in grass-roots movements. Having learned from hard experience to eschew broad-based and highly ideological strategies, they will probably continue to focus more on specific issues. Similarly, while not retreating from electoral politics, they will tend, as in recent times, to turn more to direct action. At least for the short run, the cause that seems most consonant with these trends is opposition to abortion. Calling for mass protests, activist Randall A. Terry, founder of "Operation Rescue," an activist coalition that stages sit-ins around abortion clinics, argues that the blocking and closing of clinics across the country can create enough social unrest that legislators will be forced to outlaw abortion through passage of a Human Rights Amendment:

> What politicians fear most is social unrest and upheaval. When unrest occurs in small numbers, it can be put down by force. But when unrest and upheaval begin to incorporate hundreds and thousands of people, government officials pay attention. Ultimately, they *desire* to give in to the demands of the disgruntled, so that tranquility can be restored to the realm and they can get on with the business of governing a sleeping nation.[22]

On the other hand, there are many who remain convinced that the best solutions to current social problems are personal rather than political. Among religious conservatives, this pietistic approach runs deep and strong. Furthermore, it appears to be gaining converts, as many conservative evangelicals announce their support for the concept of "dominion through service." In his *Kingdoms in Conflict,* a 1987 book, Charles Colson describes how he arrived at his own conception of the relationship between politics and personal service. A former White House counsel

who served seven months in prison for crimes related to the Watergate burglary, Colson has since his release founded and acted as chairman of Prison Fellowship, an evangelical prison ministry. Writing autobiographically, he describes how his experience as a prisoner among other prisoners led him to the realization that political power can only be made meaningful through personal and spiritual concern for others. He concludes:

> The fact that God reigns can be manifest through political means, whenever the citizens of the Kingdom of God bring His light to bear on the institutions of the kingdoms of man. But His rule is even more powerfully evident in ordinary, individual lives, in the breaking of cycles of violence and evil, in the paradoxical power of forgiveness, in the actions of those little platoons who live by the transcendent values of the Kingdom of God in the midst of the kingdoms of this world, loving their God and loving their neighbor.[23]

On one point, however, almost all of these authors agree. Although admitting differences and criticizing many of their colleagues for their mistaken views, they find common ground in the assumption that success will require long-term strategies. Thus, in looking ahead, they seem to be seeking strategies not only for the 1990s, but for the next century as well. To most of these writers, the single overriding failure of the New Christian Right was its shortsightedness, its inability to plan for the long run. Dobson and Hindson describe the most important lesson that they have learned from the last decade's experience: "If we have learned anything at all in these ten years, it is that inconsistent involvement in the political process ultimately accomplishes very little. We need to make it clear that we are here to stay and do not intend to retreat on the issues to which we are committed."[24] Working from what would seem to be a competing perspective, Gary North arrives at some of the same conclusions. Calling for a political strategy that focuses first on local government, he makes the case for long-term commitment. He writes in *Inherit the Earth:*

> Everyone wants to be in the "big time" politically. Everyone wants to run for governor. *Let them.* Meanwhile, we take over where today's politicians think that nothing important is happening. We should get our initial experience in ruling on a local level. We must prepare ourselves for a long-term political battle. We start out as privates and corporals, not colonels and generals. We do it God's way.[25]

Regardless of strategy, the authors agree that reform will take time. The New Christian Right as we have come to know it may be gone. But Christian conservatism is very much present in our politics. In a revised and restructured form, it will surely come to prominence again, recurring, according to its cyclical pattern, for as long as religious conservatives continue to hold to this remarkable and powerful blend of religion and politics. We can count on them to keep the faith. After all, says George Grant, "We have the promise of redemption."[26]

NOTES

1. See Steve Bruce, *Rise and Fall of the Christian Right* (Oxford: Oxford University Press, 1988), 190–93: See also Robert Booth Fowler, "The Failure of the Religious Right," in *No Longer Exiles: The Religious New Right in American Politics,* ed. Michael Cromartie (Washington, D.C.: Ethics and Public Policy Center, 1993), 57–74.

2. See George Marsden, "The Religious Right: A Historical Overview," in Cromartie, *No Longer Exiles,* 1–16. For an analysis of fundamentalism's adaptability, as well as its enduring appeal, see George Marsden, *Understanding Fundamentalism and Evangelicalism* (Grand Rapids, MI: William B. Eerdmans, 1991), 98–121; Joel A. Carpenter, "Revive Us Again: Alienation, Hope, and the Resurgence of Fundamentalism, 1930–1950," in *Transforming Faith: The Sacred and Secular in Modern American History,* ed. M. L. Bradbury and James B. Gilbert (New York: Greenwood Press, 1989), 105–25; and George Marsden, *Re-*

forming Fundamentalism: Fuller Seminary and the New Evangelicalism (Grand Rapids, Mich.: William B. Eerdmans Publishing Company, 1987). See also James Davison Hunter, *Evangelicalism: The Coming Generation* (Chicago: University of Chicago Press, 1987), 203–13.

3. For a similar argument, See Ted Jelen, *The Political Mobilization of Religious Reliefs* (New York: Praeger, 1991), 137–51. See also Robert Wuthnow, "The Future of the Religious Right," in Cromartie, *No Longer Exiles,* 27–46.

4. Dobson, Ed and Edward Hindson, *The Seduction of Power* (Old Tappan, NJ: F. H. Revell Co., 1988), 141.

5. Ibid., 142, 143. Dobson and Hindson continue: "Triumphalism often causes those in the New Right to claim they are winning even in the face of defeat. It is a kind of optimism gone haywire that prevents us from seeing ourselves as we really are. It is a blind hope that things are better than we ourselves know them to be. While triumphalism makes for great sermonizing, it smacks of a 'God-is-on-our-side' prejudice which hurts rather than helps our dialogue with others." Ibid., 143.

6. Ibid., 143.

7. George Grant, *The Changing of the Guard: Biblical Blueprints for Political Action* (Fort Worth, Tex.: Dominion Press, 1987), 50. David Chilton agrees: "The Christian cannot be satisfied with 'pluralism,' for his calling is to work for the dominion of Jesus Christ and His Kingdom throughout the world." David Chilton, *Paradise Restored* (Tyler, TX: Dominion Press, 1994), 226.

8. Grant, *Changing of the Guard,* 87. See also Francis Schaeffer's comment that "we must remember that although there are tremendous discrepancies between conservatives and liberals in the political arena, if they are both operating on a humanistic base there will really be no final difference between them." Francis Schaeffer, *Christian Manifesto,* Fort Lauderdale, FL: Coral Ridge Ministries, 77.

9. Grant, *Changing of the Guard,* 87.

10. Colonel V. Doner, *The Samaritan Strategy* (Brentwood, TN: Wulgemoth and Hyatt, 1988), 40, 77.

11. Dobson and Hindson, *Seduction of Power,* 125, 144, 147. They continue: "While we do everything in our power within the freedoms provided

us by a democracy to achieve our political goals, we must also be willing to insure those same freedoms to those with whom we disagree." Ibid., 147.

12. Ibid., 131, 133. Somewhat surprisingly, their arguments are echoed by the fundamentalist Tim LaHaye, who seems to sum up their prescriptions by using a miliary metaphor. He writes, "When I was assigned to a B-29 flight crew as a waist gunner, I didn't ask the other ten men whether they were Catholics, Jews, or Protestants. I merely wanted to know if they could fly the plane or shoot the 50-millimeter machine guns. Later I discovered that the other waist gunner was a Mormon, the turret gunner a Catholic, and the tail gunner a Southern Baptist. We could never have worked together on a religious project (in fact, we could barely talk about theology without heating up), but on one fundamental we were in 100 percent agreement: We were all Americans interested in preserving our country's freedom." Tim LaHaye, *Battle for the Mind* (Payson, AZ: Inspirational Tapes, 1980), 188.

13. Grant, *Changing of the Guard,* 87.

14. Ibid., 145–46. Robison would appear to agree. He writes, "It has been proven time and again that 50 to 100 dedicated volunteers actively campaigning can elect a candidate to office." James Robinson, *Save America to Save the World.* Wheaton, IL: Tyndale House Publishers, 1980, 111–12.

15. Grant, *Changing of the Guard,* 158.

16. Ibid., 88, 89.

17. Doner, *Samaritan Strategy,* 5, 132, 207. For a brief description of the strategy, see 75–96.

18. Dobson and Hindson, *Seduction of Power,* 132, 127, 141, 131.

19. Grant, *Changing of the Guard,* 51, 138. Writes Grant, "It is dominion we are after, not just influence." Ibid., 50.

20. Ibid., 131, 130–31, 133.

21. *Doner, Samaritan Strategy,* 236.

22. Randall A. Terry, *Operation Rescue* (Springdale, Pa.: Whitaker House, 1988), 198.

23. Charles Colson (with Ellen Santilli Vaughn), *Kingdoms in Conflict* (Grand Rapids, Mich.: William Morrow/Zondervan Publishing House, 1987), 371.

24. Dobson and Hindson, *Seduction of Power,* 147. Calling for "a long-range strategy for political in-

volvement," Dobson and Hindson elaborate: "We need a long-term commitment that will not allow us to give up on social-moral-political issues simply because our position is not popular or politically expedient." Ibid., 135.

25. Garg North, *Inherit the Earth: Biblical Principles for Economics* (Fort Worth, TX: Dominion Press, 1987), 160.

26. Grant, *Changing of the Guard,* 114.

DISCUSSION QUESTIONS

1. Given the fact that Christian fundamentalists continue to be a factor in American electoral politics, do you agree or disagree with Lienesch's claim that the New Christian Right "as we have come to know it may be gone"?

2. Abortion has proved to be one of the most divisive political issues in America. Discuss what you understand to be the role of the New Christian Right in defining the terms of debate on this issue.

READING 34

Four Religious Eruptions

Roger Finke and Rodney Stark

Many commentators on American religion contend that mainline religious denominations have declined precipitously since the 1960s, having been undermined by the "eruption" of new cults, Eastern mysticism, New Age religion, and conservative evangelical Christianity. Roger Finke and Rodney Stark debunk each of these claims. In the case of the first three, they attempt to show that the impact of these phenomena has been greatly exaggerated. The growth of evangelical churches, however, has not been overestimated. Nonetheless, the authors contend that this is part of a longer-term process of change in American religion, change brought about in a recurring cycle in which mainline faiths decline, to be replaced by sects, which when successful become mainline and begin their own process of decline.

The literature on cult[1] and sect formation in contemporary America is saturated with the belief that we have recently been living through strange times—through an interrelated set of cultural crises that have resulted in four major religious eruptions. The first of these is sometimes known as a "Consciousness Reformation" and refers to an "eruption" of cult formation and religious novelty during the sixties and early seventies (Wuthnow, 1976, 1978; Glock and Bellah, 1976). The second concerns an eruption within an eruption; the sudden influx of Eastern, and especially Indian, faiths, during the cult eruption of the sixties and early seventies. The third eruption involves the transformation of many of the Eastern teachings that came to the fore during the late sixties and early seventies into the New Age Movement of more recent years. Popularized by actress Shirley MacLaine and others, the movement has received a great deal of press coverage and has generated serious concern and organized opposition from evangelical Protestant groups. The fourth eruption is the "explosion" of evangelical Protestantism and the corresponding decline of mainline denominations over the past several decades. This conservative eruption is often seen as a reactionary response to the same cultural crises that produced the religious novelties of the sixties (Marty, 1979; Tipton, 1982; Berger, 1982; Marsden, 1982).

Real social crises often do have real consequences for religious culture, and the greater the degree of suffering and social disorganization, the greater the likelihood that radical changes will occur in the religious sphere (Stark and Bainbridge, 1987; Stark, 1991, 1992). Nevertheless, such moments are very rare and play no role in the birth or death of most religious movements. Indeed, we argue that whether or not there have been cultural crises in recent times, they did not prompt significant religious reactions—because the alleged eruptions of cult and sect activity never took place. We argue instead that the recent history of cults and sects is

far better characterized by stability and continuity. Although significant changes have occurred, or at least have been recently recognized, they were the result not of sudden eruptions but of gradual, long-term, linear shifts.

THE MYSTICAL SIXTIES

Everyone knows that the latter part of the sixties turned into a "magical mystery tour" during which an explosion of cult formation and importation took place and that, for the first time, the cultural climate was right for faiths from the East, and especially from India, to make significant headway. That these perceptions are accurate seem obvious. Nevertheless, we believe that these, like many other seemingly self-evident assertions about American religion, are mainly myths. That is, we intend to show that there was nothing unusual about the number of cults that formed in this era and that the sudden surge in Indian religious influence had mundane causes having little or nothing to do with deeper cultural matters.

Let us first examine the claim that the sixties were a period when there was an unusual outburst of cult formation. Consider the number of cult movements founded per year for each of the four decades, 1950–1989 (see Table 1).[2] At first glance it would seem that there was a dramatic shift between the fifties and the sixties in terms of the number of foundings, but, as will be explained shortly, this is probably an illusion. In any event, the sixties did not stand out from either the seventies or the eighties in terms of cult formation. It also seems reasonable to take population growth into account (on the assumption that the larger the population, the greater the absolute number available for recruitment). In terms of the number of cult movements founded during a decade per million population (at mid-decade), the sixties exceed only the fifties.

What these data really show is great stability over the entire period. This stability becomes even more evident when it is realized that the

TABLE 1				

FORMATION RATE OF CULT MOVEMENTS, 1950–1989

	1950–1959	1960–1969	1970–1979	1980–1989*
Number of groups founded per year	8.6	16.4	20.6	20.2
Number of groups founded per million population	0.52	0.84	0.95	0.85
Percentage Eastern	7.0	17.1	18.6	11.8

Source: Melton, (1988). Based on the files of the Institute for the Study of American Religion, University of California at Santa Barbara.

*Projected from 1980–1985 data.

data for the fifties were not assembled until the late sixties and early seventies. Many obscure and short-lived groups, having failed to leave sufficient traces so that reliable data about them could be gathered a decade or two later, would necessarily have been missed. For example, about 20 percent of the groups included in the rate for the sixties are defunct today, and little if any information would be recovered about them by a data collection campaign inaugurated now. We believe that the actual cult formation rate for the fifties was probably about the same as for the other decades.[3] For those determined to re-member the fifties as the quiet and conformist decade of Eisenhowerism, it may be worth pointing out that Scientology was founded in 1954, that Elizabeth Clare Prophet's Church Universal and Triumphant was founded in 1958,[4] and that the first American converts to the Unification Church were gathered in Eugene, Oregon, during 1959.

That an unusual number of new cults did not appear during the sixties does not rule out the possibility that far *more people actually participated* in such movements during this brief era. Were that the case, then the eruption thesis is salvaged. But there seems to be no support for this alternative. Rather, what is striking is how poorly contemporary cult movements have done in gaining converts when compared with movements from earlier times. With the exception of Transcendental Meditation—which represented nothing more than a brief experiment in self-improvement for all but the tiniest portion of those who encountered it (Stark and Bainbridge, 1985)—no cult movement of the sixties or early seventies seems ever to have attracted more than a few thousand American members, and most of even the well-publicized groups counted their true membership in the hundreds, not the thousands. For example, after more than thirty years of missionizing, it is estimated that there have never been more than 5,000 followers of the Unification Church (the Moonies) in the United States, some of whom are from abroad. After more than twenty years of operations, the membership of ISKCON (the Hare Krishnas) is estimated at 3,000 (Melton, 1989). In 1984 a Toronto magazine estimated that there were 10,000 Hare Krishna members in that city. But when Irving Hexham, Raymond Currie, and Joan Townsend (1985) checked on the matter, they found that the correct total was 80.

In 1990 Barry A. Kosmin (1991) and his colleagues at the City University of New York conducted the largest survey ever devoted to American religious affiliation. All told, 113,000 randomly sampled Americans were interviewed about their religious preference. Because such an immense sample yields very stable statistics, Kosmin projected his distributions back to the total adult population of the forty-eight contiguous states. Kosmin projected a nationwide total of 8,000 members of Wiccan groups and, nearly forty years after their founding, 45,000 Scientologists (or about 1 percent of the number of members claimed by the group in 1978).

In contrast, the Mormons grew from six members in 1830 to more than 30,000 a decade later, more than 60,000 by 1850, and more than 80,000 by 1860. In similar fashion, Christian Science grew from 27 members in 1880 to 8,724 in 1890, 65,717 in 1906, and 202,098 by

1926. Moreover, the Mormons and Christian Scientists achieved their rapid growth from a far smaller population base than has been available to recent movements.

These data are utterly at variance with the perception that an eruption of cults took place in the late sixties and early seventies. How is it possible for informed opinion to be so wrong? As we have already seen, misperceptions, even ones of this magnitude, are common in the histories of American religion. When quantitative claims are involved, the opinions of people who fail to count, shouldn't count. It is also possible that cult movements were more prominent on campuses during the sixties than had been the case earlier and therefore attracted more notice. Young adults are always the primary source of converts for such movements, and probably no cohort of young people was ever so overreported and overinterpreted as the baby-boomers, whose antics *were* the sixties.

THE EASTERN ASPECT

In their foreword to Part I of *The New Religious Consciousness,* Charles Y. Glock and Robert N. Bellah (1976, p. 1) noted: "One of the most striking characteristics of the counterculture [of the sixties] and of the movements growing out of it is the influence of Asian religions. Of course, Americans have been interested in Asian religions for over a century, but the present period seems to differ from earlier ones both quantitatively and qualitatively. . . . Most important of all was the fact that Asian religions were attracting not only the curiosity of educated youth but also serious devotion and commitment."

That same year Harvey Cox stressed the same points in his book *Turning East: The Promise and Peril of the New Orientalism.* Cox wanted to explain this phenomenon. Why was it happening? What did it all mean? In a 1983 interview he commented that Americans embraced Eastern faiths because "they've been maddened by a consumer culture." Cox continued: "In American society, I

believe we're now in the late phase, the most deteriorated, decadent phase, of consumer capitalism. When I say 'consumer capitalism,' I don't mean simply the form of our economic life; I mean our whole culture. . . . People's primal energies are fixated on commodities that are supposed to bring satisfaction of inner hungers. Through the suggestive and hypnotic power of the advertising industry, a direct connection is made from very basic and underlying needs and fears to material commodities which are touted as things which satisfy those needs; but of course they do not" (1983, p. 42). In conclusion, Cox noted a great irony, that though many critics charge that "vulnerable kids . . . are picked off the streets and brainwashed into the cults," it is only those who have not yet been brainwashed into the "existing distorted values of society" who are clear-headed enough to be "open to other life-patterns."

Underneath Cox's polemics one can detect a very common belief about the phenomenon in question: Indian religions arrived here in a sudden eruption and therefore they *must* reflect a serious cultural crisis. But such crises are, in fact, rare and have little, if anything, to do with the instance at hand.

Glock and Bellah were correct to note that there had been substantial interest in Indian and other Asian religions for more than a century. Gordon Melton (1987) has sketched the extensive involvements of Harvard professors and various proper Bostonians in Eastern religions during the latter part of the nineteenth century. The Boston Unitarian Church was responsible for the initial visits by Hindu teachers to the United States. According to Melton, the first of these was Protap Chundar Mozoomdar. In 1883 he gave his first American lecture in the Concord living room of the widow of Ralph Waldo Emerson. Other gurus soon followed.

In the wake of World War I, however, Congress passed very restrictive immigration laws that effectively excluded all Asians and thereby limited authentic Eastern religious teachers to brief visits on tourist visas. Thenceforth, Americans interested in exploring Eastern religion had to rely on books, travel abroad, or depend upon American teachers—some of whom pretended to be authentic Indians.[5]

In 1965 the exclusionary rules against Asian immigration were quietly dropped.[6] Before the year was out Swami Bhaktivedanta, founder of ISKCON, had become a resident of New York. Many other teachers of Eastern religion quickly followed, and some succeeded in attracting a following. It is their success that Cox and others were trying to explain. But it seems to us that there is much less here than meets the eye.

Given the existence of a sizable audience for books and periodicals dealing with "Eastern wisdom," it does not seem surprising that when talented gurus finally arrived and offered direct teaching they had little trouble finding at least some followers. Put another way, it was not so much that Eastern faiths suddenly struck a responsive chord in the American counterculture as that their growth had been artificially thwarted until then. With the barrier removed, normalization occurred. Given the structure of guru-based religions (Shinn, 1985), virtually each new guru who came to the United States founded a *separate* movement. Thus it took only a relatively small number of American converts to Hinduism to generate a substantial total of Hindu-based cult movements. Herein lies the explanation of the fact that an unusual number of the cult movements founded in the late sixties were of the Hindu variety. The bottom row in Table 1 indicates this increase. Only 7 percent of the groups founded during the fifties were based on Eastern faiths, but 17.1 percent of those founded during the sixties and 18.6 of those formed in the seventies were of the Eastern variety. Notice, too, that this has declined in the eighties—which supports the notion that the surge was simply a normalization of "frustrated" demand. The ability of a sudden influx of Eastern and Indian religious teachers to collectively round up a few thousand followers in the vast American religious economy was at most a blip, not an eruption.

THE NEW AGE

The term "New Age" is an old one, as is the practice of "channeling." In 1881 and 1882 John Ballou Newbrough, a New York spiritualist, "channeled" a manuscript later published as *Oahspe: A New Age Bible*. The phrase "New Age" was recurrent in the Theosophical Society at the turn of the century, and was commonly used by followers of Vedanta and the Rosicrucian Fellowship. During the 1950s, when "flying saucer cults" were popular, many spoke and wrote about the New Age that would begin when the "brothers from outer space" revealed themselves to the world. It was in the 1980s, however, that the term became widely known, largely owing to the publicity given to channelers such as J. Z. Knight and Kevin Ryerson by Shirley MacLaine (Melton, 1990).

Most observers of the American religious scene regard the New Age movement as the truly important and lasting legacy of the earlier eruptions of new mysticisms (Burrows, 1987; Babbie, 1990; Robbins and Anthony, 1990). In this they have been much abetted by the news media, for both the print and the electronic media uncritically pass along New Age press releases claiming that hundreds of thousands (perhaps millions) of Americans are sleeping in homemade pyramids and attending channeling classes. And judging from the shelf space devoted to anti–New Age materials in most Christian bookstores, the New Age is *the* cult threat of the moment.

Once again, we dissent. We believe that most people who can in any way be said to have responded to the New Age movement regard it as more of an amusement than a religion. Most are no more than casual dabblers in the various pseudo-scientific activities and techniques promoted as New Age. Indeed, we suspect that for all but a handful of committed participants, the New Age movement is an audience cult (Stark and Bainbridge, 1985) and reflects interest levels on a par with reading astrology columns.

A recent report suggests how tiny the New Age movement is. Based on Barry Kosmin's (1991) survey, discussed above, it can be estimated that 20,000 Americans regard their religious preference as New Age. Admittedly, some people who reported themselves to be Baptists or Lutherans take part in the New Age *audience*. But audiences do not constitute movements. And even this audience is probably not all that large. For example, the *New Age Journal* claimed an average circulation of fewer than 150,000 copies for 1990. It seems to us that the New Age is no more potent or relatively popular today than it was in the heyday of Theosophical Society, which claimed a total membership of 6,780 in 1926.

THE EVANGELICAL ERUPTION

In 1972 Dean M. Kelley, an executive of the National Council of Churches, provoked a storm of controversy, especially among religious liberals, with his book *Why Conservative Churches Are Growing*. His first sentence noted: "In the latter years of the 1960's something remarkable happened in the United States: for the first time in the nation's history most of the major church groups stopped growing and began to shrink." Kelley was among the very first to attempt to explain what Martin Marty (1979, p. 10) would later describe as a "seismic shift" in American religion: the sudden and very steep membership declines that began to hit the mainline denominations during the sixties. Summing up the evidence of a series of graphs showing membership figures for a number of major denominations, Kelley noted that in the sixties the "strong upward curve weakens, falters, and tilts downward like a spent skyrocket" (p. 2). As the title of his book revealed, however, not *all* denominations had hit the skids. The evangelical Protestant

bodies were still growing—many of them quite rapidly.

What was going on? According to Marty (1976, p. 71) it was another cultural crisis: "mainline churches always have the advantage . . . [when] the official culture is secure and expansive . . . [but they] suffer in times of cultural crisis and disintegration, when they receive blame for what goes wrong in society but are bypassed when people look for new ways to achieve social identity and location. So they looked good in the 1950s as they looked bad in the 1970s." Kelley disagreed. He claimed that the mainline bodies were failing to offer credible religion, that they had become so accommodated to the secular culture that people could no longer satisfy their need for the sacred by attending services at their local Methodist, Congregationalist, Episcopalian, or Presbyterian church.

As much as we admire Kelley's book, and his courage in writing it, we think the whole discussion of the sudden decline of the liberal denominations and the sudden "resurgence" of evangelical groups is based on a distorted historical perspective. Like Marty, Kelley was still trying to explain why this "sudden change took place in the 60's." Several years later Kelley (1984, p. 89) expressed continued confidence in his explanation of why the "conservatives" grew (as the "liberals" declined), but he confessed he was "less satisfied" that he had explained "why it happened at this particular time in history [the 1960s]."

But did anything akin to an eruption take place? Kelley's skyrocket image to the contrary, what is involved here is a gradual trend that has been going on for at least two centuries. The notion of a "seismic shift" is based on the fact that it was only in the sixties that this trend was finally noticed. If we are correct, all efforts by Marty and others to link the fate of the liberal churches to the "cultural crisis of the 1960s" (Marsden, 1982, p. 156) are falsified by the in-

TABLE 2

MARKET SHARES OF MAINLINE, EVANGELICALS, AND CATHOLICS PER 1,000 CHURCH MEMBERS, 1940–1985

Denomination	1940	1960	1985	Percentage loss or gain
Mainline				
United Methodists	124.7	93.0	64.3	− 48%
Presbyterian, U.S.A.	41.7	36.4	21.3	− 49%
Episcopal	30.9	28.6	19.2	− 38%
Christian (Disciples)	25.7	15.7	7.8	− 70%
United Church of Christ (Congregationalists)	26.5	19.6	11.8	− 56%
Evangelicals				
Southern Baptists	76.7	85.0	101.3	+ 32%
Assemblies of God	3.1	4.4	14.6	+ 371%
Church of the Nazarene	2.6	2.7	3.7	+ 42%
Church of God (Cleveland, Tenn.)	1.0	1.5	3.6	+ 260%
Roman Catholics	330.0	367.9	368.4	+ 12%

Source: Calculated from *Yearbook of American and Canadian Churches* (1988).

ability of consequences to precede their causes in time.

The general consensus of church historians (and most sociologists) is that the decline of the liberal Protestant churches was a product of the sixties. For example, Winthrop S. Hudson (1981, p. 439) claimed that the declines which "had begun in the 1960's . . . constituted a marked reversal after a century and a half of steady growth." Likewise, Marty (1979, p. 10) noted: "From the birth of the republic until around 1965, as is well known, the churches now called mainline Protestant tended to grow with every census or survey." But in light of the two centuries of church statistics we have examined, it is obvious that a group can add members and still fail to keep pace with the growth of the population and of other religious firms.

Social scientists who mistakenly accepted that an eruption of cult activities took place in the sixties can rightly claim that appropriate numerical estimates have been very hard to come by. But those who think there has been a "recent" surge of evangelical growth lack such a defense. Consider Table 2. The mainline denominations do not qualify as rockets that suddenly ran out of fuel in the sixties—their market shares were falling in the forties and fifties too, and throughout the century. In contrast, the evangelical groups—some of them rapidly becoming the new upstart sects of our era—do look like rockets. So much, then, for perceptions of a "seismic shift" or a sudden response to a cultural crisis. The speed of conservative growth and liberal decline will no doubt change from time to time, but the general trend has remained consistent for more than two centuries of American history. Thus, while it is true, as Hudson and Marty claim, that the total number of members of these mainline bodies increased regularly until the 1960s, each year they represented a smaller fraction of total church membership.

Even those without the slightest awareness of market share cannot long ignore an actual decline in numbers. And by the seventies the numbers were falling fast. Attempts to dismiss these declines as purely demographic (cf. Hoge and Roozen, 1979) or as symptomatic of the general decline in religiousness produced by modernity fall apart when it is noted that *only some* religious bodies were losing out. And indeed, as Dean Kelley bravely noted, the "conservative" Protestant bodies were still growing.

There have been many attempts to explain this "unwelcome" fact away. Carl Bangs (1972) charged Kelley with using "deceptive statistics." Others suggested that Kelley had fallen into the trap of confusing quantity with quality—that though the evangelicals grow rapidly by "herding insecure and frightened masses together into a superficial conformity," it is the liberal churches who are the "faithful remnant of God's people whose prophetic courage and lifestyle will truly point the way" (Miller, 1978, p. 257). Others claimed that the growth of evangelical Protestant bodies was nothing but inflated membership roles caused by people who frequently hop from one sect to another, thus being counted again and again (Bibby and Binkerhoff, 1973, 1983). Some even suggest that it was all a function of disparities in absolute size, because it is easy for small evangelical sects to have high percentage rates of growth, but virtually impossible for large denominations to keep growing rapidly (Nelson and Bromley, 1988). This excuse not only ignored the fact that the nation's largest Protestant body, the Southern Baptist Convention, was among those growing rapidly, but also ignored the huge potential for growth that actually exists in the American religious economy.

Two cases are illustrative. Between 1960 and 1970 the Assemblies of God grew by 22.9 percent to reach a total membership of 625,027. This was one of the "small" groups, thereby able to grow fast, cited by Kelley's critics. Meanwhile, the United Church of Christ (formerly the Congregationalists) declined by 12.5 percent, to 1,960,608 members, between 1960 and 1970. In 1987 the Assemblies of God numbered 2,160,667 members and the United Church of Christ had only 1,662,568. Does anyone really think that the advantage currently rests with the U.C.C., now that it has become the smaller group? It seems clear that the decline of the Protestant mainline is a long, steady

trend. It is pointless to search the 1960s for the causes of a phenomenon that was far along by the War of 1812. But the question persists: why do mainline faiths fail and why do the sects always overtake them? . . .

RATIONAL MODELS OF RELIGIOUS BELIEF AND SACRIFICE

The inevitable dilemma is clear. On the one hand, a congregational structure that relies on the collective action of numerous volunteers is needed to make the religion credible and potent. On the other hand, unless these volunteers are mobilized to a high level of participation, that same congregational structure threatens to undermine the level of commitment and contributions needed to make a religion viable.

Costly demands offer a solution to the dilemma. That is, the level of stigma and sacrifice demanded by religious groups will be positively correlated with levels of member participation.

Religious stigmas consist of all aspects of social deviance that attach to membership in the group. A group may prohibit some activities deemed normal in the external society (dancing, for example) and require other activities deemed abnormal by the world (speaking in tongues, for example). By meeting these expectations of the group, members deviate from the norms of surrounding society. In the extreme case, when the state attempts to sustain a religious monopoly, membership alone in a dissenting group can be an immense stigma.

Sacrifices consist of investments (material and human) required to gain and retain membership in the group. The requirements of some religious groups involve stigma and sacrifice simultaneously, in that stigmatized persons must often forgo rewards such as career opportunities.

On the surface it would seem that increased costs must always make a religion less attractive. And indeed the economists' law of demand predicts just that, *other things remaining equal.* But it turns out that other things *do not* remain equal when religions impose these sorts of costs on their members. To the contrary, costly demands strengthen a religious group by mitigating "free rider" problems and by increasing the production of collective religious commodities.

When high costs create a barrier to group entry, potential members can no longer reap the benefits of attendance or membership without first incurring substantial costs. To take part at all a prospective member must qualify by accepting the stigmas and sacrifices demanded for everyone. Laurence R. Iannaccone (1989, p. 9) explains: "Potential members are forced to choose: participate fully or not at all. The seductive middle-ground of free riding and low participation is eliminated." High cost serve to *screen out* potential members whose commitment and participation would otherwise be low. The costs act as nonrefundable registration fees which, as in secular markets, measure seriousness of interest in the product. As a result, the demanding sects speak of "conversions," "being born again," and "submitting their lives to the Lord." The less demanding churches refer to affiliations that are seldom life-altering events. Sectarian members are either in or out; they must follow the demands of the group or withdraw. The "seductive middle-ground" is lost.

For those who do join, high costs increase their level of involvement because it makes activities outside of the group more costly. Group members find that the temptation to free ride is weaker, not because their human nature has somehow been transformed, but because the opportunities to free ride have been reduced and the flow of rewards for displaying high levels of commitment have been substantially increased. Looked at another way, prohibiting an activity effectively increases its price, because the full cost now includes the cost of discovery and, often, the price of concealment. As the increased price of the prohibited activity reduces demand for it, the demand for substitutes rises.

If we may not attend dances or movies, play cards, go to taverns, or join fraternal organizations, we will probably look forward rather eagerly to the social activities at church.

Finally, it must be noted that the higher the costs of membership, the greater the material and social, as well as religious, benefits of membership.

At first glance it seems paradoxical that when the cost of membership increases the net gains of membership increase too. This is necessarily the case, however, when the commodity involved is collectively produced and when increased costs result in increased levels of participation in collective action, for this results in a greater supply of collective goods. An individual's positive experience in a worship service increases to the degree that the church is full, members enthusiastically participate (everyone sings and recites prayers, for example), and others express their positive evaluations of what is going on. Thus, as each individual member pays the cost of high levels of commitment, each benefits from the higher average level of participation thereby generated by the group. In similar fashion, people will value the otherworldly rewards of religion more highly to the extent that those around them do so. Or, to leave the realm of the immaterial, because Mormons are asked to contribute not only 10 percent of their income but 10 percent of their time to the church, they are able to lavish social services upon one another. Thus are the rewards of Mormon membership made tangible.

Membership in strict religions is, for many people, a "good bargain" in terms of a conventional cost-benefit analysis. We should acknowledge, however, that there are limits to the amount of sacrifice or the level of stigma people are willing to endure. Requiring members to withdraw from all secular opportunities, as some communes do, will clearly limit the growth of the organization. But most churches and sects do not increase sacrifice and stigma over time. As the circuit rider Peter Cartwright complained of the Methodists in 1856, the recurring trend over the past two hundred years has been for "expensive" sects gradually to lower the costs of membership and, by doing so, to reduce the benefits of membership as well. Thus our attention must focus on why and how the reduction of tensions with the surrounding culture weakens religious organizations.

NOTES

1. We use the term "cult" in a technical rather than a pejorative sense. A sect is a new organization of a conventional faith (conventional, that is, in the society under observation); a cult is an unconventional religion. Cults can occur because someone succeeds in attracting followers to a movement based on a new religious culture. They can also occur by importation from another society. Thus a religious group can be a cult in one society while being a conventional faith in another—Hinduism is a cult in the United States and Christianity is a cult in India. For a full discussion see Stark and Bainbridge (1985, 1987).

2. We removed atheist and adventist groups on the grounds that they were not cults, and we removed purely mail-order organizations on the grounds that they were neither cults nor sects. As it turned out, the results were unchanged by these omissions.

3. We note that Melton interprets these same data as a gradually accelerating curve—that cult formation is slowly increasing. While we disagree, Melton's interpretation is as incompatible as ours with the sixties eruption thesis.

4. Under the name of Summit Lighthouse.

5. The popular mail-order guru Yogi Ramacharaka was actually an American named William Walker Atkinson (Melton, 1987).

6. In 1965 there were 467 immigrants from India, in 1966 there were 2,293, and Indian immigration now runs at about 25,000 a year.

REFERENCES

Babbie, Earl. 1990. "Channels to Elsewhere." In Thomas Robbins and Dick Anthony, eds., *In Gods We Trust.* 2d ed. New Brunswick, N.J.: Transaction Publishers.

Bangs, Carl. 1972. "Deceptive Statistics." *Christian Century* 89: 852–853.

Berger, Peter. 1982. "From the Crisis of Religion to the Crisis of Secularity." In Mary Bibby, Reginald W., and Merlin B. Brinkerhoff. 1973. "The Circulation of the Saints." *Journal for the Scientific Study of Religion* 12: 273–283.

———. 1983. "Circulation of the Saints Revisited." *Journal for the Scientific Study of Religion* 22: 253–262.

Burrows, Robert. 1987. "A Christian Critiques the New Age." *Christianity Today* 16.

Cox, Harvey. 1977. *Turning East: The Promise and Peril of the New Orientalism.* New York: Simon and Schuster.

———. 1983. "Interview." In Steven J. Gelberg, ed., *Hare Krishna, Hare Krishna.* New York: Grove Press.

Glock, Charles Y., and Robert N. Bellah, eds. 1976. *The New Religious Consciousness.* Berkeley: University of California Press.

Hexham, Irving, Raymond F. Currie, and Joan B. Townsend, 1985. "New Religious Movements." In *The Canadian Encyclopedia.* Edmonton: Hurtig.

Hoge, Dean R., and David A. Roozen, eds. 1979. *Understanding Church Growth and Decline, 1950–1978.* New York: Pilgrim Press.

Hudson, Winthrop S. 1981. *Religion in America.* 3d ed. New York: Charles Scribner's Sons. Iannaccone, Laurence R. 1989. "Why Strict Churches Are Strong." Paper presented at the annual meeting of the Society for the Scientific Study of Religion, Salt Lake City, Utah.

Kelley, Dean. 1972. *Why Conservative Churches Are Growing.* New York: Harper and Row.

———. 1984. "Why Conservative Churches Are Still Growing." In Patrick H. McNamara, ed., *Religion: North American Style.* Belmont, Calif.: Wadsworth Publishing Co.

Kosmin, Barry A. 1991. *Research Report: The National Survey of Religious Identification.* New York: CUNY Graduate Center.

Marsden, George M. 1982. "Preachers of Paradox: The Religious New Right in Historical Perspective." In Mary Douglas and Steven M. Tipton, eds., *Religion and America: Spirituality in a Secular Age.* Boston: Beacon Press.

Marty, Martin E. 1976. *A Nation of Behavers.* Chicago: University of Chicago Press.

———. 1979. "Foreword." In Dean R. Hoge and David A. Roozen, eds., *Understanding Church Growth and Decline, 1950–1978.* New York: Pilgrim Press.

Melton, J. Gordon. 1987. "How New Is New? The Flowering of the 'New' Religious Consciousness since 1965." In David G. Bromley and Phillip E. Hammond, eds., *The Future of New Religious Movements.* Macon, Ga.: Mercer University Press.

———. 1988. "Testing the Truisms about the 'Cults': Toward a New Perspective on Nonconventional Religion." Paper presented at the annual meeting of the American Academy of Religion, Chicago.

———. 1989. *The Encyclopedia of American Religions.* 3rd ed. Detroit: Gale Research.

———. 1990. *New Age Encyclopedia.* Detroit: Gale Research.

Miller, Paul M. 1978. "Yes, Dean Kelly [*sic*], There Has Been Growth." *Gospel Herald,* March 28.

Nelson, Lynn D., and David G. Bromley. 1988. "Another Look at Conversion and Defection in Conservative Churches." In David G. Bromley, ed. *Falling from the Faith.* Newbury Park, Calif.: Sage Publications.

Robbins, Thomas, and Dick Anthony, eds. 1990. "Introduction." In *In Gods We Trust.* 2d ed. New Brunswick, N.J.: Transaction Publishers.

Shinn, Larry D. 1985. "Conflicting Networks: Guru and Friend in ISKCON." In Rodney Stark, ed., *Religious Movements: Genesis, Exodus, and Numbers.* New York: Paragon.

Stark, Rodney. 1991. "Antioch as the Social Situation for Matthew's Gospel." In David L. Balch, ed., *Social History of the Matthean Community: Cross-Disciplinary Approaches to an Open Question.* Minneapolis: Augsburg-Fortress.

———. 1992. "Epidemics, Networks, and the Rise of Christianity." *Semeia* (issue edited by L. Michael White).

Stark, Rodney, and William Sims Bainbridge. 1985. *The Future of Religion: Secularization, Revival, and Cult Formation.* Berkeley: University of California Press.

———. 1987. *A Theory of Religion.* New York and Bern: Peter Lang.

Tipton, Steven M. 1982. "The Moral Logic of Alternative Religions." In Mary Douglas and Steven M. Tipton, eds., *Religion and America: Spirituality in a Secular Age.* Boston: Beacon Press.

Wuthnow, Robert. 1976. *The Consciousness Reformation.* Berkeley: University of California Press.

———. 1978. *Experimentation in American Religion.* Berkeley: University of California Press.

DISCUSSION QUESTIONS

1. Based on the religious proclivities of your fellow students, how significant are cults, Eastern mysticism, and New Age religion for this generation of college students? Do Finke and Stark underestimate their importance?

2. Finke and Stark use a rational choice model to explain why sects grow while mainline faiths decline. Explain what their model is and discuss whether or not you think it offers a convincing explanation of religious change.

READING 35

Work in the New Capitalism

Richard Sennett

Richard Sennett is interested in examining the impact of flexible, or post-Fordist, capitalism on cultural values. In this excerpt from The Corrosion of Character, *he describes an encounter during a trans-Atlantic flight that he had with someone he had first encountered years ago when engaged in a study of American working-class culture. Rico was the son of one of Sennett's working-class subjects. Today he appears by all accounts to be a successful upper-middle-class professional, an example of intergenerational upward mobility who has proven that the America Dream still works. However, as Sennett's airline conversation with Rico reveals, the demands of contemporary capitalism serve to alienate people from community and undermine central values such as loyalty and trust. In short, Sennett sketches out the elements of the darker side of the American Dream.*

Recently I met someone in an airport whom I hadn't seen for fifteen years. I had interviewed the father of Rico (as I shall call him) a quarter century ago when I wrote a book about blue-collar workers in America, *The Hidden Injuries of Class*. Enrico, his father, then worked as a janitor, and had high hopes for this boy, who was just entering adolescence, a bright kid good at sports. When I lost touch with his father a decade later, Rico had just finished college. In the airline lounge, Rico looked as if he had fulfilled his father's dreams. He carried a computer in a smart leather case, dressed in a suit I couldn't afford, and sported a signet ring with a crest.

Enrico had spent twenty years by the time we first met cleaning toilets and mopping floors in a downtown office building. He did so without complaining, but also without any hype about living out the American Dream. His work had one single and durable purpose, the service of his family. It had taken him fifteen years to save the money for a house, which he purchased in a suburb near Boston, cutting ties with his old Italian neighborhood because a house in the suburbs was better for the kids. Then his wife, Flavia, had gone to work, as a presser in a dry-cleaning plant; by the time I met Enrico in 1970, both parents were saving for the college education of their two sons.

What had most struck me about Enrico and his generation was how linear time was in their lives: year after year of working in jobs which seldom varied from day to day. And along that line of time, achievement was cumulative: Enrico and Flavia checked the increase in their savings every week, measured their domesticity by the various improvements and additions they had made to their ranch house. Finally, the time they lived was predictable. The upheavals of the Great Depression and World War II had faded, unions protected their jobs; though he was only forty when I first met him, Enrico knew precisely when he would retire and how much money he would have.

Time is the only resource freely available to those at the bottom of society. To make time accumulate, Enrico needed what the sociologist

Max Weber called an "iron cage," a bureaucratic structure which rationalized the use of time; in Enrico's case, the seniority rules of his union about pay and the regulations organizing his government pension provided this scaffolding. When he added to these resources his own self-discipline, the result was more than economic.

He carved out a clear story for himself in which his experience accumulated materially and psychically; his life thus made sense to him as a linear narrative. Though a snob might dismiss Enrico as boring, he experienced the years as a dramatic story moving forward repair by repair, interest payment by interest payment. The janitor felt he became the author of his life, and though he was a man low on the social scale, this narrative provided him a sense of self-respect.

Though clear, Enrico's life story was not simple. I was particularly struck by how Enrico straddled the worlds of his old immigrant community and his new suburban-neutral life. Among his suburban neighbors he lived as a quiet, self-effacing citizen; when he returned to the old neighborhood, however, he received much more attention as a man who had made good on the outside, a worthy elder who returned each Sunday for Mass followed by lunch followed by gossipy coffees. He got recognition as a distinctive human being from those who knew him long enough to understand his story; he got a more anonymous kind of respect from his new neighbors by doing what everyone else did, keeping his home and garden neat, living without incident. The thick texture of Enrico's particular experience lay in the fact that he was acknowledged in both ways, depending in which community he moved: two identities from the same disciplined use of his time.

If the world were a happy and just place, those who enjoy respect would give back in equal measure the regard which has been accorded them. This was Fichte's idea in "The Foundations of National Law"; he spoke of the "reciprocal effect" of recognition. But real life does not proceed so generously.

Enrico disliked blacks, although he had labored peaceably for many years with other janitors who were black; he disliked non-Italian foreigners like the Irish, although his own father could barely speak English. He could not acknowledge kindred struggles; he had no class allies. Most of all, however, Enrico disliked middle-class people. We treated him as though he were invisible, "as a zero," he said; the janitor's resentment was complicated by his fear that because of his lack of education and his menial status, we had a sneaking right to do so. To his powers of endurance in time he contrasted the whining self-pity of blacks, the unfair intrusion of foreigners, and the unearned privileges of the bourgeoisie.

Though Enrico felt he had achieved a measure of social honor, he hardly wanted his son Rico to repeat his own life. The American dream of upward mobility for the children powerfully drove my friend. "I don't understand a word he says," Enrico boasted to me several times when Rico had come home from school and was at work on math. I heard many other parents of sons and daughters like Rico say something like "I don't understand him" in harder tones, as though the kids had abandoned them. We all violate in some way the place assigned us in the family myth, but upward mobility gives that passage a peculiar twist. Rico and other youngsters headed up the social ladder sometimes betrayed shame about their parents' working-class accents and rough manners, but more often felt suffocated by the endless strategizing over pennies and the reckoning of time in tiny steps. These favored children wanted to embark on a less constrained journey.

Now, many years later, thanks to the encounter at the airport, I had the chance to see how it had turned out for Enrico's son. In the airport lounge, I must confess, I didn't much like what I saw. Rico's expensive suit could have been just business plumage, but the crested signet ring—a mark of elite family background—seemed both a lie and a betrayal of the father.

However, circumstances threw Rico and me together on a long flight. He and I did not have one of those American journeys in which a stranger spills out his or her emotional guts to you, gathers more tangible baggage when the plane lands, and disappears forever. I took the seat next to Rico without being asked, and for the first hour of a long flight from New York to Vienna had to pry information out of him.

Rico, I learned, has fulfilled his father's desire for upward mobility, but has indeed rejected the way of his father. Rico scorns "time-servers" and others wrapped in the armor of bureaucracy; instead he believes in being open to change and in taking risks. And he has prospered; whereas Enrico had an income in the bottom quarter of the wage scale, Rico's has shot up to the top 5 percent. Yet this is not an entirely happy story for Rico.

After graduating from a local university in electrical engineering, Rico went to a business school in New York. There he married a fellow student, a young Protestant woman from a better family. School prepared the young couple to move and change jobs frequently, and they've done so. Since graduation, in fourteen years at work Rico has moved four times.

Rico began as a technology adviser to a venture capital firm on the West Coast, in the early, heady days of the developing computer industry in Silicon Valley; he then moved to Chicago, where he also did well. But the next move was for the sake of his wife's career. If Rico were an ambition-driven character out of the pages of Balzac, he would never have done it, for he gained no larger salary, and he left hotbeds of high-tech activity for a more retired, if leafy, office park in Missouri. Enrico felt somewhat ashamed when Flavia went to work; Rico sees Jeannette, his wife, as an equal working partner, and has adapted to her. It was at this point, when Jeannette's career took off, that their children began arriving.

In the Missouri office park, the uncertainties of the new economy caught up with the young man. While Jeannette was promoted, Rico was downsized—his firm was absorbed by another, larger firm that had its own analysts. So the couple made a fourth move, back East to a suburb outside New York. Jeannette now manages a big team of accountants, and he has started a small consulting firm.

Prosperous as they are, the very acme of an adaptable, mutually supportive couple, both husband and wife often fear they are on the edge of losing control over their lives. This fear is built into their work histories.

In Rico's case, the fear of lacking control is straightforward: it concerns managing time. When Rico told his peers he was going to start his own consulting firm, most approved; consulting seems the road to independence. But in getting started he found himself plunged into many menial tasks, like doing his own photocopying, which before he'd taken for granted. He found himself plunged into the sheer flux of networking; every call had to be answered, the slightest acquaintance pursued. To find work, he has fallen subservient to the schedules of people who are in no way obliged to respond to him. Like other consultants, he wants to work in accordance with contracts setting out just what the consultant will do. But these contracts, he says, are largely fictions. A consultant usually has to tack one way and another in response to the changing whims or thoughts of those who pay; Rico has no fixed role that allows him to say to others, "This is what I do, this is what I am responsible for."

Jeannette's lack of control is more subtle. The small group of accountants she now manages is divided among people who work at home, people usually in the office, and a phalanx of low-level back-office clerks a thousand miles away connected to her by computer cable. In her present corporation, strict rules and surveillance of phones and e-mail disciplines the conduct of the accountants who work from home; to organize the work of the back-office clerks a thousand miles away, she can't make hands-on, face-to-face judgments, but instead must work by formal written guidelines. She hasn't experienced less bureaucracy in this seemingly flexible work arrangement; indeed, her own decisions count for less than in the days when she supervised workers who were grouped together, all the time, in the same office.

As I say, at first I was not prepared to shed many tears for this American Dream couple. Yet as dinner was served to Rico and me on our flight, and he began to talk more personally, my sympathies increased. His fear of losing control, it developed, went much deeper than worry about losing power in his job. He feared that the actions he needs to take and the way he has to live in order to survive in the modern economy have set his emotional, inner life adrift.

Rico told me that he and Jeannette have made friends mostly with the people they see at work, and have lost many of these friendships during the moves of the last twelve years, "though we stay 'netted.'" Rico looks to electronic communications for the sense of community which Enrico most enjoyed when he attended meetings of the janitors' union, but the son finds communications on-line short and hurried. "It's like with your kids—when you're not there, all you get is news later."

In each of his four moves, Rico's new neighbors have treated his advent as an arrival which closes past chapters of his life; they ask him about Silicon Valley or the Missouri office park, but, Rico says, "they don't *see* other places"; their imaginations are not engaged. This is a very American fear. The classic American suburb was a bedroom community; in the last generation a different kind of suburb has arisen, more economically independent of the urban core, but not really town or village either; a place springs into life with the wave of a developer's wand, flourishes, and begins to decay all within a generation. Such communities are not empty of sociability or neighborliness, but no one in them becomes a long-term witness to another person's life.

The fugitive quality of friendship and local community form the background to the most important of Rico's inner worries, his family. Like Enrico, Rico views work as his service to the family; unlike Enrico, Rico finds that the demands of the job interfere with achieving the end. At first I thought he was talking about the all too familiar conflict between work time and time for family. "We get home at seven, do dinner, try to find an hour for the kids' homework, and then deal with our own paperwork." When things get tough for months at a time in his consulting firm, "it's like I don't know who my kids are." He worries about the frequent anarchy into which his family plunges, and about neglecting his children, whose needs can't be programmed to fit into the demands of his job.

Hearing this, I tried to reassure him; my wife, stepson, and I had endured and survived well a similarly high-pressure life. "You aren't being fair to yourself," I said. "The fact you care so much means you are doing the best for your family you can." Though he warmed to this, I had misunderstood.

As a boy, I already knew, Rico had chafed under Enrico's authority; he had told me then he felt smothered by the small-minded rules which governed the janitor's life. Now that he is a father himself, the fear of a lack of ethical discipline haunts him, particularly the fear that his children will become "mall rats," hanging out aimlessly in the parking lots of shopping centers in the afternoons while the parents remain out of touch at their offices.

He therefore wants to set for his son and daughters an example of resolution and purpose, "but you can't just tell kids to be like that"; he has to set an example. The objective example he could set, his upward mobility, is something they take for granted, a history that belongs to a past not their own, a story which is over. But his deepest worry is that he cannot offer the substance of his work life as an example to his children of how they should conduct themselves ethically. The qualities of good work are not the qualities of good character.

As I came later to understand, the gravity of this fear comes from a gap separating Enrico and Rico's generations. Business leaders and journalists emphasize the global marketplace and the use of new technologies as the hallmarks of the capitalism of our time. This is true enough, but misses another dimension of change: new ways of organizing time, particularly working time.

The most tangible sign of that change might be the motto "No long term." In work, the traditional career progressing step by step through the corridors of one or two institutions is withering; so is the deployment of a single set of skills through the course of a working life. Today, a young American with at least two years of college can expect to change jobs at least eleven times in the course of working, and change his or her skill base at least three times during those forty years of labor.

An executive for ATT points out that the motto "No long term" is altering the very meaning of work:

> In ATT we have to promote the whole concept of the work force being contingent, though most of the contingent workers are inside our walls. "Jobs" are being replaced by "projects" and "fields of work."[1]

Corporations have also farmed out many of the tasks they once did permanently in-house to small firms and to individuals employed on short-term contracts. The fastest-growing sector of the American labor force, for instance, is people who work for temporary job agencies.[2]

"People are hungry for [change]," the management guru James Champy argues, because "the market may be 'consumer-driven' as never before in history."[3] The market, in this view, is too dynamic to permit doing things the same way year after year, or doing the same thing. The economist Bennett Harrison believes the source of this hunger for change is "impatient capital," the desire for rapid return; for instance, the average length of time stocks have been held on British and American exchanges has dropped 60 percent in the last fifteen years. The market believes rapid market return is best generated by rapid institutional change.

The "long-term" order at which the new regime takes aim, it should be said, was itself short-lived—the decades spanning the mid-twentieth century. Nineteenth-century capitalism lurched from disaster to disaster in the stock markets and in irrational corporate investment; the wild swings of the business cycle provided people little security. In Enrico's generation after World War II, this disorder was brought somewhat under control in most advanced economies; strong unions, guarantees of the welfare state, and large-scale corporations combined to produce an era of relative stability. This span of thirty or so years defines the "stable past" now challenged by a new regime.

A change in modern institutional structure has accompanied short-term, contract, or episodic labor. Corporations have sought to remove layers of bureaucracy, to become flatter and more flexible organizations. In place of organizations as pyramids, management wants now to think of organizations as networks. "Networklike arrangements are lighter on their feet" than pyramidal hierarchies, the sociologist Walter Powell declares; "they are more readily decomposable or redefinable than the fixed assets of hierarchies."[4] This means that promotions and dismissals tend not to be based on clear, fixed rules, nor are work tasks crisply defined; the network is constantly redefining its structure.

An IBM executive once told Powell that the flexible corporation "must become an archipelago of related activities."[5] The archipelago is an apt image for communications in a network, communication occurring like travel between islands—but at the speed of light, thanks to modern technologies. The computer has been the key to replacing the slow and clogged communications which occur in traditional chains of command. The fastest-growing sector of the labor force deals in computer and data-processing services, the area in which Jeanette and Rico work; the computer is now used in virtually all jobs, in many ways, by people of all ranks.

For all these reasons, Enrico's experience of long-term, narrative time in fixed channels has become dysfunctional. What Rico sought to explain to me—and perhaps to himself—is that the material changes embodied in the motto "No long term" have become dysfunctional for him too, but as guides to personal character, particularly in relation to his family life.

Take the matter of commitment and loyalty. "No long term" is a principle which corrodes trust, loyalty, and mutual commitment. Trust can, of course, be a purely formal matter, as when people agree to a business deal or rely on another to observe the rules in a game. But usually deeper experiences of trust are more informal, as when people learn on whom they can rely when given a difficult or impossible task. Such social bonds take time to develop, slowly rooting into the cracks and crevices of institutions.

The short time frame of modern institutions limits the ripening of informal trust. A particularly egregious violation of mutual commitment often occurs when new enterprises are first sold. In firms starting up, long hours and intense effort are demanded of everyone; when the firms go public—that is, initially offer publicly traded shares—the founders are apt to sell out and cash in, leaving lower-level employees behind. If an organization whether new or old operates as a flexible, loose network structure rather than by rigid command from the top, the network can also weaken social bonds. The sociologist Mark Granovetter says that modern institutional networks are marked by "the strength of weak ties," by which he partly means that fleeting forms of association are more useful to people than long-term connections, and partly that strong social ties like loyalty have ceased to be compelling.[6] These weak ties are embodied in teamwork, in which the team moves from task to task and the personnel of the team changes in the process.

Strong ties depend, by contrast, on long association. And more personally they depend on a willingness to make commitments to others. Given the typically short, weak ties in institutions today, John Kotter, a Harvard Business School professor, counsels the young to work "on the outside rather than on the inside" of organizations. He advocates consulting rather than becoming "entangled" in long-term employment; institutional loyalty is a trap in an economy where "business concepts, product designs, competitor intelligence, capital equipment, and all kinds of knowledge have shorter credible life spans."[7] A consultant who managed a recent IBM job shrinkage declares that once employees "understand [they can't depend on the corporation] they're marketable."[8] Detachment and superficial cooperativeness are better armor for dealing with current realities than behavior based on values of loyalty and service.

It is the time dimension of the new capitalism, rather than high-tech data transmission, global stock markets, or free trade, which most directly affects people's emotional lives outside the workplace. Transposed to the family realm, "No long term" means keep moving, don't commit yourself, and don't sacrifice. Rico suddenly erupted on the plane, "You can't imagine how stupid I feel when I talk to my kids about commitment. It's an abstract virtue to them; they don't see it anywhere." Over dinner I simply didn't understand the outburst, which seemed apropos of nothing. But his meaning is now clearer to me as a reflection upon himself. He means the children don't see commitment practiced in the lives of their parents or their parents' generation.

Similarly, Rico hates the emphasis on teamwork and open discussion which marks an enlightened, flexible workplace once those values are transposed to the intimate realm. Practiced at home, teamwork is destructive, marking an absence of authority and of firm guidance in raising children. He and Jeannette, he says, have seen too many parents who have talked every family issue to death for fear of saying "No!," parents who listen too well, who understand beautifully rather than lay down the law; they have seen as a result too many disoriented kids.

"Things have to hold together," Rico declared to me. Again, I didn't at first quite get this, and he explained what he meant in terms of watching television. Perhaps unusually, Rico and Jeannette make it a practice to discuss with their two sons the relation between movies or sitcoms the boys watch on the tube and events in the newspapers. "Otherwise it's just a jumble of images." But mostly the connections concern the violence and sexuality the children see on television. Enrico constantly spoke in little parables to drive home questions of character; these parables he derived from his work as a janitor—such as "You can ignore dirt but it won't go away." When I first knew Rico as an adolescent, he reacted with a certain shame to these homely snippets of wisdom. So now I asked Rico if he too made parables or even just drew ethical rules from his experience at work. He first ducked answering directly—"There's not much on TV about that sort of thing"—then replied, "And well, no, I don't talk that way."

Behavior which earns success or even just survival at work thus gives Rico little to offer in the way of a parental role model. In fact, for this modern couple, the problem is just the reverse: how can they protect family relations from succumbing to the short-term behavior, the meeting mind-set, and above all the weakness of loyalty and commitment which mark the modern workplace? In place of the chameleon values of the new economy, the family—as Rico sees it—should emphasize instead formal obligation, trustworthiness, commitment, and purpose. These are all long-term virtues.

This conflict between family and work poses some questions about adult experience itself.

How can long-term purposes be pursued in a short-term society? How can durable social relations be sustained? How can a human being develop a narrative of identity and life history in a society composed of episodes and fragments? The conditions of the new economy feed instead on experience which drifts in time, from place to place, from job to job. If I could state Rico's dilemma more largely, short-term capitalism threatens to corrode his character, particularly those qualities of character which bind human beings to one another and furnishes each with a sense of sustainable self.

NOTES

1. Quoted in *New York Times,* Feb. 13, 1996, pp. D1, D6.
2. Corporations like Manpower grew 240 percent from 1985 to 1995. As I write, the Manpower firm, with 600,000 people on its payroll, compared with the 400,000 at General Motors and 350,000 at IBM, is now the country's largest employer.
3. James Champy, *Re-engineering Management* (New York: HarperBusiness, 1995) p. 119, pp. 39–40.
4. Walter Powell and Laurel Smith-Doerr, "Networks and Economic Life," in Neil Smelser and Richard Swedberg, eds., *The Handbook of Economic Sociology* (Princeton: Princeton University Press, 1994), p. 381.
5. Ibid.
6. Mark Granovetter, "The Strength of Weak Ties," *American Journal of Sociology* 78 (1973), 1360–80.
7. John Kotter, *The New Rules* (New York: Dutton, 1995) pp. 81, 159.
8. Anthony Sampson, *Company Man* (New York: Random House, 1995), pp. 226–27.

DISCUSSION QUESTIONS

1. What does Sennett mean when he writes that in today's flexible capitalism, "The qualities of good work are not the qualities of good charac-

ter"? Do you agree or disagree with his assessment?
2. According to Sennett, in what ways do many bedroom suburbs fail as genuine communities? Do you agree or disagree with his analysis?

READING 36

Farewell to the Factory

Ruth Milkman

What happens to the workers in manufacturing industries when their jobs are displaced or are jeopardized by economic restructuring because of deindustrialization? What is the future of such work in a postindustrial economy? These are the questions Ruth Milkman raises in Farewell to the Factory, *a study of a General Motor's plant in Linden, New Jersey. Milkman describes the varied ways workers have responded to job loss and GM's buyout plan, looking both at those workers who opted out and have attempted to forge new careers and those workers who decided to remain in the plant.*

As advanced capitalist economies shift away from manufacturing, and as the manufacturing that remains is radically restructured, what is happening to industrial workers and their way of life? This article explores that broad question through a narrow lens, focusing on the recent experiences of workers from a single factory: the General Motors (GM) automobile assembly plant in Linden, New Jersey. First opened in 1937, GM-Linden was at the core of the mass production economy that flourished over the next several decades. Like the luxury Cadillacs it built during the postwar boom, this plant was a top-of-the-line operation, with high wages, excellent fringe benefits, and a strong union—the best America had to offer to unskilled, uneducated industrial workers. The system began to unravel in the 1980s, however, as GM struggled to meet the challenge of intensified international competition. Management introduced robots and other new technologies at Linden, and began reorganizing the work process as well. The plant also shifted to small car production, and all these changes combined to generate sharp employment cutbacks. In the mid-1980s, GM negotiated with the United Auto Workers' union (UAW) to establish a buyout program offering cash payments to production workers who agreed to give up their jobs—an option that proved very popular at Linden. The pages that follow assess these unsettling developments from the perspective of the workers involved—both those who accepted the buyout and left the plant, and those who are still employed there. Their stories reveal a great deal about the dilemmas industrial workers face in the postindustrial age.

Edward Salerno (not his real name)[1] went to work as an assembler at Linden when he finished high school. His father, a lifelong GM employee, got him the job—a common arrangement in the days before the auto industry started shedding old workers rather than hiring new ones. Salerno worked at the Linden plant for eight years until he accepted the buyout in 1987. Even before that, he was restless. "Let's face it, auto workers are not in the most intelligent occupation in the world," he said, "and you kind of get hung up in that type of lifestyle." The main thing that had kept him at GM was the high pay. "You come right out of high school, and all of a sudden you're making this big money!"

A couple of years before he left, when he learned that the plant was going to be modernized, Salerno had signed up for an electronics training course, hoping it would help him get a better job. He was laid off during the year-long plant changeover, and GM paid for his training under a union-negotiated tuition reimbursement program. "After I graduated, then they started calling us back, and my mind was pretty much made up: if I didn't get a job in the computer end, fixing the new robotics and all, I was going to leave." When it became clear that he could

only return to GM as a production worker, and with his job security uncertain because of his relatively low seniority, Salerno decided to take the buyout, receiving about a year's pay, or $30,000. He got a job installing business telephone systems, but after a few months, he was laid off. So he went back to school again, this time to learn computer programming, and that led to a job in the payroll department of a large insurance company, where he works now.

The pay is less than at GM, but there is an excellent benefit package; and overall Salerno is much happier. "The working conditions and the atmosphere and the people—it's nice. It's such a great change for me, [better] than working on a line like that." He has no regrets about leaving GM:

> I'm thrilled that I'm out of there—what can I say? The place was a hellhole. I really hated it. It was very belittling. It seemed like they were always trying to play games with you, always trying to degrade you. And there was always that struggle between management and union: we're enemies. You know, it was constantly that. Each side played [its] little games. They didn't like you; they were going to do what they could to get you. Where I am now, there's never any yelling or threatening or anything like [there] was at General Motors. The relationship is better. I get along fine with my managers, and there just isn't the need for that kind of nonsense like at GM. As far as my foremen or any of my bosses there, I can't say I hated them, but I've never been brought to such anger in all my life [as] I was at that place. The things that some of the guys would try to do! It's incredible!

Salerno knew when he left GM that the auto industry's glory days were over. Only a generation before, an auto worker could make a decent living. "You could buy a house and raise a family like my father did. Now, forget it. If you're working there, your wife *has* to work." GM, and with it the UAW, had gone downhill in the 1980s:

> Let's face it, the auto workers just aren't what they used to be. They just don't have the power

they used to, because there's not as many workers and there's always that threat, well, they can just pack up and leave—which is what they're doing. No one is listening to the union anymore. What are they going to do? They have no recourse. So, I saw all that coming, and I said, "I just don't want to be a part of this anymore."

I think if the unions want to stay, they are going to have to start infiltrating the white-collar jobs, because manufacturing in this country is just going down the drain. I think that if it ever did happen, they could probably become strong again, because in this type of deal, where I work now, you could strike and you don't have to worry about picketing—because who's going to go in there and do your job? You're the one that knows what is going on. Nobody is going to walk in and take over your work, because they don't know what you're doing. In that respect it would be very easy. But where I work, you even mention the union, and they call you a communist. You start talking about that, and they get rid of you quick. But I'll tell you, I think that's their only hope for right now. I don't think that factory jobs will be around much longer.

Even though he's a lot happier now than when he worked at GM, Salerno is still keeping his eyes open for something better. "Most of the promotions come within the first two or three years over here, and then you kind of level off. I'm not learning anything new now, either." He's going to school again at night, with his employer paying the bill, working for an associate's degree in computer science. "If something else came along, I would take it."

Dan Cooper took the buyout too. He worked at GM-Linden for ten years, although he never liked it much, and like Salerno, he had not really intended to stay as long as he did. He was twenty when he was hired. "I was working at a warehouse making, I think, $5.00 or $5.25 an hour," he recalled. "They were starting up a second shift at General Motors and I heard guys talking about it and it was a lot more money. I didn't think I wanted to be an automaker, but while I was deciding what I wanted to do, I

could make more money at it. I went there, and when I first got there, I started thinking about maybe going for a foreman or trying to work up the ladder, but then I got turned off by that pretty quick."

Cooper has his own business now, as a chimney sweep, and he does other odd jobs, like stump grinding and landscaping, on a freelance basis. He started the chimney sweep business while he still worked at GM, as a second job.

> For a while my wife worked for AT&T, full-time. And so we had it made—we had money flowing out of our ears. Then the children came and she quit. All of a sudden our salary was cut in half, you know. And that's when I started my business. Working days on production, I usually got out between three and four in the afternoon, and so I could set up appointments after work or on weekends. I'd read about chimney sweeping in *Popular Mechanics* years before. I thought about it during the oil crisis, when people were going crazy buying wood stoves, but back then I didn't have the need for another job. So it had been in the back of my mind for a long time, and then I saw this ad for the equipment. I think I paid $1,600 for the vacuum, brushes, ladders, you know, basic things like that. I attacked my father-in-law's fireplace, and then I did a few for the guys at work, just free cleanings. Then I went around—I had a top hat and tails and I had flyers made up, and I'd go around on a Sunday, handing them out, looking for people working on their front lawns. And people start looking. I'd go in the liquor store and buy a six-pack of beer with top hat and tails on. Everybody in the store wants a card, you know.

For a few years Cooper built up the business while continuing to work at GM. Meanwhile, it was becoming obvious that the auto industry was in trouble. "The last five years or so before I left there, it just felt like I was giving back, I wasn't gaining anything. Once Reagan got into office, unions, organized labor went right down the drain. But before they offered the buyout, there was never any incentive to leave." When

GM did offer him the buyout, Cooper hesitated. "It was a hard thing to do. I had a house, a wife and kids, a mortgage. And benefits—picking up benefits is expensive. And security, you know, you get that weekly income. But I figured that I was young enough—I was thirty years old at the time—that I could fall on my face, you know, working for myself, and I knew I could still go out and get work."

Cooper expanded his business into a full-time operation with the help of the buyout money. "I didn't look at it as a lot of money, but it was something to help tip the scale. I looked at it more like a small business loan, rather than throwing it into our bank account, I bought a new van." He had never intended to stay at GM forever, but he realizes that if not for the buyout, he might have done so. "I was never really happy at GM, but I just never had the guts to say, 'The heck with it, I'm going to throw it in, take my ball, and go home.'" Now Cooper is much happier with his work:

To me, it's a utopia. I love when I'm doing the cleaning. . . . My main thing is getting people to love to use their fireplaces, educating them. That's how I get all the referrals, because Mrs. Jones loves to tell Mrs. Thomas any new information she finds out. And if [Mrs. Jones] can tell her this, that, and the other thing about a fireplace, Mrs. Thomas wants to know. I've got a business that—with advertising, I could probably put three trucks on the road, but I don't want the headaches.

I work probably the smallest area of any sweep in the state. I've got a circle on a map that extends out four miles, and if I go outside of there, people pay fifteen to twenty dollars extra to have me come. I try to discourage them. I don't need the whole county; I just want my little corner of the world, you know. And people love that. They like the idea that I sell myself, not my company. If you call and you have a problem, the only person you're going to talk to is me. There's not going to be a seventeen-year-old kid coming out to clean your fireplace. I like that, being a hometown boy. I grew up here, my father grew up here, and my in-laws live a half mile away.

When the economy plunged into recession, business became more uncertain, but so far Cooper has managed to hang on.

Usually, February, March, April, I keep myself semibusy; I've got maybe two jobs a day, three jobs a day, and take days off and stuff. But this year, for a while it was like I was getting two jobs a week. Everything went down, you know, all my income went down, and the bills were still there. Later the chimney cleaning picked up a little bit, and also I started the stump grinding. Now I'm working basically seven days a week. Usually, I don't get home till around eight-thirty; then I usually have about twelve calls on my answering machine. Sunday I was out from eleven until around six o'clock at night, doing stumps and running around. And before that, from like nine till eleven, I was out doing estimates. You know, I can see the end of it coming, but right now I'm working like a maniac.

Mostly he is glad he left GM, but Cooper has no illusions about the future. "I'm never sure if I did the right thing or not, because I don't know what's down the road. I could go for one slide, one fall, and never be able to climb again, you know, and that could be—whew, the whole business totally gone."

Almost a thousand GM-Linden production workers took the buyout at the same time as Salerno and Cooper. Three thousand others declined it and instead returned to work in the newly modernized plant. Susan Roberts was one of them. She thought about taking the buyout but decided against it in the end. "I was considering buying a house, and I figured that it would be a good down payment," she recalled. "But I talked myself out of it because I didn't have another job to go into. I figured if I wanted to buy a house, I don't need to put that much money down. So then I says, 'What the hell am I going to do? Where am I going to find a job that has benefits like this? Okay, the job security is a little iffy, but I'm going to hang in there.'"

When Roberts returned to the plant, she went through a two-week training program, jointly sponsored by GM and the UAW, welcoming the workforce to the "new Linden" with great fanfare. Along with the new technology, the program introduced a range of organizational innovations, many of them modeled after the practices of the Japanese auto firms that are now GM's most formidable competitors. In a dramatic reversal of past practice, for example, workers were told to "build the car in the station," meaning that they should do each job in its assigned location rather than marking problems for correction later on, as they had in the past. If extra time is needed to correct a problem, workers were told, they should simply stop the line. In addition, the plant switched to a "just-in-time" inventory system, so that parts were delivered to workers on the line as they were needed, rather than in larger quantities—a hallmark of the Japanese auto industry that is often credited with improving efficiency. The "new Linden" also had Employee Involvement Groups (EIGs) that met to discuss production and quality problems, and there were other efforts to improve communications between labor and management. Workers were promised a larger role in decision making and problem solving on the shop floor as well.

Like most Linden workers, Roberts welcomed these changes. "I feel we're going in the right direction, finally," she said.

> General Motors didn't wake up fast enough to what the Japanese were doing. They thought they were just so big that nobody could touch them. GM's a little slow; it took them a little while, but they're finally getting into it. They're finally realizing that it's not quantity—it's quality that is going to bring back the American people to buy these cars again, instead of going to Japan and Korea. And it's good that they have realized it, because they definitely got to make some changes.
>
> The union's working with management more, which, I think, helps. We have to work together. I think there's more communication now; that's the key thing to me, communication. You got to talk. And management is really doing more for the

people, you know, trying to get rid of the old dinosaurs and get them more into sync with us, 'cause we're the ones that do the job.

Roberts liked what she heard in the "new Linden" training program. She even volunteered to be an EIG spokesperson. "I like doing a good job; I like seeing a good job done. A lot of people called me Goody Two-shoes," she confessed. She was especially pleased with the just-in-time system. "The plant is cleaner; they cleared all the stock out, you know. [Before] they had racks of stock, and you couldn't even see outside. Everything was blocked up; everything was stuffy, it felt, you know, claustrophobic. Once they started doing that, it was like a whole new breath of fresh air, believe it or not. You could see sunlight, and that, that helped my day—it really did."

But her enthusiasm flagged as it became clear that the daily reality of life on the shop floor would not be quite what had been promised.

> Yeah, build-in-station. If you had a problem—let's say, sometimes on the modules the clip would be shot where I would have to snap in my rod. So, I would stop the line, go over, get a clip, stick it in there, stick the rod in, start the line up again. Which took maybe about fifteen, twenty seconds, you know, but they would go crazy, because, you know, you stop the line, and they're thinking right away they're losing money. Even though the concept was, this was how it's supposed to work. Oh man, they used to come running—unbelievable! You had the line down not even ten seconds, and, boom, they would come running, "Why's the line down.?" "Uh, a clip is missing, and I was supposed to do my job in my area, so. . . ." A lot of people were scared that they would get yelled at and so they went back to the old system where you take a job number down and eventually somebody else in another section would pick it up. They were so used to the old way that that's the way they wanted to keep it. You know, maybe to pamper us or satisfy us, they keep the buttons [to stop the line] in there, but it's kind of frustrating.

The EIG program—eventually abandoned altogether by the plant management—was another disappointment. "It didn't work well at all," Roberts reported. "And it's a shame, 'cause it was a good thing to have, but it just fell apart, and it was lack of communication, lack of interest. One of our complaints when we had EIG was to get the engineers to work with us on the line and see how these parts fit together that they say fit fine together on paper. But forget it. That never worked, we never got them in." She blamed the supervisors and middle managers for these failures. "A lot of foremen [sic], they never worked on the line, so they really don't know what it's like. And these people higher up, they just come in, they do the job, they get the money, and that's it. Sometimes I feel like they're trying to make me out like an idiot, that I don't know what I'm talking about—and that pisses me off. So I would like better communication, better understanding."

Fred Lawton also turned down the buyout and went back to work in the plant after the changeover. His assessment of the "new Linden" is remarkably similar to Roberts's, even though he is far from a Goody Two-shoes type. "It hasn't changed that much at all," he reported. "The supervisors—they always would refer to them as dinosaurs—the dinosaurs are still here. They may have been put to sleep for a while, but they're still here; they rise up every once in a while, and then they start hollering and screaming the same way they used to. You have to, I guess, put up with it. I let it go in one ear and out the other."

Like Roberts, Lawton pointed to the discrepancy between rhetoric and reality. "They [management] tell you, 'This is the way we want it; this is the way the Japanese do it.' Okay, if that's the way they do it, then let's do it that way too. But if you stopped the line, most of the time they would start the line and *then* ask what's wrong. It's going back to the dinosaurs: it's a numbers game; we need so many cars, 430 cars or whatever, and we'll do everything to get them out.

They don't want that line to stop for any reason." He also questions the level of commitment on the part of both managers and workers to the EIG program: "I think it was just done to make it look good, as a show. I really don't think they were serious about it. Everybody would go to the meetings because they got a half-hour's overtime pay, so that's why people took part. We used to come up with some good ideas for them, but they didn't want any. You know, 'Okay, okay, okay.' They didn't want to hear us, you know. They would want numbers, not ideas."

In the 1970s, Lawton had been active in a dissident faction of the local union, and through his father, who worked in the plant for forty years, he was familiar with its entire history. He deeply regrets the union's recent loss of power:

> My belief is that in the past five years [there have] been less grievances filed than were filed in, say, all of '77 or all of '78. Our local used to be considered the rebels, going way back. We were the ones! The metropolis, this city that this plant is in, has such a wide variety of people. They don't have the hicks from, you know, come off the farm; they got an intelligent workforce up here. But now, our local is just going along with everything. The union is playing more of a management role. Their whole attitude has changed. They seem to be too cooperative, and I think all labor unions are getting that way. I think they're all dying. They say you can't have the militance, but you need something there; otherwise, things are going to fall too easy, and that's when things go downhill. That's what happened to our union.

To him, this is part and parcel of the decline of the auto industry as a whole. Despite Lawton's negative evaluation of recent developments, he remains a loyalist in some respects:

> It bothers me that we have engineers who pull up to work in Nissans. There's something wrong; there's got to be some loyalty somewhere. I mean, I have two cars; they're General Motors cars. I had a Plymouth before that—I felt uncomfortable buying it at first. I cannot see, especially these engineers and upper management, driving these

other cars. People in union-appointed positions, too—[there are] guys driving Mercedes. "Hey, Mercedes is a great car; so is my other car, my wife's car, a Chevy." I said, "Well then, do me a favor; keep your Mercedes home; drive your Chevy to work. Park your Chevy in the lot; don't park your Mercedes here. If everybody bought Mercedes, where would you be working?" But nobody cares.

Although Lawton turned down the buyout, he has long aspired to leave the blue-collar world. He attended college at night and got a degree in accounting back in 1981, "with an understanding that I would be moved into a financial department position" at GM:

> But then, when the time came, they said, "Go and be a foreman." Their major concern was "We don't move anybody from the hourly line into the front office."
>
> I said, "Why not?"
>
> They said, "We don't do that; you have to be a foreman first." I had three kids; I did not want to work six weeks days, six weeks nights, like the foremen do. I like to have some time for my home life. I mean, I coach two soccer teams; I coach baseball. I couldn't do that as a foreman, but as a straight salary worker, I wouldn't have a problem.
>
> I was hurt and disappointed, and was ready to leave then. I even had gone to an employment agency, looking for other jobs. At the time, in '81, we were probably making $21,000 or $22,000 a year. I went looking for junior accountant jobs, and they were all starting at $13,000 and $12,000 and no benefits.
>
> So that was tough, but they don't move from the line in. You have to go and be a supervisor first, and that bothered me.

Lawton continues to dream of leaving the plant to become an accountant. He thought hard about taking the buyout. But "I couldn't just do it; I would have to have something to go into. All my résumés went out, and I got nothing back. I have a whole folder in there, probably about two hundred responses back, and they were all: 'Very sorry, we'll keep your résumé on file. If something comes up, we'll let you know.'"

So for Lawton, leaving the plant remains a fantasy, at least for now.

THE LACK OF NOSTALGIA

Social commentators in the past often lamented the destructive effects of capitalist industrialization on ordinary people; today, however, the focus of critical inquiry has shifted to the results of *de*industrialization. Despite the irony of this reversal, there is ample basis for concern—particularly from a labor perspective—about the structural transformations now under way. Radical economic restructuring inevitably renders less powerful groups newly vulnerable, and it threatens whatever forms of self-protection they have developed. Indeed, as manufacturing has moved to regions with cheaper, more tractable labor, and as GM and other American firms have seen their formerly unchallenged market position dramatically eroded by foreign competition, millions of people have been thrown out of work, and employers have launched bold attacks on labor organizations. Particularly in monoindustrial communities where alternative sources of work are few or nonexistent, many victims of plant closings or mass layoffs who once enjoyed middle-class incomes have been forced into long-term unemployment or into marginal, poorly paid jobs and have suffered a radical decline in their standard of living. Discarded, like obsolete machinery, by their former employers, they face a bleak future of economic deprivation and social humiliation. A considerable literature already exists documenting the devastating social effects these developments have produced in recent years.[2]

Even if this proves a transitional phenomenon limited to a single, lost generation of "displaced" workers, it represents a tragic and inexcusable failure of social policy. Without denying its importance, however, one can also recognize that this is only part of the story of industrial decline and restructuring. Some former high-wage factory workers like Edward Salerno and Dan Cooper have been able to make a relatively smooth transition into other types of employment; others, like Susan Roberts and Fred Lawton, are still employed in basic industry, although technological and organizational innovations have transformed their work. To be sure, neither those who left GM-Linden under the buyout program nor those still employed there are representative of the industrial labor force, past or present. The buyout takers are a self-selected, relatively youthful group who are in many ways atypical of the larger population of displaced workers; those who remain at GM-Linden are dependent on a firm that is undergoing extensive internal restructuring and whose survival, given the continuing shake-up in the global automobile industry, is far from assured.

But it is precisely their peculiar yet strategic social locations that make these two groups of workers particularly interesting. The buyout takers' post-GM employment trajectories suggest the problems and possibilities confronting young workers in the growing service-based "postindustrial" economy, whereas the situation of their co-workers who stayed at GM exposes the complexities of the process of work reorganization now under way in the shrinking, but still important, manufacturing sector. The recent experiences of workers like these may be more relevant for understanding the prospects for future generations of non-college-educated workers than the more dramatic stories of emiseration among former industrial workers in other settings that are so extensively documented in the literature on deindustrialization.

For both those who left and those who stayed at GM-Linden, the future is extremely uncertain, and they are painfully aware of this fact. Although so far, both groups have escaped the long-term unemployment, downward mobility, and accompanying social distress that has afflicted so many other workers, they know very well that they remain vulnerable to such a fate. As Dan Cooper put it, "I don't know what's down the road." And yet surprisingly few GM-Linden workers, past or present, express any desire to restore the old industrial system that is now collapsing around them. Their lack of nostalgia highlights a sad fact that is all too often forgotten in the age of deindustrialization: factory work in the golden age of mass production was deeply problematic in its own right. However much it fascinated some left-wing intellectuals, workers themselves never romanticized the assembly line—instead they mostly yearned to escape its relentless and dehumanizing rhythms.

NOTES

1. The life histories recounted in the text are based on interviews with actual GM-Linden workers; only names and other identifying information have been altered to protect the privacy of individuals. All direct quotations are reproduced verbatim from tape-recorded interviews conducted by the author, unless otherwise indicated.

2. See, among many others, Barry Bluestone and Bennett Harrison, *The Deindustrialization of America: Plant Closings, Community Abandonment, and the Dismantling of Basic Industry* (New York: Basic Books, 1982); Katherine Newman, *Falling from Grace: The Experience of Downward Mobility in the American Middle Class* (New York: Free Press, 1988); Kathryn Marie Dudley, *The End of the Line: Lost Jobs, New Lives in Postindustrial America* (Chicago: University of Chicago Press, 1994); Carolyn C. Perrucci, Robert Perrucci, Dena B. Targ, and Harry R. Targ, *Plant Closings: International Context and Social Costs* (New York: Aldine de Gruyter, 1988); and Daniel S. Hamermesh, "What Do We Know about Worker Displacement in the U.S.?" *Industrial Relations* 28 (winter 1989): 51–59.

DISCUSSION QUESTIONS

1. What are the major risks for workers who decided to accept GM's buyout plan and leave the plant? What are the main risks for those who decided to remain in the plant?

2. Milkman notes that workers, whether they left or stayed in the plant, exhibit little nostalgia for the old industrial system. Why is this the case?

Television's Anti-Politics: Surveying the Wasteland

Todd Gitlin

Todd Gitlin offers a critical assessment of the role of television in shaping the peculiar antipolitical sentiments of a growing sector of the American population. Its alienation and disengagement from active political participation occurs at a time when one might contend that there are more and more possibilities to be both informed and engaged because of the advances in communications technologies. Gitlin is suspicious of technological solutions to social problems, and he reviews a range of claims about the positive role played by such phenomena as talk radio and television, the news coverage of CNN and C-SPAN, and Internet linkages. He concludes that the emphasis on tabloid journalism is a reflection of a deeper underlying erosion of a democratic public sphere.

Democratic politics in the world's oldest democracy is losing popular appeal. Public cynicism about what government, or politics, can accomplish is rampant. American voting turnout has been declining for decades, though with occasional upticks. At the same time, Americans are overwhelmed with imagery and information. What is the relation, if any, between the scandalous obsessions of American news media and the glut of entertainment, on the one hand, and the declining participation and rising demagoguery in American politics?

For more than a decade, American news media have been roundly and loudly criticized for degrading politics. Since 1980, many painstaking empirical studies have established that the principal subject covered during political campaigns is the so-called "horse race"—the question of who is leading, who is behind, who is gaining. To this obsession with polls and competitive strategies has been added a strategic obsession—intense, half-cynical, half-admiring coverage of the maneuvers of the politicians and campaign strategists as they attempt to "position" themselves and manage their images. This tendency is not strictly American, of course. Comparable fascinations and criticisms could be seen in the recent French presidential campaign— a glut of polls coexisting with a skeptical attitude toward them, as expressed in the headline of one critical *feuilleton* piece: "Do you think there are too many, just enough, or not enough polls?"

The press treatment of politics emulates the "postmodern" fascination with backstage tactics in sports and entertainment. The point of much entertainment coverage is to make the audience privy to Hollywood marketing calculations, casting tactics, career moves, and box office figures. We are invited to understand Hollywood not only as a machine for dreams but as a game through which we, the spectators, are dreamed of.

Similarly enthralled by the machinery by which images are manufactured, the press—not only television and radio—treats politics as a game, giving only limited coverage to the positions and records of the candidates. The same is largely true of the coverage of politicians in office. Here, for example, is the lead to a *New York Times* article of July 1994: "Speaking at a heavily scripted community forum here, Hillary Rodham Clinton today previewed the sales pitch she will take on the road this fall to make her case for extensive changes in the nation's health care system." *Previewed the sales pitch.* The media themselves have amplified the observation, first made by academics, that the "discourse" of politics has been crippled by the compression of speeches into ten-second "sound bites," rendering serious debate of public issues impossible. They claim as a warrant for ten-second sound bites the declining attention span of the American public—a declining attention span to which, of course, they contribute.

These are far from the only criticisms to be leveled at news coverage of political life. Critics of various persuasions accused the news media—especially television—first, in the Reagan years, of permitting the White House's smooth-running public relations apparatus to command the national agenda; then, in the case of George Bush, of inflaming racial suspicions through demagogic appeals; and in the case of the hapless Bill Clinton, of failing to manipulate television adroitly enough. Neither of Reagan's successors has proved nearly as adept as he in coaxing the media into his embrace, and so the recent emphasis in media criticism has been on the degradation of media coverage into a scurrilous obsession with scandals. The mass media are charged with casting such discredit upon elected officials as to raise public cynicism to the boiling point and to make it difficult for any government to govern.

The American right accuses the news (and entertainment) media of disrespect for "family values" and an excess of sympathy for multiculturalism. The left, such as it is, finds in the media signs of racism, sexism, and homophobia. There is warrant for both views. But the howls of outrage are scarcely limited to partisan and academic circles. Disgust at the spectacle of the mass media is a popular sentiment. At a time when public confidence in American institutions is almost uniformly low, the press is scarcely exempt from popular dissatisfaction. The background is, of course, the widespread feeling that social problems are intractable unless, perhaps, extreme measures are taken. The rise of demagogic pseudosolutions—severe jail sentences, an end to immigration, not to mention the lunatic terrorism of the ultraright—is fueled by the pervasive sense that business as usual has not worked. Television is blamed for bringing bad news, but the blame is frequently cast by precisely

the same people who rely on television news for their everyday social bearings.

Contrary to the assumptions of contemporary nostalgia, the media obsession with scandalous accusations is nothing new in the history of American democracy. From the early nineteenth century onward, blatant charges of sexual, financial and other forms of personal malfeasance were the conventional stuff of American political life as recorded in the press. The highmindedness of the Lincoln-Douglas debates of 1860 was exceptional. But during the last halfcentury, the ideal of press objectivity drowned out the memory of the old conventions. A standard of fair-mindedness and sweet reasonableness has jelled, and it is this that seems to many people to have been transgressed in recent years—especially by the tabloid press and related television "reality shows." A considerable portion of the public is plainly angry at what it feels to be the media's trivialization of political life.

In 1992, this anger was so thunderous as to arouse media coverage itself. Never before, at least not in the twentieth century, has the American press been so vociferously attacked, and so defensive about the attacks. In the aftermath of each widely reported scandal, the major media have indulged in massive and public selfscrutiny, in which influential figures in the news media confess to excesses, express doubt about whether they are discharging their debt to democracy, and promise to be more judicious the next time. We saw this cycle at work with respect to the reporting of the Clintons' "Whitewater" and other scandalous investments, along with the charge that President Clinton was guilty of sexual harassment.

The pattern reached something of its high— or low—point during the 1992 presidential campaign, when presumably legitimate media picked up from scandal-mongering weeklies Gennifer Flowers's charge that she had a longterm affair with then-governor Bill Clinton. The established media quickly became obsessed with these charges on the ground that once they had been made public, even by disreputable media, the charges were "in the public domain" and therefore deserved to be taken seriously. Thus the agenda for the "quality press"—the *New York Times* and *Washington Post* and *Wall Street Journal,* the *Los Angeles Times* and *Philadelphia Inquirer,* the three major television networks, public television and radio—was set by the quantity press. And so, in February of 1992, the same issue of the supermarket weekly called *Star,* whose front page offered "FOUND! Ted Danson's forgotten first wife" and "I was Stevie Wonder's secret lover for 24 years," commanded America's respectable outlets with "MY 12-YEAR AFFAIR WITH BILL CLINTON." That the *Star* and later, the syndicated television "magazine" sensation show *A Current Affair* paid for Gennifer Flowers's story (dollars in the estimated six figures) went barely noted. Soon CBS's prestige news "magazine" *60 Minutes* was airing the Clintons' response to the charges, and CNN was carrying Gennifer Flowers's press conference live. Thus do the quality media have great difficulty resisting market pressures. Competition leads not to variety but to uniformity.

Again and again, what begins as a sensational accusation quickly becomes mainstream. A strong motive is, not surprisingly, economic. In the last two decades, the three major television networks have lost roughly one-third of their audience to cable-satellite networks and independent stations, which, in turn, have succeeded in recruiting audiences to "real-life crime" programs and scandalous talk shows among other offerings. Moreover, in general, the local stations and major networks have felt pressed to compete with the purveyors of lurid crime stories. One consequence is popular crime panic and the lust for instant solutions—longer sentences, cancellation of parole for repeat offenders ("three strikes and you're out"), and so on.

The abdication of news judgment to the "low-end" press is one more development in the general elevation of celebrity chatter, with the concomitant expectation that politics shall be another branch of the unending entertainment spectacle. In the eyes of most of the news media—I notice that this is true in France and Britain as well—the market certifies what is worth attention. The "upscale" newspapers now regularly report television ratings and movie box-office receipts, and fawn over movie stars; it is no surprise that this fascination with entertainment values has drawn the once more austere news operation in its wake. The president is the Celebrity-in-Chief, fair game for adulation when he plays the part as smoothly as Ronald Reagan, fair game for contempt when he is as young and perplexing as Bill Clinton.

As in the early nineteenth century, when scurrilous charges against politicians were also the order of the day, the eruption of petty scandals has left candidates—and officials—with few good choices. If they stand silent, they are accused of "stonewalling." If the candidate at first tries evasion and later decides to answer the charges, he or she gets accused of "flip-flopping." Having admitted any transgression, he or she seems guilty of bad character.

Political news coverage has become at times an accomplice of demagoguery, at times a branch of the sports and entertainment industries, and at times an exercise in cynicism, keeping Americans diverted, perhaps, but failing to help them govern themselves.

SALVATION BY NEW MEDIA?

Is the American media system self-remedying? There are two wings to this hope. First, it is argued that reforms in the traditional media may eliminate, or at least temper, the abuses of recent years. Second, it is argued that new media are emerging, and that they may rectify the situation.

Certainly, popular disgust at the news media's obsession with scandal has pushed the media to an unusual search for self-reform. The established news media have been busily trying to rectify their conduct since 1988. Responding to the charge that the press has given credence to deceptive political advertising, newspapers now routinely evaluate the truthfulness of political candidates' television commercials. Responding to the charge that they have permitted irresponsible candidates to set a distracting agenda by exchanging reckless and misleading charges, several local newspaper, television, and radio enterprises have taken some initiative, asking the public to say what they think the issues should be, attempting to keep political campaigns focused on the most significant questions. The media's attempts at self-rectification may be attributed to good will; they should also be attributed to self-interest, since television networks and newspapers alike are aware that the audience for news is declining steadily. With readership and viewership in seemingly irreversible decline, especially among the young, the major media have a strong interest in appearing to be responsive.

By far the more important reaction to the recent waves of media criticism comes, however, from outside the established media. It comes in the form of new media organizations, new formats, and new technologies, often with new audiences. There is so much novelty, one conventionally hears that America has entered a "new media age." There is incessant talk about the democratic potential of "new news." It is declared that radio and television talk shows have made it possible for citizens to widen the range of opinion publicly expressed; that they permit citizens to mobilize on issues of deep concern, and thus make politicians more responsive; that they even permit the organization of an independent presidential campaign like that of Ross Perot in 1992. It is argued that the "deliberative opinion poll" and other links between polls and the media can make politicians more responsive to public sentiment. It is argued that telephone technology permits the financing of new political campaigns. It is argued that computer-telephone hookups—the Internet—nurture political community.

In my view, the democratizing potential of the new media has been drastically exaggerated. Most of the hopes laid on new electronic developments belong in the American tradition of looking to the technological fix for political, spiritual, economic, and social troubles. Technological improvements heighten uniformity more than they challenge it. Let me address these potentials in the course of a review of recent and impending developments in the news media.

Radio Talk Shows One of the major uses of AM radio in the United States today is the circulation of angry political talk. Daily talk shows are available at all hours of the day and much of the night. Most of these are local, many have fundamentalist Protestant affiliations, and some have been at work for decades, but one of the new developments is that several now have national hookups, of which the main one in public appeal is Rush Limbaugh's, available for three hours every day (with an additional half-hour television program in much of the country). Limbaugh has become enormously successful serving up a mixture of fierce right-wing views, self-promotional bombast, and nasty humor.

In this ideological enterprise he is not unprecedented: in the 1930s, Father Charles Coughlin, the Catholic "radio priest," offered a potent stream of populist rhetoric, with an undercurrent of anti-Semitism—though as his anti-Semitism grew more ferocious, Coughlin lost a good deal of his following. Limbaugh's right-wing populism focuses anger on government bureaucrats, intellectuals, feminists, and liberals. His devotees pride themselves on being "dittoheads." There are "Rush Rooms" at restaurants and bars around the country, where the faithful gather to listen to their hero in the company of co-believers. What is his influence? It is hard to know exactly. He may well have helped kill health insurance legislation in 1994. But he has certainly impressed the strong Republican opposition that he speaks for them and for the alienated multitude they aspire to represent.

Most of the talk show talk is unfocused anger, but some has a practical import. Some of the hosts invite their listeners to lobby their representatives or flood the president with mail and faxes. In a few cases, talk show hosts have even coordinated their efforts and had direct political impact—the first successful case was a campaign to keep members of Congress from voting themselves a pay increase. Such symbolic crusades against government privilege are of little material consequence, and display a Republican bias—they are the perfect issues for talk show hosts and their constituencies.

One of the most successful of radio talk hosts, Larry King, is a centrist of no discernible political passion. But one of the striking things about radio talk shows in general is how predictably they tilt toward the right. According to one survey, 70 percent of the hosts, and the callers they attract, occupy positions considerably to the right of American public opinion. This is even true in the San Francisco Bay Area, the most liberal metropolitan area in the country. Former governor and quixotic presidential candidate Jerry Brown, who did a talk show based in Sacramento, was unable to acquire an outlet in the Bay Area. One San Francisco AM station, after trying out several liberal hosts, abandoned them for right-wingers, one of whom, according to Howard Kurtz's forthcoming book, *Hot Air: All Talk, All the Time,* had been fired by another station for denouncing "the stinking Japanese." His new employer proceeded to fire him six weeks later for calling gays "sick" and "pathetic."

The tilt to the right bears some reflection. There are several causes. First, station owners tend to be Republicans. Consider the cancellation by ABC of Jim Hightower's show, syndicated to some 150 stations, although not in the largest markets, after Hightower started ragging on Disney's purchase of the network—"I work for a rodent." ABC said its concern was strictly low ratings; and whether venality or politics was the prime cause is known only to the network's

bookkeepers. (At this writing, the substitute show is left-of-center.) Second, the audience during commuting hours, when talk radio has its largest audience, is disproportionately male. (Women are concentrated in the audience for *television* talk.) Third, right-wing talk is more theatrical than left-wing talk. It overflows with emotion, particularly spleen and rancor. It has a more compelling dramatic structure. Liberals, who at least superficially value tolerance and reconciliation, do not compete well, for entertainment purposes, with the party of rancor and unreason. Therefore the latter starts with an advantage. Fourth, the counterpart melodrama that Democrats could, in principle, muster would be directed against the rich and the corporations, but they are reluctant to mobilize a populist fury—partly because of their own dependence on corporate funds, partly because their leading figures are comfortable, partly because the union base is so weak.

Without doubt, radio talk shows provide outlets—principally for the angry and prejudiced, whose vulgarity they legitimize. They keep in circulation a rage targeted against immigrants, minorities, welfare programs, feminists, and so on. They are considerable instruments of demagoguery, and a power base for future politicians in the Republican party, especially on its right fringe. President Clinton's denunciation of the radio demagogues after the Oklahoma City bombing was long overdue—and of course was counter-denounced in turn—but did nothing to reduce their significance.

Television Talk Shows This genre, popular in the afternoon with women at home, has been a strong presence in American life since the early 1980s. The guests are frequently victims of some sort of abuse—crime in the family, sexual molestation, and so on. Studio audiences are joined by phone callers. The display of curiosity and judgment provides an audience of millions certain assurances of their own normality by giving them a safe, brief, vicarious acquaintanceship with deviance. Phil Donahue's talk show, which pioneered the format, has at times lent itself to explicit political discussion, and indeed, Bill Clinton, under fire from mainstream media, turned to Donahue's program for relief during the 1992 campaign. The in-studio audience format was adopted for one of the candidate debates during that campaign, at Clinton's behest, and he used it to great effect, while George Bush demonstrated only that he was out of touch with popular concerns.

The television talk show is also available as a non-party conduit for political mobilization. The dramatic case in point was Ross Perot's use of the Larry King talk show on CNN to declare his candidacy. Perot proceeded to use another technological novelty to convey the impression that his crusade was a public campaign—he collected funds through an 800 number in a method previously used by Jerry Brown. But such a method is most compelling when the candidate is a billionaire to start with. Had Perot not been a man of enormous wealth, neither his views nor his intentions would have been of interest to Larry King in the first place, nor would his use of the 800 number have carried him to the degree of success he eventually attained, with almost one-fifth of the votes in the general election. Perot's purchase of tremendous blocks of network time for long lectures conveying his views is obviously incapable of emulation by anyone but the super-wealthy.

C-SPAN, CNN, Court TV For the past ten years, dedicated followers of American politics have been able to feed their appetites by watching two public affairs channels available twenty-four hours a day on cable. C-SPAN, financed by the commercial cable companies, presents the daily deliberations of the two houses of Congress, along with campaign events, academic conferences, book interviews, and so on. The real-time coverage of campaigns has the virtue

of eliminating the interpretive middleman, though following this coverage requires a considerable investment of time.

CNN carries considerable coverage of breaking stories, supplemented by occasional talk, daily debates, Washington gossip. But CNN is not nearly so novel as its devotees have claimed. For one thing, its forms of news coverage are largely conventional. (The main exceptions: international reports; extensive coverage of press conferences and congressional hearings; occasional investigative reports; protracted coverage of breaking stories—wars, crimes, natural disasters.) Routine CNN broadcasts have the standard forms to which the older networks have accustomed us—the parachuting reporter, the shallow reportorial stand-up, the posture of balance, the truncated debate, the presentation of the world in snippets, the clutter of sound bites. Its political debates compress opinion into the range running from the deeply conservative to the mildly liberal. (The contrast with the BBC World Service, with its extended analytical reports, is stark.) During the Gulf War, thanks to the courage of Peter Arnett, CNN did offer useful though obviously restricted coverage of Baghdad, but otherwise was no more independent of military surveillance and a Washington-centered worldview than the rest of American television. The C-SPAN and CNN audiences are normally small, less than a million a day, though these numbers spike upward in the case of extraordinary events.

For the last several years, Court TV has offered continuing coverage of trials, most famously—or notoriously—the O. J. Simpson saga. What is accentuated by Court TV, and related crime obsessions, is the American tendency to treat reality as a soap opera. It can be argued that it is only *as* soap opera that Americans are willing to consider issues like sexual harassment (the Clarence Thomas/Anita Hill hearings) and marital violence (the Simpson case). Insofar as this is so, it is a terrible judgment on the state of democratic discourse.

Agenda-Setting through Poll Feedback Since 1992, some news organizations have attempted to intervene directly in the agenda-setting process during campaigns. In 1994, the *San Francisco Chronicle,* KQED public radio, and KRON commercial television cooperated in what they called a "Voice of the People" project. Citizens were polled for their sense of the important questions that the candidates should address in the party primaries. The questions were put to the principal gubernatorial candidates. The answers appeared in the newspaper and over the radio. But the answers were brief and frequently evasive. Moreover, many of the issues designated as "important" by the public—for example, crime and immigration—were the products of a positive feedback loop, in which the public embraces those issues defined by the media to be the burning questions of the moment. (The Republicans developed the "Contract With America" in the same manner.) This process recognizes that the candidates frequently have a vested interest in evading important questions, but instead of requiring journalists to take independent positions on the important issues, turns the job over to public opinion polls. This mechanism is therefore not free of demagogy.

Let me add a word about the proposed deliberative opinion poll. This idea has been promoted by the political scientist James Fishkin, and was on the brink of adoption by American public television during the 1992 campaign. (Subsequently it has been used in England.) The idea is that randomly selected persons are brought together for debate over a period of several days. Experts are called in to bid for the allegiance of the group. The entire process is publicly televised, giving the designated citizens a chance to affect each others' views, in the spirit of full-blooded democratic discourse, and giving the rest of the electorate a chance to observe.

Public Sphericules: The Internet and Other Linkages Not a week passes without popular articles claiming that computer-telephone linkages—fax, computer electronic mail, the Internet, and so on—make possible such a rapid torrent of information that they create vital community, expedite the organization of social protest, popular lobbying, and so on. The claim is that by bringing quasipublic links into the private space of the home and the office, the ensemble of these relations—what the writer Howard Rheingold has called "virtual community"—enables people to move their concerns into public life with an unprecedented vigor and intensity.

It is true that there are now thousands of worldwide linkages among citizen groups organized by political affinity. There are linkups for groups like Amnesty International, PeaceNet, and the Rainforest Action Network. (These are not all on the left by any means: a Rush Limbaugh fan places a summary of the daily Limbaugh conversation on the Internet, and racist groups recruit members there as well.) There are global contacts of a more informal sort, including news from Bosnia and other republics of the former Yugoslavia, electronic exchanges among readers of magazine articles (one can converse with the author) and listeners to radio talk (one can converse with other listeners). There are the faxes and electronic mail networks that linked dissident Chinese students with their opposite numbers in the United States during the democracy movement of 1989. There are the huge data-bases that enable journalists and private citizens to conduct rapid research.

Indeed, electronic linkages have lubricated the operations of many grass-roots groups. By bridging the physical gulf between nations, they contribute to the growth of cosmopolitanism—the understanding that one lives in a globally interconnected world. To some degree, the new communication forms expedite the development of what Charles Nathanson has called, perhaps too optimistically, an international civil society. They heighten a global ecological awareness just as, put to different uses, they expedite global flows of capital, finance, resources, and merchandise. The same technologies that have given capital unparalleled mobility also further movements that seek to limit the prerogatives of capital. But there is one problem the new means of communication do not address and may even worsen: the existence of a two-tier society. To those who are information-rich shall more information be given. At present, about one-quarter of American homes have personal computers. About one-fifth of these have modems that enable them to enter the "cyberspace" of computer networks. In other words, five percent of Americans can get onto the computer "superhighway." Without doubt, this five percent includes scholars who wish to collaborate across the oceans; journalists wishing to expedite their research; graduate students who wish to chat, or procrastinate, with like-minded specialists; and activists in search of affinity groups. But at the same time, the gulf deepens between the information-saturated and the information-deprived. Technology, in other words, aggravates a certain class division—the division between the political class and the rest.

This point bears on a theoretical problem. Does democracy require a public or publics? A public sphere or separate public sphericules? The diffusion of interactive technology surely enriches the possibilities for a plurality of publics—for the development of distinct groups organized around affinity and interest. What isn't clear is that the proliferation of publics contributes to the creation of *a* public—an active democratic encounter of citizens who reach across their differences to establish a common agenda of concern and to debate rival approaches. To put the question crudely: are we headed toward a public square or toward a series of segregated secessionist movements?

FABRICATED IDENTITIES

The significance—even the political impact—of the contemporary media extends far beyond

their treatment of formal politics, for American society is saturated by television. The average American watches (or inhabits a room with) television more than four hours a day, most of it entertainment. Watching is second only to work as the primary activity, or inactivity, that Americans undertake during their waking hours. One sign of how thoroughly television has been assimilated, even among the more literate, is that it has become a sign of inverse snobbery to proclaim affection for a pet series. Whole generations of popular-cultural scholars now unashamedly rhapsodize on the stellar qualities of their favored habits. Television is so thoroughly accepted that, however difficult it may be to assess its effects, the effort must still be made.

Without doubt, television has served as an instrument for the nationalization of American culture. In the years of maximum network dominance, when Americans tended to be watching the same programs, television furthered tolerance while eroding ethnocentrism and other forms of parochialism. For good reason did Edward R. Murrow choose to inaugurate the first coast-to-coast broadcast, on November 18, 1951, with a split screen showing the Statue of Liberty and the Golden Gate Bridge simultaneously—for simultaneity is the enemy of cultural heterogeneity. It was no small blow against white supremacy, in the 1950s and 1960s, to bring into the living rooms of white America images of the brutal treatment of blacks—or, for that matter, in the 1980s, to convey to a white audience that professional-class blacks like Bill Cosby were effectively identical to their white counterparts. Distinctions that were formerly sacrosanct—urban/suburban, Northern/Southern, public/private, national/local, naughty/nice—have blurred. To use Joshua Meyrowitz's terms, themselves borrowed from Erving Goffman, the "frontstage" world of formal American life is more tolerant—there is a growing degree of gender and racial integration at many professional levels; gay figures pass across the evening news without scandal; African-American stars have their talk-show billings; suburban white teens thrill to African-American rappers. Meyrowitz has argued, in *No Sense of Place,* that television has brought to public view the "backstage" of social life, educating the public to see through appearances, cultivating a knowledgeable skepticism, contributing to the spread of egalitarian sentiments.

Whether one endorses this view or a darker one, it is clear that television has filled a space left vacant by the demise of traditional authority. Television purveys identities, especially for the young, in a fluid, unsettled society where neither work, religion, nor family is stable or compelling enough to do the traditional job. Cultural identity has become modeled accordingly on peers and celebrities. Growing numbers of families are recombinant, so that one (or one's sub-self) belongs to more than one family at a time. In this setting, where people are members of many clubs at once, people increasingly look to popular culture—especially to television—for a vocabulary they can use to identify themselves.

Indeed, to call television a medium of communication seems to miss a good deal of the point. It is somewhat like calling a family a system of communication. Family therapists do so, but their descriptive power is not Tolstoy's. Television is a medium of cultural power. Television may not compel, but it compels attention—this, after all, is its *raison d'être.* But to speak of television as if it were nothing but a sequence of images is to miss a crucial feature, namely how much of it there is and how easily it enters the house.

Television is more than an amusement bank, a national bulletin board, a repertory of images, an engine for ideas, a classification index, a faithful pet and a tranquilizer. It is all of these, but one of its principal impacts is as a school for manners, mores, and styles for repertories of speech and feeling, even for the gestures and experiences of self-presentation that we call per-

sonality. Again, this is not simply because television is powerful, but because other institutions are less so; and as work, family, and religion lose their capacity to teach us how we are expected to behave, television takes up much of the slack. Yet ideologically minded critics of the right (the *Wall Street Journal,* for example) or the left (Noam Chomsky, for example), obsessed with the power of ideas over benighted citizens, have perhaps distracted us from recognizing the deepest workings of television because their own rationalist bias impoverishes their social imagination—they cannot imagine that there might be any other reason for wrongheaded policies than the misinformation of influential publics.

Television creates a certain texture of experience. I am struck, in particular, by the growth of "knowingness" to which I referred at the beginning of this paper: a quality of self-conscious savvy that often goes by the name "sophistication." But knowingness is not simply access to knowledge; knowingness is a state of mind in which any particular knowledge is less important than the feeling that one knows and the pleasure taken in the display of this feeling. It is the conviction that it is possible to be "in the know"; it is the demonstration that one hasn't been left behind, that one is hip, with it, cool; it is a mastery of techniques by which to reveal that one has left the sideshow and made it into the big tent.

The content of television is not simply one story after another. As Raymond Williams pointed out, one remarkable thing about television is the sheer profusion of stories it delivers. No previous generation of human beings has been exposed to the multitude of narratives we have come to take for granted in everyday life. The impact of each one may be negligible, but not the impact of the totality.

Because the stories of television exist in sequence, their significance bleeds from one story into another. Television, Williams wrote, has "flow." One thing leads to another. Most people watch swathes of television—they watch *television,* not discrete narrative units. But television not only flows, its flow is both rapid and interrupted. A story begins with credits. A few minutes of story take place. The story is interrupted for commercials—probably more than one per commercial break. There may be previews of news bulletins, promotions, previews of other shows. The story resumes. There are more commercials, more announcements. The story resumes. And so on. At the hourly or half-hourly station break, there may be scenes from the following week's episode, scenes from shows later that night, announcements of coming events. Each segment, moreover, comes attended by a distinct bundle of sounds. Since the segments and their sounds are juxtaposed, not simultaneous, what results may be experienced as an extended "horizontal" cacophony. As the remote-control-equipped viewer zaps or grazes through dozens of cable channels—to the delight of postmodernist theorists celebrating the juxtaposition as a freedom—cacophony is in the nature of the pastiche. In the wonderful world of television, anything is compatible with anything else. But even short of remote-control zapping, the paradox is that each particular segment comes immersed in a context that, while multiform, is also reliable. The one continuity is discontinuity.

Now, obviously, rapidity and interruption are not brand-new features of Western civilization. Television is a caricature of what, before television, was already a way of life. The ideals and sins it depicts are those of America's formulaic modernity. The picture may be sepia but the frame glitters. Thanks to slick visuals ("high production values") and crisp movement, glibness rules. Glibness, in fact, is the tribute formula pays to sophistication. The slickness of television, and of popular culture more generally, carries a sense of the tumult and velocity of a commercial version of urban life, the cornucopia of desire, the lure of consumable things and "lifestyles." Commercials don't simply announce the wonders of goods and the lives they

promise, they also bring energy and novelty—news of what passes for fun, freedom, and security these days. They invite one to think of oneself as a consumer—or, if one is poor or estranged, an enrage—but not as a citizen.

Moreover, for the most part, the style of speech that cuts across commercial (and most public) television is predictable. Its common currency consists of slogans and mockery. Thanks to the wonders of editing, no one on television is ever at a loss for words. Not even the bereaved parent asked "How do you feel?" about the death of a child is seen to hesitate. Speech is stripped down, designed to *move.* (Thus "Coke is it!" or Nike's equally meaningless invitation to associate its shoes, which *you* can buy, with achievements of the athlete's body: "Just do it.") The one-liner, developed by advertising, is television's stock element. Situation comedies and morning shows are obsessed with this form of speech: the jokey comeback. The put-down is the universal linkage among television's cast of live and recorded characters. A free-floating hostility mirrors, and also inspires, the equivalent conversational style among the young. And it serves as a template for political advertising. None of these styles contribute to the reflectiveness or the passions of political life. Instead, they contribute to a corrosive cynicism.

As Mark Crispin Miller has memorably observed, the knowing attitude is so widespread and automatic, it deserves to be called "the hipness unto death." Relentless if superficial self-disclosure is one of the conventions of television today. The audience is simultaneously alerted to the contrivance, transported behind the scenes, and pleased by both—and by the possibility of enjoying both. In one commercial of the late 1980s, a man in a white coat looks you in the eye and says, "I'm not an doctor, but I play one on TV." The audience is expected to recognize him as a soap opera actor. (He goes on to say that other people also think they can "play doctor" and as a result may take the wrong medicine. He has come to sell the right one.)

The equivalent process operates in our thinking (and feeling) about politics. As I mentioned above, coverage is dominated by inside analysis of the stratagems of campaigns and governance. The audience is flattered that it is superior to the corruption, dishonesty, and hypocrisy of public servants. The viewer has been brought into the know. He or she is treated as an "inside-dopester," savvy to spin-doctors, speech writers, electorate-pleasing "positioning," and all manner of practical calculations. In one sense, what is going on is democratic unmasking: let the politicians remember that they are hired hands! But the cynicism that has become so widespread in politics is more likely to generate withdrawal than political engagement.

I am suggesting that the glibness, relentless pace, sloganeering and shrinking attention spans of private life filter into television, via the selective antennae of the television-industrial complexes of Hollywood and New York, only to be reinforced there. The free-floating nastiness of sitcom existence may well be cultivating an equivalent show of popular sentiment, so that the endless put-downs of popular comedy penetrate into the rest of everyday life in the form of bumper stickers and T-shirt slogans, which then recycle into the popular domain. All in all, the sensibilities that television cultivates are inimical to people's engagement in the activities of a political life.

A CORNUCOPIAN CULTURE?

In summary, then: television has nationalized American culture and made it both knowing and thin. Yet this conclusion seems to fly in the face of predictions that television's homogenizing days are waning. Basic cable service now enters 62 percent of American homes, bringing an average of thirty-two channels. The profusion of new cable networks and independent stations has eroded the three-network share of the total audience from its high of 91 percent in 1975 to some 60 percent today. Surely the new age looming before us is an age of wondrous variety—or so promoters of new channels have been assuring us since the early 1980s.

On the surfaces of culture, distinctions do multiply. But the point I argued above with respect to the coverage of political activity also holds for the culture as a whole. Over the course of the decades when a three-network oligopoly dominated television, certain uniformities penetrated deeply into contemporary culture—so much so that they are unlikely to be flooded out by the possibly hundreds more channels soon to pour into the cabled home. Corporate pursuit of new niches ends up exaggerating tendencies already present in the previous system. Postoligopoly "niche" novelties like popular music, home shopping, evangelical Christianity, African-American music, and Spanish language soap operas have in common that they thrive on undiminished enthusiasm for slick entertainment. Advances in interactive technology will probably not divert from the main tendencies; they will be used primarily to render more efficient services that people already use—whether banking, video games, gambling, or quiz shows. Among the many things Americans can feel knowing about will be the sheer array of channels available and the routine surrealism, the normal strangeness, of America's culture of artless juxtapositions—the standard national mall/strip sequence of Taco Bell, Kentucky Fried Chicken, Pizza Hut, Fish 'n' Chips, Burger King. Pride in the national cornucopia will become a cornerstone of orthodox American identity in the next century. White bread has already ceased to be the symbol of national unity; it has been supplanted by the new standard supermarket shelf with seventy-two different loaves, each bland in its different way.

The uniformities in present-day American style are not simply the creatures of television or of corporate culture more generally. They build on cultural uniformities observed in

1831–32 by Alexis de Tocqueville, who pointed out, long before Sylvester Stallone, Arnold Schwarzenegger, Roseanne Arnold, or MTV, that America's cultural products "substitute the representation of motion and sensation for that of sentiment and thought. . . . Style will frequently be fantastic, incorrect, overburdened, and loose, almost always vehement and bold."

That television is popular does not make it less demagogic, but rather more so. The odds are that the rule of the slick, the glib, and the cute will prevail. Most of what is circulated through the new cornucopia is old television entertainment recycled—television episodes from earlier years, and old movies. The once-over-lightly glibness of American culture prevails not only on television but in the movies and magazines, among sports announcers and talk show hosts, in politics and psychotherapy alike. It is difficult to resist the conclusions that America's culture of distraction and convenience, of the quick fix and fast relief, of mass-manufactured labels of individuality, has acquired in television a useful technology to reduce the spectrum of life to a pale center glittering with multicolored sequins.

DISCUSSION QUESTIONS

1. What does Gitlin mean when he distinguishes "public sphericules" from a genuine democratic public? Do you agree or disagree with his distinction?
2. Talk radio and talk television obviously afford individuals opportunities to be heard and to debate with others. Why does Gitlin think that this is not a positive development in facilitating public discourse?

From Citizens' Army to Social Laboratory

Charles Moskos

The composition of the military has changed in recent decades, in part because of the end of conscription, which Charles Moskos sees as calling into question the very notion of a citizens' army. At the same time, because of the end of the Cold War, a rethinking about the proper role of the military is underway. In this context of a changing institution, Moskos examines the military as the social laboratory it has become, first looking at the ways that racial divisions have been handled since the integration of the military after World War II. This leads to an analysis of the changing place of women in the military. Finally, Moskos looks at the issue of homosexuals in the military prior to when the controversial Clinton "don't ask, don't tell" policy (which Moskos helped formulate) went into effect.

These are uncertain times for the armed forces of the United States. How could they not be? With the Cold War over, the very foundations of our thinking about national security have undergone profound changes. Short of a terrible accident, the likelihood of a nuclear war between major powers is slim. Indeed, wars among any major powers appear unlikely, though terrorism and internal wars triggered by ethnic and religious animosities will be with us for some time, if not forever. More to the point, nonmilitary threats—economic competitiveness, environmental pollution, and crime—have now moved to the fore of our national-security preoccupations.

Of course, no serious observer sees the imminent end of warfare. Clausewitz's dictum about war being the extension of politics by other means remains in the back of any thinking person's mind. Nevertheless, we are witnessing the dawn of an era in which war between major powers is rejected as the principal, much less inevitable, means of resolving conflict. At the same time, the citizens of the United States, like those of other advanced industrial nations, are increasingly reluctant to become engaged in uncertain, protracted wars in parts of the world where no vital interests appear to be at stake. In the absence of traditional threats, political support for military spending has slowly given way to expectations of a "peace dividend" for domestic social expenditures—a phenomenon that is as pronounced in Moscow as it is in Washington.

In this most unprecedented of historical epochs, we are also seeing important changes in the relations between the military and American society, changes that have been under way for at least two decades but that are now being accelerated by the end of the Cold War. Among these, perhaps the most consequential is the demise of military service as a widely shared coming-of-age experience for American males. Another change, more diffuse in shape and possible consequences, is a redefinition of the military's role in society. Once thought of as the institution through which citizens—at least male citizens—discharged their basic civic obligation, the military is now coming to be seen as a large and potent laboratory for social experimentation. Such changes and others are part of a larger movement, a trend toward what I call the postmodern military.

Postmodernism is not one of those words that tend to win friends or influence people, at least outside the academy. Indeed, its overuse by the tenured classes makes it seem, variously, pretentious, empty, or imprecise. That said, the concept has its uses. From its humble origins as the name of an architectural style blending whimsy, pastiche, and playful historical allusion, it has been generalized into an all-embracing theory of society. Simply put, this theory posits a world in which the old verities are thrown into question, social institutions become weak or permeable, and uncertainty everywhere reigns.

In matters military as well as cultural, the adjective postmodern implies a modern precursor. In America, as in most of the Western world, the military acquired its distinctively modern form with the rise of the nation-state in the late 18th and early 19th centuries, reaching a kind of zenith during the two world wars of this century. The modern military was distinguished by two conditions. The first was sharp, clear distinctions between military and civilian structures. The second was universal male conscription. Both conditions allowed military leaders to stress the more traditional martial virtues, the virtues of combat. Some fraying of the modern military occurred during the last decades of the Cold War with the rise of a military establishment driven as much by technical and information imperatives as by those of the trenches. Still, the modern military remained recognizable, in form and mission, right up to collapse of the Soviet Union.

Since then—and particularly since the end of the Persian Gulf War in March 1991—American armed forces have been deployed in more than 20 different operations, few of which had traditional military objectives. The list includes two operations related to the Gulf War: the multinational Operation Provide Comfort in Kurdistan and Operation Southern Watch in southern Iraq. The American military has taken part in Operation Sea Angel for flood relief in Bangladesh, in the rescue of civilians following the volcano eruptions of Mount Pinatubo in the Philippines and of Mount Etna in Italy, in drug interdiction along U.S. borders as well as in Latin America, in a domestic mission to restore order after the Los Angeles riot, and in disaster relief following hurricanes in Florida and Hawaii. The United States has also joined other nations in rescuing foreign nationals in Zaire and it is now spearheading relief efforts in Somalia. To the success of most of these operations, administrative and logistical skills, not to mention health-care and social-work skills, were far more important than tactical insight, marksmanship, or courage under fire.

To be sure, Western militaries have performed nonmilitary roles in times past, but what is different about these post–Cold War missions is their frequency and multinational character. Although it may be hard to imagine a U.S. soldier becoming misty-eyed about duty served under the aegis of the United Nations or the Conference on Security and Cooperation in Europe, the move toward multinational forces will gain momentum. The next step may well be the formation of a genuine international army with its own recruitment and promotion systems, as outlined in the 1991 "Agenda for Peace" written by United Nations Secretary General Boutros Boutros-Ghali.

In the postmodern setting, the legitimacy of conscription has progressively weakened. The draft has either been abolished—as it was in the United States in 1973 and 10 years earlier in the United Kingdom—or severely cut back, as in various European countries during the last 15 years. The political forces pushing for an end to conscription, though unlikely bedfellows, constitute a formidable bloc. They include traditional peace organizations, assorted religious groups, political radicals who dislike the military establishment, libertarian conservatives, policy specialists who seek to transfer military spending to social programs, young people imbued with individualism and materialism, and even some military leaders.

In America specifically, the abandonment of conscription jeopardizes the nation's dual-military tradition, one-half of which—and truly its heart—is the citizen soldiery. This institution antedates the Revolutionary War. The first colonists came to the shores of the New World anticipating conflict, and they prepared for it. Each colony formed its own militia on the principle that fundamental liberties entailed individual responsibilities. The militia, it must be stressed, was not a voluntary force. Every able-bodied man was obliged to possess arms and to train periodically. And every such man was subject to call-up when military needs dictated.

The military requirements of the Revolutionary War led to the creation of America's first professional army. This force remained small because of Americans' deep distrust of a standing army, but it marked the beginning of America's dual-military tradition. Henceforth, a citizen soldiery of varying sizes was balanced by a permanent and professional force. Large forces consisting of short-term volunteers, draftees, or draft-induced volunteers came into being during the Civil War and World War I. But it was World War II that shaped our most recent understanding of military service.

In 1939, 340,000 men were serving in the U.S. military. By June 1941—six months before Pearl Harbor—American mobilization was well under way. America's first peacetime draft raised U.S. military strength to 1.8 million men. Shortly after it entered the war, the United States raised the largest military force in the nation's history. At war's end, more than 12 million people were in uniform.

By 1946, the number of servicemen had shrunk to three million. The draft was suspended in 1947, and the number of active-duty military personnel fell to 1.5 million. The draft was resumed in 1948, as the Cold War heated up, and though the Korean War never resulted in total mobilization, there were some 3.7 million Americans in uniform in 1952. During the ensuing decade, America's military posture was based on "nuclear deterrence" and large troop deployments abroad, notably in Europe and Korea. Between 1955 and 1965, the number of people in uniform hovered around 2.5 million, more than during any other peacetime period in American history.

A clear conception of the place of military service in American society survived from early in World War II right up to the beginning of the Vietnam War. According to this view, service in the military, and particularly the army, was almost a rite of passage for most American males. Eight out of 10 age-eligible men served during World War II, the highest ratio in U.S. history. From the Korean War through the early 1960s, about half of all men coming of age served in the armed forces. But the proportion began to fall—to roughly four out of 10—during the Vietnam War, as the children of privilege found ways to avoid service in an unpopular and ill-defined military quagmire. Since the suspension of the draft in 1973, only about one in five eligible males has been entering the military. And when the post–Cold War "drawdown" to the projected base force of 1.6 million is reached in 1995 (though it will likely be smaller), the proportion of young men serving will be down to one in 10, if that.

The changing social composition of the military—evident first in the Vietnam War—became even more obvious during the first decade of the all-volunteer force, when the military began to draw disproportionately from among racial minorities, particularly blacks and Hispanics, and from lower socioeconomic groups. By 1979, 40 percent of army recruits were members of minorities, and half of the white entrants were high-school dropouts. This shift in social makeup corresponded with a tendency on the part of Defense Department policymakers to redefine military service as an attractive career option rather than the fulfillment of a citizen's obligation.

Perhaps the best example of the loosening hold of the military experience in the United States is seen in the changing background of America's political leaders. For at least the first three decades after World War II, military service (or at least a very good reason for having missed it) was practically a requirement for elective office. The unpopularity of the Vietnam War and the termination of the draft both chipped away at this attitude. In 1982 the proportion of veterans fell below half in Congress for the first time since before Pearl Harbor. And as the Vietnam War generation replaced the World War II cohort, it brought with it a highly ambivalent view of military service. Not surprisingly, this view reflected the electorate's changed attitude toward the importance of military experience to service in elective office. In

1988, the nomination of Senator Dan Quayle as a candidate for vice president created a stir because of his avoidance of active duty in the Vietnam War. In 1992, Governor Bill Clinton, who not only avoided all forms of duty but protested against the war, was elected to the nation's highest office.

The changed composition of the military and new attitudes toward military service raise the inevitable question: What has been lost? The answer is simple. Universal military service was the one way in which a significant number of Americans discharged a civic obligation to their nation. If this fact is obvious, its significance has been obscured by a political culture that ignores the importance of individual obligations while virtually enshrining individual rights—possibly to the detriment of our civic health. Universal military service did something else: It brought together millions of Americans who otherwise would have lived their lives in relative social and geographic isolation. No other institution has accomplished such an intermingling of diverse classes, races, and ethnic groups.

The racial dimension of this social intermingling—the integration of the armed forces and the impressive record of African-Americans in the services—is often cited as the great success story of the American military. Unfortunately, many people forget that this success came only at the end of what is in fact a rather ugly story, one that too faithfully reflects the larger national tragedy of racism. Until relatively recent years, African-Americans were a group resolutely excluded from equal participation in the armed forces. Even though they have taken part in all of America's wars, from colonial times to the present, they have usually done so under unfavorable and often humiliating circumstances, typically serving in all-black units with white commanders. And though they have served bravely, they often received less than glowing reviews from condescending, unsympathetic white officers. (By contrast, black units that served directly under the French in World War I received high praise from their commanders.)

The plight of blacks in uniform did not even begin to change until World War II. On the eve of that global struggle, there were only five black officers in the entire American military, and three of them were chaplains. Black soldiers during the war continued to serve in segregated units, performing mainly menial labor. Strife between black and white soldiers was common. Despite these conditions, blacks proved themselves when given the chance— none more so than the all-black 99th Fighter Squadron, whose performance in combat over Italy won the highest plaudits of the previously skeptical commander of U.S. tactical air forces.

In December 1944, during the Battle of the Bulge, African-American soldiers were finally given the chance to prove that segregation was not only unjust but militarily inefficient. Desperately short of combat troops, Lt. General John C. H. Lee, General Eisenhower's deputy for logistics, asked for black volunteers to fill the thinned-out ranks of white combat units. The soldiers who stepped forward performed exceptionally well in battle, gaining the respect of the white soldiers they fought next to and the high regard of the white officers under whom they served. Notably, there was none of the hostility that usually existed between white officers and black soldiers in the all-black units and none of the fighting that often broke out between whites and blacks in segregated units.

The unqualified success of this small experiment in racial integration was cited after the war to support arguments for integrating the military. Those arguments prevailed in 1948, when President Harry S. Truman abolished segregation in the military. Little happened at first, but when the Korean War erupted manpower requirements in the field led to many instances of ad hoc integration. By 1955, two years after the end of the Korean War, the last remnants of military Jim Crow were gone.

Integration alone did not bring an end to the problem of race in the military. Between the wars in Korea and Vietnam, African-Americans made up about 11 percent of the enlisted ranks but less than three percent of the officer grades. Racial tensions mounted dangerously during the Vietnam War, the outcome of both real and perceived discrimination in the military and of spillover from the racial and political turmoil in society at large. Even after the war and the termination of the draft, there were frequent outbursts of hostility between blacks and whites in the all-volunteer force.

Thanks to decisions made by the military leadership in that "time of troubles," things have changed markedly for the better. Today, in terms of black achievement and a general level of interracial harmony, few civilian institutions approach the army. In 1992, blacks made up 30 percent of the enlisted force, over a third of the senior noncommissioned officers, 12 percent of the officer corps, and six percent of the generals. General Colin L. Powell became chairman of the Joint Chiefs of Staff in 1989, the first African-American to head the American military. The army is still no racial utopia. Beneath the cross-race bantering, an edge of tension often lurks. Still, the races do get along remarkably well. Under the grueling conditions of the Gulf War, for example, not one racial incident was brought to the attention of the military police. Certainly the racial climate is more positive than that found on most college campuses today.

What has made the military in so many ways the vanguard of racial progress? I suggest three factors. The first is a level playing field, dramatized most starkly by basic training. For many black youths from impoverished backgrounds, basic training is the first test at which they can outshine Americans coming from more advantaged backgrounds.

The second factor is the absolute commitment of the military leadership to nondiscrimination, regardless of race. One sign of this commitment is the use of an "equal-opportunity box" in officer evaluation reports. While such a box may not eradicate deep prejudices, it alters outward behavior, for any noted display of racism will prevent an officer's promotion. Just as effective have been guidelines for promotion boards—"goals" that are supposed to approximate the minority representation in the eligible pool. If this looks like a quota by another name, one should note that the number of blacks promoted from captain to major, a virtual prerequisite for a full military career, is usually below goal. (The most plausible explanation for this is that about half of all black officers are products of historically black colleges, where a disproportionate number of more recent graduates fail to acquire the writing or communication skills necessary for promotion to staff jobs.) By contrast, promotions through colonel and general ranks come far closer to meeting goals. Significantly, the military has avoided the adoption of two promotion lists, one for blacks and one for whites. While the army's system satisfies neither the pro- nor anti-quota viewpoints, it works.

Third, the armed forces developed an equal-opportunity educational program of unparalleled excellence. Courses with specially trained instructors were established throughout the training system during the time of racial troubles in the 1970s, and these courses stressed not who was at fault but what could be done. Mandatory race-relations courses sent a strong signal to black soldiers that the military was serious about equal opportunity.

The attractions of the military to African-Americans are worth pondering. To begin with, blacks find that there are enough other African-Americans in the military to provide a sense of social comfort and professional support. Just as important, though, they know that they are not in a "black-only" institution. They appreciate the fact that the military provides uplift in the form of discipline, direction, and fairly meted-out rewards—and does so without the stigma of a social uplift program. The justification of the

military remains—at least to date—national defense, not welfare or social engineering.

One cannot exaggerate the importance of this last point in evaluating the lessons of recent black success in the military. For the driving force behind formal and actual integration of the armed forces was *not* social improvement or racial benevolence but necessity (notably manpower shortages in World War II and the Korean War) and the belated recognition of the military superiority of an integrated force to a segregated one. Put another way, it was the imperative of military effectiveness that led to equal opportunity, not the imperative of equal opportunity that led to greater military effectiveness. Overlooking this fact, political leaders and scholars have come to think of the military as a social laboratory, in which charged debates over gender roles and homosexuality and national service can not only be addressed but possibly resolved. This lack of clarity about the military's primary function is indeed a cardinal characteristic of the postmodern military. It is also potentially harmful to the long-term security interests of the nation.

The issue of women in the military—and particularly in fighting roles—is important. Recent history sets the stage of the current controversy.

When World War II broke out, the only women in the armed services were nurses. By the end of World War II, some 350,000 women had served in the various female auxiliary corps of the armed forces, performing duties that ranged from shuttling aircraft across the Atlantic to breaking enemy secret codes. Following the war, a two-percent ceiling on the number of women in the military was set, and most women served in administrative, clerical, and health-care jobs. This situation remained basically unchanged until the advent of the all-volunteer force in 1973. Finding it difficult to recruit more than a few good men, the military allowed good women to fill the ranks. Today, women make up about 12 percent of the total armed forces.

Both before and after the draft was abolished, a number of important gender barriers within the military began to fall. Women entered the Reserve Officer Training Corps on civilian college campuses in 1972. Female cadets were accepted by the service academies in 1976. (Today, about one in seven academy entrants is a woman.) Congress abolished the separate women's auxiliary corps in 1978, and women were given virtually all assignments except direct combat roles. This meant that they were excluded from infantry, armored, and artillery units on land, from warships at sea, and from bombers and fighter planes in the air.

The combat exclusion rule, already opposed by feminist leaders and many women officers, came under renewed attack in the wake of the Gulf War. The performance of the some 35,000 women who served in that conflict received high praise from both the media and Pentagon officials. But surveys of soldiers who served in the Persian Gulf yield a murkier picture. Forty-five percent of those who were in mixed-gender units reported that "sexual activity had a negative impact" on unit morale. Over half rated women's performance as fair or poor, while only three percent gave such ratings to men. Nevertheless, almost as a direct result of the Gulf War, Congress lifted the ban on women in combat planes, even though service regulations effectively kept the ban in place.

The usual response to a thorny social impasse is a presidential commission, and, true to form, one was established late in 1991: the President's Commission on the Assignment of Women in the Military. The 15-member panel (on which I served) took up three areas of consideration. The first was primarily factual. What, for example, were women's physical capabilities, and what would be the cost of modifying equipment or quarters to accommodate a woman's size or need for privacy?

A trickier area concerned questions of how mixed-gender groups would perform in combat. Here definitive answers are harder to come by, because apart from the defense of the homeland, no military force has ever used women in combat roles. Just as difficult to determine were matters related to the last area of concern: culture and values.

In addition to hearing opposing arguments, the commission sponsored a poll to determine whether the American public was willing to accept women in combat roles for the sake of equal opportunity. The answer that the Roper Organization came up with was a qualified yes. Three findings deserve mention. First, the public was split pretty much down the middle on the question of whether the combat-exclusion rule should be lifted. A large majority favored giving women the option to volunteer for combat arms, as long as no woman was ever compelled to assume a combat role. Second, most people believed that women already served in combat roles. Third, most respondents were more concerned with family status than with gender limitations. Three-quarters opposed mothers serving in combat; 43 percent felt the same way about fathers doing so.

By contrast with the general public, army women are much more wary about women in combat roles. One 1992 survey found that only four percent of enlisted women and 11 percent of female officers said they would volunteer for combat. But like the larger population, most military women favored a voluntary option.

The same survey disclosed that almost all army women—by a margin of 15 to one—opposed the adoption of uniform physical standards for men and women. Ironically, it was in support of such standards that two opposed groups within the policy community were rapidly coming to a consensus. Feminists supported it because of its egalitarian purity. Conservatives liked it because they believed it would reduce the number of women in the military across the board. Focusing on a strength definition of capability, both groups scanted the social and psychological problems that would likely arise with men and women fighting together in life-or-death situations.

Feminists and female senior officers do come together on the question of the *categorical* exclusion of women from direct combat roles. They believe that such exclusion is a limit on full citizenship. More recently, opponents of the exclusion rule, notably Representative Patricia Schroeder (D.-Colo) of the House Armed Services Committee, have argued that if women were included in combat roles, sexual harassment would decline. But according to the 1992 survey of army women cited above, most respondents think the opposite is true—that sexual harassment would increase if women served in combat units. And in fact sexual harassment is far more common in the Coast Guard, the only service with no gender restrictions, than in any of the other services, at least as measured by reported incidents at the respective service academies.

Less dogmatic opponents of the exclusion rule favor trial programs, which on the surface sounds reasonable. Trial programs are not the same as combat, but they would tell us more than we now know. Yet even the most carefully prepared trials would not address the biggest question: Should every woman soldier be made to take on the same combat liability that every male soldier does?

If the need arises, any male soldier, whether clerk-typist or mechanic, may be assigned to combat. True equality should mean that women soldiers incur the same liability. To allow women, but not men, the option of entering or not entering combat is not a realistic policy. As well as causing resentment among men, it would be hard to defend in a court of law. To allow both sexes to choose whether or not to go into combat would be the end of an effective military. Honesty requires that anti-ban advocates state openly that they want to put all female soldiers at the same combat risk—or that they do not.

By a one-vote margin last November, the presidential commission arrived at a surprisingly conservative recommendation: While approving of women's service on most warships (except submarines and amphibious vessels), it advised keeping women out of combat planes and ground combat units. President Bill Clinton has said that he will take the recommendation under consideration, but debate will surely continue before the matter is settled.

The vexed issue of homosexuals in the armed forces draws the postmodern military into another heated social controversy. And some of the solutions proposed would present just as great a problem to the military's combat effectiveness as do those proposed in the gender arena.

Again, some historical background. Up to World War II, the military treated homosexuality as a criminal act, punishable by imprisonment. During the war, however, service leaders came to adopt a psychiatric explanation of homosexuality: Discovered gays were either "treated" in hospitals or given discharges "without honor." From the 1950s through the 1970s, gays—defined almost always as people who had engaged in homosexual activity—were discharged under less than honorable circumstances. In 1982, in an effort to bring about a more uniform policy, the Department of Defense issued new guidelines that for all practical purposes made stated sexual orientation, rather than behavior (unless it was overt), the defining quality of homosexuality. The policy stipulated that a service member who declared that he or she was gay would receive an honorable discharge if his or her record was otherwise unsullied. However, if a gay service member was caught in a compromising situation, he or she might receive a less than honorable discharge.

The exclusion of homosexuals from the military has come under intense criticism not only from gay-rights groups but from civil libertarians and champions of equal opportunity. The 1992 Democratic platform pledged to remove the gay ban. And a threshold was crossed when the 102nd Congress introduced House Resolution 271, which called for the Department of Defense to rescind the ban. Editorials in the national press and sympathetic television accounts of gays in the military have added pressure to abolish the restriction.

Public-opinion polls show that the number of Americans favoring the admission of gays into the armed forces has been creeping upward. By 1992, about two-thirds of those surveyed favored abolishing the ban. Support for repeal is strongest among women and whites, and weakest among males and minorities. Without question, the growing support for ending the ban reflects a generally more tolerant attitude among the general public, but it may also be a sign of how distant most of the citizenry has become from the realities of military service.

Certainly, some of the reasons for excluding gays do not stand up to scrutiny. The argument that homosexuals are susceptible to blackmail is illogical. (If there were no ban, a gay service member could not be manipulated by the threat of exposure.) No evidence exists that homosexuals, under present rules, have been greater security risks than anyone else. Furthermore, no one can prove that homosexuals are any less effective than heterosexuals as soldiers, sailors, airmen, or marines.

What is at issue today, however, is whether or not *declared* gays should be allowed to serve in the military. This is different from the question of tolerating the service of discreet homosexuals in uniform (though with some 1,000 gays being discharged each year, it is clear that not all are discreet). To condone discreet homosexuality in the services while opposing the official acceptance of declared homosexuals is to set oneself up for the charge of hypocrisy. And it probably does no good to say that a little hypocrisy may be the only thing that allows imperfect institutions to function in an imperfect world.

Whatever is done, policymakers should think twice before they invoke a misleading analogy between the dynamics of racial integration in the military and the proposed acceptance of overt homosexuality. Racial integration increased military efficiency; the acceptance of declared ho-

mosexuals will likely have the opposite effect, at least for a time. In a letter to General Powell last year, Representative Schroeder invoked the race analogy. His response was direct:

> Skin color is a benign, non-behavioral characteristic. Sexual orientation is perhaps the most profound of human behavioral characteristics. Comparison of the two is a convenient but invalid argument. I believe the privacy rights of all Americans in uniform have to be considered, especially since those rights are often infringed upon by conditions of military service.

At the very least, the lifting of the ban will create a controversy over the issue of privacy, which in turn could make recruitment (particularly among minorities) even more difficult than it is today. Just as most men and women dislike being stripped of all privacy before the opposite sex, so most heterosexual men and women dislike being exposed to homosexuals of their own sex. The solution of creating separate living quarters would be not only impractical but an invitation to derision, abuse, and deep division within the ranks.

There is also the problem of morale and group cohesion. Voicing the conservative position, David Hackworth, a highly decorated veteran who writes on military affairs for *Newsweek,* acknowledges that equal-rights arguments are eloquent and theoretically persuasive. The only problem, he insists, is that the military is like no other institution. "One doesn't need to be a field marshal to understand that sex between service members undermines those critical factors that produce discipline, military orders, spirit, and combat effectiveness."

Foes of the ban point to the acceptance of homosexuals in the armed forces of such countries as the Netherlands, Sweden, Denmark, and Israel. In the Netherlands, an alleged 10 percent of the military is gay (though nine out of 10, studies say, remain undeclared), and a four-day seminar stressing sensitivity toward minorities, including gays, is mandatory in all Dutch services. Harmony is said to reign throughout the tolerant ranks of the Dutch army.

Those who object to the validity of national comparisons charge that the Dutch and Scandinavian cultures are far more progressive and tolerant than is mainstream American culture. Furthermore, they say, neither the Dutch nor Scandinavian armies have been in the thick of combat in recent decades. These objections are partially invalidated by the example of Israel's military, which inducts declared homosexuals. Israel is a conservative society, and its troops are among the most combat-seasoned in the world. Yet while it is true that gays in Israel are expected to fulfill their military obligation, it is also true that they receive de facto special treatment. For example, gays are excluded from elite combat units, and most sleep at their own homes rather than in barracks.

It is likely that the United States will soon follow the example of these and other nations and rescind the gay ban, despite widespread resistance within the U.S. military. One can of course argue that the United States now has such a decisive strategic advantage over any potential enemy that it can well afford to advance the cause of equal opportunity at possible cost to military effectiveness. Still, such a risk must be acknowledged.

Because we live at a time when the combat mission of the armed forces appears to be of secondary importance, it is easy for citizens and their leaders to assume that the military can function like any other private or public organization. But we must face certain realities if we accept this assumption. We must decide, for one, whether we will be willing to restore compulsory national service if dropping the gay ban makes recruitment even more difficult than it now is. (Most nations without such a ban do have obligatory national service, the military being an option in many cases.) Unless such realities are faced, we can only hope that our postmodern military never has to face the uncivil reality of war.

DISCUSSION QUESTIONS

1. Moskos believes that the military has handled racism better than other American institutions. Why does he think this is the case?
2. Whether women should be allowed into combat situations is one of the most contested aspects of their role in military life. What are the pros and cons of allowing women into combat situations?

SOCIAL MOVEMENTS

In December of 1999, the members of the World Trade Organization met in Seattle. Much to their surprise, they were greeted by a massive protest. Tens of thousands of people gathered in the streets of that city to express their disapproval of the policies of the organization. Specifically, protesters were displeased with the WTO's stands on human rights and environmental and labor issues. Although the media tended to rivet attention on anarchists smashing the plateglass windows of Niketown and Starbucks, this was not on the whole an irrational or spontaneous collective action. Rather, the marches were the result of considerable coordination and planning on the part of a range of existing social movement organizations. Moreover, the protest could not have taken place if these organizations did not have at their disposal the kinds of resources—money, communication networks, leadership, willing participants, and so forth—that were required for such a mobilization to be possible.

As this example suggests, social movements are the products of discontent with some facet or facets of the status quo, and can be defined simply as a collective effort to remedy the problems at the source of that discontent. Social movements constitute one type of collective behavior. Unlike other types—such as panics, crazes, and mass delusions—social movements operate within the frameworks of formal organizations. These organizations, with some level of leadership, networks of communication, coherent tactics, and so forth, arise only when sufficient resources can be effectively and efficiently mobilized. When mobilization efforts succeed, social movements can be potential vehicles for social change.

But not all social movements are alike. They differ in two ways. First, they differ regarding the scope of change they want to see effected. Revolutionary social movements want to see a dramatic transformation of existing social arrangements. The Russian or Chinese revolutions are examples. On the other hand, reformist movements want to see changes occur, but essentially within the framework of an existing society. Thus, the American civil rights movement wanted to see the expansion of rights guaranteed to white Americans expanded to include blacks as well. Second, social movements differ insofar as they can be described as left-wing or radical on the one hand and right-wing or reactionary on the other hand. The former tends to use the future as their point of reference. Thus, gay and lesbian activists who want to extend the right to marry to same-sex couples want to legitimate a novel form of family unit. The changes they promote would make the world different from the way it has been in the past or is at present. On the other hand, the latter tends to use the past as a point of reference. Thus, a conservative movement such as Promise Keepers wants to return to a world where the divorce rate is low and men are viewed as the heads of households.

Sociologists are interested in a range of issues surrounding social movements. These include a concern with the factors generating sufficient levels of discontent to stimulate people to act. They include an interest in who does and who does not join a social movement. They include a desire to understand the nature of social movement leadership and the varieties of organizational forms. They include an effort to understand social movements in the larger context of the societies in which they arise. Finally, sociologists seek to advance our understanding of the ways social movements relate to other social movements, whether that be as potential allies or as potential adversaries. In a variety of ways, each of these concerns is reflected in the four essays contained in this section.

The Beijing Spring, 1989

Craig Calhoun

By chance, Craig Calhoun was in Beijing in 1989 during the height of the student pro-democracy movement that ended with the massacre in Tiananmen Square, and he had an opportunity to engage in an unplanned participant observation study of the movement. In this essay, Calhoun examines the context within which such a movement became possible, shaped by the desire of the Chinese political leadership to restructure the economy and to encourage foreign investment, while at the same time warding off political liberalization when it threatened the power of the ruling elite. Calhoun discusses the nature of the student organizing efforts, the character of the movement's leadership, the shifting objectives of participants, and the internal conflicts that beset the movement. The failure of the movement raises questions about the potential for genuine political reform in China.

The climax of China's spring 1989 student protest movement is well known, at least outside of China. Troops acting to clear Tiananmen Square of protesters and enforce martial law succeeded in their charge, firing automatic assault weapons on unarmed citizens and sometimes wildly into neighboring buildings. People were crushed under the tracks of armored personnel carriers as they moved in to smash the statue of the "Goddess of Democracy" that had come almost overnight to symbolize the movement. Some students tried nonviolent protest tactics, sitting in before the troops. They were shot. Eyewitness reports emphasized the frenzied activity of the soldiers, their excessive and sometimes almost aimless violence. But though some may have run amok, there is no doubt that the overall attack was consciously planned.

Some of the soldiers were killed, mainly burned as crowds torched their vehicles. A few were beaten. Though dead students cannot be mourned publicly, China's government has gone to great length to honor the soldiers as martyrs, and to publish graphic accounts of their deaths. Student leaders had urged nonviolence, but the crowds by this point were not composed primarily of students.

Though these stark outlines of the massacre are known, it is much harder to make sense of it. We can only make educated guesses as to what the government was doing. Even harder to ferret out is clear evidence for just who was acting as the government at that point, what combination of the various factions that had used the student movement as an occasion for their own power struggles. We know that Zhao Ziyang and many of his associates and fellow "liberalizers" were toppled, but we do not know and probably never will know exactly the course of events that brought this about. We know that the government had been almost incapacitated by its internal struggles in the preceding weeks. But we do not know to what extent the events of the night of June 3 and morning of June 4 represented the policy of factions that had already succeeded in gaining power, or to what extent they were themselves tactics in the power struggle. Certainly they eliminated the argument that the Chinese government should use moderation to avoid inflaming world opinion. After the massacre, world opinion was already forfeit.

Since June 4 attention has been focused, ironically, on the killers not the killed, on the Chinese government and not the student protesters. It is important, however, not to let geopolitical considerations or the practical concerns with who has emerged on the top rung of Chinese leadership obscure the movement itself. Even our horror at the massacre should not make us forget just how remarkable an event this protest was. For the Chinese people, it has value as an inspiration, not just a cautionary tale.

I want here to look at some of the conditions and tactics that made the protest movement possible. My comments are based mainly on six weeks of "participant observation." They are not a final evaluation or a comprehensive report. They are an attempt to draw out certain key themes from the vantage point of the student activists. They leave many gaps, but, I hope, add a few points not always made in recent Western discussions. In particular, I do not try here to go very much into the question of students' ideology or goals in the movement. The present essay is not a comprehensive narrative, or still less analysis, of the student movement as a whole.

A SUPPORTIVE STRUCTURE

The student protest of 1989 was in many ways a tactical triumph. It did not produce the outpouring of new ideas, the creation of newspapers and journals, or the level of reflective thought that had been part of the democracy wall movement of 1979–80. It did give rise to a number of innovations in struggle itself and to the largest popular mobilization independent of the government that the People's Republic has ever seen.

From the beginning, the "Beijing Spring" of 1989 bore testimony to the fact that even a relatively spontaneous movement depends upon organization. Neither feature necessarily contradicts the other. This is partly because spontaneity is not always a radically individual phenomenon, some of the current Western-influenced ideology of Chinese youth notwithstanding. Their spontaneous participation was nurtured in group discussions. They came forward organized by schools and within schools by classes. Small clusters of friends and classmates had discussed their complaints about the government and the state of Chinese culture for months; they had debated various ideas in the privacy of dormitory rooms and in semi-public gatherings at restaurants and campus hangouts. Indeed, one of the striking features of the protest movement from the very beginning was its ability to generate organization without requiring much bureaucratic apparatus or formal hierarchy.

At many levels, this ubiquity of organization was an achievement of Chinese Communism; every class had its monitor, for example, and they were as prepared to organize food for hunger strikers as circulation of course materials. Traditional Chinese culture also encouraged this sense of the primacy of the group. But at its base in 1989 was a more novel feature that helped to change the meaning of the whole process of solidarity. This was a strong ideology and actuality of friendship. Personalties among individuals, created voluntarily rather than by the system, were highly valued and emotionally charged. Students debated, for example, whether the friendship bond—something perhaps closer to the strongest senses of Australian mateship than to the usual American sense of the word—should take primacy over marriage. They stressed high ideals of loyalty. They shared everything. Students well aware that the black-market rate for foreign exchange was some 50 percent above the official rate nonetheless exchanged money among friends at face value—even though foreign exchange was an extremely prized commodity for those who hoped to go abroad since everything from tests to application fees had to be paid for in foreign exchange certificates. One student I knew, eventually a minor leader in the protest, housed a friend in his dormitory room, even providing money for his friend's meals out of his own meager income (a standard tiny stipend augmented by teaching English to students preparing for exams). The friend was a graduate student at another university, but came to think of himself as a "professional revolutionary."

The institution of friendship had not always overridden ascribed group membership—kinship, *danwei* (work unit), class—in China. Previous policies of the Communist regime had in many ways specifically undermined it, calling for a commitment to ideology and party above such personal ties, creating powerful ritual occasions for friends and relatives to betray and criticize each other. Friendship, and also kinship and other directly interpersonal relationships, seemed of central importance to students' lives. Yet they are poorly grasped by either the notions of individualism or the equation of society with the large collectivity and/or the state. Students identified strongly with various bits of individualistic ideology, from Western writings on capitalism and freedom to the simple idea of the primacy of romantic self-expression (personified in China by the poet Xu Zhimo). A vaguely Rousseauian (or Californian) idea of the ultimate value of expressing one's internal feelings was very widely shared. The government's common taunt of "bourgeois individualism" seemed to hit it rather accurately. But the strong feeling for friendship, practiced with a level of loyalty that put most Westerners to shame, was not individualistic. It was truly social. I wondered how many students thought about whether their own espousal of individualism might be at odds with this other fundamental value. In any case, the resurgence of friendship was one of the most basic manifestations of the emergence of society beyond the reach of the state, and thus of a capacity for genuine insurgency and an independent public sphere.

One could see other manifestations of the development of "civil society," perhaps most notably the growing numbers of small entrepreneurs. Many of these were merchants. Some were to be found filling every free market (and lining quite a few sidewalks), their capital limited to the merchandise they could fit on a single table or the back of a pedicab—pots and pans, books and magazines, belts, bicycle bells, or postcards. A few of these *getihu* (small entrepreneurs) came to be owners of substantial businesses, operating a chain of market stalls, for example, or entering the wholesale trade. Some other kinds of enterprises contributed more directly to the beginnings of a public sphere in Chinese cities.

Restaurants, for example, flourished at all price levels, bringing a range of regional cuisines into Beijing and providing at least partially free public spaces. Some of these were operated on university campuses, using leased buildings. Perhaps not surprisingly, they offered the best, though not the cheapest, food on campus. Others, often much smaller, were located nearby, providing at four or five tables the opportunity for free discussion over Xinjiang noodles or Szechuan soups. Of course still others catered to a more upscale clientele of businesspeople, party officials, and foreigners, and charged prices which meant that most students would never see the inside of them. Owners of all these sorts of businesses contributed money to the protest movement; many joined in the marches of late May.

The spread of a private market in publications was a powerful direct influence on the rise of dissenting, pluralist thought. Gradually, since the early 1980s, independent booksellers had carved a major niche for themselves in China's intellectual life. To be sure, their most popular publications were sex manuals and salacious or gory novels. On the same tables, however, one could sometimes find such foreign works as Freud's *New Introductory Lectures,* C. Wright Mills's *The Power Elite,* or Locke's *Second Treatise.* One could also find, in between the government's periodic efforts to purge the market of counterrevolutionary materials, the publications of Chinese thinkers grappling with questions of national identity, the problems of bureaucratization, and the possible virtues of stock markets and private ownership of industry. The most influential works were probably works of fiction, a genre (or set of genres, from satire to realism) well-suited to raising controversial questions in less than explicit forms, posing problems without having to advocate solutions that might be at variance with party policy, giving expression to individual feelings and thus encouraging the idea of their primacy.

Various journals made a similar impact, both introducing Western ideas (in translation and summary or commentary form) and providing for an independent Chinese discourse. Those that were too independent were often short-lived, flowering mainly during such periods of democratic activity and apparent government openness as the 1979–80 democracy movement. They were especially likely to be suppressed, or to fail of their own internal problems, if they were published without institutional sponsorship and/or aimed at a relatively broad readership. Academic periodicals, on the other hand, were more stable. Though their openness to free expression varied with the political climate, they continued to publish discussions of new and often controversial ideas fairly continuously through the 1980s. Journals of philosophy called tenets of official Marxism into question, encouraging a flowering of interest in Western Marxists and critical theory. Sociological publications examined stratification in Chinese society. Perhaps the most influential were literary journals. These not only reinforced the influence of some fiction writers, they sponsored a discourse on Chinese culture. This was a discourse heavily influenced (in its more academic versions) by Western postmodernists, rhetoricians, and new wave literary scholars; Jacques Derrida, Wayne Booth, and Frederic Jameson all had Chinese fans, though based generally on a fairly fragmentary understanding of their French or English works and especially of their discursive contexts.

At the same time that it sought currency by international standards (or almost pathologically pursued Western trendiness), however, this discourse also sometimes found new inspiration in older (but for the most part still modern) Chinese writings, most especially those of Laing Qichao, Lu Xun and the protagonists of the May 4th movement. It addressed in original and important ways the problem of how Chinese culture—traditional and Communist—would fare in the twenty-first century. What were the cultural implications of importing Western technology? Was China's generally postulated economic and political backwardness due to fundamental cultural weaknesses? How would

Chinese culture have to be strengthened (echoing Kang Youwei and the self-strengtheners of 1895) to provide for modernization, perhaps including democracy? These questions were not always posed straightforwardly, but they were debated by readers.

Perhaps the most striking semipopular manifestation of this was the television series *River Elegy,* shown in the fall of 1988. This was produced by a group of well-educated young men, heavily influenced by this literary-cultural discourse. They took their occasion and a good bit of their footage from a Japanese-produced travelogue about the Yellow River. Adding their own commentary and a wide variety of archival footage, however, they transformed the genre of travelogue into a critical cultural analysis. The Yellow River is traditionally seen as the heart and source of Chinese life. They portrayed it as the focus of an inward-looking culture, characterized by mud and soil erosion, disastrous floods, and unfortunate human interventions. A dominant motif was the challenge posed when the Yellow River met the blue sea; striking aerial cinematography imprinted this visually into the viewers' minds. Chinese culture was compared to that of "primitive" Africa—a shocking statement for proud and racist Chinese. The heritage of four thousand years of civilization was shown as more a trap than a resource. Mao Zedong was pictured facing the Yellow River but silent; this man who always had so much to say was quiet before the problems it posed.

River Elegy was also technically sophisticated by Chinese standards. It worked mainly through montage, with extremely rapid cuts from scene to scene (influenced I suspect by Hong Kong film fashions and reminiscent of recent trends in American television advertisements and music videos). In the space of a minute, a viewer might see Mao, the river, the Egyptian pyramids, the Great Wall, and a rally of the People's Liberation Army. Intentionally, it purveyed more information than any viewer could take in at one showing, and especially more than he or she could assimilate within received categories. It left the viewer with a welter of unresolved impressions. The voiceover provided only a partial framework for understanding. The film's real message was left just below the explicit, and heavily dependent on the visuals.

The film attracted a remarkably large audience on Chinese television, and was shown a second time before the authorities had second thoughts about allowing it to be shown at all. It also sparked a wide discussion among viewers. This reveals, first of all, that a much larger public than university-trained intellectuals was prepared to engage in a critical discourse about Chinese culture and China's future (though surely many found the film's more unkind comparisons and evaluations shocking, even offensive). In addition, the episode reveals that the government was not united in its stance on either Chinese culture or the limits of permissible public expression. The film could only have been made with the backing of fairly powerful figures, and its repeated showings indicated their strong support. A genuine liberalization in public expression helped to pave the way for the protest movement of Spring 1989. On the other hand, *River Elegy's* third broadcast was stopped (as was a film planned by the same group on the May 4th movement).

River Elegy's popularity dramatized the centrality of the problem of culture for thoughtful Chinese in the late 1980s. Few doubted the desirability of economic "modernization," though what form it should take was debated. But how was economic change to relate to culture? What did it mean to be Chinese in a world of computers and FAX machines, tourists and joint ventures, the internationalization of commodity flows and culture? Maoist Communism had offered an alternative source of pride and a version of national identity (incorporating some aspects of tradition while rejecting others). What elements of Maoism or Confucianism could provide a vision for the future? Or had both de-

cisively failed the tests of modernity? Did that mean wholesale Westernization or were there still the resources for an authentic Chinese path? In short, all but the most technocratic or cautious and party-loyal Chinese intellectuals, and a good many others besides, felt that China's modernization was in need of a cultural vision. However real the economic gains might be, they were either in jeopardy or even pernicious if not accompanied by a sound vision of Chinese society and culture.

This was the point where most students and intellectuals thought they had a crucial role to play. Some were primarily trained to play technical roles in modernization, as engineers, doctors, or demographers. Even they might have worries about vision. For humanists and the more culturally oriented of social scientists these worries were much more acute. And they were coupled with a sense that the government lacked respect for them and failed to provide for their role in China's modernization. Not all of these students had a strongly political conception of what to do, of how far an insurrection could go, of what role the Communist party might play or whether multiparty elections were possible or good, or of what form decentralization of bureaucratic power should take. But the political ideas of nearly all the active leaders, as well as the sentiments of more "rank-and-file" participants in the protest, were deeply shaped by this sense of cultural crisis and impoverishment. It was at the heart of the students' talk of democracy, at least as centrally as any imported Western specifics about the mechanics of liberal democratic rule.

These ideas and this sense of crisis had been so widely disseminated before the protest movement actually got going in April that they could be taken for granted among the core of student participants. This was simultaneously a strength and a weakness. It helped to make the substantial early mobilization possible. It also impeded the development of both the ability to spread the movement's message beyond its original student base and internal discourse about goals, methods, and priorities. This cultural concern informed both the students' initial very moderate message—essentially "take us and our ideas seriously, give us a voice"—and their subsequent determination to persist, as government recalcitrance made their movement more radical.

AN OPPORTUNITY FOR PROTEST

The immediate occasion for protest was the death of Hu Yaobang. Though some Chinese students, especially in the United States, have since suggested that this was a deep, spontaneous, and heartfelt outpouring of sadness over a beloved leader, I think some skepticism is in order. Hu was indeed a relative liberal, but more important he was a symbol of the party's repression of political reform and his death a pretext for demanding more such reform. Hu, after all, had been no great advocate of free speech as head of the propaganda ministry, and he was ousted as party chief less for befriending students than for failing to contain their prodemocratic protests.

Hu's death, however, provided the students with a splendid opportunity and they made the most of it. It would be awkward if not impossible, they knew, for the government completely to forbid mourning the death of a sitting Politburo member who was also a past General Secretary of the Communist party. Activists decided to see how far they could stretch official tolerance. Their calls for demonstrations drew thousands of students carrying photographs of Hu and wearing signs of mourning. The government recognized the implicit protest but apparently decided to try to appease the students or demonstrate its tolerance by allowing them to carry on. Unappeased, the students added broader slogans to the signs of mourning and their numbers grew. Every Chinese observer read clearly the echoes of the public demonstrations that followed Zhou Enlai's death in 1976 and produced the notorious Tiananmen incident

(the repression of the protest that created popular martyrs and was a key moment in the fall of the Gang of Four and return of Deng Xiaoping). The potential potency of such protests was thus unquestioned.

Hu Yaobang also provided a powerful, multivocal symbol. He was not only a liberal, but a clear Westernizer who had made a stir while I was in China in 1984 by (apparently impulsively) suggesting that chopsticks should be abandoned for forks. He was also Deng Xiaoping's personally picked and publicly designated successor. Deng had made providing for an orderly succession one of the centerpieces of his reform campaign. The sacking of Hu thus suggested that China had not shaken its "feudal" tradition of rule as fully as Deng claimed. Hu was a sponsor as well as a predecessor of Zhao Ziyang, the current party chief. Hu died during a Politburo meeting, apparently suffering a heart attack. This allowed for discreet rumors that he had either been humiliated by his colleagues or shocked by some action they contemplated.

By late April, after nearly two weeks of protest in the guise of mourning, senior officials began to lose patience with the students. Crowds now numbered in the tens of thousands and the use of Hu's death as pretext was wearing thin. A number of students thought the government would probably wait until after the end of the official month of mourning to ban further marches. In fact, those cadres who had already had enough apparently gained the upper hand and secured Deng's approval for a crackdown on April 25. This resulted in the now-infamous *People's Daily* editorial of April 26 which warned students none too delicately to stop creating disorder; the editorial implied that the government was ready to use military force (though as soon as it was published a variety of senior leaders including Zhou Enlai's widow were said to begin lobbying for more restraint).

Far from calling their protests off, students drew new fervor from the government's condemnation, seeing it as provocation rather than warning. They were particularly incensed that their own patriotic inclinations had been called into doubt, that they were being labeled trouble-makers rather than good citizens exercising their constitutionally guaranteed rights of remonstration and free speech. Student leaders feared the worst, however, and several melodramatically made wills the night of April 26. The next morning, they were joined by the largest crowd yet, perhaps a quarter of a million people (though estimates vary widely and extend up to more than half a million). There are at most about 160,000 university students in Beijing, so any numbers beyond that suggest substantial participation from other groups—teachers, secondary school students, and the general public.

The march of April 27 was one of the most remarkable successes in China or elsewhere, and one of the most striking cases of bad government tactics I know of. As the column of marchers approached Tiananmen Square along several routes they met large contingents of military police. Anxiety grew amid the sense that the government meant to crush them. On Chang'an Boulevard, the immediate approach to the Square, protesters confronted blockades of policemen, apparently intending to halt the march. But the policemen were unarmed, and stood only a few rows deep against the massive crowd. They attempted briefly to hold their ground then gave way; a few scuffles followed. The crowd cheered as marchers pushed through. To compound its apparent madness, the government had arrayed several such police blockades a few hundred meters apart along the boulevard. The students pierced each one easily, and each time their confidence and enthusiasm grew. The government's intention may have been to provide a symbolic warning that the protesters were breaking the law. They ended up giving the students the feeling of having won a victory against the military!

As Chinese protesters have done at least since 1919, the students marched in rows with arms linked. But this time they added another

bit of organization. Students around the perimeter of each group also linked their arms, providing a neat definition to each marching unit—class, school, and so on—and simultaneously keeping out *agents provocateurs*. This was not a trivial issue, because disorder of any type would delegitimate the students' cause in the eyes of the public. The government was apt not only to call the protesters hooligans but to employ some real hooligans to lend credence to the charge. This seemed to have happened only days before in Xian where a protest was marred by a small rampage of attacks on property.

The April 27 march galvanized popular attention and brought the first phase of student protest to its climax. This was no longer a protest confined narrowly to university students, nor could it rest any more on the pretext of mourning Hu Yaobang. It had taken on an autonomous significance. And the attention it galvanized was not limited to Beijing or even to China. From this point on, the protest began to be echoed in a growing number of other Chinese cities. Within a week, the first of eventually enormous contingents of students from around the country began to come to Beijing to join the protest. And the April 27 march made front page and first item television news around the world. The students were well aware of this international interest and had organized specifically to turn it to their advantage. They carried signs in English, French, and other Western languages. "Vive la liberté" and "Give me liberty or give me death" established links to the year's two famous bicentennials (albeit loosely in the second case, since the reference was revolutionary and not constitutional). They also, and perhaps more important, gave foreign photographers shots that were more likely to hold the attention of folks back home than were signs in Chinese. At this point too, at least some student leaders began to become much more visible in the press, precisely because they made themselves accessible to the press. Thus Wu'erkaixi's dormitory room at Beijing Normal University became a regular stop for journalists. But at the same time a few leaders from smaller schools—including the very active University of Politics and Law—began to chafe a little at the appropriation of this aspect of the leadership role by leaders at Beijing Normal and Beijing Universities.

The next big event was a march on May 4, the anniversary of the 1919 student movement. Though the government again brought out the military police, this time it had them discreetly withdraw to the sides of the streets rather than challenge the students directly. Deprived of the drama of breaking through police lines, the occasion was curiously anticlimactic. The demonstration was as large as on April 27, and the crowd of bystanders larger, but there was no tension and there were no events, music, or even major speeches to hold people's attention once they made it to Tiananmen Square. For a week afterward, students watched the protests dwindle as they waited to see what response the government would make to their demands. Most returned briefly to classes. The protest was a constant topic of discussion on campuses, but no one seemed to know what the next move was.

LEADERSHIP

The next move was unclear for three main reasons. First, the protest had moved beyond the range of lessons available from experience. Although protesters had posed implicit challenges to the government before, none had ever acted against direct instructions—backed apparently by military force—and gotten away with it. Students talked frequently with teachers and others who remembered earlier movements and who had thought at length about possible courses of action; they gave advice, but this mobilization escaped both their expectations and experience. Second, it was not clear what the government was going to do. The possibilities the students saw ranged from harsh crackdown to taking the

students seriously and massively accelerating reform. Uncertainty about the government's actions stemmed from lack of knowledge of which factions in the government were in the ascendant, though most students did not yet know just how deeply divided the government was. It seems that some partisans of the reform faction may have talked with student leaders, or informed them of their views indirectly through senior intellectuals (and on the other side, Li Peng met with senior professors to try to get them to encourage calm and faith in the government on campuses). But though this may have affected actions at various points it does not seem to have been extensive enough to say that the movement was either substantially encouraged by any party faction or helped by access to much significant inside information. Third, the student leadership was itself both somewhat amorphous and unable to make and communicate decisions except by word of mouth and *dazibao* (large character posters).

Students had initially become leaders primarily by leading. That is, there was no prior stage of selection, a procedure by which individuals became officially sanctioned leaders. On a few occasions formal elections were held, but they were not the primary source of authority for leaders. Most were after-the-fact ratifications of leaders who had emerged in the course of practical activity. Some involved more or less fanciful positions—like the election of Beijing Normal University student Chai Ling as "Commander of Tiananmen Square." In the case of this election as of most others in China (whether as part of government officialdom or in a protest movement) the outcome was not in doubt when the voting took place; the vote-count ratified a decision that had already become more or less consensual. And being nominal "Commander" for a moment gave Chai Ling little opportunity to command, for the movement was not organized in a hierarchy of ranks.

Not only were leaders less official than Western media reports have frequently suggested, leadership was spread much more widely through the movement. Many different groups of students made innovations in protest simply by deciding that some particular slogan or line of action was a good idea and then putting it into practice. Others might copy or not. Important decisions were often taken by small groups; they did not all percolate up from the "masses." But the small groups were not always identical to or part of a centralized leadership. It is important to realize how rapidly the movement developed from bases on campuses of about ten thousand or fewer students to include hundreds of thousands of participants coming from various backgrounds with varying degrees of knowledge and commitment. The level of organization achieved was quite remarkable. Marches were orderly, not rag-tag affairs; in mid-May there was a notable increase in pageantry, with new banners and flags and matching T-shirts for a few groups. In the Square itself crowds were orderly, there was virtually no crime, health services were set up and when it became necessary, paths were made for ambulances. A system of passes was devised and enforced fairly effectively by student guards. But though linked, leadership and organization are not exactly the same. A lot of this organization came through the borrowing of templates from other settings (as with the role of class monitors) and from lateral interactions among groups. Only a portion was centrally initiated. As time went on, however, leadership became simultaneously more important and harder to organize and provide.

In late May, for example, leaders tried repeatedly to move slogans from an almost exclusive preoccupation with persons—"Down with Li Peng," "Deng Xiaoping step down"—to a renewed emphasis on democracy as such and other systemic changes. They failed. The earlier emphasis on systemic rather than personnel changes in government was all but lost as the movement broadened, anger grew, and confrontation intensified.[*] At the same time that such ideological leadership was relatively ineffective, organization remained fairly strong. There was a crisis over managing and accounting for donations from abroad, but considering the pressure students were under, the fact that they could not even open a bank account, and that the sums were huge by the standards of their daily lives, this was minor. Supplies that arrived were circulated effectively. Tents from Hong Kong were distributed and arranged in orderly ranks. Couriers maintained contacts between students in the Square and their home campuses. Loudspeakers were set up. Troop movements were monitored.

There were two great triumphs of inspirational leadership. The first was the decision of May 12 to begin a hunger strike; the second was that which resulted in the erection of the statue

---

[*]An aspect of this that struck me especially forcefully was the students' refusal to use Marxist and/or Maoist rhetoric in any of their slogans. Even students who did use some Marxist categories in their analyses during small group discussions, and who might acknowledge abstractly the rhetorical force of using the government's own language against it, never made any effort to develop this in their public pronouncements. Whether this was simply because Marxism had been made boring by mandatory political study classes taught from translated Soviet manuals, or because it had been deradicalized by its use as an offical ideology, or because it had been more deeply discredited by its role in Maoist rule I was never certain. But protesters did not accuse elites of class rule. Students who in the classroom were keen to discuss Marx's writings on alienation (and who regarded the government's dismissal of these "immature works" as merely an attempt to avoid the charge that alienation continued under socialism) did not use this language in movement gatherings. In this, the 1989 protesters differed substantially from those of 1979–80 who made considerable use of Marxist texts, including Marx's writings on the Paris Commune, as a basis for conceptualizing democracy. Perhaps the most important reason was simply the much readier availability of other languages of discourse after a decade of Western influence and internal reform.

of the "Goddess of Democracy" exactly two weeks later. Each involved an interaction between (a) a widespread sense that something needed to be done, (b) initiative from some particular individuals and/or small groups, and (c) a sort of ratification by the core leadership of the movement. In the case of the hunger strike, the initiating and ratifying groups were more closely linked, indeed heavily overlapping at the major universities—Beijing, Beijing Normal, People's, and Qinghua. With regard to the statue, however, the key role was played by students at the Central Academy of Fine Arts, people for the most part outside the "established" core of student leadership.

Both the hunger strike and the statue, however, were successful symbolic acts. They bolstered the enthusiasm and commitment of student activists when these were flagging, and they communicated about the movement to far-flung audiences. Each brought a new period of exhilaration to a movement that swung rapidly between emotional highs and lows.

The hunger strike was the more important, though the statue became an enduring symbol. Several tactical considerations guided the hunger strike, though it also followed some historical examples and was based in emotional expression. Most obviously, perhaps, those who planned the hunger strike were well aware of the impending visit of Soviet Premier Gorbachev. Not only would his visit inhibit the Chinese government from taking overt repressive action, it would bring an even larger flock of international reporters and focus more media attention on China. The protesters' message would be heard (and seen) more widely, and that itself would have an impact, perhaps, on the Chinese regime. But the students had to offer the reporters newsworthy events; the hunger strike provided both a focus of attention and numerous concrete events and photo opportunities as students collapsed and were carried unconscious to hospitals while others rallied to their support. And it was during the hunger strike that

the largest of all the protest marches was held. More than a million people converged on Tiananmen Square on May 17. The impact of sheer scale was multiplied by the diversity of banners proclaiming the different units in attendance or offering witty or piercing slogans. And the marchers wore a rainbow of colors, one of the most visible signs of the freedom people felt in the midst of this brief relaxation of government control being a delight in more expressive clothing.

The hunger strike also aroused enormous sympathy on the part of ordinary people who heard of it. This meant at least most of the residents of China's larger cities and probably a fair part of the rest of the country. Scenes from the hunger strike were broadcast on Chinese Central Television and printed in *People's Daily,* but it cannot simply be assumed that these sources reached the whole of their routine audiences throughout the country. Constant reporting was also beamed back via the BBC and Voice of America, both of which can be heard widely in China (although the government jammed them with at least middling efficacy for some of this time).

Ordinary people felt drawn to and protective of the hunger strikers; they were prepared to see the latter as suffering on their behalf. This was partly because they were moved by the spectacle of relatively privileged university students worrying not only about their personal careers but about China's future, putting their health, future prospects, and possibly lives at risk. It was also because they could identify readily with some of the students' complaints—notably about corruption. And while political democracy was apparently a less pressing concern outside intellectual ranks, other people were prepared to see the student protest as speaking also for their more economic anxieties and demands.

The hunger strike quickly turned into an occupation of Tiananmen Square. This ultimately became problematic, as student leaders found that they could not end the occupation in a way that saved face, satisfied the full range of participants, and still avoided an intolerable confrontation with the government. But at the start it was a fine tactical move. Aside from the strike's successful communication to the Chinese people and abroad, the occupation of Tiananmen Square gave the movement a focal point. This was important not just for those reporting on it from outside but for the protesters themselves. Previously there had been no "neutral" turf on which activists from all the different universities gathered to discuss their plans and ideas. Now the Square became not only a symbol of success and an object of defense, it became the scene of nightly meetings of the student leadership.

OCCUPYING THE SQUARE

On May 22, I sat in Tiananmen Square with a group of the occupying students. The sun was mercilessly hot and the pavement absorbed the heat and radiated it back at us. The Square had been occupied for ten days, and garbage disposal was a problem (though students worked hard to keep it under control). Banners that had been bright and fresh a week before were a little bedraggled. So were the students. On the other hand, the chronic water shortage was lessening. Pedicabs were wheeled around the Square with barrels on the back; protesters came and filled their own bottles, usually one- or two-liter plastic drink bottles of a sort that had only arrived in China during the last five years. Merchants were now donating food in more than ample supplies. I ate steamed rolls with my student friends and then shared their disappointment when a more tempting meal of sliced pork over rice arrived, just after we had taken the edge off our appetites. The pork dishes came in styrofoam containers, just as they might from any Chinese take-out restaurant in the United States, fifty at a time. Only three days before, many of these same students had ended a week-long hunger strike. One had made six round-trips to a hospi-

tal to be revived by intravenous drip and back to the Square to continue his fast.

Now he ate well, but talked of disarray and discouragement in the leadership. The previous day had seen crisis at the top, even while the "broad masses" of students were still savoring the support of Beijing's ordinary people and the government's inability to impose martial law. The three most prominent leaders, Wu'erkaixi, Wang Dan, and Chai Ling, had differences of their own (notably a clash of male egos between the first two) but had agreed that it was time to call for a withdrawal from Tiananmen Square. From the massive and festive May 4 demonstration, just a week after the April 27 triumph, to just before the massacre a month later, students occasionally suggested. "It's time to consolidate our gains; let's declare victory and return to classes." They didn't mean to give up, of course, only to step back from the most provocative tactics, and to put the ball in the government's court for a response to the democratic challenge.

At first this suggestion came mainly from older graduate students, somewhat less radical and more cautious in their overall approach. By the end of May, it had been voiced by key leaders of the student movement. Some thought a declaration of victory and organized withdrawal would bolster Communist party General Secretary Zhao Ziyang's chances to stay in power, and thus enhance the forces of liberal reform. Others worried that if the occupation were too prolonged, crowds would grow smaller and the movement would look gradually weaker. Still others simply wanted to avoid violent repression. By June 4 it looked like the last argument, at least, had had significant merits.

Nonetheless, in the May 21 midnight caucus of the leadership, the leaders sharing this view were outvoted by a substantial majority. Wu'erkaixi had retreated to collect his thoughts and recover his strength. Wang Dan sat for hours with his head in his hands, sometimes crying in frustration. The problem was not just that the occupying students were not following his leadership but that there was no coherent alternative. The decision had been made, it seemed, to stay in the Square. But there was no alternative organization to that which seemed to be losing its efficacy and no particular plan about what to do while the occupation was continued.

What would the American Students for a Democratic Society have done under similar circumstances, asked my friend, the main student leader of one of the smaller but prestigious Beijing universities? I wasn't sure, I said, In retrospect, however, it seems to me that the SDS quite likely would have done, and over the long run did do, pretty much the same thing. Though comparisons with the Western student movement of the 1960s were often misleading about the Chinese students' struggles in 1989, there was a striking similarity here. The SDS (and more generally the leadership of the sixties struggles) dissolved in factional fighting (even before one faction launched a takeover) and lost its ability to lead a movement that had grown rapidly both beyond the core that had been a part of the long discussions leading up to it, and beyond the movement's organizational capacity. So too in Beijing. There were clashes of egos and ideologies among the leaders. Protesters who came from outside of Beijing now rivalled and would soon pass the numbers of those from the capital's universities. Those who came later often felt a need to demonstrate their own commitment to the struggle by taking stronger positions or engaging in more extreme tactics than those who began the fight. At the same time, their understanding of the slogans and goals that guided the movement was often fuzzier and shallower.

At various points, some students tried to push the movement ahead by more radical measures. The most striking of these was the declaration of a handful of hunger strikers that they planned to burn themselves to death if the government did not meet key student demands. This threat was made repeatedly during the week after May 13. On at least one occasion the would-be martyrs got so far as dousing themselves with kerosene before they were prevented by other protesters from completing their threatened immolation.

This incident made me think of the comments Lu Xun (China's greatest modern writer) made on the death of Qiu Jin some eighty years before. Qiu Jin had been one of the first women to rise to importance among China's radical modernizers, and had studied in Japan at the same time as Lu Xun. There she had developed a reputation as a fiery orator and drew large and admiring crowds. Her fame continued to grow when she returned to China. She played a key role in building a school and joined with her lover and others in planning an insurrection. Eventually their plot was uncovered. She was warned by friends that the army was coming for her but chose to remain at her school, hoping to make a dramatic last stand with the arms which had been stockpiled there. She was captured and ultimately beheaded. Lu Xun wrote, however, that she had been "clapped" to death. In other words, the crowds that had urged on her speeches and applauded her protestations against the government had implicitly pushed her to ever more radical positions. She could neither pause to consolidate her gains nor escape when the troops came without humiliation and betrayal of her own sense of direction. The complicity of the crowd in her death went further. Their applause was not just the product of agreement with her complaints, but of a pleasure in the entertainment her protest provided. A crowd would also gawk at her execution.

So too in the "Beijing Spring" of 1989 and in varying degrees—so too always. A crowd of a quarter of a million people is impressive when observers and participants expected only a hundred thousand. But it quickly establishes a new norm. To maintain a sense of momentum, to remain newsworthy, activists must increase the numbers in the crowd. Or they must do something more dramatic than merely marching. Attention will always be focused on the apparent leaders and the core activists, but the crowd on the fringes shares implicitly in responsibility for the actions taken. Those who cheer encourage those who demonstrate. Those who merely watch still swell the crowd counts. Simply by attending, every one of us, Chinese or foreign, upped the ante for the protesting students.

So, almost invisibly, the stakes kept being raised throughout the month of May and the first two days of June. The government tried concessions. State Council spokesman Yuan Mu, for example, met with some students for a televised dialogue. It was not open enough and he was not senior enough (or forthcoming enough) to satisfy many people. It encouraged further action, however, not just by failing to satisfy but by seeming to prove that protest could bring results. The government tried condemnation and the imposition of martial law. Li Peng's speech declaring martial law was like gasoline on a fire; students who previously were unsure of how far to go or whether some moderation might bolster the cause of reform immediately took to the streets, insulted by his tone and angered by his denial of everything they called for. And of course the imposition of martial law failed, at least for two weeks, with troops stalled on the periphery of Beijing. The soldiers' inability or unwillingness to enforce martial law was widely felt as another triumph. But just as it prevented short term repression it raised the stakes of action yet again. However orderly they might be, the students and their allies among the citizens of Beijing were now engaged in what the government would clearly see as a sort of illegal occupation of the city.

The flow of students from outside of Beijing into Tiananmen Square contributed to a sort of radicalization in a different way. These students had started coming in large numbers and to stay for an extended period of time shortly after the hunger strike began. They established camps under the banners of their various schools. They

had not been involved in the early stages of protest, and so may have felt an extra need to prove their commitment to the cause, to match or top the actions taken by the Beijing students. They were also cut off from various potentially moderating influences. Only those most committed to the struggle had made the trip to Beijing. Where local students constantly mingled with less committed or less radical classmates, and thus were reminded that their views were particularly strong, those from outside Beijing had few such contacts. Local students also talked more often to family members and to teachers. Perhaps most important, the students from outside of Beijing were not well integrated into the leadership of the movement. They had no voice in the most prominent ranks of leaders, and there were fewer strands of communication spreading information, views, and instructions among them.

These students from outside Beijing played a central role in the decision not to withdraw from Tiananmen Square at the very end of May, a few days before the massacre. They had not been in the protest as long, and so were perhaps not as tired of it. More to the point, withdrawing from the Square meant returning to their own homes or campuses. This might expose them to retaliation from local officials (many of whom were less sympathetic to the protests than were leaders of some of the Beijing campuses, nearly all of which had at least large and powerful prore-form factions). It would also cut them off from the center of protest. Beijing students could stay intensively involved after a withdrawal; at best those from other cities could try to carry on with local protests but out of both the limelight and the main lines of communication.

Many of the non-Beijing students did leave during the first three days of June, but this may have meant that those who stayed were all the more determined. In any case, on the fateful night of June 3, as the army approached Tiananmen Square, the students from outside Beijing are reputed to have decided for the most part to stay put while large numbers of local students withdrew to the south.

Leaving Tiananmen Square was important not just to avoid a massacre. At the time, no one expected a massacre of the sort wrought June 3 and 4. Students expected tear gas and rubber bullets. Rather, the issue was how to reorient the movement towards long-term struggle rather than short-term protest. Even among those who shared this view, there were reasonable arguments for staying in Tiananmen Square—the need for a focal point, for example, and for continuing to show the citizens of Beijing that their support was necessary. The point is not to judge whether withdrawal would have been the right move or wrong. Rather, it is to see how hard it is for a movement like this to transform itself into the sort of organization that can carry out a long-term struggle, shifting as necessary from what Gramsci would call the war of position to the war of maneuver—or in this case back again.

One of the difficulties faced by the Chinese student protesters in 1989 was that they lacked the luxury of building a movement gradually, carrying on discussions, and building solidarities over a period of months or years. It is true that the movement had grown out of months of complaint about China's current situation, not sprung full blown into action after Hu Yaobang's death. It is true also that it is not an isolated event but the latest in a series of prodemocratic protests including those of 1979–80 and 1986–87—and stretching back also to the mourning of Zhou Enlai, the Chinese Revolution of 1949, the May 4th movement of 1919, the Republican Revolution of 1911, and the examination candidates' remonstration and repression of 1895. Nonetheless, at least in recent years, prodemocracy protests have been relatively brief incidents, not long-term movements. The government has repeatedly shown its capacity to stifle public discussion. China is remarkably lacking in free spaces for such discourse. Compared even to the Soviet Union and Eastern Europe, China is short on institutions of "society" separate from the state, and short on privacy. A bit more of either of these would allow more publication of an unofficial press, for example, or more links to be forged between members of different potentially oppositional groups, such as workers and students.

Without either free public spaces or privacy, democracy is unlikely to get very far. It is possible that reform will bring more of each to China over the next few years. It is likely that there will be more flowerings of dissent like the student movement of this past spring. But until deeper roots are laid, such protests will continue to echo the old Confucian idea of the people (or the intellectuals) remonstrating with the ruler. They will not be manifestations of alternative bases for government so much as attempts to remind those in power of their responsibilities. One of the main significances of the tactical difficulties I have described, and of the particular pattern of success the movement achieved, is that they do not suggest a capacity to supplant the government so much as to deliver it a kick in the rear. The government has responded so far mainly by kicking back. It may also try to clean up its act, for example by policing corruption more closely. This kind of popular movement can hope mainly for concessions. Its strengths are its ability to make life difficult for leaders, and especially to play leaders off against each other.

The long scope of Chinese history can breed depression over the slow pace of progress or optimism because martyrs are not forgotten. In trying to further the cause for which people died this year, a key issue will be whether ties can be forged among different groups—intellectuals, students, workers, entrepreneurs, officials, and peasants. For all but the last there were at least the beginnings of joint efforts in this spring's protest. If these can begin to be secured, or even institutionalized, then there will be a stronger basis next time. That there will be a next time seems almost certain. Whether it will be in two years, five years, or ten is less clear. At some point in the not too distant future, Deng Xiaoping will die; at that time a new power struggle within the government will quite likely create an opening for protest from without. In the meantime, the way will be paved for the next struggle if discussion improves ideas, if associational links are strengthened, and if the memory of this movement is kept alive. None of these, however, is an easy task.

DISCUSSION QUESTIONS

1. As was the case with the New Left in the United States during the 1960s, the core of the Chinese pro-democracy movement consisted of university students. Why?
2. Based on Calhoun's discussion about the conflicts that emerged within the movement, do you think that the massacre at Tiananmen Square might have been avoided without necessitating a complete capitulation on the part of students?

READING 40

Volunteers and the "Lessons of Mississippi"

Doug McAdam

Evoking C. Wright Mills's sociological imagination, Doug McAdam listens to the way Freedom Summer volunteers describe retrospectively the way that participation in this major episode in the civil rights movement shaped the subsequent course of their lives. In 1964, over 1,000 student volunteers from the North headed for Mississippi to work in community centers, teach in Freedom Schools, and assist with black voter registration. Local law enforcement and extremist groups such as the KKK responded aggressively to this threat to white supremacy, resulting in murders, beatings, arrests, and the burning of black churches. The experience

radicalized volunteers and alienated them from the mainstream of American society, with implications that are discussed by McAdam.

All of our lives represent, in C. Wright Mills' (1959) phrase, the "intersection of biography and history." While we may be only dimly aware of the historical currents that are shaping our lives, we can rest assured they are. For most of us, however, the confluence of biography and history is somewhat prosaic. That is, if not seamless, there is a certain predictable match between each of us as social products and the historical era in which we grow to maturity. Who we are raised to be is relatively consistent with the broader social world we encounter as adults.

For some few others, the course and texture of the interface between their own biographies and the history of their era is less predictable. Faced with historical circumstances unanticipated by those who helped socialize them, these individuals suddenly confront new possibilities for social action and self-conception. The interplay between history and biography takes on a disjunctive quality, as the orderly progression toward adulthood is interrupted by historical events and processes. The result is often a period of thoroughgoing resocialization, as biographies and identities are modified in accordance with the newly perceived historical imperatives. Among those rare few whose biographies fit this description are many who came into young adulthood at the time of the Depression, many World War II or Vietnam War veterans, and to a less dramatic extent, the Freedom Summer volunteers.

Ignoring differences for the moment, several generalizations can be made about the volunteers. By and large, they were the sons and daughters of American privilege. They came from comfortable, often wealthy, families, some of them patrician. They applied to the project while attending the top elite colleges or universities in the country. The volunteers had known few limits in their lives, least of all those imposed by race or class. The generally liberal, and occasionally radical, political views of the volunteers' parents stamped the volunteers as more leftist politically than most children of class privilege. Still, on the eve of the summer, they remained reformers rather than revolutionaries, liberals rather than radicals. Their narrative statements, written on the project applications, reflect a generally idealistic view of America, based on the liberal imagery characteristic of the era. The United States certainly had its imperfections, but they were less the product of flaws inherent in the system than they were remedial aberrations stemming from our failure to fully realize the humane and egalitarian values on which the nation had been founded. Neither their experiences nor their generally liberal political views prepared the volunteers for what they were to find in Mississippi. The education they were to receive there was to have profound and enduring consequences. To quote Gren Whitman, one of the volunteers, "it was simply the most important experience of my life. It really set me on a course in my life that I'm still on."[1] Such assessments remain commonplace among the volunteers, who nearly a quarter of a century later continue to view the summer as a watershed in their lives, a point in time around which to reorganize their biographies in "before" and "after" terms. It was the moment when they climbed aboard a barely discernible political and cultural wave that would later crest as the "Sixties experience," sweeping up much of their generation as it went. But the volunteers would be among the first.

Therein lies their significance. For historical currents do not irresistibly propel themselves and everyone in their path. No matter what their broader structural or ideological roots, they both carry along and are carried along by people, who are not merely the passengers of history, but its pilots as well. In the end, social history is little more than the sum of countless individual choices aggregated over time. That it appears otherwise may owe to the fact that although we can do as we choose, we can seldom choose as we please. Ordinarily, people's choices have the effect of reconfirming and reinforcing the "nor-mal order of things." What was remarkable about the Sixties was that large numbers of people began, through their choices, to challenge all manner of longstanding social, political and cultural arrangements. This process did not proceed in random fashion, however. Instead, as in all diffusion processes, the objects of change—attitudes about the war, styles of dress, tastes in music, etc.—spread outward in ever-widening circles from an initial core of innovators. The broader societal significance of Freedom Summer lies in the stimulus it afforded this process. Through its radicalization of many of the volunteers, the project created a nucleus of political and (counter) cultural pioneers who returned to their respective colleges and communities outside the South intent on "bringing the message of Mississippi to the rest of the nation." Though it differed from volunteer to volunteer, that message variously embraced conceptions of the United States, politics, community, human relationships, and sexuality clearly at odds with mainstream values. In short order, these conceptions would attract a wide following, especially among those of the baby-boom generation. That these conceptions would, in turn, be supplanted by even more radical ones many times before the "Sixties wave" began to recede is of little importance. What is important is the role the volunteers played in the formative stages of this process.

However, to more fully appreciate this role we will want to know more about the mix of biography and history that produced it. In this reading we focus on the diverse historical contexts that confronted the volunteers on the eve of the summer. It was a volatile mix. . . .

THE VOLUNTEERS AND THE "LESSONS OF MISSISSIPPI"

Notwithstanding all the political turbulence, the Sixties were not simply about politics. Nor were they exclusively about experimenting with new lifestyles. What made the era unique was the combination of these two emphases. Personal transformation came to be wedded to political and social change as a rhetoric of liberation suffused the New Left and the later counterculture. Only after 1968 or 1969 did the cultural and political components of the "Sixties experience" diverge. Thereafter, the political left came to be more exclusive and sectarian while elements of the counterculture—dress and hairstyles, music, drug usage—diffused through a wider public. But early on, the two impulses were clearly joined.

Much of the significance of Freedom Summer derives from the impetus it furnished this process of fusion. For most of the volunteers, the "lessons of Mississippi" were as much personal as political. Returning North, they carried with them the seeds of a new culture, equally attuned to personal and political change as necessary components of a broader transformation of American society. In effect, the twin themes of political and personal change received early expression in Mississippi and the volunteers came away clearly committed to both.

Political Radicalization

Above all else, the volunteers became more political as a result of their experiences in Mississippi. In their interviews the volunteers returned to this theme over and over again. Said Heather Tobis Booth, "It [the summer] had an enormous effect on me . . . it made me really feel [that] I want to do this kind of thing for the rest of my life."[2] Another said, "The summer moved me light years beyond where I had been politically . . . I went from being a liberal Peace Corps-type Democrat to a raging, maniacal lefty."[3] Yet another put it even more succinctly, "I *became* political in Mississippi. I began to see the world strictly in political terms."[4]

The sources of this radicalization were numerous. Chief among them were the events of the summer. Given their advantaged and generally sheltered backgrounds, it would be hard to imagine the volunteers *not* being powerfully affected by the things they saw in Mississippi.

Those who had been raised in leftist homes may have been ideologically familiar with the concepts of oppression and inequality, but few of the volunteers had ever experienced them directly. But it wasn't the discrimination alone—the "colored only" drinking fountains and KKK billboards—that made such an impact; the volunteers had expected those things. It was the depths of the problem and the broader implications of what they saw. It was the poverty of black Mississippi and what that said about the inherent goodness of America. It was the endemic quality of official lawlessness and the blatant contradiction it posed to their "law and order" upbringings. But perhaps what shocked the volunteers most was the depths of federal complicity in maintaining Mississippi's system of segregation. If the SNCC veterans had grown increasingly dubious of Washington's commitment to civil rights, the majority of volunteers arrived in Mississippi with generally positive images of the federal government. It was the redneck farmer, Southern sheriff, and Dixiecrat politician who were the enemy. For many, the events of the summer upset this simplistic distinction between "good guys" and "bad guys." All too often, the "good guys" were linked to the "bad guys" in ways that were no less disturbing for their subtlety. In a long essay written during the summer, a volunteer named Brian Peterson attempted to delineate these connections.

> The Klansman-assassin at the local gas station has close connections with the local sheriff, who in turn has connections with the legislature and governor, who in turn have connections with Congress and the President. The implications of this aren't always clear: the FBI will find the murderers of Schwerner, Chaney and Goodman, but they won't find out who killed the six other Mississippi Negroes since January and they won't interfere with the constant police brutality.
>
> Similarly, the Negro sharecropper is bossed by a plantation manager, who is employed by the local bank to run the land it owns, this bank is controlled by a bank in Memphis, which is largely owned by a bank in Chicago or New York. (Other

TABLE 1

EFFECT OF FREEDOM SUMMER ON THE VOLUNTEER'S PERCEPTION OF VARIOUS BRANCHES OR AGENCIES OF GOVERNMENT

	President		Congress		Justice Dept.		FBI	
	%	No.	%	No.	%	No.	%	No.
Lowered estimate	42	(81)	40	(77)	50	(98)	73	(143)
Raised estimate	12	(23)	9	(18)	26	(51)	6	(12)
Estimate unchanged	46	(87)	51	(98)	24	(46)	21	(42)
Total	100	(191)	100	(193)	100	(195)	100	(197)

large owners of sharecrop land include life insurance companies, most notably Metropolitan of New York, and Northern universities, most notably Harvard, that citadel of liberalism.) Thus the highest financial (and intellectual) levels of this country have a direct interest in exploiting the Negro sharecropper and seeing to it that he does not gain political power by which he could end that exploitation.[5]

A sign on the wall of many of the Freedom Houses put the matter of federal complicity in Mississippi a bit more ironically. The sign read:

> There's a street in Itta Bena called FREEDOM
> There's a town in Mississippi called LIBERTY
> There's a department in Washington called JUSTICE

Though the volunteers lagged behind the SNCC veterans, they too were beginning to redefine who the enemy was. The radicalizing effect of Freedom Summer is reflected in the answers the volunteers gave to one item on the follow-up questionnaire. They were asked whether their estimate of various branches or agencies of the federal government was raised, lowered, or remained unchanged as a result of their experiences in Mississippi. Their answers are given in Table 1. The direction of change in the volunteers' perceptions is the same for all branches or agencies of government. Overwhelmingly, the volunteers report Freedom Summer lowering their opinion of federal officials.

Their strongest criticisms were reserved for the FBI and the contacts they had with individ-

ual agents. Time and again, FBI agents called to investigate violence against the projects either never showed up or were uncooperative or hostile when they did. The worst of the incidents recounted during the interviews was one provided by David Gelfand, a volunteer who had been severely beaten on August 21, 1964, near Laurel, Mississippi. As bad as the beating was, the failure of the FBI to take action during the attack, to pursue the investigation following the attack, or to cooperate in the prosecution of those involved was even more damning to Gelfand:

> The bottom line was the federal government never did anything. . . . [It] was another interesting fiasco with the FBI . . . we had been assured by our local congressman, Ogden Reed . . . that the local FBI in Jackson and Laurel would be very cooperative . . . [it] turned out [that] the head of the Laurel FBI was . . . related to the [local] sheriff and this Klan guy. . . . I wound up totally disenchanted with the FBI and the Justice Department.[6]

Nor was the FBI seen as some anomaly in relation to an otherwise responsive federal government. The entire federal establishment came in for criticism. At the height of the summer one volunteer took angry aim at a variety of targets:

> Coming from lunch the other day to the COFO office we noticed a hush unusual for the place. A boy in a bloody shirt was reporting a brutal beating via phone to the FBI. . . . The FBI will "investigate" and no more.
> Where is the USA? It is a violation of FEDERAL LAW to harass voter registration workers.

Where are the Federal Marshals to protect these people? How do the Negroes defending "democracy" in Vietnam feel about the defense that democracy gets in Mississippi? (Quoted in Sutherland, 1965: 147)

Others singled out specific targets for criticism. By its timidity and reluctance to aggressively prosecute civil rights violations, the Justice Department earned the enmity of many volunteers. So too did Lyndon Johnson and his supporters for the tactics they employed at the Democratic Convention in Atlantic City. Said one volunteer, "the convention challenge was kind of a last straw for me. . . . When I went to Mississippi I was a Kennedy Democrat. After Atlantic City I didn't really feel like I had . . . [a party]."[7] Other liberal standard bearers came in for criticism as well. Marion Davidson remembered "complaining to [then Attorney General] Robert Kennedy that our mail was being opened. His response was formal and . . . cold . . . and it was clear that he didn't care all that much and [that he] couldn't really do anything about it."[8] Wouldn't do anything about it is probably closer to the truth. Based on evidence uncovered by the late Senator Frank Church's Select Committee on Government Intelligence Activities, we now know that Kennedy himself authorized wiretaps on Martin Luther King Jr.'s home and several SCLC offices.[9] Finally, another volunteer described as "shocking and depressing" a meeting he had during the summer with yet another hero of the Democratic left.

[A] group of us . . . were sent for a few days to Washington to lobby among senators and congressmen . . . for some immediate action on their [Chaney, Goodman, and Schwerner] disappearance and [on] the more general question [of civil rights]. . . . Paul Douglas [D-Ill.] was still a senator in those days . . . he was this sort of liberal hero of mine but this was a very disillusioning meeting. . . . I'll never forget this, he said, "you young people want to play you're great and . . . [that] this is a wonderful thing you are doing, but," he said, "the main thing," and he'd repeat

this over and over again, "is watch out for the Commies." . . . that word is indelible in my memory; it was like something [from a] comic book . . . very sad and very disillusioning.[10]

Consistently, then, their encounters with federal officials left the volunteers frustrated and disillusioned. This was especially true for those whose political socialization had been fairly conventional.[11] The government they had been led to believe was powerful and essentially just was proving itself to be cowardly and amoral in its dealings with segregationists. For many, this contrast was profoundly radicalizing. Long-time SNCC staffer, Mary King, describes the effect the summer had on many of the volunteers: "there were certain feelings of betrayal, particularly, I suspect, this was true for the white kids involved, the feeling that you couldn't count on your own government. A sort of suspension of values, almost, that the things I had grown up believing were constants; were just of dust" (quoted in Sinsheimer, 1983: 139).

Another source of radicalization for the volunteers was their interaction with the project staff. There was even a phrase—the "SNCCizing of the volunteers"—to describe this process. Several volunteers touched on it during their interviews.

Lots of the volunteers sort of sat at the feet of the SNCC guys, and it was the [SNCC] guys, not the girls. It was sort of pathetic, everybody trying to out SNCC each other. But it was also hard not to. They [the male SNCC staffers] were tremendously charismatic . . . very forceful and frankly, their rap made sense. It was hard not to start seeing the world through their eyes.[12]

It's hard to say this now, but I wanted to be like them [the SNCC staff]. Not to the point where I started to talk and dress like them; some of the others almost become [sic] like groupies . . . I mean politically, I wanted to be like them. . . . More than anything else I guess I admired their courage and their commitment to political *action*.[13]

This latter point is especially important. It was not simply that the volunteers had their political *attitudes* changed by their experiences in Mississippi. Indeed, a good many of the volunteers arrived in Mississippi with a relatively sophisticated and sometimes radical political view of the world. This was especially true of the sizeable number of volunteers whose parents had been socialists or communists. Even these "red diaper babies," however, found their politics changed by the experience.

> Well, I wouldn't say I was politicized by it [Freedom Summer]. I had always been political, but in what strikes me now as a very detached, academic sense. . . . Shit, I could debate Trotsky's position against Lenin when I was ten . . . I was the classic arm chair radical . . . smug, self-congratulatory . . . I always prided myself on having the "correct analysis." . . . But I didn't become an *actionist* until Mississippi. I came to see that you could talk till you were blue in the face, but at some point, if you were really committed to the stuff, you had to act on what you were saying.[14]

Heather Tobis Booth described the political legacy of the summer for her as "the positive impulse to action."[15] So it was not only the attitudes of the volunteers that were changed by the summer, but their willingness to act on those attitudes. This is not a trivial point. When we speak of the Sixties as a "political" era we are really making a statement about the level of political action during the period rather than the content of political attitudes per se. In this sense, the most important legacy of Freedom Summer may lie in the "positive impulse to action" it furnished the New Left. While collective action had been more or less continuous among blacks since 1955, and especially 1960, the predominantly white Northern colleges and universities had remained very quiet over the same period of time. While there were stirrings of political life before the summer, the dramatic upsurge in campus activism corresponded with the return of the volunteers to school in the fall.

The confluence is no coincidence. Freedom Summer had served as a kind of activist "basic training" for some 1,000 people, nearly all of whom returned North following the summer. With them went not only the ideological "lessons" of Mississippi, but the desire to act on those lessons. The radicalization of the volunteers, then, had important behavioral as well as attitudinal implications. It was the former that was to prove so important in the emergence of an activist subculture in the North. The volunteers were among the first activist role models for an entire generation.

Personal Liberation

The impact of Freedom Summer on the volunteers was not exclusively political. If it had been, the volunteers presumably would have had little trouble returning to the lives they were leading prior to the summer. In fact, this transition proved difficult for most of the volunteers. For some, there was no desire to even attempt it. They had been changed in too fundamental a sense to think about resuming their previous lives. Two processes at work here. The first was an outgrowth of the political radicalization the volunteers had undergone. Their experiences in Mississippi had led them to see the world in more starkly political terms than they had previously. In turn, this heightened political awareness made them more critical of American society and the lives they had led before. But this was only half the story. Even as the volunteers were rejecting certain aspects of their previous lives, they were embracing new images of the world and of themselves. Mississippi had exposed them to a way of life and a vision of community that most of the volunteers found enormously appealing. The trick now was to recreate this alternative way of life and community in the North. On the personal front, then, Freedom Summer moved the volunteers in two directions: away from various aspects of mainstream society, and toward an alternative vision of America and of themselves.

Alienation from Mainstream Society

For many of the volunteers the immediate effect of the summer was to leave them feeling disoriented, depressed, and alienated. Having spent eight to ten weeks isolated from mainstream white society, it was inevitable that the volunteers would have some trouble readjusting to life outside of Mississippi. Some of the difficulties were of a temporary, even humorous, nature. One volunteer remembers "almost missing how much I stunk in Mississippi . . . it was this kind of earthy badge of courage or something. When I got back home I remember [being] . . . depressed by all the sterility."[16] Another spoke of how, on returning to New York City, he found himself monitoring white passengers on the subway more closely than black because of the distrust of whites he had developed in Mississippi.[17] These adjustments were fleeting, but there were others that suggested more basic changes in the values and attitudes of the volunteers. Their summer in Mississippi had put considerable distance between themselves and the privileged worlds they had previously inhabited. To the extent that the perceived superiority of any world depends on its insularity, the Freedom Summer experience was bound to raise questions and plant doubts in the minds of the volunteers. There were other worlds, other ways of life out there; and the view from those other worlds did not necessarily confirm the assumptions the volunteers had previously taken for granted. Late in the summer, Ellen Lake wrote home challenging her parents' objections to her plan to stay on in Mississippi. She wrote:

> You speak of losing focus from spending a year in Mississippi; but what kind of focus do I have? All of my nineteen years I have shuttled between Westchester, Martha's Vineyard, the Virgin Islands, summer camp and Radcliffe—how can I help but gain a new perspective from Mississippi?[18]

While provocative, this "new perspective" was also confusing and generally alienating. In the in-terviews, more than half of the volunteers acknowledged some degree of estrangement from their previous lives immediately following the summer. For Pam Parker, these problems began the day she left the project to begin a vacation with her parents. She describes what happened:

> my folks had a station wagon and they were all in the front seat and I was in the back seat lying down . . . we were driving up in New Hampshire and I totally freaked out that we were going to crash . . . there had been one civil rights worker killed on our project in an automobile accident [Wayne Yancy] and . . . that was intense dealing with his death . . . so I always thought that [my freaking out] was a reaction to the pressure and fear of being in Mississippi and then having come out and things having lightened up, I . . . [could finally let] this fear . . . come up. . . . [But] a couple of years ago I realized that that probably was not the case, that more likely . . . what had happened to me was that I was confronting the reality of going into northern white society with all its deadness and that I was on a subconscious level feeling the fear of dying and being a walking zombie.[19]

Several months later Parker was featured in a documentary done by a local television station in Philadelphia on two of the returning project workers. The segment on her featured sunny, upbeat shots of her strolling around the grounds of her parents' large home in the rolling horse country of eastern Pennsylvania. Against this idyllic visual backdrop, however, her voice-over narration provides a somber, chilling contrast. The last line of the segment captures the mood nicely. "I feel," she says, "like . . . a marginal person. I am not happy nor comfortable in white society any longer nor am I fully comfortable in Negro society, and I know, at least for myself, it's been a very lonely, isolated year because of this."[20]

Other volunteers recalled similar difficulties in adjusting to life after Mississippi. Len Edwards remembers

> not [being] in control of my emotions for at least a year [afterward], I was consumed by what I had

seen; what [I] had been exposed to . . . and had a very difficult time . . . relating to people. . . . Here I am . . . [coming] out of this very intense summer and then suddenly I'm back reading law books again and sitting with guys drinking beer and they want to talk about how the Cubs are doing and talk b.s. and talk about girls and somebody casually says, "well, what was happening down there in Mississippi?" . . . And I started talking and I said about two sentences and I started crying; I just burst out crying and it wasn't just . . . a little trickle down the cheek . . . I just sobbed . . . I had other times that were bad. I remember dating a girl . . . and she asked me about it once and the same thing happened to me and she didn't know what to do . . . and I didn't know what to do . . . it was embarrassing, but I couldn't control myself.[21]

The confusion and alienation the volunteers were feeling spilled over into all aspects of their lives. Some felt estranged from their parents, either because they viewed them as somehow morally culpable for the situation in Mississippi or because they had come to redefine their parents' lifestyle as amoral or excessive. After returning home late in the summer, one of the volunteers expressed her new-found reservations in a letter to a friend:

> Coming out of Mississippi and into the "civilized white" world was hard. It was like cultural shock or something. Like I didn't feel like talking to anyone. I was in a kind of daze . . . I don't know quite what I am saying except that I am against much of what my family stands for. I realize that four families could live comfortably on what my father makes—comfortably Miss. Negro style. . . . He's worked for what he's got. But it hurts me.[22]

The interviews afforded a certain historical perspective on the long-term effect of Freedom Summer on the volunteers' relations with their parents. They made it clear that, in most cases, whatever conflict the summer precipitated was only temporary. For at least four of the volunteers, however, the summer marked the begin-

ning of a prolonged or even permanent estrangement between volunteer and parents.[23]

In other cases, it was the volunteers' school or career plans that came to be questioned. The doubts started well before the summer ended. The alienation the volunteers were feeling is clearly evident in their letters home.

> Hell, Ollie, I'm scared to death to leave this place next month . . . what am I going to do with myself. I really think that I've changed on what is important in life and what I want to do in life. What am I going to do sitting in the halls of Chicago reading taxation and corporation cases when I hear that one of the people I have lived with and fought with and loved has been shot?[24]

Another wrote to inform friends that she would not be going on to graduate school in the fall as she had originally planned.

> Maybe the immediacy of the sufferings and dangers here is overwhelming me and blurring out the essential "larger view," but I can simply no longer justify the pursuit of a Ph.D. When the folks in Flora have to struggle to comprehend the most elementary of materials on history and society and man's larger life, I feel ashamed to be greedily going after "higher learning." And when I feel the despair of youngsters who can't even get through high school because cotton planting prevents them, I almost feel ashamed of my college diploma. And when I reflect on the terrors and deprivations in daily lives here, I cannot return to the relative comforts and security of student life. (Quoted in Sutherland, 1965: 228)

Those who did return often found themselves at a loss socially and academically. Writing nearly a year after the summer, the parents of one volunteer described the change they had witnessed in their daughter.

> It's been an unhappy year for her at college. She didn't want to go back. It had lost its meaning, but she'd promised her father. She's having trouble with identification and relating to others. She graduates this June and doesn't know what she wants to do. Our very normal, bright, young child has changed.[25]

Finally, Freedom Summer precipitated religious crises for a number of Christian volunteers. In some cases the crisis stemmed from a general sense of betrayal on the part of the volunteer. One remembers the summer as the point at which "I started questioning everything . . . I was never told about this [the situation in Mississippi] in my history classes, and in my family. [I wondered] what else haven't I been told. . . . I used to wear a cross and I ripped it off and said 'this is it' . . . I had it with religion."[26] For others, the crisis was a specific response to the "good Christian" reception accorded the project by members of the volunteers' own congregations.

> We had to raise a certain amount of money—300 or 500 dollars, something like that—and I knew there was no way I was going to get it from my parents . . . so I went to him [her minister] and asked if he would make an announcement to the congregation . . . he said "no" and proceeded, in the sleaziest way to [try to] talk me out of going. . . . I was just stunned. His whole rap seemed to be "good Christians don't rock the boat." I figured either he was nuts or Christ was a bad Christian.[27]

On all fronts, then, the volunteers were feeling the alienating effects of the summer. Their experiences in Mississippi seriously undermined the volunteers' faith in the American political system and undercut their relationships to church, school, and family. This wholesale rejection of mainstream values and institutions created a dilemma for the volunteers. If they could no longer incorporate their lives into mainstream society, what alternative identities and forms of community were they prepared to substitute? Freedom Summer had provided them with the broad contours of an answer.

NOTES

1. Interview with an anonymous Freedom Summer Volunteer, April 14, 1984.
2. Interview with Heather Jobis Booth, May 7, 1985.
3. Interview with an anonymous Freedom Summer volunteer, April 18, 1985.
4. Interview with an anonymous Freedom summer volunteer, August 19, 1985.
5. This excerpt is taken from an unpublished essay entitled, "Thoughts about Mississippi," written by Brian Peterson; included in papers (hereinafter cited as Peterson papers) on file, SHSW.
6. Interview with David Gelfand, February 7, 1985.
7. Interview with an anonymous Freedom Summer volunteer, June 8, 1985.
8. Interview with Marion Davidson, March 21, 1985.
9. See U.S., Congress, Senate, Select Committee to Study Governmental Operations with Respect to Intelligence Activities, *Final Report—Book III, Supplementary Detailed Staff Reports on Intelligence Activities and the Rights of Americans*, 94th Congress, 2d session, 1976. Kennedy's role in authorizing the wiretaps on King are also carefully documented in David Garrow's excellent book, *The FBI and Martin Luther King, Jr.* (1981: 64–65, 72–73, 91–95, 201–202).
10. Interview with an anonymous Freedom Summer volunteer, April 22, 1985.
11. The following table shows that those volunteers who described themselves as more politically moderate prior to Freedom Summer were also more likely to report a drop in their estimate of federal officials as a result of their experiences in Mississippi.

PERCENT OF THE VOLUNTEERS REPORTING A LOWERED ESTIMATE OF VARIOUS BRANCHES OR AGENCIES OF GOVERNMENT, BY POLITICAL ORIENTATION, PRIOR TO FREEDOM SUMMER

Orientation prior to summer	President		Congress		Justice Dept.		FBI	
	%	No.	%	No.	%	No.	%	No.
Radical (1–3)	34	(34)	28	(28)	47	(48)	64	(65)
All other (4–10)	51	(47)	53	(49)	54	(50)	82	(78)

12. Interview with an anonymous Freedom Summer volunteer, April 28, 1985.
13. Interview with an anonymous Freedom Summer volunteer, May 9, 1985.

14. Interview with an anonymous Freedom Summer volunteer, June 8, 1985.
15. Interview with Heather Tobis Booth, May 7, 1985.
16. Interview with an anonymous Freedom Summer volunteer, April 12, 1985.
17. Interview with Robbie Osman, August 13, 1984.
18. Letter written by Ellen Lake to her parents, August 12, 1964; Lake papers, SHSW.
19. Interview with Chude Pamela Allen, August 14, 1984.
20. From a taped transcript of the voice-over narration of the television show in question; in author's possession.
21. Interview with Len Edwards, August 17, 1984.
22. Letter written by Pam Parker to a friend, August 30, 1964; Allen papers.
23. The interviews in question took place on: 8/14/84; 2/5/85; 3/21/85 and 6/6/85.
24. Letter written by Len Edwards; included in papers given to the author by Len Edwards (hereinafter cited as Edwards papers).
25. Letter written by Mrs. Jeannette Parker; Allen papers.
26. Interview with an anonymous Freedom Summer volunteer, August 14, 1984.
27. Interview with an anonymous Freedom Summer volunteer, April 28, 1985.

REFERENCES

Mills, C. Wright. 1959. *The Sociological Imagination.* New York: Oxford University Press.
Sinsheimer, Joe. 1983. *Bring the Country to White Heat: The 1964 Mississippi Project and Its Volunteers.* Duke University: Unpublished Manuscript.
Sutherland, Elizabeth, ed. 1965. *Letters from Mississippi.* New York: McGraw-Hill Book Company.

DISCUSSION QUESTIONS

1. Not all university students were likely candidates for participation in Freedom Summer. What types of people would you expect to be willing to take the risks involved in challenging the racism of the segregated South?
2. Part of the transformation of the volunteers entailed what McAdam refers to as "personal liberation." What does he mean by this term?

READING 41

Half a Revolution: The Second Wave of Feminism and the Family

Arlene Skolnick

The first wave of contemporary feminism, early in the 20th century, won women the right to vote, but left unchallenged the notion that women's lives were fundamentally tied to the private, domestic realm. As Arlene Skolnick points out in this selection from Embattled Paradise, *second-wave feminism, which took off in the 1960s, differed from its predecessor insofar as it called into question notions about femininity, the family, and sexuality. She traces the movement from its heady days to the late 1970s, when a conservative countermovement, mobilized around opposition to the ERA and to the legalization of abortion, gained ground while the movement waned. Skolnick concludes with an assessment of the lasting impact of the second wave.*

For many of us, the initial feminist understanding came as a kind explosion: shattering, scattering, everything tumbling about, the old world splintering even as the new one was collecting.
— Vivian Gornick
Essays in Feminism

In September 1968 a group of radical women staged a demonstration against the Miss America Pageant in Atlantic City. The event appeared on millions of television sets all over the country, and gathered much more space in newspapers than did the contest itself.[1] The second wave of feminism had burst into American consciousness.

About two hundred women took part in the demonstration, aided by the media and a crowd of hecklers. Outside the convention hall, they marched and sang, bearing signs with messages such as: "Welcome to the Miss America Cattle Auction"; "I am a woman—not a toy, a pet, or a mascot"; and "Can make-up cover the wounds of our oppression?" The women crowned a live sheep Miss America, "to parody the way the contestants . . . are appraised and judged like animals at a county fair." Though the media described the protesters as "bra burners," nothing was actually burned. But the demonstrators did dump bras, girdles, high-heeled shoes, dishcloths, false eyelashes, and other "instruments of torture to women" into a "freedom trashcan."[2]

The climax occurred inside the Convention Hall after the new Miss America was crowned; a white bedsheet floated down from a balcony bearing the message "Women's Liberation" to viewers across America. Denouncing "the Libs" for desecrating one of America's most beloved rituals, the writer Frank Deford observed: "To the women's liberation movement, the skirmish at Convention Hall is roughly analogous to the Boston Tea Party."[3]

He was more prophetic than he realized, or would have wished. The Atlantic City demonstration did amount to a call for a new American revolution. Of all the movements of the 1960s, the one with the most lasting and profound influence on both public and private life in America has been the second wave of feminism. Despite its shocking arrival on the scene, and although it is far from complete, the new feminist movement has brought about changes as dramatic and far-reaching as any that have occurred in the twentieth century.

TAKING OFF: REBIRTH OF A WOMEN'S MOVEMENT

The roots of the feminist revival reach back into the 1950s. Despite that decade's glorification of domesticity and togetherness, there was a growing gap between the public images of smiling, home-all-day suburban housewives and the private realities of everyday family life. Behind the rhetoric of domestic bliss seethed a vast, only partly hidden reservoir of frustration and discontent.

The Atlantic City demonstration and other events like it marked a turning point. Although

the women's movement had been stirring for years before these eruptions, the public was largely unaware of it. Miss America protesters came from the more radical wing of the women's movement, younger women whose political style and rhetoric had been shaped in the protests and confrontation of the 1960s. A second branch consisted for the most part of older, established professionals with a more mainstream political style, who focused on legal and policy changes as the route to equal rights for women.

Eventually the movement grew beyond these two distinct categories into a vast collection of groups, large and small, devoted to different purposes—political action, consciousness raising, child care, rape crisis centers—and split along a variety of dividing lines: radical versus liberal, straight versus lesbian, those seeking gender equality versus those centered on women's differences from men.

Whatever their internal conflicts, feminists shared a common core of beliefs. Feminism in the 1960s and 1970s was, in essence, as much an emotional and intellectual understanding as a political movement. It was like a psychoanalytic insight, or the "aha" experience in problem solving—the shift in perception that enables a person to see a problem differently. It was "a profoundly new way of interpreting human experience . . . . a vital piece of information at the center of a new point of reference from which one both reinterprets the past and predicts the future."[4] The journalist Jane O'Reilly described the "click" of what she called the "housewife's moment of truth"—the shock of recognizing that the everyday assumptions and patterns of behavior governing sex roles were unfair and arbitrary.[5]

To those who heard the click, women's oppression was seen as being as pervasive and crushing as that of other disadvantaged groups. Ranging from vast inequities in the workplace to the seemingly inescapable constraints and expectations in private life, women's second-class status was suddenly recognized not as natural and inevitable but as a social construct, based on power and the assumption that women are naturally inferior to men. As O'Reilly put it, "We have suddenly and shockingly perceived the basic disorder in what had been believed to be the natural order of things."[6]

The new wave of feminism challenged cultural understandings of home, family, femininity, masculinity, and sexuality in a more profound way than its earlier counterparts had. Few of the first wave of feminists in the nineteenth century had directly challenged the family. They were willing to accept celibacy and spinsterhood as the price of carving themselves a place in the world outside the home.[7]

In the second wave, however, even moderate feminists were calling for a transformation of marriage and family life. The NOW manifesto of 1966 declared:

> We do not accept that a woman has to choose between marriage and motherhood on the one hand, and serious participation in industry and/or the professions on the other. . . . We believe that a true partnership between the sexes demands a different concept of marriage, an equitable sharing of the responsibilities of home and children and of the economic burdens of their support.[8]

More radical voices in the movement argued for more extreme solutions and attracted a great deal of media attention. Shulamith Firestone called for artificial reproduction to free women from the oppression of their biology; Ti-Grace Atkinson called for communal child rearing, arguing that women could not be free "unless you get the childrearing off their backs." Others argued that marriage was a central part of the "total oppression" of women: "We are exploited as sex objects, breeders, domestic servants and cheap labor," declared the 1969 manifesto of the Redstockings, a radical feminist group in New York City. "We are considered inferior human beings whose only purpose is to enhance men's lives."[9]

News of the women's liberation movement spread with incredible speed. Within five years of the Atlantic City protest and its spectacular breakthrough into public awareness, feminism had become a grass-roots mass movement. But the ideas of the movement spread far beyond activists and those who identified themselves as "feminists." In the 1970s and 1980s, the general public would come increasingly to support the aims of the women's movement. And despite the successes of the antifeminist New Right, feminist positions have continued to represent the views of the majority of Americans.[10]

But widespread acceptance was a gradual process.[*] Initially, news of the movement was greeted with humor or puzzlement. Even years of student protest, civil rights marches, and antiwar demonstrations had not prepared Americans for this. The media often treated the movement as a joke, focusing on the sensational side, like the alleged Miss America "bra burning." The Feminist was often portrayed as a frustrated, unfulfilled man hater. Many people, women included, were confused, and reiterated Freud's question: "What do women want?" Many men felt themselves under attack; indeed, some feminists had declared men "the enemy," though most simply challenged the age-old custom of male privilege and power. At the very least, observed the sociologist William Goode, men experienced "a loss in centrality, a decline in the extent to which they are the center of attention."[12] At worst, they saw the feminist challenge as a threat to their very identity.

Meanwhile, women who had settled comfortably into traditional domesticity, who had staked their lives on the traditional marriage bargain by which a woman traded her service as a wife and mother for a lifetime of support, felt that the movement had nothing to say to them.

---

[*] Jo Freeman points out that like other successful innovations, the spread of movement ideas followed a bell-shaped curve. At first, a few people, the Innovators, advance the new idea; a larger group of Early Adopters comes next, followed by Early and Late Majorities, and finally, Laggards—a small group of late acceptors. The critical point is where the curve shoots upward—the "take-off" point.[11]

Worse, it seemed to be telling them that they had wasted their lives or, worse still, that men no longer had to keep their end of the marriage bargain.

Early converts to feminism often found themselves out of step even with close friends. In 1969 the journalist Vivian Gornick was astonished at her friends' response when she mentioned she favored the women's liberation movement. One man asked, "Jesus, what is all this crap about?" while his wife, a scientist who had given up her work to stay home and raise their children, said, "I can understand if these women want to work and are demanding equal pay. But why on earth do they want to have children, too?"[13]

Yet soon large numbers of Americans were rethinking sex roles both inside and outside the family. In 1969, when the editor of *Harper's Bazaar* traveled the country interviewing married American women, hardly anyone had heard of radical feminism; a year later, she found hardly anyone "whose thinking about herself in relation to men had not been shaken up or altered by the widening feminist clamor for women's rights."[14]

The takeoff point for the women's movement was in the early 1970s (the sociologist Jo Freeman pinpoints the date to 1970). Surveys taken at the time confirm it as a dramatic turning point in sex role beliefs as well as in the acceptance of the women's movement itself.[15] Traditional concepts of sex roles in family and marriage—for example, the notion that married women, especially mothers, should confine their activities to the home—gave way to more "modern," egalitarian attitudes. In a 1973 survey of its readers by *Redbook* magazine, two-thirds favored the movement, and less than 2 percent believed that women could fulfill their potential through marriage and motherhood alone.[16] A Gallup poll tracking women's answers to a question about sex discrimination reveals the movement's influence: in 1962 two out of three women denied having been treated unequally; in 1970 half said

they had been discriminated against; in 1974 two-thirds reported unequal treatment and were in favor of efforts to improve women's status.[17]

Underlying attitudes on particular issues was a sea change in perceptions of women, a new view of women as individuals able to make choices about their lives—working, marrying, child rearing—along with a new tolerance for whatever choices they might make. These changes showed up first among the college-educated and college students themselves, but eventually crossed class, educational, and regional lines.

The shift, of course, was not unanimous. The 1970s also witnessed the rise of antifeminism. Spurred by the Supreme Court's legalization of abortion in *Roe v. Wade*, as well as by the early success of the Equal Rights Amendment (and the prospect of its passing if three more state legislatures voted for it), the backlash against the women's movement grew into a powerful political force. It was both an ironic sign of the movement's success[18] and a measure of the deep anxieties and cultural conflicts aroused by the ideas, as well as the reality, of family and gender role change. . . .

"THE NEXT GREAT MOMENT IN HISTORY IS THEIRS"

By the middle of the 1970s, the second wave of feminism had reached its crest. For millions of women who had heard the "click" of feminist insight, it was a time of high hopes; it seemed as if the dream of equality in the workplace and equal partnership in the home might be coming true. Dramatic changes in the law symbolized a transformation of women's place in the social order. In 1972 the Senate passed the Equal Rights Amendment by a vote of 84 to 8. By the end of 1973, the ERA had been passed by twenty-two state legislatures and seemed on its way to early ratification. In January of the same year, the Supreme Court, by a 7 to 2 vote, had made abortion legal, on the grounds that the right to privacy, "whether it be found in the Fourteenth Amendment's concept of personal liberty . . . or in the Ninth Amendment's reservation of rights to the people, is broad enough to encompass a woman's decision whether or not to terminate her pregnancy."[19]

In retrospect, the hopes of the heady days of the early to middle 1970s look naive and misguided. After its initial success, the ERA began to lose in state legislatures across the country. Feminists became painfully aware that their movement did not speak for all women; instead, it had begotten its own antithesis—a powerful grassroots movement of women opposed to the ERA and the right to abortion, and dedicated to preserving the family and traditional female roles.

By the end of the decade, antifeminism, allied with other "pro-family" conservative movements, helped to sweep Ronald Reagan into the White House. The election of 1980 was widely seen as marking a realignment in American politics, the onset of a new conservative era that would roll back the social changes of the 1960s and 1970s. This expectation was not fulfilled, but the election did reflect a change in the national mood. By the end of the 1970s, the rhetoric of equality and liberation had lost much of its appeal even to feminists. The movement experienced its own internal backlash, as some feminists began to have "second thoughts about the second wave."[20]

Yet, if we look back at the golden age of feminism in the mid-'70s, the great expectations of gender equality do not seem so naive. Apart from the legal victories, evidence of a sex role revolution was everywhere—on the newsstands, on television screens, in the movies, in the bookstores, on the street, in the small rituals of everyday life: Should men open doors for women, light their cigarettes, pick up the check for dinner or lunch?

Ms. became the first mass-circulation feminist magazine in history. Appearing in January 1972, it was intended to be a one-time-only publication. It sold out practically all 250,000

copies in eight days, and gathered 35,000 paid subscriptions, enabling the magazine to publish as a monthly. Over the course of the 1970s the mainstream media became increasingly receptive to feminist views: in 1975, *Time* magazine's Man of the Year was twelve women; in 1979 thirty-six American women's magazines ran pro-ERA articles; in 1976 Dr. Spock revised his best-selling *Baby and Child Care* to eliminate sexist biases.

The ideal of women's equality advanced across the national landscape, seeming to dismantle, brick by brick, the still imposing structure of disadvantage. Women ran for the first time in the Boston Marathon. Girls joined the Little League. Rape crisis centers and battered women's shelters opened all over the country. Women entered politics, as well as medical, law, and business schools in record numbers. As women's roles shifted, new kinds of male roles appeared in the media, including the sensitive, non-macho "new man."

Public opinion polls confirmed that the ideas of the movement had passed from heresy to acceptance in a remarkably short time. Men pushing baby carriages and wearing infants in Snugglis on their chests became common sights on city streets. Newspapers showed President Ford making his own toast for breakfast. In 1975 Ford created a national commission on the observance of International Women's Year. In 1977 the first National Women's Conference was held in Houston. It was attended by 15,000 women as well as three First Ladies—Betty Ford and Roslyn Carter, who were avowed feminists, and Lady Bird Johnson.

For women who had been touched by the movement or its insights, there was a sense of momentum, of riding the wave of the future. The title of a 1969 essay by Vivian Gornick—"The Next Great Moment in History Is Theirs"—had turned out to be prophetic.[21] In 1975 Robin Morgan, who had organized the Miss America demonstration, looked back at how her own life had been changed by the women's movement:

"Ten years ago, I was a woman who believed in the reality of the vaginal orgasm (and had become adept at faking spiffy ones). I felt legitimized by a successful crown roast and was the fastest hand in the east at emptying ash trays." Then came the "radical chic" of the late 1960s: "I learned to pretend contempt for monogamy as both my husband and I careered . . . through the fake 'sexual revolution.' " Then came the women's movement:

> years of . . . joy, misery and daily surprise; my first consciousness raising group . . . the marches, meetings, demonstrations. . . . And all the while, the profound "interior" changes: the tears . . . and laughter and despair and growth wrought in the struggle with my husband. . . . There are millions of us now . . . we've only just begun, and there's no stopping us.[22]

THE MOMENT PASSES

But the momentum of the movement did stop. The event that symbolized the movement's failure for both its supporters and opponents, was the failure of the Equal Rights Amendment. What went wrong? Theories about the alleged "failure of feminism" abound, especially among feminists themselves. The movement was charged with neglecting the needs of working-class, poor, ethnic, and minority women; with not speaking to women who were happy to stay home and take care of their kids. It was charged with pouring too much money and effort into the ERA struggle and other equal rights issues, emphasizing equality at the expense of women's special needs—child care, child support, maternity leave. If only the movement had not been so strident about the family, so beset by feuding factions, so farout, so lesbian. . . .

Whatever the validity of these specific charges, it seems misguided to assume that the difficulties the movement encountered were due to the wrong language or the wrong tactics. Nor is it clear that by using a different rhetoric, the women's movement could have forestalled the growth of an antifeminist backlash. The historical record shows that social change itself, as well as movements that push for social change, gives rise to backlash movements aimed at reversing its effects. Change that affects the family, and women's roles in the family, is profoundly disturbing, touching on deeply rooted cultural anxieties.

It is therefore not surprising that the women's movement would provoke hostility and sharp cultural anxiety. Gender, along with race and class, is one of the fundamental organizing principles of American society. Even the seemingly modest proposal NOW put forth for a true partnership between the sexes—the "equitable sharing of the responsibilities of home and children and the economic burdens of their support"[23]—constitutes a fundamental challenge to the social order. Any change in women's place affects men, children, the economy, conceptions of human nature—and, above all, the family.

The antifeminist backlash was a response not just to feminism itself but to the same changes that had led to feminism in the first place. A similar sequence had occurred in earlier women's movements: socioeconomic and cultural change alters women's lives, especially the lives of middle-class women; a women's movement arises, led largely by middle-class women most affected by the changes; women who see their interests threatened by a shift in women's roles and by feminist arguments join with conservative clergymen and business interests to oppose the changes and the demands of the women's movement. In the late nineteenth century, women were becoming increasingly literate, attaining higher education (many women's colleges were established at this time), entering professions such as schoolteaching and social work, as well as the commercial and industrial segments of the economy. The "New Woman" appeared on the scene—the highly educated professional woman who challenged traditional gender roles and fought for suffrage and other rights for women, as well as a host of other social reforms. Still, in the nineteenth century, the socioeconomic trends favoring a women's movement were much less strong than they would be later. The New Woman was a tiny, if vocal, minority among American women.

Like their nineteenth-century counterparts, the supporters of the modern antifeminist backlash were responding to realistic threats to their own self-interests and identity. Then as now, women were divided into two antagonistic groups: "traditional" women, who remain "encapsulated" in the home and find fulfillment there, with a vested economic interest in their roles as wives and mothers; and women with "expanded" roles, which bring them into the public world outside the home.[24]

A 1984 study of pro-choice and right-to-life activists shows the contrast clearly. The pro-choice group tended to be highly educated working women with small families; the pro-life group tended to invest their self-esteem mainly in their large families, rarely working outside the home or, if they did, in low-paying jobs.[25] But some prolife women were middle- to upper-middle-class housewives, often well educated. Usually religiously and politically conservative, antifeminist women, whatever their economic situation, feel threatened by feminism's challenge to the economic bargain embodied in the breadwinner/homemaker marriage.

Traditional women have been threatened not just by feminist rhetoric but by the social fact of the massive entrance of women, especially middle- and upper-middle-class women, into the labor force. In the 1970s, it became "déclassé" to be "just a housewife."[26] The homemaker/breadwinner bargain was also being undone by the other dramatic changes in the family that took place in the 1960s and 1970s, especially rising divorce rates.

Of all the shifts in family life, skyrocketing divorce rates caused the most widespread alarm. Antifeminists blamed the women's movement for the general breakdown of the family. In fact, divorce rates had been rising steadily since the middle of the nineteenth century. The decade or so that followed World War II, however, departed from this long-term trend: 1950s divorce rates were relatively low, and the generation of couples who married in the postwar years was the only one in the last hundred years that would undergo fewer divorces than the historical trend would predict. By the early 1960s, however, divorce rates began to resume their upward course. This increase in divorce came well before public attitudes toward divorce became liberalized.[27] It also came well before the rise of "women's liberation." In fact, the growing instability of marriage may have helped set the stage for the reemergence of feminism.

Because of the divorce revolution and other changes in the family, feminism came to confront a dramatically different social landscape than the one that had inspired it in the first place. The problem with no name was transformed into a set of problems with various names: single motherhood, the displaced homemaker syndrome, the double day of work, the loneliness of the single life.

While women suffered from new conflicts arising from family change, they faced persisting disadvantages that legal changes favoring women's rights had not been able to address. The feminist movement shared the tragic fate of other "successful" movements for dramatic social change; after the moment of elation and utopian hopes passes, reality catches up. The same sequence occurred when women won the right to vote in 1920. To many women at the time, the victory signaled that the long battle for equality had been won. Now that women had the vote, they would have the power to sweep away the remaining barriers to full equality.[28]

Then as now, the formal equalities granted by the law did not change the difficult realities most women faced in everyday life. Feminists after the mid-1970s also had to contend with the fact that the barriers to equality in the workplace and the home were much more formidable than they first appeared. The number of women in the workplace continued to rise during the 1970s, but so did the discrepancy between men's and women's incomes.[29] Most women remained confined to low-wage, gender-segregated occupations. Despite some headway in the 1980s, women's overall economic well-being has not improved since the 1960s.[30]

Women did not fare much better in the home. Despite all the talk of equal partnership, men ultimately proved reluctant to take up their share of the household work. No matter how sympathetic to feminist ideals their husbands might be, most working women continued to do the bulk of family chores. Even in the glory days of the early 1970s, few feminists believed it would be easy to alter the sexual division of labor within the family. "I cannot imagine anything more difficult than incurring the kind of domestic trauma I describe," admitted Jane O'Reilly in "The Housewife's Moment of Truth." A "liberated woman," she observed, is in danger of losing not only the role she has been taught all her life but her man as well: "The more we try, and argue, and change, the more we will realize that the male ego will be the last thing in the world to change. . . . Men do not want equality in the home. A strong woman is a threat, an inconvenience, and she can be replaced."[31]

Finally, the shift in the women's movement from elation to despair coincided with a shift from one historical era to another. Feminism was born in a time of economic expansion and restrictive family and sex role norms; it was the last act in the postwar drama of affluence and optimism. Both reformers and radicals had assumed that change could come easily, as, in fact, it appeared to with the ERA and *Roe v. Wade*. It did not seem farfetched to think the dream of equality might come true.

But the golden years of the feminist movement overlapped with the beginning of economic decline. "The year 1973," declared one economist, "should probably be taken as a watershed, sharply dividing the second half of the 20th century."[32] Not just in America but also in England and other Western countries, the long postwar boom came to an end. Just as the crash of 1929 and the Depression had sobered the Roaring Twenties, so did the various crises of the 1970s help put an end to the freewheeling era of "liberating" social change.

CONCLUSION

The feminist movement has been through a complex and paradoxical time since the 1970s. The Reagan revolution came to power on a wave of antifeminist backlash, yet was unable to reverse the social and cultural transformations that had already taken place: women's new roles in the workplace; freer sexuality; demographic shifts in marriage, divorce, and childbearing. Further, the antifeminist movement itself empowered conservative women in ways that undid the gender stereotypes of the prefeminist era that claimed women were irrational, unserious, not quite fully adult. The fact that it was Reagan who appointed the first woman to the Supreme Court testifies to the ways feminism had reshaped conceptions of gender in America.

By the end of the Reagan era, issues such as equal pay, child care, abortion, rape, and domestic violence were no longer "feminist" issues; they had become "women's" issues. Yet feminism emerged in surprisingly good shape after the Reagan years. Opinion polls carried out in the late 1980s showed that a majority of women identified themselves as feminists and believed a feminist movement was still necessary to improve women's situation in society.[33] In the wake of a Supreme Court decision threatening abortion rights in the summer of 1989, a powerful pro-choice movement had been mobilized.

To those who remembered the prefeminist era, it was clear that there had been a sea change in the unconscious sexism that once pervaded everyday life. For example, put-downs masked as flattery—"You think like a man"; "Don't bother your pretty little head about it"—and the assumption that victims of rape or wife battering had "asked for it" were no longer tolerated.

As the writer Ellen Willis observes, there is a "profound difference between a society in which sexism is the natural order, whether one likes it or not, and one in which sexism is a problem, the subject of debate, *something that can be changed.*"[34]

But if the old order had crumbled, the nonsexist future seemed a long way off. It had been only half a revolution: women had changed, the family had changed—but other institutions, and men, had not fully accepted or adapted to the changes. Further, the shape of the ideal future seemed unclear. Debates among feminist women were as fierce as those they had with their opponents. Should feminists pursue gender equality or celebrate female difference? Is heterosexuality a pleasure or a source of oppression? The dilemmas raised by the new reproductive technologies—dramatized in the legal battle over the custody of "Baby M"—opened up new fault lines among feminist women.

Whatever the difficulties and frustrations of an unfinished revolution, feminism has irreversibly transformed the social and cultural landscape. Yet the image of a genderless, androgynous world that some early feminists had hoped for, and their opponents had feared, never came to pass. On the other hand, in the Persian Gulf War, Americans did see a scene few could have imagined only a decade or two ago: women saying goodbye to husbands and children and going off to battle.

Paradoxically, as feminism freed women to say no to 1950s assumptions about women's place, it also freed them to embrace what had been devalued, to choose what had been obligatory—to say yes to motherhood, to domesticity, even to femininity. One card-carrying feminist, staying home with a newly adopted baby after "years of 'achievement' in the working world," recently observed: "There is a seductive grace to focusing all your efforts on making a few people happy, creating order and beauty on a small scale, bending to natural rhythms rather than time clocks or deadlines."[35] For some, the

reaction against the glorification of motherhood during the years of the feminine mystique had come almost full circle. In 1987, an article in a feminist journal noted an "obsession with maternity and children that seems to pervade aging feminist circles, a romanticization of motherhood that occasionally rivals that of the fifties."[36]

For younger women, the so-called postfeminist generation, the gains of the movement—expanded employment opportunities, the decline of the sexual double standard,[*] a more symmetrical version of family—have been taken for granted. Today's young women are fervent believers in a new version of the American dream; they want both family happiness and success at work.[38] The difficulty they will have in fulfilling the dream on their own is eventually likely to set the stage for a restructuring of American institutions to meet to new realities of women's—and men's—lives.

NOTES

1. Cohen 1988, pp. 149–53; Echols 1989.
2. Filene 1986, p. 204.
3. Quoted in Cohen 1988, p. 153.
4. Gornick 1978.
5. O'Reilly 1972.
6. Ibid.
7. Filene 1986, pp. 205–6.
8. Cited in Hole and Levine 1971.
9. Ogden 1986, p. 209.
10. Fleming 1988.
11. Freeman 1975, p. 147.
12. Quoted in Astrachan 1988, p. 201.
13. Gornick 1978.
14. Gittelson 1972.
15. McLaughlin et al. 1988.
16. Cited in Degler 1980, p. 448.
17. Chafe 1986, p. 434; Fleming 1988.
18. Chafetz and Dworkin 1987.
19. *Roe v. Wade* 1973.
20. Rosenfelt and Stacey 1987.

---

[*]Lillian Rubin offers evidence, however, that the double standard still persists.[37]

21. Gornick 1978.
22. Morgan 1975/1987.
23. Cited in Hole and Levine 1971.
24. Chafetz and Dworkin 1987.
25. Luker 1984.
26. Mansbridge 1986.
27. Cherlin 1981.
28. Mathews 1982.
29. Ibid.
30. Fuchs 1983.
31. O'Reilly 1972.
32. Chafe 1986.
33. Belkin 1989; Destefano and Colesanto 1990.
34. Echols 1989, p. xv.
35. Solomon 1991.
36. Rosenfelt and Stacey 1987, p. 351.
37. Rubin 1990.
38. Sidel 1990.

REFERENCES

Astrachan, Anthony. 1988. *How Men Feel: Their Response to Women's Demands for Equality and Power.* New York: Anchor Press/Doubleday.

Belkin, Lisa. 1989. "Bars to Equality of Sexes Seen as Eroding, Slowly." *New York Times.* August 20, pp. A1, A16.

Chafe, William H. 1986. *The Unfinished Journey: America Since World War II.* New York: Oxford University Press.

Chafetz, Janet Saltzman, and Anthony Gary Dworkin. 1987. "In the Face of Threat: Organized Antifeminism in Comparative Perspective." *Gender and Society* 1, no. 1. New York: Sage.

Cherlin, Andrew. 1981. *Marriage, Divorce, Remarriage.* Cambridge: Harvard University Press.

Cohen, Marcia. 1988. *The Sisterhood: The True Story of the Women Who Changed the World,* pp. 149–53. New York: Simon and Schuster.

Degler, Carl. 1980. *At Odds: Women and the Family in America from the Revolution to the Present.* New York: Oxford University Press.

Destefano, Linda, and Diane Colesanto. 1990. "Most Believe U.S. Men Have a Better Life." *San Francisco Chronicle.* 5 February, pp. B3, 5.

Echols, Alice. 1989. *Daring to Be Bad: Radical Feminism in America 1967–1975.* Minneapolis: University of Minnesota Press.

Filene, Peter G. 1986. *Him / Her / Self: Sex Roles in Modern America.* Baltimore: Johns Hopkins University Press.

Fleming, Jeanne J. 1988. "Public Opinion on Change in Women's Rights and Roles." In *Feminism, Children and the New Families.* Edited by Sanford M. Dornbusch and Myra H. Strober. New York: Guilford Press.

Freeman, Jo. 1975. *The Politics of Women's Liberation.* New York: McKay.

Fuchs, Victor R. 1983. *How We Live: An Economic Perspective on Americans from Birth to Death.* Cambridge and London: Harvard University Press.

Gittelson, Natalie. 1972. *The Erotic Life of the American Wife.* New York: Delacorte Press.

Gornick, Vivian. 1978. *Essays in Feminism.* New York: Harper & Row.

Hole, Judith, and Ellen Levine. 1971. *Rebirth of Feminism.* New York: Quadrangle Books.

Luker, Kristin. 1984. *Abortion and the Politics of Motherhood.* Berkeley: University of California Press.

Mansbridge, Jane. 1986. *Why We Lost the ERA.* Chicago: University of Chicago Press.

Mathews, Jane De Hart. 1982. "The New Feminism and the Dynamics of Social Change." In *Women's America: Refocusing the Past,* pp. 397–421. Edited by Linda K. Kerber and Jane De Hart Mathews. New York: Oxford University Press.

McLaughlin, Steven D., Barbara D. Melber, John O. G. Billy, Denise M. Zimmerle, Linda D. Winges, and Terry R. Johnson. 1988. *The Changing Lives of American Women.* Chapel Hill: University of North Carolina Press.

Morgan, Robin. 1975/1987. "Rights of Passage." In *A History of Our Time: Readings on Postwar America,* pp. 229–30. Edited by William H. Chafe and Harvard Sitkoff. New York: Oxford University Press. (Originally published in *Ms.* magazine, November 1975.)

Ocden, Annegret. 1986. *The Great American Housewife: From Helpmate to Wage Earner, 1776–1986.* Westport, CT: Greenwood Press.

O'Reilly, Jane. 1972. "The Housewife's Moment of Truth." *Ms.* magazine (Spring): 54–59.

Rosenfelt, Deborah, and Judith Stacey. 1987. "Second Thoughts on the Second Wave." *Feminist Studies* 13, no. 2 (Summer): 341–61.

Rubin, Lillian B. 1990. *Erotic Wars: What Happened to the Sexual Revolution?* New York: Farrar, Straus & Giroux.

Sidel, Ruth. 1990. *On Her Own: Growing Up in the Shadow of the American Dream.* New York: Viking Penguin.

Solomon, Deborah. 1991. "New and Improved?" Review of *Ms.* Magazine. *Women's Review of Books* 8: 9–10.

DISCUSSION QUESTIONS

1. Skolnick compares the typical women's movement activist to those most likely to be active in the conservative countermovement. What are the differences and in what ways do they help account for the different reactions to the goals of the woman's movement?

2. At the end of the selection, Skolnick notes that some second-wave feminists have embraced motherhood and domesticity. Is this a rejection of the goals of the movement? Why or why not?

READING 42

Democracy and the Culture Wars

James Davison Hunter

In the aftermath of the 1960s counterculture, the liberalizing demands of that movement were challenged by a conservative countermovement. As a result, the debates surrounding a number of moral issues have become increasingly polarized as groups on either end of the political spectrum have mobilized to advance their particular positions. James Davison Hunter notes in this passage from Before the Shooting Begins *that some of the most controversial debates focus on the body, with the most obvious examples involving the debates over abortion and homosexuality. Hunter raises concerns about the ability of our society at the moment to engage in actual dialogue over these controversial topics.*

Every generation has its struggles. People being what they are, such struggles are inevitable. In this, of course, we are hardly immune. But in our time, a large region of public contention has opened up that is peculiar for both its moral character and its historical significance.

Think about it for a moment.

At the very center of contemporary cultural conflict in our society—the "culture war," as it has been called—are a cluster of public issues concerned, ironically, with the most private of all matters: the body. Controversies about abortion, sexual harassment, pornography, "vulgar" art or music, sex education, condom distribution, homosexuality, AIDS policy, or euthanasia and the "right to die" all trace back to the human body. Those issues that do not relate to the body deal, more often than not, with the social institutions that claim authority over the body (family, church, school, law and the like). The body, it would seem, is the underlying symbolic of the culture war. This being the case, the politics of the culture war is, in large part, a politics of the body.

But why the body?

Clearly the human body is more than just a biological organism. It also has social meaning and significance. In short, how we understand the body—its functioning, its representation, and its discipline—reveals a particular cultural understanding of nature, what the so-called natural order of things will allow or not allow, and human nature (what it means to *be* human). Indeed, as Michel Foucault has instructed us, the body is ultimately a reflection of, and a central metaphor for, the implicit order that prevails in a civilization.[1]

If the body is indeed a metaphor of the social order, then a conflict over our understanding of the body—latent within all of the issues just mentioned—signals a conflict about (if not a turning point in) the ordering of our social life, and perhaps civilization itself. This is why abortion, to mention the most prominent case, has been and remains so deeply contested. The controversy over abortion carries many layers of meaning, to be sure, but at root it signifies different propositions about what it means to be human. As such, the controversy contains within it a metaphor for two different civilizational ideals in conflict.

In this light we begin to see the significance of the contemporary culture war. Cumulatively, the various issues of cultural conflict point to a deeper struggle over the first principles of how we will order our lives together; a struggle to define the purpose of our major institutions, and in all of this, a struggle to shape the identity of the nation as a whole. In a broader historical perspective, however, this culture war may also mark an epoch-defining moment—although in what sense is still unclear. One thing, though, is certain: when cultural impulses this momentous vie against each other to dominate public life, tension, conflict, and perhaps even violence are inevitable.

Conflict and violence? This observation is not made lightly, if only because *culture wars always precede shooting wars*—otherwise, as Philip Rieff reminds us, the latter wars are utter madness: outbreaks of the most severe and suicidal efforts to escape the implications of any kind of normative order.[2] Indeed, the last time this country "debated" the issues of human life, personhood, liberty, and the rights of citizenship all together, the result was the bloodiest war ever to take place on this continent, the Civil War. There is little doubt that we are in the midst of a culture war of great social and historical consequence, and thus the possibility of conflict and violence should not surprise us. The memory of the shooting murder of abortion provider, Dr. David Gunn of Pensacola, Florida, in February 1993 should stick in our mind as a poignant symbol of just this.

The question this article takes up is whether American democracy can face up to conflict of this subtlety, significance, and potential volatility. Can democratic practice today mediate differences as deep as these in a manner that is in keeping with the ideals set forth in the founding documents of the American republic?[3] Or will one side, through the tactics of power politics, simply impose its vision on all others?

The question is not an idle one—for the simple reason that cultural conflict is inherently antidemocratic. It is antidemocratic first because the weapons of such warfare are reality definitions that presuppose from the outset the illegitimacy of the opposition and its claims. Sometimes this antidemocratic impulse is conscious and deliberate; this is seen when claims are posited as fundamental rights that *transcend* democratic process. The right to have an abortion and the right to life, for example, are both put forward as rights that transcend deliberation. Similarly opposing claims are made on behalf of gay rights, women's rights, the rights of the terminally ill, and so on.

More often than not, though, the antidemocratic impulse in cultural conflict is implicit in the way in which activists frame their positions on issues. This is what is meant by the popular phrase *political correctness*—a position is so "obviously superior," so "obviously correct," and its opposite is so "obviously out of bounds" that they are beyond serious discussion and debate. Indeed, to hold the "wrong" opinion, one must be either mentally imbalanced (phobic—as in *homophobic*—irrational, codependent, or similarly afflicted) or, more likely, evil. Needless to say, in a culture war, one finds different and opposing understandings of the politically correct view of the world.

Consider, by way of illustration, the way in which both sides of the cultural divide in America attempt to identify the other's agenda with the deadly authoritarianism of Germany's Third Reich. One is first tempted to dismiss such associations as the stuff of a cheap polemic merely intended to discredit one's opposition. But such associations are not only found in the purple prose of direct mail or in the sensationalism of demagogues. Below are two compelling statements made by serious intellectual players on—in this case—the issue of abortion. The first was made by novelist Walker Percy in a letter he wrote to the *New York Times* in 1988:

Certain consequences, perhaps unforeseen, follow upon the acceptance of the principle of the destruction of human life for what may appear to be the most admirable social reasons.

One does not have to look back very far in history for an example of such consequences. Take democratic Germany in the 1920s. Perhaps the most influential book published in German in the first quarter of this century was entitled *The Justification of the Destruction of Life Devoid of Value.* Its co-authors were the distinguished jurist Karl Binding and the prominent psychiatrist Alfred Hoche. Neither Binding nor Hoche had ever heard of Hitler or the Nazis. Nor, in all likelihood, did Hitler ever read the book. He didn't have to.

The point is that the ideas expressed in the book and the policies advocated were the product not of Nazi ideology but rather of the best minds of the pre-Nazi Weimar Republic—physicians, social scientists, jurists, and the like, who with the best secular intentions wished to improve the lot, socially and genetically, of the German people—by getting rid of the unfit and the unwanted.

It is hardly necessary to say what use the Nazis made of these ideas.

I would not wish to be understood as implying that the respected American institutions I have named [the *New York Times,* the ACLU, NOW, and the Supreme Court] are similar to corresponding pre-Nazi institutions.

But I do suggest that once the line is crossed, once the principle gains acceptance—juridically, medically, socially—innocent human life can be destroyed for whatever reason, for the most admirable socioeconomic, medical, or social reasons—then it does not take a prophet to predict what will happen next, or if not next, then sooner or later. At any rate, a warning is in order. Depending on the disposition of the majority and the opinion polls—now in favor of allowing women to get rid of unborn and unwanted babies—it is not difficult to imagine an electorate or a court ten years, fifty years from now, who would favor getting rid of useless old people, retarded children, anti-social blacks, illegal Hispanics, gypsies, Jews. . . .

Why not?—if that is what is wanted by the majority, the polled opinion, the polity of the time.[4]

Consider now a second observation made by legal scholar Laurence Tribe:

> The abortion policies of Nazi Germany best exemplify the potential evil of entrusting government with the power to say which pregnancies are to be terminated and which are not. Nazi social policy, like that of Romania, vigorously asserted the state's right to ensure population growth. But Nazi policy went even further. Following the maxim that "Your body does not belong to you," it proclaimed the utter absence of any individual right in the matter and made clear that abortion constituted a governmental tool for furthering Nazi theories of "Aryan" supremacy and genetic purity.
>
> Nazi propaganda constantly emphasized the duty of "Aryans" to have large families. Family planning clinics were shut down, often on the ground of alleged ties with communism. The Third Reich made every effort to control contraception, ultimately banning the production and distribution of contraceptives in 1941. The state, largely at the behest of SS leader Heinrich Himmler, abandoned its commitment to "bourgeois" marriage and undertook to promote the "voluntary" impregnation of "suitable women." Allowances were paid to women, married, or not, for having children.
>
> Abortion and even its facilitation were, in general, serious criminal offenses in Nazi Germany; a network of spies and secret police sought out abortionists, and prosecutions were frequent. By 1943 the penalty for performing an abortion on a "genetically fit" woman was death; those on whose premises abortions were performed risked prison sentences.[5]

Clearly more is involved in these two statements than mere rhetorical posturing. Each passage conveys a deep and well-thought-out suspicion that their opponents embrace an authoritarianism that can only exist at the cost of human liberty and ultimately, perhaps, human life. The perception and the fear of this kind of authoritarianism, reinforced by the quest of both sides to force a *political* solution to these controversies, may be a measure of the extent to which democratic practice has become a thin veneer for the competing "will to power."

Thus, on one side we hear a senior writer for *Christianity Today* "reluctantly praise" the "extremism" of the pro-life movement. Drawing wisdom from the abolitionist movement of the nineteenth century, he concludes that the Civil War (precipitated by the activism of the abolitionists) was ultimately justified because "the nation was redefined as one built on liberty and equality, not compromise."[6] Shall we do the same with abortion or, say, homosexuality? On the other side of the cultural divide we hear Andrew Sullivan of the *New Republic* come to a similar conclusion: "The fracturing of our culture is too deep and too advanced to be resolved by anything but coercion; and coercion . . . is not a democratic option."[7] Indeed!

To be sure, the exercise of state power, even if through conventional politics, can never provide any democratically sustainable solution to the culture war. We must come to terms with the underlying issues of these controversies at a deeper and more profound level. But in a vital democracy, the means to that end are serious public reflection, argument, and debate.

I have used the terms *discussion, debate,* and *argument* loosely in the past few pages to describe how much of the social conflict on the contemporary American scene takes shape. In fact, it would seem as though there is very little real discussion, debate, or argument taking place. Debate, of course, presupposes that people are talking *to* each other. A more apt description of Americans engaged in the contemporary culture war is that they only talk *at* or *past* each other. If it is true that antagonists in this cultural struggle operate out of fundamentally different worldviews, this would seem inevitable. Is it not impossible to speak *to* someone who does not share the same moral language? Gesture, maybe; pantomime, possibly. But the kind of communication that builds on mutual understanding of opposing and contradictory claims on the world? That would seem impossible. And then, too, there is not really much talking, even if it is only past one an-

other. What is heard is rather more like a loud bellowing, in the clipped cadences of a shouting match.

The irony in the way we Americans contend over these issues is striking to say the least. America embodies the longest-standing and most powerful democracy in the world. The principles and ideals that sustain it, not to mention the very founding documents that articulate those ideals, are a source of national pride and a model that many nations around the world strive to imitate. Yet the actual manner in which democratic discussion and debate are carried out in this country has become something of a parody of those ideals: obnoxious, at the very least; dangerous at the worst. In short, the most important and consequential issues of the day are presented through (and all too often based upon) what amounts to slogan, cliché, and aphorism—observations and opinions rendered within a ten-second "sound bite" and manifestos published in the latest direct mail copy or in a paid political advertisement in the *New York Times*. To be honest one would have to admit that advocates on all sides of the issues contested are culpable. And so it is that grave social concerns about the status and role of women are fashioned as anti-family; ethical concerns about the act of abortion are labeled anti-choice; policies rooted in the desire to redress the agelong oppression of minorities are dismissed as quotas; people who are nervous about the social effects of affirmative action risk being called racist; the severe problems of the criminal justice system are represented by the pathos of a Willie Horton or Charles Manson; deep moral quandaries about homosexuality are reduced to pseudopsychoanalytic categories like homophobia; art that questions social mores is decried as smut or blasphemy; and the enduring work of generations of intellectuals and writers is dismissed as the sexist, racist, and heterosexist claptrap of dead white males. The cacophony that too often marks contemporary public "debate" skreighs on.

The problem is not that positions on complex issues are reduced to caricatures, even if the latter are ugly and slanderous. In political discourse this has long been a practice. Rather, the problem is that democracy in America has evolved in such a way that public debate now rarely seems to get beyond these caricatures. Democratic discourse becomes a trade in accusation, an exchange in vilification, and all of this occurs in a context where the first principles of our life together are at stake. The discord taking place in public life, then, goes beyond mere political disagreement following the collapse of consensus over these matters. It is very much a war to impose a new consensus by virtually any political and rhetorical means possible.

What of the average American in all of this? Ordinary Americans greet the bellowing of what now passes as public "discourse" with an attitude something akin to dread. Indeed, there is an exhaustion that characterizes the national spirit when the controversies recur. Surely the rhetoric of public debate is more polarized than we are as a people. And so it is that many Americans wish that these battles would just go away.

Private life, of course, can be a refuge for us. Heaven knows that between finding and keeping a job, making ends meet, holding a marriage together, raising kids, and the like, we have enough to occupy our time and attention. But our biographies invariably intersect the skirmishes of the larger culture war. We are discriminated against in getting a job or in receiving a promotion, a teenage daughter becomes pregnant and pleads for an abortion, a nephew "comes out of the closet," a local group of citizens wants to remove the textbooks from the neighborhood school because they are not multicultural enough—and private life is no longer much of a refuge at all.

And so we find ourselves embroiled in controversy that we seem helpless to influence or change. The terms of the so-called debate have already been set for us by powers and processes over which we have no control. Thus, for all of

the diversity of belief, opinion, and perspective that really does exist in America, diversity is not much represented in public debate. Rather than pluralism, democratic discourse tends to reflect the dualism of opposing extremes. Clearly most Americans do have opinions on the critical issues of our day, but most of the time those opinions conform to neither of the reigning positions. Indeed, the majority of voices that would dissent from either credo are for all practical purposes drowned out by the rhetoric of ideologues. Voices in the middle—of a perplexed or even a well-conceived ambivalence—are rarely if ever given a hearing. Here again, the life and spirit of democratic practice suffers.

There are those who say that the conflict of which I speak—the culture war—is not terribly important in the final analysis. Cultural issues, these critics say, are tangential to the "real" issues: labor law; the allocation of tax burdens and government expenditures; the struggle for limited resources in the workplace, in neighborhoods, and in schools; the emergence of a predominantly black underclass and its relation to welfare, crime, and illegitimacy; and so on. It is these more basic issues, they say, that really challenge democracy. Culture is epiphenomenal—a silly national sideshow.

No one would deny the importance of economics, labor, international finance, and the like, but is it not unwise and ultimately artificial to draw a line separating the "hard" issues of economics or the state from the "soft" issues of culture? (This is what Marx tried to do in his unfortunate distinction between economic "substructure" and the legal/political/cultural "superstructure.") Surely the way that we cope with these so-called hard issues is a function of our normative assumptions and ideals (and our interests, justified by these ideals). What issue is *not* filtered through an ideal grid of how things should be? It is these normative assumptions, principles, ideals, and interests—often unspoken and unaccounted for—that define us as a nation. It is these ideals that are in conflict, and it is for this reason that issues seemingly unrelated to those of the culture war are nevertheless affected by it.

Even some who recognize the significance of contemporary cultural conflict nevertheless say that the system for dealing with it is fine as it is. Those who take this position, in my opinion, are ignoring, not listening to—or, more likely, repressing—that which is counter to their own interests. It is the perspective of those sitting on top, like the industrialists of the past (and some even today) who ignored the voices of the workers they employed. Then, as now, there is a disenfranchisement that those in power refuse to acknowledge. As Rieff teaches us, such "repression is the Freudian word for lying to oneself without ever quite knowing it."[8]

Still others would contend that the conduct of democratic debate today may not be perfect, but it is certainly as robust as it ever has been in the past. This, too, misses the point. What haunts us about the character of contemporary public discourse is not so much a distant legacy of high democratic conduct deep within American experience. It is always a mistake to elevate the past as though it were some gilded age of life as it should be—an Edenic time from which we have fallen and that we now yearn to regain. The harsh details of the historical record insist that such a past never really existed. The memory that invokes this imagery is selective and fragmented; its effect is nostalgia, but its purpose is usually ideological. What haunts us, rather, is not a legacy of past experience but an ideal: the ideal that a just and democratic order that we all aspire to requires that somehow we do it a little bit better.

To realize fully the promise of the democratic ideal, of course, is a fantasy of utopian proportions. "Do not expect Plato's ideal republic," Marcus Aurelius said long ago, "be satisfied with even the smallest step forward, and consider this no small achievement."[9] The old Stoic's words chide us for any unwarranted idealism we might secretly cherish. His warning should indeed be the epigraph of this entire essay. Even so, one might think that with more than two hundred years of practice we would be wise to new problems that arise and how they might be addressed. If this is not an unreasonable assumption, then why does public discourse in the world's most powerful democracy continue to be so dangerously shallow at such a critical time in its history?

Struggle is inevitable, to be sure. Our predicament is that the stakes of the struggle we are in are so very high, while our ability to cope with the realities—not just the symbols—of that struggle is notably wanting. Let me be clear: democracy will not emerge phoenix-like from the ashes of the culture was. It will either be trivialized or revitalized. This book is a search for the common ground in American life where a more substantial and robust debate about the public good/goods can be engaged and sustained.

Why is such debate relevant? *If the culture was is really a war over first principles of how we will order our lives together, then the only just and democratic way beyond the culture war is through it—by facing up to the hard, tedious, perplexing, messy, and seemingly endless task of working through what kind of people we are and what kind of communities we will live in.* If we say the cleavages are too deep to resolve any other way, then it is time to choose sides and set up the barricades. If, however, we say they are not—if we choose to be democrats, pledging to face up to our deepest differences without harming each other, and to resolve them in a manner fitting the ideals of democratic governance—then it behooves us to look carefully not for the middle ground of compromise, but for common ground in which rational and moral suasion regarding the basic values and issues of society are our first and last means to engage each other. This is the democratic imperative.

The culture war will be with us for some time to come. Racial conflict, gays in the military (and in the rest of society), multiculturalism, text-book controversy, condom distribution to school-age children, arts funding, fetal tissue research, the tense relationship between church and state, reproduction technology, and the like all will be flash points in the coming years for this deeper conflict. Yet rather than deal with this larger matter through the entire range of controversies, I focus here on one controversy in particular—the one surrounding abortion—as a window into the relationship between democratic practice and the culture war as a whole. The special significance of the abortion controversy has been mentioned already. It not only mirrors the culture war as a whole, it has been a centerpiece of our postmodern politics (the politics of the body) for many years. Abortion remains the knottiest moral and political dilemma of the larger culture war, contested now for more than two decades with little hope of a satisfying resolution. Pitting the basic human concerns of life and liberty against each other, it brings home to most Americans the stakes of the entire cultural conflict. It is, then, an ideal case—a prism, if you will—through which to explore how democratic practice faces up to the larger challenges of our time. If the common ground of democratic argument can be found here, it can be found anywhere.

NOTES

1. See Michel Foucault, *The History of Sexuality, Volume I* (New York: Vintage, 1990).
2. Philip Rieff, "The New Noises of War in the Second Culture Camp: Notes on Professor Burt's Legal Fictions," *Yale Journal of Law and the Humanities,* 3, no. 2 (Summer 1991), 324.
3. As my colleague G. W. Sheldon has written, "If we wish to continue flattering ourselves as 'the nation of Jefferson,' every generation of Americans is obliged to determine how well its society and values measure up to Jefferson's hope for the new American republic" G. W. Sheldon, *The Political Philosophy of Thomas Jefferson* (Baltimore: Johns Hopkins University Press, 1991), 147. This book is written in the spirit of that obligation.
4. The letter was unpublished and was unacknowledged. He wrote again three weeks later with a copy enclosed. In his follow-up he said, "The pur-

pose of this letter is to establish for the record that you did in fact receive the first letter. For if I do not receive an answer to this letter, it is fair to assume that you did." Percy received no reply. The original letter and his follow-up note are published in Walker Percy, *Signposts in a Strange Land,* ed. Patrick Samway (New York: Noonday Press, 1991).

5. Laurence Tribe, *Abortion: The Clash of Absolutes* (New York: Norton, 1990), 58. Several endnotes in his text have been deleted here for the sake of readability.
6. Tim Stafford, "In Reluctant Praise of Extremism," *Christianity Today,* 26 October 1992, 18–24. Some pro-life advocates *would* sanction violence. The response of some grass-roots pro-life supporters to the murder of David Gunn was chilling in this regard. "Obviously, not all killing is murder," said one woman from Grants Pass, Oregon. "The Bible is full of instances where God told people to kill other people. . . . Griffin did not shoot Mother Teresa; he shot a mass murderer no different from the likes of Hitler or Saddam Hussein. I do not rule out the possibility that when a government refuses to stop mass murders, God raises up people who will." Said another, "Even President Lincoln realized that God demands a price from a nation that prizes such 'national offences,' and that . . . price is war and death, not love and peace." (These statements were taken from the letters-to-the-editors section of *World,* 17 April 1993, p. 5. The letters were all in response to an editorial by John Seel entitled "Killing the Baby Killers.")
7. Andrew Sullivan, "Washington Diarist: Losing Ground," *New Republic,* 14 December 1992, 46.
8. Rieff, "New Noises of War," p. 354.
9. Marcus Aurelius Antoninus, from his *Meditations,* Book IX, 29 (Indianapolis: Hackett Publishing Company, 1988), pp. 92–93.

DISCUSSION QUESTIONS

1. Do you agree or disagree with Hunter's charged language in describing current conflicts over issues such as abortion and homosexuality as "culture wars"? Why or why not?
2. Choose one of the several conflicts Hunter notes in the article and attempt to define what might be a middle ground between the two polar extremes.

SOCIAL CHANGE

Sociology arose in the 19th century during a period of unprecedented social change. The classic founders of the discipline—Karl Marx, Émile Durkheim, Max Weber, and Georg Simmel—were preoccupied with change, so much so that one might say with some justice that sociology is first and foremost the study of change. Sociology was both the product of and an attempt to make sense of what historian E. J. Hobsbawm has referred to as the "Age of Revolution." What he had in mind was the combined impact of the economic transformation brought about by the Industrial Revolution, the rise of modern democracy as a consequence of the American and French Revolutions, and the emergence of modern culture, with its profound impact on all facets of life, including religion, the arts, and science. Thus, sociology was premised on the idea that contemporary societies—or at least those of western Europe and North America—were experiencing profound shifts: from agrarian to industrial economies, from aristocratic to democratic polities, and from traditional to modern cultures. The task of sociology was, simply, to comprehend the contours and the impacts of social change.

Out of this tradition, sociology has consistently sought to understand the implications of change in all realms of social life. If in the 19th century there was an interest in assessing the impact of such technological innovations as the steam engine, the new machinery used in the textile industry, the blast furnace, and electricity, contemporary sociologists are interested in the societal impact of nuclear reactors, petrochemicals, television, and computers. If 19th-century political analysts were interested in the expansion of democracy in nation-states, today's political sociologists are interested in what democracy means in an increasingly globalized world. If 19th-century analysts of culture studied the effect of the innovative character of Beethoven on the classical tradition, their 20th-century counterparts are preoccupied with entirely new musical genres, such as rock and jazz. In short, although the particulars change, there is a remarkable continuity about the kinds of concerns to which sociologists past and present have devoted their energies.

Sociologists ask, In what ways have these macrosocial patterns of change transformed the major institutions of society? What are their implications for organized social life? What do they mean for social relations? What are the positive consequences of change? What are the negative implications?

Gradually during the past quarter of a century a growing chorus of sociologists has become convinced that we have entered yet another era of profound change. As a result, we increasingly hear attempts to define the present in relation to the immediate past. Some see the shift as one that occurred gradually. Thus they speak of the shift from industrial to advanced industrial society. On the other hand, others think the changes have been more dramatic, and thus they use terms that imply a break with the immediate past, with the two most commonly used terms in this regard being postindustrial and postmodern. The four articles in this section address topics that point to various aspects of contemporary social change that have created new possibilities and new problems.

When Work Becomes Home and Home Becomes Work

Arlie Hochschild

For millions of Americans, balancing the time demands of work and family has proved to be a difficult and frustrating task, one that leaves many feeling that they are experiencing "time famine." In this case study of a large corporation that has been given the pseudonym Amerco, Arlie Russell Hochschild explores the ways employees try to juggle work and family, and how they feel about their situations. In this passage from The Time Bind, *she discusses the perception on the part of some workers that they, in effect, feel more at home at their jobs than when they are with their families, and provides insights into why this situation has arisen.*

Amerco, a highly profitable, innovative company, had the budget and the will to experiment with new ways to organize its employees' lives. Its Work-Life Balance program could have become a model, demonstrating to other corporations that workforce talents can be used effectively without wearing down workers and their families. But that did not happen. The question I have asked is: Why not? The answer, as we have seen, is complex. Some working parents, especially on the factory floor, were disinclined to work shorter hours because they needed the money or feared losing their jobs. Though not yet an issue at Amerco, in some companies workers may also fear that "good" shorter-hour jobs could at any moment be converted into "bad" ones, stripped of benefits or job security. Even when such worries were absent, pressure from peers or supervisors to be a "serious player" could cancel out any desire to cut back on work hours. The small number of employees who resolved to actually reduce their hours risked coming up against a company Balashev. But all these sources of inhibition did not fully account for the lack of resistance Amerco's working parents showed to the encroachments of work time on family life.

Much of the solution to the puzzle of work-family balance appeared to be present at Amerco—the pieces were there, but they remained unassembled. Many of those pieces lay in the hands of the powerful men at the top of the company hierarchy, who had the authority and skill to engineer a new family-friendly work culture but lacked any deep interest in doing so. Other pieces were held by the advocates of family-friendly policies lower down the corporate ladder, who had a strong interest in such changes but little authority to implement them. And the departmental supervisors and managers, whose assent was crucial to solving the puzzle, were sometimes overtly hostile to anything that smacked of work-family balance. So even if the workers who could have benefited from such programs had demanded them, resistance from above would still have stymied their efforts.

But why *weren't* Amerco working parents putting up a bigger fight for family time, given the fact that most said they needed more? Many of them may have been responding to a powerful process that is devaluing what was once the essence of family life. The more women and men do what they do in exchange for money and the more their work in the pubic realm is valued or honored, the more, almost by definition, private life is devalued and its boundaries shrink. For women as well as men, work in the marketplace is less often a simple economic fact than a complex cultural value. If in the early part of the century it was considered unfortunate that a woman had to work, it is now thought surprising when she doesn't.

People generally have the urge to spend more time on what they value most and on what they are most valued for. This tendency may help explain the historic decline in time devoted to private social relations,[1] a decline that has taken on a distinctive cultural form at Amerco. The valued realm of work is registering its gains in part by incorporating the best aspects of home. The devalued realm, the home, is meanwhile taking on what were once considered the most alienating attributes of work. However one explains the failure of Amerco to create a good program of work-family balance, though, the fact is that in a cultural contest between work and home, working parents are voting with their feet, and the workplace is winning.

In this respect, we may ask, are working parents at Amerco an anomaly or are they typical of working parents nationwide? In search of an answer, I contacted a company called Bright Horizons, which runs 125 company-based childcare centers associated with corporations, hospitals, real estate developers, and federal agencies in nineteen states.[2] Bright Horizons allowed me to add a series of new questions to a questionnaire the company was sending out to seven thousand parents whose children were attending Bright Horizons Children's Centers. A third of the parents who received questionnaires filled them out. The resulting 1,446 responses came from mainly middle- or upper-middle-class parents in their early thirties.[3] Since many of them worked for Fortune 500 companies—including IBM, American Express, Sears, Roebuck, Eastman Kodak, Xerox, Bausch and Lomb, and Dunkin' Donuts—this study offers us a highly suggestive picture of what is happening among managers and professional working parents at Amerco's counterparts nationwide.

These parents reported time pressures similar to those Amerco parents complained about. As at Amerco, the longest hours at work were logged by the most highly educated professionals and managers, among whom six out of ten regularly averaged over forty hours a week. A third of the parents in this sample had their children in childcare forty hours a week or more.[4] As at Amerco, the higher the income of their parents, the longer the children's shifts in childcare.

When asked, "Do you ever consider yourself a workaholic?" a third of fathers and a fifth of mothers answered yes. One out of three said their *partner* was workaholic. In response to the question "Do you experience a problem of 'time famine'?" 89 percent responded yes. Half reported that they typically brought work home from the office.[5] Of those who complained of a time famine, half agreed with the statement "I feel guilty that I don't spend enough time with my child." Forty-three percent agreed that they "very often" felt "too much of the time I'm tired when I'm with my child." When asked, "Overall, how well do you feel you can balance the demands of your work and family?" only 9 percent said "very well."

If many of these Bright Horizons working parents were experiencing a time bind of the sort I heard about from Amerco employees, were they living with it because they felt work was more rewarding than family life? To find out, I asked, "Does it sometimes feel to you like home is a 'workplace'?" Eighty-five percent said yes (57 percent "very often"; 28 percent "fairly often"). Women were far more likely to agree than men. I asked this question the other way around as well: "Is it sometimes true that work feels like home should feel?" Twenty-five percent answered "very often" or "quite often," and 33 percent answered "occasionally." Only 37 percent answered "very rarely."

One reason some workers may feel more "at home" at work is that they feel more appreciated and more competent there. Certainly, this was true for many Amerco workers I interviewed, and little wonder, for Amerco put great effort into making its workers feel appreciated. In a large-scale nationwide study, sociologists Diane Burden and Bradley Googins found that 59 percent of employees rated their family performances "good or unusually good," while 86 percent gave that rating to their performances on the job—that is, workers appreciated *themselves* more at work than at home.[6] In the Bright Horizons national survey, only 29 percent felt appreciated "mainly at home," and 52 percent "equally" at home and work. Surprisingly, women were not more likely than men to say they felt more appreciated at home.

Often, working parents feel more at home at work because they come to expect that emotional support will be more readily available there. As at Amerco, work can be where their closest friends are, a pattern the Bright Horizons survey reflected. When asked, "Where do you have the most friends?" 47 percent answered "at work"; 16 percent, "in the neighborhood"; and 6 percent, "at my church or temple." Women were far more likely than men to have the most friends at work.[7]

Some workers at Amerco felt more at home at work because work was where they felt most relaxed. To the question "Where do you feel the most relaxed?" only a slight majority in the Bright Horizons survey, 51 percent, said "home." To the question "Do you feel as if your life circumstances or relationships are more secure at work or at home?" a similarly slim majority answered "home." I also asked, "How many times have you changed jobs since you started working?" The average was between one and two times. Though I didn't ask how many times a person had changed primary loved ones, the national picture suggests that by the early thirties, one or two such changes is not unusual. Work may not "always be there" for the employee, but then home may not either.

I should have asked what arena of life—work or family—was most engrossing. Amerco parents loved their children but nonetheless often found life at work more interesting than life at home. The workplace, after all, offered a natural theater in which one could follow the progress of jealousies, sexual attractions, simmering angers. Home, on the other hand, offered fewer actors on an increasingly cramped stage. Sometimes, the main, stress-free, "exciting" events at home came during the time Americans spend watching television. (According to one study, Americans spend about 30 percent of their free time in front of the television.)[8]

For this sample, then, we find some evidence that a cultural reversal of workplace and home is present at least as a theme. Unsurprisingly, more people in the survey agreed that home felt like work than that work felt like home. Still, only to half of them was home a main source of relaxation or security. For many, work seemed to function as a backup system to a destabilizing family. For women, in particular, to take a job is often today to take out an emotional insurance policy on the uncertainties of home life.

The Bright Horizons parents—middle- and upper-middle-class employees of large corporations who had children in childcare—are a good match for many Amerco parents, and the results of the survey confirm that much of what we have seen in Spotted Deer is in fact happening across the nation. Obviously, however, many working parents do not resemble those in the Bright Horizons group. What kinds of families might be omitted from this sample, and what are *their* experiences of work and home and the relation between the two? As a start, we need to recognize at least four other models of family and work life, each based on the relative emotional magnetism of home and work. Most real families, of course, blend aspects of more than one of them.

There would be a "haven model," for instance, in which work *is* a heartless world and family still a haven. Amerco workers who fit this traditional "haven model" to any extent tended to be factory hands, who did jobs that were relatively unpleasant and lacked on-the-job community. For many blue-collar men and even more women, home is still often—though as Deb and Mario Escalla's story indicates not always—far more of a haven than work. When I asked women whether they would continue to work if they did not need the money, the proportion who answered "no" rose as occupational level fell. This, in part, may reflect the fact that, over the last decade as the rich have become richer and the poor poorer, those with "desirable" jobs have generally found their jobs to be ever more inviting (with more carefully engineered workplace cultures and more impressive corporate perks). Those with "undesirable" jobs, on the other hand, have generally found them ever less welcoming (with little cultural engineering, growing vulnerability to technological displacement, greater insecurity, and declining pay). Many of these "have-nots" may still look to home as a haven, no matter what the realities of their actual home lives.

Bill and Emily Denton fit another "traditional" model, in which home and work each exhibit gender-specific pulls. Bill, and men like him at the top of the corporate ladder, flee neither a dismal workplace nor a stressful home. They make pleasurable "homes" for themselves at an office to which they devote most of their waking hours, while their real homes become like summer cottage retreats. Wives like Emily are then left to manage home and children. For them, home is not a refuge from the workday world, but a potentially fulfilling world in its own right. This old-style model of work-family balance in which each sphere of life is given to one gender is on the decline even among top executives at corporations like Amerco. The magnetic pull of work is drawing some executive wives out of the house; while for those who remain the appeal of housewifely and motherly duties and pleasures has probably diminished.

There is also a "no-job, weak-family" model, in which neither work nor home has any strong attraction for the individual. Poor people who can't find work and to whom a job may be the economic and emotional prerequisite for a reasonable family life would fit this model. In his book *When Work Disappears,* focusing on the plight of African Americans, the sociologist William Julius Wilson has argued that without a New Deal–style national public works program many blacks will find themselves living in a spreading economic desert.[9] Inner city street corner and gang life, buoyed by an underground economy, loom ever larger as substitute sources of appreciation, relaxation, and security, while

drugs help provide the temporary illusion that these ideals are really within one's grasp.

Finally, there is the "work-family balance" model in which parents take advantage of family-friendly options at work and do not crave time on the job so much that they are tempted to steal it from time allotted to their children. Such parents might begin to break the time-deficit cycle and so escape the need for a third shift at home. This model was a reality for a small minority at Amerco, and probably a larger minority nationwide.

If families matching the "haven" and "traditional" models are on the decline, and families matching the "no-job, weak-family" model fluctuate with the economic times, families that fall into the reversal model in which home is work and work is home have been on the increase over the last thirty years. But what social conditions have been fostering this change? The takeover of the home by the workplace is certainly an unacknowledged but fundamental part of our changing cultural landscape.

BEHIND REVERSING WORLDS

Although work can complement—and, indeed, improve—family life, in recent decades it has largely competed with the family, and won. While the mass media so often point to global competition as the major business story of the age, it is easy to miss the fact that corporate America's fiercest struggle has been with its local rival—the family. Amerco company officials worry about their battles for market share with companies in Asia and Europe. But they take for granted their company's expanding share of domestic time. For where the workplace invests in its employees, as at Amerco, it often wins the emotional allegiance of its workers—and so ever more of its workers' time.

The ascendancy of the corporation in its battle with the family has been aided in recent years by the rise of company cultural engineering and, in particular, the shift from Frederick Taylor's principles of scientific management to the Total Quality principles originally set out by W. Edwards Deming.[10] Under the influence of a Taylorist worldview, the manager's job was to coerce the worker's mind and body, not to appeal to his heart. The Taylorized worker was deskilled, replaceable, cheap, and as a consequence felt bored, demeaned, and unappreciated.

Using more modern participative management techniques, companies now invest in training workers to "make decisions" and then set before their newly "empowered" workers moral as well as financial incentives. Under Taylor's system, managers assumed that workers lacked the basic impulse to do a good job. Under Total Quality, managers assume workers possess such an impulse. Under Taylorism, the worker was given no autonomy. Under Total Quality, the worker has a certain amount of autonomy and is drawn further into the world of work by the promise of more.

As the Amerco work environment illustrates, the Total Quality worker is invited to feel recognized for job accomplishments. The company publishes a quarterly magazine, *Amerco World,* that features photos of smiling workers credited with solving problems, anticipating bottlenecks, inventing new products, reducing errors, and otherwise "delighting the customer." In describing its application of the Total Quality system before the House Subcommittee on Science, Research, and Technology, an Amerco vice president noted that the company preferred to reward quality work with personal recognition rather than money. Personal recognition, he pointed out, has proved an extremely effective motivational tool, one far less likely to create the jealousies that often result from giving financial rewards to some workers and not others. Company surveys confirm this.

At Amerco, employees are invited to feel relaxed while on the job. Frequent recognition events reward work but also provide the context for a kind of play. Amerco's management has, in fact, put thought and effort into blurring the distinction between work and play (just as that distinction is so often blurred at home). Fridays during the summer, for instance, are "dress down" days on which employees are urged to dress "as though" they are at home; and the regular rounds of company picnics, holiday parties, and ceremonies are clearly meant to invest work with celebratory good feeling. For white-collar workers at Amerco headquarters, there are even free Cokes, just as at home, stashed in refrigerators placed near coffee machines on every floor.

Amerco has also made a calculated attempt to take on the role of helpful relative in relation to employee problems at work and at home. The Education and Training Division offers employees free courses (on company time) in "Dealing with Anger," "How to Give and Accept Criticism," "How to Cope with Difficult People," "Stress Management," "Taking Control of Your Work Day," and "Using the Myers-Briggs Personality Test to Improve Team Effectiveness." There are workshops in "Work-Life Balance for Two-Career Couples" and "Work-Life Balance for Single Adults." At home, people seldom receive anything like this much help on issues so basic to family life. At home, there were no courses on "Coping with Your Child's Anger over the Time Famine" or "Dealing with Your Child's Disappointment in You or Yours in Him."

As a result, many Amerco managers and professionals earnestly confessed to me that the company had helped them grow as human beings in ways that improved their ability to cope with problems at home. Even in the plants, training in team building sometimes instills similar feelings in the workers. One Amerco handout for its managers lists a series of "qualities for excellence at work" that would be useful at home—an employee would be judged on whether he or she "seeks feedback on personal behaviors," "senses changes in attention level and mood," or "adapts personality to the situation and the people involved." Amerco is also one of about a hundred companies that enrolls its top executives in classes at the Corporate Learning Institute. There, managers learn how to motivate and influence others and manage conflict. The Institute offers an open-ended "personal focus program designed for people from all walks of life who have a genuine desire to explore and expand their unique possibilities." One can, at company expense, attend a course on "Self-Awareness and Being: The Importance of Self in the Influence Process."[11]

The Total Quality worker is invited to feel committed to his company. When, in *Modern Times,* a speedup finally drives the Taylorized Charlie Chaplin crazy, he climbs into a giant complex of cogs and belts and is wound around a huge wheel. He has become part of the machine itself. How could he feel committed to a company that had turned him into a machine part?

Under Total Quality at Amerco, the worker is not a machine; he's a believer. This became clear to me when I witnessed a "Large Group Change Event," held in a high school cafeteria one summer morning in 1992. The event, Amerco's response to losing customers to a growing competitor, was staged somewhat like a revival meeting. Its purpose was to convince each worker to renew his commitment not to his spouse or church but to his workplace. It was one of a series of such events held at underproducing plants in the valley. Two banners hanging at the entrance said, "Show Our Commitment." Four hundred workers, most of them white men between the ages of twenty and forty, were assembled eight to a table. They tended to sport tee-shirts, blue jeans, and baseball caps worn back to front. One young man in sunglasses casually lifted his leg over the back of his chair as if mounting a horse and sat down to join his group. "What's frustrating about your job?" the group leader asked.

"A few supervisors don't have anything to do but watch for you to make a mistake," one man responded. "Why don't they just get to work themselves?"

Talk soon turned to the effect the morning's proceedings might have on life at home. George, twenty-two, his hair in a Mohawk, volunteered, "Me and my wife just got back together. We were going down to New Orleans for a trip; but now this event comes along."

"If we keep this plant open," another worker replied wryly, "that will help keep your family together more than going on some trip."

The organizer of the event then introduced three people, a plant manager, an investor, and a union representative, each emphasizing the need to improve production in the next six months. As a revivalist minister might plumb the depths of sin, the plant manager described how "low down" plant production had sunk, how many fewer defects per million parts Amerco's competitors had, and how many more employee-initiated ideas (or, as they were calling them, Corrective Action Requests) their plants were generating each year. He went on to bemoan Amerco's declining share of the market.

The union representative, who had been a mold maker at another company for twenty-six years, told how his plant had merged with another, then closed. "We lost over 400 jobs in a town of 2,000," he said. "This is what American industry and labor face today." To think up good ideas, to concentrate harder, to be more careful, to cooperate with the coworkers on your team—these were, he suggested, patriotic as well as pro-labor acts.

Workers were then handed pads of Post-its and asked to write down good ideas, which would be stuck on a large wall in the cafeteria under the heading, "Action Ideas." Typical Post-its read: "Don't throw safety goggles away." "Recycle the water." "Don't need to wax the floor three times a day—save money." Each eight-person group was then given twenty-one adhesive gold stars and asked to vote for the best suggestions by sticking stars on the wall next to the action ideas of which they most approved. Back at their tables, workers discussed the stars their groups, now renamed "Worker-Manager Improvement Teams," had given out.

Each team was then asked to consider the question "What am I willing to commit to?" Men at one table talked about quitting their horseplay, their back talk, their slowdowns. They vowed to "cast out the devil" of taking petty revenge on the company for the tediousness of their jobs.

The event organizer then asked all the workers to take a Meyers-Briggs Personality Test using pamphlets and pencils set out on the tables.[12] This test focuses on one's capacity for teamwork, one's tendency to lead or follow, to stand up or hide, to work fast or slow. "Who here is an introvert? Who is an extrovert?" People volunteered and were then asked, "Is your personality getting in the way of committing yourself to improvement?" As was the intent of the whole meeting, the test tacitly invited these blue-collar workers to take on a managerial viewpoint in which people skills matter more than brawn, in which you and the company both should care about what type of personality you have and how it best suits the workplace. They were invited to leave their individual fates behind and try, like any executive, to envision, care about, and plan for the fate of the company.[13]

At the end of the event, to signify their new "commitment," workers inscribed their names on one of the immense red banners that hung at the cafeteria entrance. They signed with fancy long g's and tall t's, with lines under their names, and curlicued s's. Under some names they bracketed nicknames, others as in a high school yearbook were cleverly written inside one of the banner's larger letters that corresponded to the beginning letter of a name.

The event had climaxed with a promise of redemption. Workers had offered themselves up, name by name, to be "saved" from unemployment, and to save the company from falling profits. Amerco, too, wanted these workers to be saved, not laid off. It had already spent four million dollars to get the "mission" of Total Quality out to the plants—and now it was spending even more to save plants and jobs. That said something in itself, the workers felt: Amerco cared.

This sense of being cared for encouraged workers to adopt a more personal orientation toward work time. If, in *Modern Times,* Chaplin, like millions of real factory workers of his era, found himself the victim of a company-initiated speedup, Amerco's professionals, managers, and even factory workers were being asked to envision themselves as their own time strategists, their own efficiency experts. They were to improve their own production, to manage their own intensified work pace at their own plants, even in their own lives. Under the moral mantle of Total Quality, however, workers weren't being asked to consider the speed of their work—not directly anyway—only its "quality." Meanwhile at home, the same workers were finding that quality was exactly what they had to let go of in order to do a certain quantity of chores in the few hours left to them.

THE TAYLORIZED FAMILY

If Total Quality called for "reskilling" the worker in an "enriched" job environment, capitalism and technological developments have long been gradually deskilling parents at home. Over time, store-bought goods have replaced homespun cloth, homemade soap and candles, home-cured meats and home-baked foods. Instant mixes, frozen dinners, and take-out meals have replaced Mother's recipes. Daycare for children, retirement homes for the elderly, wilderness camps for delinquent children, even psychotherapy are, in a way, commercial substitutes for jobs a mother once did at home. If, under Total Quality, "enriched" jobs call for more skill at work, household chores have over the years become fewer and easier to do.

Even family-generated entertainment has its own mechanical replacement—primarily the television, but also the video game, VCR, computer, and CD player. In the Amerco families I observed, TV cartoons often went on early in the morning as a way to ease children into dressing and eating breakfast. For some families in the evening, CNN or network news lent an aura of seriousness to the mundane task of preparing dinner. After dinner, some families would sit together, mute but cozy, watching sitcoms in which *television* mothers, fathers, and children talked energetically to one another. TV characters did the joking and bantering for them while the family itself engaged in "relational loafing." What the family used to produce—entertainment—it now consumes. Ironically, this entertainment may even show viewers a "family life" that, as in the sitcoms *Murphy Brown* and *Ink,* has moved to work.[14]

The main "skill" still required of family members is the hardest one of all—the ability to forge, deepen, and repair family relationships. Under normal circumstances the work of tending to relationships calls for noticing, acknowledging, and empathizing with the feelings of family members, patching up quarrels, and soothing hurt feelings.

In the wake of the "divorce revolution," this sort of emotional work, always delicate, has become even more complicated and difficult. Two-thirds of the marriages that end in divorce involve children. In *Second Chances,* Judith Wallerstein and Sandra Blakeslee report on a fifteen-year study of sixty middle-class parents and children. Within ten years, half of the children whose parents had divorced had gone through a parent's second divorce; typically, one parent happily remarried and the other did not. Only one child in eight saw both parents remarry happily. Half the women and a third of the men were still intensely angry at their ex-spouses a decade later.

The study provided other insights as well. For one thing, parents and children often saw divorce differently. Two-thirds of the women and half of the men claimed they felt more content with the quality of their lives after divorce,

but only one in ten children felt the same way. Three out of four children felt rejected by their fathers. Yet Wallerstein and Blakeslee found, poignantly enough, that these "rejecting" fathers often maintained phantom relations with the children they didn't see or support, keeping their photographs near at hand. One national study found that half of children aged eleven to sixteen living with a divorced mother had not seen their fathers during the entire previous year.[15]

Family life can be baffling under the best of circumstances. But in a society based on the nuclear family, divorce creates extra strains. Blending and reblending people into remarriage "chains" can be much harder than the word "blend" implies. Stepsiblings in such families are rarely as close as biological siblings—and that's only one of many problems such new families face. One divorced Amerco employee complained that his stepchildren refused to obey him and instead confronted him with the challenge "You're not my *real* Dad!" On the other hand, many divorced mothers also deeply resented the ways their remarried ex-husbands favored their new families. One divorced wife, for instance, observed bitterly that her ex-husband had managed to buy a new car and boat while remaining in arrears on his child support payments. Faced with such issues and in need of emotional "reskilling" few parents at home have the faintest idea where to look for "retraining."

At Amerco, successful completion of on-the-job training is rewarded with a recognition ceremony, a Total Quality pin, and possibly even a mention in the company magazine. At Amerco, large sums of money are spent to stage "commitment ceremonies" between the company and its workers whenever a "divorce" seems to threaten. But who rewards a difficult new kind of emotional work or watches for declining profit margins at home?[16] Who calls for renewed vows of commitment there? . . .

NOTES

1. Those whose time is not compensated by money—housewives, children, the elderly—are held in lower regard than those whose time is compensated by money, everything else held equal. (This holds true only for jobs that are not subject to moral censure; a prostitute is not more highly valued than a housewife because she has a paying job in public life.) For many paid workers themselves, the trade of time for money can take on very different cultural meanings depending on the societal context. (Thanks to Deborah Davis for clarification on the relation between work for money and time.) See Helga Nowotny, *Time: The Modern and the Postmodern Experience* (Cambridge: Polity, 1994); and Staffan Linder, *The Harried Leisure Class* (New York: Columbia University Press, 1974).

2. Founded in 1986, Bright Horizons was named the nation's leading work-site childcare organization in 1991 by the Child Care Information Exchange. The company offers a range of services: drop-in care, weekend programs, and programs for infants, toddlers, preschoolers, and school-age children. Bright Horizons pays its teachers 10 percent more than whatever the going rate may be at nearby childcare centers and has a rate of teacher turnover that averages only half of the industry-wide 40 to 50 percent a year.

3. Thirty-five percent of parents responded (9 percent were male and 90 percent female; 92 percent were married and 7 percent single). Percentages may not add up to 100 for some questions either because some respondents didn't answer that question or because the percentages that are reported were rounded to the nearest whole number.

4. Twenty percent of parents reported that their children were in childcare 41–45 hours a week; 13 percent, 46–50 hours; 2 percent, 51–60 hours. In the lowest income group in the study ($45,000 or less), 25 percent of parents had children in childcare 41 hours a week or longer. In the highest income group ($140,000 or higher), 39 percent did.

5. Parents were asked how many hours they spent doing work they brought home from the office "on a typical weekday." Eighteen percent didn't answer. Of those remaining, half said they did bring work home. The largest proportion—19 percent—brought home "between six and ten hours of work [per week]." They estimated even longer hours for their partners.

6. Diane S. Burden and Bradley K. Googins, "Boston University Balancing Job and Homelife Study" (Boston: Boston University School of Social Work, 1987), p. 30.

7. Yet friends may not be a working parent's main source of social support. When asked which were the "three most important sources of support in your life," nine out of ten men and women mentioned their spouses or partners. Second came their mothers, and third "other relatives." So people turned for support to kin first. Among *friendships,* however, those at work proved more significant than those around home. As sources of emotional support, 10 percent of the respondents also mentioned "books and magazines," the same percentage as mentioned "church or temple"; only 5 percent mentioned neighbors. Thirteen percent turned for support first to friends at work—as many as turned to their own fathers.

8. Jim Spring, "Seven Days of Play," *American Demography* 15 (March 1993): 50–54. According to another study, in the average American home, a television is on for almost half of all waking hours. Teenagers watch approximately twenty-two hours of television each week (Anne Walling, "Teenagers and Television," *American Family Physician* 42 [1990]: 638–41), and children watch an average of two to three hours each day (Althea Huston, John Wright, Mabel Rice, and Dennis Kerkman, "Developmental Perspective of Television Viewing Patterns," *Developmental Psychology* 26 [1990]: 409–21).

9. William Julius Wilson, *When Work Disappears: The World of the New Urban Poor* (New York: Knopf, 1996).

10. W. Edwards Deming. "Improvement of Quality and Productivity through Action by Management." *National Productivity Review,* Winter 1981–82, pp. 2–12. See Mary Walton, *The Deming Management Method* (New York: Dodd, Mead & Co., 1986); Frederick Taylor, *The Principles of Scientific Management* (New York: Harper, 1911). While the Total Quality move-

ment has come to many corporations, the influence of Frederick Taylor is hardly dead. Many low-skill workers are vulnerable to Taylorization of their jobs. In her book *The Electronic Sweatshop* (New York: Simon and Schuster, 1988), Barbara Garson describes a McDonald's hamburger cook whose every motion is simplified, preset, and monitored.

11. Hugh Mulligan, "Employers Foster Friendly Workplaces [Associated Press release]," *Louisville Courier Journal,* 1991. In some companies, such as Hudson Food Inc.'s processing plant in Noel. Missouri, the company hires chaplains as company counselors. As Barnaby Feder describes in his *New York Times* article,

As the workers chop and package the birds' carcasses, others talk about their battles with drinking or drugs, marital tensions, sick parents, runaway children and housing crises. Such chats (with the chaplain) frequently lead to private counseling sessions, hospital visits and other forms of pastoral ministry.

Companies hiring chaplains are, in a sense, offering themselves as sources of the spiritual help that workers need to cope with problems at home (Barnaby J. Feder, "Ministers Who Work around the Flock," *New York Times,* 3 October 1996).

12. The Myers-Briggs Type Indicator (MBTI) is a "self-report questionnaire designed to make Carl Jung's theory of psychological types understandable and useful in everyday life." An Amerco manual states that, among many uses, understanding your type on the MBTI "enhances cooperation and productivity." Types are based on various dimensions of personality extroversion, introversion, sensing, intuition, thinking, feeling, judging, and perceiving. Each type is assumed to make a different kind of contribution to a work team and to need a different kind of support. See Isabel Myers-Briggs, *Introduction to "Type": A Guide to Understanding Your Results on the Myers-Briggs Type Indicator* (Palo Alto, Calif.: Consulting Psychologists Press, 1993), p. 1.

13. Just as Total Quality *expands* workers' authority at work, the declining size of the family and, for men, pressure to share the second shift at home *diminish* their authority at home. On the other hand, women who already have a low degree of

authority in marriages with traditional men sometimes relish jobs where they can at last speak up and be heard. For very different reasons, then, both men and women can feel that their authority is curtailed at home and enhanced at work.

14. As Ella Taylor observes, over the years many television situation comedies have centered on "fun" family-like relationships between coworkers at a workplace. *The Mary Tyler Moore Show* featured a work-family that ran a television news operation; *M*A*S*H* depicted a work-family that operated an army medical unit during the Korean War; and the "familial" coworkers in *Taxi* worked at a cab company. See Ella Taylor, *Prime-Time Families: Television Culture in Postwar America* (Berkeley: University of California Press, 1989); see also Gerard Jones, *Honey, I'm Home! Sitcoms: Selling the American Dream* (New York: St. Martin's Press, 1992).

15. Andrew J. Cherlin, ed., *The Changing American Family and Public Policy* (Washington, D.C.: Urban Institute Press). See Judith Wallerstein and Sandra Blakeslee, *Second Chances: Men, Women, and Children a Decade after Divorce* (New York: Tichnor and Fields, 1989). The authors, unfortunately, do not compare the children from divorced families with those from intact marriages, so we do not know to what degree the children of intact families have comparable experiences. See also P. Bohannon, *Divorce and After: An Analysis of the Emotional and Social Problems of Divorce* (New York: Anchor Books, 1971): and William Goode, *World Revolution and Divorce* (New York: Free Press, 1956).

16. One partial sign of the devaluation of home life is the low status of the homemaker. A national 1981 Harris poll asked. "If you had to place a dollar value on the job of a homemaker, what do you feel fair wages for a year's work would be?" Men said $12,700, women $13,800. Those women who did *paid* work gave homemaking a higher dollar value ($24,000) than homemakers themselves ($13,400), and feminists gave it a higher value ($21,500) than traditionalist women ($19,600). In particular, the value of caring for children seems to have declined. A Harris poll asked adults and teenagers whether they agreed

that "parents today don't seem as willing to sacrifice for their children as parents did in the past." Two-thirds of men and women forty years old and over agreed, as did half of those aged eighteen to thirty-nine (Louis Harris and Associates, *The General Mills American Family Report 1980–81,* conducted by Louis Harris and Associates Inc., Minneapolis, 1981).

DISCUSSION QUESTIONS

1. Compare and contrast the family you grew up in with the families portrayed by Hochschild. Was there evidence of the "time bind" in your family? If so, in what ways did family members respond to it? If not, how did they prevent this situation from arising?
2. Given the reality of large numbers of dual-income households and working single parents, what can be done to provide people with ways to combat the "time bind"?

Toxic Reckoning: Business Faces a New Kind of Fear

Kai Erikson

New threats to the well-being of people have arisen as the unintended negative consequences of scientific and technological developments, constituting what Kai Erikson refers to as a "new species of trouble." The risk of various forms of toxic poisoning, be it from a failed nuclear reactor at Chernobyl or Three Mile Island or chemical poisoning at Bhopal or Love Canal, constitutes a major source of anxiety among the public, even though far fewer people have been killed or injured by these "troubles" than by automobile accidents. This has led some observers to conclude that this reaction on the part of the public is irrational. Erikson disagrees with this assessment and offers a rationale for his position and a call to take seriously the potential dangers of toxic accidents.

On the morning of March 28, 1979, one of two generating units of a nuclear power plant called Three Mile Island experienced an odd sequence of equipment failures and human errors, resulting in the escape of several puffs of radioactive steam. It was a moment of considerable potential danger, as we all were soon to learn. It was a moment of considerable uncertainty as well.

At the height of the uncertainty, Pennsylvania's governor, Richard Thornburgh, issued a calm and measured advisory suggesting that pregnant women and preschool children living within five miles of the plant might want to evacuate and that all other people within ten miles ought to consider taking shelter in their homes. In effect, the governor was recommending that 3,500 persons living in the shadow of the reactor relocate for at least the time being and that everyone else stay put.

Instead, some 200,000 persons were alarmed enough to take to the public highways, and they fled, on average, a remarkable 100 miles. For every person advised to leave home, almost 60 did. This was not the largest evacuation in human history by any means, but it involved the widest discrepancy on record between the scale of an advisory and the scale of an actual evacuation.

Three young geographers from Michigan State University called this the "evacuation shadow phenomenon," meaning the gap between what official wisdom called for and what the people at risk, acting on wisdoms of their own, actually did. Specialists and laypeople alike often try to bridge such a gap with a string of makeshift terms. "Overreaction" is much in vogue these days. So is "irrationality." But to describe the gap in that way, after the fact, is to give it a name without saying anything useful about it. The questions we need to ask are: Of what did that shadow consist? What were the wisdoms on which the evacuees acted? To that we can almost surely answer, a deep and profound dread.

The accident at Three Mile Island is a particularly instructive one, since we know only approximately how much radiation was released and how much harm, if any, it did. So in one sense the feeling generated there was pure dread, perfect dread, the very essence of dread. It was not a reaction to anything the senses could apprehend—the sight of falling bodies, the sound of breaking timbers, the smell of smoke, the sensation of burning eyes, or, in general, the contagious alarm that erupts among people who share a time of danger. There was no panic, just quiet withdrawal over several hours. Each of those 200,000 people (or at least those who made the decision to withdraw on behalf of their families) was reacting to an individual reading of whatever portents could be found in a mute landscape.

What the evacuees feared in this instance was radiation, but it might well have been some other toxic substance. Radiation is but one strain of a whole new species of trouble that we are fated to see more and more of in years to come. Recent events at Three Mile Island and Chernobyl, both of them involving radiation, are of a kind with recent events at Love Canal and Bhopal, both of them involving toxic substances of another sort.

The first thing to say about this new species of trouble is that it is a product of human hands. The ancients dreaded pestilence, drought, famine, flood, plague, and all the other scourges that darken the pages of Revelations. These miseries trouble us today, to be sure, but it is fair to say that we have learned to defend ourselves against many of the worst of them. Some (certain epidemics, for example) we can now arrest or even prevent altogether. Others (like last fall's Hurricane Hugo) we can see far enough in advance to allow people to move out of their paths, thus neutralizing much of their lethal force.

The irony, though, is that technological advances, which have afforded us this degree of protection from *natural* disasters, have created a whole new category of disasters, what specialists have come to call *technological disasters*— what happens when systems fail, humans err, designs prove faulty, engines misfire, and so on.

Earthquakes, tornadoes, floods, hurricanes, volcanic eruptions, and tidal waves belong in the natural category; collisions, explosions, breakdowns, collapses, and crises like those at Chernobyl and Bhopal belong on the technological roster.

Technological disasters have clearly grown in number as we humans test the outer limits of our competence, but, more to the point, they have also grown in scale. Events of local origin, for example, can have consequences that reach across huge distances—as was the case with Chernobyl. And news of an event is broadcast so quickly and so widely that it becomes a moment in everyone's history, a part of our collective consciousness—as was the case with Three Mile Island.

The distinction between natural and technological disasters is sometimes hard to draw exactly. The collapse of a mine shaft in Appalachia is often a collaboration between restless mountain and careless people; an epidemic that spreads across Central Africa owes its virulence both to tough new strains of bacillus and to stubborn old human habits.

However hard it may be to draw, though, that line is usually distinct to victims. Natural disasters are almost always experienced as acts of God or caprices of nature. They happen *to* us. They *visit* us, as if from afar. Technological disasters, however, being of human manufacture, are at least in principle preventable, so there is always a story to tell about them, always a moral to draw, always a share of blame to assign. They provoke outrage rather than acceptance or resignation. They move people to a feeling that this thing should not have happened, that someone is at fault, and that the victims deserve not only compassion and compensation but also something akin to what lawyers call punitive damages. So to understand the feelings and responses that technological disasters provoke, it is crucial to draw the line between crises that are the work of nature and those that are the work of humankind.

The second thing to be said about these new troubles is that they involve toxics. They contaminate rather than merely damage; they pollute, befoul, and taint rather than just create wreckage; they penetrate human tissue indirectly rather than wound the surface by assaults of a more straightforward kind.

At their worst, these disasters can have a malevolence that even the authors of Revelations would have found hard to imagine. And there is growing evidence that they scare human beings in new ways, that they elicit an uncanny fear in us. One of the surest findings to emerge from the new field of risk assessment is that people find radiation and other toxic substances significantly more threatening than most natural hazards and nontoxic technological hazards.

Example: The incident at Three Mile Island gave rise to a round of discussions about evacuation plans at other nuclear power plants, among them the Shoreham plant on Long Island. In the course of that debate, a survey was commissioned by Suffolk County officials to ask Long Island residents how they would react to a mishap at Shoreham. If an accident occurred, one question read, and everyone living within five miles of the plant were advised to stay indoors, what would you do? More than 40% of those residents living within ten miles of the reactor and 25% of all Long Island residents answered that they would flee. And if pregnant women and young children were advised to evacuate? Then 55% of the people within ten miles and more than 33% of the total Long Island population would leave. These are the mildest possible advisories, and the latter was the one officials broadcast at Three Mile Island. More urgent warnings, the survey indicated, would further swell the number of evacuees, adding to the severity of what would surely already be gridlock.

It is important to note that these are expressions of intent and not reports of actual behavior, so they need to be viewed with caution. But the percentage of people who expect to evacuate Long Island and the percentage of those who did in fact evacuate the neighborhood of Three Mile Island are nearly equal, and that degree of corroboration compels an additional measure of respect.

The conclusion that people have an uncommon dread of toxic substances is clearly supported by the few experiences we have to draw on in recent history. In a number of places where radiological and other toxic disasters have struck, the sense of dread lingers long after the incident itself is officially declared over. Fear of radiation was so prevalent in the regions surrounding Chernobyl more than two years after the accident that the Soviet government spoke (scornfully) of "radiophobia." In Goiânia, Brazil, where a small release of cesium-137 killed four persons and contaminated hundreds, officials were surprised to discover that apprehensions seemed to grow rather than decline with the passing of time. Even at Three Mile Island, where there is still no evidence of lasting physical damage, levels of anxiety remain a good deal higher than the experience of other kinds of disasters would suggest. The same is true of Love Canal, which has been extensively studied, and other sites around the world where toxins released into the environment have found their way into human tissues.

This evidence, added together, is still far from decisive. Risk assessment studies remain few and scattered. Surveys like the one conducted on Long Island are both infrequent and inconclusive, and the world can count itself fortunate that accidental laboratories like Goiâniay, Bhopal, and Chernobyl are as rare as they are. In that sense, the information available to us has to be seen as a few brief glances into the heart of things. What we have are not hard scientific conclusions, then, as much as hints, intimations, and auguries, but they are nonetheless important because they may be the leading edge of a wave building just beyond the sight of shore.

Most technical experts seem to assume that increased experience and familiarity will reduce the sense of dread and mystery over time. After all, some 50,000 persons are killed every year in traffic accidents without provoking any widespread public aversion to automobiles; so why should we be so afraid of nuclear power plants and toxic-waste dumps, which, on the face of it, do much less damage? This thought encourages a hope on the part of some experts that people will one day resign themselves to radiological accidents as they have to hurricanes or earthquakes. One of the most thoughtful pronuclear physicists notes how much easier it is to "scare" people than to "unscare" them, but his reading of human history persuades him that people will sooner or later overcome this apprehension, as they did their initial fear of electricity.

Perhaps. But as we wait for the passing of years to deliver that remote verdict, we have many reasons to suppose that toxic emergencies simply nourish dread, that they are, by their very nature, a thing of darkness and foreboding, and thus that over time, the fear may grow rather than diminish. We will dismiss this fear as irrational if, like most experts, we assess the danger by calculating the odds of an accident and then estimating the number of casualties likely to result from it. But there are other reasonings and other reckonings at work in the world. Maybe we should understand radioactive and other toxic substances as naturally loathsome, inherently insidious—horrors, like poison gas, that draw on something deeper in the human mind. That is odd conceptual terrain for a sociologist to be wandering around in, but I want to offer the proposition that toxic emergencies really are different, that their capacity to induce a lasting sense of dread is a unique—and legitimate—property.

I have been describing a generalized feeling of dread that research has found common among laypeople across this country. I want now to consider how these feelings are expressed by people who have experienced toxic emergencies and have reason to believe they have been exposed to potentially dangerous levels of toxicity. I will be calling on the voices of a handful of people who lived through the emergency at Three Mile Island because they lend immediacy to the abstractions that tend to dominate this subject. The voices are those of plaintiffs in a legal action speaking several years after the event, so we have no right to assume that they represent the feelings of everyone in the neighborhood. We do know, however, that the outlooks expressed here are widely shared by residents at Three Mile Island and, moreover, are common to other toxic accidents studied by social scientists—and Love Canal is only the most prominent of several.

The first of two questions I want to ask is: Why do toxic emergencies create so much alarm? Let me note two of their distinguishing characteristics.

For one thing, they are unbounded; they have no frame. We generally use the word "disaster" in normal conversation to refer to distinct events that interrupt the flow of everyday life. Disasters, in that sense, seem to adhere to Aristotle's rules of drama in *Poetics*. They have "a beginning and a middle and an end." They "do not begin and end at random." They have "a certain magnitude" and yet are "easily taken in by the eye." They have *plot*, in short, which is "the first principle and as it were the soul of tragedy."

An alarm sounds the beginning. It is a signal to retreat, to take to storm cellars, to move to higher ground, to crouch in the shelter of whatever cover presents itself. A period of destruction follows, which may be no more than a brief, shattering moment or may last many days. Sooner or later, though, the disaster comes to an exhausted close. The floodwaters recede, the smoke clears, the winds abate, and an "all clear" is sounded, literally or figuratively. Officials announce that the emergency is over and that the time is now at hand for cleaning up. The time has also come for a fire marshal or a sheriff or whoever is in charge of such ceremonies to cast a shrewd eye over the desolation and estimate for the press the dollar value of the property damage. The pain may last, of course; nightmares may continue to haunt, wounds may prove difficult to heal. But the event itself is over, and we will call what happens next the "aftermath." "In the wake of the flood," we will say.

Toxic disasters, however, violate all the rules of plot. Some of them have clearly defined beginnings, such as the explosion that signaled the emergency at Chernobyl or the sudden moment of realization that began the drama of Bhopal; others begin years before anyone senses that anything is wrong, as was the case at Love Canal. But toxic accidents never end. Invisible contaminants remain a part of the surroundings—absorbed into the grain of the landscape, the tissues of the body, and, worst of all, into the genetic material of the survivors. An "all clear" is never sounded. The book of accounts is never closed.

The feeling of uncertainty—the sense of a lack of ending—can begin, paradoxically, the very moment that the event ought logically to be over. Here is the report of a family who heard the advisory, left Three Mile Island, and traveled some 300 miles:

> "So we got in the car and headed south, and we got as far as—I believe it was Durham, North Carolina, where we stopped first. And we didn't know how bad we were hurt. I remember when we went to the motel, I remember sleeping with my hands between my knees, and I was just trembling, worried sick about what this had done to our family and the ones who were still back there.

The uncertainty can continue for months, years, even generations. Others may look on the scene from a safe remove in time or place and consider the emergency over. But those who were there reckon the situation differently.

> What damage would it have on me or on my unborn child? What damage was done to the ground, the surrounding areas? What damage was done to the people who lived around the area at the time and still do? What effect did it have on my daughters, my sons? What took place there that we are not aware of?
>
> I felt sure at that time that we had gotten quite a bit of radiation, and at that point you don't know if you're going to die next week. But because of this, was our life going to be cut short? Just exactly what was going to happen? We still don't know. Are the kids going to get it? Is my husband going to get it? It's nothing to dwell on, I can tell you, because if you dwelled on it every day, you'd be crazy.

Note how often vague referents like "it" or "this" appear in these passages, as if to indicate a nameless bane. To be exposed to radiation or other toxins—in many cases, anyway—is to be contaminated in some deep and lasting way, to feel dirtied, tainted, corrupted. "It will always be there, the contamination," said a 60-year-old woman, speaking of both herself and her environment. A neighbor, a 48-year-old man, added, "I don't feel that the stuff is going to leave. It's still here with us. It's in our bodies, in our genes, and later on, we're going to pay for it."

The second characteristic of radiation and most other toxic substances is that they are without form. You cannot apprehend them through the unaided senses; you cannot taste, touch, smell, or see them. That makes them especially ghostlike and terrifying. Moreover, they invert the process by which disasters normally inflict harm. They do not charge in from outside and batter like a gust of wind or a wall of water. They slink in without warning, do no immediate damage so far as one can tell, and begin their deadly work from within—the very embodiment, it would seem, of stealth and treachery.

The widely observed prohibition against chemical warfare is instructive. Chemical weapons have a special place on the human list of horrors, but it is not immediately obvious why. In World War I, shrapnel proved a good deal more lethal than poison gas, but it earned a much higher public approval rating because it only rips through flesh and tears bodies apart. So the moral case must lie in the way the two work rather than in the amount of damage they do. "Gas is a perfidious, impalpable, and cruel abomination," said an Allied report shortly after the war; "that hellish poison," Winston Churchill called it. Gas is furtive, invisible, and unnatural. In most forms, it moves for the interior, turning the process of assault inside out, thus seeming to violate the integrity of the body. It is evil.

Mary Douglas and Aaron Wildavsky ask in their influential book *Risk and Culture*: "Why is asbestos poisoning seen to be more fearsome than fire?"[1] And Henry Fairlie asks in a recent issue of the *New Republic*: "Why do Americans seem to be more concerned about the risks of pollution than about the budget deficit, economic stagnation, and even war?"[2] The mood of these questions is puzzled disapproval, but the best answer to both would have to draw on the considerations I have just raised. Toxic poisons provoke a special dread because they contaminate, because they are undetectable and uncanny and so can deceive the body's alarm systems, and because they can become absorbed into the very tissues of the body and crouch there for years, even generations, before doing their deadly work. A number of people from Three Mile Island, as elsewhere, noted separately that it is as if they had "a time bomb ticking" within them.

The knowledge that these catastrophes are the work of other humans only intensifies the dread they inspire. They are brought on not by declared enemies but by compatriots, even neighbors, many of whom respond by denying the importance of such crises or by ignoring them. This is an understandable reaction, but it can be devastating to people who consider themselves victims. They feel adrift, devalued, demeaned, robbed of a measure of their human-

ity. Consequently, they often come to see life with an almost corrosive skepticism.

With that in mind, we ought to ponder my second question: What happens to people who experience this dread over long stretches of time? Feelings of helplessness and vulnerability are so common in moments of crisis that they are recognized as one of the identifying psychological symptoms of "trauma" and are a prominent feature of what is widely called "the disaster syndrome." These insecurities, however, can broaden into something more ominous, for survivors of severe disasters can experience not just vulnerability but a feeling of having lost immunity to misfortune, a feeling, even, that something terrible is almost *bound* to happen. If this dread does find a more permanent place in the human imagination, what will be the consequences to society—and to people in positions of managerial authority?

One of the crucial jobs of culture, let's say, is to help people camouflage the actual risks of the world around them—to edit reality so that it seems manageable, so that the perils pressing in on all sides are screened out of our line of vision as we pursue our everyday rounds. Daniel Defoe has *Robinson Crusoe* muse:

> This furnish'd my thoughts with many very profitable reflections, and particularly this one, how infinitely good that providence is, which has provided in its government of mankind such narrow bounds to his sight and knowledge of things; and though he walks in the midst of so many thousand dangers, the sight of which, if discovered to him, would distract his mind and sink his spirits, he is kept serene and calm, by having the events of things hid from his eyes, and knowing nothing of the dangers which surround him.

In most severe disasters, this kind of emotional insulation is stripped away, at least for the moment. But in toxic crises, it happens with a special sharpness, because you can never assume that they are over. What must it be like to have to look these dangers in the eye, without blinders or filters?

---

[1] Mary Douglas and Aaron Wildavsky (Berkeley: University of California Press, 1982), p. 7.
[2] Henry Fairlie, "Fear of Living," January 23, 1989, p. 14.

Scary. You pull in the driveway, and it's like the twilight zone. You think, When I walk into the house, will there be some kind of radiation lingering? It came into your house, and it's going to stay there. You think, Is the food in the refrigerator safe to eat? So you still have that insecure feeling of wondering what is going to happen at TMI [Three Mile Island]. Are they telling us everything? You always have that insecure feeling. I'll always have it.

People stripped of the ability to screen out signs of peril are not just unusually vigilant and unusually anxious. They evaluate the data of everyday life differently, read the signs differently, see patterns that the rest of us are spared from seeing.

My mind is like a little computer. It's always ticking. I figure it even ticks when I'm asleep. I listen more to what people say to me. It's hard to trust. It seems you can trust only the ones close to you. I'm not being paranoid. It's not like that. It's just that these last couple of years I see more, I listen more. I read between the lines more.

When victims reach that level of awareness, evidence that the world is a place of constant peril appears everywhere. It is a rare morning paper or evening broadcast that does not contain news of acid rain, polluted waters, tank-car derailments, toxic-waste dumps, or malfunctions at nuclear power plants (all of which are stories in the news as I write these pages). And even the back pages are full of items to alarm the wary. The following stories were among scores I clipped from two newspapers within a few days: "Plutonium Hazard Found at Nuclear Power Plant," "Dioxin Found in Milk from Paper Cartons," and "Oil Spill Shuts 30-Mile Stretch of Hudson River." If this is the kind of data your mind is sensitive to—the kind of data your eye, made sharp and canny by events of the recent past, is good at taking in—the gloomiest of forecasts seem amply supported.

It will come as no surprise that people who share such an outlook can easily lose confidence in officialdom, not only in designated spokespersons but in certified experts as well. For one thing, officials and experts can lie. Here's a prim, middle-aged woman made blunt by a sense of urgency:

I think—should I say it?—I think that's bullshit. I really do. I think it is. "Everything's under control." Bullshit. Nothing's under control. I don't believe anything they say, if you want to know the truth. I do not believe anything I hear from them.

To make matters worse, however, it is not at all certain that "they" can tell the truth even when they want to, for they don't know what's going on either. They too are out of control.

It's like a child with a grenade in his hand. Sooner or later, he'll figure how to pull the pin and blow his brains out. That's what they're doing down there with nuclear. Just playing with it.

So victims can lose faith not only in the good intentions—that's common enough—but also in the good sense of those in charge of a dangerous universe. Nor is this sensation confined to the immediate neighborhood. The *New Yorker*, reporting ten weeks after Bhopal, when the casualty estimates had reached 2,000 dead and 200,000 injured, put it well:

What truly grips us in these accounts is not so much the numbers as the spectacle of suddenly vanishing competence, of men utterly routed by technology, of fail-safe systems failing with a logic as inexorable as it was once—indeed, right up until that very moment—unforeseeable. And the spectacle haunts us because it seems to carry allegorical import, like the whispery omen of a hovering future.[3]

The most important point to be made here, however, is that when the dread is lasting and pronounced, the spectacle of a failed technology can become the spectacle of a failed environment as well. This outlook is born of the feeling

---

[3] "Talk of the Town," February 18, 1985, p. 29.

that poisons are lodged in the body, that the surrounding countryside is contaminated, that the natural envelope in which people live has become defiled and unreliable. "Dead ground," said one person from Three Mile Island, describing the land he was standing on. He did not mean it was inert and lifeless, like a moonscape. It was, for him, alive with dangers, a terrain in which fresh air and sunshine and all the other benevolences of creation are to be feared as sources of toxic infection. Imagine having to see the natural world through so dark a glass as these four:

I don't even hang wash out anymore, and usually I'm a fanatic on hanging wash out. I don't want to bring in what might be out there.

I used to lie out in the sun, but ever since TMI, I don't. Because I'm thinking about the radiation. What's to say that the stuff isn't coming over and just coming right down on me?

Well, one of the things was you always felt that to get out into the fresh air was so much better than to be inside. Well, it's healthier inside now than outside. So we just spend more time inside. And when you do go out, you have the feeling, Should you be there? Is it going to harm you?

I do not want my grandchildren romping in my backyard. I just don't know what's there. I can't see what's there.

Indeed, everything out there can seem unreliable and fearsome. The vegetables in the garden are no longer dependable: "I went down there and I cut [the asparagus] off and threw it into the weeds. The stuff around here that was growing in the ground was not fit to eat because it was radiated." Nor is the river dependable: "The water's polluted and doesn't even freeze up anymore." Nor is the ground: "We had a very nice yard. Now nothing grows. The land is bad."

People ask them, "Why don't you move to a safer location?" But that is to misunderstand, for there is no safer location. The point is not that a particular region is now spoiled but that the whole world has been revealed as a place of danger and numbing uncertainty.

The whole country. There's no place in this country that you could go that isn't slopped up. There isn't a safe place that you could go where the drinking water isn't bad. The food you get is all poisoned. There's radiation. It isn't like it was when we were kids.

It is important for me to note (once again) that these voices express a fear and a view of the world shared by but a portion of the people at Three Mile Island. I am not suggesting that all survivors of a toxic emergency see things as they do. Those who do, however, are many by any measure and are very likely a majority in some affected places. The fact that waves of people share a common dread not only in such well-known places as Love Canal and Three Mile Island but also in lesser known disaster sites like Centralia (Pennsylvania), Grassy Narrows (Ontario), Northglenn (Colorado), Times Beach (Missouri), and Woburn (Massachusetts)—never mind Bhopal and Chernobyl and Goiânia—should tell us that something important may be happening. The apprehension that seems to preoccupy so much of the population can easily erupt into the feelings expressed above. At the very least, this feeling ranks as another "whispery omen of a hovering future."

Two final thoughts. First, Mary Douglas and Aaron Wildavsky write in *Risk and Culture:*

We turn to a cultural change that has taken place in our own generation. We begin with a sense of wonder. Try to read a newspaper or news magazine, listen to radio, or watch television; on any day some alarm bells will be ringing. What are Americans afraid of? Nothing much, really, except the food they eat, the water they drink, the air they breathe, the land they live on, and the energy they use. In the amazingly short space of fifteen to twenty years, confidence about the physical world has turned into doubt. Once the source of safety, science and technology have become the source of risk. What could have happened in so short a time to bring forth so severe a reaction? How can we explain the sudden, widespread, across-the-board concern about environmental pollution and personal contamination that has arisen in the Western world in general and with particular force in the United States?[4]

Good question. How indeed? Douglas and Wildavsky suggest that environmental movements like the Sierra Club and the Clambake Alliance have helped induce this modern strain of "irrationality" by provoking an unnecessary sense of fear. And there may be something to that thought: environmental groups, feeling they have a world to save, certainly draw on and perhaps even fan the public's fear. But they did not *create* it.

The fear is real, its roots deep, its effects lasting. If science and technology have become the source of risk, as Douglas and Wildavsky assert, it is because toxic peril has moved people so far up the scale of suspicion that they come to distrust not only public officials and experts, not only the social order and the natural world, but also the very ethos of science and technology. And people who begin to doubt the findings of scientists and the inventions of engineers can also begin to lose confidence in logic and reason themselves—a frightening prospect by any reckoning.

Second, the discussion so far has focused on particular crises, incidents that become known as "accidents," "disasters," "events," "catastrophes." In a sense, however, those kinds of incidents are really no more than events of unusual intensity, moments of unusual publicity involving perils that are essentially everywhere. An acute disaster offers us a distilled, concentrated look at something more chronic and widespread.

Sooner or later, the public discussion will have to turn to broader concerns—the fact that radioactive wastes with half-lives measured in the thousands of years will soon be implanted in the body of the earth; that modern industries release toxic matter of the most extraordinary ma-

lignancy into the atmosphere; that poisons that cannot be destroyed or even diluted by the technologies responsible for them have become a permanent part of the natural world. All of which can only add to the level of dread.

Are there lessons here for those who manage modern technologies? My task in this essay has been to note some of the long-term consequences of the chemical age we have entered, not to count its obvious blessings; and I do not suggest for a moment that the costs outweigh the benefits. Still, it seems to me very important that we measure those costs accurately, and toward that end, I would note that the growing sensitivity to matters toxic is *not* some exotic form of hysteria that will subside once the media stops fanning the flames and calm returns to public discourse.

An important role for managers, therefore, may be to become a more credible part of the educational process where toxic dangers are concerned. Increasingly, laypeople expect managers to stonewall in the event of crisis and to underestimate systematically the dangers of the toxic products they are responsible for. Managers do so, I suspect, probably partly in recognition of the fact that the best defense may, after all, be a defense and partly because they fear that open admonitions of danger will only increase what seems to them an irrational public reaction in the first place.

Let me offer two reasons for bending over backward when it comes to informing people of toxic dangers. The first is a matter of raw calculation. When the public channels its dread into organized expression, it can take the form of "toxic torts"—now exploding into legal prominence, much as product liability litigation did some 20 years ago. And this dread can also be channeled into quasi-political movements that virtually become a voice against technology itself. The second reason—far more important—is a matter of common humanity. Toxic accidents damage in special ways. So it goes entirely without saying that everything possible

[4] Douglas and Wildavsky, p. 10.

should be done to prevent them. But to *understand* the dread that people experience may be as important.

The extraordinary number of people who turn to litigation in the hope of repairing a sense of damage caused by noxious substances or who engage in political actions of one kind or another are acting on the basis of an honest and deeply felt sense of injustice and injury. The one thing we cannot afford to assume as we consider how to deal with this new species of trouble is that the fear it evokes is either a passing whim or a fever that can be cooled by the calculations of experts. This dread has its own reasons; it must be respected.

DISCUSSION QUESTIONS

1. What is new about the "new species of trouble"? Describe Erikson's characterization of the differences between natural disasters and disasters of human origin, and discuss the implications of the distinction.
2. Some have accused environmental groups of fostering an irrational fear among the public, a charge that Erikson disputes. Do you agree or disagree with his position? Why?

READING 45

The Theming of America

Mark Gottdiener

The shopping mall and the fast-food chain restaurant are central features of our everyday landscapes, and are emblematic of new modes of consumption. In this postmodernist analysis of contemporary consumer culture, Mark Gottdiener uses malls and chain restaurants in exploring a phenomenon he refers to as the "theming of America." Dating the rise of themed environments to the 1960s, Gottdiener links this trend to the suburbanization of America, and with it the emergence of new forms of what he refers

to as "symbolic differentiation." One of his central claims is that themed environments are simulations essentially devoid of meaning.

Since the end of World War II, our everyday environment has been altered in profound ways. Before the 1950s there was a clear distinction between the city and the country (Williams 1973). Cities grew as compact, dense industrial environments usually laid out along right-angled grid lines. They possessed a central sector of office towers and an adjacent area of factories tied to rail spurs and roads. Residential areas comprised the classic contrast of the "gold coast and slum." Wealthy, privileged areas of housing were juxtaposed in close proximity with the more modest, sometimes squalid, neighborhoods of industrial workers. Lying in contrast directly beyond the limits of the city was the country—the fields of farm lands, wooded acres and occasional houses of families separated by open space. Cultural styles of life that were either urban (urbane) or rural reflected this dichotomy of land uses as did depictions of city and country dwellers in novels and films (see Redfield 1947).

Beginning with the 1950s the trend toward suburbanization, which had been operating in the United States for over 100 years, began to accelerate and break down the urban/rural dichotomy. Between 1950 and 1970 the plurality of the U.S. population took up residence in the new space created by the large-scale housing development of rural land next to our biggest cities. Decades of suburban growth eradicated the clear distinction between the city and the country, although its vestiges continue to echo in the popular media. Novels and films, for example, are still produced that focus exclusively on cities. They give the impression that the cities are somehow isolated from both the surrounding suburban region and the global forces that influence virtually all places on the earth.

Along with these population shifts, people changed the ways they imputed meaning to their daily environment. Before the 1950s, fundamental class differences between capitalists and workers organized the land use of the industrial city. Neighborhoods, for example, were working class and the local community reflected ethnic, racial and religious solidarity dedicated to the task of raising families. The center of the city, in contrast, belonged to business. During this period the symbols that provided meaning to daily life were quite limited and *understated*. Buildings reflected their functions with a minimum of symbolic trappings. People in neighborhoods signified their culture through the sometimes subtle markings of churches and store signs, often using foreign languages. Symbols of these kinds gave the ethnic enclaves their distinctive style.

After the 1950s, a new theme emerged in the burgeoning spaces of suburbia. People moving to these areas abandoned religious and ethnic markers characteristic of the inner city, replacing them with signs of prestige centering on the status of home ownership. For over a century a residence outside the city signified high status (Veblen 1899). Until the 1950s, this social position was reserved almost exclusively for the wealthiest people who could afford the land and construction costs of a custom-made home or estate. Now, suburban status increasingly characterizes the majority of Americans and the single-family house is our principal sign of prestige. The present-day suburban home is vested with a host of status symbols that anchor daily life in a culture of affluence. Two- or three-car garages, expansive front lawns, separate eating and family rooms, and extensive square footage are just a few of these structural features that also signify prestige.

In sum, the urban environment of the nineteenth and early twentieth centuries was marked by limited thematic content. Symbols were used almost exclusively to denote ethnic enclaves or religious institutions and the business function of buildings. The thematic differentiation of the built environment increased during the turn of

the century because of the popularity of suburbanization among the wealthy, who established the norm of prestige associated with their country estates. Most of the symbolic activity at the time, therefore, involved designating class or ethnic status as the major social markers of the population.

Since the 1960s, a new trend of symbolic differentiation within the built environment has appeared that contrasts graphically with the earlier period. More frequent use of symbols and motifs characterizes the space of everyday life in both the city and the suburb. Signification involves not only a differentiation of particular material objects, but also a constant reworking of facades and interior spaces by overarching motifs drawing on a broad range of symbols. These new modes of thematic representation organize daily life in an increasing variety of ways. Social activities have moved beyond the symbolic work of designating ethnic, religious or affluent status to an expanding repertoire of meanings. More important, and in contrast to previous historical periods, today's environmental symbolism is derived from our popular culture—from common themes that can also be found in films, popular music and novels. In turn, today's themed environments constitute, in fact, a part of our popular culture as well. Consequently, while symbolic elements were muted in the settlement spaces of the early 20th century, construction of metropolitan places today reverses that trend. Our present themed environment merges fluidly with contemporary, commercialized popular culture and the entertainment media. . . .

THE THEMED ENVIRONMENT

The domination of marketing considerations above other aspects of commodity production and the increasing use of market segmentation to keep up with a highly differentiated consumer public contributes to the proliferation of themed environments. Themes are direct marketing appeals. They reduce the product to its image and the consumer experience to its symbolic content. The purpose of all commercial places, as we have seen, is the realization of capital—the selling of goods and/or services. These spaces cannot, however, make this function the prime focus of their appeal to potential consumers, because profit-making benefits corporations or commercial retailers alone. Instead, businesses must disguise the instrumental exchange relation of money for a commodity as another relation between commercial place and the consumer.

Our society bathes the consumer purchase in a benevolent light of nurturing and advertised self-fulfillment. In addition, commercial spaces try to entertain while they promote consumption. People *expect* to be entertained by the commercial environment. Perhaps the theme park illustrates this phenomenon best with its mixture of amusement rides, merchandizing outlets and food courts. As some observers have noted (Postman 1985), a focus on the need for entertainment articulates with every aspect of our society, including politics, education, work, and the serious discussion of social issues. With this cultural change has come changes in our expectations that make entertainment a premium of social encounters, thereby reinforcing the saturation of commercialized entertainment throughout our culture.

Thus, the commercial environment, taken as a whole, has increasingly been designed as a sign itself, as some symbolic space that *connotes* something other than its principal function—the realization of capital through the stimulation of consumer desires and the promotion of sales. It provides a form of entertainment while stimulating the transformation of individuals to commodity-craving selves. All establishments dependent on the attraction of paying customers, therefore, have progressively resorted to overarching thematic devices that disguise the space's fundamental purpose with some general motif or theme. The theme not

only promises the realization of desire, but also advertises producer "benevolence" through a facade of nurturing that suggests it has the best interests of people at heart. In addition to the production of desire through the connection with mass advertising, the themed environment promotes deals, discounts, rebates, sales, special purchasing arrangements, easy credit, customization, and care that are all part of the seller's marketing strategy for the daily seduction of the consumer.

There are many themed environments in our society. Restaurants divide themselves between specifically promoted images and according to the type of food they serve; museums specialize in particular artifacts and advertise special exhibits with overarching themes; department stores sell symbols along with goods, such as through the use of designer clothing labels; malls adopt general design motifs; and theme parks proliferate as the preferred form of family entertainment. Even the interior of the home has been commodified through thematic devices and incorporated into the cyclical sphere of fashion. Some of these themed environments, such as home interiors or restaurants, are designed to be used daily, that is, they are part of our everyday life. Others are meant for special occasions, such as the theme park destination of family vacations or holidays. All of these environments, however, share a common link in the promotion of commercial sales, the blending of entertainment with other cultural experiences, and the melding of material space with the media-scape of television, advertising, movies, cyberspace, and commodity marketing. Let us consider some examples.

In what follows I shall emphasize the function of spaces as themed environments and pay special attention to the symbolic devices used to differentiate otherwise similar commercial places from each other. My discussion of motified milieus to follow has two propositions. The first asserts that, due to increased competition among producers and distributors of goods and services, businesses increasingly use themes and symbolic appeals. In the past they relied more on direct demonstrations of the intrinsic use-value of the goods they produced. In the second case, I suggest that, while symbols and motifs were commonly used in the past by commercial establishments to advertise their goods or services, now businesses are increasingly building environments completely designed as themed spaces. These typically consist of some overarching motif complemented by corresponding thematic details throughout the constructed space that together create an entertaining, themed environment. People increasingly enjoy these symbol-filled milieus, such as large malls, for their own sake as entertaining spaces, and not simply as locations for the easy purchase of commodities.

The appearance of such spaces harkens back to earlier history when people lived within environments completely structured by cosmological, religious, or political codes. The important difference now is that our themed environments are imitations or *simulations* of substantive symbols. Today's signs possess superficial rather than deeply felt meanings. They are *fundamentally* disconnected from the use-value of the commodities with which they are associated. As pure images, their major source of inspiration is the fickle and rapidly changing fashionable world of mass advertising, television and Hollywood culture. Thus, there is both a positive and a negative side to the proliferation of themed environments. In the former case, they have emerged as a qualitatively new source of entertainment in the history of human civilization. In the latter, their essential purpose of merchandising and profit-making, their control by *private* commercial rather than public interests, and their reduction of all meanings to superficial surface images, compels us to examine closely the significance of the increasingly popular experience they offer. I shall deal in more detail with these pros and cons in the last chapter.

THEMED ENVIRONMENTS OF EVERYDAY LIFE: RESTAURANTS AND MALLS

The Themed Restaurant

Until quite recently, Americans rarely ate in restaurants. The norm was to cook meals at home. Dining out was reserved for a special occasion. Eating at the local community diner was an exception to this practice, because it offered a substantial breakfast or meat and potatoes dinner for reasonable prices. Frequenters of diners were mainly people on the move, such as truck-drivers, traveling salespeople, delivery men, or single adults, especially bachelors.

The roadside diner was an important place during the 1930s and 1940s, at the first blossoming of our now mature automobile culture. Many of these structures were simple affairs that restricted their advertising to the daily specials (Jakle 1995). They counted on traffic and the sparsity of competition to bring customers their way. Nevertheless, a few of these establishments exploited advertising in competition for business and some managed to develop thematic devices. One classic case was the original McDonald brothers' roadside hamburger stand located in 1955 on Route 66 just west of San Bernardino, California (Cartensen 1995). The brothers embellished their simple diner with a golden logo in the shape of a large "M." Over the years, as the original stand grew into the multi-national, multi-billion dollar corporation under new, franchise thinking owners, this arched logo would undergo many stylistic transformations as it melded with the *theme* of the "McDonald's" experience (Ritzer 1993).

Between 1930 and 1960 other roadside hamburger stands developed themes, although none duplicated the success of McDonald's franchising. Burger Chef, Burger Queen, Burger Jet, all tried their luck as chains, in addition to Wendy's, Burger King, and ice cream stores, such as Dairy Queen. On the East Coast a diner called the Red Apple Rest, located on a well-traveled route of vacationers leaving New York

City for the upstate Catskill Mountains, expanded into a thematic built environment. For a time, it was the most popular stopover point on the family trip between mountains and the city. In the Midwest and parts of the South, the Stuckey Corporation opened franchised strings of roadside restaurants that offered pecan products, surgary confections, and the usual fare of hamburgers and fries to weary automobile passengers. Other examples of multipurpose roadside restaurants, such as the Hadley Farms truckstop outside of Palm Springs, California, abound throughout the motorized American landscape. Many gas stations have also become "one stop" convenience stores servicing transportation with light shopping needs in a new version of the local roadside stand.

As Venturi, Brown and Izenour (1972), observed, the diner is essentially a simple shed adorned with symbols. The *decorated shed* became the forerunner for the themed restaurants of today. Competition among fast-food franchises or restaurants, coupled with increasing affluence and the new consumer norms that support frequent meals outside the home, have pushed eating establishments into competition through the use of thematic devices. Some restaurant chains utilize totally themed environments. Typical of the new trend are the dining places constructed by the Specialty Restaurant Corporation (Wright and Hutchinson 1996). They often renovate failed factories. The Cannery in Newport Beach, California, processed sea food from 1921 to 1966, when pollution from suburbanization forced its closure. The interior of the factory was gutted and converted into the Cannery Restaurant. Instead of throwing out the original machinery, however, the designers recycled it as sculpture. Artifacts from the manufacturing process became part of the decor. Thematic elements, including photographs, ship's compasses, and navigational equipment, were pinned to the walls. Employees dress in uniforms that recall a version of the 1920s. The elements of the cannery motif,

therefore, pervade the entire space as a totally themed environment. Of course, the current cannery is only a simulation—not a real fish processing plant, but a fish restaurant disguised as a factory.

Most themed restaurants are synonymous with the image of their franchise chain. The symbolic concordance of a McDonald's carries the exterior theme into its interior. The Cannery looks like a factory on the outside, and continues that theme throughout the interior. The use of themed environmental design, however, is so common today that even places with limited exterior signification often resort to fully themed decor for their interiors. I found one example of this phenomenon while searching for a place to eat in a suburban area outside Pittsburgh, Pennsylvania. I had been staying on a motel row between the city and the regional airport and was dissatisfied with the food prepared by the local motel restaurants. On a quick drive to locate a more promising place to eat, I saw a sign from the highway advertising the "Hacienda" restaurant inside a typical motel. I tried it less out of hunger than of curiosity at finding an anachronistic Mexican eatery on the motel row outside of Pittsburgh.

The place was fully themed in a mass cultural version of Tex-Mex design. Earth-tone painted walls, Aztec printing on the menu, sombreros, cacti, painted chairs and tables, and hot sauce on the counter combined to create that ambience of simulated southwest America familiar from restaurants in Arizona, New Mexico, and places west. After ordering a lunch of typical Mexican fare, I was pleasantly surprised to find that the food was as good as in any other franchised restaurant of that kind in the Southwest. The suburban Pittsburgh "Hacienda" had delivered from simulation to reality with a decent hot meal of burritos, beans and salsa. Furthermore, since I was from southern California at that time, I also enjoyed a reminder of home and was entertained by the simulated space. Themed environments have the capacity of providing enjoyment for their own sake beyond the attractions they contain.

Perhaps the best-known fully themed franchise is the Hard Rock Cafe, which was launched in England. Catering to young adults and serving comparatively simple meals centering on the staple of hamburgers and french fries, this restaurant chain has become so successful that it can be found in the capital cities of several countries. A Hard Rock Casino has recently opened in Las Vegas. The thematic motif of this franchise derives from the rock music industry, including nostalgic elements from its origins in the 1950s. Two signature logos comprise the decor. The exterior of the restaurant is framed by a large guitar outlined in neon. Part of a 1950s Cadillac convertible is embedded in one interior wall where it is easily seen by patrons in all corners of the restaurant. The walls are decorated with both facsimiles and original memorabilia of the rock industry, including gold records, concert posters, tour jackets, photographs, and the guitars of famous singers encased in special displays. Waiters and waitresses wear standard restaurant uniforms and the menu is virtually the same whether you dine at the Cafe in London, Los Angeles, or Tel Aviv. The distinctive motif, fed constantly by the connection to the rock industry, is developed further by ambitious merchandising made available at all restaurant locations, including sales of Hard Rock Cafe T-shirts with the location on the logo, jackets and Hard Rock Cafe tote bags.

Because the totally themed environment proved successful for the Hard Rock Cafe franchise, its form has been copied more recently by other operations. Perhaps the most spectacular example is the chain called Planet Hollywood started by several movie superstars—Arnold Schwarzenegger, Sylvester Stallone and Bruce Willis, among others. As with the Hard Rock Cafe, Planet Hollywood commodifies its connection to a popular culture industry—movies. Its walls are decorated with Hollywood memorabilia. Once inside a typical franchise, the cus-

tomer can order virtually the same type of fare as at the Hard Rock Cafe—basic American diner food. Other than the themed environments of these two examples, there is little to differentiate them from any other local American diner in nearly every town in the United States.

The *themed* environment makes the difference. Judging from the examples of the Hard Rock Cafe, linked to the rock industry, and Planet Hollywood, linked to the movie industry, popular culture themes can be successfully incorporated by mundane consumption-stimulating environments. Now there is even a new chain based on the fashion industry and started by several superstar models. In all these cases, the ordinary but always highly functional American diner has been transformed through a successful popular culture theme—rock, film, or fashion—into a successful international restaurant franchise.

Other restaurant franchises that have been less successful feature French village motifs, southwestern decor, and New York City deli style. A diverse development of nostalgia themes include 1950s "oldies," farm houses, and mechanically replicated ethnic symbols such as the quasi-Italian "Olive Garden" restaurants (more successful than most). A typical nostalgia-themed restaurant is the "Ruby Tuesday" chain. I find it particularly interesting for its postmodern *implosion* of times and places that stretch over almost an entire century while the decor manages to integrate the varied referents in the exploitation of popular nostalgia. Its walls are lined with reproductions of ads and public signs from the 1920s, 1930s, and 1940s. The decor of the booths, however, reaches further back to the last century. The booths are illuminated by a remarkable display of imitation Tiffany lamps (originally dating to the 1890s) and stained glass windows. The nineteenth and early twentieth century implosion is complemented by "old tyme" ceiling fans and Victorian-era style of hanging plants. Lastly, no Ruby Tuesday's Restaurant would be complete without its authentic looking, but simulated plastic tin roof.

Along with these more dramatically themed environments, famous franchises such as McDonald's, Kentucky Fried Chicken, and Burger King stylize and abstract their identifying logos into equally pervasive motifs that add to the array of signs and symbols within the built environment. One case of abstraction, for example, is the recent alteration of the Kentucky Fried Chicken logo to the stylized letters "KFC" that the company reproduces as part of the decor and as a logo in packaging. More comprehensive examples can be found in the mass production of virtually identical interiors by the McDonald's Corporation. McDonald's capitalizes on the many thematic elements it has produced in advertising over the years, such as the cartoon characters associated with Ronald McDonald and his friends (Ritzer 1993). These signs and McDonald's interior are found around the globe. Anyone familiar with the local hometown McDonald's can successfully negotiate those in Rio de Janeiro, Brazil, Paris, France, Tokyo, Japan, and London, England. Because franchises like Kentucky Fried Chicken and McDonald's are so famous in their own right, promotional advertising develops their names as a corporate theme that functions along with the efficiently designed fast-food interior scheme as a total environment.

The marketing of a restaurant as a thematic environment also deploys aspects of merchandizing to attract customers. Fast-food places often run promotions by providing special gifts that reflect corporate motifs or representative characters. Even when not engaging in special promotions, themed restaurants carry through their coordinated designs down to their napkins, plates, cups, and table decor. As we have seen for the Hard Rock Cafe, they may also extend merchandising to clothing such as T-shirts and jackets that can be a lucrative business in their own right. In addition, stores play matching themed Muzak in the background. There is a close relation between the commercialization of our material environment and the development of commercialized musical environments within work and leisure interiors in our society (Lanza 1993).

Ordinary eateries will liven up menus, like illuminated medieval manuscripts, by designs that represent restaurant symbols or logos. Diners that lack exploited advertising symbols, often bring their decor into concordance with the type of food they serve. Restaurants owned by ethnics—Greeks or Italians for example—include dishes from those cultures along with the standard American fare and commonly have ethnic signs mixed in with generic decorations on tables and menus. A prevalent example of this more subtle theming is the paper hot-cup for take-out coffee (embellished with Greek designs printed in the Greek national colors) used by diners around the country.

The Themed Mall

Malls, just like the restaurants I have discussed, vary regarding the extent to which they carry through thematic designs. Yet, they, too, increasingly use overarching motifs and coordinated design schemes in total environments. As we have seen, restaurants compete with each other for cash customers. Malls began, however, in competition not with other malls, because only recently have they proliferated, but with the downtowns of cities. Their direct competition was for many years the large department stores located in the center of the metropolis. Consequently, they had to advertise themselves as a *place* to go, and they still do. This kind of advertising for a particular space or location within an urban region is, besides the ads placed by individual department stores, aimed at attracting customers to a specific retailing center. As a particular destination, malls require some overarching means of identification. Consequently, as a whole, they often adopt an image meant to be attractive to potential consumers who always have the choice of where to do their shopping. In this way they are different than the city downtown, which is not a unified commercial space and does not advertise itself as a location.

There is another reason malls adopt a unified image. The central city remains a public space that allows free interaction among a variety of people for any number of purposes. The mall is a highly regulated, *private* commercial space that is expressly designed to make money. This instrumental function of the mall, for realizing capital, must be disguised because it would not be attractive to consumers. As a result, almost every mall has an overarching motif that attempts to convey it as a unique and desirable location for its own sake. As with restaurants, the mall theme is a simulation, a facade, but as a motif for the entire space it sets the symbolic tone for the interior.

There are several motifs commonly adopted by malls around the country. One type, called "ye old kitsch," is exemplified by the Olde Towne Mall in Orange County, California. The interior space contains a pedestrian path lined with artificial gas lamps and park benches. Each store confronts the customer in an image of some old-style emporium of the past. There is even a sign, "police," using nineteenth-century graphics for the mall security office. This kind of conformity between overarching mall motif and the particular facades of interior stores is characteristic of the totally themed environment. The latter is rare among restaurants, as we have seen, and is more commonly characteristic of malls because of the importance of advertising them as a particular place in competition with other locations. Franchise competition is different, because individual stores are not in competition as locations.

Another frequent motif is called "high tech urban" (Gottdiener 1986). Malls of this type are several stories high. They have skylighted ceilings that recall the parisian arcades once studied by Walter Benjamin (1969; Frisby 1985). They strive for a clean, modern look that accentuates chrome, large plate-glass windows, and flashy

neon writing. Perhaps the most famous high tech mall is the Galleria in Milan, Italy. It became so popular as a means of marketing commodities that many mall developers in other countries copied its form. The United States alone has many malls called "The Galleria"— one in Houston, Texas, one in Buffalo, New York, one in Glendale, California, and so on. The original galleria, however, is the Palazzo Vecchio in Florence, Italy, which was constructed during the middle ages. The original galleria is a two-story building with a large interior space without a roof and with the second story open to the interior space. Galleria malls in the United States are all enclosed spaces and may have more than two stories.

Malls have been very effective as commercial spaces. They account for over half of all retailing sales in the United States. In many metropolitan areas, competition from malls has been so severe that they have forced downtown shopping districts out of existence. Buffalo, New York, for example, has several large suburban malls ringing the central city, but the last large department store located downtown closed in 1995. During the 1960s, suburbanization and mall development were so devastating to central cities that they required large infusions of cash from federal government renewal programs to float schemes that would bring customers back downtown. Few of these efforts were successful.

Despite their commercial accomplishments, malls are now locked in fierce competition with each other, because their customers can commute to a variety of alternatives. As a result, owners have resorted to thematic appeals in both the outer design of the mall and its advertising to attract business. Typical of this process is the Galleria, in Riverside, California, a medium-sized city 50 miles east of Los Angeles. Riverside had a one-story mall, built in 1970, that serviced the local area. As the community gained more affluent residents over the next few decades, the mall could not compete with more fashionable "upscale" places in

Orange County such as the large South Coast Plaza less than one hour away. In 1990 a consortium of developers invested $100 million to transform the Riverside Mall into "The Galleria." The new mall is two stories high, contains over 120 stores, including four large, "anchoring" department stores, has a cinema and a dual-level parking structure able to accommodate almost 10,000 cars. These specifications are typical of the large suburban shopping mall.

The most important aspect of the new Riverside Galleria was the advertising campaign for the mall itself as a competitive location. This campaign used thematic elements in its core appeal to customers that had once forsaken local shopping for the flashier sites of Orange County. According to the local paper,

> Riverside's regional mall reopens tomorrow with a new theme, new promise and new stores. . . . The lofty marketing theme for the grand reopening of the Galleria is "Reaching New Heights." But the subliminal message could easily be "Reaching New Customers." . . . . The Galleria Gurus are confident that their dolled-up, classed up, two-storied showcase will lure Riverside County shoppers who had defected to the hallowed malls of Orange County (Lucas 1991:1).

Besides creating pressure on cities by competitive retailing locations, malls often use symbolic design devices that expressly recall the central city through simulations. That is, malls have always competed with the urban downtown, but recently suburban malls attempt to replicate these downtowns in design motifs recreating a simulated "urban" environment. First, they have destroyed the inner city's monopoly on retailing, then they proceeded to co-opt the very image of urban life for mall themes. According to one of the leading southern California architects of malls,

> In essence, the difference between what malls are trying to look like now versus what they were trying to do 10 years ago is that now they're trying to create more of a street scene with a variety of store fronts and architecture. . . . And they're also trying to create an interplay of store merchandise from store to store—which is like a department store with different kinds of merchandise in each section, only now you would consider the whole mall as a large department store and each store is one of those separate departments. . . . behind this kind of mall design is the idea of going back to the old sense of community, where there used to be the general store where everyone met and knew each other's name (Knaff 1991:4).

In at least one case, fierce competition has produced a mall that advertises itself as an "anti-mall." This Orange County, California, shopping area, also known as The Lab, caters to young adults who find no use for typical mall stores such as Waldenbooks or The Nature Company, and features retailers known for their alternative clothing or accessory styles. In addition, while many malls around the country discourage teenage loitering, this anti-mall welcomes it and offers places to hang out. Other mall owners are also aware of segmented marketing (discussed above). They aim for a mix of stores among their tenants that appeal to different class and status groups.

As the above discussion implies, suburban malls introduced the dimension of spatial location to retailing competition. In the past, when central city department stores dominated all commerce, only individual stores had to advertise. Once suburbanization reached a mass level, after World War II, and malls were introduced as retailing outlets dispersed within the larger metropolitan region, the downtown of the city became only one location among several alternate destinations for shoppers. Each retailing center, suburban or urban, had to compete with every other center as a possible shopping location of commuters. Besides advertising that expresses competition among stores, therefore, mall advertising also expresses competition among the alternate locations of retailing centers. The latter kind of promotion takes the form of thematic appeals, especially for malls that project a special image of their own. Lately, even central cities have begun to advertise themselves to shoppers. Thus, competition leads to a greater use of themes, and the success of certain malls leads to a preferred form that is a self-contained, total environment like the galleria form. In addition, because of place competition, there is a tendency over time for malls to be bigger and bigger so that more store possibilities are offered to potential visitors.

The largest mall in the United States is the Mall of America in Bloomington, Minnesota, outside the city of Minneapolis. It opened for business August 21, 1992. In many ways, this "megamall" is a separate small city. Developers, therefore, pushed the total environment form of the galleria a step further by constructing a closed but immense interior space (sometimes called a "hyperspace" because of its size, see Jameson 1984). The Mall of America covers 78 acres with over 4 million square feet of floor area that includes 2.5 million of actual retailing space, has over 400 specialty shops and four large department stores, contains a 14-screen movie theater, nightclubs, bars, 9 areas of family entertainment, over 22 restaurants and 23 more fastfood outlets. But that is not all. At the center of this three-story complex, beneath an immense hyperspace of skylights, mall developers located a seven-acre theme park that is run by Knotts Berry Farms of southern California. The park has trees and bushes, a controlled climate, 23 amusement rides including a roller coaster, 14 places to eat, and high tech virtual reality simulations.

Promotion literature for the megamall says that it is as big as 88 football fields, can contain 20 of Rome's St. Peter's Basilicas and is five times as large as the famous Red Square in Moscow. According to its Canadian developers, the megamall site in Minnesota was chosen among alternatives in several states because of key factors, including the presence of 27 million people in the surrounding region, and their above average household income. In addition, local governments put up over $100 million in transportation upgrades for the surrounding area, including the construction of large multi-storied parking ramps.

The Mall of America cleverly ties its overarching theme to the grand symbol "America." Developers made up the exterior facade in stars and stripes of red, white and blue. Its patriotic decor can mean so many things to so many different people that it serves as a consummate mass marketing device. Ironically, the original developers of the mall were Middle-Eastern immigrants to Canada, but that did not prevent them from feeding an "all American" simulation to the hungry consumers of the Minneapolis–St. Paul region. The interior of the megamall articulates the polysemic patriotic theme with others shaping the major shopping sections. Restaurants are often like the ones analyzed in the last section with individual themes of their own. Most of them are chain franchises such as Hooters (featuring skimpily clad waitresses), Tony Roma's (a chain of rib restaurants), Ruby Tuesday's, Fat Tuesday, the Alamo Grill (Southwest food), the California Cafe (a simulation of southern California style), and Gators (another diner food chain), among others. Each of these themes relates to each other only in the loosest possible sense as belonging to the tapestry of American folklore simulations.

Retailing activities within the mall subdivides space into four main areas. Each, however, returns to the old standby simulation—a recapturing of urban ambience in a varied version of the city street scene. It seems, so far, that malls cannot escape from their main competitor—the downtown, truly public space of the classic central city. The four shopping areas of the Mall of America are: North Garden: Main Street USA; West Market; South Avenue; East Broadway. The mall's inaugural brochure describes the North Garden area as follows: "This lushly landscaped, serpentine walk extends from the venerable Sears to the eagerly waited Nordstrom. With plant-covered balconies, wooden trellises, gazebos, bridges, and airy skylights, North Garden is Main Street, USA" (Mall of America 1992, p.10). Why North Garden is like a typical main street of this country is not at all clear from the above description, but the Mall promoters make that connection anyway.

The second area, West Market, is a simulated representation of a European style marketplace: "From Nordstrom to Macy's, West Market bustles like an old-fashioned European marketplace. You'll make your way past a variety of carts, street venders, shops and eateries to the fancifully painted shop fronts" (p.11). The urban metaphor continues as the brochure describes the third area, South Avenue. "This upscale promenade between Macy's and Bloomingdale's just might become the Rodeo Drive of the Twin Cities," reads the brochure. "Its sophisticated storefronts recall the great shopping streets of Europe" (p. 12). This description has reached the realm of mixed references and geographical confusion. First compared to Rodeo Drive in Beverly Hills, California, South Avenue (named for its directional location in the mall) is then described as recalling streets of Europe.

It is possible to ask whether South Avenue is that distinct from West Market and whether the entire mall description as recalling or representing a type of place merely exists as advertising discourse with no real basis in reality. This supercession of reality is typical of other themed environments that are also mere simulations of distinct cultural places. The simulated environment is simply a cartoonish facade produced to disguise an ordinary retailing establishment. Aside from the skillful deployment of images it has no relation to any real places or cultures around the globe.

Finally, the last area of the Mall is known as East Broadway. "From Bloomingdale's to Sears, this upbeat district features sleek storefronts, bright lights and the latest looks from the hottest shops" (p.15). At last, we have escaped the European street. However, we find ourselves in an area just as amorphous and as hard to pin down with any degree of uniqueness. It is clear that the ambience of the Mall of America is produced less by careful re-creation of urban street scenes from this country and Europe, than general designs meant to fit in with the style of stores located in each of the four sections. Thus, the two large department stores, Sears and Nordstrom, dominate North Garden. West Market contains several small shops and places to eat besides the department stores. South Avenue is denoted as the "upscale" section of the Mall with the most expensive stores, while East Broadway possesses shops specializing in glitter, current fashions and more youthful clothes.

Despite its sometimes overreaching metaphors that try to connect with urban spaces in real cities, this mall's decor is only a thinly veiled disguise for what is an immense indoor commercial shopping area. This is true of other malls, too. The grand themed environment of the mall functions as a sign-vehicle that aids its role as a container of many commercial enterprises because it is also attractive as a desirable destination. What makes the Mall of America different are its large scale and overabundance of family entertainment opportunities, including the 7-acre theme park. It represents a consummate linkage between retailing and the effort to attract and entertain families in competition with the downtown of the city, which has little family entertainment. This mall is a totally themed environment, but its motifs, like other malls, are subservient to the principal need of conformity with the decor of its tenant shops. Commercialism and not the overarching themes of the classical city—religion, cosmology, or politics—dominates the contemporary mall form.

Finally, the mall form with its themed restaurants and retailers had been imported onto university campuses. A recent report notes the following:

They stood eye to eye and nose to nose for almost 40 minutes, exchanging heavy talk, soulful looks and angry glares outside Mrs. Field's Cookies at the food court entrance. . . . It was the kind of minor mall world melodrama that plays out all the time whenever kids gather over their Whoppers, Pizza Hut personal pan pizzas, and Freshen's Premium Yogurt—everywhere from Tysons Corner Center in suburban Washington to the Galleria in Dallas and Phipps Plaza in Atlanta. The only differences was that this was no shopping center, it was the student union at Boston University (Applebome 1995:16).

The report goes on to contrast this scene with the one at Harvard University across the Charles River. There, students prefer the elite facilities of elegant dining areas, such as Dunster Hall. "No one expects a Jack in the Box or a Taco Bell in Harvard Yard, though even Harvard will offer an upscale grazing emporium on campus this fall that includes a familiar name or two" (Applebome 1995:16–17).

According to those interviewed, campus administrations find the mall form a promising way of raising revenues. The University of South Carolina, for example, constructed a 14-store shopping center for its students and faculty over 10 years ago. Recently, other campuses also see the virtues of blending a university environment with the commercial attractiveness of the mall. As this report argues, "Increasingly, the culture and values of the mall are coloring the culture and values of the university. . . . Let's face it, Main Street America doesn't exist anymore. Mall America exists. Why should collegiate life be the last bastion of something that doesn't exist anymore?" (Applebome 1995:17) As elsewhere, franchising of food and retailing takes over commerce because of the success of the mall form—the enclosed, themed space of quasi-public communion. . . .

REFERENCES

Applebome, P. 1995. "Franchise Fever in the Ivory Tower." *New York Times Educational Life Supplement,* 2 April, sec. 4A, p. 16.

Benjamin, W. 1969. *Reflections.* NY: Schoken Books.

Cartensen, L. 1995. "The Burger Kingdom," pp. 119–128, in G. Carney, ed. *Fast Food, Stock Cars and Rock-n-Roll.* Lanham, MD: Rowman and Littlefield.

Frisby, D. 1985. *Fragments of Modernity.* Oxford: Polity Press.

Gottdiener, M. 1986. "Recapturing the Center: A Semiotics of the Shopping Mall," in Gottdiener and Lagopoulos, eds. *The City and the Sign.* New York: Columbia University Press.

Jakle, J. 1995. "Roadside Restaurants and Place-Product-Packaging," pp. 97–118, in G. Carney, ed. *Fast Food, Stock Cars and Rock-n-Roll.* Lanham, MD: Rowman and Littlefield.

Jameson, F. 1984. "Postmodernism or the Cultural Logic of Late Capitalism." *New Left Review,* 146:53–92.

Knaff, D. 1991. "Shopping Centers Have Become World, Culture of Their Own." *Galleria Supplement, The Riverside (Calif.) Press-Enterprise,* 16 October, p. 4.

Lanza, J. 1993. *Elevator Music.* New York: Picador Press.

Lucas, L. 1991. "The Galleria." *Galleria Supplement, The Press-Enterprise,* 16 October, p. 4.

Mall of America 1992. *Guide.* Minneapolis, Minnesota.

Postman, N. 1985. *Amusing Ourselves to Death.* New York: Penguin.

Redfield, R. 1947. "The Folk Society." *American Journal of Sociology* 3 (January): 293–308.

Ritzer, G. 1993. *The McDonaldization of America.* Newbury Park, CA: Pine Forge Press.

Veblen, T. 1899. *The Theory of the Leisure Class.* New York: Macmillan.

Venturi, R., D. S. Brown, S. Izenour, 1972. *Learning from Las Vegas.* Cambridge, MA: MIT Press.

Williams, R. 1973. *The Country and the City.* New York: Oxford.

Wright, T. and R. Hutchinson. 1996. "Social-Spatial Reproduction and the Built Environment." *Research in Urban Sociology,* v. 4, New Perspectives in Urban Sociology Series. JAI Press.

DISCUSSION QUESTIONS

1. Describe in your own words what Gottdiener means by "theming." Based on the examples he uses in the reading or examples you suggest, do you agree or disagree with his portrayal of the themed character of consumer culture?

2. What does Gottdiener mean by simulation? Collect some examples of popular advertisements and examine them to determine whether he is correct in claiming that the symbolic content of the advertisement is disconnected from the use value of the product.

The Third Technological Revolution

Daniel Bell

Over a quarter of a century ago, Daniel Bell introduced the term "postindustrial society" in an attempt to distinguish contemporary developments in advanced industrial societies from the preceding phase of industrial development. In this essay, he contends that three technological revolutions have shaped each phase of industrialization, beginning with the centrality of steam power and moving to the revolution brought about by the harnessing of electricity and chemistry for use in production. Finally, the present age is characterized by the centrality of electronics, especially as seen in the computer and telecommunications arenas. Key to Bell's thesis is the claim that this third revolution is not simply located in the high-tech sector of the economy, but rather pervades the entire economy and as such has had a profound impact on all social relationships.

We are today on the rising slope of a third technological revolution. It is a rising slope, for we have passed from the plus-minus stage of invention and innovation into the crucial period of diffusion. The rates of diffusion will vary, depending upon the economic conditions and political stabilities of societies. Yet the phenomenon cannot be reversed, and its consequences may be even greater than the previous two technological revolutions that reshaped the West and now, with the spread of industrialization, other parts of the world as well.

NB: I make a distinction between a technological revolution and its socioeconomic consequences. The early phrase "the industrial revolution" obscures two different things: the introduction of steam power as a new form of energy and the creation of factories to apply that energy to machines for the production of goods. The reason for the distinction is that there is no necessary, determinate single path for the use of the new technologies. The ways in which technologies can be organized vary widely, and these are social decisions, which can be made in a conscious way. No one "voted in" the first industrial revolutions—in the way that political revolutions, such as the French and the Russian Revolutions, were shaped by active minorities. The industrial revolution moved along the path of least resistance because it generated profits and provided goods at cheaper prices. Yet the social costs were rarely reckoned or dealt with. Today we have a greater awareness of the forces of change and the possible outcomes; and, given our values, we try to enact policies that will create different social matrices to encapsulate these changes and deal with the transitions they provoke.[1]

What I hope to do in this article is to identify the salient aspects of the "third technological revolution," sketch a number of social frameworks that may allow us to see how this technological revolution may proceed in the reorganization of basic structures, and describe the choices we may have.[2]

THREE TECHNOLOGICAL REVOLUTIONS

Any dating or numbering is somewhat arbitrary, yet if we look at the nature of the technological changes and their consequences, we are justified, I believe, in speaking of three major technological revolutions in the Western world in modern times.

The first is the introduction of steam power, more than two hundred years ago, an innovation identified largely with the name of James Watt. The pleasant story goes that as a boy Watt saw the kettle boiling on his mother's hearth and the heavy iron top being raised by the rising steam, and he wondered what would happen if that steam could be enclosed within a chamber and used to push shafts and drives. Yet one cannot underestimate the extraordinary nature of that simple idea.

One can take, as a contrast, the visions of Leonardo da Vinci, who was not only a great painter but, as we know, a civil engineer, a military engineer, and a gifted inventor. In his *Notebooks,* da Vinci imagined an airplane, a submarine, a threshing machine, and refrigeration, and he drew the machines to embody these ideas with extraordinarily painstaking accuracy: the wheels, the gears, the shafts, and so on. Models of these have been made today, and they show how prescient he was. Yet, even with his astonishing imagination, da Vinci could not imagine the one necessary element to make these work: a source of continual and repeatable power strong enough to drive them. He could think of human muscle power, draft animal power, natural wind power, but these were insufficient. Steam provided a quantum jump in our ability to apply energy to machines.

With steam power we could achieve a variety of technological feats impossible before. One was to have steam pumps. England was an island bedded on coal, but one could not dig down very far because of the large pools of underground water, which hand pumps could not extract. With steam pumps, the water could be expelled and coal dug out to create an iron and steel industry. With steam, we could create railroads that could go faster (and longer) than any known animal, steamships that could sail faster, and more steadily, than any wind-driven sails, machines that could card and spin and thus create cloth faster than the nimble fingers of a trained woman. More important than these, the first technological revolution introduced, and made possible, a vast new conception in the cre-

ation of wealth: the idea of productivity, the simple proposition of greater output with less effort, as a result of investment. Prior to modern times, wealth had been gained largely by direct exploitation, such as slavery; or by tithes on work, such as in serfdom; or by plunder and conquest; or by direct political levies, such as tax farming, and so on. For the first time, there existed a peaceful means of generating wealth, a means that was not primarily a zero-sum game but one whereby all might benefit, albeit differentially. That has been the promise of the new methods of production. This is the decisive break with the modes of production of the past. This is the continuing promise of technology.

The second technological revolution, only a hundred years or so ago, can be identified with two innovations: electricity and chemistry. Electricity gives us a new, enhanced form of power that can be transmitted hundreds of miles, as steam cannot, thus permitting new kinds of decentralization that the bunching of machines in a factory, to minimize the loss of steam heat, could not. Electricity gives us a new source of light, which changes our rhythms of night and day. Electricity allows us to code messages on wires or to transform voice electric signals, so as to create telephone and radio. Chemistry, for the first time, allows us to create synthetics, from dyes to plastics, from fibers to vinyls, that are unknown in nature.

And now, the third technological revolution. If we think of the changes that are beginning to occur, we think, inevitably of things and the ways we seek to use them: computers, telecommunications, and the like. But to think in these terms is to confuse applications or instruments with some underlying processes that are the crucial understandings for this revolution, and only by identifying the relevant underlying processes can we begin to "track" the vast number of changes in socioeconomic and political structures that may take place. Four technological innovations underlie this new technological revolution, and I shall describe each briefly:

(1) *The change of all mechanical and electric and electromechanical systems to electronics.* The machines of industrial society were mechanical instruments, powered first by steam and later by electricity. Increasingly, electronic systems have taken over and replaced mechanical parts. A telephone system was basically a set of mechanical parts (e.g. a dial system) in which signals were converted into electricity. Today, the telephone is entirely electronic. Printing was a system in which mechanical type was applied, with inked surfaces, to paper; today, printing is electronic. So is television, with solid-state circuits. The changes mean a reduction in the large number of parts, and an incredible increase in the speed of transmission. In modern computers, we have speeds of nanoseconds, or one-billionth (10^{-9}) of a second (or thirty years of seconds, if one sought to add these up), and even picoseconds, or one-trillionth (10^{-12}) of a second, permitting "lightning" calculation of problems.

(2) *Miniaturization.* One of the most remarkable changes is the "shrinkage" of units that conduct electricity or switch electrical impulses. Our previous modes were vacuum tubes, each, as in the old-fashioned radios, about two or three inches high. The invention of the transistor is akin to the invention of steam power, for it represented a quantum change in the ability to manufacture microelectronic devices for the hundreds of different functions of control, regulation, direction, and memory that microprocessors perform. We had 4k (k = a thousand) bits on a chip, the size of a thin fingernail, then 32k, 64k, and now we begin to construct megabits, or a million binary digits, or bits, on a chip.

In the past two decades we have seen an exponential growth in components per chip, by a factor of one hundred per decade. Today the limit is almost a million components; by 1990 it will be about five million; and by the year 2000 between ten and one hundred million.

Today a tiny chip of silicon contains an electronic circuit consisting of hundreds of thousands of transistors and all the necessary inter-connecting conductors, and it costs only a few dollars. The circuitry on that chip, now made by printed boards, is equivalent to about ten years' work by a person soldering discrete components onto that printed wiring board. A single chip can itself be a microcomputer with input/output processing capability and random-access memory and be, like the AT&T WE* 32100, smaller than an American dime.

(3) *Digitalization.* In the new technology information is represented by digits. Digits are numbers, discrete in their relation to one another, rather than continuous variables. A telephone, for example, was an analogue system, for sound is a wave. Through digital switching a telephone becomes converted to the use of binary systems. One sees this in sound recordings, as on musical discs. The third technological revolution involves the conversion of all previous systems into digital form.

(4) *Software.* Older computers had the instructions or operating systems wired into the machine, and one had to learn a programming language, such as Cobol or Fortran, or the more specialized languages such as Pascal or Lisp, to use the machine. Software, an independent program, frees the user to do various tasks quickly. In distributed processing the software directing the work of a particular computer terminal operates independently of software in other terminals or in the central processing unit. Micro or personal computers have specific software programs—for financial analysis or information data-base retrieval—that tailor the system to particular user needs and become, in the argot of the computer, "user-friendly."

Software—the basis of customization—is still a developing art. It takes a programmer about a year to produce a few thousand lines of code. In telecommunications, large electronic switching machines (to route the hundreds of thousands of calls onto different lines) use more than two million lines. Breaking the "bottleneck" of software programming is the key to the rapid spread of the personal computer into the small business and the home.

(One can point to a significant development that promises the enlargement and enhancement of the new technology: photonics. Photonics is the key technology for transmitting large amounts of digital information through laser and ultrapure glass or optical fibers. Combined, they provide a transmission capability that far exceeds the copper wire and radio. In laboratory experiments, the AT&T Bell laboratories set a "distance record" by transmitting 420 million bits per second over 125 miles without amplification, and two billion bits per second over eighty miles without amplification. The pulse rate can transmit the entire thirty-volume *Encyclopedia Britannica* in a few seconds. But these are still in the development stage, and we are concerned here with already proven technologies that are in the process of marketing and diffusion.)

The most crucial fact about the new technology is that it is not a separate domain (such as the label "high-tech" implies), but a set of changes that pervade all aspects of society and reorganize all older relationships. The industrial revolution produced an age of motors—something we take for granted. Motors are everywhere, from automobiles to boats to power tools and even household devices (such as electric toothbrushes and electric carving knives) that can run on fractional horsepower–motors of one-half and one-quarter horsepower. Similarly, in the coming decades, we shall be "pervaded" by computers—not just the large ones, but the "computer on a chip," the microcomputer, which will transform all our equipment and homes. For automobiles, appliances, tools, home computers and the like, microcomputers will operate with computing power of ten MIPS (million of instructions per second) per computer.[3]

We can already see the shape of the manifold changes. The old distinctions in communication between telephone (voice), television (image), computer (data), and text (facsimile) have been broken down, physically interconnected by digital switching, and made compatible as a single unified set of teletransmissions. This is what my colleague Anthony Oettinger calls "compunications" and what Simon Nora and Hilary Minc, in their report to the president of France several years ago, called "télématique." The introduction of computer-aided design and simulation has revolutionized engineering and architectural practices. Computer-aided manufacturing and robotics are beginning to transform the production floor. Computers are now indispensable in record-keeping, inventory, scheduling, and other aspects of management information systems in business, firms, hospitals, universities, and any organization. Data-base and information-retrieval systems reshape analysis for decisions and intellectual work. The household is being transformed as digital devices begin to program and control household appliances and, in the newer home designs, all aspects of the household environment. Computers, linked to television screens, begin to change the way we communicate, make transactions, receive and apply information.

The intellectual task is how to "order" these changes in comprehensible ways, rather than just describing the multitude of changes, and thus to provide some basis of analysis rooted in sociological theory. What I intend to do, in the following sections, is to present a number of "social frameworks," or matrices, which may allow us to see how existing social structures come under pressure for change, and the ways in which such changes may occur. I repeat one caveat stated earlier: Technology does not determine social change; technology provides instrumentalities and potentialities. The ways that these are used are social choices. The frameworks that I sketch below, therefore, indicate the "areas" within which relevant changes may occur.

THE POSTINDUSTRIAL SOCIETY

The postindustrial society is not a projection or extrapolation of existing trends in Western society: it is a new principle of social-technical organization and ways of life, just as the industrial system (e.g., factories) replaced an agrarian way of life. It is, first, a shift in the centrality of industrial production, as it was organized on the basis of standardization and mass production. This does not mean the disappearance of manufacturing or the production of goods; the production of food and products from the soil does not disappear from the Western world (in fact, more food is produced than ever before), but there is a significant change in the way food is produced, and, more significantly, in the number of persons engaged in agricultural production. But more than all these, the idea is a "logical construct," in order to see what is central to the new social forms, rather than an empirical description. Postindustrial developments do not replace previous social forms as "stages" of social development. They often coexist, as a palimpsest, on top of the others, thickening the complexity of society and the nature of social structure.

One can think of the world as divided into three kinds of social organization. One is preindustrial. These are primarily extractive industries: farming, mining, fishing, timber. This is still the lot of most of Africa, Latin America, and Southeast Asia, where 60 percent or more of the labor force is engaged in these activities. These are largely what I call "games against nature," subject to the vicissitudes of the weather, the exhaustion of the soils, the thinning out of forests, or the higher costs of the recovery of minerals and metals.

Similar sections of the world have been industrial, engaged in fabrication, the application of energy to machines for the mass production of goods. These have been the countries around the Atlantic littoral: those of Western Europe and the United States, and then the Soviet Union and Japan. Work, here, is a game against fabricated nature: the hitching of men to machines, the organized rhythmic pacing of work in a highly coordinated fashion.

The third type is postindustrial. These are activities that are primarily processing, control, and information. It is a social way of life that is, increasingly, a "game between persons." More important, there is a new principle of innovation, especially of knowledge and its relation to technology.

Let me describe some of the lineaments of the postindustrial society. It is, first, a society of services. In the United States today, more than 70 percent of the labor force is engaged in services. Yet "services" is inherently an ambiguous term and, in economic analysis, one without shape because it has been used primarily as a "residual" term.

In every society there is a high component of services. In preindustrial society, it is primarily domestic or personal service. In a country such as India, most persons with a middle-class income would have one or two servants, because many persons simply wish for a roof to sleep and a place to eat. (In England, until 1870, the largest single occupational class was that of domestic servants.)

In an industrial society services are those activities auxiliary to industry: utilities, transportation (including garages and repairs), finance, and real estate.

In a postindustrial society there is an expansion of new kinds of service. These are human services—education, health, social work, social services—and professional services—analysis and planning, design, programming, and the like. In the older conceptions of classical economics (including Marxism), services were thought of as inherently unproductive, since wealth was identified with goods, and lawyers and priests or barbers or waiters did not contribute to the national wealth. Yet surely education and health services contribute to the increased skills and strengths of a population, while professional services (such as linear programming in the organization of production, or new modes of layout of work and social interaction) contribute to the productivity of an enterprise and society. And the important fact is that the expansion of a postindustrial sector of a society requires the expansion of higher education and the education of many more in the population in abstract conceptual, technical, and alphanumeric skills.

In the United States today more than 30 percent of the labor force (of more than one hundred million persons) is professional, technical, and managerial, an amazing figure in social history. About 17 percent of the labor force does factory work (the industrial proletariat, in the older Marxian sense of the term), and it is likely that this will shrink to about 10 percent within a decade. If one thinks this is small, consider the fact that fewer than 4 percent of the labor force are farmers, producing a glut of food for the United States—as against 50 percent in 1900.

An equally important change is in the role of women. In 1950 the "typical" picture for 70 percent of the labor force was a husband at work and his wife and two children at home. Today that is true of only 15 percent of the labor force. Today more than 50 percent of all wives are working outside the home.

Any social change is an intersection of cultural attitudes with the ability to institutionalize those attitudes in market terms. The cultural attitudes regarding equal rights of women go back a hundred years. But the ability to institutionalize those sentiments in market terms goes back only to the past twenty-five or so years—with the expansion of postindustrial employments, particularly in the "quinary" sector of services (health, education, research) and then back into the "quaternary" areas (trade, finance, real estate). The reason is, broadly, that industrial work has been largely considered men's work (including the corporate sectors of management). Postindustrial employments are open, in skills and capacities, to women.

The decisive change—what I call the axial principle of organization—is a change in the character of knowledge. Now, every human society has always existed on the basis of knowl-

edge. The sources go far back, lost in the vistas of time, when the human animal was able, because of the voice box in the larynx, to take the sounds of communication made by all birds and animals, and to codify these into distinct vocables that could be combined, differentiated, and organized into complex meanings, and, through voice, to make intelligible signals that could be transmitted through an oral tradition. With the creation of alphabets we could take a few ideographic scratches and combine these into thousands of words that could be written in stylized forms, to be learned and read by others.

But what is radically new today is the codification of theoretical knowledge and its centrality for innovation, both of new knowledge and for economic goods and services. In his pathbreaking book, *Invention, Growth and Welfare: A Theoretical Treatment of Technological Change* (M.I.T. Press, 1969), William Nordhaus lays out an analytical framework in which, "for the purposes of economic analysis, it is important to distinguish two kinds of knowledge, general and technical. The distinction refers to the usefulness of knowledge in producing either more knowledge or more goods." On the higher level, there is general knowledge, such as the laws of nature, liberal arts, and language, knowledge "not particularly useful for the specialized problems of producing goods." And there is a second tier of technical knowledge, in which he includes computer programs and engineering formulas, which is useful in producing goods but not additional knowledge.

Whatever utility that distinction may have had for the measurement of inventions and the rate of technological change, it is increasingly diminished and even misleading in understanding the way innovation now increasingly proceeds with the new technology. Let us take the relation of technological invention to science in the major sectors of industrial society. If we look at the major industries that were developed then and that still carry over today—steel, electricity, telephone, radio, aviation—we can see that they are all "nineteenth-century" industries (though steel was begun in the eighteenth century by Darby with the invention of the coking process and aviation in the twentieth century by the Wright brothers) created by "talented tinkerers," men who were adroit with the nature of equipment, but who knew little about, or were indifferent to, the developments of science, and in particular the theoretical aspects taking place at the time.

Sir Henry Bessemer, who invented an oxidation process to reduce the impurities in molten metal and to produce stronger structure steel (and to win a prize from Louis Napoleon for a better cannon), knew little of the work of the metallurgist Henry Sorby on the properties of metals. Alexander Graham Bell, one of the inventors of the telephone, was originally a speech teacher who sought to transmit amplified voice on a wire in order to enable deaf people to hear better. Thomas Alva Edison, one of the great geniuses among inventors—he invented the long-lasting filament for the electric-light bulb, the phonograph, and the motion picture—was a mathematical illiterate who cared little about the work of Clerk Maxwell in uniting electricity and magnetism into a combined theoretical set of equations. (It was Maxwell who started us off, thus, on the search that continues today for the unification of all the forces that hold matter together in the universe.) When Edison became head of the U.S. Navy Consulting Board during World War I, he said that there ought to be someone on the board who knew some mathematics, in the event they encountered some problems that had numbers or equations, and the Navy hired a physicist; but since the Navy personnel slots had no designation at that time for a physicist, the man was paid as a chemist. This gives us some indication of the magnitudes of change from World War I to the present. Similarly, Guglielmo Marconi, who invented wireless communication, knew little of the work of Hertz on radio waves.

But all of that has now changed radically. Let me take three instances for dramatic effect:

In 1905 Albert Einstein, at age twenty-eight, wrote three papers for *Annalen der Physik* (plus his Ph.D. thesis on a new theoretical method for determining molecular radia and Avogadro's number), any one of which would have won him eponymous fame in the history of science. One paper was on the Brownian motion, which not only "proved" the "reality of molecules," but provided exact computations that demonstrated the correctness of Boltzmann's interpretation of thermodynamic laws. The second paper dealt with "special relativity" and described how the invariance of the velocity of light held in different moving frames of reference, thus showing the limiting nature of the Newtonian view of the universe, putting space and time into a single continuum and the pregnant equation $E = mc^2$, which exploded into the atomic age. And the third paper was on the so-called "photo-electric effect." In many respects, the latter paper has been of lesser importance in the arcane theoretical literature of physics (quoted less than others), yet it has had the most extraordinary technological importance and, in 1922, was the basis for Einstein's Nobel Prize.

Einstein's paper on the photoelectric effect flouted the concepts of classical physics, which held that light (like sound) was a wave. The paper postulated, hypothetically, that light was a *quanta,* or a stream of discontinuous particles. This paper met with extraordinary resistance among experimental physicists, was not vindicated experimentally until a decade later, and was finally resolved theoretically by the complementary principle of wave-particle dualism. Yet the crucial point is that Einstein's paper was the starting point for much twentieth-century work in optics, from such simple things as we now see in the application of photoelectric effects, in breaking light beams, to the work of Charles Townes in creating lasers (an acronym for "light amplification stimulated by the emission of radiation"), Dennis Gabor on holography, and the development of photonics as the new frontier for telecommunications.

The second illustration is the revolution in solid-state physics. The contemporary conceptions of solid-state physics play no role, and to some extent are unthinkable, within the purview of classical physics. Our shifts in the conception of matter go back to the model of the hydrogen atom that Niels Bohr constructed in 1912, with the idea of the nucleus and the orbits of electrons around the nucleus. The basic step forward was taken in 1927 with the picture of the lattice structure of matter, by Felix Bloch, in which one could show how electrons, in their spins, "jumped" from orbit to orbit as energy is given off. These "pictures" of the structures of matter led to the discovery of the transistor at Bell Labs by Bardeen, Brittain, and Shockley in the late 1940s and to the revolution in solid-state technology that is the basis of modern-day electronics and the computer.

And, finally, an innovation of an entirely different sort, Alan Turing's mathematical paper in 1937, "On Computable Numbers," which is the fundamental basis for programming, storage, and the creation of the digital computer. In 1928, the great German mathematician David Hilbert, at the World Congress of Mathematics, had laid down three questions in order to see whether a complete formulization of mathematics was possible. He asked whether mathematics could be complete, consistent, and decidable. Two years later, in 1930, the Czech mathematician Kurt Gödel had produced his theorems, which showed that, given the problems of providing a complete and consistent set of axioms, if mathematics was complete it could not be consistent, and if consistent it could not be complete.

When Alan Turning wrote his paper, which showed that there could be a principle of decidability (whether in principle a problem was solvable or not) if the numbers were computable, he invented a tape that would be a "table of behavior" that could through binary rules compute any possible configuration of finite numbers. The

idea of a computer goes back to the work of an earlier Cambridge mathematician, Charles Babbage, who in 1837 conceived of a "difference engine" that could mechanize any mechanical operation. What Turing's innovation did was utilize binary numbers (Boolean algebra) with internal program storage, to allow for the development of an automatic electronic digital computer. Thus, theory preceded artifice.[*]

One consequence of this is that invention, or the "talented tinkerer," disappears from the horizon. There will always be innovations and changes in "things" that will create new products. But the basic point remains that fundamental innovations in theoretical knowledge—not just in physics, as in the illustrations above, but in biology (going back to the discovery of the double helix of the DNA molecule by Crick and Watson, and to the branching structure of molecular biology by Monod, Jacobs, and Lwoff) or in cognitive psychology (as the basis for expert inference systems)—become the new principle of innovation in society.

I said before that one has to distinguish technological changes (even when they are now not only in machine technology but in intellectual technology) from the more valuable changes in social structure. Changes in technology, as I have insisted, do not determine social changes; they pose problems that the political controllers of society have to deal with. It would take a book to begin to explore the many problems suggested by the possible changes we have seen. Some of these are explored in the following two sections on changes in infrastructure, or the social geography of societies, and changes in the nature of production systems. Let me briefly, however, with the more delimited framework of a postindustrial hypothesis, pose a number of questions.

---

[*]One should distinguish this innovation of Turing's from his later creation of the "Turing Machine problem": Could a human being distinguish an answer to any set of problems whether given by another human being or by a "computer"?

1. The shrinkage of the traditional manufacturing sectors—augmented, in these instances, by the rising competition from Asia and the ease whereby the routinized, low-value-added production can be taken up by some of the Third World societies—raises the question whether Western societies (all or some) can reorganize their production to move toward the new "high-tech, high-value-added" kinds of specialized production, or whether they will be "headquarter economies" providing investment and financial services to the rest of the world.

2. The costs of transition. Can these be managed? And if so, by the "market," or by some kind of "industrial policy"?

3. The reorganization of an educational system to provide a greater degree of "alpha-numeric" fluency in larger portions of the population who would be employed in these postindustrial sectors.

4. The character of "work." If character is defined by work, then we shall see a society where "nature" is largely excluded and "things" are largely excluded within the experience of persons. If more and more individuals are in work situations that involve a "game between persons," clearly more and more questions of equity and "comparable worth" will arise. The nature of hierarchy in work may be increasingly questioned, and new modes of participation may be called for. All of these portend huge changes in the structures of organization from those we have seen in the older models of the army and the church, or the industrial-factory organization, which have been the structures of organization (if not domination) until now.

SOCIETAL GEOGRAPHY AND INFRASTRUCTURES

Historically every society has been tied together by three kinds of infrastructure: These have been the nodes and highways of trade and transactions, of the location of cities and the connections between peoples. The first has been transportation: rivers, roads, canals, and, in modern times, railroads, highways, and airplanes. The second is energy systems: hydropower, electricity grids, oil pipelines, gas pipelines, and the like. And the third has been communications: postal systems (which moved along highways), then telegraph (the first break in that linkage), telephone, radio, and now the entire panoply of new technological means from microwave to satellites.

The oldest system has been transportation. The breakdown between isolated segments of a society comes when roads are built to connect these, so that trade can commence. The location of human habitats has come with the crossing of roads or the merging of rivers and arms of lakes: traders stop with their wares, farmers bring their food, artisans settle down to provide services, and towns and cities develop.

Within the system of transport, the most important has been water routes. They are the easiest means for carrying bulk items; waterways weave around natural obstacles; tides and currents provide means of additional motion. It is striking to realize that almost every major city in the world, in the last millennia (leaving aside the fortified hill towns that arose during the breakdown of commerce and provided a means of protection against marauders) is located on water: Rome on the Tiber, Paris on the Seine, London on the Thames, not to mention the great cities located on the oceans, seas, and great lakes.

If one looks at industrial societies, the location of cities and the hubs of production come from the interplay of water and resources. Consider a map of the United States and look at the north-central area of the country. In the Mesabi range of Minnesota there was iron ore; in the fields of southern Illinois and western Pennsylvania there was coal. And these were tied together by a Great Lakes and river-valley system that connected them with ports on the oceans: the lakes of Superior, Huron, Michigan, Ontario, and Erie, the St. Lawrence waterway through Canada reaching out to the Atlantic, the Erie Canal across New York reaching down the Hudson River, and the Ohio River wending its way down to the Mississippi and the Gulf of Mexico.

Given the iron ore and coal, one has a steel industry and from it an automobile industry, a machine-tool industry, a rubber industry, and the like. And given the water-transport system tying these together, we get the locational reasons for the great industrial heartland of the United States, the bands of cities along the lakes and rivers of Chicago, Detroit, Cleveland, Buffalo, and Pittsburgh. Thus the imprint of economic geography.

Now all this is changing, as industrial society begins to give way. Communication begins to replace transportation as the major node of connection between people and as the mode of transaction.

Water and natural resources become less important as locational factors for cities, particularly as, with the newer technology, the size of manufacturing plants begins to shrink. Proximity to universities and culture becomes more important as a locational factor. If we look at the major development of high-tech in the United States, we see that the four major concentrations respond to these elements: Silicon Valley, in relation to Stanford University and San Francisco; the circumferential Route 128 around Boston, in relation to M.I.T. and Harvard; Route 1 in New Jersey, from New Brunswick to Trenton, with Princeton University at its hub; and Minneapolis-St. Paul in Minnesota, clustering around the large state university and the Twin City metropolis.

What we see, equally, with communication networks becoming so cheap, is a great pull toward decentralization. In the past, central business districts concentrated the headquarters of large enterprises because of the huge "external economies" available through the bunching of auxiliary services. One could "walk across the street" and have easily available legal services, financial services, advertising services, printing and publishing, and the like. Today, with the increasing cheapness of communication and the high cost of land, density and the external economies become less critical. So we find that dozens of the major U.S. corporations, in the last decade or so, have moved their basic headquarters from New York to the suburban areas where land is cheaper, and transport to and from work easier: northeast to Fairfield County in Connecticut; north to Westchester County in New York; and west and southwest to Mercer County in New Jersey.

In Japan we see a major effort now under way, the Technopolis project, to create large, far-flung regional centers for the new computer and telecommunications industries. For status reasons, many corporations maintain a display building in New York or Tokyo; but the major managerial activities are now decentralized.

As geography is no longer the controller of costs, distance becomes a function not of space but of time; and the costs of time and rapidity of communication become the decisive variables. And, with the spread of mini- and microcomputers, the ability to "down-load" databases and memories, and to place these in the small computers (as well as give them access to the large mainframes) means there is less of a necessary relation to fixed sites in the location of work.

As with habitats, so with markets. What is a market? Again, it is a place where roads crossed and rivers merged and individuals settled down to buy and sell their wares. Markets were places. Perhaps no longer.

Take the Rotterdam spot market for oil. It was the place where tankers carrying surplus oil would come so that oil could be sold "on the spot." They came to Rotterdam because it was a large, protected port, close to the markets of Western Europe; it had large storage capacity; there was a concentration of brokers who would go around and make their deals. It is still called the Rotterdam spot market for oil, but it is no longer in Rotterdam. But if not in Rotterdam, where? Everywhere. It is a telex-and-radio system whereby brokers in different parts of the world can make their deals and redirect the ships on the high seas to different ports for the sales they have made. In effect, markets are no longer places but networks.

And this is true for most commodities, especially for capital and currency markets. Today one can get in "real time" quotations for dollars, D-marks, Swiss francs, yen, French francs, sterling, Italian lire, in Tokyo, Singapore, Hong Kong, Milan, Frankfurt, Paris, London, New York, Chicago, San Francisco, and money moves swiftly across national lines. Capital flows in response to differential interest rates or in reaction to news of political disturbances.

What we have here, clearly, are the nerves, nodes, and ganglia of a genuine international economy tied together in ways the world has never seen before. What this means—and I shall return to the question at the close of this article—is a widening of the arenas, the multiplication of the numbers of actors, and an increase in the velocity and volatility of transactions and exchanges. The crucial question is whether the older institutional structures are able to deal with this extraordinary volume of interactions.

THE SOCIAL ORGANIZATION OF PRODUCTION

The modern corporation—I take the United States as the model—is less than a hundred years old. Business, the exchange of goods and services, is as old as human civilization itself. But the modern corporation, as a social form to coordinate men, materials and markets for the mass production and mass consumption of goods, is an institution that has taken shape only in the past century.

There are three kinds of innovators who conjoined to create the modern industrial system. The greatest attention has been paid to those who have been the organizers of the production system itself: Eli Whitney, who created standardized forms and interchangeable parts in production; Frederick Taylor, who designed the measurement of work; and Henry Ford, who created the assembly line and mass production. (There were of course other forebears, and there were European counterparts: Siemens, Bedeaux, Renault, etc.)

Those who achieved the greatest notoriety were the capitalists, the men who by ruthless means put together the great enterprises: the Carnegies, the Rockefellers, Harriman, the men who initiated the large quasi-monopoly organizations, and the financiers, such as J. P. Morgan, who assembled the monies for the formation of such great corporations as U.S. Steel, General Electric, and the like.

But there was also a different social role, often unnoticed even in the history of business, played by men who, curiously, were probably just as important, and perhaps more so: the organizers of the corporate form, those who rationalized the system and gave it an ongoing structural continuity. I will discuss three individuals who symbolize the three crucial structural changes: one was Walter Teagle, of Standard Oil of New Jersey, who created vertical integration; another was Theodore N. Vail, who fashioned the American Telephone and Telegraph Co. and imposed the idea of a single uniform system; and the third was Alfred P. Sloan, of General Motors, who created the system of financial controls and budgetary accounting that still rules the corporate world today.

These three men created modern industrial capitalism. It is my thesis, implicit in this article and which can be stated only schematically here, that this system, marvelously adaptive to a mass-production society, is increasingly dysfunctional in today's postindustrial world.

Vertical integration, the control of all aspects of a product—in the case of Teagle, from oil in the ground, to shipping, refining, and distribution to industrial customers and retail outlets—

was created for the clear reasons of economies of scale, reduction of transaction costs, the utilization of information within the entire process, and the control of prices, from raw materials to finished goods. What vertical integration did, as Alfred Chandler has pointed out in his book *The Visible Hand,* was to destroy "producer markets" within the chain of production and impose uniform controls. In the previous system, one of merchant capitalism, production was in the hands of independent artisans or small-business companies, and all of this was funneled through the matrix of the merchant capitalist, who ordered the goods he needed, or contracted production to the small workshop, and sold finished products to the customers. But the creation of large-scale, mass-produced, identical goods made vertical integration a functional necessity.

The idea of a single system arose when Vail, seeking to build a telephone utility, beheld the railroad system in the United States, where railroad systems grew "higgledy-piggledy," without plan, and often for financial reasons, to sell inflated stock. Franchises were obtained from corrupt legislatures or from congressional land grants, and the roads were built in sprawling ways. Before the advent of coast-to-coast air flight, if a traveler wanted to go from New York to the West Coast by train, he could not do so on a single system. He could take one of two competitive railroads from New York to Chicago, where he changed trains and then took one of three competitive systems to the Coast. (If one wished to ship a hog, or freight, it was not necessary to change trains. Animals or freight goods, unlike human beings, could not pick themselves up and move to another freight car; it was cheaper to shuttle the freight car onto different lines.) Even today there is no unified rational rail system in the United States.

Vail, in building a telephone network, decided that if there was to be efficient service between a person calling from any point in the United States to any other point, there would have to be a single set of "long lines" connect-

ing all the local telephones to one another. Until the recent federal court decision which broke up the American Telephone and Telegraph Co., it was a unified, single system.

Alfred P. Sloan's innovations came about when he took over the sprawling General Motors from William C. Durant, a Wall Street speculator who had put together the different automobile companies (named for their early founders: Chevrolet, Olds, Cadillac, and the like) into a single firm, General Motors. But Durant had little talent for creating a rational structure. Alfred P. Sloan, the MIT-trained engineer who was installed as head of the company by the Du Pont interests (the largest block of stockholders until the courts forced them to divest their holdings about twenty-five years ago), installed unit cost accounting and financial controls with a single aim: to obtain a clear return on investment for the monies given to the different divisions. Durant never knew which of the companies was making money, and which not; he did not know whether it was cheaper to make his own steel or buy outside, make his own parts or buy outside. Sloan rationalized the company. His key innovation was a pricing system for the different lines of automobiles that would provide a 20 percent return on investment based on a stipulated capacity, a break-even point based on overhead and fixed costs, and a market share for the particular line of car.

Together, these innovations were the corporate principles of modern industrial capitalism. Why are they now dysfunctional?

In the case of production, the older standardized, routinized, low-value-added forms of production are being increasingly taken over by the newly industrializing societies, where cheap wages provide the crucial cost differential in competition. More than that, the newer technologies—particularly computer-aided design (CAD), numerical-control machine tools (NC), and computer-aided manufacturing (CAM)—now make possible *flexible,* shorter-run, batch productions that can be easily adapted to different kinds of markets, and which can be responsive to specialized products and customized demands.

One of the great success stories in this respect is Italy, in such an "old-fashioned" industry as textiles. The textile district of Prato—the group of towns in Central Italy in the provinces of Florence and Pistoia—was able to survive and flourish because it could adapt. As two MIT scholars have pointed out (relying, of course, on Italian studies), "Prato's success rests on two factors: a long-term shift from standard to fashionable fabrics and a corresponding reorganization of production from large integrated mills to technologically sophisticated shops specializing in various phases of production—a modern *systeme* Motte."[4]

But what holds true for textiles is true for a wide variety of industries as well. In steel, integrated production is now cumbersome and costly, and it is the minimills, with their specialized, flexible production, and the specialty steels that have become the basis for survival in the Western world. It is not, thus, deindustrialization, but a new form of industrialization, which is taking place.

In the case of telecommunications—to be brief—the breakdown of the old distinctions between telephone, computer, television, and facsimile (Xerox) means that new, highly differentiated systems—private branch exchanges, local area networks, "internal" communication networks between firms, international satellite communication—all emphasize diversity rather than uniformity, with many specialized systems rather than a single product such as the telephone.

In the case of Sloan's system of a return on investment through budgetary controls, the assumptions he made were those of a quasi monopoly or oligopoly in a "steady-state" market, and that kind of financial planning can scarcely adapt to a changing world where old product lines are breaking down (one need simply consider the old distinctions between banks, insurance companies, brokerage houses, credit firms,

real estate investment, all of which become to some extent interchangeable under the rubric of financial-asset management), where substitutions of products provide price challenges, where market share and cash flow may be more important momentarily, and a long-term commitment necessary technologically, than the simple unit-cost accounting that Alfred Sloan introduced.

In effect, the world of the postindustrial society requires new modes of social organization, and these are only now being fashioned by the new entrepreneurs of the new technology.

THE QUESTION OF SCALE

The crucial question, as I have indicated, is how new social structures will be created in response to the different values of societies, to the new technological instruments of a postindustrial world. Beyond the structural frameworks I have tried to identify, there is one crucial variable that must be taken into account—the change in scale.

It is a cliché of our time that ours is an era of acceleration in the pace of change. I must confess that I do not understand what this actually means. If we seek to use this concept analytically, we find a lack of boundary and meaning. To speak of "change" is in itself meaningless, for the question remains: change of what? To say that "everything" changes is hardly illuminating. And if one speaks of a pace, or of an acceleration in pace, the words imply a metric—a unit of measurement. But what is being measured?

However, one can gain a certain perspective about what is happening by thinking of the concept of scale. A change in the scale of an institution is a change of form. Metaphorically, this goes back to Galileo's square-cube law: If you double the size of an object, you triple its volume. There is consequently a question of shape and proportion. A university with fifty thousand students may still be called by the same name it had thirty years before, with five thousand students, but the increase in numbers calls for a change in the institutional structure. And this is true of all social organizations.

What the revolutions in communication are doing is changing the scale of human activities. Given the nature of "real time" communication, we are for the first time forging an interdependent international economy with more and more characteristics of an unstable system in which changes in the magnitudes of some variables, or shocks and disturbances in some of the units, have immediate repercussions in all the others.

The management of scale has been one of the oldest problems in social institutions, whether it be the church, the army, or economic enterprise, let alone the political order. Societies have tended to function reasonably well when there is a congruence of scale between economic activities, social units and organization, and political and administrative control. But increasingly what is happening is a mismatch of scale. As I stated in an essay several years ago,[5] the national state has become too small for the big problems of life, and too big for the small problems. The national state, with its political policies, is increasingly ineffective in dealing with the tidal waves of the international economy (coordination through economic summitry is only a charade) and too big, when political decisions are concentrated in a bureaucratic center, for the diversity and initiative of the varied local and regional units under its control. To that extent, if there is a single overriding sociological problem in the postindustrial society— particularly in the management of transition—it is the management of scale.

NOTES

1. There are important consequences for sociological theory in these distinctions. My division can be seen as corresponding to the Marxist distinction between "forces of production" (technology or technique) and the "social relations of production" (property, organization of work, etc.). Yet

in Marxist theory the two are yoked into a single form, the "mode of production." Social change is seen as "holistic" changes from one form of production to another.

Yet this is patently not true. In *The Poverty of Philosophy,* Marx remarks that the hand mill or windmill gives us feudalism and the steam mill capitalism. But the technologies of wind and steam are compatible with many different kinds of social formation. To couple the two terms is to distort social analysis.

In my book *The Coming of Post-Industrial Society* (New York: Basic Books, 1976; original edition 1973), what I sought to do was to "decouple" the two terms, and to treat them analytically, as two independent variables. Given that distinction, we can then see, along the axis of technology, societies that we can call preindustrial, industrial, and postindustrial. Along the axis of social relations, we can have feudal, capitalist, and state-collectivist societies. (I reserve the term "socialism" for more humane societies.) None of the social forms is complete or is a "total" description of a society. Any particular society would be a combination of several forms, depending on its own historical evolution. Yet if we treat these as "ideal types," we can make relevant comparisons, depending on which axis we use.

When one speaks of the "convergence" of societies, one would have to ask, along which axis? On the axis of technology, both the United States and the Soviet Union are industrial societies, as against, say, Indonesia and China, which are preindustrial. But along the axis of social relations, the Soviet Union and China are state-collectivist societies while the United States and Indonesia are capitalist.

2. A simple methodological point: Most discussions of technological change have focused on a single, major item and then sought to trace the social effects. Thus we have had many studies of "The Social Effects of the Railroad," of radio, of the automobile, of aviation, etc. The problem with such a strategy is that it is increasingly difficult to understand the technological changes in terms of single major innovations, and even more difficult to trace the multiple effects. It is clearly quite different to trace the effects, say, of

the plough on medieval agriculture or the stirrup on war, than the interacting ways that automobiles, trucks, railroads, ships, and airplanes change a transportation system. For this reason, I begin with social matrices and try to see how they may change with the introduction of the new technologies. (For a contrast with the older modes of analysis and the hazards of their contemporary use, see Lynn White, Jr., *Medieval Technology and Social Change* [Oxford: Clarendon Press, 1962] and W. F. Ogburn, *The Social Effects of Aviation* [Boston and New York: Houghton Mifflin, 1946].)

3. For a convenient summary of these technologies, see "*Information Technologies and Social Transformation.*" The National Academy of Engineering (Washington D.C.: National Academy of Science, 1985).

4. Michael J. Piore and Charles Sabel. *The Second Industrial Divide* (New York: Basic Books, 1984).

Piore and Sabel cite the various studies of Gianni Lorenzi, Ezio Avigdor, Danielle Mazzonis, and others, and the OECD study of textile and clothing, 1983.

5. "The Future World Disorders," reprinted in my book of essays, *The Winding Passage* (Cambridge, Mass.: Abt Books, 1980).

DISCUSSION QUESTIONS

1. What is the significance of the shift from mechanical, electric, and electromagnetic systems of production to one in which electronics is central? Do you agree with Bell that this constitutes a bona fide revolution?

2. According to Bell, one of the features of postindustrial society is the decline in manufacturing jobs and the growth of the service sector. If looked at in a global perspective, and not simply in national terms, do you think Bell is right?

PERMISSIONS